Professional Visual Basic 6
The 2003 Programmer's Resource

Jerry Ablan

Fabio Claudio Ferracchiati

Steven Livingstone-Perez

Ryan Payet

Larry Steinle

Kent Tegels

Rick Weyenberg

Vincent Varallo

Donald Xie

wrox

Wrox Press Ltd. ®

Professional Visual Basic 6
The 2003 Programmer's Resource

First printed January 2003

Published by Wrox Press Ltd,
Arden House, 1102 Warwick Road, Acocks Green,
Birmingham, B27 6BH, UK.
Printed in the USA
ISBN 1-86100-818-X

Trademark Acknowledgments

Wrox has endeavored to adhere to trademark conventions for all companies and products mentioned in this book, such as the appropriate use of capitalization. Wrox cannot however guarantee the accuracy of this information.

Credits

Authors
Jerry Ablan
Fabio Claudio Ferracchiati
Steven Livingstone-Perez
Ryan Payet
Larry Steinle
Kent Tegels
Rick Weyenberg
Vincent Varallo
Donald Xie

Original Material
Chris Blexrud
Matt Bortniker
Jon Crossland
Rockford Lhotka
Stephen Mohr
Scott Short
Charles Williams

Additional Material
Rockford Lhotka
Karli Watson

Commissioning Editor
Ian Blackham

Technical Editors
Richard Deeson
Michelle Everitt
Devin Lunsfor

Technical Reviewers
Jason Follas
Mark Horner
Sean Medina
Mike Perrin
Ranga Raghunathan
David Schultz
Don Udawattage

Production Coordinator
Neil Lote

Cover Design
Natalie O'Donnell

Series Editor
Dan Richardson

Proof Reader
Dev Lunsford

Indexer
Martin Brooks

Project Manager
Darren Murphy

Managing Editor
Joanna Mason

About the Authors

Jerry Ablan

Jerry is the consummate computer nerd. His first computer experience was on a TRS-80 Model I in a branch of Radio Shack. It was all downhill from there. After school, Jerry ventured forth to work for various companies until settling in to the financial industry. He joined FutureSource, a commodities quotation vendor, as a systems designer and engineer building high-volume financial transaction reporting systems. He then moved to the Chicago Board Options Exchange building those same high-volume financial transaction reporting systems but on a larger scale. Later at the CBOE, Jerry became Manager of Internet Application Development and led the charge to put CBOE on the Net.

In 1997, Jerry left the CBOE to co-found MindBuilder, a multimedia training company. There he designed and implemented a unique system of delivering multimedia training content over the Internet. In 2000, Jerry left MindBuilder for another start-up, Auctionworks.com. Auctionworks provides online inventory and auction management services for sellers big and small. Jerry designed and implemented the entire Auctionworks infrastructure and front end. He now enjoys the role of Chief Scientist there.

Fabio Claudio Ferracchiati

Fabio Claudio Ferracchiati is a software developer and technical writer. In the early days of his ten-year career, he worked with classic Microsoft tools such as Visual Basic and Visual C++. After five years, he decided to dedicate his attention to the Internet and its related technologies. In 1998, he started a parallel career writing technical articles for Italian and international magazines, and he now works in Rome for CPI Progetti Spa (http://www.cpiprogetti.it) where he develops Internet/intranet solutions using Microsoft technologies.

> I dedicate my work on this book to my nephew Nico: I hope to be always your "best friend of the whole universe". I love you, "big puzzetta" boy!

> Also to Danila: my muse, my air, my love. Thank you for your patience and your love. I love you.

> I'd also like to thank everyone at Wrox for the chance to write on this book.

Steven Livingstone-Perez

Steven Livingstone-Perez is a freelance author, consultant, and entrepreneur. He currently lives in tropical Glasgow, Scotland where he maintains the web sites http://www.sightkeys.net, http://www.deltabis.com, and http://www.venturetogether.com. In addition, he continues to work on projects using XML and .NET.

He recently married Loreto, who is expecting their first baby (Cochi) in March 2003. He can be contacted at steven@venturetogether.com.

Ryan Payet

Ryan N. Payet (BSc Computer Science, MCP) is a system analyst working as software development team leader and system administrator for Victoria Computer Services (VCS), a leading IT company based in the Seychelles. His main role is software development, primarily for the tourism industry, and he is also responsible for maintaining and enhancing a variety of in-house software packages.

His interests include development of n-tier systems including the development of XML Web Services. Ryan has extensive experience of database design and development, including data warehousing and online analysis systems. He also has much experience of various Microsoft products including Visual Studio .NET, Internet Security and Access Server, MS SQL Server, and Windows 2000 Server.

Ryan likes good humor, science fiction, and scientific documentaries, not necessarily in combination. He has a varied taste in music, ranging from classical to heavy metal.

Dedicated to "sweet M". To live is to risk. To love is to risk even more. Life is neither kind nor cruel. It is what we make of it.

Larry Steinle

Larry Steinle is a software analyst for HDR Inc, a nationally recognized architecture, engineering, and consulting firm. He graduated with a certificate in Biblical Studies, an Associate in Computer Programming, and a Bachelor Degree in Management Information Systems. He has experience in JCL, COBOL, Visual Basic, Microsoft SQL Server, and Active Server Pages.

I would like to thank my parents, Duane and Karen, for their patience, encouragement, and guidance (Proverbs 3:1-12; 29:17). Above all, I wish to thank my lovely wife, Melissa, for her faithful support (Proverbs 18:22).

Kent Tegels

Kent Tegels is a Senior System Analyst for HDR. He is a contributor to a number of Wrox Press offerings on web and .NET development. He is also a Microsoft Certified System Engineer and Database Administrator. When not swamped with work, Kent loves to be with his family.

Wow, there's a lot of people I need to thank. First and foremost, I want to dedicate my efforts on this title to my significant other, Janell. Words just can't express how thankful I am that you are part of my life or how much you mean to me every day. Same to Kevin and Lizzie for being with us and stronger than ever as we make the transitions we have together. I'd also like to thank Ian and Darren at Wrox for all they've done for me on this title. Gents, I owe you one.

Finally, I'd like to thank Angelo, Rod, and Gary of the HDR Information Service department for giving me the opportunity to work on our .NET migration efforts instead of more drudgerous things.

Rick Weyenberg

Rick Weyenberg is a Microsoft Certified Solutions Developer (MCSD) and works for Cornerstone Consulting in Minneapolis, MN as an IT Consultant. He began programming in BASIC on the Apple II at the age of 10. One of the first programs he wrote was a simplistic version of the game "Global Thermonuclear War" from the movie *War Games*. He also wrote a program for learning-disabled students that helped them learn arithmetic.

Currently, Rick is involved in architecting n-tier applications with an emphasis on web-based solutions using the latest Microsoft technologies: .NET, COM+, IIS, MSMQ, XML, and XSL. He is excited about pursuing his Microsoft Certified Application Developer (MCAD) certification and looks forward to the challenges that lay ahead.

I would like to thank my parents for their support and encouragement throughout the years, and, more recently, my wife Jenny and new son Lucas for their patience throughout the writing process.

Vincent Varallo

Vincent Varallo is Senior Software Engineer for FXpress Corporation where he develops treasury workstation software for large multinational companies. He has been developing applications in Visual Basic and ASP for six years, ranging from fat client Windows applications to n-tiered web apps. Recently he has taken a liking to C# and is now developing for the .NET platform. He is a fully fledged Microsoft follower and has enjoyed the success that this company has made possible. When not pounding away at the keyboard, he likes to pound away at the golf ball.

I would like to thank my wife Vicki and my two daughters Madison and Courtney for being my inspiration.

Donald Xie

Donald Xie is a software consultant specializing in object-oriented application development on the Microsoft platform. Over the past ten years, he has worked as programmer, designer, analyst, architect, and project leader in various sectors and government agencies. Donald has co-authored several books on Visual Basic, C++, and recently .NET. You can contact Donald on donald@xies.net.

p2p.wrox.com
The programmer's resource centre

ASP Today

wrox.com

wrox

wroxdirect

Table of Contents

Table of Contents

Table of Contents

Table of Contents

Table of Contents

Table of Contents

p2p.wrox.com

The programmer's resource centre

ASP Today

wrox.com

Foreword

Rockford Lhotka has over 15 years of experience in software development and has been working with Visual Basic since the release of VB 1.0. He is also the author of Professional VB.NET (1-86100-497-4) and Visual Basic 6.0 Business Objects (1-86100-107-X), among many other titles.

When I left college, my first job involved working on the rewrite of a large PDP-11 application onto the VAX/VMS platform. The VAX/VMS platform was the successor to the PDP-11, and while there were many similarities there were also dramatic differences.

Several years later, there were still PDP-11 production applications being used by customers – despite the fact that the superior VAX/VMS product had been available for some time. Those applications were maintained even though it was long past the point that the PDP-11 was considered a vibrant platform.

We face a similar situation today with .NET. While .NET will undoubtedly become the dominant platform in a few years' time, we are now merely at the start of the period of transition. During this period, VB6 will remain a viable, living platform even as .NET grows. Once we reach the point that .NET is truly dominant, VB6 and COM applications will continue to be used, maintained, and even enhanced for some years.

Long-time PC developers might recall the DOS-Windows transition, or the Win16 to Win32 transition. As a consultant, I encountered clients working in VB3 when VB6 was introduced. They saw no reason to change – VB3 apps ran *really fast* on VB6-era hardware!

The corporate world is nothing if not pragmatic. "If it ain't broke, don't fix it, don't touch it, don't even mess with it" often seems to be the slogan. The broader industry, including hardware vendors, software vendors, and service vendors, don't abide by this slogan – if they did, there'd be nothing new to buy, and thus no revenue for them.

What this meant for PDP-11 developers then, and what it means for VB6 developers now, is that we need to plan for the future while being productive today. Yes, .NET is coming and it is exciting, but for many people it isn't here yet. We still need to be productive with the tools we have. Even if your aim is to migrate to .NET soon, remember that .NET is an evolutionary step for the typical Visual Basic programmer. It is a different way of doing things, and allows us to do more complex things more easily. However, it is evolutionary, and is merely the last in a long line of gradual changes that have emerged in the Visual Basic world. The better your skills in VB6, the easier you will find the transition.

The pressure to be productive is higher now than ever. New systems development is justified through return on investment (ROI), but maintenance and enhancement of existing systems is typically measured by the much stiffer total cost of ownership (TCO) measure. As VB6 development becomes increasingly devoted to maintenance and enhancement of existing systems, we will be under increasing pressure to perform with maximum productivity and minimal cost.

Most experienced VB6 developers know how to approach and solve development problems based on the types of application they've created or worked on in the past. When confronted with a new type of application or problem, we don't need coddling or hand-holding – we need answers. That's exactly why we wrote this book – to provide a valuable resource of techniques and knowledge that developers need today in order to make the best use of Visual Basic 6.

Who Is This Book For?

This book aims to provide a resource for intermediate and advanced VB6 developers. It brings all the programming techniques and practices required for producing modern production level applications together into one place.

What Does This Book Cover?

Starting with a quick rundown of where VB6 is now, and where it's come from, we move quickly on to cover all the techniques that professional VB6 developers will need to be confident in today. We look at various aspects of data manipulation and display, COM, VB6's transactional support, web applications and web services, XML, and more.

The book's chapters can be summarized as follows:

Chapter 1 – *"Classic" Visual Basic in the .NET World:* This chapter sets the scene with a quick history of the Visual Basic language, and provides an analysis of its likely future role as .NET becomes more widely adopted.

Chapter 2 – *Visual Basic Designs:* This chapter starts with a look at how the design process might go in the ideal world, and how that process often needs to be compromised in the real world. Next, we cover issues faced when we select our application architecture. The second half of the chapter introduces the concept of Design Patterns, taking a look at which of these can be applied in VB6 applications.

Chapter 3 – *The Basics of Data Access:* This, our first chapter on data access, examines the objects that we can use in VB6 to access and manipulate data, and the properties, methods, and events of those objects. We look at the details of connecting to databases, and running queries to retrieve or alter data.

Chapter 4 – *Working with the ADO Data Control:* The ADO Data control is a very powerful and flexible means for connecting to databases and provides a built-in UI for navigating through records. This chapter investigates its workings by working through a sample application.

Chapter 5 – *Views, Stored Procedures, and Triggers:* This chapter looks at the advanced features and capabilities of database products such as SQL Server to see how these can allow our applications to support hundreds of concurrent users and to provide far more advanced features and capabilities.

Chapter 6 – *Data Validation, Transactions, and Error Trapping:* The value of data is dependent on its quality and integrity, and this chapter looks at techniques that can ensure that our applications handle data appropriately.

Chapter 7 – *Advanced ADO:* This chapter is aimed at those developers who wish to learn how to apply advanced ADO techniques in the Windows DNA architecture. We look at ADO disconnected recordsets, Remote Data Services (RDS), and finally examine ADO's support for XML as a means of exchanging information between different processes and operating systems.

Chapter 8 – *COM+:* Implementing distributed applications requires different parts of an application to run in isolation from one another, possibly in different processes on the same server or in different processes on different – and perhaps poorly connected – computers. The key technology to such applications is COM+ and in this first chapter on the topic, we examine exactly what COM+ is.

Chapter 9 – *Component Development:* Carrying on from the previous chapter, we move on to look at the issues involved in the design and development of effective COM+ components.

Chapter 10 – *COM+ Transactions:* Objects hosted under COM+ can be configured to support or require transactions. This chapter covers the topic in depth, starting with the requirements for transactional support, moving on to see how to implement them in COM+, and finishing with a look at the more advanced topic of building a Compensating Resource Manager.

Chapter 11 – *COM+ Distributed and Queued Components:* COM+ components can be distributed over multiple servers through the technology of DCOM, an integral part of COM+. This chapter quickly gets you up to speed in the founding principles, including configuration and deployment. We also have an in-depth look at Microsoft Message Queue, MSMQ.

Chapter 12 – *VBScript and ASP:* This chapter looks at some of the key differences between VBScript and VB proper, and looks at how it is used in ASP. We create some sample applications to illustrate usage of the principle objects in ASP applications.

Chapter 13 – *Essential XML:* This chapter examines XML, and how to use it from VB6. We learn how to create valid XML documents with DTDs and XML Schema, how to make use of the Document Object Model (DOM), and how to output an ADO recordset as XML. We also see how to convert XML to HTML on the server, and upload an XML file from the client.

Chapter 14 – *SOAP and XML Web Services for VB6:* This chapter investigates the new and exciting world of XML Web Services. Once we've covered the concepts and standards that web services are built on, we get practical as we implement and consume web services in VB6 using the Microsoft SOAP Toolkit.

Chapter 15 – *Looking Forward to .NET:* The last chapter looks at what you might expect as you migrate applications from VB6 to VB.NET. While Microsoft has done a good job with the upgrade tool, we discuss when it might be better to rewrite instead.

Appendix A – *Visual Basic Tips and Tricks:* The first appendix is a collection of useful hints and techniques to help the VB programmer. All the code given is included on the CD for you to copy and paste into your own applications.

Appendix B – *Visual Studio Installer:* This appendix guides developers through the process of creating reliable installation files using Microsoft's Visual Studio Installer tool. This software can help avoid many of the problems of "DLL Hell" when deploying software.

Appendix C – *Deployment Techniques – Wise Installation System:* This appendix provides a guide to the installation software offered by Wise, which can be used as an alternative to the Visual Studio Package and Deployment Wizard.

Appendix D – *ADO Object Summary:* ActiveX Data Objects (ADO) are central to the data access model as conceived by Microsoft. This appendix describes the objects, along with their properties, return types, and descriptions. There is also a quick reference guide to method calls.

Appendix E – *SQL Reference:* SQL (Structured Query Language) lets us manipulate and retrieve data from a relational database, and this appendix describes the syntax of the most common SQL commands for the database engines you are most likely to encounter.

Note that Chapters 3, 4, 5, and 6 are revised versions of material that originally appeared in **Professional Visual Basic 6 Databases** *(ISBN 1-86100-202-5), and Chapters 7, 8, 9, and 10 are updated material from* **Professional Windows DNA** *(ISBN 1-86100-445-1). Chapters 12 and 13 are updates of material that originally appeared in* **Professional Visual Basic 6 Web Programming** *(ISBN 1-86100-222-X).*

What Do I Need To Use This Book?

The software requirements for using this book are:

- ❑ Windows 2000 or XP (with IIS)
- ❑ Visual Basic 6.0
- ❑ Visual Interdev 6.0
- ❑ SQL Server 7 or higher. For many examples MSDE will be fine, but there are areas where we discuss features of SQL Server, such as Enterprise Manager.

Conventions

We've used a number of different styles of text and layout in this book to differentiate between different kinds of information. In this section, you'll find examples of the styles used along with an explanation of what they mean.

Code has several fonts. If we're talking about code in the text, we use a non-proportional font like this: For...Next. If it's a block of code that can be typed as a program and run, then it will also appear within a gray box:

```
<asp:TextBox id="txtNameBox" runat="server" />
<asp:Button id="btnSubmit" onclick="btnSubmit_Click"
                        runat="server" Text="Click Here!" />
```

Sometimes we'll see code in a mixture of styles, like this:

```
Private Sub calDates_SelectionChanged(ByVal sender As System.Object, _
        ByVal e As System.EventArgs) Handles calDates.SelectionChanged
    lblMessage.Text = _
            "Current Date: " & calDates.SelectedDate.ToLongDateString()
End Sub
```

When this happens, code with a white background is code we are already familiar with, while that highlighted in gray is a new addition since we last saw it.

Advice, hints, and background information come in this type of font.

> **Important pieces of information are placed inside boxes like this.**

❏   **Important Words** are in a bold type font.

❏   Words that appear on screen, or in menus like File or Window, are in a similar sans serif font to that used by default on the Windows desktop.

❏   Keys that you press on the keyboard, such as *Ctrl* and *Enter*, are in italics.

Customer Support

We always value hearing from our readers, and we want to know what you think about this book: what you liked, what you didn't like, and what you think we can do better next time. You can send us your comments, either by returning the reply card in the back of the book, or by e-mail to feedback@wrox.com. Please be sure to mention the book title in your message.

How to Download Sample Code for this Book

Visit the Wrox site at http://www.wrox.com/, and locate the title through our Find a Book facility. Open the book's detail page and click the Download Code link. Alternatively, click the DOWNLOAD CODE link at the top of the Wrox homepage, and select the book in the text box there.

Before you download the code for this book, you may register your book by providing your name and current e-mail address. This is a purely optional step which allows us to contact you should issues with the code download arise, or should the code download package be updated at a later date. Be assured that Wrox will never pass any details supplied during registration to any third party. Full details are contained in our Privacy Policy, linked to from the download page.

Download files are archived using WinZip, and need to be extracted with a decompression program such as WinZip or PKUnzip. The code is typically arranged with a suitable folder structure, so ensure your decompression software is set to use folder names before extracting the files.

Errata

We've made every effort to make sure that there are no errors in the text or in the code. However, no one is perfect and mistakes do occur. If you find an error in one of our books, such as a spelling mistake or a faulty piece of code, we would be very grateful to hear about it. By sending in errata, you may save another reader hours of frustration, and of course, you will be helping us provide even higher quality information. Simply e-mail the information to support@wrox.com, where your information will be checked and posted on the errata page for the title, or used in subsequent editions of the book.

To view errata on the web site, go to http://www.wrox.com/, and locate the title through the Find a Book search box. Clicking the View errata link that appears below the cover graphic on the book's detail page brings up a list of all errata for that book reported to date.

E-mail Support

If you wish to directly query a problem in the book with an expert who knows the book in detail then e-mail support@wrox.com, with the title of the book and the last four numbers of the ISBN in the subject field of the e-mail. A typical e-mail should include the following things:

❑ The **title of the book**, **last four digits of the ISBN**, and **page number** of the problem in the Subject field.

❑ Your **name**, **contact information**, and the **problem** in the body of the message.

We **won't** send you junk mail. We need the details to save your time and ours. When you send an e-mail message, it will go through the following chain of support:

❑ Customer Support – Your message is delivered to our customer support staff, who are the first people to read it. They have files on most frequently asked questions and will answer anything general about the book or the web site immediately.

❑ Editorial – Deeper queries are forwarded to the technical editor responsible for that book. They have experience with the programming language or particular product, and are able to answer detailed technical questions on the subject.

❑ The Authors – Finally, in the unlikely event that the editor cannot answer your problem, he or she will forward the request to the author. We do try to protect the author from any distractions to their writing; however, we are quite happy to forward specific requests to them. All Wrox authors help with the support on their books. They will e-mail the customer and the editor with their response, and again all readers should benefit.

The Wrox Support process can only offer support to issues that are directly pertinent to the content of our published title. Support for questions that fall outside the scope of normal book support is provided via the community lists of our http://p2p.wrox.com/ forum.

p2p.wrox.com

For author and peer discussion, join the P2P mailing lists. Our unique system provides **programmer to programmer™** contact on mailing lists, forums, and newsgroups, all in addition to our one-to-one e-mail support system. If you post a query to P2P, you can be confident that it is being examined by the many Wrox authors and other industry experts who are present on our mailing lists. At p2p.wrox.com you will find a number of different lists that can help you, not only while you read this book, but also as you move on and develop your own applications.

To subscribe to a mailing list just follow these steps:

1. Go to http://p2p.wrox.com/

2. Choose the appropriate category from the left menu bar

3. Click on the mailing list you wish to join

4. Follow the instructions to subscribe and fill in your e-mail address and password

5. Reply to the confirmation e-mail you receive

6. Use the subscription manager to join more lists and set your e-mail preferences

Why This System Offers the Best Support

You can choose to join the mailing lists or you can receive them as a weekly digest. If you don't have the time, or facilities, to receive the mailing list, then you can search our online archives. Junk and spam mails are deleted, and your own e-mail address is protected by the unique Lyris system. Queries about joining or leaving lists, and any other general queries about lists, should be sent to listsupport@p2p.wrox.com.

p2p.wrox.com
The programmer's resource centre

ASP Today

wrox.com

wroxdirect

1

"Classic" Visual Basic in the .NET World

Back in 1991, Microsoft saw an opportunity to innovate. At this time, producing meaningful programs on a microcomputer was not straightforward. Although we had a variety of languages like C, C++, and Pascal to choose from, none were as easily learned by the layperson as BASIC. However, BASIC wasn't attractive to developers because as an interpreted language, it ran much slower than fully compiled code. Enter VB1 with its introduction of functions and subroutines. For all of its shortcomings, VB1 did introduce many to event-oriented programming, the idea of a form engine for displaying User Interfaces, and the use of visual design. However, the code was all still executed by a runtime. This meant that it was faster than interpreted code, but still lagging behind the compiled languages.

In late 1992, Microsoft brought the relational database to the personal computer with the advent of Access. Around the same time, VB2 came out, featuring support for the then emerging Open Database Connectivity (ODBC) standard and most of the VB2 language core was exposed for use with Access as Access Basic. This split in the BASIC language used by the Office Product suite would take different forms over the years.

Then in 1993, Microsoft introduced VB3. The integration with Access grew into integration with Jet, and interaction with the Operating System was finally possible due to Object Linking and Embedding (OLE) automation.

Things on the VB scene entered a lull until the fall of 1996 when Microsoft released Internet Explorer 3.0 with its VBScript language. VBScript was a subset of Visual Basic, so it provided a familiar vocabulary to enable scripting without the pain or pleasure of a forms engine. It still used the virtual machine, however. In October of 1996, VB4 introduced us to "classes", OCXs, and the ability to create Dynamic Linked Libraries (DLLs). These were the first signs that Visual Basic was moving towards the adoption of object-oriented programming. Within a few months, Microsoft introduced the "Option Pack 4" upgrade for WindowsNT and developers were given Active Server Pages (ASP) to play with. Using VBScript, ASP opened up server-side web programming to the masses. Within a couple of months, Microsoft releases Office97 wherein all of the products in the office suite – except Outlook – ran Visual Basic for Applications (VBA). Outlook used VBScript.

> **Why VBScript in Outlook?**
>
> That's a question that some have been asking for a long time. Was it simply that it couldn't technically be done with VBA? Probably not. The real answer seems to be that all of the Office products were on slightly different development tracks. Outlook was probably mostly completed before the VB for Applications platform was ready to work with its internal object model. At the same time, the lack of sophistication in VBScript made developing Outlook-based applications far more tedious.
>
> Of course, the more cynical of us would point out that, with dolor induced by Melissa and ILOVEYOU, aren't we glad we didn't get all of VB in Outlook...

Over a year passes before VB5 is introduced in April of 1997. VB5 in turn added `WithEvents` to the language, along with the ability to build ActiveX controls. ActiveX controls were thought to be important because they provided a way to achieve rich functionality over the Internet, so long as you were using Internet Explorer. And as long you trusted the downloaded code. See a problem here? But the real turning point in the evolutionary course of VB was that for the first time, you could actually compile VB into binary code. In a sense, the VB virtual machine changed gears a bit and became more of a functional library of code than a pure runtime. This concept – combining the runtime environment with a feature rich library – is fundamentally what .NET is all about. However.....

So up to this point, we really have two VB languages: VB5 and VBA in Office – feature rich with reasonably robust development environments – and VBScript for web-based client and server applications. The core design elements of VB – events, forms and the runtime – got tweaked and stretched to better fulfill their role. The big changes were under the hood with the move from a runtime-hosted language to a compiled language. VBScript, in comparison, stagnated.

A year and a half later – October 1998 – VB6 debuts. Its release was aimed at making developer productivity enhancements rather than attempting to break new ground, with the exception that is of the ill-fated Web Classes. Web Classes were really an attempt to bring the rich development environment of VB6 to the development of Web Applications. This was very much needed as developing and debugging ASP is a fairly painful process. But more than anything, it's my opinion that Microsoft misjudged the Web Development space at the time. Most of the folks using VB at this point were predominately working on desktop, forms-based applications, while the folks writing web applications were comfortable with scripting language programs invoked via CGI. For many, Web Classes were simply too much of a mindset shift to make. But the concept of Web Classes – compiled classes created and debugged in a rich environment yet with markup files that are processed into HTML output – is really the genesis of ASP.NET.

> **Why will ASP.NET succeed when Web Classes didn't?**
>
> It isn't so much that the technology of ASP.NET is so much more developer-friendly than Web Classes. It is more that Microsoft has done a good job of getting those of us who despised the VB nature of Web Classes to see their value. Microsoft's push of Server Objects, and then *n*-tier distributed architectures, have been the ways of us getting us comfortable with writing components in the VB environment, then using ASP to call on these objects. Fundamentally, that's what Web Classes did and that's the architecture of preference for ASP.NET.

Fast forward to 13 February 2002, the day that Visual Studio .NET was launched. All of the evolution we've seen in VB since 1991 reached critical mass. The forms engine was completely overhauled and updated, the language itself was brought up to date (did we really need both TRIM and TRIM$?), and the VB-specific runtime is replaced with the Common Language Runtime (CLR). The importance of VBScript begins to fade in importance now as well as on the server-side, the use of VBScript for ASP is given a decent burial. More importantly, VB joined the ranks of SmallTalk, Java, and C++ with substantial support for key object-oriented concepts like class. And VB finally has a foundation of classes to draw on equal to C++ without (much) invocation of Win32 API calls. It seems clear that this trend of unification will continue. Although Microsoft is being understandably quiet about .NET's integration with future products, there's been mention of replacing VBA with VB.NET in future versions of the Office Suite. There's even talk of exposing .NET-compliant languages for use in stored procedures with the next version of the SQL Server product.

Visual Basic has undergone a gradual process of changes into a different and usually more complex and improved form. That's evolution by definition. But has that evolution been spontaneous or has it been caused by the environment in which VB "lives"? It's important to answer that question because it sheds light on how we can best design highly sustainable applications – those that withstand continuous evolution.

VB – A Product of its Environment?

I'll put forward the hypothesis that the evolution of VB has been driven by the environments in which it is used. We've just surveyed the major changes that VB has undergone and have talked about some of the environmental factors that drove those changes. But not all of the changes in VB caused by environmental changes have manifested themselves as marketed features.

Take Memory Models for example. In previous years, I wrote a lot of DOS applications using Microsoft C/C++ 6.0. We had to write code for both 16-bit and 32-bit CPUs. One design consideration we had to make was what memory model we would use. If we knew that our code and data was going to use less than 16k of memory, we could use the Tiny Memory Model. Such applications ran faster than other programs in other models because more of the work could be done directly on the CPU registers and the stack itself. Changing the memory model after the first build was a chore because all of the linked libraries also had to be of the same model. VB developers were somewhat luckier because the runtime took care of minutia like this, but it imposed harsher limits on CPU flexibility. Ask anybody that tried upgrading VB1 or VB2 to VB4 how much fun that was!

But even now, nearly a decade later, we're at the same crossroads again. The 64-bit processor looms on the horizon casting a long, foreboding shadow on our applications. It's important to understand that while such processors do run our existing code in emulation mode, we can't expect that support to last forever because doing so defeats the purpose of having bigger, faster and more powerful CPUs. The fact is that if you want to make the best use of the CPU, you have to write code that is specific to it.

Or you have to cheat...

It has been suggested that the real motivation for .NET is to address precisely this problem. Microsoft needs a way to abstract its applications (and ours as well) from any particular CPU model, yet they need a way to take full advantage of the hardware available. They also need the unified development environment for all platforms. .NET uses a two-step compile approach. The first compile produces output in the form of Microsoft Intermediate Language (MSIL). MSIL is an abstract assembler-like language of primitive moves, jumps, and function calls that can be mapped to native machine operations on virtually any computer. The second compile, executed when the program loads into memory, produces binaries that are specific to the hardware platform on which the program is executing. This concept is hardly new to VB, however. Before version 5, compiled VB was simply "P-code" that the Runtime knew how to execute. .NET simply evolves that model.

The issues with migrating to 64-bit CPUs aren't the only shadow-casters that Microsoft hopes to banish with .NET. Over the past few years, we've seen the population of computing-intensive gadgets explode: cellular phones, PDA's, video games, and even the family car all have more computing power than the supercomputers of just a few dozen years ago. And you can probably safely bet that we're just experiencing the first one percent of how things will be in a few dozen years from now.

The key point to take away from this is that your approach to code optimization may need to change. For example, you may have a policy that says "pass numeric values as singles instead of doubles where possible" because singles take half the memory of doubles and the loss of precision is negligible. In the future, the probability of that assumption remaining correct is probably likely to be less, so spending a great deal of time optimizing this sort of thing is wasteful. Trust the runtime to do the right thing on things it can understand. Spend your time optimizing higher-level logic that the compiler isn't likely to catch. It will also make upgrading your code to .NET easier too.

Another consideration is the operating system. Microsoft is in the operating system business and, every few years, we can count on them rolling out a new OS for us. Other vendors will do the same. As anybody who has had to upgrade from a DOS application to a Windows application or port a Windows Application to Linux will tell you, it's not much fun and its definitely not something you want to slug through every other year. To their credit, Microsoft has been reasonably good about maintaining application compatibility between their Windows operating systems but there will also be some changes. The differences between Windows 2000 Professional and Windows CE are dramatic (and frequently traumatic) for developers.

We've seen how Visual Basic has coped with different operating systems by isolating those things that can get you into corners. Take the Event Logging support as an example. This functionality is smart enough to know to behave differently on operating systems that support an Event Log from those which don't. For the most part, you can write code that ignores these details and lets the runtime determine the best way to do what you want.

In virtually every software development project I've worked on, by focusing my optimization efforts on solving higher-level logic problems that the compiler won't catch, and by using an isolate and interface approach, I've found that my solutions tend to weather much better than those where I didn't stick with these principles. I think it's been fairly easy to see these principles in action in VB as it has developed too. As the VB developer community has applied the various disciplines to developing solutions in VB, the product has been changed to keep up with us. We're free to think in terms of forms and events rather than GDI objects, handles, and so on. This means that we're much more free to focus on solving business problems rather than coming up with the best way to implement a Collection class.

Another change in VB that owes itself to environmental change is the shift of focus from Data Access Objects (DAO) to Active Data Objects. The reasons for that are clear: Microsoft's first steps into the world of relational database-centered application development were squarely focused on making the best of their *database du jour* – Access. The best technology at the time to work with Access was DAO. However, as developers started to apply the power of VB as a general tool for working with any database and standards like ODBC and then OLE DB grew in importance, something other than DAO was needed. Enter ADO and its more generic approach to working with any data source. VB6 really made an effort to work with ADO via the various tools and wizards offered.

But ADO is just a window on the larger picture of what Microsoft calls its Universal Data Access (UDA) Strategy. The idea is to abstract all of the messy bits of dealing with a database into a single, consistent interface for developers to use. The hard work of matching native database behaviors to the abstract interfaces is left to the driver provider. The other parts of the UDA strategy are the Microsoft Data Access Components (MDAC). MDAC is more or less the container for ADO, ODBC and OLE DB. The essential difference between ODBC and OLE DB is how much protocol they define and require in order to work with a database. Most of the time by just by using the right driver, ADO will sufficiently take care of these details appropriately for the VB Developer.

> **Enter ADO.NET**
>
> A question I'm frequently asked is: what's the relationship between ADO and ADO.NET? As Mark Twain might say, "...the difference between lightning and a lightning bug."
>
> Both technologies serve the same purpose – to make it easy to work with data. ADO was initially designed to work with Relational Databases. ADO.NET was initially designed to work with data regardless of its source. This allows ADO.NET to treat virtually any type of data as though it were from a well-structured data source even though it may come from something as semi-structured as an Exchange Public folder. ADO.NET is conceptually similar enough to ADO, however, that most VB developers won't have problems learning it quickly.

So what can we learn from how VB has adapted to changes in Data Access technologies? I think the most important lessons are:

❑ **Expect change**: I've lost count of how many times something that started out as a simple Access application burgeoned into a SQL Server backend with an ASP User Interface and an Access ADP editing tool collage. I now regularly encourage developers to design their projects with the assumption that the database could be moved to Oracle at any time. Not that we necessarily will, but we might have to. The isolate and interface philosophy makes these sorts of designs much more manageable.

❑ **When making a change, make the best long-term change you can**: When Microsoft found themselves running into the limits of DAO, they didn't try to push it outward to fit the problem. Instead, they went to ADO. Granted, it's a very substantial change, but in the long-term it's worked out better. The same is true of ADO.NET. Rather than continue to stretch ADO to work better with non-relational data in a disconnected manner, they came up with an entirely different approach that is far more appropriate. Similarly, when you find yourself at the point where expanding a class or library to do something just doesn't seem like the best long-term example, don't be afraid to push forward in a new direction.

❑ **Change the technology, but keep the techniques conceptually similar**: Going back to previous example, as ADO developers, we've become comfortable with the concepts of connections, transactions and commands. Although ADO.NET changes the internals of these concepts, they serve pretty much the same purpose in both ADO.NET and ADO. This makes it easier for new developers to associate what they already know with what they have to learn.

One of the big changes we saw over time was the ability to generate real dynamic link libraries (DLLs). This was a significant change for VB in that it removed the form as the focus of the development effort. However, the use of VB and Visual Studio didn't really change that much. With VB4, it became common practice to use classes within our forms-based applications. The bits of our programs that weren't directly concerned with the User Interface could be coded as classes and these classes could be reused between projects. Our code became much more modular.

It was this evolutionary step of having classes that allowed us to take the next step to using components – ActiveX DLLs. In principle, the "ActiveX DLL" is simply a collection of compiled classes that can be invoked through COM. VB is a blessing for many of us because it automatically and quietly deals with the intricacies and idiosyncrasies of COM, freeing us to focus on higher-level problems. At the same time, it's a potential curse because it makes it possible for us to write what seem like reasonable solutions that have endless problems in production because we've not been exposed to what's going on under the covers. ActiveX DLLs made it possible to achieve component-sharing applications. For example, a developer could write an entire set of classes to encapsulate the logic needed with SQL Server databases, and other developers' higher-level business applications could reuse that component. Component libraries were free, of course, to call on other component libraries. ASP developers found that by moving much of their logic into ActiveX DLLs and using them as Server Components, they could achieve much better application performance and higher levels of productivity.

It certainly didn't take long for developers to realize that COM could be stretched in a number of ways. From its inception, COM used OLE to expose functionality across process boundaries. That is, one COM-enabled process – like a VB application – could invoke functionality from any other OLE enabled process on the same computer but running in different processes. The next step – Distributed COM or DCOM – allowed a "client" application to call "server" processes on a completely different computer. Although DCOM was certainly a powerful tool, it frequently proved too cumbersome for VB developers to leverage effectively. What did arise from DCOM was a technology known as Microsoft Transaction Server (MTS). MTS was effectively a container from which COM components could be called upon to do certain tasks. These components were also able to listen and raise signals for tasks that had succeeded or failed, and the component would be able to undo any of the partially completed work involved in the complete task. MTS also proved to be a much more hospitable environment for VB developers when compared to DCOM.

The early version of MTS was essentially limited to hosting transactional processes. While this met the need at the time, Microsoft quickly recognized that the idea of a container for hosting processes had much more potential. Enter COM+ with Windows 2000. Although COM+ shed the appearance of being just a transaction processing system, it certainly filled that role. It also enhanced the container concept to better management of the contained objects and greater security control. The best thing about COM+ (at least so far) is that it's fairly straightforward to write good VB applications that leverage COM+ in desktop applications, in component libraries, and within ASP. And again, VB developers are mostly shielded from the convoluted details of how it actually all works.

> **Wag the Dog?**
>
> There was initial sentiment in the industry that COM+ was really just a lot of marketing flair to help sell Windows 2000 Server as a viable Application Server. Although the previous version of Windows Server – Windows NT Server – was reasonably good at supporting client/server (2-tier) applications, critics and competitors could fairly point out that it failed to provide a suitable or sufficient infrastructure for use as an applications server in 3-tier and n-tier architectures. Windows 2000 Server had to do a much better job in order to compete in that market space. COM+ proved to be much more than hype, particularly when you look at how well it provides a simple to set up, simple to administer, simple to develop in, robust environment for application components.

The real problem with COM+ is that it took a long time for VB developers to see its uses. This seems to have the been the result of two factors:

❑　The mindset of developers and others that VB is limited to being a tool for developing client/server applications.

❑　The lack of accumulated knowledge and techniques of how to use VB to build larger, multi-tier applications.

Client/server architectures went from *haute* to *passé* as we came to realize that the amount of burden that is frequently laid on the server meant an ultimate limit to the total performance of the application. What was needed was a way to distribute the total work needed to be done over many different computers with each computer doing smaller amounts of work. This resulted in synergy: more total work could be done by a distributed application than could be done in total by each of the individual computers. Thus the concept of three-tier (clients, a flat hierarchy of middleware components, and servers) came to be. This approach to architecting systems and solutions created a number of quantum leaps within the development community. First, it became possible to not only serve mere scores of clients at a time with a single pool of components and a single server, but hundreds. Second, by creating more component pools talking to more servers, thousands of clients could be concurrently supported. So-called "n-tier architectures" were introduced to add depth to the middle component hierarchy. That spawned more reuse of components, better isolation of processes and generally made the distributed application seem better.

The problem with all of this is that for every positive gain, developers were hit with nearly equal costs. Obviously the total complexity of such systems is much greater than of simple client/server applications. There is a lot more opportunities for something to break. High quality documentation and exhaustive testing of such systems was virtually required before the program would ever be supportable in a production mode.

Sadly, a lot of developers blamed VB, believing for whatever reasons that it just wasn't up to the challenge of being used for more than the client portions of such applications. But it really wasn't VB's fault. VB wasn't a good choice for such applications because Microsoft lacked a solid environment for hosting distributed components. That left us with choices, such as writing everything in a lower-level language like C++ or looking at different development and hosting environments. C++ just wasn't an option for many because it forced the developer to wrestle with the minutiae of COM and MTS.

Small groups of developers pushed ahead anyway and, quite soon, a critical mass of knowledge about building distributed applications with VB was accumulated. Microsoft still needed a catalyst to help VB catch on as a valid tool for developing distributed applications. So they wrapped this knowledge up in a concept called Distributed interNetwork Architecture or DNA.

> **In all fairness, I shouldn't give you the impression that DNA was strictly a way to promote VB as the tool of choice for developing distributed applications. DNA applied just as much to C++ or J++. However, it is clear that VB was the biggest benefactor of the DNA push from this group.**

Later chapters in this book will explain the DNA concept in more detail. The important thing to remember here is that DNA addressed the problems of VB's role as a client/server tool. It gave developers a road map for using COM+ and VB together to build distributed applications.

So, what lessons can we learn from this evolutionary step of VB? A key one would seem to be that the more we can fragment our solutions into discrete units of work, the more likely we are to be able to reuse them as components. It very much reinforces the idea of isolating functionality and providing interfaces to it. Another useful concept that COM+ and DNA can teach is that no matter how great an idea or component is, if other developers don't understand why it's great they won't use it. In practice then, it might be wise to use your documentation as an opportunity to "wag the dog" yourself.

Three other technologies have shaped the evolution of VB as well, and one other pushed it past its breaking point. They also offer us some food for thought.

Access

We noted earlier in this chapter that Access and VB have lived symbiotic lives. The earliest versions of VB were very much about providing rich client interfaces into Access databases via Jet and DAO and Access needed a language for developing applications within itself. Over time, Microsoft has pushed us away from Jet and DAO, which are specific to Access to more general components like ODBC, OLE-DB, and ADO. This allows VB to interact with data from virtually any Relational Database Management System (RDBMS).

Going forward, it seems clear that VB's role of being the best high-level programming language tool for working with databases is not likely to change. Nor is the need for localized data storage likely to go away. ADO.NET provides VB.NET with a great environment for doing just that.

SQL Server

Although Access is an ideal RDBMS in many ways, its design makes it far from ideal for use by large numbers of concurrent users. Access shares another common problem with VB: since it is primarily based on a form-driven concept, it's difficult to make it work in other ways. That makes sharing table designs (or data schemas as I also refer to them) much harder than it needs to be. But probably the most serious limitation of Access is that it tends to create numerous islands of repeated data in different locations, which may even have different schemas. Trying to bring even a few such databases together for combined use frequently becomes a Herculean task.

The best way to deal with problems like this is with an RDBMS product that supports large numbers of concurrent users over a network and uses common industry-standard approaches to doing tasks. Such products use the Structured Query Language (SQL) to do virtually everything from defining table schemas to the querying of data. Having a centralized data source tends to make the desirability of and need for isolated islands of data (like Access databases) far less common because it's easier to share important data with multiple users. In the Microsoft portfolio, that product is SQL Server. This product was first introduced in 1990 for OS/2 as the result of collaborations between Microsoft and Sybase. Clearly the rise in the importance of working with data in RDBMS is what drove the integration of MDAC into the VB developer's realm.

A key lesson learned from dealing with numerous Access and SQL Server Databases over the years is that the two should be seen as more complementary than competitive. Access, as an RDBMS, is used at its best when the amount of data to be dealt with is fairly small (a few megabytes in total) and only one or two users need to concurrently work with the data on a Local Area Network (LAN.) In just about every other case, it's proven best to move to a SQL Server based solution as soon as possible. The longer you leave valuable data in place, the more difficult it becomes to ever cleanly and simply move that data into a centralized data source.

Another completely acceptable use of Access in my opinion is to use it as an "administrative" front end to SQL Server data in the classic client/server architecture. This saves you a great deal of development effort so long as you don't need to enforce a lot of rules about the data and those rules are codified in COM+ hosted components.

ASP

It is hard to say that ASP has had a direct impact on VB as we know it today, short of Web Classes. Although ASP is commonly based on the VBScript dialect of VB, VB itself is seldom used in a web application. Very early on, there were techniques to invoke VB applications without form UIs via the Common Gateway Interface (CGI). That seemed to fizzle quickly when ASP came along and really hasn't been heard of since. Another seldom-used option was to write Internet Service Application Programming Interface (ISAPI) extensions and filters in VB. This API was really intended to be used only by C++ developers and, as such, provided endless challenges for the VB developer.

Indirectly, however, ASP has helped push VB from being a tool for just building the client parts of client/service applications to being a useful distributed component-building language.

In the long run, it appears that .NET blares out the death knell of ASP as we know it today and VB.NET might well be the cause of ASP's demise. In much the same way that VB1 effectively killed QBASIC and QuickBasic, the superior development environment offered by Visual Studio .NET's form-based approach has superceded the Visual Interdev approach to server-side web programming.

Simple Object Access Protocol – SOAP

If VB.NET's better development environment was the straw that broke the back of ASP, SOAP may very well be what will break Classic VB's back. To understand why, you need to understand why SOAP changes everything for the better. To understand the changes, you need to know a bit about SOAP and the problems that it tries to solve.

I've previously said that VB was a good thing to use to develop distributed multi-tier applications because it shields you from having to deal with a lot of things. A couple of those things are the messages that components use to communicate with each other and the "plumbing" in which the messages flow.

In a nutshell, when one component needs to interact with another, it must first work out where on the hosting computer the application is. It then needs to send information to and get information from the target component. The discovery process normally involves a registry lookup. In COM and the current versions of COM+, the messages and the messaging mechanism is based on either Interprocess Communication (IPC) if the target component is hosted on the same server, or Remote Procedure Calls (RPCs) otherwise. Both IPCs and RPCs in turn are based on very specific standards and protocols expressed into a binary form. IPC is generally quite fast and highly reliable. The performance and reliability of RPC is dominated by the performance and the reliability of the network connection between the involved computers. Given the characteristics of how RPC behaves on the network, it's normally only feasible to use RPC on local network segments.

OK, so if we have an explicit binary format, a registry dependence and poor network performance then how do we get RPC to work over a large network of poorly connected heterogeneous computers like, say, the Internet? To be blunt: You don't.

That's where SOAP comes in. In principle at least, SOAP is "RPC for Internetworks." Instead of having a binary standard for messages, SOAP uses XML. Instead of using network RPC calls only, SOAP is flexible enough to be transported over virtually any networking protocol. At the moment the protocol of preference is HTTP – the protocol of the World Wide Web.

SOAP is also the foundation of XML Web Services. What a Web Service amounts to is a distributed component hosted in COM+ with an HTTP interface. In the same way that we make an RPC to talk to an application component on a remote computer, we use SOAP and HTTP to do that to a Web Service.

So how exactly is SOAP going to break the back of VB then? You can really only appreciate this answer if you've actually tried writing a VB component that's intended to be a Web Service. It's a hard row to hoe because you have to deal with a lot of the messaging issues that VB hides for other components. You also have to deal with setting up a communications endpoint for your application to listen on. It is far more work than we're used to doing as VB programmers. From Microsoft's point of view, the harder they make something to do, the slower the developer community adopts it. That's just not an option in their minds when it comes to Web Services. However, since .NET was designed from the ground up with Web Services in mind, writing Web Services in VB.NET is a blissfully detail-ignorant thing.

> **I have a friend in Seattle who likes to make his own light bulbs.**
>
> Well, sort of anyway. More accurately, he really enjoys digging into the nuts and bolts of how everything works. We were having a discussion about the serialization of .NET classes so that they could be transported over an XML Web Service and then reconstructed on the client-side for use. At one point I said that while I could explain how passing a certain electrical current through a thin metal filament would excite that filament into emitting energy in the form of light and heat, it didn't mean that I should make my own light bulbs.
>
> In VB.NET, the generation of XML Web Services is more or less as simple as screwing a light bulb into the socket and flipping the power switch on. For most us, we'll be able to live our programming lives comfortably without knowing much more than that.
>
> However, if blissful ignorance isn't really your thing and you want to learn more about "how to make an XML Web Service light bulb" with VB6, the place to start is with the "SOAP Toolkit" in the MSDN download area. You can download both the toolkit and the example programs from:
>
> **http://msdn.microsoft.com/downloads/default.asp?url=/downloads/
> sample.asp?url=/msdn-files/027/001/948/msdncompositedoc.xml**

What Else is Important to Learn Now?

If there is any one thing that the professional VB programmer of today will need to learn to stay "in the game" for the next few years, it has got to be the Extensible Markup Language (XML) and its allied technologies. Microsoft has made working with XML in VB rather easy and feature-rich. For more information on this, see
http://msdn.microsoft.com/downloads/default.asp?url=/downloads/sample.asp?url=/msdn-files/027/001/766/msdncompositedoc.xml

Why so? First, it appears likely that XML will be a meaningful standard for expressing data in a universal way. Consider all of the sources of data you cope with today: Text files, SQL Server query results, Excel worksheets and just about anything else. The beauty of XML is that it allows virtually any data to be expressed in a consistent, well-formed way that's easily read into memory, parsed and worked with. In a fashion, XML is the ultimate format for importing and exporting data to and from an application. Second, thanks to the Extensible Stylesheet Language with Transformations (XSLT), it is possible to very quickly and easily transform one XML document format to another. XSLT allows you to generate virtually any other non-binary file format from an XML document. The most common application of that today is XML to HTML for display in a web browser, but I've also used XSLT for virtually everything from generate Perl scripts to do System Administration tasks to generating recipes for that cookbook I'm going to get around to writing someday. Understanding enough about how XML Schemas (XSD) generate a schema is also important. Schemas describe the proper syntax and semantics of an XML document and are used to validate XML documents to ensure that they meet all of the syntactic and semantic rules required to say the data is probably useful.

> **For a more detailed look at the differences between VB6 and VB.NET and a more thorough examination of the transition process between the two languages, please see Chapter 15.**

Summary

So now do you agree that the world as we know it today – at least as it applies to VB6 programming – will be dominated by .NET? And do you agree that it's a good thing?

The reason is that the VB6 world can evolve no further as it is. No matter how hard Microsoft tries to keep the VB we know and love today together, too many external forces are acting upon it. While VB has been unbelievably resilient, Microsoft's goal has always been to keep it simple. There is just no way to keep doing that with the advent of .NET and the coming era of Web Services. COM just isn't the right answer for the Internet-connected age. So VB needs to be reborn for this brave new world – what's familiar will become new again.

But what is new will also be what is familiar. We'll still have forms to work with. We'll have a depth of object-oriented techniques to employ and we'll have a great IDE to make our work easier. And our good knowledge of design patterns, event-driven programming, and good practices like isolation and interfacing will be around for us to take advantage of. As much as anything, this book will bring you up to speed on developing applications in VB6 while you plan and prepare for your evolving into a VB.NET programmer.

Knowing what events have caused the evolution in classic VB will help you see, predict, and react to future environmental changes better. Key ones have been:

- Changes to the hardware environment have signaled a change in what we look at when optimizing the code for performance.

- Changes in how data is stored and queried have resulted in the development of new data access technologies. That indicates that it's best to isolate the data access parts of programs to enable us to easily change those functions without disturbing the interfaces to those functions that our programs expect to be consistent.

- The change from client/server to multi-tier distributed components resulted in a whole new recommended architecture for our applications. Spending the time and effort to plan, write, document, and test componentized code will help position us best for future architectural preference changes.

- We can expect that Microsoft is going to keep introducing "new and improved" operating systems for us to contend with on a regular basis. That should tell us that we need to be careful to isolate those parts of our programs that are highly dependent on OS-specific functionality in such a way that they can be easily changed without affecting the rest of the application.

- Knowing what's in store will help you write applications that will either migrate smoothly or at least be highly sustainable in the future. We should expect change and design our applications to be reasonably flexible. When we have to make a change, we should make the change that gives the application the best long-term results. And when we make a change, try to constrain the change to a technological rather than a methodological one. Just because we went from DAO to ADO didn't mean that we shouldn't have a thoroughly documented understanding of how the data flows through our application.

- If you haven't already, most definitely add a solid understanding of XML, XSLT, and XML schemas to your portfolio.

p2p.wrox.com
The programmer's resource centre

ASP Today

wrox.com

wrox

wroxdirect

2

Visual Basic Designs

When creating software, there is nothing more important than choosing the right architecture and design. Even the best developers in the world will fail if they are given a faulty design or architecture. Windows DNA is a powerful tool for application design, but it is misunderstood and misused all too frequently.

It is critical to understand that n-tier applications are **logically** divided into tiers, not necessarily **physically** divided into tiers. A great many Windows DNA applications make use of extra physical tiers where none are needed – decreasing performance, increasing cost of maintenance, and generally resulting in poorly working, if not totally failed systems.

A solid understanding of logical versus physical architectures and how they relate is critical. Along with this, it is important to apply solid design principles to our software. A good way to do this is through design patterns, which embody the collective experience of those who have come before. Don't reinvent the wheel – take an existing wheel and adapt it to meet your needs.

Design in Visual Basic is more important now than it ever was. With Visual Basic 6 and Windows DNA, we have the ability to develop enterprise-scale applications that can have a lifespan of several years. Because of this, it is important that we, as developers, are disciplined and think ahead when approaching a new project. We will need to start by outlining our chosen methodology, moving on to determine the architecture most suitable for our needs, so that we are able to deliver a solution that meets the present and future requirements of the end user. Odds are, we will also be responsible for maintaining the application, fixing bugs, and developing its capabilities further, so good design can be of direct benefit to us as well. This chapter aims to help in this process, and we begin with a refresher of formal and informal methodologies. Next we discuss architecture choices, and finally, we finish up with design patterns, concentrating on those that work well with VB6.

Development Methodologies

Incorporating a methodology into the development process is crucial for success. Our methodology establishes the approach that we follow when building applications. It helps identify lengths and costs of tasks, and can expose potential roadblocks that may be missed otherwise.

We won't have a full discussion here, as you will probably already have a preferred application development methodology, either from your personal programming experience, or because your company has an established methodology of its own.

In this section, we will simply take a quick overview of the Structured Formal Methodology (SFM), which outlines phases that can be applied to any development task. Afterwards, we'll have a quick look at its more practical cousin, the Unstructured Casual Methodology, or UCM.

A Structured Formal Methodology

In the ideal world, we would have adequate funds, resources, and time to complete any given project. We would be able to invest plenty of time to the early design stages, and we would be able to implement a well-defined methodology at every stage.

Such a well-defined methodology would typically cover five key phases in sequence:

1. Gathering

2. Suggesting

3. Developing

4. Implementing

5. Maintaining/Evolving

Gathering Phase

The first phase is a period where we gather rules and requirements for the application. We need to determine exactly who the end users are to be, including occasional users along with those that will use the product every day. We need to create a clear idea of their expectations and requirements, in order to quantify the application's goals and intended deliverables. The technology and architecture that might be most appropriate are consciously left out of the thinking at this stage.

Suggesting Phase

The suggesting phase is when a practical course of action is established and appropriate technology and architecture for implementing the solution are recommended. The User Interface (UI) might be prototyped at this point to give the project sponsors an idea of what they can expect. Functional and technical specifications are established as well as the precise business requirements. A timetable with estimated delivery dates is drawn up.

Developing Phase

For most developers, the developing phase is the highlight of the process. It is when we start constructing the individual tiers (more on this later), and implement the data, business, and UI rules for the application. This phase includes debugging and testing, and making revisions and tweaks to overcome shortcomings that are highlighted.

Implementing Phase

Most developers will agree that the implementing phase is less exciting than the developing phase. It is when the application is deployed into the production environment for release. Final documentation for the application is also created at this time, and helpdesk scripts are created if required. Last of all, a post mortem is conducted with all concerned, to discuss what parts of the process went well and what areas could have been improved upon.

Maintaining/Evolving Phase

The maintaining and evolving phase is of course an ongoing process. Most applications require maintenance from time to time, such as shrinking a SQL Server database, clearing out caches, and fixing bugs that were not caught in the developing phase.

Updates that are required to reflect changing business requirements or user feedback are considered more of an evolution. Generally, minor revisions will be considered as part of the maintaining and evolving phase, while major changes are usually best treated as a new project.

The Casual Methodology

As you have probably experienced by now in your development career, we usually lack the time, resources, or money to follow the structure of the methodology introduced above. In such cases, we scale back the idealized case, and cut certain phases from the process.

The suggesting phase is usually the first to go, and we often move directly to the developing phase, relying on our experience from previous projects. The implementing phase may also be altered. While the application will still have to be deployed, documentation can often be generated as we progress through the developing phase. Frequently, the post mortem is skipped, leaving the developer to learn from their experience on their own. This cut-down methodology really only consists of three phases:

- ❑ Gathering
- ❑ Developing
- ❑ Implementing

Each of these phases is roughly the same when following a casual methodology as for the more formal methodology discussed above, except that the Gathering and Suggesting phases are combined and simplified. Feedback is still crucial to the application, but the architects and designers make more assumptions. Also, the implementing phase is reduced, as mentioned above.

Architecture Considerations

Visual Basic applications have evolved greatly over the last 10 years. For my part, I started developing in Visual Basic 3, when every application was a cumbersome, standalone executable that required users to install the VBRUN.DLL runtime, which weighed in at what seemed to be a decadently large 400 Kb (!).

Over the years since then, Visual Basic has come a long way, offering more sophisticated architectures, design possibilities – and headaches – for developers to contend with. Two different strategies for application design have emerged – we either dive straight in using a rapid application development (RAD) methodology, or we follow a more measured formal approach.

The RAD approach, which some might call "winging it", involves addressing design issues on the fly, as and when we encounter them. This strategy will usually get you into trouble sooner or later, and in general, it is preferable to take the formal approach. While this is more complex, as we need to weigh up the options in advance, picking the optimum architecture on the basis of an analysis of the problem at hand, it offers benefits as we'll see later in the chapter.

"Winging It"

Visual Basic is a procedural language that has been designed for RAD solutions. We don't have to spend precious time modeling components or objects; we can simply start developing. We sacrifice quality for speed of development. Very few developers can use this approach successfully, but it has definite value for prototyping an application, as it doesn't take much time and the code doesn't have to be "pretty". To get a clearer idea of the pitfalls, let's consider a simple fictional application.

An application is required for a Human Resources department to edit personnel files. Following a RAD design, the application was produced as a web-based UI with all of the functionality for business rules mixed in with UI code in ASP pages. Each ASP page has its own code to communicate with an Access 2000 database on a server, selecting, inserting, updating, and deleting employee data via recordsets. Such an application may well work fine up to a point. However, what if the database gets too big, and needs to be migrated to SQL Server, residing on a different server? The developer would have to trawl through each page, updating every reference to the database to the new configuration. Similarly, what if too many users start using the application and it becomes slow and unresponsive? A solution would be to rewrite the business and data logic as ActiveX components and stored procedures that can be placed on different server to share processing. Again, the task would be an arduous and error-prone one for the hapless developer. The same would be true for any changes that might be required – such an application is doomed to become a nightmare both for the developer and the users, as changes will often not be practical to implement.

As such applications grow, they become harder and harder to maintain and debug. Such code will rarely scale well, and it is being used very inefficiently, as most of it is scrapped each time the requirements changed. As you can see, this type of approach can be a real nightmare, and can often consume more man-hours in the long run than a similar application built on a more formal and robust design.

The problems of this sort of design led to the idea of modularity, where applications are divided into several modules, each module with a clear and distinct purpose. This is altogether a much more efficient use of programmer's time – modules are easier to debug, and can be reused in multiple applications. In addition, the approach makes applications more extensible, as new features can be added much more easily. Modular applications are inherently more scalable, as modules can readily be deployed to different servers.

Application Architectures

Application architecture represents the high-level design that an application will follow, and the choice made must aim to satisfy the business requirements as best as possible given the limitations of the system available. It is also important to factor in the limitations of the development team itself; for instance, a VB team with no experience of building ActiveX components will probably have trouble with anything beyond the one-tier.

The basic server architecture is the well-known client-server model, where a client computer interacts with an application running on a single remote server. The client-server model extends naturally to a more sophisticated model, where the server application is itself distributed over several locations, or **tiers**. Each tier encompasses a logical grouping of services. For instance, the presentation services tier contains functionality that relates to the user interface, and the business services tier houses components that apply business logic to application data.

The Three-Tier Model

The three-tier model is one of the most common architectures found in business applications today. Each of the three tiers is responsible for performing presentation, business, or data services.

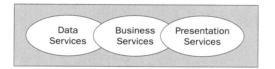

The data tier handles all access to application data. The data services typically return data to the services residing in the business tier, but they can return data directly to the presentation services as well.

The business tier encapsulates all of the business logic that the application can apply. For example, for an employee application like that mentioned above, the business tier would perform services such as calculating wages and vacation time. It might include logic such as `Vacation = x days after y years of service`, which in turn uses queries that reside in the data services tier, such as `SELECT * FROM Employees`. The business tier takes data from the data tier, manipulates it, and sends it to the presentation tier for display.

The presentation tier handles the application's UI, through which the end user navigates and manipulates data. Data validation also occurs in this tier. For example, if the user is manipulating an employee's profile, before the data is passed to the business services, the presentation services validate the data to make sure the user has entered all necessary fields and has also entered the proper value types for appropriate fields. This avoids an unnecessary call to the business services.

Splitting functionality into services that have a distinct purpose like this makes debugging and maintaining these applications much more manageable. If an error is detected where a database table is being updated incorrectly, it is much simpler to track down the offending component, as we would know it would reside in the data tier.

The services can all run on a single machine, or be distributed according to the systems they interact with. For instance, it may be more appropriate to have a separate server for the data tier, another for the business tier, and so on. This flexibility lets us create applications that are scalable, extensible, and which perform well. Applications can reside on one physical tier, two physical tiers, three physical tiers, or *n* physical tiers. An *n*-tier application simply means that one of the three tiers of the three-tier model is broken down further into smaller, but still distinct, tiers.

Logical vs. Physical

The tiers can reflect the physical network topography of the application. From a Visual Basic design perspective, it makes more sense for us to talk about the logical architecture implementation. We are more concerned with the modularity of our code than where it will physically reside. Before we can select the best logical architecture for a project, we need to define a few parameters first.

We need to determine where the data will be persisted (if at all). Will it be persisted at the client or at the server? How the users will interact with the system needs to be determined. Will we have a rich or thin client? Will the client be a Windows-based application, or a browser-based application? There are other considerations as well, such as scalability, security, reliability, multi-platform, and deliverables, which will be discussed later. Once these considerations have been dealt with, we can begin the process of choosing our logical architecture.

Single-Tier Physical Model

One option is to place all three services in the same physical tier. In this model, no special protocol is necessary to communicate between the services. Note, though, that even though the services exist on the same physical tier, the actual database may exist on a separate machine.

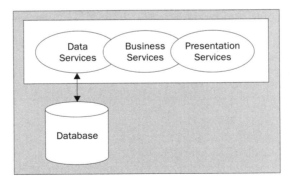

Below is an example of a web-based application in which all of the functionality resides in the same module on the same tier:

```
<%@ Language=VBScript %>
<%
dim objCmd : set objCmd = Server.CreateObject("ADODB.Command")
dim objRS : set objRS = Server.CreateObject("ADODB.Recordset")
dim intI : intI = 0
dim intCurrRow : intCurrRow = 1
dim strHTML : strHTML = vbNullString
```

```vb
dim strBG : strBG = vbNullString
dim strOrder : strOrder = vbNullString

  'Beginning of code that belongs in the data tier
  if StrComp(Request.QueryString("Order"), vbNullString) <> 0 then
    strOrder = "ORDER BY " & Request.QueryString("Order")
  end if

  'Set the command object properties
  objCmd.ActiveConnection = "Provider=SQLOLEDB.1;Initial
   Catalog=Northwind;Data Source=localhost;uid=sa;"
  objCmd.CommandText = "SELECT EmployeeID, LastName, FirstName FROM " _
                    & "EMPLOYEES " & strOrder
  objCmd.CommandType = adCmdText

  'set the recordset object properties and retrieve the records
  objRS.CursorLocation = adUseClient
  objRS.Open objCmd, , adOpenForwardOnly, adLockReadOnly

  'destroy unused objects
  Set objCmd.ActiveConnection = Nothing
  Set objCmd = Nothing


  'Beginning of code that belongs in the presentation tier
  if not(objRS.EOF and objRS.BOF) then
    objRS.MoveFirst
    'loop through the recordset and create the table rows for output
    do until objRS.EOF
      'alternate background colors for the rows to make them more readable
      if intCurrRow mod 2 = 0 then
        strBG = "#ffffff"
      else
        strBG = "#cccccc"
      end if
      'create the html string
      strHTML = strHTML & "<tr bgcolor='" & strBG & "'><td>" _
              & objRS.Fields("EmployeeID").Value & "</td>"
      strHTML = strHTML & "<td>" & objRS.Fields("LastName").Value & "</td>"
      strHTML = strHTML & "<td>" & objRS.Fields("FirstName").Value _
              & "</td></tr>"
      objRS.MoveNext
      intCurrRow = intCurrRow + 1
    loop
  end if

  Set objRS = Nothing
%>
<html>
<head>
<meta name="GENERATOR" content="Microsoft Visual Studio 6.0">
</head>
<body>
```

```
<!-- Start table to display the employee information -->
<table cellpadding="0" cellspacing="0" border="1" width="600">
  <tr>
    <th><a href="DisplayEmployees2.asp?Order=EmployeeID">
        Employee ID</a></th>
    <th><a href="DisplayEmployees2.asp?Order=LastName">Last Name</a></th>
    <th><a href="DisplayEmployees2.asp?Order=FirstName">First Name</a></th>
    <%= strHTML %>
  </tr>
</table>
<!-- End table to display the employee information -->

</body>
</html>
```

To run this sample, simply copy the source code below into a Visual Studio project ASP page and name the page `DisplayEmployees.asp`. Select **Project | Project References** from the Visual Studio menu, and check the **Microsoft ActiveX Data Objects 2.6 Library**. Then save your changes and point your browser to the page you created:

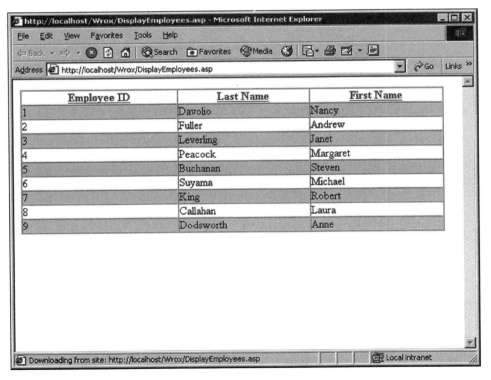

Two-Tier Physical Model

The two-tier physical model, or client-server model, is probably the most common. There are two variations on this theme, depending on the sophistication of our client. In the case of the **rich client**, the client contains the presentation services and the business services, while the server houses the data services and the database.

If the business services co-exist with the data services on the server, we have a **thin client**. The communication mechanism between the two tiers is typically the database connection, which typically uses the TCP/IP protocol:

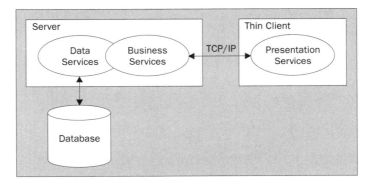

Three-Tier Physical Model

In a three-tier model, the three service layers are separated into three physical tiers. This architecture gives developers a tremendous amount of flexibility when architecting an application. The three-tier approach also gives developers:

❑ More scalability, extensibility, and reusability in an application

❑ Enhanced maintainability compared to a one- or two-tier application

❑ More granular security options for a developer within the different tiers

This physical model does carry a potential performance penalty, as communication between the tiers of an application can now become subject to network delays.

The three-tier physical model is often confused with the three-tier logical model. Developers sometimes refer to an application as a three-tier logical model when in fact they mean a three-tier physical model. I have also heard developers also make the mistake of equating the three-tier logical model with the three-tier physical model. As the preceding two diagrams show, it is possible to have a three-tier logical model built on a one- or two-tier physical model.

N-Tier Physical Model

The *n*-tier model is an extension of the three-tier physical model. This architecture splits up the three tiers into additional tiers, to create another degree of separation. This architecture is the most extensible and scalable of all of the models we looked at.

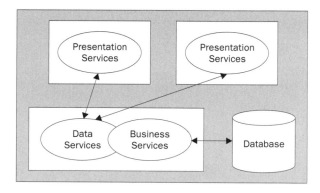

Microsoft Windows DNA

The Microsoft Windows Distributed interNet Architecture (DNA) is a multi-tiered distributed model, which emphasizes **cooperating components** (common, component-based application architecture). Its primary benefits are:

❑ Applications can utilize the Internet's communication capabilities.

❑ Application architecture tiers are even more extensible.

❑ Other applications are more easily integrated into your application.

When following the Microsoft Windows DNA approach, we have available to us some services that enhance our applications that are otherwise unavailable in a non-Microsoft solution. COM+ (Component Services) helps to create more scalable and transactional components. MSMQ (Messaging Services) can be used for reliable, asynchronous communications. Finally, IIS (Web Application Services) helps us create reliable, robust Internet-based applications. These are just a few advantages to using the DNA architecture.

Integration Considerations

When modeled and built properly, applications can distribute processing over many machines. This encourages scalability, manageability, and maintainability.

Component Object Model (COM+)

Creating reusable components is the underlying concept of COM+, the Component Object Model. The compiled binary modules that COM+ produces are the basis for most multi-tier applications currently in service in enterprise. These modules encapsulate related functionality into logical objects exposed through interfaces that communicate with each other and other services and applications. We discuss COM+ in detail in Chapter 8.

It is COM+ that enables VB developers to build multi-tier applications with components that can exist on any tier. COM+ components can be written in one of several languages, including Visual Basic and C++, and yet still work seamlessly with applications written in any other language. COM+ components use a local inter-process communication method to "talk" to one another, and DCOM extends this idea to allow components to reside on remote tiers yet integrate seamlessly.

Distributed Component Object Model (DCOM)

The Distributed Component Object Model (DCOM), discussed in Chapter 11, dictates how COM+ components on one physical tier can communicate with COM+ components on another physical tier and in separate processes. In essence, DCOM intercepts calls to a component and forwards those requests to the proper tier and component, using a standard network protocol. If DCOM is not permissible between the components (perhaps due to firewall restrictions or other reasons) XML and web services may help you.

XML

The Extensible Markup Language (XML) is a data format that allows developers to deliver rich, flexible data to applications running on just about any platform. We cover it and some key related standards in detail in Chapter 13, but in short, XML is a markup language that describes data, using tags similar to those found in HTML. Unlike HTML, the tags are really only useful to a developer or an application that has the knowledge to interpret a particular set of tags. Below is an example of a typical XML file:

```xml
<?xml version="1.0"?>
<employees>
  <employee id="1" type="full-time" FirstName="Joe" LastName="Smith">
    <phone type="home">952.555.1212</phone>
    <phone type="cell">612.555.9300</phone>
    <address type="home">
      <street>123 Main Street</street>
      <city>Anytown</city>
      <region>MN</region>
      <postalcode>55355</postalcode>
    </address>
  <employee>
  <employee id="2" type="part-time" FirstName="Sam" LastName="Wells">
    <phone type="home">952.555.0400</phone>
    <address type="home">
      <street>456 Harbor Road</street>
      <city>Anytown</city>
      <region>MN</region>
      <postalcode>55455</postalcode>
    </address>
  <employee>
  <employee id="3" type="full-time" FirstName="Joe" LastName="Smith">
    <phone type="home">952.555.7782</phone>
    <phone type="cell">612.555.1120</phone>
    <address type="home">
      <street>9001 Corner Road</street>
      <city>Anytown</city>
      <region>MN</region>
      <postalcode>53455</postalcode>
```

```
    </address>
  <employee>
</employees>
```

XML can be used to pass different data types from tier to tier, regardless of the protocol required by the intervening network connections. XML's text format allows it to be interpreted by a very wide range of applications, making it ideal for situations where you do not know the exact nature of applications that will use your components.

Web Services

Web services are leading the charge in the distributed computing movement's invasion of the Internet. Web services, specifically XML Web Services, are quickly surpassing DCOM and ORB to become the medium of choice for passing data in distributed applications, and we'll look at them in Chapter 14. When disparate applications (applications written in a different language and/or on multiple platforms) cannot communicate via traditional methods, XML and web services become a very viable solution. Visual Basic makes it easy to implement XML Web Services, built on the Simple Object Access Protocol (SOAP). IIS listens for incoming requests for the web service, which are transmitted over HTTP using SOAP. When such a request comes in, the web service's Web Service Description Language (WSDL) file associates web service methods to their underlying COM+ component interfaces. The association helps SOAP to translate the web service request into a call to COM+ components. The response from the COM+ component is then sent back to the originator of the request, with all communications being made in various formats of Internet-friendly and firewall-friendly XML over HTTP.

Design Patterns in Visual Basic 6

Design patterns are typically reserved for object-oriented programming languages. While Visual Basic 6 is not a true object-oriented programming language, there are some design patterns that are nevertheless very applicable. In this section, we investigate those patterns that can assist development of VB6 applications.

What is a Design Pattern?

A **design pattern** can be defined as a common answer to an object-oriented design problem that can be applied when modeling application objects. The patterns help to persist relationships between objects and their classes and interfaces. Each unique design pattern has a purpose – it solves a specific object-oriented design problem.

Don't forget that a design pattern is simply a *conceptual* solution to a problem, *not an actual* implementation of the solution. So for instance, if we've decided to create a database component using the **singleton** design pattern to limit the number of times it can be instantiated to one, we would have a clearer idea of how our design will go, but the details of implementing the pattern are up to us.

Design Pattern Origins

Design patterns are relatively new, having origins that can be traced back to the early 1990s. In 1994, a group of four people – Erich Gamma, Richard Helm, Ralph Johnson, and John Vlissides – wrote a book called *Design Patterns, Elements of Reusable Object-Oriented Software* (Addison-Wesley, ISBN 0-201-63361-2), which has become a pattern "bible" among object-oriented developers. Due to the success of this book, the authors eventually became known as the *Gang of Four* (or *GoF*) – the patterns defined in this section are commonly referred to as **GoF patterns**.

Benefits of Design Patterns

There are several benefits that design patterns can bring when modeling applications. They can make an object model more extensible and maintainable. Without using design patterns, code classes tend to multiply as we add functionality to satisfy requirements, making them difficult to keep track of and update. Design patterns help keep the code base down and avoid redundancy. Design patterns also give the developer more control over object creation. There are a few patterns that specifically address different object creation.

Applying Design Patterns to Visual Basic

Design patterns are intended to be implemented within the context of object-oriented programming, and as we all know, Visual Basic 6 is *not* a truly object-oriented programming language. Therefore, some patterns do not work at all, while others are somewhat of a work-around implementation. A good example of a design pattern that does work well in Visual Basic 6 is the Singleton design pattern.

The Singleton Design Pattern

The intent of this design pattern is to ensure that a specified class can only be instantiated once, and to provide global references to that one class. There is no built-in functionality in Visual Basic 6 to prohibit a calling component from creating multiple instances of a class. However, if we implement the Singleton design pattern, we can limit the number of class instantiations to one. After the class has been instantiated, a reference to the existing class is returned.

One of the best examples of where a Singleton design pattern is useful is in handling database connections. Let's pretend for a minute that you have a database application and that you want to limit the number of connections to one. How could you control the number of connections in this way? The sample code below shows how the Singleton design pattern can be applied to this end:

```
Option Explicit

'Global module that is accessed by many classes that need to
'communicate with the database.
Private m_objConn As ADODB.Connection

'Implementation of the GetConnection method in the module that is called
'by any class that need to make a db call
Public Function GetConnection() As ADODB.Connection

  'Check to see if the connection objects exists
  'If it does, return a reference to it instead of creating
```

```
      'a new one
   If m_objConn Is Nothing Then
     Set m_objConn = New ADODB.Connection
   End If

     Set GetConnection = m_objConn

End Function
```

With a Visual Basic client, this Singleton design pattern works adequately. With a non-Visual Basic client, the Singleton design implementation may fail. If a client for your object may be written in a language other than Visual Basic, it is recommended that you set the Threading Model option of the ActiveX DLL to Single Threaded on the General tab of the Project Properties dialog box, shown in the screenshot below. This ensures that all instances will exist in the same COM+ apartment.

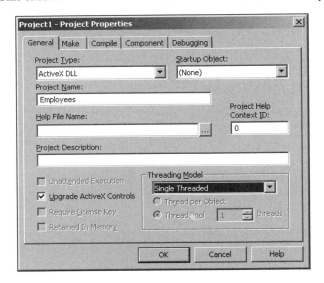

The Repository Design Pattern

With the introduction of concepts such as distributed computing, web-farms, and load balancing, came the issue of maintaining object state. How do we maintain state information between calls to an object that is state unaware? The Repository design pattern emerged to handle that exact problem. While the Repository design pattern is not specifically a GoF pattern, it still requires our attention as a decent design pattern for Visual Basic 6 development. This design pattern models interfaces that allow an object's state to be persisted to a data store, which is especially useful for web-based applications. There are three main objectives of the Repository design pattern:

1. To persist object state at a given moment in time

2. To retrieve object state from a given moment in time

3. To abstract implementations required to persist and retrieve the state of an object from a data store to make it reusable across applications

State management can be difficult to implement in a load-balanced environment in Visual Basic 6, especially when server requests are based on a least-connection or round-robin rule. The Repository design pattern removes the state management process from the presentation layer into a separate one, greatly simplifying the developer's task. In web applications, this means replacing session variables with a custom session management component or components. For instance, we may have a component that would insert, update, delete, and fetch session data from a data store, using a Globally Unique Identifier (GUID) stored on the client's computer in the form of a cookie. An example of this concept can be seen in the code sample below.

This sample ASP could be used to maintain state for a web-based application. The code references an object named objState. Towards the beginning of the code, a GUID is created if need be and a variable is used to handle some "session" data (pre-populated for the purpose of this example with a dummy XML string). The XML string is then passed off to a function, persistSessionData, for processing. Finally, the function executes a method on the objState object to persist the string to the database. Notice that no session variables are used. This allows the client to maintain state without having a constant connection to the web server.

```vbscript
<%@ Language=VBScript %>
<object id="objState" runat="server" scope="page"
progID="userState.clsStateMgt"></object>
<%
option explicit
dim m_strGUID    : m_strGUID = vbNullString
dim m_strSession : m_strSession = vbNullString

  'Retrieve the user's GUID
  m_strGUID = Trim(Request.Cookies("GUID"))

  'Create the user's GUID
  if (m_strGUID = vbNullString) then
    m_strGUID = objState.createGUID
  end if

  m_strSession = "<state><name>Bill Smith</name></state>"

  'Persist GUID to the client's cookie
  Response.Cookies("GUID") = m_strGUID


  Call persistSessionData(m_strGUID, m_strSession)

'*****************************************************************
sub clearSessionData()
'Executes the object's method that deletes data from the database
  objState.clear(strGUID)

end sub
'*****************************************************************
sub persistSessionData(strGUID, strData)
'Executes the object's method that writes data to the database
  objState.persist(strGUID, strData)
```

```
end sub
'*****************************************************************
function readSessionData(strGUID)
'Executes the object's method that retrieves data from the database
  readSessionData = objState.read(strGUID)

end function
'*****************************************************************
%>
```

Below is an example of the objState component and the interfaces it may need to handle the state management for the ASP page above. This code would reside in an object named userState, with a class named clsStateMgt. As you can see by the interfaces defined, the state is maintained in a database and is referenced via a GUID.

```
Option Explicit

Public Function persist(ByVal strGUID As String, ByVal strData As String) As
Boolean
'Function that persists data to the database by passing in the state
'string (formatted in XML) and the user's GUID for later reference

    ' functionality to persist data to the database ...

End Function

Public Function read(strGUID) As String
'Function that returns data to the client as an xml string
'based on the user's GUID

    ' functionality to retrieve data from the database ...

End Function

Public Function createGUID() As String
'Function that creates a new GUID and returns
'it to the client

    ' functionality to create GUID ...

End Function


Public Function clear(strGUID) As Boolean
'Function that clears the state "session" data from
'the database

    ' functionality to delete data from the database ...

End Function
```

The Adapter Design Pattern

The Adapter design pattern converts one interface to another, in order to make it consistent with related objects. This is necessary when we have a group of objects with a single interface, and we then introduce a new object with a different interface, but which accomplishes the same task. Let's illustrate this with a simple example.

Say you have built a component named `objEmployees` that lets us interact with employee data in the data store through a class it exposes called `clsEmployee`. It contains a function named `Update` that takes the following parameters: `lngID`, `strFirstName`, `strLastName`, and `dblHourlyWage`:

```
Option Explicit

Public Function Update(ByVal lngID As Long, ByVal strFirstName As String, _
                       ByVal strLastName As String, _
                       ByVal dblHourlyWage As Double) _
                       As Boolean

   ' code to update employee information in the database here...
   Update = True

End Function
```

You have been told that your new parent company will want you to eventually be able to update their employee database as well. Without knowing the interface for their object, how can this be done?

First, you would create a single COM+ component, perhaps called `EmployeeUtils`, with a class called `clsEmployeeUtils`, as shown below.

```
Option Explicit
Private m_strCompanyName As String
```

This class would have a property named `CompanyName`:

```
Public Property Get CompanyName() As String

   CompanyName = m_strCompanyName

End Property

Public Property Let CompanyName(ByVal strNewValue As String)

   m_strCompanyName = strNewValue

End Property
```

and a method called `Update`:

```
Public Function Update(ByVal lngID As Long, ByVal strFName As String, _
                       ByVal strLName As String, ByVal dblWage As Double) _
                       As Boolean
```

```
Dim objEmployees As Object
Dim blnSuccess As Boolean

'Instantiate the proper object based on the CompanyName object
If m_strCompanyName = "XYZ" Then
  Set objEmployees = New clsEmployee

'Instantiate the class that acts as the adapter to the objAcmeEmployee
'component class
ElseIf m_strCompanyName = "Acme" Then
  Set objEmployees = New clsPCEmployee
End If

blnSuccess = objEmployees.Update(lngID, strFName, strLName, dblWage)

Update = blnSuccess

End Function
```

Depending on what the CompanyName property is set to, the component will instantiate either your component, or the parent company's component. However, instead of interfacing directly with the parent company's component, which may or may not have an Update method, you apply the Adapter design pattern to this problem and create an intermediate component, called, say, objPCEmployees:

```
Option Explicit

Public Function Update(ByVal lngID As Long, ByVal strFirstName As String, _
                ByVal strLastName As String, _
                ByVal dblYearlyWage As Double) _
                As Boolean

  Dim dblNewWage As Double
  Dim objAcmeEmployee As New objAcmeEmployees.clsAcmeEmployee
  Dim blnSuccess As Boolean

  'Create an approximate hourly wage based on the average number of hours
  ' worked per year
  dblNewWage = dblYearlyWage / 1920
  blnSuccess = objAcmeEmployee.UpdateEmployees(lngID, strFirstName, _
                                      strLastName, dblNewWage)

  Update = blnSuccess

End Function
```

This new component will also have an Update method, taking the same parameters as the one in the objEmployees component. If the parent company's component has a different interface or parameters, the adaptation will occur within the objPCEmployees.Update method, which would then instantiate the parent company's component (using the reference to objAcmeEmployees shown above) and execute its UpdateEmployees method:

```
Option Explicit

Public Function UpdateEmployees(ByVal lngID As Long, _
                                ByVal strFirstName As String, _
                                ByVal strLastName As String, _
                                ByVal dblYearlySalary As Double) _
                                As Boolean

    'Code to update Acme companies employees database here
    UpdateEmployees = True

End Function
```

A shortcoming of applying the Adapter design pattern to a Visual Basic component is that the adapted class (objAcmeEmployees in this case) can still be instantiated. Unfortunately, we cannot control the component's creation. We can and should, however, control who instantiates the clsEmployee and clsPCEmployee classes by setting the Instancing property to 1 – Private, so only clsEmployeeUtils can instantiate the two classes:

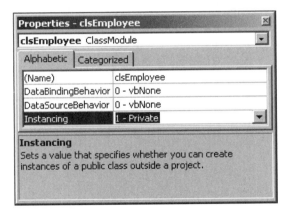

Thus, except for the one caveat of instantiation, the Adapter pattern can be reasonably implemented in VB6.

The Abstract Factory Design Pattern

The purpose of the Abstract Factory design pattern is to create an interface for instantiating components that are very similar to each other. The instantiating of the components actually occurs in the classes that implement this interface. The pattern can be beneficial in the following scenarios:

❑   When the client needs to be unaware to the classes of components that represent an interface used by the client.

❑   When control over the component creation process is required. This process is normally out of our control because the New keyword or the CreateObject method allow other code to instantiate our component almost anywhere.

The Abstract Factory design pattern allows the client to use classes that implement an interface without knowing full details of the class's properties in advance. As a result, classes can be modified to introduce new functionality into the client, without any changes being required on the client. This type of implementation represents the ideal for real-world production applications.

Summary

To be a successful developer, you need a disciplined approach or methodology to how you handle development tasks. It all starts with the methodology. The design can follow a formal, structured plan, or you can follow a less formal, unstructured approach. Which you choose for any given situation will be a tradeoff between doing things properly and by the book, with the safeguards and future-proofing that that offers, and just getting things done acceptably in the time you have available. Making the correct choice when deciding which right design considerations to forego for a project can be make-or-break.

For an application to be successful, one of the determining factors is to pick the right architecture. Which architecture is the most suitable will depend on how scalable, extensible, and maintainable the application needs to be. While the most common architecture is the two-tier application, the most scalable and extensible is the n-tier approach.

We can make use of established patterns to aide us in solving development problems that arise. Design patterns are very useful when modeling an application's objects. We looked at a few of the patterns that have arisen out of work done by the GoF to categorize recurrent object modeling problems. The patterns we described can help in building solutions that are maintainable as well as highly extensible, and they can help our applications become useable and reliable tools in our clients' workplaces.

p2p.wrox.com

The programmer's resource centre

ASP Today

wrox.com

wroxdirect

3

The Basics of ADO

Throughout the existence of Visual Basic, Microsoft has come out with a new data access technology every two to three years. First we had DAO, then RDO, then various versions of ActiveX Data Objects (ADO). The next step is ADO.NET. Of all the data access technologies to date, ADO has had the longest reign, trouncing even DAO from the days of VB3.

This chapter gives a whirlwind introduction to ADO. We'll focus on the objects exposed, and on the properties, methods, and events of those objects. There is a lot of value to be had in learning and understanding the basic model of ADO – almost all business applications use data, and ADO encapsulates access to that data. The key to successful implementation of a business system often lies directly with effective implementation of data access code.

In this chapter, we will cover:

- ❑ The ADO object model
- ❑ How to open a connection to the database (and how to close it when you've finished!)
- ❑ Using a command to query the database
- ❑ Using a recordset to manipulate data
- ❑ Cursor types and lock types
- ❑ Using VB controls with ADO

A Quick History of ADO

When Microsoft Visual Studio 98 was released, a new data management mechanism was introduced, called Universal Data Access. Part of this ambitious project included the ActiveX Data Objects classes created to facilitate database management. It was the first ADO library, version: 2.0.

During the following years, the needs of developers induced Microsoft to release new ADO library versions. The first was ADO 2.1, released with Microsoft SQL Server 7.0. This brought significant new features such as ADOX components, an OLE DB Remote Provider to retrieve data from a remote server using DCOM and the HTTP protocol, and a new ODBC driver for Microsoft Access.

> *The ADOX library contains a set of classes that are useful for executing Data Definition Language (DDL) instructions. It contains everything needed to change a database schema, create and modify tables, stored procedures and so on.*

The next ADO release was version 2.5, shipped with Microsoft Windows 2000. It introduced two new classes: Record and Stream. The former is a sort of lightweight recordset that can contain just a one-row record. It is really useful when your query to the database returns just one record such as when using an aggregate function like SUM or COUNT. The latter manages streams of text and binary bytes and is particularly useful in managing XML streams retrieved from recent OLE DB providers such as the Microsoft SQL Server 2000 one. A lot of work has been accomplished by Microsoft developers in an effort to integrate XML with the ADO recordset. This version allows developers to save recordsets into streams and persist hierarchical recordsets into XML format.

With Microsoft SQL Server 2000, a new ADO library version was released: 2.6. Other than resolving some previous version bugs this version improved Stream class and ADO MD object functionalities.

> *Microsoft ActiveX Data Objects Multidimensional (ADO MD) object extends the ADO library to manage multidimensional data such as CubeDef and Cellset objects.*

The ADO library has now reached version 2.7, which ships with Microsoft Windows XP. The unique new feature of this version is support for 64-bit systems.

There is a lot to learn about ADO, but this chapter should give you enough to get you underway. You can use the complete ADO object model description in Appendix D to get a better idea of the full set of keywords and functionality offered by ADO – and as you get to use it more, you'll become familiar with the syntax. Before long, you should be well placed to use ADO quite effectively.

The ADO Object Model

There's a good chance that you've already seen the ADO object model in one form or another. Lots of developers have copies of the ADO object model poster hanging up in their offices and cubicles. And yet, folks seem not to understand how it works or how they can use it to their advantage. If you have one of those posters, don't tear it down yet. By the end of this chapter, that poster will make sense to you, and you will be able to use it as a reference.

There are three main objects in ADO:

- ❑ The Connection object, which is designed to handle the connection to the database
- ❑ The Command object, which is designed to help us handle SQL commands
- ❑ The Recordset object, which we use to hold data and to manipulate it

In addition to these three main objects, ADO makes use of four subsidiary objects – `Property`, `Error`, `Parameter` and `Field` – and four associated collections, which are used to access these subsidiary objects.

The following diagram should give you an idea of how all these objects and collections relate to one another. We'll take a closer look at each of the objects in turn later in the chapter:

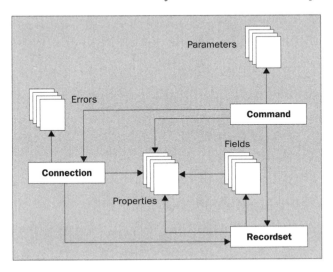

Object Hierarchy

It's probably most effective to think of ADO as having a 2-level hierarchy, with the three main ADO objects in the top layer and the four subsidiary objects in the bottom layer.

Connection, Command and Recordset Objects

Essentially, in order to talk to the database, you need to establish a connection to it. Therefore, the `Connection` object is sometimes perceived to be alone at the very 'root' of the hierarchy, with the `Command` and `Recordset` objects coming after it.

In practice, however, you can connect to the database without creating an explicit `Connection` object in your code. For example, you can use a `Recordset` object to fetch some data from a database. In this case, instead of using an explicit `Connection` object in your code, you can simply tell the `Recordset` what the connection details are – and the `Recordset` will go away and create an implicit connection behind the scenes.

And later, you can make that implicit connection into an explicit `Connection` object in your code (by using the `Recordset` object's `ActiveConnection` property). So, in terms of using the three main ADO objects in your code, the hierarchy is essentially flat. It's designed so that your code doesn't need to contain any more objects than you need.

Property, Error, Parameter and Field Objects

So what about the remaining four objects? It doesn't really make sense for them to exist independently, because the information that they contain relates directly to the other ADO objects. So, for example, when you create a `Connection` object you'll also get an `Errors` collection. The `Errors` collection gives you access to all of the `Error` objects that relate to that `Connection`, and indeed, you can only access this collection through the `Connection` object.

Similarly, the `Command` object gives you a `Parameters` collection, which in turn gives you access to the `Parameter` objects pertaining to that command. And the `Recordset` object gives you a `Fields` collection, by which you can access the individual `Field` objects.

Finally, the `Properties` collection contains a number of `Property` objects, each of which represents an OLE DB property. There are many of these properties, and they're not all supported by all OLE DB providers.

> *The OLE DB properties are sometimes known as dynamic properties. Be careful of the ambiguous terminology – the OLE DB properties are not the same as the properties of an ADO object!*

Setting a Reference to ADO

Before attempting to connect to any database using ADO, you will need to add a reference to ADO in your project. Visual Basic 6 was released with version 2.0 of ADO (but you will most likely have a later version installed). This reference gives your project the functionality that you need to connect to a database and work with its data.

To add the ADO reference to your project, open your Visual Basic project and select **Project | References...** from the main menu bar. The References dialog will open, allowing you to view all registered references. Scroll down and find the latest version of the ADO library installed on your machine, and check it:

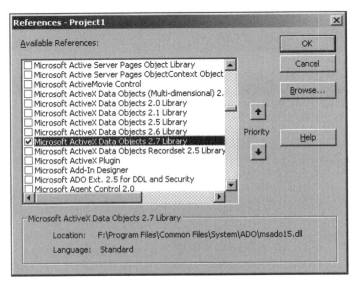

When you select the reference, you'll notice that the location, filename and language are displayed at the bottom of the dialog box. The name of the latest ADO DLL happens to be `msado15.dll` (don't let this name confuse you – it really is the library version you have chosen!). With the new ADO reference checked off, click **OK**, and you have successfully added the reference to your project. Your project will look just the same as it did prior to adding the reference as the reference doesn't include any viewable components. If you compile your project into a setup process, the reference will be automatically added to your project by the setup wizard.

This highlights a significant difference between using the ADO Data Control (discussed in the following chapter) and the ADO reference – namely that the former is an `.ocx` file with a viewable component, while the latter is a `.dll` file, which does not have a viewable component. When you set the reference to this DLL, your project will act as if the code in the DLL were part of the project. Your project code can call functions from the DLL, and it's just as though it were running locally to the project. If you fail to add this reference to your project, your code will fail because it won't be able to locate the functions.

> **In short, setting this reference exposes the ADO object model to your project.**
>
> **You'll need to add this reference to every new project that connects to a database using ADO. Forgetting to add the reference is one of the most common errors in ADO VB programming.**

In the following sections we'll look at the ADO objects. We will cover some of the properties and methods of the ADO Data Control (such as `AddNew`, `MoveNext`, and `Delete`) in the following chapter, and so these will become very familiar to you. The methods and properties you see here (and in Appendix D) are not only applicable when you use ADO in your VB code – you can also use them in the ADO Data Control (and indeed in any COM-compliant programming language).

Connecting to a Database

In order to access a database, we need to establish a connection to it. In ADO, the connection is represented by a `Connection` object.

Because the connection is fundamental to database access, the `Connection` object is sometimes considered to be the most important item you use while working with your database. With previous data connection mechanisms, such as the DAO, establishing the database connection was the real challenge – particularly when dealing with remote databases and databases such as Oracle. However, ADO really has taken much of the work out of establishing the connection.

Creating a Connection Object

The first task is to declare and create the `Connection` object. The following code declares and creates a `Connection` object called `objConn`:

```
Dim objConn As ADODB.Connection
Set objConn = New ADODB.Connection
```

These two lines of code will be fairly standard from one project to another. Keep in mind that if you're connecting to more than one database, you may have more than one Connection object.

Note that we could have declared the connection with this line:

```
Dim objConn as Connection
```

This is a little dangerous, because previous data access technologies (like DAO) also used a Connection object. Therefore, it's safer to explicitly state that you want an **ADO** Connection object, by specifying ADODB.Connection.

Implicit Connection Objects

As we mentioned in the introduction, we can choose not to create a Connection object explicitly. Instead, we can supply the necessary connection details direct to a Recordset or Command object – in this case, when we open the recordset (or run the command) a nameless Connection object will be created under the covers.

If we subsequently need to refer to this Connection object, we can get a reference to it through the ActiveConnection property exposed by the Command and Recordset objects like so:

```
Dim objRec As ADODB.Recordset
objRec.Open "OrderDetails", "Provider=Microsoft.Jet.OLEDB.4.0;" & _
    "Data Source=C:\Program Files\Microsoft Visual Studio\VB98\Northwind.mdb"
    .
    .
    .
Dim objConn As ADODB.Connection
Set objConn = objRec.ActiveConnection
```

In fact, we can also use the ActiveConnection property in the opposite direction – assigning an existing Connection object to the ActiveConnection property of a Command or Recordset object.

Setting the Connection String

Now that we have created a Connection object, we need to prepare the object for a connection to the database. Amongst other information, we must provide the location and name of the database. This information is provided in a semicolon-delimited string known as the **connection string**. When connecting to a database programmatically through ADO, we'll build the connection string ourselves.

The connection string is constructed of a number of arguments. The most important of these arguments is Provider – this dictates the OLE DB data provider that will be used for the connection. The following OLE DB providers are supplied with the data access components:

Provider	Description
MSDASQL	Connects to ODBC data sources
Microsoft.Jet.SQLOLEDB.4.0	Connects to MS Access databases
SQLOLEDB	Connects to SQL Server databases
MSDAORA	Connects to Oracle databases
MSIDXS	Connects to MS Index Server
ADSDSOObject	Connects to Active Directory Services
MSDataShape	Connects to hierarchical recordsets
MSPersist	Connects to locally saved recordsets
MSDAOSP	For creating custom providers for simple text data
MSDAIPP.DSO	Connects to Internet Publishing resources
MS Remote	Connects from a client to a remote data providers

The form of the connection string depends upon which data provider we choose, because different providers need different information in order to connect you to the database. We'll have a look at some different connection strings in a moment.

The most direct way to assign a connection string to the Connection object is to assign it directly to the Connection object's ConnectionString property, like this:

```
objConn.ConnectionString = "Provider=SQLOLEDB; Data Source=bigsmile;" & _
                           "Initial Catalog=Northwind; User Id=sa; Password="
```

Alternatively, you could build up a character string (like strConn in the next example), and then assign that string to the ConnectionString property:

```
Dim strConn
strConn = "Provider=SQLOLEDB; Data Source=bigsmile;"
strConn = strConn & "Initial Catalog=Northwind; User Id=sa; Password="

objConn.ConnectionString = strConn
```

Now, let's look at how connection strings are constructed.

OLE DB Provider for ODBC Drivers

The OLE DB Provider for ODBC is the default provider, so if you don't specify a Provider argument, this is what you'll get. Of course, you should specify the provider, and to specify the OLE DB Provider for ODBC you'll need to give the rather obscure name MSDASQL.

Having specified this provider, connecting through ODBC requires that we give the desired `Driver` (we enclose this in curly brackets). If we're connecting to a desktop database, we also need to specify the path and filename of the database:

```
Provider=MSDASQL;Driver={Driver_Name};DBQ=Database_Filename
```

If we're connecting to a database that's hosted on a database server, we must provide the server name (using `server`), the database name (`database`), a user ID (`uid`) and a password (`pwd`):

```
Provider=MSDASQL;Driver={Driver_Name};"server=Server_Name;
                database=Database_Name;uid=User_ID;pwd=Password
```

The `Driver Name` might be one of those that are usefully displayed in the **Drivers** tab of the ODBC Control Panel applet (this can be found in the Control Panel, from the Start Menu):

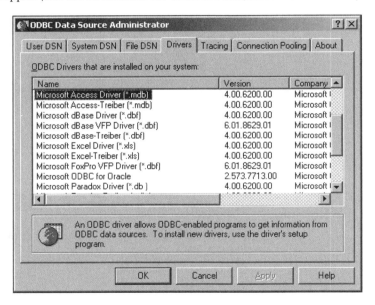

To connect to a desktop database through a previously created ODBC Data Source Name, we need only supply the DSN itself:

```
Provider=MSDASQL;DSN=Data_Source_Name
```

To connect to a database server through a DSN, we also need to supply a user name and password:

```
Provider=MSDASQL;DSN=Data_Source_Name;uid=User_ID;pwd=Password
```

Examples

Let's look at some examples. A simple connection string might specify just the OLE DB provider and the data source. For an Access database, this might be as simple as follows:

```
objConn.ConnectionString = "Provider=MSDASQL;" & _
                           "Driver={Microsoft Access Driver (*.mdb)}" & _
                           "DBQ=C:\Databases\MyDataBase.mdb"
```

In the next few examples, we connect to a SQL Server Northwind database, hosted on a server called bigsmile, through the ODBC driver:

```
objConn.ConnectionString = "Driver={SQL Server};server=bigsmile;" & _
                           "Database=Northwind;uid=sa;pwd="
```

This format can be abridged slightly if we have set up an ODBC Data Source Name for the database. The following example connects to the Northwind database using an ODBC DSN with ODBC tags:

```
objConn.ConnectionString = "DSN=Northwind;UID=sa;PWD=;"
```

Other OLE DB Providers

Among the other data providers, it's usually (though not always) necessary to specify the Provider and the Data Source. For a desktop database, the Data Source is the path and filename to the database to which the connection will be made:

```
Provider=Provider_Name;Data Source=Database_Filename
```

If we're connecting to a database server, the Data Source is the name of the server; we can also supply the name of the database to connect to (this is the Initial Catalog), and a user ID and password if necessary (alternatively, these can be supplied later when the connection is open):

```
Provider=Provider_Name;Data Source=Server_Name;Initial Catalog=Database_Name;
User ID=User_ID;Password=Password
```

Examples

A couple more examples will make this a bit clearer. Here's an example that will use the Microsoft Jet provider to connect to an Access database:

```
objConn.ConnectionString = "Provider=Microsoft.Jet.OLEDB.4.0;" & _
    "Data Source=C:\Databases\MyDataBase.mdb"
```

To connect to a SQL Server database through OLE DB, we must specify the OLE DB provider, the name of the server, the name of the database, and the name and password of the user who is logging on to the database:

```
objConn.ConnectionString = "Provider=SQLOLEDB; Data Source=bigsmile;" & _
    "Initial Catalog=Northwind; User Id=sa; Password="
```

If you need to check that you're creating your connection string correctly, you can add the ADO Data Control to your project and use the wizard to create your connection string. Then copy it over to your code and remove the ADO Data Control.

Opening the Connection

So the database and provider have been specified and the database is in place (and the DSN has been set up, if we're using one). Now we're in a position to make the connection. The most straightforward way to do this is to call the `Connection` object's `Open` method:

```
objConn.Open
```

When this method is called, the `Connection` object attempts to connect to the database that you specified in the `ConnectionString` property. If it fails, an error message will be returned. If it's successful, you have your connection and are ready to work with your database.

Note that the line above doesn't specify any connection details – so the `Connection` object assumes that you want to use the connection details that you specified in the `ConnectionString` property. It is also possible to call the `Open` method without having specified the connection string in advance – we simply pass the connection string as a parameter to the method:

```
objConn.Open ConnectionString, UserID, Password, OpenOptions
```

As you can see, we can also specify a user ID and password (if they're not included in the `ConnectionString` parameter or specified in the `Connection` object's `ConnectionString` property), as well as additional options for the connection.

`OpenOptions` may be one of the `ConnectOptionEnum` constants. One of the two permissible values is `adAsyncConnect`, which specifies that the connection be opened asynchronously. This means that, instead of waiting for the connection to open before proceeding to the next line of code, the application will continue to run while the connection is being made. The other value, `adConnectUnspecified`, represents a synchronous connection and is the default value.

Closing the Connection

For completeness, we should really also know how to close a connection – so let's quickly look at that now. When we've finished using our open connection, we can close it by using the `Connection` object's `Close` method:

```
objConn.Close
```

Note that this does not uninstantiate the object. If you want to destroy the `Connection` object completely, and release its memory, we must also set the object to `Nothing`:

```
objConn.Open strConn1
...     ' do some data manipulation
objConn.Close
Set objConn = Nothing
```

Alternatively, you can re-open a closed `Connection` object with different settings:

```
objConn.Open strConn1
...     ' do some data manipulation on database #1
objConn.Close
objConn.Open strConn2
...     ' do some data manipulation on database #2
objConn.Close
Set objConn = Nothing
```

Later in this chapter we'll look at events, and at the `Error` object and the `Errors` collection. We'll look at how we can use these in harness with events to do some basic error handling. Before that, let's get at the data in those databases!

Querying the Database

So we know how to create a `Connection` object, and how to use it to open and close database connections – but we still don't have any records to view or edit. ADO works by capturing a recordset from the database and caching it locally. We query the database by asking it to return all the data that matches our desired criteria – the data that we get back is placed into a recordset.

The query itself may be a SQL statement or a stored procedure, and is represented in the ADO object model by the `Command` object. In addition, the `Command` object allows you to execute batch operations, and even modify the structure of your database.

Creating a Command Object

When creating a `Command` object, we must first declare an instance of the object, just as we did with the `Connection` object. It's generally best to declare this in the `General Declarations` section of your form or module. Here, we'll declare a `Command` object with the name `objComm`:

```
Dim objComm As ADODB.Command
```

Once the `Command` object has been declared, we can create the object by setting it to a new instance of the `ADODB.Command` object:

```
Set objComm = New ADODB.Command
```

The `Command` object's methods and properties can then be invoked. Note that parameters can be used in conjunction with `Command` objects to execute stored procedures with parameters, or parameterized queries.

There are other ways to assign a reference to a `Command` object. For example, we can use a `Recordset` object's `ActiveCommand` property to get a reference to the `Command` object that was used to create that recordset:

```
Dim objRec As ADODB.Recordset
'... use the recordset object to query the database
Dim objComm As ADODB.Command
Set objComm = objRec.ActiveCommand
```

Building the Command Text

The actual command that is to be executed against the database is held in the CommandText property of the Command object. This property is where we place our SQL statement, stored procedure, table name, or file name before executing the command. For example:

```
objComm.CommandText = "SELECT * FROM Employee"
```

We need to be sure that our data provider is able to interpret the text of our command efficiently. Therefore, we also use the CommandType property, which specifies the type of command in question. The CommandType property tells the provider whether the CommandText contains a text command (such as a SQL statement), or the name of a table or stored procedure, or the path and filename of a persisted recordset. The value of this property may be any of the following CommandTypeEnum constants:

- ❏ adCmdFile – The command text is to be evaluated as the path and filename of a recordset persisted on the local hard drive.

- ❏ adCmdStoredProc – The command text is to be evaluated as a stored procedure.

- ❏ adCmdTable – The command text is to be evaluated as a SQL statement, which will return all rows from the named table.

- ❏ adCmdTableDirect – The command text is to be interpreted as a table name.

- ❏ adCmdText – The command text is to be interpreted as a text command, such as a SQL statement.

- ❏ adCmdUnknown – The type of command is unknown.

- ❏ adCmdUnspecified – Does not specify the command type argument.

For example, if we want to retrieve the entire Authors table as a recordset, we would need to set the CommandText and CommandType properties as follows:

```
objComm.CommandText = "Authors"
objComm.CommandType = adCmdTable
```

When this command is executed, the query "SELECT * FROM Authors" will be sent to the provider, and the table will be returned as a recordset.

Commands that Return No Records

Sometimes, we'll want to execute commands that don't return any records – for example, if we intend only to add records, but not to view or edit existing ones. In this case, we can also specify the command type adExecuteNoRecords in conjunction with adCmdText or adCmdStoredProc:

```
objComm.CommandType = adCmdStoredProc + adExecuteNoRecords
```

Executing the Command

Before we can execute the command defined in the CommandText, we must specify the connection to be used. This involves setting the Command object's ActiveConnection property, either to a valid connection string, or to an existing Connection object. For example:

```
objComm.ActiveConnection = "Provider=SQLOLEDB;Data Source=bigsmile;" & _
                           "Initial Catalog=pubs;User ID=sa;Password="
```

Alternatively:

```
objConn.ConnectionString = "Provider=SQLOLEDB;Data Source=bigsmile;" & _
                           "Initial Catalog=pubs;User ID=sa;Password="
objComm.ActiveConnection = objConn
```

There is a subtle difference in the way these two code fragments work. The first creates a new connection (with an implicit Connection object, running under the surface of your code). The second reuses an existing connection, and is therefore a more efficient use of resources.

Now we're ready to execute the query. The Command object has an Execute method, which applies the command text to the database, and returns any resulting data to the assigned Recordset object:

```
Set objRec = objComm.Execute(RecordsAffected, Parameters, Options)
```

If we know that the command will not return any data (that is, if CommandType was set to adExecuteNoRecords), or if we don't wish to capture the rows returned by the command, then we can simply miss out the part that assigns the results to a recordset – like this:

```
objComm.Execute RecordsAffected, Parameters, Options
```

The Execute Method's Optional Arguments

You'll see that there are three arguments that can be used with the Execute method. They're all optional, and are described as follows:

❑　RecordsAffected – You can specify a variable name here. If specified, the provider returns the number of affected records to that variable.

❑　Parameters – This is an array of any Parameter objects, which represent parameters that are to be passed to the command.

❑　Options – Specifies how the provider should evaluate the CommandText property of the Command object. This parameter can contain one of the CommandTypeEnum constants identical to that in the CommandType property seen above. In addition, to this can be added adAsyncExecute to specify that the command is to be executed asynchronously, and adAsyncFetch or adAsyncFetchNonBlocking to specify that the recordset is to be returned asynchronously.

An Example

The following snippet of code illustrates the usage of the `RecordsAffected` parameter. A `Long` variable is passed into the `Execute` statement as a parameter. The value of this variable is set to the number of records affected by the operation after the command has been executed.

```
Set objConn = New ADODB.Connection
objConn.Open "Provider=SQLOLEDB;Initial Catalog=pubs;User ID=sa"

Set objComm = New ADODB.Command
objComm.ActiveConnection = objConn
objComm.CommandText = "UPDATE titles SET royalty=royalty * 1.10"
objComm.CommandType = adCmdText

objComm.Execute lngRecs
MsgBox lngRecs & " records have been updated."
```

Note that recordsets with a firehose (read-only, forward-only) cursor do not support the
`RecordsAffected` argument. The firehose cursor is the default cursor type for a recordset. We'll
look at cursor types and lock types later in this chapter.

Other Command Object Functionality

In this section we'll briefly mention a couple of other useful things that the `Command` object can do.

Sometimes, the execution of a command can take longer than you expect – for example, if the application has a problem communicating with the database server. In situations like this, it's useful to be able to limit the length of time to wait before terminating the operation and generating an error. This functionality is provided by the `Command` object's `CommandTimeout` property. This is set to a `Long` value, specifying the number of seconds after which the command will be timed out:

```
objComm.CommandTimeout = 20
```

Setting it to zero causes ADO to wait indefinitely (or until the command has been executed). The default value is 30 seconds.

We can programmatically cancel an asynchronous command at any point during its execution, up to the point when it has completed executing. This is achieved through the `Cancel` method. This method only works if the command was executed asynchronously (that is, with `adAsyncExecute` added to the `Options` parameter of the `Execute` method), and it must be called before the execution of the command has been completed.

Executing a Command Without a Command Object

So far we have only seen how to execute a query against a database using a `Command` object. But, just as we can open a connection without explicitly creating a `Connection` object, we can also execute a command without creating a `Command` object. In fact, there are two ways to do this. First, we can execute the command directly through the `Connection` object; second, we can open a pre-created `Recordset` object by querying it directly against the database.

Using a Connection Object

To execute a command directly from the `Connection` object, we use that object's `Execute` method. This is similar to the `Command` object's `Execute` method, but we must also pass in the command text as a parameter. Here's the syntax:

```
Set Recordset = Connection.Execute(CommandText,[RecordsAffected],[Options])
```

The optional `RecordsAffected` and `Options` arguments are identical to those for the `Command` object's `Execute` method. The `CommandText` argument is a string value, equivalent to the `Command` object's `CommandText` property – so it might be a text command (such as a SQL statement), or a stored procedure or table name.

For example, to open the `Authors` table from the SQL Server pubs database asynchronously:

```
Dim objConn As ADODB.Connection
Dim objRec As ADODB.Recordset

Set objConn = New ADODB.Connection
objConn.ConnectionString = "Provider=SQLOLEDB;Data Source=bigsmile;" & _
                           "Initial Catalog=pubs;User ID=sa;Password="
objConn.Open
Set objRec = objConn.Execute("authors", , adCmdTable + adAsyncExecute)
```

As with a query executed through the `Command` object, we have the ability to cancel the operation and to set a limit to the length of time the application will wait for the command to be executed. To cancel a command executed through a `Connection` object, we use the same `Cancel` method that we would use to cancel the opening of a connection. Again, only an asynchronously executed command (with the argument `adAsyncExecute` added to the `Options` parameter of the `Execute` method) can be cancelled.

To set a timeout limit for a command executed through the `Connection` object's `Execute` method, we can use the `Connection` object's `CommandTimeout` property. This property performs the same task as the `Command` object's `CommandTimeout` property. However, the two properties are entirely independent – and neither property inherits its value from the other.

Using a Recordset Object

We can use the `Recordset` object's `Open` method with or without a `Command` object. In the former case, the `Command` object is passed as a parameter to the `Open` method; in the second, the command text is passed in instead. The syntax for the `Open` method is:

```
Recordset.Open([Source],[ActiveConnection],[CursorType],[LockType], _    [Options])
```

The `Source` argument can be either a valid command text or a `Command` object; `ActiveConnection` may be a connection string or an existing `Connection` object. Thus, if we choose, we can open a recordset and query a database without explicitly creating a `Command` object or a `Connection` object

In fact, the `Source` and `ActiveConnection` arguments are both optional – because we can set them prior to calling the `Open` method with the `Recordset` object's `Source` and `ActiveConnection` properties.

The CursorType and LockType arguments define what type of recordset will be returned; lock and cursor types will be discussed later in this chapter. Note that this is the only way of specifying lock and cursor types: recordsets opened with a Connection or Command object are limited to the defaults. Finally, Options specifies the type of the command in the Source parameter, and is identical to the Options argument of the Command object's Execute method.

For example, to retrieve the Authors table from the SQL Server Pubs database with existing Connection and Command objects:

```
Dim objConn As ADODB.Connection
Dim objComm As ADODB.Command
Dim objRec As ADODB.Recordset

'Create and open the Connection object
Set objConn = New ADODB.Connection
objConn.ConnectionString = "Provider=SQLOLEDB;Data Source=bigsmile;" & _
                           "Initial Catalog=pubs;User ID=sa;Password="
objConn.Open

'Create and set the Command object
Set objComm = New ADODB.Command
objComm.CommandText = "authors"
objComm.CommandType = adCmdTable

'Create and set the Recordset object
Set objRec = New ADODB.Recordset
objRec.ActiveConnection = objConn
Set objRec.Source = objComm

'Open the Recordset object, thus executing the command
objRec.Open
```

The following code retrieves the same table, but without explicitly creating Connection or Command objects:

```
Dim objRec As ADODB.Recordset

Set objRec = New ADODB.Recordset
objRec.Open "authors", "Provider=SQLOLEDB;Data Source=bigsmile;" & _
            "Initial Catalog=pubs;User ID=sa;Password=", , , adCmdTable
```

While the second sample is clearly more concise, it can be more efficient to create the objects explicitly. This allows us to reuse connections, rather than creating a new Connection object each time we want to connect to the database, and to pass parameters into the command.

Like the Command and Connection objects, the Recordset object provides a Cancel method to halt the execution of an asynchronous command. Unlike the other objects, however, the Recordset object does not provide a CommandTimeout property.

Parameters

One important point to note is that neither the `Connection.Execute` nor `Recordset.Open` methods provide a means of passing return or output parameters back from a stored procedure. In order to do that, we must explicitly create a `Command` object. Then, each parameter of the stored procedure can be represented in the form of a `Parameter` object: these parameter details are passed with the other command details to the provider when the command is executed.

The `Parameter` objects reside in the `Parameters` collection of the `Command` object, which can be accessed via the `Parameters` property of the `Command` object:

```
Set colParam = objComm.Parameters
```

We'll take a closer look at the `Parameters` collection in a moment. First, let's find out about the individual `Parameter` objects.

Creating a Parameter Object

To create a new `Parameter` object, we must use the `CreateParameter` method of the `Command` object. The following demonstrates the syntax of the `CreateParameter` method:

```
Set Parameter = Command.CreateParameter([Name],[Type],[Direction],[Size], _
                                                              [Value])
```

The `CreateParameter` method has five optional arguments:

- ❑ `Name` – The name of the `Parameter` object
- ❑ `Type` – The data type of the `Parameter` object. The constants for these are listed below
- ❑ `Direction` – The type of `Parameter` object: input, output, both, or the return value of a stored procedure. The constants for these are listed below
- ❑ `Size` – The maximum length for the value of the parameter in characters or bytes
- ❑ `Value` – The value of the parameter

Here's an example, in which we declare an `ADODB.Parameter` object, then create an input parameter of type integer with the name `percentage`:

```
Dim objParam As ADODB.Parameter
Set objParam = objComm.CreateParameter("percentage", adInteger, adParamInput)
```

The arguments for `CreateParameter` are all optional, as they can be supplied later by setting properties on the `Parameter` object. For example:

```
Dim objParam As ADODB.Parameter
Set objParam = objComm.CreateParameter
objParam.Name = "percentage"
objParam.Type = adInteger
objParam.Direction = adParamInput
```

The Name Property

Note that the Name property or Name argument (which is used to identify the parameter) does not have to be the same as the name given in the stored procedure or query, although it does make sense to keep them the same.

The Type Property

The data type for the parameter can be set through the Type property. This is set to one of the DataTypeEnum constants. The following table shows some of the data types available, and the data types of the SQL Server and Access providers that they map to:

Constant	SQL Server type	Access type
adBoolean	bit	Yes/No
adCurrency	money, smallmoney	Currency
adDate		Date/Time
adDBTimeStamp	datetime, smalldatetime	
adDouble		Double
adEmpty		Value
adGUID		Replication ID
adInteger	int	Long Integer
adSingle	float, real	Single
adSmallInt	smallint	Integer
adUnsignedTinyInt	tinyint	Byte
adVarBinary	binary, varbinary, timestamp, image	Binary, OLE Object
adVarChar	char, varchar, text	Text, Memo

The Direction Property

The Direction property specifies whether the parameter is an input parameter, an output parameter, an input/output parameter or a return value. It may be set to any of the ParameterDirectionEnum constants:

- ❑ adParamUnknown – Indicates that the parameter direction is unknown.
- ❑ adParamInput – Default. Indicates an input parameter.
- ❑ adParamOutput – Indicates an output parameter.
- ❑ adParamInputOutput – Indicates both an input and output parameter.
- ❑ adParamReturnValue – Indicates a return value.

The distinction between `adParamOutput` and `adParamReturnValue` is quite subtle. A return value is returned from the SQL stored procedure in much the same way that a Visual Basic function returns a value. By contrast, output parameters are populated during the execution of the procedure. In many cases, there will be little practical difference between the two.

> **Be aware that MS Access does not support output parameters or return values.**

The Size Property

In addition to specifying the data type of the parameter, we can specify its size – either its maximum possible length in characters (for a text parameter) or the maximum number of bytes it can hold (for a numeric parameter). The `Size` property indicates the maximum size allowable in the `Value` property of a `Parameter` object. This is a required property if the specified data type is of variable length, such as `VarChar`.

If this property is not set when it is required, an error will be generated when the parameter is appended to the `Parameters` collection. For example, consider the following code, which defines the `Type` as `adVarChar`, but does not specify the `Size`:

```
Set objParam = objComm.CreateParameter("strDescription", adVarChar, _
                                        adParamInput, , "Quite Tasty")

objComm.Parameters.Append objParam
```

Here, note that the fourth parameter has deliberately been left blank. If we try to execute this, we generate the following error:

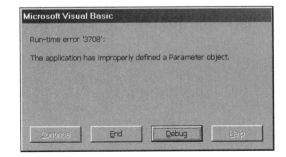

The Value Property

The final property we can set when we create a parameter is its value – that is, the value that will be passed into the stored procedure when the command is executed. The `Parameter` object's `Value` property can be used to set or return the data in a `Parameter` object. Note that the data populated in the `Value` property must have the same data type as declared in the `Type` property.

The Parameters Collection

The `Parameters` collection exposes a number of methods and properties that allow us to manage the parameters for a given command. We can add an existing `Parameter` object to the collection using the `Append` method (we will see a little later how to create a `Parameter` object):

```
objComm.Parameters.Append objParam
```

The `Parameters` collection also exposes a `Delete` method, which removes a specified `Parameter` object from the collection. The `Delete` method has one parameter – the index value of the object you want to remove. This zero-based value indicates the position of the `Parameter` object within the collection. For example, to delete the second parameter in the collection, we would write:

```
objComm.Parameters.Delete 1
```

We can also retrieve a specific parameter from the collection. In this case, we use the `Parameters` collection's `Item` property – employing the index value once again. For example, to set a reference to the first `Parameter` object in the collection:

```
Set objParam = objComm.Parameters.Item(0)
```

> *Note that, when retrieving or deleting parameters, an error will be returned if you give an index value of an object that does not exist.*

We can also retrieve parameters by using the `Item` property in conjunction with the `Parameter` object's `Name` property. To do this, we simply specify the name of the parameter that we want to retrieve. For example:

```
Set objParam = objComm.Parameters.Item("MyParam")
```

There's one more `Parameters` method, `Refresh`, which updates the `Parameter` objects in the collection, retrieving information from the provider:

```
colParam.Refresh
```

In addition to these methods, the `Parameters` collection also has a property – the `Count` property – that returns a `Long` value indicating the number of `Parameter` objects in the collection. If the value is 0, there are no objects in the collection. The following example displays the number of `Parameter` objects in a message box:

```
MsgBox "There are " & objComm.Parameters.Count & _
       "parameters in the collection.", vbInformation
```

Passing Parameters into a Stored Procedure

Now let's see all this in action. The SQL Server `pubs` database is supplied with a stored procedure named `byroyalty`, which selects (from the `titleauthor` table) the `au_id` field for every author with a specified royalty percentage. The SQL for this stored procedure is:

```
CREATE PROCEDURE byroyalty @percentage int
AS
select au_id from titleauthor
where titleauthor.royaltyper = @percentage
```

The royalty percentage to be matched is passed into the stored procedure as the parameter @percentage. So, we must supply a value for the @percentage parameter when we execute this procedure – otherwise an error will be generated. We will execute this stored procedure by creating a Command object with its CommandType set to the procedure name (byroyalty). In order to pass in the parameter information, we'll create a new Parameter object and add this to the Parameters collection of our Command object.

First we must dimension our Connection, Command, Recordset and Parameter objects, and open the connection:

```
Dim objConn As ADODB.Connection
Dim objRec As ADODB.Recordset
Dim objComm As ADODB.Command
Dim objParam As ADODB.Parameter

Set objConn = New ADODB.Connection
objConn.Open "Provider=SQLOLEDB;Data Source=bigsmile;" & _
             "Initial Catalog=pubs;User ID=sa;Password="
```

Now we instantiate the Command object and set its CommandText and CommandType properties. CommandText will be the name of the stored procedure, "byroyalty", and CommandType will be set to adCmdStoredProc, to indicate that the command is a stored procedure. We also set the Command object's ActiveConnection property to our existing Command object, objComm:

```
Set objComm = New ADODB.Command
objComm.CommandText = "byroyalty"
objComm.CommandType = adCmdStoredProc    ' the command is a stored procedure
objComm.ActiveConnection = objConn       ' use the existing connection
```

We can now create our Parameter object. We'll call it percentage (for convenience, since that's the name of the parameter used in the stored procedure), and indicate that it's an integer input parameter with a value of 40. Once we've created the parameter, we can add it to the Parameters collection:

```
Set objParam = objComm.CreateParameter("percentage", adInteger, _
                                       adParamInput, , 40)
objComm.Parameters.Append objParam
```

Finally, we instantiate and open the recordset. The only parameter we need to pass into the Open method is our Command object, objComm, since this contains references to the Connection and Parameter objects:

```
Set objRec = New ADODB.Recordset
objRec.Open objComm
```

This last line will open the recordset based on the stored procedure with the parameter that we passed into it.

Now, the requested data is contained in the recordset and ready for use to analyze and manipulate. This is the subject of the next section.

Viewing and Editing Records

Once we have retrieved a recordset from the database, we can start to view and manipulate that data. We can retrieve the value of a named field of the current record using the exclamation mark syntax. To access the value, we simply place an exclamation mark and the field name after the name of the `Recordset` object. For example, to display a message box containing the first and last names of the current author from the `Authors` table of the `pubs` database, we would write:

```
MsgBox "Current author is: " & objRec!au_fname & " " & objRec!au_lname, _
    vbInformation
```

The fields that we want to access in this case are named au_fname (the author's first name) and au_lname (the author's last name). We can also use a slightly longer notation with the `Recordset`'s `Fields` property, specifying the field either through an index value or through its name (note that the index is zero-based, so the first field returned into the recordset has an index value of 0):

```
MsgBox objRec.Fields(0).Value
MsgBox objRec.Fields("au_fname").Value
```

Each of these lines uses a reference to an object representing the field, and generates a message box containing the value of that object. The `Field` object has a `Value` property, which we use to extract the value of the field for the current record.

In fact, `Value` is the default property for an ADO `Field` object, so it can be omitted from the code. Thus, the following two lines of code therefore have exactly the same effect:

```
MsgBox objRec.Fields(0)
MsgBox objRec.Fields(0).Value
```

> We will look more closely at the **Field** object later in this chapter.

We can now retrieve the value of a record's fields, but to access specific records we will need to know how to find our way around the recordset.

Navigating through the Recordset

We have already met some of the most important methods for navigating through the recordset and moving from one record to another. The simplest way of doing this is with the `MoveFirst`, `MoveLast`, `MoveNext` and `MovePrevious` methods. These methods take no arguments and simply move the record pointer to the appropriate record. For example, to move the record pointer to the beginning of the recordset and make the first record the current one, we simply write:

```
objRec.MoveFirst
```

Similarly, `MoveLast` moves the record pointer to the end of the recordset.

The `MoveNext` and `MovePrevious` methods work in a similar way, but (as we will see in the next chapter, when using the ADO Data Control) we must be careful not to go beyond the beginning or end of the file. We can do this by checking the `BOF` or `EOF` properties of the `Recordset` object.

The best way to think of this is to imagine a BOF 'pseudo-record' that sits before the first record of the recordset, and an EOF pseudo-record that sits just after the last record. While the record pointer is placed before the first record of the recordset, on the BOF pseudo-record, the `BOF` property will be `True`. While the record pointer is placed past the last record, on the EOF pseudo-record, `EOF` is set to `True`.

The record pointer can reside at these BOF and EOF pseudo-records without generating an error, but any attempt to move beyond them will generate an error. An error will also be raised if we attempt to access the current record while the record pointer is set to `BOF` or `EOF`. Therefore, it's a good idea to check the `BOF` property after every `MovePrevious` method call and `EOF` after every `MoveNext`. If the property returns `True`, we can then move the record pointer back to a valid record. For example:

```
objRec.MoveNext
If objRec.EOF Then
  objRec.MoveLast
End If
```

> **Not all cursor types support all types of movement within the recordset. We shall look at the implications of different cursor types later in this chapter.**

We can also move directly to a specific record by specifying its position in the recordset with the `AbsolutePosition` property. Note that this property is one-based (not zero-based), so, for example, to move to the fifth record, we would write:

```
objRec.AbsolutePosition = 5
```

We can use this property to return the current position of the record pointer in the recordset. We use this property to update the status label in the application developed in the next chapter. Here, the label gives the number of the current record and the total number of records in the recordset (for example, "Record 1 out of 4"). The other property used is `RecordCount`, which returns the total number of records in the recordset.

The `RecordCount` property only works with static and keyset cursors (see later in this chapter).

Bookmarks

Of course, we sometimes want to move straight to a record without knowing its position in the recordset – particularly since its position may change as records are added or deleted. We can do this by assigning a **bookmark** to the record. A bookmark will uniquely identify the record, and we can use it to jump to the record whenever we want.

To assign a bookmark to a record, we first move the record point to that record; then we set a variant to the `Bookmark` property of the `Recordset` object. For example, this code sets a bookmark named `varBkmrk` to point to the first record of the recordset:

```
Dim varBkmrk As Variant

objRec.MoveFirst
varBkmrk = objRec.Bookmark
```

That's it. We can move around the recordset, visiting other records, and when we want to move the record pointer to this record, we simply have to set the Bookmark property of the Recordset to our bookmark variant:

```
objRec.Bookmark = varBkmrk
```

> **Bookmarks are generally only supported on keyset and static cursors, although some providers also support bookmarks on dynamic cursors.**

We will see, in the next chapter, how we can use this property temporarily to store the current position in the recordset, so we can return to that record if any operation is canceled or is unsuccessful.

Moving by More than One Record

We've seen that we can move backwards and/or forwards through the recordset by one record at a time (as long as the cursor type allows!). In addition, we can move by a specified number of records using the Recordset object's Move method. We must supply as a parameter the number of records we wish to move from the current record; a positive value indicates forward movement, a negative value backward movement. So, for example, to move to a record five records before the current one:

```
objRec.Move -5
```

Furthermore, we can also specify the starting point from which we want to move by the given number of records, by supplying a bookmark as a second argument. So, to move forwards three records from our varBkmrk bookmark, we would use:

```
objRec.Move 3, varBkmrk
```

As well as using our own bookmarks as a starting point, we can use any of the BookmarkEnum constants in the second argument:

- ❑ adBookmarkCurrent – Move from the current record by the specified number of records.
- ❑ adBookmarkFirst – Move from the first record by the specified number of records.
- ❑ adBookmarkLast – Move from the last record by the specified number of records.

For example, to move to the antepenultimate record in the recordset:

```
objRec.Move - 2, adBookmarkLast
```

Recordset Pages

Because a recordset will frequently contain a large number of records (often an entire table), ADO gives us the ability to subdivide the recordset into a number of **pages**. This makes record handling more manageable, and allows for faster navigation within the recordset.

We can specify or determine the number of records contained on each page by using the `PageSize` property. For example, to limit each page to five records, we would use:

```
objRec.PageSize = 5
```

We can determine the number of pages in the recordset using the `PageCount` property. For example, the following line displays a message box indicating the number of pages of data returned by a query and the number of records on each page:

```
MsgBox objRec.PageCount & " pages of " & _
       objRec.PageSize & " records were returned."
```

Finally, the `Recordset` object also exposes an `AbsolutePage` property. This allows us to determine the current page in the recordset for the current record, or to move to a specific page within the recordset. We could use these properties to navigate quickly through the recordset, jumping *x* records at a time (where *x* can be chosen by setting the value of the `PageSize` property). For example, the following two snippets of code could be used for command buttons to move backwards and forwards through a recordset by one page at a time:

```
Private Sub cmdPrevPage_Click()
  Dim intPage As Integer
  intPage = objRec.AbsolutePage
  intPage = intPage -  1
  If intPage > 0 Then objRec.AbsolutePage = intPage
End Sub
```

```
Private Sub cmdNextPage_Click()
  Dim intPage As Integer
  intPage = objRec.AbsolutePage
  intPage = intPage + 1
  If intPage <= objRec.PageCount Then objRec.AbsolutePage = intPage
End Sub
```

We set a variable to equal the current value of `AbsolutePage` and increase or decrease by one – then we check that we won't move by moving before the first page or after the last page when we set `AbsolutePage` to its new value. When moving forwards, we check the new page value against `PageCount` to ensure that we don't move beyond the end of the recordset.

Locating Records in the Recordset

Even though the recordset is returned from a query against a database – and as such is a subset of the full set of database data – it can still be very large, and could contain many thousands of records. For this reason, ADO provides methods to search, filter and sort the recordset.

Finding Specific Records

The Recordset object's Find method will search for the next record that matches the given SQL criterion. The syntax for this method is:

```
Recordset.Find(Criteria, [SkipRecords], [SearchDirection], [Start])
```

The Criteria argument is a string containing an expression against which the records will be matched. This expression takes the form of a SQL WHERE clause, without the WHERE keyword. For example, to find the next author whose last name begins with R in the Authors table of the SQL Server pubs database, we could use the following line:

```
objRec.Find "au_lname LIKE 'r*'"
```

This expression will usually consist of the name of a field, a comparison operator and a value against which the field is to be compared. It is not permitted to combine multiple expressions with AND or OR operators.

By default, the search begins at the current record. However, this can be modified by specifying a value for the SkipRecords argument. This argument specifies an offset value from which the search will start. For example, a value of 0 (the default) indicates that the search will commence at the current record; a value of 1 causes the search to begin at the next record in the recordset, and a value of – 1 at the previous record.

The SearchDirection parameter specifies whether the search is to run forwards or backwards from the current record. This parameter must be one of the SearchDirectionEnum constants: adSearchBackward (or – 1) for a backwards search, or adSearchForward (or 1) for a forward search. The default is adSearchForward.

It is also possible to specify a bookmark from which the search is to commence. This is useful if we wish to search from a specific record, but we don't know the offset of that record from the current record. This is indicated in the Start argument, which may hold a valid bookmark or one of the three BookmarkEnum constants:

❑ adBookmarkCurrent – The search will start from the current record.

❑ adBookmarkFirst – The search will start from the first record.

❑ adBookmarkLast – The search will start from the last record.

For example, to search backwards from the last record through a recordset based on the sales table of the pubs database for sales orders with a quantity greater than or equal to 30, we would use:

```
objRec.Find "qty >= 30", 0, adSearchBackward, adBookmarkLast
```

Note that the Find method simply moves the record pointer to the **first** record that matches the specified criterion, and thus returns only a single record. If we want to execute a search that returns more than one record, we should apply a filter to the recordset using the Recordset object's Filter property.

Filtering the Recordset

This property temporarily filters the recordset. While a filter is active, only the records that meet the given criteria are visible to the user of the recordset. The filter may be a valid filter string, an array of bookmarks or one of the `FilterGroupEnum` constants:

❑ `adFilterNone` – The filter is reset, and the full recordset restored.

❑ `adFilterPendingRecords` – The recordset is filtered to show only the records that have been modified but not yet sent to the server (batch update mode only).

❑ `adFilterAffectedRecords` – The recordset is filtered to show only records affected by the last `Delete`, `Resync`, `UpdateBatch` or `CancelBatch` method call.

❑ `adFilterFetchedRecords` – The recordset is filtered to show the records in the current cache only.

❑ `adFilterConflictingRecords` – The recordset is filtered to show only records that caused a conflict in the last batch update attempt.

The filter is applied simply by setting the `Filter` property to the desired value. For example, to view the records that caused a problem during an attempt to update the database, we would use the `adFilterConflictingRecords` constant:

```
objRec.Filter = adFilterConflictingRecords
```

A filter string is similar to the criteria used by the `Find` method. However, unlike the `Find` method, `Filter` does allow you to string together multiple criteria, using the `AND` and `OR` keywords, and you may use parentheses to group them. For example:

```
objRec.Filter = "qty > 30 AND ord_date >= 1/1/01
```

We can filter our recordset to show only selected records that need not match a specific criterion. The best way to do this is by setting the `Filter` property to an array of bookmarks. The bookmarks in the array are defined individually, and the filter is then set to the entire array. For example, to filter the recordset to contain only the first and last records:

```
Dim arrBkmark(1)

objRec.MoveFirst
arrBkmark(0) = objRec.Bookmark
objRec.MoveLast
arrBkmark(1) = objRec.Bookmark
objRec.Filter = arrBkmark
```

To reset the filter and restore the full recordset, set `Filter` to an empty string or to `adFilterNone`:

```
objRec.Filter = ""
```

or:

```
objRec.Filter = adFilterNone
```

Retrieving Rows into an Array

We can retrieve records into an array using the GetRows method of the Recordset object. The first dimension of the returned array corresponds to the columns of the recordset, the second to the rows (although this is not particularly intuitive, this system is preserved for compatability with DAO and RDO). The syntax for this property is:

```
Variant = Recordset.GetRows([Rows], [Start], [Fields])
```

The Rows argument specifies how many records are to be retrieved. The default is adGetRowsRest, which specifies that all the remaining records are to be retrieved into the array.

By default, rows are retrieved from the current record, but it is possible to move the start point by setting the Start parameter to any valid bookmark in the recordset, or to one of the BookmarkEnum constants:

❑   adBookmarkCurrent – The operation will start at the current record.

❑   adBookmarkFirst – The operation will start at the first record.

❑   adBookmarkLast – The operation will start at the last record.

We can also specify which fields are to be retrieved, by using the Fields parameter. This can be set to a single field name or an array of field names, or to the index position of a field in the Recordset's Fields collection or an array of index values. For example, to retrieve the au_lname field from the first 10 records of the recordset, we would use:

```
Dim varRows As Variant
varRows = objRec.GetRows(10, adBookmarkFirst, "au_lname")
```

To retrieve both the au_fname and the au_lname fields, these values must be held in a variant array, which is passed in as the final parameter to the GetRows method:

```
Dim varRows As Variant
Dim varFlds(1) As Variant

varFlds(0) = "au_fname"
varFlds(1) = "au_lname"
varRows = objRec.GetRows(10, adBookmarkFirst, varFlds)
```

Alternatively, we can pass the index number for the field into the method:

```
Dim varRows As Variant
varRows = objRec.GetRows(10, adBookmarkFirst, 1)
```

Or, to retrieve more than one field:

```
Dim varRows As Variant
Dim varFlds(1) As Variant
```

```
varFlds(0) = 2
varFlds(1) = 1
varRows = objRec.GetRows(10, adBookmarkFirst, varFlds)
```

Because the first dimension in the array represents the columns in the recordset, to display the full name in a message box, we would use:

```
MsgBox varRows(0, 0) & " " & varRows(1, 0)
```

Note that the fields are placed in the array in the order that they are passed into the method, not in the order in which they occur in the recordset.

Sorting the Recordset

In addition to filtering the recordset, it's often useful to sort the records into a specific order. This can be achieved with the `Recordset` object's `Sort` property. This works in a similar way to the `Filter` property: the property is set to a string, which indicates the fields on which the sort is to take place, and the order for the sort for each field:

```
objRec.Sort = "ord_date ASC, qty DESC"
```

If we choose to sort by multiple fields, we can separate the fields using commas. The sort order is indicated by the keywords `ASC` for ascending order (the default) and `DESC` for descending order.

In order to use the `Sort` property you have to set the `CursorLocation` property to `adUseClient`.

Modifying the Data

We can retrieve data from a database into our recordset, and we can manipulate the recordset in order to find the records that we're interested in. Now, we need to know how to modify the data in the recordset – by editing the values of individual fields, and by adding and deleting records.

The first thing to note is that, if the `Recordset` object's `LockType` property is set to `adLockReadOnly`, then the recordset is a read-only recordset. This means that the data in the recordset can only be viewed; it cannot be modified.

> **Recall that the `Recordset` object's lock type is set when the `Recordset` is created. We'll discuss lock types in greater detail later in this chapter.**

Editing Records

Editing records through ADO does not require a special method. We simply modify the value of the appropriate field. We can access the field value for editing using much the same ways that we could retrieve it for viewing. So, to change the value of the `au_fname` field for the current record, we might use any of the following lines:

```
objRec!au_fname = "Archibald"
```

```
objRec.Fields("au_fname") = "Roderick"
```

```
objRec.Fields(2) = "Herbert"
```

In all of the above lines, we've left out the .Value part of the syntax because Value is the default property of a Field object. But we can make it explicit if we want to:

```
objRec!au_fname.Value = "Friedrich"
```

Of course, it's not often that the new value will be hard-coded into the application. More commonly, it will be generated dynamically or input by the user into a text box or input box:

```
Dim strName As String

strName = InputBox("Please enter new name:", "Edit record")
objRec!au_fname = strName
```

It is also possible to modify the data in a database using the SQL UPDATE statement. However, this causes the database itself to be updated, not just the cached recordset. In this case, we place the SQL statement in the CommandText property of a Command object and then execute the command, as we did when opening a recordset:

```
Dim objComm As ADODB.Command

Set objComm = New ADODB.Command
objComm.ActiveConnection = objConn
objComm.CommandText = "UPDATE authors SET au_fname='Archie' " & _
                      "WHERE au_fname='Archibald'"
objComm.CommandType = adCmdText
objComm.Execute
```

Adding Records

To add a new record to the recordset, we call the Recordset object's AddNew method. This creates a new record, which we can populate with data in two ways. The first technique is to pass the field names and values for the new record, as arguments to the AddNew method:

```
objRec.AddNew "au_lname", "Schmidt"
```

The example above creates a new record, and assigns the string Schmidt to the new record's au_lname field.

In fact, this technique also allows us to assign values to more than one field: to do this, we must pass in two arrays containing the field names and the values:

```
objRec.AddNew Array("au_id", "au_lname", "au_fname", "contract"), _
    Array("123-45-6789", "Schmidt", "Johannes", True)
```

The second technique to populate the new record is to assign values to the fields individually:

```
objRec.AddNew
objRec!au_id = "123-45-6789"
objRec!au_fname = "Johannes"
objRec!au_lname = "Schmidt"
objRec!contract = True
```

This works because the `AddNew` call leaves the record pointer pointing to our new record – which allows us to populate the fields immediately without having to move around the recordset.

> **Remember that you must assign values to all required fields before updating the database. We'll look at how to update the database from a recordset shortly.**

We can, of course, also add a new record using a `Command` object and a SQL `INSERT` statement:

```
Dim objComm As ADODB.Command

Set objComm = New ADODB.Command
objComm.ActiveConnection = objConn
objComm.CommandText = "INSERT INTO authors(au_id,au_lname," & _
                                          "au_fname,contract) " & _
                      "VALUES('245-43-5432','Schmidt','Johannes',1)"
objComm.CommandType = adCmdText
objComm.Execute
```

Deleting Records

The `Recordset` object's `Delete` method allows us to delete a single record or a group of records. This method takes a single parameter, which can have any of the following `AffectEnum` constants:

- ❑ `adAffectAllChapters` – All child recordsets of the current record or group of records will be deleted.

- ❑ `adAffectCurrent` – Only the current record will be deleted.

- ❑ `adAffectGroup` – All records in the current filter will be deleted.

- ❑ `adAffectAll` – All records in the recordset will be deleted.

If none of these values is given, the default `adAffectCurrent` will be assumed. Therefore, to delete only the current record we simply need the line:

```
objRec.Delete
```

To delete a selected group of records, we must first set the `Recordset`'s `Filter` property to the criterion by which we want to delete records. For example, to delete all records for which the `ord_date` field has a value earlier than 1st January 1993, we would use:

```
objRec.Filter = "ord_date < 1/1/93"
objRec.Delete adAffectGroup
```

Not all recordsets support this option.

75

Refreshing the Recordset

If we want to cancel any changes we have made to the recordset, or if we want to re-check the data in the database (in case it has been updated by another user), we must refresh the recordset from the underlying database. ADO provides two ways to do this: the `Requery` method and the `Resync` method.

The `Requery` method re-executes the query on which the recordset is based, and is thus equivalent to closing and reopening the recordset using the original command. Its syntax is quite simple:

```
Recordset.Requery Options
```

This method takes a single optional argument, `Options`. Because the original command cannot be changed, this will only have any effect if it is used to specify that the recordset is to be cached asynchronously, using either `adAsyncFetch` or `adAsyncFetchNonBlocking`. An error will be generated if `Requery` is called while a record is being edited or added.

The `Resync` method does not re-execute the query, and allows specific records to be updated, whereas `Requery` always updates all records. The syntax for `Resync` is:

```
Recordset.Resync [AffectRecords], [ResyncValues]
```

The `AffectRecords` argument allows us to specify which records will be refreshed. It can be set to one of the following `AffectEnum` constants:

❑ `adAffectCurrent` – Only the current record will be refreshed.

❑ `AdAffectGroup` – All records in the current filter will be refreshed.

❑ `AdAffectAll` – If no `Filter` property is set then all records in the recordset will be refreshed otherwise only the filtered records will be treated.

❑ `AdAffectAllChapters` – All records in the recordset will be refreshed.

`ResyncValues` may be one of the `ResyncEnum` constants:

❑ `adResyncAllValues` – All of the value properties will be refreshed.

❑ `adResyncUnderlyingValues` – Only the `UnderlyingValue` property will be changed.

We have seen already that each `Field` object has a `Value` property, which contains the value of the field for the current record in the recordset. In fact, there are also two closely related properties, called `UnderlyingValue` and `OriginalValue`. The `UnderlyingValue` property holds the current value of the field in the database, while `OriginalValue` contains the original value of the field at the time before any changes were made to the recordset. When changes are made to the `Value` of a field, the `UnderlyingValue` and `OriginalValue` remain unchanged until the database is updated or the recordset is refreshed.

When we call `Resync` with `adResyncAllValues`, the `Value`, `OriginalValue` and `UnderlyingValue` properties are all updated to the current value in the database. This means that any pending updates to the value of the field will be lost. However, when we use `adResyncUnderlyingValues`, only the `UnderlyingValue` property is changed, leaving the `Value` and `OriginalValue` intact. This means that any pending updates are retained.

Updating the Database

Once changes have been made to the cached recordset, we need to save these changes to the database itself. ADO provides two methods to do this, depending on whether the recordset is in update or batch update mode.

> Batch update mode is set by opening the recordset with a lock type of **adLockBatchOptimistic**. We will be discussing lock types shortly.

The difference between these two modes is this:

❏ In update mode, the database will automatically be updated to reflect changes to a record as soon as the user moves off that record or calls `Update`

❏ In batch update mode, the database will only be updated when an explicit method call is made

Note that, even in update mode, we may need to call the `Update` method after changing a record, in order to update the `UnderlyingValue` and `OriginalValue` properties, or update the database without moving to another record.

We can also use the `Update` method to assign new values to given fields. For example, to change the value of the `au_fname` field to `"Vitezslav"`, we could write:

```
objRec.Update "au_fname", "Vitezslav"
```

If we wish to update more than one field, we can pass both the field names and the new values in arrays (as we did when we added a new record with the `AddNew` method):

```
objRec.Update Array("au_fname", "au_lname"), Array ("Vitezslav", "Novak")
```

The corresponding method for batch update mode is `UpdateBatch`. This takes one optional parameter, to specify which records will be updated. This may be one of the `AffectEnum` constants:

❏ `AdAffectAll` – If no `Filter` property is set then all records in the recordset will be updated else only the filtered records will be modified.

❏ `AdAffectAllChapters` – All records in the recordset will be updated.

❏ `adAffectCurrent` – Only the current record will be updated.

❏ `adAffectGroup` – All records in the current filter will be updated.

Canceling Updates

A pending update can be canceled using the `CancelUpdate` method, or, for a batch update, the `CancelBatch` method. The `CancelUpdate` method can only affect the current record, and therefore takes no parameters:

```
objRec.CancelUpdate
```

CancelUpdate cancels any changes made to the current record since the last Update method call.

In batch update mode, we must instead use the CancelBatch method, which cancels any changes made to records since the last UpdateBatch method call. This method has the single parameter AffectRecords, which specifies which records are to be affected by the operation:

```
Recordset.CancelBatch AffectRecords
```

This parameter may be one of the AffectEnum constants:

- ❑   adAffectAll – If no Filter property is set then all records in the recordset will be affected else only the filtered records will be canceled.

- ❑   AdAffectAllChapters – All records in the recordset will be deleted.

- ❑   adAffectCurrent – Only updates to the current record will be canceled.

- ❑   AdAffectGroup – Updates to all records in the current filter will be canceled.

Cursor and Lock Types

When we open a recordset with the Recordset object's Open method, we have the option of specifying a cursor type and a lock type. We have, up to now, treated the recordset as an ordered sequence of records; in fact, the records are ordered not by the recordset, but by a **cursor**. Cursors expose the entire recordset, but present the records as though they were sequentially ordered, and allow us to iterate through the records one at a time.

Cursor Types

There are a number of different types of cursor available, and the cursor we choose impacts dramatically on the features available to us and the performance of the application. ADO provides four types of cursor:

- ❑   **Forward-only** (adOpenForwardOnly) – This cursor only allows forward movement through the recordset, one record at a time.

- ❑   **Keyset** (adOpenKeyset) – This cursor supports both forward and backward movement through the recordset. The records are up-to-date with the underlying data, but added records are not visible.

- ❑   **Static** (adOpenStatic) – Both forward and backward movement is permitted. The data in the recordset is fixed at the time the cursor is created; no changes, additions or deletions by other users will be visible.

- ❑   **Dynamic** (adOpenDynamic) – Both forward and backward movement is permitted. Changes, additions and deletions by other users are visible. This cursor type is not supported by the MS Access provider.

- ❑   **Unspecified** (adOpenUnspecified) – Does not specify the cursor type.

Because a forward-only cursor only supports movement forwards through the recordset by one record at a time, we can only use MoveNext or Move with a value of one with this cursor. RecordCount is also not supported. It should be noted that the forward-only cursor is the default, so this is the cursor that will be returned if no cursor type is specified in the Recordset's Open method, or if the recordset is opened with the Execute method of the Connection object or the Command object.

As well as being specified when the recordset is opened, the cursor type may be defined in the Recordset object's CursorType property. For example, to set the cursor type as keyset:

```
objRec.CursorType = adOpenKeyset
```

However, this can only be done before the recordset is opened: once the recordset has been opened, the cursor cannot be changed. We can, however, use this property to verify the type of cursor in use. This is useful because, if we request a cursor type that is not supported by the provider being used, another cursor type will automatically be substituted.

Cursor Location

As well as specifying the type of cursor to use, we may also specify the location of the cursor – that is, whether the cursor is to be situated on the client or on the server. To do this, we use the Connection object's CursorLocation property. To specify a client-side cursor, we use:

```
objConn.CursorLocation = adUseClient
```

And for a server-side cursor:

```
objConn.CursorLocation = adUseServer
```

There is also an option adUseNone, to specify that no cursor services are required, but this is obsolete and appears solely for the sake of backward compatibility. The default is adUseServer.

Server-side cursors are supplied by the data provider or driver. These cursors are sometimes very flexible and allow for additional sensitivity to changes others make to the data source. However, some features of the Microsoft Client Cursor Provider (such as disconnected recordsets) cannot be simulated with server-side cursors and these features will be unavailable with this setting.

Client-side cursors are supplied by a local cursor library. Local cursor engines often allow many features that driver-supplied cursors may not, so using this setting may provide an advantage with respect to features that will be enabled. However, only the static cursor type is supported.

> The **CursorLocation** property can only be set while the connection object is closed. It should therefore be set before the **Open** method is called.

Lock Types

The LockType property indicates the type of locking that applies to records while they are being edited: for example, how the provider will attempt to prevent multiple users editing the same record simultaneously, and thus avoid data integrity conflicts. This can be an important part of your client-server environment. It's important to specify the limits to prevent one application being able to edit a record while another is editing the same record. The available lock types are:

- ❑ adLockReadOnly – Read-only: the data cannot be modified. This is the default.

- ❑ AdLockPessimistic – Pessimistic locking. This shifts control to the provider, which will attempt to lock edited records.

- ❑ AdLockOptimistic – Optimistic locking. The provider only locks records as they are being updated.

- ❑ adLockBatchOptimistic – Optimistic batch updates. Used to specify batch update mode.

- ❑ adLockUnspecified – Does not specify the lock type. If a recordset is cloned then the same lock type will be created.

For example, to specify pessimistic locking:

```
objRec.LockType = adLockPessimistic
```

Specifying pessimistic locking is a safe way of avoiding data conflicts, since the record is locked as soon as one user starts to edit it: no other user can edit the record until the first user's edit has been completed. With optimistic locking, the locking occurs only when the user attempts to update the database. This means that another user may already have edited the record by this time, and a conflict can arise. This is clearly less satisfactory if avoiding conflicts is the main priority, but it is more efficient in its use of resources, since pessimistic locking implies a permanent connection to the database.

Batch optimistic locking is typically used with client-side cursors and disconnected recordset. In batch update mode, updates are cached locally until the UpdateBatch method is called.

Working with Fields

We have already seen that every field in the recordset is represented by a Field object. These Field objects are contained in the Recordset object's Fields collection.

The Fields Collection

If we want to obtain a reference to this collection, we use the Fields property of the Recordset object:

```
Set colFields = objRec.Fields
```

The Fields collection has three methods and two properties used for managing the fields of the recordset. The Item property is used to return a specific Field object from the collection and can be used in conjunction with either the index position of the Field object in the collection or the name of the field:

```
Set objField = objRec.Fields.Item(1)
```

or:

```
Set objField = objRec.Fields.Item("au_lname")
```

Since Item is the default property we can also use either of the following:

```
Set objField = objRec.Fields(1)
```

```
Set objField = objRec.Fields("au_lname")
```

But Fields is also the default property for the Recordset object, so in fact, either of the following will do the same job:

```
Set objField = objRec(1)
```

```
Set objField = objRec("au_lname")
```

This is, of course, equivalent to the familiar exclamation mark syntax:

```
Set objField = objRec!au_lname
```

The other property exposed by the Fields collection is Count, which returns the number of Field objects in the collection. This can be used as an alternative to the For Each construction to iterate through the collection:

```
For intCount = 0 To objRec.Fields.Count - 1
   Set objField = objRec.Fields.Item(intCount)
   ' Do something with the field...
Next
```

Like other ADO collections, the Fields collection is zero-based, so the first field has an index value of zero, and the last of Fields.Count - 1.

The Fields collection also provides methods to refresh the collection, add fields to, and delete fields from the collection. However, the Refresh method has no visible effect: the Recordset object's Requery method should be used instead. And note that fields can only be added to or deleted from recordsets that you have created yourself.

The Append method adds a Field object to the collection. We must supply as parameters the name of the field and its data type (one of the DataTypeEnum constants); we can also supply a defined size (in characters or bytes) for the field, and attributes for the new field (such as whether the field can contain Null values). This can be any of the FieldAttributeEnum constants. This method can be used to create recordsets programmatically:

```
Dim objRec As New ADODB.Recordset

objRec.Fields.Append "Name", adVarChar, 25, adFldMayBeNull
objRec.Fields.Append "Age", adInteger, 8, adFldFixed
```

This method cannot be used on an open recordset (even a disconnected one), or one for which an `ActiveConnection` has been set. In addition, the `CursorLocation` must be set to `adUseClient`.

The final method, `Delete`, allows us to remove fields from a programmatically created recordset. The field to be deleted can be specified by its index value or by its name:

```
objRec.Fields.Delete(1)
```

```
objRec.Fields.Delete("Age")
```

The Field Object

The `Field` object exposes a number of properties that define what kind of data can be held in that particular field. Some of these are identical to the parameters passed into the `Fields` collection's `Append` method. The `Name` property simply specifies the field's name, and can be used, as we have seen, to retrieve a specific field object. For example, this line makes use of a `Field` object whose `Name` property is `au_lname`:

```
Set objField = objRec("au_lname")
```

The `Type` property indicates the data type for values in the field, and may be one of the `DataTypeEnum` constants. A list of these constants and the corresponding data types in SQL Server and Access can be found in the section on *Creating a Parameter Object* above.

The `Attributes` property contains one or more of the `FieldAttributeEnum` constants. For example, to specify that a field may be updated and also that it can contain Null values:

```
objField.Attributes = adFldUpdatable + adFldIsNullable
```

The `Attributes` property can contain more than one of these values – they are compounded by bitwise addition. Thus, when reading this property, we can use the logical AND to check the `Attributes` property for the attribute that we seek:

```
If (objField.Attributes AND adFldUpdatable) = adFldUpdatable Then
    ' Field can be updated
End If
```

The other parameter passed into the `Append` method, indicating the maximum size in bytes or characters for values in the field, corresponds to the `Field` object's `DefinedSize` property. Related to this is the `ActualSize` property, which returns the actual size of a specific entry in the field. For fixed length fields, `ActualSize` and `DefinedSize` will have the same value.

> Remember that these properties of the **Field** object can only be set when creating a recordset. For an open recordset, they will be read-only.

Disconnected and Persisted Recordsets

While it is possible to keep open the connection to the database for the whole time that the application is running, this is clearly inefficient in its use of resources: it requires the connection to be open even when no data is being passed between the client and the server, and more network traffic is used when the database is updated every time a record changes than is needed for batch updates.

The solution to this is to use **disconnected recordsets**. These are recordsets that are not actively connected to the database server. They can be manipulated on the client, and batch updates can be sent in one go when required. To disconnect a recordset, we must:

- ❑ Set the CursorLocation to adUseClient
- ❑ Set the Recordset's ActiveConnection to Nothing
- ❑ Set the LockType to adLockBatchOptimistic

To update the recordset, we must call the UpdateBatch method. We can specify whether all records are to be marshaled back to the server, or only those that have been modified, by setting the Recordset object's MarshalOptions property. If this is set to adMarshalAll (the default), all rows will be returned to the server; if it is set to adMarshalModifiedOnly, only those records that have been altered will be returned. This can greatly improve performance.

As well as disconnecting a recordset temporarily from the server, we can create a more permanent local copy of the recordset on the hard drive. In order to create a **persisted recordset**, we use the Save method of the Recordset object. This takes two parameters: the path and filename under which the recordset is to be saved, and the format in which the recordset is to be saved. In ADO 2.0, the only possible value for this second parameter is adPersistADTG. So, to save a recordset with the filename Recordset.adtg in the My Documents folder, we would use:

```
objRec.Save "C:/My Documents/Recordset.adtg", adPersistADTG
```

When we wish to open this persisted recordset, we pass the path and filename into the Recordset's Open method, and use a command type of adCmdFile:

```
objRec.Open "C:/My Documents/Recordset.adtg", , adOpenStatic, _
            adLockOptimistic, adCmdFile
```

ADO 2.1 and later also permits files to be saved in XML format. To do this, we specify a persist format of adPersistXML:

```
objRec.Save "C:/My Documents/Recordset.xml", adPersistXML
```

This will cause the recordset to be saved as an XML file, in which each recordset is represented by an XML element and each field as an attribute of that element. For example, the first record in the SQL Server pubs database will appear as:

```
<z:row au_id="409-56-7008" au_lname="Bennet" au_fname="Abraham" phone="415 658-
9932" address="6223 Bateman St." city="Berkeley" state="CA" zip="94705"
contract="True" />
```

ADO Events

In the next chapter, we will write some code that changes the caption of a label whenever the user moves to a different record. In order to be able to react to this change, we will place the code in an event handler for the `Recordset` object's `MoveComplete` event. ADO supports a number of such events. These events are raised when an operation is executed against an object or when one of its properties changes, and they allow us to react to changes as they occur, rather than having to check whether something has happened before we execute code that is dependent on the change.

ADO events fall into two classes – events that are fired immediately before an action occurs, and events that are fired after the operation has taken place. The former always has names beginning `Will...`, the latter frequently (but by no means always) ends with `...Complete`. Although many of these events fall into pairs, such as `WillConnect` and `ConnectComplete`, the first occurring just before the action and the second just after it, many of the events fired after an action have no corresponding `Will...` event. In this chapter, we will only look at a few of the more important events.

Accessing ADO Events

Two of the ADO objects support events: the `Connection` object and the `Recordset` object. To access the events of one or other of these objects, we must first dimension the `Connection` or `Recordset` object `WithEvents` in the `General Declarations` section of a class module or form:

```
Dim WithEvents objConn As ADODB.Connection
```

The events now become available and appear in the **Procedure** drop-down box of the code window:

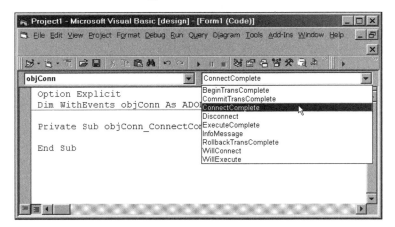

Connection Object Events

The events exposed by the `Connection` object relate to changes in the state of the connection, such as when a connection is opened or closed. There are also events that are fired whenever a command is executed against the connection, and events that relate to transactions performed against the connection.

The WillConnect Event

The first event to be fired in an ADO session is the `WillConnect` event, which is raised immediately before a connection is made to the database. The event handler supports six arguments, which expose connection details to the code in the event handler:

Name	Data type	Description
ConnectionString	String	The connection string for the current connection.
UserID	String	The user ID for the current connection. This will be empty if the user ID was passed in as part of the connection string, rather than as a separate parameter.
Password	String	The password for the current connection. Again, this will be empty if the password was entered as part of the connection string.
Options	Long	The options specified in the method call for opening the connection.
adStatus	EventStatusEnum constant	The status of the operation. Setting this to adStatusCancel or 4 cancels the operation, and causes the connection not to be opened.
pConnection	Connection object	The Connection object for the event.

This event could be used to check the user's details or the connection string before making the connection. If any of these details are invalid, they can be corrected or the operation can be halted. For example, we could use this event to prevent any attempt to log on as the systems administrator:

```
Private Sub objConn_WillConnect(ConnectionString As String, _
      UserID As String, Password As String, Options As Long, _
      adStatus As ADODB.EventStatusEnum, _
      ByVal pConnection As ADODB.Connection)
   If UserID = "sa" Then
     MsgBox "Sorry. It is not permitted to log on as the " & _
            "Systems Administrator.", vbExclamation
     adStatus = adStatusCancel
   End If
End Sub
```

This code checks the `UserID` argument to see if it is equal to `"sa"`, the default user name for the Systems Administrator in SQL Server. If it is, we display a message box informing the user that they are not permitted to log on as the SA and cancel the operation by setting `adStatus` to `adStatusCancel`. This code assumes that the user ID and password were passed in separately as parameters to the `Open` method; if they were included in the connection string, we need to parse the `ConnectionString` argument instead:

```
If InStr(UCase(ConnectionString), "USER ID=SA") <> 0 Then
```

We use the UCase function to capitalize the connection string to ensure that the comparison does not fail due to case sensitivity. Of course, if we did not know how the user details were passed in, we would have to check both these methods:

```
If UserID = "sa" Or InStr(UCase(ConnectionString), _
          "USER ID=SA") <> 0 Then
```

The ConnectComplete Event

The ConnectComplete event is fired when the connection has been made, or when the attempt to connect fails. It allows us to halt the application until the connection is complete and to check that the connection was successful, or to handle any errors that occurred. The event has three arguments:

Name	Data type	Description
pError	Error object	An object representing any error, which occurred.
adStatus	EventStatusEnum	The status of the operation.
pConnection	Connection object	The Connection object for the event.

Since the user could be waiting a few seconds for the connection to be made, it is a good idea to use this event to inform the user either that the connection was successful, or that an error occurred. If the mouse pointer was set to vbHourglass before making the connection, we could reset it here. For example, the following code sets the mouse pointer to the hourglass and opens the SQL Server Northwind database when a command button called cmdOpen is clicked, and informs the user of the result when the ConnectComplete event fires:

```
Option Explicit
Dim WithEvents objConn As ADODB.Connection


Private Sub cmdOpen_Click()
  Me.MousePointer = vbHourglass
  Set objConn = New ADODB.Connection
  objConn.Open "Provider=SQLOLEDB;Data Source=bigsmile;" & _
             "Initial Catalog=Northwind;User ID=sa"
End Sub


Private Sub objConn_ConnectComplete(ByVal pError As ADODB.Error, _
          adStatus As ADODB.EventStatusEnum, ByVal pConnection As _
          ADODB.Connection)
  Me.MousePointer = vbArrow
  Select Case adStatus
    Case adStatusOK
      MsgBox "Connection successful."
    Case adStatusErrorsOccurred
      MsgBox "Error occurred: " & pError.Description
    Case Else
```

```
        MsgBox "Connection status unknown."
    End Select
End Sub
```

This ensures that the user is aware of what's happening until the connection is made, and will be less likely to assume that the system has hung.

The Disconnect Event

When a connection is closed, either because the Connection object's Close method was called, or because of a network problem, the Disconnect event is fired. This event takes only two arguments:

Name	Data type	Description
adStatus	EventStatusEnum	The status of the operation.
pConnection	Connection object	The Connection object for the event.

This event could be used to inform the user and perform error handling when a connection drops unexpectedly, or to track users as they log into and out of the database. The following code shows how we might achieve the latter. When the Disconnect event is fired, an entry is added to a log file (called Pubs.log) in a directory named Database Log, indicating that the current user has logged out at the current time. The user ID for the current user is returned by the User ID property in the Connection object's Properties collection.

```
Private Sub objConn_Disconnect(adStatus As ADODB.EventStatusEnum, _
                               ByVal pConnection As ADODB.Connection)
    Dim intFileHandle As Integer
    intFileHandle = FreeFile
    Open "c:/Database Log/Pubs.log" For Append As intFileHandle
    Print #intFileHandle, "User '" & objConn.Properties("User ID") & _
                    "' logged out at " & Now() & "."
    Close #intFileHandle
End Sub
```

Recordset Object Events

The events exposed by the Recordset object are raised when a property of the Recordset object is altered or when one of the Recordset's methods is called. For example, events are fired when changes are made to the recordset, when the user navigates to a different record, and when the recordset is refreshed.

The MoveComplete Event

The MoveComplete event is fired after the record pointer has been moved from one record to another. This event has four arguments:

Name	Data type	Description
adReason	Long	The reason why the event was fired. This is one of the EventReasonEnum constants, and indicates whether the event was fired because of a Move, MoveFirst, MoveLast, MoveNext, MovePrevious or Requery method call. This will also be adRsnMove if the event was fired due to the Bookmark or AbsolutePosition properties being set.
adStatus	Long	The status of the operation.
pError	Error object	An object representing any error that occurred.
pRecordset	Recordset object	The Recordset object for the event.

We will see in the next chapter how this event can be used to update the caption of a label indicating the position of the current record in the recordset:

```
Private Sub objRec_MoveComplete(ByVal adReason As ADODB.EventReasonEnum, _
        ByVal pError As ADODB.Error, adStatus As _
        ADODB.EventStatusEnum, ByVal pRecordset As ADODB.Recordset)
    lblStatus.Caption = "Record " & objRec.AbsolutePosition & " out of " & _
                    objRec.RecordCount
End Sub
```

The RecordChangeComplete Event

The last event we'll look at in this chapter is RecordChangeComplete. This is fired, as its name suggests, whenever the value of a record has been changed. Its arguments are:

Name	Data type	Description
adReason	EventReasonEnum	The reason the event was fired
cRecords	Long	The number of records which changed
pError	Error object	An object representing any error which occurred
adStatus	EventStatusEnum	The status of the operation
pRecordset	Recordset object	The Recordset object for the event

We could use this event for auditing. For example, to record the ID of the user who made the changes, the number of records affected and the time the changes were made to a log file named Pubs.log in the Database Log folder, we could use the following code:

```
Private Sub objRec_RecordChangeComplete(ByVal adReason As _
        ADODB.EventReasonEnum, ByVal cRecords As Long, ByVal pError _
        As ADODB.Error, adStatus As ADODB.EventStatusEnum, ByVal _
        pRecordset As ADODB.Recordset)

    Dim intFileHandle As Integer
    intFileHandle = FreeFile

    Open "c:/Database Log/Pubs.log" For Append As intFileHandle
    Print #intFileHandle, "User '" & objRec.ActiveConnection.Properties _
        ("User ID") & "' changed " & cRecords & " records at " & Now() & "."
    Close #intFileHandle

End Sub
```

Error Handling

We can use the `Connection` object's events to perform error handling when errors occur, such as whenever a connection fails or is broken. ADO provides an `Error` object to facilitate this. Each `Connection` object contains an `Errors` collection with information on any errors that occurred. Each error is represented by an `Error` object, which is used to hold a description and other information for the error. Note that an `Error` object represents an error from the OLE DB provider, and not an ADO error. ADO raises runtime errors, which must be handled using the normal `On Error GoTo` or `On Error Resume Next` line. In contrast, provider errors do not necessarily halt the execution of the program.

The Errors Collection

In order to access a specific `Error` object, we must first get a reference to the `Errors` collection, using the `Errors` property of the `Connection` object:

```
Dim colErrors As ADODB.Errors

Set colErrors = objConn.Errors
```

The `Errors` collection provides methods and properties for accessing the individual `Error` objects exposed by the connection. To retrieve a specific `Error` object, we can use the `Item` property with the index value specifying the position of the object in the collection. This index value is zero-based, so, for example, to retrieve the first `Error` object, we need to write:

```
Dim objError As ADODB.Error

Set objError = objConn.Errors.Item(0)
```

We can determine the number of `Error` objects in the collection (that is, the number of errors returned from the provider for a given connection) using the `Count` property of the `Errors` collection:

```
MsgBox objConn.Errors.Count & " errors occurred."
```

We can use these two properties in conjunction to iterate through the `Errors` collection:

```
For intCount = 0 To objConn.Errors.Count -1

  Set objError = objConn.Errors.Item(intCount)

  '
  ' Error handling goes here.
  '

Next
```

Because the `Errors` collection is zero-based, its first member has an index value of zero, and its last member an index of `objConn.Errors.Count -1`, not `objConn.Errors.Count`. Alternatively, we can of course use the `For Each` construction:

```
Dim colErrors As ADODB.Errors
Dim objError As ADODB.Error

For Each objError In colErrors

  '
  ' Error handling goes here.
  '

Next
```

The `Errors` collection is automatically cleared every time a new error occurs, so any information about previous errors is lost when a new error occurs. This does not mean that the `Errors` collection can only ever contain one object, since providers can return multiple errors. In addition, providers sometimes return warning information, and these warnings are represented by `Error` objects in the `Errors` collection. For this reason, ADO provides a `Clear` method to clear the `Errors` collection programmatically:

```
objConn.Errors.Clear
```

This allows us to reset the `Errors` collection when desired, so that we know the collection is empty at that point. We consequently know that any errors or warnings in the collection occurred subsequently to that line. Finally, the `Errors` collection also has a `Refresh` method. This method can be called before working with an `Error` object, to ensure that we have access to the latest information from the provider.

The Error Object

The `Error` object has a number of properties that provide specific information about the error that the object represents. Perhaps the most useful of these is `Description`, which returns a string describing the error. This can be returned directly to the user when an error occurs:

```
On Error GoTo Err_handler

.
.
.

Err_handler:
Dim objError As ADODB.Error

For Each objError In objConn.Errors
  MsgBox objError.Description, vbExclamation, "ADO Error"
Next
```

Alternatively, we can provide our own, more user-friendly error messages. To do this, we can use the `Error` object's `Number` property to identify the error that occurred, and match that with our custom description:

```
On Error GoTo Err_handler

.
.
.

Err_handler:
Dim objError As ADODB.Error

For Each objError In objConn.Errors
   Select Case objError.Number
     Case -2147217843
       MsgBox "SQL Server could not authenticate you. Please check" & _
               vbCrLf & "that your user name and password were " & _
               "correctly entered.", vbExclamation, "ADO Error"

       ' etc. ...

     Case Else
       MsgBox "An unknown error has occurred:" & vbCrLf & _
               objError.Description, vbExclamation, "ADO Error"
   End Select
Next
```

Here we use Visual Basic's `Select Case` construction to enumerate through the codes for any errors we want to trap for, including a final `Case Else` clause, in case any errors occur which we were unable to foresee.

The other properties provide further information about the cause of the error. Perhaps the most important is the `NativeError` property, which returns a provider-specific error code: that is, an error code returned by the OLE DB provider in use, and defined by that provider. These error codes are therefore not generic to ADO or OLE DB, but vary according to the provider in question. For this reason they may be more specific than the generic errors. For information on these error codes, consult the provider's documentation.

We will be looking at the subject of error handling in more detail in Chapter 5.

Binding to VB Controls with ADO

When we use the ADO Data Control in the next chapter, we will bind the other controls in our form via that control to the data provider, and so avoid populating them with data programmatically. We can do the same with ADO, binding controls directly to the recordset or to a middle-tier data component. This is done by setting the control's `DataSource` and `DataField` properties. We can illustrate this with a very simple, minimalistic database application. Design a form with two text boxes, named `txtFirst` and `txtLast`, and two command buttons, `cmdFirst` and `cmdLast`:

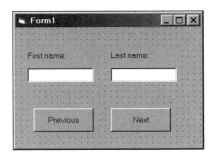

When the form loads, we will connect to the SQL Server `pubs` database, selecting the `au_fname` and `au_lname` fields from the `authors` table. We set the `DataSource` property for the two text boxes to our recordset (named `objRec`), and the `DataField` property to the fields that they will represent, `au_fname` and `au_lname`:

```
Private Sub Form_Load()

    Set objConn = New ADODB.Connection
    objConn.Open "Provider=SQLOLEDB;Data Source=julians;" & _
                 "Initial Catalog=pubs;User ID=sa;Password="

    Set objRec = New ADODB.Recordset
    objRec.Open "SELECT au_fname,au_lname FROM authors", objConn, _
                adOpenStatic, adLockOptimistic, adCmdText

    Set txtFirst.DataSource = objRec
    txtFirst.DataField = "au_fname"
    Set txtLast.DataSource = objRec
    txtLast.DataField = "au_lname"

    objRec.MoveFirst

End Sub
```

And that's all there is to it! When the user navigates through the recordset, the text boxes will automatically be updated, just as they were when we used the ADO Data Control. Two command buttons provide the basic functionality for this navigation through the recordset (for simplicity's sake, we have only included `Previous` and `Next` buttons):

```
Private Sub cmdNext_Click()
  objRec.MoveNext
  If objRec.EOF Then objRec.MoveLast
End Sub
```

```
Private Sub cmdPrev_Click()
  objRec.MovePrevious
  If objRec.BOF Then objRec.MoveFirst
End Sub
```

Notice that we check the EOF and BOF properties after MoveNext and MovePrevious calls, to avoid generating an error if the record pointer goes beyond these markers.

Finally, when the form is closed, we update the database with the new values, and uninstantiate our Recordset and Connection objects:

```
Private Sub Form_Unload(Cancel As Integer)
  objRec.Update
  objRec.Close
  Set objRec = Nothing
  objConn.Close
  Set objConn = Nothing
End Sub
```

Summary

In this chapter, we took a tour of all the objects – and many of the methods, properties and events – of the ADO object model. As I mentioned at the beginning of the chapter, it's through using these that you will learn them. Additionally, most of the basic concepts of connections, commands, parameters, and resultsets found in ADO are carried forward in ADO.NET. Certainly ADO.NET is quite different in some ways, but the underlying concepts remain largely consistent and in our industry, a solid understanding of concepts is often the best we can hope for.

We have deliberately avoided trying to cover every little detail about ADO here – that would be impossible in a chapter of this size, and indeed, there are probably some methods, properties and events you will never use. However, now that you have a good knowledge of the most important of them, you will be able quickly to find the methods and properties you need to accomplish any given task in Appendix D.

p2p.wrox.com

The programmer's resource centre

ASP **Today**

wrox.com

wrox

wrox*direct*

4

Working with the ADO Data Control

In this chapter, we'll examine the flexible ADO Data Control, to see how it facilitates connecting to a database, and inputting and retrieving data through VB forms. The aim of this chapter is to provide a solid understanding of the Data Control and how it allows us to connect to databases without having to worry too much about its object model.

In this chapter:

- ❑ We begin by using the Visual Data Manager to build a database, which will contain addresses and phone numbers.

- ❑ Then we'll build an application that allows us to view the data present in our database. We'll extend our application to include a navigation bar that allows us to add, delete, modify, and search for data.

- ❑ Finally, we'll take a look at some of the other controls that we didn't use in the example, but are readily available for you to use in your projects.

Application Walk-Through

The application that we will build in this chapter consists of a form that houses the ADO Data Control. This control connects to a database containing addresses. The database doesn't exist yet, so we'll build it using Visual Basic's Visual Data Manager (VisData) program. This database will have one table, which holds address information such as name, phone number, and address. The application will be able to:

- ❑ Navigate and locate records
- ❑ Update records

❑ Indicate the current record and the record count in a status label

❑ Add and delete records

❑ Locate a record, given a search string

Building the Database

As already mentioned, we are using our own database, rather than a ready-made one, so building this database is the first thing we need to do. SQL Server, Oracle, or other high-end database servers are undeniably powerful data stores, yet many applications do not require their level of sophistication or security, and Visual Basic has shared a very long and rich history with Access and its Jet database engine. From the days of VB3, there have been close ties between Jet and VB, allowing us to quickly, easily, and cheaply integrate basic data management into our applications.

Even looking forward to .NET, the Jet engine remains a viable and attractive option for some applications. It is the only database engine from Microsoft that doesn't have complex or expensive licensing requirements. Although SQL Server 2000 has its Personal Edition, more commonly known as MSDE, its license is quite restrictive. Jet's license is simple, and the technology is even more usable in VB6 than it was in earlier versions.

So we'll create a Jet database using Microsoft's VisData. Note that Jet databases do not require Access; any database that uses Jet as its database engine is a Jet database, and VisData lets us create them without Access installed.

VisData can:

❑ Build and maintain Jet databases and tables (as well as other formats)

❑ Create indexes on tables

❑ Enter/edit data in tables

❑ Create queries

❑ Repair or compact any Jet database

❑ Create and test SQL statements

Although Jet is inexpensive and easy to use, it is quite limited in its capabilities and can only support a handful of concurrent users, unlike SQL Server. The ADO Data Control is quite capable of connecting to SQL Server data stores, and the procedures involved are very similar to those for Jet that we'll look at as we work through this chapter.

Our database will be fairly simple with just one table, called Address, with the following fields: AddressID, Last_Name, First_Name, Street, City, State, Zip, Phone, and Comments. The AddressID will be created as a long number, with an auto counter activated. This field will also be our primary key. The Last_Name and First_Name fields will be created with indexes attached. Although we won't be using SQL commands in this chapter, it's always better to plan for future sorting and data selection requirements.

Let's get started. Open Visual Basic, and choose Visual Data Manager from the Add-Ins menu. When the VisData program opens, select File | New | Microsoft Access | Version 7.0 MDB.

> **Versions of Access prior to Access 95 use version 2.0 MDB, so if you have such a version and wish to view the database from Access (which isn't necessary for our application), choose version 2.0 instead of 7.0.**

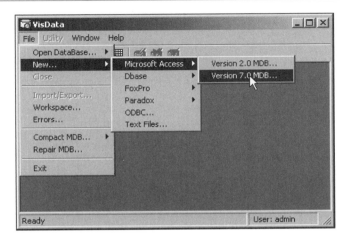

We are now prompted to choose a location and name for our database. Create a folder called `wrox`, and create the database in this new folder as `Address`. The extension `.mdb` will automatically be appended.

VisData creates an Access database without any tables, so the next thing to do is add one. Right-click the Properties node in the Database Window and select New Table.

> **The Properties item of the Database Window pane allows you to view any associated properties of the database that is currently opened. These properties include database location, the version that the database was created in and time-out parameters for queries. Properties exist on databases, tables, and even fields. They are an intricate part of the schema of the database as a whole.**

This opens the Table Structure dialog, which allows us to create a new table. Enter Address in the Table Name box, and we can start adding the fields by clicking the Add Field button to bring up the Add Field dialog.

Type AddressID in the Name box for our first field. This field will store a long number and will automatically increment when a new record is added, so select Long from the Type drop-down and check the AutoIncrField box. Lastly, click the Required checkbox. Although the database assigns a value automatically, this ensures the user won't remove the value later. The dialog should look like the following screenshot:

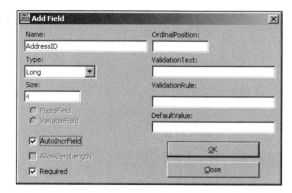

For reference, the other options on this dialog are:

❑ Size: The maximum number of characters the user can enter. Primarily for text data types.

❑ FixedField/VariableField: Specifies if the data in the field can be less than the maximum allowed, or if it is fixed. Text fields only.

❑ AllowZeroLength: Indicates if a zero length value is acceptable, such as empty strings or nulls.

❑ OrdinalPosition: The order of the fields in the table. This is zero-based, so the first field is zero, the second is one, and so on. This is significant if you reference the field based on its ordinal position (although it's not a common practice) rather than field name. Additionally, this is the default tab order, and the order that your fields will be added to the form when you use form wizards.

❑ ValidationText: The error message that will be shown if the user breaks the validation rule.

❑ ValidationRule: A rule that limits the acceptable values for the field. For example, a rule of >10 would cause an error for values below 11.

❑ DefaultValue: The value to use if the user leaves the field blank.

For this example, we won't add any validation text or descriptions, so just click **OK** and the field will be added. Add a further eight fields, according to the following table:

Name	Type	Size	Required	FixedField/VariableField
Last_Name	Text	35	No*	Variable
First_Name	Text	25	No*	Variable
Street	Text	50	No	Variable
City	Text	20	No	Variable
State	Text	2	No	Variable
Zip	Text	10	No	Variable
Phone	Text	10	No	Variable
Comments	Memo	N/A	No	Variable

Although this would be the best place to ensure the Last_Name *and* First_Name *fields are populated, we'll leave this unchecked for now so that later we can demonstrate how to implement business rules in code.*

Once you have finished adding the fields, click the **Close** button, and the **Table Structure** dialog should now appear as in the following screenshot. As you click each field, the corresponding properties are presented:

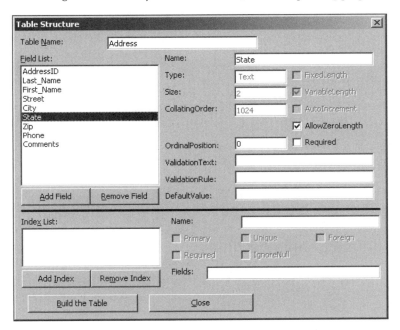

The final step before building the table is to specify the indexes by clicking the **Add Index** button. When the **Add Index to Address** dialog appears, click the **AddressID** field to add it to the **Indexed Fields** list box. Then copy and paste it into the **Name** box as the name for the index. This way, you won't accidentally misspell it (if you need to rationalize being lazy!). In this table, the AddressID field will be classified as a primary key and will always be unique, so leave both boxes checked:

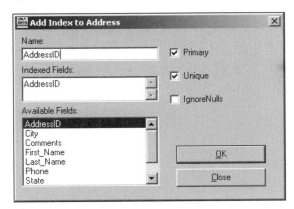

Build two more indexes as follows:

Index Name	Fields Added	Primary Key	Unique	Ignore Nulls
First_Name	First_Name	Unchecked	Unchecked	Unchecked
Last_Name	Last_Name	Unchecked	Unchecked	Unchecked

After adding these indexes, we're ready for the final step of building the table. Click the Build the Table button at the bottom of the Table Structure dialog.

Once the table has been built, you'll be able to review the properties of the table, fields, and indexes in the Database Window pane. Double-clicking the properties of the various fields in the Database Window allows you to modify them where possible.

We can insert the first record in the database using VisData's graphical user interface. Select Open from the table's context menu in the Database Window, or simply double-click the table name, and then click Add on the dialog that appears. Enter some data and click Update:

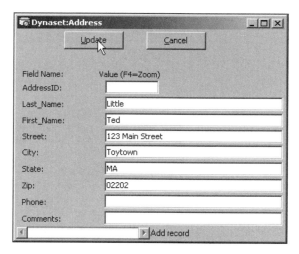

Alternatively, you could create the record by typing a SQL statement, such as that shown below, into the SQL Statement pane and clicking the Execute button:

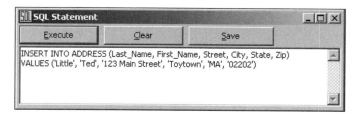

Click No when asked if the statement is a SQLPassThrough query. Such queries are for databases that handle SQL themselves, perhaps in a slightly modified dialect of SQL. Clicking No allows the client application to optimize the query if appropriate.

Now that we've built the table and added a record, let's add some more data. Click on the **Use DBGrid Control on New Form** button (the sixth from left button on the VisData toolbar). When you now open the `Address` table, it will appear in a grid format:

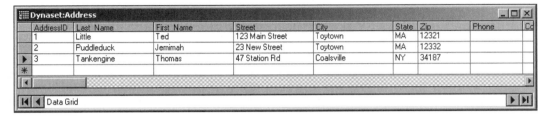

Add two or three records for use later when testing our interface. You can now close VisData and return to Visual Basic.

Building the Front-End Application

Now that we have built our database, we can build the interface that will connect to it. Return to Visual Basic. You should already have a new Standard EXE project opened. Follow the steps below:

1. Change the name of the project to `prjAddress`.

2. Change the name of the form to `frmAddress`.

3. Change the `Caption` property of `frmAddress` to **Address Database**.

4. Save the form and project as `Address.vbp` and `Address.frm` in a suitable folder off the `wrox` one we created earlier.

The ADO Data Control

The ADO Data Control is not included in the Toolbox for Standard Executable projects by default. To add it, select **Project** from Visual Basic's menu bar and then select **Components**. The **Components** dialog will open, allowing you to choose which components you want to add to the project. Locate **Microsoft ADO Data Control 6.0** in the list and check it. If you are unable to locate the control, you may need to reinstall Visual Basic, ensuring that the Database options are selected (if using a custom install).

To open the Components dialog, you can also right-click the toolbox and select Components.

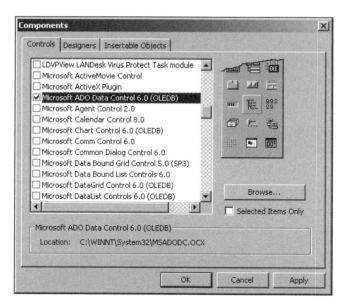

After selecting this, click **OK** and the ADO Data Control will be added to the Toolbox. It looks like a horizontal scrollbar with a yellow database symbol attached.

Add an ADO Data Control to your form, and set its `Align` property to `vbAlignBottom`:

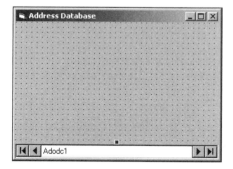

The ADO Data Control requires a connection string, which allows it to connect to virtually any database server. In fact, the ADO Data Control can access data sources other than databases, such as LDAP data sources, e-mail data sources, text data sources, and so on. The connection string contains the information required to connect, such as the drivers to use, security details, and the location of the data source.

Building the Connection String

To build a connection string, open the **Properties** window for the ADO Data Control and locate the `ConnectionString` property. Selecting this property causes an ellipsis button to appear (a button displaying three consecutive dots). Clicking this opens a wizard which walks you through the process of building a string:

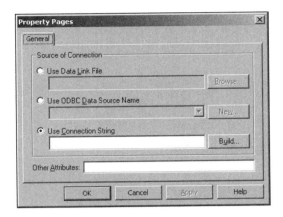

This dialog prompts you to choose one of three mechanisms for connecting to the database:

❑ **Use Data Link File:** Allows you to specify a file that contains the connection information. These files are can be created in Windows Explorer by choosing **Microsoft Data Link** from the list of **New** items. When saved, the file will have an extension of .UDL.

❑ **Use ODBC Data Source Name:** Allows you to specify an ODBC Data Source Name (DSN). DSNs are created from the **ODBC Data Source Administrator** located in the **Control Panel**.

❑ **Use Connection String:** Allows you to build a connection string that specifies drivers, database location and password information.

Ensure the **Use Connection String** option button is selected and click **Build**. The next dialog prompts you to select the database provider:

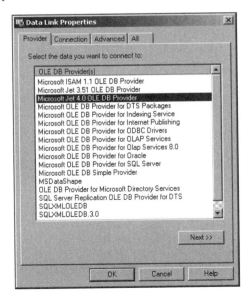

This dialog lists all the OLE DB providers installed on your system, so you may have a different number available. If you have Access 2000 or greater installed on your machine, select Microsoft Jet 4.0 OLE DB Provider; otherwise select Microsoft Jet 3.51 OLE DB Provider. Then click Next to move to the Connection tab:

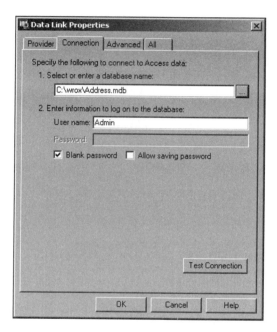

The Connection tab is where you specify the location of the database, and the username and password if required. Click the ellipsis button and locate the Address.mdb database. You can leave the username and password as they appear.

Click the Test Connection button and the wizard will attempt to connect to the database. If everything is configured correctly, the following message box should appear:

Click the OK button to close the message box.

While we're here, click the Advanced tab. This tab allows you to set protection levels for database servers using a network, the time-out for the connection attempt in seconds, and the access permissions for the database. Finally, open the All tab. This displays all properties relevant to your data source, and varies according to the source you are connecting to. To modify a property, select it and click the Edit Value button.

Click the OK button at the bottom of the dialog and the connection string now appears in the Use Connection String textbox:

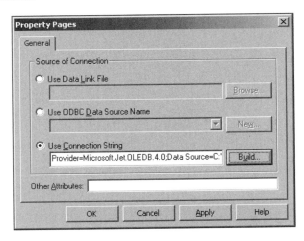

Notice that the connection string details the provider, security, and data source. We could have manually typed in this connection string had we wanted, but the wizard does prevent typos that can sometimes be hard to track down.

Setting the RecordSource Property

The RecordSource property specifies from where in the database the data will come, and is very flexible. We can specify a single table, or use a SQL statement to join several tables, select criteria, and even sort the data. As we work through examples in the book, we'll see how we can apply SQL to this property to extract the data we want.

Click the ellipsis button for the RecordSource property which opens the following Property Pages dialog. Select adCmdTable from the drop-down at the top, which should enable the Table or Stored Procedure Name listbox:

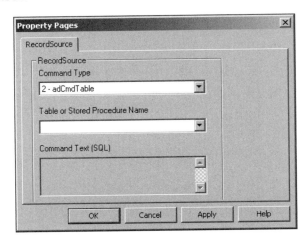

Select **Address** in the second drop-down, to make our control connect directly to this specific table.

The other command types are:

- ❏   adCmdUnknown – Use if you intend to specify the RecordSource in code.

- ❏   adCmdText – The RecordSource is determined by the SQL command given in the lower **Command Text** textbox.

- ❏   adCmdStoredProc – The stored procedure named in the second drop-down will determine the RecordSource.

Click **OK**, and our ADO Data Control is now configured to connect to the Address table of the Address database on startup.

Setting the Other Properties

Change the EOFAction property of the ADO Data Control to adDoAddNew, indicating that if the 'End of File' (the end of the recordset in this case) is reached, a new record should be created for entry.

Finally, ensure the BOFAction property is set to adDoMoveFirst, which will prevent the user passing the beginning of the recordset and causing an error.

Building a User Interface

We now need to add more controls that will bind to the ADO Data Control. Each of these will represent a field for a specific record in the recordset. Follow these steps:

1.   Add a label to the form, and a textbox immediately below it.

2.   Name the label lblField, and set its BorderStyle property to Fixed Single, its Alignment property to Center and its BackColor property to pale yellow.

3.   Name the textbox txtField, and clear its Text property. Set its DataSource property to Adodc1. All textboxes that we add will be bound to this data source. Later, we'll assign specific fields in the DataField property of each.

Your form should now look as shown:

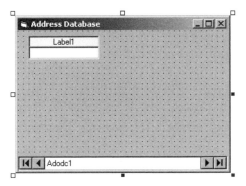

We'll need nine textboxes in total to display each of the fields in our database. To achieve this, multiselect both the label and textbox we have already, and copy and paste eight more instances of them. The textboxes will have duplicate names, so we are asked if we wish to create a control array when we paste. Click **Yes**, and our controls will then be distinguished by a unique index value in the array. Copying them at this stage means we don't have to set the properties of each individual control. Paste and arrange the controls as shown, working from left to right, and top to bottom:

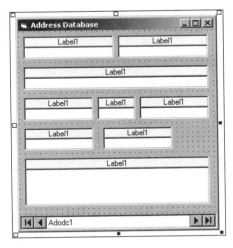

Although all labels have the name `lblField` and the textboxes are all called `txtField`, we can specify one particular control using its index value, ranging from 0 to 8. This allows us to manipulate the controls in our code by using a loop. The alternative of giving each control a unique name can often, depending on your functional requirements, require you to write more code as this array approach wouldn't be possible. For example, to change the `BackColor` property of all nine labels at run time, we can easily loop through all of them through their indices in the control array.

Saying this though, if we chose not to create a control array, we could loop through each controls with a `For Each` loop, which is fairly simple if we wish to change all controls that are of type 'Textbox'. If only a few of the textboxes were to be changed, we could use the `Tag` property to 'mark' those controls and check this value as we loop through them. The control array is more elegant I feel, but it's really down to personal preference.

Now change the `Caption` properties of the labels, again working from left to right, and top to bottom. Make sure the index matches that shown in the table below:

Index Property	Caption Property
0	Last Name
1	First Name
2	Street Address
3	City

Table continued on following page

107

Index Property	Caption Property
4	State
5	Zip Code
6	Phone
7	Address ID
8	Comments

The Comments textbox will need to accommodate multiple lines of text so change its `MultiLine` property to `True`, and its `ScrollBars` property to `Vertical`.

As you recall, the `AddressID` field is automatically generated by the database, so we don't want to allow the user to change its value. Change the following properties of the Address ID textbox:

Property	Value
Enabled	False
TabStop	False
Locked	True

The next step is to specify which field each textbox will be bound to. Let's begin with the first textbox, which will contain the surname. Select Last_Name from the `DataField` property drop-down.

Using the following table, change the `DataField` properties of the remaining textboxes:

Index Value	DataField Property
1	First_Name
2	Street
3	City
4	State
5	Zip
6	Phone
7	AddressID
8	Comments

Although we don't need to in this example, the `DataFormat` property brings up a useful dialog for customizing how numbers and dates are presented.

We're now ready to test the application. Save your work and run the project. You'll notice that the application opens with the first record displayed in the textboxes. Navigate through the records using the data control and modify some of the fields. Test out the Comments box by adding multiple lines of text.

By navigating to the end of the records, we can even add new records simply by filling in the empty form that appears and moving back to the previous record when done:

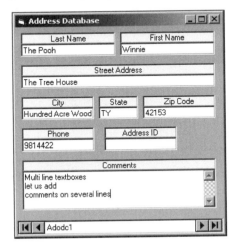

You may notice hard drive activity as you edit and move through the records. This is because each record is saved as you move off an edited record, a feature of the Jet Database Engine.

Without writing a single line of code, we have successfully built an application that connects to a database, allows us to navigate through the records, updating fields and adding new records. We'll continue our exploration of ADO by adding to this functionality later in the chapter.

What's Going On

Thankfully, this is all taken care of for us, and we can simply set the required properties and have the control handle the details.

The ADO Data Control we added is capable of navigating through the records of the database that we configure it to connect to. The records are stored in memory in a recordset; a subset of records from a table (or group of joined tables) based on a very specific criteria. The size of the recordset depends on how many records are returned by the query, the cache size limit, and the ADO's MaxRecords property. When a change is made to a record in the recordset, that change is made in the database if there is a call to the Update method of the ADO Data Control's Recordset object, which happens implicitly when the user navigates off the current record.

Once connected to a database, the ADO Data Control takes on the responsibility of passing data back and forth between the database and all the bound controls. In the case of our project, the first textbox is bound to the Last_Name field of the Address table. Thus, ADO uses the current record's Last_Name field to populate that textbox, and conversely, if any changes are made to the textbox, ADO uses the new value to update the appropriate field in the database accordingly.

109

The Masked Edit Control

One enhancement we can make to our project would be to mask certain fields that require a fixed format. For example, the phone number field should always be a specific length and we could use hyphens and parentheses to indicate the desired format, as in (555) 555-5555.

The Masked Edit Control lets us accomplish this, and it can be added by opening the Components dialog and checking Microsoft Masked Edit Control 6.0 to add it to the Toolbox. It appears after the ADO Data Control as the text ##|.

To create a mask for the phone number field, delete that textbox, and add a Masked Edit Control in its place. Name the new control mskPhone, and bind it to the ADO Data Control by setting its DataSource property to Adodc1 and its DataField property to Phone.

Open the property pages of the Masked Edit Control by right-clicking it and selecting Properties. Uncheck the PromptInclude checkbox, and type (###) ###-#### in the Mask text box. Type the same into the Format box (or just copy and paste):

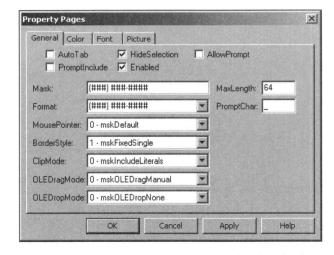

It's important to configure this control correctly, as it may not bind to the data source properly if you set a property erroneously.

The PromptInclude checkbox indicates whether the literals and prompt values, such as underscores and hash characters, should be included as part of the text to be passed to the database when the value is not populated.

The Mask property is a sort of template for text entered in that textbox. You can probably work out that our mask will display hyphens and brackets to separate numeric values represented by the hash character. The valid placeholders are:

❑   # – Digits only

❑   ? – Letters only

❑   & – Any character allowed

The `Format` property defines how the data should be displayed once the value has been entered, and the `PromptChar` property specifies the character that will take the place of values before anything has been entered. We'll just keep it as the underscore.

Click the **OK** button.

Change the `TabIndex` of the Masked Edit Control so that it replaces the removed textbox in the *Tab* order.

Run the application and you'll see that blank phone numbers appear filled in with underscores. The Masked Edit Control can give your application a professional look and feel, and help in validating data for certain fields.

Creating a Navigation Bar

The next thing we'll do is build a custom navigation bar. This is not always necessary, but it does have several advantages, including:

❑   Your navigation bar can reflect your GUI style. Command buttons can contain images or any caption that fits your needs.

❑   You can enable and disable portions of the navigation bar as required.

❑   It provides more flexibility for custom error trapping.

❑   It lets you apply business rules such as validation against the data before moving to the next record.

Because we're no longer using the ADO Data Control to navigate, the first thing to do is change its `Visible` property to `False` to hide it at run time. It will still be there to do our work for us, but we don't want to show it.

Add a single command button named `cmdNavigate` and set its `Font` property to **Arial, 10, Bold** – place over the top of the ADO control. Copy the command button and paste it on the form three times, creating a control array as before. Add a new label to the form, and set its `BackColor` property to pale yellow. Arrange the command buttons and label below the **Comments** textbox as shown in the next screenshot:

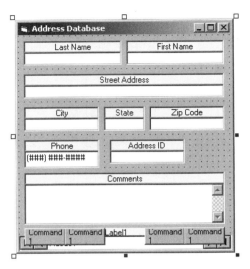

Change the other properties of the new controls according to the following table. Note that the buttons are ordered from left to right:

Object	Property	Value
Label	Name	lblRecord
	Caption	*blank*
	BorderStyle	Fixed Single
Command Button	Index	0
	Caption	|<<
Command Button	Index	1
	Caption	<
Command Button	Index	2
	Caption	>
Command Button	Index	3
	Caption	>>|

Navigating the Recordset

Recordset navigation will be taken care of by a single handler for the Click event of all the cmdNavigate buttons. When any of the buttons are clicked, the Index property will be used to determine the appropriate code to execute.

The next, previous, first, and last records can be located with a single line of code calling the MoveFirst, MoveLast, MoveNext, or MovePrevious method on the ADO Recordset object. These methods retrieve the specific record and refresh the bound controls. If an error occurs during the navigation, we'll display an error message in a message box.

When locating the next record or the previous record, we need to check to see if the EOF has been reached after we call the MoveNext method. If we have reached EOF, we move to the last record by stepping back one position. The same applies after we call the MovePrevious method, except we check for BOF, and call MoveFirst if so. If we didn't do this, we'd get an error on passing the start or end of records. Although we could handle this with our error handler, we should always avoid an error situation if we can.

Click on one of the command buttons, and enter the following code for the handler:

```
Private Sub cmdNavigate_Click(Index As Integer)

    On Error GoTo goNavigateErr

    With Adodc1.Recordset

      Select Case Index
        Case 0  'First Record
          .MoveFirst
        Case 1  'Previous Record
          .MovePrevious
          If .BOF Then .MoveFirst
        Case 2  'Next Record
          .MoveNext
          If .EOF Then .MoveLast
        Case 3  'Last Record
          .MoveLast
      End Select

    End With

  Exit Sub


goNavigateErr:

    MsgBox Err.Description

  End Sub
```

Updating the Status Label

After the ADO Data Control has completed navigating to a specific record, an event is fired called `MoveComplete`. We'll create a handler for this event to determine the current position in the recordset and the total number of records altogether.

View the code for the form, and select **Adodc1** from the **Object** drop-down. Then select **MoveComplete** from the **Procedure** drop-down box on the right, and add the following code to the event handler:

```
Private Sub Adodc1_MoveComplete(ByVal adReason As ADODB.EventReasonEnum, _
                                ByVal pError As ADODB.Error, _
                                adStatus As ADODB.EventStatusEnum, _
                                ByVal pRecordset As ADODB.Recordset)

    lblRecord.Caption = CStr(Adodc1.Recordset.AbsolutePosition) & _
                     " of " & Str(Adodc1.Recordset.RecordCount)

End Sub
```

This code updates the label with the absolute position of the current record in the recordset and the total number of records using the following two properties of the ADO `Recordset` object:

- ❑   `AbsolutePosition` – the current record position within a recordset.

- ❑   `RecordCount` – the total number of records within a recordset.

> *If we were still using the ADO Data Control to navigate through our recordset, we could have assigned the same concatenated string to its `Caption` property.*

Now we can test the new form. Our new command buttons should navigate through the recordset just as the ADO Data Control buttons did. Note that navigation does not need to use command buttons, as we can call the `MoveFirst`, `MoveNext`, and related methods from anywhere in code.

Further Enhancements

We're almost done with our first sample application. First, we will add code to:

- ❑   Add new records
- ❑   Delete records
- ❑   Locate records through a find function
- ❑   Update changes made to the fields
- ❑   Restore data fields, aborting any changes made

To begin, add a single command button to the form and name it `cmdAction`. As you might have guessed, we'll create a control array to handle our logic. Copy the command button and paste it four more times. Arrange the new command buttons as shown below, changing the captions to match, and making sure the indices go left to right from 0 to 4. Again, place the controls over the ADO Data Control as it will be invisible at run time:

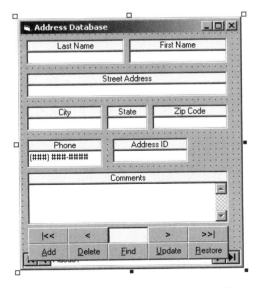

Now add the following code for the `cmdAction_Click` event handler:

```
Private Sub cmdAction_Click(Index As Integer)
```

```
    On Error GoTo goActionErr

    With Adodc1

        Select Case Index

            Case 0    'Add
                If cmdAction(0).Caption = "&Add" Then
                    varBookMark = .Recordset.Bookmark
                    .Recordset.AddNew
                    txtField(0).SetFocus
                    cmdAction(0).Caption = "&Cancel"
                    SetVisible False
                Else
                    .Recordset.CancelUpdate
                    If varBookMark > 0 Then
                        .Recordset.Bookmark = varBookMark
                    Else
                        .Recordset.MoveFirst
                    End If
                    cmdAction(Index).Caption = "&Add"
                    SetVisible True
                End If

            Case 1    'Delete
                If .Recordset.EditMode = False Then
                    .Recordset.Delete
                    .Recordset.MoveNext
```

```
            If .Recordset.EOF Then .Recordset.MoveLast
        Else
            MsgBox "Must update or restore record before deleting!"
        End If

    Case 2  'Find
        frmFind.Show

    Case 3  'Update
        .Recordset.Update
        varBookMark = .Recordset.Bookmark
        .Recordset.Requery
        If varBookMark > 0 Then
            .Recordset.Bookmark = varBookMark
        Else
            .Recordset.MoveLast
        End If
        cmdAction(0).Caption = "&Add"
        SetVisible True

    Case 4  'Restore
        varBookMark = .Recordset.Bookmark
        .Restore
        If varBookMark > 0 Then
            .Recordset.Bookmark = varBookMark
        Else
            .Recordset.MoveLast
        End If

    End Select

End With

Exit Sub


goActionErr:

    MsgBox Err.Description

End Sub
```

Adding New Records

When we add a record, the ADO Data Control will do the dirty work of creating the new record. However, the programmer must protect the record until it is either updated or cancelled. The best way to do this is to disable the other options, which we'll do in a simple procedure that sets the Enabled property of each command button.

With the form's code window open, select Tools | Add Procedure from Visual Basic's menu, and supply a name of SetVisible. Modify the procedure to receive a Boolean argument called blnStatus, and type the following code as the procedure body:

```
Public Sub SetVisible(blnStatus As Boolean)

    Dim intIndex As Integer

    For intIndex = 0 To 3
        cmdNavigate(intIndex).Enabled = blnStatus
    Next intIndex

    cmdAction(1).Enabled = blnStatus ' Delete
    cmdAction(2).Enabled = blnStatus ' Find
    cmdAction(4).Enabled = blnStatus ' Restore

End Sub
```

We'll call this procedure to disable command buttons when we call the Add method, and to re-enable them once the new record is finished or canceled.

In the General Declarations section of your code, add a new variable called varBookMark. This variable will be used by a few of our command buttons to return to the record that we were working with prior to the Add method being called. Add Option Explicit too if it's not there already:

```
Option Explicit
Dim varBookMark As Variant
```

In this application, the **Add** command button (cmdAction index 0) will be used as a toggle to add or cancel a new record. When we click the command button, we'll check the Caption and if it's &Add, we'll set varBookMark to the current record position and then call the AddNew method.

In the AddNew method, we set the focus to the **Last Name** textbox, ready for the user to enter data, change the button caption to &Cancel, and disable all buttons except **Add** (now **Cancel**) and **Update**.

On the other hand, if the button caption isn't &Add, then it must be &Cancel, and we call the CancelUpdate method. We revert back to the original record that the user was viewing before they clicked the **Add** button by setting the Bookmark property to the value of varBookMark. Finally, all command buttons are re-enabled.

Deleting Records

When the user clicks the **Delete** button, we check to see if they have modified any data fields using the EditMode property of the Recordset, which is True whenever the user has edited a bound control. If the user attempts to delete a record which they have changed, the Update or Restore method must be called first. Once we've deleted the record, we move to the next record.

Updating Records

The Update method propagates any changes made to the database. In this sample, we follow the Update method with the Requery method. The only reason for this is so that we can display the value of the AutoNumber field once the new record has been submitted.

Again, we set a bookmark when updating so that the user is returned to the current record. The last step is to ensure the cmdAction(0) button's Caption is set to &Add, as it may have been &Cancel, and re-enable all command buttons by calling the SetVisible procedure.

Restoring Records

To abandon changes and restore the data in the database table, we use the `Restore` method. This is called against the ADO Data Control, not against the `Recordset` object, and it reloads the data as it is in the database table. The `Restore` method moves us to the first record, just as when first connecting to the database, which could be quite annoying if a user has already located a specific record. Thus, we'll avoid this by bookmarking the current record before the call.

> **Note that if another user has deleted the record, it will not be possible to move back to the bookmark, and an error would be returned. In a production application, you may wish to code for such an eventuality.**

The `Restore` method can also be useful in situation where more than one user modifies the same record. When one has made updates, the second can call the `Restore` method to view their changes.

Finding Records

If the user clicks the Find button, we open a new form called `frmFind` where the user can enter their search text. We could use Visual Basic's `InputBox` command, but we'll implement a second form for greater flexibility. This form will have several buttons, allowing the user to locate the first occurrence of the string, the next occurrence of the string, or cancel the operation.

Select **Project | Add Form** from the menu. Save the new form as `Find.frm` in the same directory as `Address.frm`. Add three buttons and a textbox, setting their `Caption/Text` properties as shown:

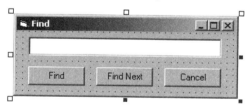

Name the controls as described in the following table:

Item	Name
Form	frmFind
Textbox	txtSearch
Command Button	cmdFind
Command Button	cmdFindNext
Command Button	cmdCancel

We now need a procedure to scan through the records, searching for a match. Add a procedure to the `frmFind` form named `FindString`. It starts off by declaring variables and error handling:

```
Public Sub FindString()
    Dim strFind As String
    Dim intFields As Integer

    On Error Goto FindError
```

Next, we initiate a loop to search for the requested text until the end of the ADO Data Control Recordset is reached:

```
strFind = Trim(txtSearch)
With frmAddress.Adodc1.Recordset
    Do Until .EOF
```

The procedure only searches the first and last name textboxes, txtField(0) and txtField(1):

```
For intFields = 0 To 1
```

We use the InStr function to look for the string in any part of the field. It returns an integer indicating the start position of the substring if found, or else it returns zero, so if it is greater than 0, we highlight the text and exit the search routine. Note that we use a search type of vbTextCompare, which provides a more general search, avoiding misses due to case sensitivity and other anomalies:

```
If InStr(1, frmAddress.txtField(intFields), strFind, _
    vbTextCompare) > 0 Then
```

To highlight the string we're searching for; we use the SelStart and SelLength properties of the textbox. First, we establish where the highlighted text begins by finding the start position and subtracting 1 from it. To find the start position, we use the InStr function in exactly the same way as above. We must subtract one because InStr will return the text position and the SelStart property needs to be set equal to the value just before the character we want to highlight:

```
frmAddress.txtField(intFields).SelStart = InStr(1, _
    frmAddress.txtField(intFields), strFind, vbTextCompare) - 1
```

The Len keyword is used to determine the length of the string we're looking for. Once we have this, we highlight the string by setting the SelLength property of the textbox equal to the length of the string that was searched for:

```
frmAddress.txtField(intFields).SelLength = Len(strFind)
frmAddress.txtField(intFields).SetFocus
Exit Sub

        End If

    Next

    .MoveNext

DoEvents
```

119

```
        Loop
      MsgBox "Record not found"
      .MoveFirst

      End With

  Exit Sub


  FindError:

    MsgBox Err.Description
    Err.Clear

  End Sub
```

The search could be easily modified to include other textboxes by changing the start and end values of the `For` loop. However, don't forget that we deleted the textbox for the phone number, so it can't be accessed using that index, which was 6. We could either re-index the control array, or add a line to skip over `Index` 6. Alternatively, we could use a `For Each` loop to run through all textboxes, or check all fields individually.

Next, add the handler for the click event of the `cmdFind` button. If the search string is not empty, the above method is called to locate the first instance of the string. If the `RecordCount` property of the `Recordset` is less than one, there is no need to continue. To ensure that the data is searched from the beginning, we need to move to the first record before calling the `FindString` procedure:

```
  Private Sub cmdFind_Click()

    If Trim(txtSearch) = "" Then Exit Sub

    If frmAddress.Adodc1.Recordset.RecordCount > 0 Then
      frmAddress.Adodc1.Recordset.MoveFirst
      Call FindString
    Else
      MsgBox "Recordset is Empty"
    End If

  End Sub
```

When searching for the next instance of the string, we don't need to move to the first record, but we do need to move to the next record so that the `FindString` procedure doesn't find the same record again. Of course, if we call the `MoveNext` method, we need to check for the `EOF` marker. In this scenario, if we reached the end of the file, there's no need to continue searching:

```
  Private Sub cmdFindNext_Click()

    With frmAddress.Adodc1.Recordset
      .MoveNext
      If .EOF Then
        .MoveLast
        MsgBox "End of File Reached!"
```

```
      Else
         Call FindString
      End If
   End With

End Sub
```

Finally, if a user clicks the Cancel button, we can close the form by calling its `Unload` method. The `Me` keyword refers to the object containing the current code, which in this case is `frmFind`:

```
Private Sub cmdCancel_Click()

   Unload Me
   Set frmFind = Nothing

End Sub
```

We could have used `Unload frmFind` instead, or even called `frmFind.Hide`. However, to save resources, it's better practice to unload the form out of memory.

Testing the Search Mechanism

Run the application and click the Find button. Type in a name, or a portion of a name, when the Find dialog appears and click Find:

The application will search through the records until a match is found, or EOF is reached. If a match is made, the search string will appear highlighted:

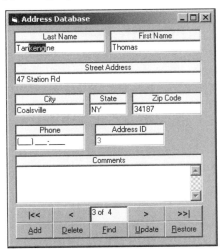

121

Moving sequentially through all records looking for a match works well in this case because the table size is small, but for a larger table, it would be better to apply a SQL statement to the `Recordset`, or use the `Filter` property of the `Recordset` object.

Other Databound Controls

In this section we'll look at other controls that can be bound to a data source to display information. Note that not all of these will be in the Toolbox by default, and many need to be added through the Components dialog just as we did for the ADO Data Control.

These are just a few of the controls that can be bound to an ADO Data Control. Don't forget that if you don't find a control that suits your needs, you can always build a custom one. In addition, a great number of vendor controls are available, although these do vary greatly in price. But if the control fits your needs and is cheaper than building it in-house, it's worth the investment.

The Label

Binding to a label control works similarly to the textbox, with the difference that it prevents the user entering, selecting, or copying the displayed value. If you bind a label to a data source, the user would only be able to view that data.

The Checkbox

A checkbox offers a neat way to let the user enter Boolean data, and really makes an app seem more professional when used for appropriate fields. The checkbox can take one of three possible values:

❑   `Unchecked` = 0

❑   `Checked` = 1

❑   `Grayed` (not applicable) = 2

The Picture and Image Controls

Both the picture and image controls work in very similar fashion. Both can be bound to an image field in a database, but each control has certain advantages. The image control, for example, can alter to the size of the image to stretch or shrink it, while a picture box requires knowledge of the image size. There are other similar advantages and disadvantages for each control.

DataGrid Control

The `DataGrid` control has been around for some time, and allows the user to view and edit multiple records at once. It works and looks similar to the table view of Access, so many non-technical people will already be comfortable with using it as an interface to data:

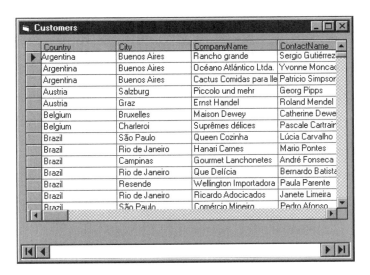

The Hierarchical FlexGrid Control

This control is an enhancement to the `DataGrid` control, and offers a variety of layout options for how data should be presented to the user. As the screenshot below demonstrates, the control can condense records that have repeating fields:

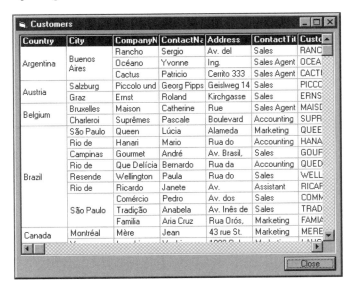

The control also allows many display formats to be applied to data it contains, with shading and font styles. Due to its complexity, the Hierarchical FlexGrid control is probably best set up and configured by running the Data Form Wizard to create the form where it will live. This wizard can be found in the Add-Ins menu.

The DataList and DataCombo Controls

The DataList and DataCombo controls offer the user mechanisms for selecting an item from a list of choices. Each control pulls data from one record source, and populates a field in another record source when an item is selected. It's not always a good idea to use them when there are thousands of possibilities, as they tend to slow down somewhat. This is especially true when you have several boxes on a single form.

The DataCombo provides a drop-down that can be used to select one of many options from a database with minimal wasted space. The DataList on the other hand offers the user a range of choices at once:

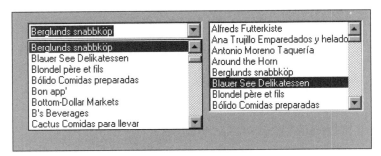

There are four data-binding properties for both of these two controls, which are used to set up the record sources mentioned above:

❑   RowSource – The data control from which the DataCombo or DataList will be filled.

❑   ListField – The field from which the DataCombo or DataList will be filled.

❑   DataSource – The ADO data control that specifies where the selected data will be stored.

❑   DataField – The field that will be populated with the selected data.

The OLE Container Control

This control can be bound to any OLE object within a database table, such as a bitmap image, Excel worksheet, or even a Word document. Once embedded, the user can double-click the object to enter edit mode and change it as required. Any changes can then be propagated to the original source file.

The Rich Textbox Control

This control works in a similar way to the textbox. However, it allows for more varied content, and it is suitable for displaying and editing fields that allow underlining, specific font types, bold, and so on.

The MS Chart Control

With the MS Chart Control, we can build a wide range of charts generated from data in an ADO data control. The available chart types include pie, line, area, step, scatter, and bar. There's a wizard to assist with creating charts, and the property pages of the control define color types, titles, footers, and more.

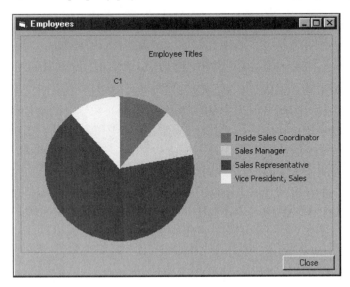

The Data Repeater Control

This control is very flexible in that you can design a data form (as an ActiveX control) and use the Data Repeater control to display that form a number of times simultaneously, each showing a different record.

Summary

In this chapter, we've reviewed the basics of the ADO Data Control, and some of the controls that can be bound to it. We also demonstrated that even if you don't have a database program on your computer, you can create a database quickly with the VisData add-in. In particular we looked at:

- ❏ The Visual Data Manager (VisData)
- ❏ The ConnectionString property
- ❏ The RecordSource property
- ❏ The Masked Edit Control
- ❏ Creating our own navigation bar
- ❏ Other data bound controls, including the DataGrid, Hierarchical FlexGrid, DataList, DataCombo, OLE Container, Rich Textbox, MS Chart, and Data Repeater

p2p.wrox.com

The programmer's resource centre

ASP Today

wrox.com

 **wrox**direct

Views, Stored Procedures, and Triggers

More complex or widely used applications really need powerful database engines such as SQL Server, Oracle, or DB2, and ADO works quite happily with these more advanced database servers. The basic concepts and techniques apply no matter what data store is in use.

Effective use of SQL Server and similar database products requires an understanding that these *are* servers, and that our SQL statements are processed in the server itself rather than in the client application as with Jet. It is this fundamental difference that allows these servers to support hundreds of concurrent users and to provide far more advanced features and capabilities. It also means that we need to understand not only how to connect to the database, but how to create and use server-side capabilities such as views, stored procedures, and triggers.

As time goes on, our applications tend to get larger and more complex, and their user base expands. From a career perspective, taking the time to understand and leverage these database features is worth its weight in gold.

Previous chapters have discussed architectures and the considerations for designing successful client-server applications. We've covered database design, ADO data access technology, and we'll now look at some ways of creating efficient, secure, high-performance client-server applications.

The key point is that the client should not perform low-level data manipulation – this processing is taken care of by the server. The client sends requests for data, through a network, to the server and the server does not merely send back data for the client to work with, but is capable of processing complex SQL commands and returning highly specific sets of data. In this chapter we take this further and discuss some key issues in multi-user client-server systems:

❑ How can we make retrieval of specifically focused data as easy and efficient as possible?

❑ How can we minimize network traffic and improve performance?

❑ With potentially hundreds of people wanting access to the database, what steps can we take to ensure that the data does not become corrupted?

Views, stored procedures, and triggers are SQL queries that are stored *on the server* and can be called from the client with simple, short SQL commands. Not only does this make database access simpler and less error-prone to the coder, but it also reduces network traffic and speeds up data retrieval.

In this chapter, we'll look at each of these topics in detail. We'll start with views – SQL queries that can allow users easy access to highly specific information in the database and can be used in a security context. We'll then move on to stored procedures and triggers – precompiled SQL statements that provide vital functionality relating to data integrity and performance issues.

Typically, a database administrator would be the one to create these views, stored procedures and triggers for us. However, times are changing quickly and these are just some of the many tasks that programmers may find themselves required to do.

Looking at Views

A view is a SQL query that is stored on the database server. When a view is executed, an object is created – a *virtual* table – that allows us to retrieve and work with data in the underlying base tables.

> **It is important to understand that data in the base database tables is *not* duplicated and stored in the virtual table. When the query is terminated the virtual table is destroyed. However the view remains on the server and can be called the next time a client wishes to view the data.**

Some of the main benefits that views bring are:

❑ *They can be used for security purposes.* A view extracts and displays in a virtual table *only* the records and fields that are defined in the view. A user can be assigned permission to a view in the same way they can be assigned permission to a normal table. Thus, a user may be granted access only to a certain view and, in effect, denied access to other confidential data stored elsewhere in the database.

❑ *They can be used to extract only the information that is relevant to the user's needs.* Different groups of people within an organization require frequent access to different data from the database. Furthermore, large and complex SQL statements are often required in order to provide access to highly specific data, often drawn from multiple tables. This complex SQL statement can be defined as a view and a 'special purpose' view can be created to suit each requirement. The clients that require data from the view may then execute a simple SQL statement to retrieve the same data, over and over.

❑ *Views confer the ability to modify field names and aliases on the server rather than on the client.* If, for example, a field is renamed in a table, the view can then allow the clients to call the field name by its old name. In addition to this, there are many other changes that can be handled by a view in order to avoid having to modify all of the client applications.

SQL Server has many existing views for us to have a look at as well as providing an environment for the quick and easy creation of views.

Views in the Northwind Database

First, let's take a look at an existing view. This will help provide a solid understanding of the SQL code required to build a view.

We'll need to use the SQL Server Enterprise Manager, so from the Start menu select Programs | Microsoft SQL Server (or Microsoft SQL Server 7.0) | Enterprise Manager. Once it has opened, navigate to Databases | Northwind | Views under the node for the server you wish to connect to.

Double click the view called Products Above Average Price amongst the views listed in the right hand pane. The View Properties dialog will appear, showing the SQL statement which generates the view. This dialog allows you to design new views and modify existing ones:

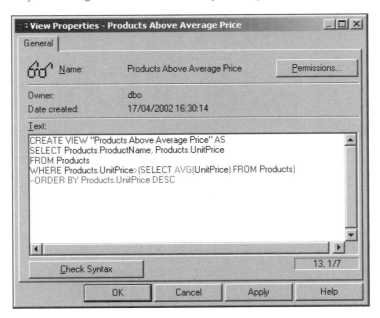

Views start with a CREATE VIEW *<viewname>* AS statement, which is followed by a SELECT query specifying what the view is to contain. You may have already seen the AS keyword used to define fields as aliases, and here, it defines a view as an alias for a SQL statement.

Creating a New View with SQL

As we can see, a view is really just a SELECT statement set as a view by the CREATE VIEW command. Let's create a simple view for the Northwind database by entering a SQL statement directly. The following code creates a view restricting the visible fields of the Employee table, and only includes records for sales reps:

```
CREATE VIEW SalesContactDetails AS
SELECT EmployeeID, LastName, FirstName, TitleOfCourtesy, Extension
FROM Employees
WHERE Title = 'Sales Representative'
```

Launch the SQL Query Analyzer tool by selecting **Tools | SQL Query Analyzer** from the Enterprise Manager menu bar, and type in the above SQL code. Make sure that the Northwind database appears in the dropdown box in the toolbar shows the Northwind database, and press *F5*, or click the **Execute Query** button with the green 'Play' icon:

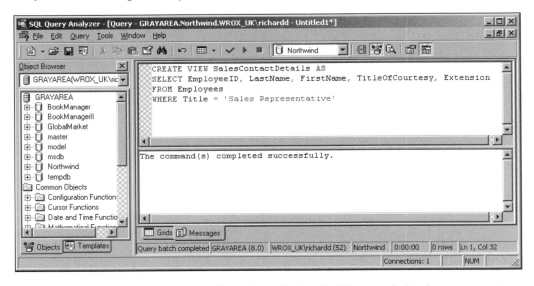

The new view is then created, as you will see if you look at the **Views** node for the Northwind database. If the view does not appear immediately, right-click the **Views** folder and select **Refresh**.

To actually see the data that our new view returns, we can execute a query in Query Analyzer as shown below:

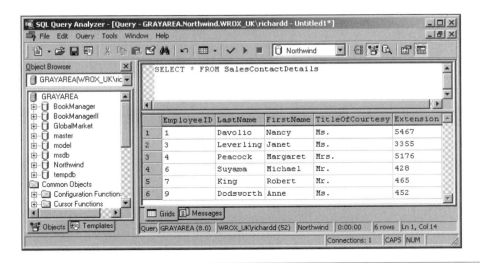

> A view acts just as a table in its own right, but do remember that the data for a view is not stored in its own location. If you change the data in a virtual table, you are in fact altering the base tables.

A view such as this is a first step to the implementation of field-level security, where we prevent certain users from accessing certain confidential or sensitive information. For this to be effective of course, we would also have to restrict users from viewing the Employees table directly, but for now it's a good start.

A point to bear in mind is that we cannot implement an ORDER BY clause when creating a view, but we can apply one to the virtual table created for the view. The following statement refines the virtual table to display the records in ascending order of surname:

```
SELECT * FROM SalesContactDetails
ORDER BY LastName
```

Creating a New View Graphically

Now that we've covered the basics of view design, let's create a view to hide a complex SQL statement using the graphical tool in Enterprise Manager. We'll pull fields from several tables to create a single virtual table of related data.

Right-click the Views node in Enterprise Manager, select New View, and four panes will appear. The first thing to do is choose the tables that our view will draw on. Click the Add table button on the far right of the Enterprise Manager toolbar, and add the Orders, Order Details, and Products tables. As you do so, the tables will appear in the top pane, along with a graphic to indicate relationships between them. Click on the box to the left of each field name that you want to include in the view – a check will appear and the field will pop up in a column cell in the second pane. Select OrderId, OrderDate, and RequiredDate in the Orders table, UnitPrice and Quantity in Order Details, and ProductName, UnitsInStock, and UnitsOnOrder in the Products table.

Also note that as you select tables and fields, a SELECT statement is built up in the third pane, defining the records and fields included in the view. Finally, click Run (the button with a red exclamation mark), and the resulting virtual table (the view itself) is created and displayed in the bottom pane:

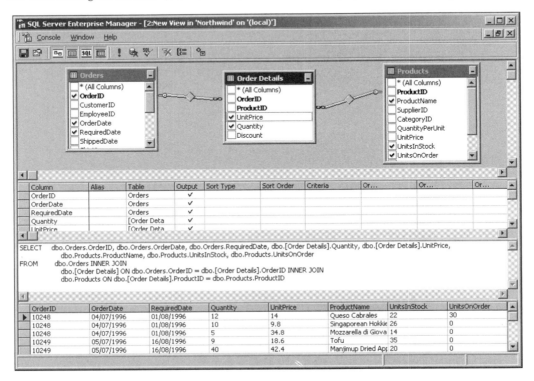

Save the view with an appropriate name, such as OrderInfo, by clicking the Save button. We can then access it in our SQL statements run on the Northwind database using this name:

```
SELECT * FROM OrderInfo
```

Modifying Data Using a View

When working with a view, we can use UPDATE and INSERT commands to modify data in the base tables, via the view. Remember though, that all constraints and keys of each view are enforced just as though we were editing the base table directly. There are a couple of other things to remember:

❑ We can only update and insert data into fields that are included in the SELECT statement of our view. So, the SalesContactDetails view would not allow us to update the Title field, for example.

❑ We can only update fields from one table at a time. For instance, in the OrderInfo view, we would not be able to update the RequiredDate and the Quantity fields at the same time.

The main point is that, once a view is created, we don't have to look at the SQL code again: we simply call the view from our statements without needing to think of what exactly it specifies. While this makes it simpler to use, it also makes it easier to make mistakes. For instance, say our `SalesContactDetails` view were to return the `Title` field. We would then be perfectly free to update that field using the view – we could change all occurrences to, say, 'Customer Harassment Technician'. However, if we did this, the next time we called the view we would receive an empty table, because our view only returns records where this field is 'Sales Representative'! In order to prevent this sort of occurrence, we can add `WITH CHECK OPTION` to our view creation code:

```
CREATE VIEW SalesContactDetails AS
SELECT EmployeeID, LastName, FirstName, TitleOfCourtesy, Extension, Title
FROM Employees
WHERE Title = 'Sales Representative'
WITH CHECK OPTION
```

`WITH CHECK OPTION` makes the DBMS check the `WHERE` clause (and any other conditions) to ensure that only modifications that can be seen in the virtual table are permitted. This would prevent users changing the `Title` and other fields later.

Stored Procedures

Stored procedures are precompiled SQL statements that take parameters with the capacity for automating a wide range of tasks. They can also provide return values to inform the caller of the success or failure of the execution process. Stored procedures are compiled into an object stored on the RDBMS and can be called by a client program, or by a **trigger**, which we'll come to later.

Stored procedures bring many benefits to distributed systems, and the main ones are listed below. As you'll see, they mainly relate to performance enhancement and the preservation of data integrity:

❏ Stored procedures are maintained on the server side; therefore, they can be modified quickly without needing to be redistributed to each client.

❏ Stored procedures allow us to place the code for a wide variety of tasks, such as purging data, archiving data, and creating tables, on the server. Instead of sending complex SQL queries over the network, which can easily contain hundreds of lines of code, an application need only send a single command to invoke a stored procedure on the RDBMS, drastically reducing network traffic for busy data-backed systems.

❏ Stored procedures run much faster than standard SQL queries. When a stored procedure is first called, the RDBMS parses the code, validating syntax, and compiling. So while the first execution may take some time, subsequent runs will be much faster. Many RDBMSs allow pre-compilation of stored procedures before first use. Additionally, once the procedure has been executed once, it is stored in RAM for the duration of that particular session, making it even quicker.

❏ Complex business logic governing how data may be stored in the database, legal ranges for certain fields, and so on, can be encapsulated in a stored procedure. These procedures can then protect the database from queries that would disrupt data integrity, or from modifications by users with insufficient security levels.

Basic INSERT, UPDATE and DELETE commands are embedded in complex SQL code that themselves may call other stored procedures in order to validate proposed modifications before permanent changes are made. In some cases, the DBA may provide such stored procedures as the *only* interface to the data. Additional security can be applied by granting users access only to the stored procedures rather than to the database tables.

❑ Error handling can be conducted at database level. For example, if the server detects an error while validating a stored procedure, a custom error message can be sent to the calling application, describing precisely why the procedure failed.

Database servers also offer numerous variables that can return useful information to calling applications, such as @@rowcount, which returns the number of rows affected by the execution of a stored procedure.

Stored Procedures in the Northwind Database

Before we create our own stored procedure, let's get an idea of what they look like. In Enterprise Manager, select the **Stored Procedures** node for the Northwind database. From the right-hand pane, double-click the **CustOrderHist** stored procedure. The Stored Procedure Properties window opens, showing the SQL code that this stored procedure comprises:

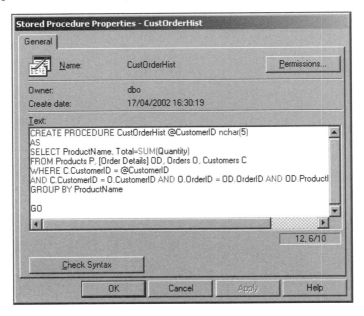

The syntax is very similar to that for creating views. We start by specifying the name for the stored procedure, followed by any arguments it may take, along with their data types. In this example, the procedure takes a string in an argument called @CustomerID. Next, we define a SELECT statement for the stored procedure, using the view we created before. This stored procedure will return the totals for all products ordered by the specified customer. Before we move on to the details of how to execute these stored procedures from our application, let's create a couple of our own.

Creating Stored Procedures Using SQL

Creating elementary stored procedures using a CREATE PROCEDURE statement is a relatively straightforward process. We'll create four simple stored procedures in this section, each applying either a SELECT, INSERT, UPDATE, or a DELETE statement, and in the next section, we'll make use of them from a VB project.

In this section, we'll create a procedure that takes one argument, @searchStr, which is a string (varchar) of up to 40 characters. We'll use this parameter in a SELECT statement in conjunction with the LIKE keyword to locate product records that contain the string in the ProductName field. Run the following statement in the query analyzer:

```
CREATE PROCEDURE findProducts @SearchStr varchar (40)
AS
SELECT ProductID, ProductName, UnitPrice, UnitsInStock
FROM Products
WHERE ProductName LIKE '%' + @SearchStr + '%'

GO
```

Once this has completed successfully, we can run it with the EXEC command, specifying a valid value for the search string argument as shown below:

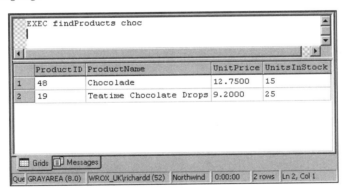

In this next example, we create a stored procedure that contains an UPDATE statement, which takes three parameters, an integer called @ProdID, a string called @name, and @price which is a money type. The procedure updates the record for the product with the ID given in @ProdID with the name and price given by the other two parameters:

```
CREATE PROCEDURE updateProduct @ProdID int,
                               @name varchar(40),
                               @price money

AS
UPDATE Products
SET ProductName = @name,
    UnitPrice = @price
WHERE ProductID = @ProdID

GO
```

Let's now create a simple INSERT stored procedure. This one receives two arguments which are used to create a new product record. Note that we assume the new product is not discontinued:

```
CREATE PROCEDURE insertProduct @name varchar(40),
                               @category int
AS
INSERT INTO Products
   (ProductName, CategoryID, Discontinued)
   VALUES(@name, @category, 0)

GO
```

Finally, here's a DELETE stored procedure that takes a parameter called @prodID, and deletes all products with a ProductID field equal to that value:

```
CREATE PROCEDURE deleteProduct @ProdID int
AS
DELETE FROM Products
WHERE ProductID = @ProdID

GO
```

As you can see, building stored procedures is not hard. Make sure you run all of the above statements, because in the next section, we create a Visual Basic project that calls them.

Executing Stored Procedures from Visual Basic

ADO makes it relatively easy to execute stored procedures from VB code. Let's walk through the code we need to call a stored procedure. Don't enter any of it yet, just follow along.

When executing stored procedures, the first step is to declare a new Command object which we can then use to execute our stored procedure:

```
Dim objSPCommand As ADODB.Command
```

If we want to pass more than one parameter to our stored procedure, we'll need to declare an array to hold the values. However, our array *must* be declared as a variant and *must* be designed to hold exactly the number of parameters that your stored procedure requires. Remember, Visual Basic arrays are zero-based, so the following code will hold three parameters, not two:

```
Dim pr_insert(2) As Variant
```

Next, we instantiate the Command object and set its ActiveConnection property to a Connection object. Ideally, we should create a Command object and destroy it after each stored procedure call. This is because new parameters tend to append themselves to the existing ones, causing an imbalance in the number of parameters passed. Once we have specified the Connection, we let ADO know that the command to be executed is a stored procedure by setting the CommandType property to adCmdStoredProc:

```
Set objSPCommand = New ADODB.Command
objSPCommand.ActiveConnection = objActiveConnection
objSPCommand.CommandType = adCmdStoredProc
```

The `CommandText` property should be set to the name of the stored procedure, and then the array is populated with the parameters to be passed. The array must be populated in the *exact* order in which the arguments are specified by the procedure, otherwise it will not be able to match them up correctly.

We're then ready to execute the stored procedure against the `Command` object. The comma immediately after the `Execute` method acts as a placeholder for the `RecordsAffected` argument of the `Execute` method. It is followed by the `Parameters` argument, which specifies the input parameters that we will pass to our stored procedure:

```
objSPCommand.CommandText = "insert_jobs"
pr_insert(0) = "President"
pr_insert(1) = 50
pr_insert(2) = 250
objSPCommand.Execute , pr_insert
```

The last step is to destroy the `Command` object by simply setting it to `Nothing`:

```
Set objSPCommand = Nothing
```

Simple, right? Let's create a project and put it to practice.

Our project will use both ADO standalone code and the ADO Data Control. The ADO code will create a connection and a command object then execute the specified stored procedure. The ADO Data Control will display the contents of the `Products` table, showing the changes effected by the stored procedure.

To begin, create a new standard EXE project and add a command button to the form. Name the command button `cmdExecute`, then copy the new button and paste it three times, creating a control array. Add a listbox, an ADO Data Control, and a `DataGrid` control. If necessary, add the `DataGrid` and the data control components using the dialog opened by selecting **Project | Components**, as described in the previous chapter. Arrange and label the form and controls as shown:

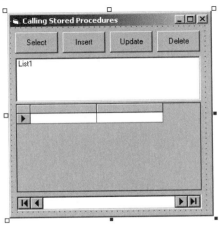

Leave the form, data control, DataGrid and listbox with their default names (which should be Form1, Adodc1, DataGrid1 and ListBox1 respectively). Set the DataSource property of the grid to Adodc1. Open the property pages for the RecordSource property of the ADO Data Control, select a command type of adCmdText and enter SELECT * FROM Products. Also set the ConnectionString property of the ADO control to connect to the Northwind database (refer to the previous chapter if you aren't sure how to do this).

Now open the form's code, and declare a Connection object, a Command object, and a Recordset object in the General Declarations section. Follow by declaring an array for the parameters of each stored procedure we'll be calling. The SELECT and DELETE stored procedures only require one parameter each, so we could have put them in the same array. However, for the sake of clarity and organization, we'll keep them separate:

```
Option Explicit
Dim objActiveConnection As ADODB.Connection
Dim objSPCommand As ADODB.Command
Dim objSPRecordset As ADODB.Recordset

' Declare an array of variants for parameters
Dim pr_Select(0) As Variant
Dim pr_Insert(1) As Variant
Dim pr_Delete(0) As Variant
Dim pr_Update(2) As Variant
```

We'll establish our connection to the Northwind database in the Form_Load event:

```
Private Sub Form_Load()

    Set objActiveConnection = New ADODB.Connection
    objActiveConnection.ConnectionString = "Provider=SQLOLEDB.1;" & _
            "Persist Security Info=False;User ID=sa;Initial Catalog=Northwind"
    objActiveConnection.Open

End Sub
```

Next, in the Click event of the command button array, we set up our connection and specify the CommandType property. Now, we're ready to execute each of our four stored procedures. We use the Select Case statement to query the index value of the command button array and find out which button was clicked:

```
Private Sub cmdExecute_Click(Index As Integer)

    ' Create a new Command object and set the active
    ' connection and CommandType
    Set objSPCommand = New ADODB.Command
    objSPCommand.ActiveConnection = objActiveConnection
    objSPCommand.CommandType = adCmdStoredProc

Select Case Index
```

We'll deal with the buttons from left to right, so we start with the Select button. Since this stored procedure may generate several records we need a recordset in which to store them:

```
Case 0 ' SELECT statement requested
  List1.Clear

  ' Create a new recordset object
  Set objSPRecordset = New ADODB.Recordset
```

An input box then pops up in which the user must enter an appropriate search string for the stored procedure:

```
  ' Get the parameters and specify the SP name
  pr_Select(0) = InputBox("Search Text", "Search", "choc")
  objSPCommand.CommandText = "findProducts"
```

We pass the string entered by the user to the stored procedure, which populates the recordset:

```
  ' Call the stored procedure
  Set objSPRecordset = objSPCommand.Execute(, pr_Select)
```

We then navigate through the recordset, populating the listbox with the ProductID and ProductName for records that matched the search string:

```
  ' Pull the results from the RS
  Do Until objSPRecordset.EOF
    List1.AddItem objSPRecordset("ProductID") & " - " & _
                  objSPRecordset("ProductName")
    objSPRecordset.MoveNext
  Loop
```

Lastly, we destroy the recordset object:

```
  Set objSPRecordset = Nothing
```

Now we come to the code to insert new data into the table. To keep the example simple, we have hard-coded this data, but you may wish to modify this to grab values from a textbox or file:

```
Case 1 ' INSERT statement requested
  ' Get the parameters and specify the SP name
  objSPCommand.CommandText = "insertProduct"
  pr_Insert(0) = "Yummy Muck"
  pr_Insert(1) = 3

  ' Execute the SP
  objSPCommand.Execute , pr_Insert
```

139

Once we execute the stored procedure, we call the `Refresh` method on the ADO Data Control so that the data grid displays the new entry:

```
' Refresh the ADO Data Control with the results
Adodc1.Refresh
```

The UPDATE button allows the user to change any job description. We use three input boxes, the first to get the ID of the product that is to be changed, the second providing the new name, and the last to get the new price:

```
Case 2 ' UPDATE statement requested
  ' Get the parameters and specify the SP name
  objSPCommand.CommandText = "updateProduct"
  pr_Update(0) = Int(InputBox ("Please enter the ID of the product", _
                               "Update Product"))
  pr_Update(1) = InputBox("Please enter the new name", "Update Product")
  pr_Update(2) = Int(InputBox("Please enter the price", _
                              "Update Product"))

  ' Execute the SP
  objSPCommand.Execute , pr_Update

  ' Refresh the ADO Data Control with the results
  Adodc1.Refresh
```

The DELETE code is very similar to the INSERT and UPDATE code. The user supplies the appropriate parameter to be passed to the stored procedure (in this case, the `ProductID` to be deleted). The query is executed and the ADO Data Control refreshed:

```
Case 3 ' DELETE statement requested
  ' Get the parameters and specify the SP name
  objSPCommand.CommandText = "deleteProduct"
  pr_Delete(0) = Int(InputBox ("Enter ID of Product to delete", _
                               "Delete"))

  ' Execute the SP
  objSPCommand.Execute , pr_Delete

  ' Refresh the ADO Data Control with the results
  Adodc1.Refresh

End Select

' Destroy the Command object
Set objSPCommand = Nothing

End Sub
```

In order to keep the code simple, I've not included any error handling. I'll leave that to you – I'm sure you can find plenty of suitable places!

Now run the project and test the buttons. From left to right, the buttons should:

❑ Populate the listbox with values specific to your request

❑ Insert a new record

❑ Update a record of your choosing

❑ Delete a record of your choosing

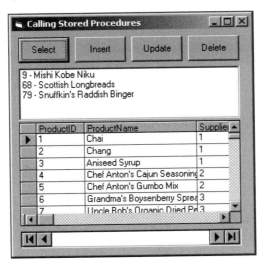

Output Parameters

A stored procedure can generate a return value or several output parameters as a result of its execution. This output is not necessarily data from the database; it could be, for example, an error message or a server variable (such as @@rowcount), and such output can be stored in a parameter object.

In the previous section, the data set generated by our SELECT stored procedure was stored in a recordset object and displayed in a listbox. Sometimes, however, a user may wish to supply an input parameter (such as a product ID) to a stored procedure and receive only one or two specific values, such as the name and quantity in stock. Such a situation does not require a Recordset object, and we can instead use VB's Parameter object to hold the return values for the single record. The following stored procedure takes a single parameter (@ProdID) and returns two **output parameters** containing the name and quantity of the matching record from the Products table:

```
CREATE PROCEDURE prodInStock @ProdID int,
                            @name varchar (40) output,
                            @quantity int output

AS
SELECT @name=ProductName, @quantity=UnitsInStock
FROM Products
WHERE ProductID = @ProdID
RETURN
```

Let's create an application to see how we could this procedure from code by displaying the output parameters for a product specified by the user. Create a new standard EXE project, and add a button and two textboxes to the form. Clear the Text properties of the textboxes, and set the Caption property of the button to Get Info. Add a reference to Microsoft ActiveX Data Objects library. Next, double-click on the button, and enter the following code:

```
Private Sub Command1_Click()
    Dim strID As String
    Dim objConn As ADODB.Connection
    Dim objComm As ADODB.Command
    Dim objParam1 As ADODB.Parameter
    Dim objParam2 As ADODB.Parameter
    Dim objParam3 As ADODB.Parameter

    Set objConn = New ADODB.Connection
    objConn.Open "Provider=SQLOLEDB;Data Source=localhost;Initial Catalog=" _
            & "northwind;integrated security=sspi"

    Set objComm = New ADODB.Command
    Set objComm.ActiveConnection = objConn
    objComm.CommandText = "prodInStock"
    objComm.CommandType = adCmdStoredProc

    strID = InputBox("Enter ID of product to find:")
    Set objParam1 = objComm.CreateParameter("ProdID", adVarChar, _
                                        adParamInput, 11, strID)
    objComm.Parameters.Append objParam1

    Set objParam2 = objComm.CreateParameter("name", adVarChar, _
                                        adParamOutput, 40)
    objComm.Parameters.Append objParam2

    Set objParam3 = objComm.CreateParameter("quantity", adVarChar, _
                                        adParamOutput, 20)
    objComm.Parameters.Append objParam3

    objComm.Execute
    Text1.Text = objParam2
    Text2.Text = objParam3

    Set objParam1 = Nothing
    Set objParam2 = Nothing
    Set objParam3 = Nothing
    Set objComm = Nothing
    Set objConn = Nothing

End Sub
```

This code is fairly straightforward, and should be familiar from previous examples. The user supplies the input parameter as a String via an input box. We then create a parameter object to store this value and pass it to the stored procedure. The CreateParameter method accepts five arguments, as described in Chapter 3 (remember that the third argument specifies the direction of the parameter). We then create two more Parameter objects for the output parameters, which we then display in the textboxes:

System-Level Stored Procedures

SQL Server has many built-in **system-level stored procedures** to assist in your database maintenance and administration needs. These procedures perform tasks such as adding and removing database users, and modifying user access. They are executed in the same manner as user-defined stored procedures, and are identified by a prefix of sp_. With this in mind, you should avoid using this prefix when naming your own stored procedures.

The first system stored procedure we'll explore is sp_addlogin, which allows a new login ID and password to be added to SQL Server. It takes five arguments, the only mandatory one being login_id. The others are:

❑   password

❑   default_db

❑   default_language

❑   login_suid

Create a new standard EXE project, add a button to the form, and enter the following code:

```
Option Explicit
Dim objActiveConnection As ADODB.Connection
Dim objSPCommand As ADODB.Command

Private Sub Form_Load()
   Set objActiveConnection = New ADODB.Connection
   objActiveConnection.ConnectionString = "Provider=SQLOLEDB;" _
                   & "integrated security=sspi;Initial Catalog=Northwind"
   objActiveConnection.Open
End Sub

Private Sub Command1_Click()
   Dim pr_Login(1) As Variant

   Set objSPCommand = New ADODB.Command
   objSPCommand.ActiveConnection = objActiveConnection
   objSPCommand.CommandType = adCmdStoredProc
   objSPCommand.CommandText = "sp_addlogin"
   pr_Login(0) = "CharlieB"    ' new login ID
   pr_Login(1) = "Snoopy"      ' new password
```

```
    objSPCommand.Execute , pr_Login
    Set objSPCommand = Nothing
End Sub
```

If you wish, you can simply add the button to an existing project, and include all the code in the handler for the command button.

Run the code and `CharlieB` will be added as a new login on SQL Server. Another system level stored procedure, `sp_password`, allows the password for a specified user to be updated. The procedure receives three arguments, the last of which is optional:

❑   `old_password`

❑   `new_password`

❑   `login_id` (optional)

The default value for `login_id` if it is not specified is your Server ID. You must also ensure that you are logged in with proper access to change the specified password. If you are not authorized, the request will be rejected.

Change the code for the handler to that given below, which changes CharlieB's password from "Snoopy" to "Woodstock":

```
Private Sub Command1_Click()

    Dim pr_password(2) As Variant

    Set objSPCommand = New ADODB.Command
    objSPCommand.ActiveConnection = objActiveConnection
    objSPCommand.CommandType = adCmdStoredProc

        objSPCommand.CommandText = "sp_password"
        pr_password(0) = "Snoopy"        ' old password
        pr_password(1) = "Woodstock"     ' new password
        pr_password(2) = "CharlieB"      ' login id

        objSPCommand.Execute , pr_password

    Set objSPCommand = Nothing

End Sub
```

Other commonly used system level stored procedures and their parameters include:

❑   `sp_addgroup` – adds a new group to the current database.

    `group_name` – group name to be added

- ❑ `sp_addUser` – adds a new user to the current database.

  `login_id`

  `user_name` (optional)

  `group_name` (optional)

- ❑ `sp_droplogin` – removes a login from SQL Server.

  `login_id`

- ❑ `sp_dropuser` – removes a user from the current database.

  `user_name`

- ❑ `sp_help` – returns information about a specific database object.

  `object_name`

- ❑ `sp_helptext` – displays information about Triggers, Stored Procedures, and Views.

  `object_name`

- ❑ `sp_helpuser` – displays information about a specified user's security.

  `user_name`

The above list summarizes the system stored procedures that I have found most useful, but there are many more available. For further information, consult the documentation for your specific RDBMS.

Triggers

A trigger is a special type of stored procedure that responds to specific events. It is a collection of SQL commands that is stored as an object on the RDBMS. Unlike normal stored procedures, triggers *cannot* be called directly from within Visual Basic. A trigger is associated with a database table and is automatically invoked whenever a user attempts to modify (`UPDATE`, `DELETE`, or `INSERT`) data on the table that is "protected" by the trigger. It cannot be circumvented.

A trigger is executed only once, even if the modification that invoked it involves the alteration of hundreds of records. As you can imagine, the code encompassed by a trigger can be extremely complex.

The key aim of a trigger is to maintain integrity of data by preventing unauthorized or inconsistent changes. Triggers are executed immediately before the data is changed, so the data can be validated and the changes can be "rolled back" if they threaten data integrity.

> **As an aside, do be aware that triggers *cannot* be invoked against views.**

Triggers are commonly used to:

❏ **Enforce Business Rules**
They can enforce complex business logic, validate data, and ensure proper security clearance for alterations to a database table. This might include capturing an UPDATE, INSERT, or DELETE statement for a specific table, and validating the changes made, possibly even comparing the values to those found in another table. A trigger forms part of a **transaction** and can be programmed to accept or roll back attempted changes. Transactions are covered in detail in the next chapter, and we'll look at an example of a ROLLBACK later in this chapter.

❏ **Log Transactions**
Every time certain data in the database is altered, a trigger can query the user's login ID and write the changes to another table for later reference. We will implement a transaction log later in the chapter.

❏ **Maintain Data Integrity**
A trigger can ensure that a field value conforms to value or format restrictions and that the value is in accordance with related values in other tables. A trigger can cascade changes made in one table down to other tables in the database.

❏ **Call User-Defined and Other Stored Procedures**
This allows repetitive use of tried and tested stored procedures.

You will have noticed that the functionality provided by a trigger overlaps that available through the server's inherent referential integrity constraints. Triggers should not be used to perform tasks that can easily be handled using normal constraints (such as setting simple default values). However, triggers do provide a much more flexible environment in which to handle business rules. For example, if a rule relating to data integrity is transgressed, a check constraint will simply return an error message. A trigger can check the rule, and execute further logic based on the value passed. A trigger can handle much more complex business logic due to the procedural extensions to SQL provided by the database server.

A Note on the Mode of Operation of Triggers

In the previous section we discussed how triggers could be used to enforce restrictions on data modification processes. You may have asked yourself: How does the trigger know exactly what rows were affected by the modification? The answer is through *virtual* tables – the inserted table and the deleted table. When an INSERT command is executed, the new rows are added to the table on which the trigger acts and, simultaneously, are copied to the inserted table. When a DELETE command is executed, records are deleted from the base table and copied to the deleted table. An UPDATE command is treated like a DELETE command followed by an INSERT command so the records containing the old values are copied to the deleted table and the new records are copied to the inserted table. The trigger refers to records in these tables as it performs data validation.

Triggers provide complex functionality but can be difficult to program. There's a lot to learn about them and in this chapter we'll just be covering the basics. It's only through practice and the examination of existing triggers that you can perfect the art of creating and executing them.

Creating Triggers

We'll create a trigger to monitor transactions that are applied to the `Order Details` table in the `Northwind` database. If a user updates data in this table or creates a new record, the values will be stored in a new table, which will let us know what changes were made, when they were made, and who made them.

We're pushing any changes made into a new table, which needs to be created. The following SQL statement creates a table entitled `changed_orderdetails`, that has fields that would be relevant to an audit process, such as the user ID of the person who modified the table. Run this statement in SQL analyzer:

```
CREATE TABLE changed_orderdetails (
     OrderID int NOT NULL,
     ProductID int NOT NULL,
     UnitPrice money NOT NULL,
     Quantity smallint NOT NULL,
     Discount real NOT NULL,
     modify_date datetime NOT NULL,
     modify_user char (10) NOT NULL
)
```

Check the **Tables** node of `Northwind` to ensure the new table is listed. Now we can set up the trigger. Right-click on the `Order Details` table in Enterprise Manager, and choose **All Tasks | Manage Triggers**.

The first part of the code uses a `CREATE TRIGGER` statement to create a trigger; we'll name ours `orderdetails_insupd`:

```
CREATE TRIGGER orderdetails_insupd
```

Next, the `ON` keyword specifies the table on which the trigger is to execute:

```
ON [dbo].[Order Details]
```

The `FOR` keyword specifies the commands that will cause the trigger to execute. We just want `INSERT` and `UPDATE` here, to make the trigger execute when order details are inserted or updated:

```
FOR INSERT, UPDATE
AS
```

Next, we declare the variables that will be populated using values taken from the virtual `inserted` table:

```
DECLARE @OrderID int,
        @ProdID int,
        @quantity smallint,
        @discount real
SELECT @ProdID = inserted.ProductID,
       @OrderID = inserted.OrderID,
```

```
        @quantity = inserted.Quantity,
        @discount = inserted.Discount
FROM inserted
```

Once we have all the data we need, we can apply some business rules. For this example, we're just going to apply a simple rule which ensures that any orders for 20 or more items have a discount greater than zero, as we'll pretend this is one of Northwind's great offers, keeping customers coming back to buy their Knäckerbrot. If this is not the case, we raise an error that is sent back to the user, and the transaction is rolled back with no changes being saved to the database:

```
IF (@quantity >= 20) and (@discount = 0)
BEGIN
  RAISERROR ('Orders of 20 or more items are discounted', 16, 1)
  ROLLBACK TRANSACTION
END
```

Finally, we populate our changed_orderdetails table. We use the built-in SQL Server functions GETDATE(), which returns the current date and time, and USER_NAME() which returns the ID of the current user, to add information about who modified the table:

```
ELSE
BEGIN
INSERT INTO changed_ orderdetails
     (OrderID, ProductID, UnitPrice, Quantity, Discount,
      modify_date, modify_user)
VALUES
     (@OrderID, @ProdID, 0, @quantity, @discount, GETDATE(), USER_NAME())
END
```

Click OK, and the trigger will be created.

Trigger Happy

Now we have our trigger in place, any modification of the Order Details table will be logged in the changed_orderdetails table. Run the following SQL statement to check:

```
UPDATE Order Details
SET Quantity = 190
WHERE OrderID = 10264 AND ProductID = 2
```

When the command is sent, the trigger executes and the modified row is copied to the virtual inserted table. The trigger then proceeds as described above, and it should prevent the update, returning the error message we set and rolling back the transaction:

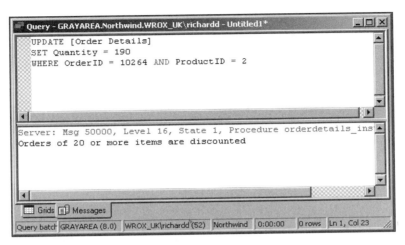

A more common use for triggers is as a mechanism for implementing referential integrity where tables are not explicitly joined. After a record is added, updated, or deleted, a trigger can execute a SELECT statement against related tables in order to check for the existence of related records. If all is OK, the changes are forwarded throughout the database, otherwise an error is returned to the user.

Summary

Views, stored procedures and triggers are not, strictly speaking, *necessary* for the successful implementation of all client-server systems. However, each is capable of greatly enhancing the reliability, efficiency, performance, and security of a system. Just a few of the benefits gained from using these methods include maintaining data integrity, implementing security with views, enforcing business logic and automating tasks.

This chapter has demonstrated how to create views, stored procedures, and triggers in SQL Server, and how to call them from a Visual Basic application. You may find the syntax and scope of these three advanced features varies slightly for other vendors' RDBMS, but nevertheless, the basic principles will be the same.

One of the great advantages of triggers is the ability to rollback the changes, and send the user an informative error message as we've just seen.

If not properly documented, views, stored procedures, and triggers can cause real headaches during programming and testing. Remember to design and implement them according to a logical plan, and most of all, be sure to keep detailed and up-to-date documentation available to all members of the team.

p2p.wrox.com
The programmer's resource centre

ASP Today

wrox.com

wroxdirect

Data Validation, Transactions, and Error Trapping

This chapter brings together a number of further topics which you will need to consider when designing your client-server system. These will help you ensure that your data conforms to the specifications required for your business, and they do so with minimal network traffic. The topics covered here are:

❑ **Data Validation**: This is the process of ensuring that data entered into your tables conforms to your business rules. For example, you wouldn't want to allow a user to enter a date of birth value after today's date into a database holding people's details. If such a value were provided, you would want to alert the user of the error.

❑ **Transactions**: Transactions give the user the ability to execute a number of SQL statements as a single entity. If any one of the statements fails, the entire transaction fails. This can be critical to ensuring that data is not lost, especially for accounting systems where money is transferred from one account to another.

❑ **Error trapping**: While error trapping is usually fairly easy to incorporate into your project, it takes time and plenty of thought. Just forecasting all of the conditions that could occur is half the battle. Once you know what conditions to expect, you need to have a plan of action to handle the errors. This may include ignoring the error, writing the error to an error log or notifying the user.

Data Validation

As we have already discussed, data validation is performed to ensure that the data entered into your database conforms to your business specification. The list of possible rules is nearly endless. Some of the common validation criteria include:

- ❑   Values must be greater or less than a specific number
- ❑   Text must be a specific length or no more than x characters long
- ❑   Values cannot be null
- ❑   Text must be in upper or lower case
- ❑   Values must exist in another table
- ❑   Values must be one of several specific possibilities, such as M or F to record a person's gender
- ❑   Dates must be in a specific range or format
- ❑   If one field is populated, another must be as well
- ❑   If one field is populated, another field must not

The impact of trapping data that doesn't conform to your rules can be essential to a successful implementation. Remember, the data that goes into the database will eventually come back out. This may be in the form of a report, or displayed on a form. There's nothing more frustrating than seeing invalid data in a field (such as a value of 'L' in the gender code field).

Data validation can occur at one or more of the following three places:

- ❑   On the client
- ❑   On the server
- ❑   In the middle-tier objects

There's no absolute rule stipulating where to put this business logic. You may find that it's practical to place the logic on both the client and the server. There are benefits to each.

Placing the business logic on the client reduces network traffic because the data is validated before it is sent to the server. The downside of this is that updating your logic rules can be quite cumbersome.

Data Validation on the Server

When the business logic resides on the database server, the client sends a request to insert a new record or update or delete an existing record. The server receives this request and validates the data according to all validation criteria or **constraints** that have been placed on the table. If a constraint rule has been broken, the server will send an error notification back to the client. The client should then interpret the error message and display a useful message to the user. At this stage, the user can make changes to the data and attempt to re-send the request:

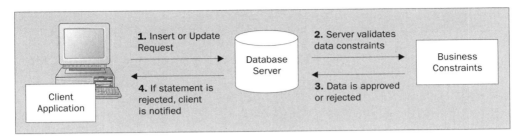

As the figure shows, this causes more network traffic and the server has to spend more time validating the data received. For this reason, you may choose to place the business logic on the client. Just remember that the greater the number of clients, the greater the number of upgrades that must be made each time your logic changes.

> **Business logic does not necessarily equate to data validation. Validation such as ensuring all zip codes are entered as numbers and have no letters does not constitute a business rule. This type of validation should be placed on the client to minimize network traffic.**

Exploring Constraints in SQL Server

Now that you understand how data is validated on the server, let's examine the types of constraints available in SQL Server and then we'll look at an existing constraint on the pubs database in SQL Server.

SQL Server supports five different types of constraint. These types restrict in different ways the possible values that the columns on which they are placed can take:

❑ **Primary Key** – Designates the constraint as a primary key. This causes the column(s) on which the constraint is placed to be the primary key for the table and creates a unique index for the column(s). There may be only one PRIMARY KEY per table and the value of the column(s) must be unique in the table.

❑ **Foreign Key** – Designates the constraint as a foreign key. Each entry in the column must have a corresponding entry in the column of the table to which the FK refers.

❑ **Unique** – Similar to a PRIMARY KEY, in that each entry in this column must have a unique value. However, there may be more than one UNIQUE constraint per table.

❑ **Check** – This is the usual type of constraint for data validation; it stipulates specific limits for the values of the entries in the column.

❑ **Default** – This constraint specifies the value that is to be inserted into the column if no other value is supplied.

In this chapter, we will be concentrating solely on the CHECK constraint – the others are concerned more with referential integrity than with data validation.

Constraints are typically created during the creation of a table; however, they can also be created with an ALTER TABLE SQL command and, in some RDBMSs such as Oracle, with a CREATE CONSTRAINT command. There are a number of methods for creating SQL Server tables and constraints. One of the most practical methods is to use scripts. A script is simply a text file containing one or more sets of SQL commands to be executed by SQL Server; scripts can be saved and then reused at a later time. When minor changes need to be made to a table, or a new constraint needs to be added, the script can be modified and re-executed. SQL Server provides a wizard to generate scripts automatically, without writing any SQL statements ourselves.

To see this in action, let's look at a script that recreates the jobs table on the pubs database, including any constraints. Open the SQL Server Enterprise Manager and navigate to the jobs table in the pubs database as shown. Right-click on the jobs table name and select All Tasks | Generate SQL Scripts from the pop-up menu:

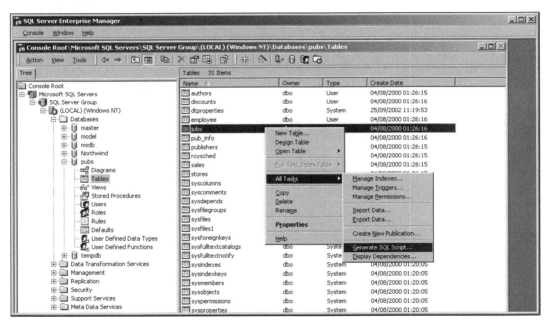

The Generate SQL Scripts dialog will appear. This dialog allows you to create a script to recreate the table specified. In this case, we'll use it to generate a script capable of recreating the jobs table:

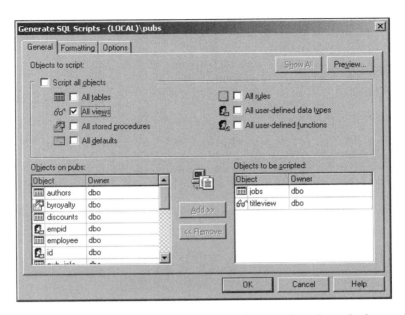

The script builder is capable of creating scripts that include everything from the basic table definition to indexes, keys, and dependencies. For now, we just want to generate the commands to drop the table if it already exists, to recreate the table, and to recreate any constraints. To do this, ensure that the following check boxes are selected: Generate the CREATE <object> command for each object and Generate the DROP <object> command for each object on the Formatting tab, and Script PRIMARY Keys, FOREIGN Keys, defaults, and check constraints on the Options tab (in SQL Server 6.5, this option appears as Table Keys/DRI):

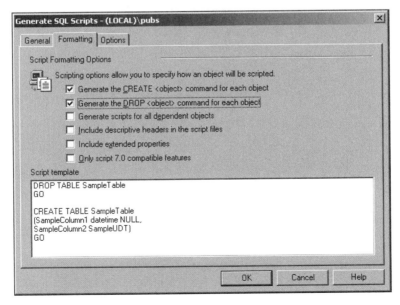

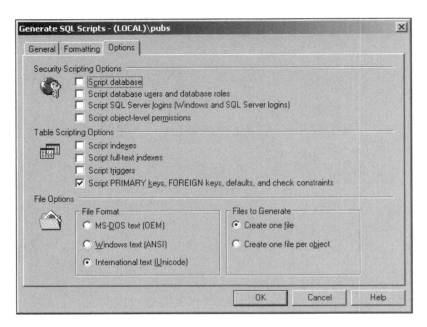

You may select more than these three options, but they are unnecessary at this point. We're more interested in seeing the script stripped down with just table constraints and the table definition. Once you have made your choices, click on the OK button:

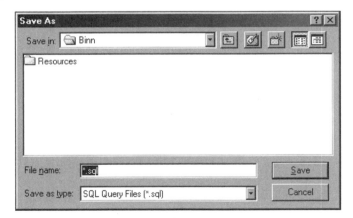

You will be prompted to save your script. You may place it in the default directory or another directory if you prefer. Remember the location for later use. When the script is created, it may be viewed and modified in any text editor such as Word or Notepad. Specify the filename jobs.sql and click on the Save button. After some processing you should receive a message indicating that the script was successfully created:

Now that we have our script generated, let's take a look at its contents. From the main menu, select
Tools I SQL Query Analyzer. This is an ideal tool to view your script because the script that you built is
a SQL statement, but you may use Notepad to view the script if you prefer. Click on the **Load SQL
Script** icon (or hit *Ctrl + Shift + P*) and select the jobs script from the **Open Query** dialog. The script
will load into the Query window:

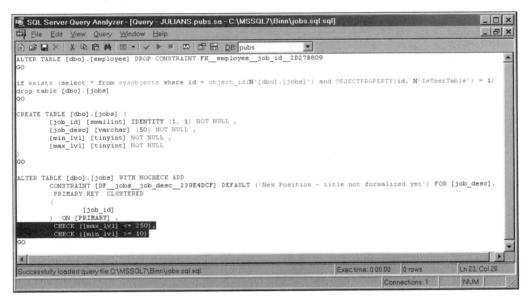

In the above image, there are four constraints: the PRIMARY KEY constraint on the job_id column, a
DEFAULT constraint on the job_desc column, and CHECK constraints on the max_lvl and min_lvl
columns. However, here we are interested only in the CHECK constraints; they are as follows:

❑   The max_lvl field must be less than or equal to 250

❑   The min_lvl field must be equal to or greater than 10

In SQL Server, each constraint must have a unique name. For this reason, it's preferable to use a
naming convention that includes the type of constraint (such as CK for CHECK), the name of the table,
and the name of the field. We'll explore creating constraints in more detail a bit later.

> **Further on in the chapter, we'll explore how constraints are added to a table using the
> CREATE TABLE SQL command. But first, let's see how an application reacts to
> a constraint.**

Testing Constraints

Now that we know of these constraints, we can build an application to test their validity. Open Visual Basic and create a new standard executable project. Add a reference to the Microsoft ActiveX Data Objects 2.x Library and enter the following code in a command button or the Form_Load event:

```
Dim objConn As ADODB.Connection
Set objConn = New ADODB.Connection
objConn.ConnectionString = "Provider=SQLOLEDB.1;" _
                        & "Persist Security Info=False;" _
                        & "User ID=sa;Initial Catalog=pubs"
objConn.Open
objConn.Execute "INSERT INTO jobs (job_desc,min_lvl, max_lvl)" _
            & "VALUES ('Programmer',0,210)"
```

> **Your connection string may differ from the above code, depending on the configuration of your database server and the version of SQL Server or other database you are using. If you have trouble connecting, use the Connection Wizard as outlined in Chapter 3 to create the connection string.**

This code is no different from any other you have seen to this point. The first section establishes a connection to the pubs database and the second section executes a SQL INSERT statement. This INSERT statement has been designed with the intention of breaking the CK_jobs_min_lvl constraint. Notice that the value that corresponds to min_lvl is 0. This is an invalid value because the value passed must be greater than or equal to 10.

When you run the project, the following error dialog appears:

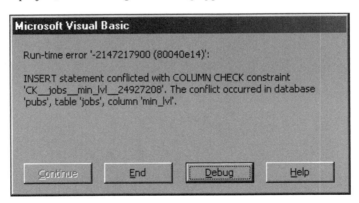

The error raised has a number and description, just as any other error. This allows you to trap any anticipated constraint errors such as this one.

> **Depending on the database server, you may be able to return a message to the user (such as an error description) when a constraint is violated.**

Exploring Constraints in Microsoft Access

Microsoft Access also allows you to set up constraints. To view the constraints in an Access database, open the table in Design View:

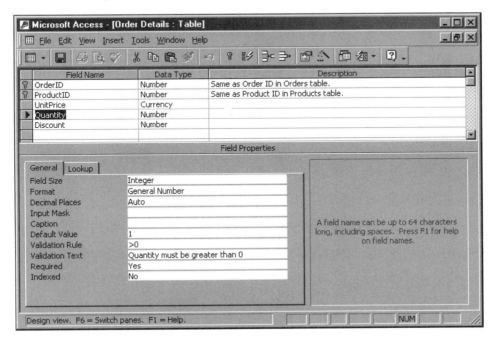

The following properties concern the constraints applicable to a given field:

❑ Validation Rule – the actual constraint

❑ Validation Text – the descriptive text passed to a user when a constraint is violated

In the image above (showing the Order Details table of the Nwind database), notice that the Quantity field has a constraint specifying that the value must be greater than zero. If this rule is broken, the user will receive the message in the validation text: Quantity must be greater than 0. These properties can also be changed in this screen.

Adding Validation Constraints with SQL

As we have seen, validation constraints are also known as CHECK constraints. A CHECK constraint allows us to compare the values that are about to be saved to a specific field in the table with rules applied to the table. The syntax for a CHECK constraint is similar to that for a primary key. As you recall, when we learned how to create primary keys in tables, we used the CONSTRAINT clause. We'll now use that same keyword to create a CHECK constraint. The syntax is:

```
CONSTRAINT Constraint_Name CHECK (Expression)
```

`Constraint_Name` is the name of the constraint and `Expression` is the formula that will be used to validate the data. Usually this will consist of the name of a field, an operator and a value against which the column's data is to be matched. This clause can be added to a CREATE TABLE or ALTER TABLE statement.

The following SQL statement is designed specifically for a SQL Server database. It creates a table titled `Employer` with three fields:

- ❑ emp_id – a small integer acting as a unique identifier

- ❑ emp_name – a varchar (max 50 characters long) used to store a name

- ❑ emp_commission – a tinyint used to store commission percentages on sales

The last line of the SQL statement creates a constraint titled `CK_Commission`. The word CHECK identifies the constraint as a CHECK constraint. The validation criterion is then placed inside parentheses. In this example, we ensure that all commission payoffs are less than or equal to 25 percent:

```
CREATE TABLE Employer(
   emp_id smallint IDENTITY (1, 1) NOT NULL ,
   emp_name varchar (50) NOT NULL,
   emp_commission tinyint NOT NULL ,
CONSTRAINT CK_Commission CHECK (emp_commission <= 25))
```

The following code is another example of a CHECK constraint. As you can see, many of the operators you learned when we first covered SQL are valid. This example applies a CHECK constraint to the emp_name field. Its purpose is to ensure that all names entered begin with the letters se. While this has little practical application, it nicely illustrates the use of the keyword LIKE and % as a wildcard:

```
CREATE TABLE employer1(
   emp_id smallint IDENTITY (1, 1) NOT NULL ,
   emp_name varchar (50) NOT NULL,
   emp_commission tinyint NOT NULL,
CONSTRAINT CK_Name CHECK (emp_name like 'se%'))
```

Try running these SQL statements, then enter data that breaks the rules. You should receive an error message with specifics of which constraint was violated:

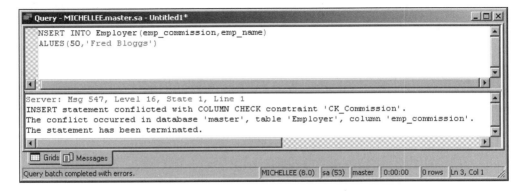

When a field has been identified as an automatically generated field (such as using IDENTITY), you should NOT attempt to populate it. The RDBMS is responsible for ensuring that a unique value is stored in the field, and you may disrupt the integrity of the field's unique values.

Data Validation at the Application Level

Data validation can take place at the client level in a number of ways. As I'm sure you have discovered with Visual Basic, there is usually more than one way to accomplish any given task. Data validation is no exception. However, there are two basic methods for performing client-side data validation. The first is to validate data whenever the user attempts to update the database; the second is to perform the validation as the user types the data. To demonstrate these two methods, we will revert back to our sample Address application from Chapter 4, the ADO Data Control chapter. As you recall, the application connected to a table that stored names and addresses:

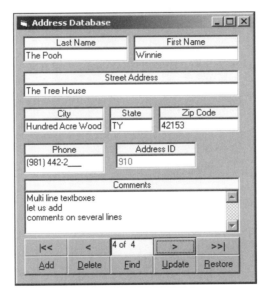

We'll implement field validation in the following ways:

- ❑ Ensure the last and first name fields are not blank
- ❑ Ensure the zip code does not include any letters (A–Z)

Let's begin with the name fields. To implement this restriction, we need to ensure that the first and last name text boxes are both populated with data. The question is when we should test this condition. In this case, we cannot validate the data as it is typed, because we only want to check that there is *something* in the fields. We must therefore perform the validation when the user attempts to update the database. There are two possible points at which this might happen: when the Update button is pressed, and after the fields have been modified and the user attempts to move to a new record.

To begin, create a new function called `ValidateFields`. This function will return a Boolean value indicating whether either of the two name fields breaks the validation rule. Inside this procedure, we check the contents of the two text boxes. If either is blank, we return a message box to the user and then return `False` to the calling procedure:

```
Public Function ValidateFields() As Boolean

  If Trim(txtField(0).Text) = "" Then
    MsgBox "Last Name field cannot be empty"
    Exit Function
  End If

  If Trim(txtField(1).Text) = "" Then
    MsgBox "First Name field cannot be empty"
    Exit Function
  End If

  ValidateFields = True

End Function
```

We'll first call the new procedure from the **Update** command button. The code that updates the database table is embedded inside an `If` statement that evaluates the result of `ValidateFields`. This causes the record to update only if the function returns `True`; otherwise, the remaining code is ignored. Apply the following changes to the `cmdAction_Click` event procedure:

```
Private Sub cmdAction_Click(Index As Integer)
    On Error GoTo goActionErr
  If ValidateFields = True Then
    With Adodc1
              ...

      End With
  End If
Exit Sub

goActionErr:
  MsgBox Err.Description
End Sub
```

The other point in our code where we want to call our `ValidateFields` procedure is when the user is attempting to navigate from the current record. The goal is to prevent the record from being saved if the fields are empty. For this, we need to trigger an event that indicates that we're about to change the record. The appropriate event we need is `Adodc1_WillChangeRecord`. This event only fires when a change has been made to the current record and it is about to be saved due to navigation. In the code for this event, we call the `ValidateFields` function again. If the function returns `False`, then we set the `adStatus` property to `adStatusCancel`, which cancels the record change:

```
Private Sub Adodc1_WillChangeRecord(ByVal adReason As _
              ADODB.EventReasonEnum, ByVal cRecords As Long, _
              adStatus As ADODB.EventStatusEnum, _
              ByVal pRecordset As ADODB.Recordset)
```

```
      If ValidateFields = False Then
        adStatus = adStatusCancel
      End If

   End Sub
```

The second validation task is to prevent letters from being entered in the zip code text box (although in some countries, letters are used in zip codes, so this validation rule is geographically specific). Since we know which specific characters can be entered into this field, we can perform validation as the keys are pressed, and ignore any 'illegal' characters (such as letters) the user attempts to enter. To restrict letters from being entered, we can capture the KeyPress event of the zip code text box and reject any letters passed. Because we have several boxes with the same name, we need to ensure this logic only applies to the zip code box (the text bound to the "ZIP" field). To implement this, we simply check the DataField property of the text box. If this is not set to "ZIP", no validation is required. The KeyPress event takes an argument KeyAscii which returns the ASCII value corresponding to the key pressed. The character value is pulled from this ASCII value with the Chr$ function; this is then evaluated to check whether it is a number or not. If the value is not numeric, the KeyAscii value is set to 0, which prevents any text from being entered.

```
   Private Sub txtField_KeyPress(Index As Integer, KeyAscii As Integer)
      If UCase(txtField.Item(Index).DataField) = "ZIP" Then
        If Not IsNumeric(Chr$(KeyAscii)) Then
          KeyAscii = 0
        End If
      End If
   End Sub
```

> **Another method to achieve the same result is to compare the KeyAscii value with the ASCII values of the numeric characters (48 - 57).**

Test the new code. As you can see, client-side validation is essentially quite easy. You simply need to know where to place your code; the rest is simple Visual Basic coding logic.

What Are Transactions?

One of the important concepts you must understand as a client-server developer is that of **transactions**. Transactions consist of one or more SQL statements that are processed together as a single unit of work. If any one of those SQL statements fails, the entire batch of statements fails. When you understand this, you might wonder why you would want to do this.

The primary reason for using transactions is to avoid the loss of data integrity; that is, to ensure that no discrepancies occur in our data (for example, due to a systems failure). To illustrate this more clearly, let's walk through a scenario. Let's assume that we have two accounts in a XYZ Bank, called Checking and Savings. If we wanted to move $500 from one account to the other, it would involve four steps:

1. Request a deduction from the Checking account.

2. Wait for a response that the action completed successfully.

3. Request that our Savings account be credited.

4. Wait for a response indicating that the action completed successfully.

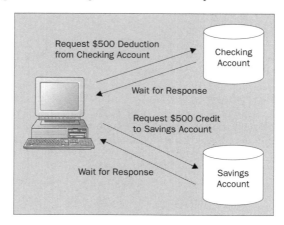

Now, let's assume that when we requested that the Savings account be credited, an error was returned. We're now left in a situation where $500 has been deducted from the Checking account, but not placed in the Savings account. This discrepancy needs to be accounted for. There are a number of ways to handle this. If you didn't know about transactions, one solution might include the redeposit of $500 to the Savings account and alerting the user that an error occurred. The problem with this is that it causes confusion as to where the initial $500 went to and where the second $500 came from, not to mention the additional network and server traffic.

The optimal solution is to use a transaction. Transactions allow you to mark the beginning of a transaction. Then the transaction is either **committed** (that is, all the operations within the transaction are confirmed and actually performed) upon the successful completion of the final SQL statement or it is **rolled back** (that is, the transaction and all operations within it are aborted), which will cancel any SQL statements executed prior to the error. Let's walk through this same problem using transactions.

1. Mark the beginning of the transaction.

2. Request a deduction from the Checking account.

3. Wait for a response that the action has completed successfully.

4. Request that our Savings account is credited.

5. Wait for a response indicating that the action has completed successfully.

6. If all SQL statements succeed, commit the transaction and save changes. Otherwise, rollback the transaction and abort any changes made.

If the transaction does fail, the error will need to be logged with the transaction information. This will allow the user to track down the cause of the error and correct the situation. No data is lost and because the transaction is rolled back, no trace of the changes exists in the database.

BeginTrans, CommitTrans and RollBackTrans

ADO has three methods for handling transactions:

- ❑ `BeginTrans`
- ❑ `CommitTrans`
- ❑ `RollBackTrans`

These three methods are applied to the `Connection` object at the appropriate times. We'll now build a sample application that uses these methods.

Create a new **Standard EXE** project, and add three command buttons to the form. Arrange the command buttons and change their captions to resemble the following image:

The three command buttons should be named as follows:

- ❑ `cmdConnect` – connects to the appropriate database
- ❑ `cmdUpdate` – creates a new table, populates it with data, updates the data, then commits the transaction
- ❑ `cmdCommit` – manually pushes changes through a table, then allows the user the ability to cancel all changes

We'll first build the code to connect to the `pubs` database. Begin by adding a reference to the Microsoft ActiveX Data Objects:

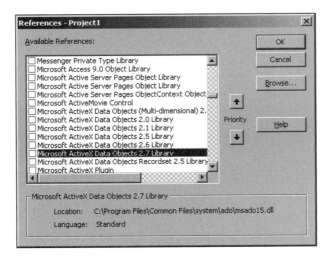

Then add the following code to the General Declarations section of your form. We will call our Connection object objConn, and our recordset object objRec, allowing us to return recordsets from the database:

```
Option Explicit
Dim objConn As ADODB.Connection
Dim objRec As ADODB.Recordset
```

Next, add the code to your cmdConnect button. This will connect to the pubs database located in Microsoft SQL Server (you might of course need to alter the connection string to suit your own database setup):

```
Private Sub cmdConnect_Click()

  On Error GoTo Connection_Error

  Set objConn = New ADODB.Connection
  objConn.ConnectionString = "Provider=SQLOLEDB.1;" _
                        & "Persist Security Info=False;" _
                        & "User ID=sa;Initial Catalog=pubs"
  objConn.Open
  MsgBox "Connection successful!", , "Connect"

  Exit Sub

Connection_Error:
  MsgBox "Unable to connect:" & vbCrLf & Err.Description, , "Connect"

End Sub
```

The code for the cmdUpdate button is broken out into a number of functions. Initially, we DROP the Employee_BK table if it already exists. The reason for this is that if the table already exists, an error will be generated when we attempt to build it, unless we have first used the DROP TABLE statement. The line On Error Resume Next is added at the top of the DROP TABLE code. This is to handle the possibility that the table may not exist, generating an error when we attempt to DROP it.

After ensuring that we don't already have a table called Employee_BK, we create a table of that name. When we're sure we have our new table Employee_BK, we call the BeginTrans method of our newly established connection. This will mark the beginning point of our transaction. After this, we pass any errors to an error handler located at the bottom of the procedure. Any SQL statements after this point will be rolled back if an error should occur. Inside the error handler, we pass the user a message box with the reason for the error and rollback the transaction using RollbackTrans. Inside the transaction, we pass two SQL statements, which add all records from the Employee table and then modify any records with a job_id of 5. If all three statements succeed, we commit these three transactions using CommitTrans:

```
Private Sub cmdUpdate_Click()

  Dim strSQL As String

  objConn.CommandTimeout = 15
```

```
' DROP the table if it exists. We'll ignore any errors
' that might occur if the table doesn't exist
On Error Resume Next
strSQL = "DROP TABLE Employee_BK"
objConn.Execute strSQL

' Create a backup table to work with
strSQL = "CREATE TABLE Employee_BK "   _
        & "(emp_id    empid          NOT NULL ," _
        & "fname      varchar (20)   NOT NULL , " _
        & "minit      char (1)       NULL ," _
        & "lname      varchar (30)   NOT NULL ," _
        & "job_id     smallint       NOT NULL ," _
        & "job_lvl    tinyint        NOT NULL ," _
        & "pub_id     char (4)       NOT NULL ," _
        & "hire_date  DateTime       NOT NULL)"
objConn.Execute strSQL

objConn.BeginTrans
On Error GoTo Update_Error

' Populate it with backup data
strSQL = "INSERT INTO Employee_BK "  _
        & "SELECT * FROM Employee"
objConn.Execute strSQL

' Update the new salary information
strSQL = "UPDATE Employee_BK "  _
        & "SET job_lvl = job_lvl + 3 "  _
        & "WHERE job_id = 5"
objConn.Execute strSQL

MsgBox "Completed Successfully!" & vbCrLf  _
      & "Committing Changes.", ,"Update"

objConn.CommitTrans

Exit Sub

Update_Error:

MsgBox "Error occured - " & Err.Description & vbCrLf  _
      & "Rolling Back the last transactions.", , "Update"

objConn.RollbackTrans

End Sub
```

Run the application and click on the **Connect** button. Once you have connected, click on the **Update** button. If you have made no errors with your code, the following message should appear:

To confirm the successful execution further, apply a SELECT SQL statement to the Employee_BK table. You can use the SQL Server Query Analyzer from SQL Server's Enterprise Manager to view the results, making sure that you select **pubs** from the **DB** drop down.

Now, let's try to break the code. In the section that populates the table with data, create an error in your SQL statement by changing the table name from Employee_BK to Employee_B. This will generate an error, rolling back all SQL statements:

```
' Populate it with backup data
strSQL = "INSERT INTO Employee_B "   _
        & "SELECT * FROM Employee"
objConn.Execute strSQL
```

When you rerun the project, the following error is returned:

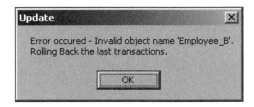

The last command button is designed to demonstrate how transactions can be used while you are manually stepping through your recordset. In this example, we set the objRec recordset's Locktype property to adLockOptimistic, which allows us to prevent other users from modifying the records to be updated after the Update method has been called. We call the BeginTrans method just as in the **Update** command button. Once the table is open, we call the MoveFirst method to set the current record to the first record in the recordset. The loop allows us to navigate through the records until we reach the end of the recordset. As we navigate through these records, we check the value of the job_id field for each record. If the job_id is 5, we reassign its value to 3 and increment intCounter. The final stage is to ask the user if they would like to commit or rollback the changes:

```
Private Sub cmdCommit_Click()
   Dim strSQL As String
   Dim intRetval As Integer
   Set objRec = New ADODB.Recordset
   Dim intCounter As Integer

   objRec.LockType = adLockOptimistic

   objConn.CommandTimeout = 15
   objConn.BeginTrans
```

```
On Error GoTo Update_Error

' Navigate through all Employees and count affected records

objRec.Open "Employee_BK", objConn, , , adCmdTable
objRec.MoveFirst

Do Until objRec.EOF
  ' Get the Job code & update
  If objRec("job_id") = "5" Then
     objRec("job_id") = "3"
     intCounter = intCounter + 1
  End If
  'Move to the next record
  objRec.MoveNext
Loop

' Ask the user if the information is correct
intRetval = MsgBox(intCounter & " records are about to be modified." & _
        " Commit Changes? ", vbQuestion + vbYesNo, "Commit Changes?")

If intRetval = vbYes Then
  ' If so, commit the changes
  objConn.CommitTrans
Else
  ' Otherwise, rollback the changes
  objConn.RollbackTrans
End If

Exit Sub

Update_Error:

MsgBox "Error occured - " & Err.Description & vbCrLf & _
      "Rolling back the last transactions."

objConn.RollbackTrans

End Sub
```

Run the project and click on the **Connect** button followed by the **Commit** button. The following message should appear:

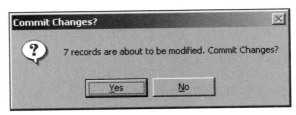

Click on **Yes**. You can confirm that the changes worked by running the code again. This time there should be 0 records in the count. This is because all records with a `job_id` of 5 have already been changed to a 3 the first time you ran the project:

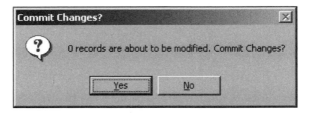

If you want to continue with more testing, rerun the project and click on the **Update** button. This creates a fresh copy of the table.

ADO and OLE DB Provider Errors

Capturing errors will be one of the most important chores of developing your application. As I mentioned at the beginning of this chapter, it's a long and time-consuming task to consider all of the possible errors that can be encountered. For this reason, you should attempt to log these as you think of them, right from the beginning stages of your project. Many of the errors you encounter will become apparent during your testing phase. However, a number of them may not be apparent until your product is released and live data is filtered through it.

The next project we build will work specifically with errors. We'll attempt to apply a number of invalid commands to a database, and handle the error messages that are returned.

Create a new project and add one new command button to the form. Name the button `cmdError`. We want to create an array of command buttons, so copy the command button and paste it five more times. Set the properties of the form and the command buttons as described in the following table:

Object	Property	Value
Form	Name	frmError
	Caption	Errors
Command Button	Name	cmdError
	Index	0
	Caption	Invalid Table
Command Button	Name	cmdError
	Index	1
	Caption	Invalid Field

Object	Property	Value
Command Button	Name	cmdError
	Index	2
	Caption	Locked Record
Command Button	Name	cmdError
	Index	3
	Caption	Deleted Record
Command Button	Name	cmdError
	Index	4
	Caption	No Current Record
Command Button	Name	cmdError
	Index	5
	Caption	Wrong Data Type

When finished, your form should look like this:

Add a reference to the Microsoft ActiveX Data Objects Library, and then declare a `Connection` and `Recordset` object in the `General Declarations` section. We'll also declare some constants to refer to error codes, to make our code more readable:

```
Option Explicit

Dim objConn As ADODB.Connection
Dim objRec As ADODB.Recordset
```

```
Const INVALID_TABLE = -2147217865
Const INVALID_FIELD = 3265
Const TABLE_LOCKED = 3251
Const DELETED_RECORD = -2147217885
Const NO_CURRENT_RECORD = 3219
Const WRONG_DATA_TYPE = -2147352571
```

For simplicity, we'll connect to the database when the form loads:

```
Private Sub Form_Load()

    Set objConn = New ADODB.Connection
    objConn.ConnectionString = "Provider=SQLOLEDB.1;" _
                             & "Persist Security Info=False;" _
                             & "User ID=sa;Initial Catalog=pubs"
    objConn.Open

End Sub
```

When each of the command buttons is clicked, the `Index` value is passed with it. Each command button has a specific task associated with it. We have purposely created errors for each. Some have invalid table and field names, while others have errors such as the record being locked. Regardless of the case, the error is passed to an error handler at the bottom of the procedure. The error handler queries the error for its number (using the constants we defined earlier in place of the actual values of the error codes) and handles it by calling another procedure called `ErrorLog`. This procedure presents a message to the user and writes an entry describing the error to a log file. It is designed to receive one argument, a customized (user-friendly) error message:

```
Private Sub cmdError_Click(Index As Integer)

    Set objRec = New ADODB.Recordset

    On Error GoTo errHandler

    Select Case Index

        Case 0
          ' Error caused by invalid Table Name
            objRec.Open "FakeTableName", objConn, , , adCmdTable
            MsgBox "This line of code is called after calling 'Resume Next'"

        Case 1
          ' Error caused by invalid Field Name
            objRec.Open "Employee", objConn, , , adCmdTable
            MsgBox objRec("InvalidField")

        Case 2
           ' Error caused by failing to unlock the table
            objRec.Open "Employee", objConn, , , adCmdTable
            objRec.Delete adAffectCurrent
```

```
    Case 3
      ' Error caused by calling a field of a deleted record
      objRec.LockType = adLockOptimistic
      objRec.Open "Employee_BK", objConn, , , adCmdTable
      objRec.Delete adAffectCurrent
      MsgBox objRec("emp_id")

    Case 4
      ' Error caused by navigating beyond the BOF marker
      objRec.Open "Employee", objConn, , , adCmdTable
      objRec.MoveFirst
      objRec.MovePrevious

    Case 5
      ' Error caused by entering data of the wrong type
      objRec.LockType = adLockOptimistic
      objRec.Open "Employee_BK", objConn, , , adCmdTable
      objRec("job_id") = "EM"

  End Select
Exit Sub


NextLine:
  MsgBox "This line is only called after calling 'Resume NextLine'"
Exit Sub

errHandler:

  Select Case Err.Number

    Case INVALID_TABLE        ' Table not found
      ErrorLog "Table not found in database! "
      Resume Next

    Case INVALID_FIELD        ' Field not found
      ErrorLog "Field not found in table! "
      Resume NextLine

    Case TABLE_LOCKED         ' Table Locked
      ErrorLog Err.Description & " Use Optimistic Locking!"

    Case DELETED_RECORD       ' Deleted Record
      ErrorLog "The requested field of the current record" & _
               " has been deleted!"

    Case NO_CURRENT_RECORD    ' No Current Record
      ErrorLog "There is no current record!"

    Case WRONG_DATA_TYPE      ' Wrong data type
      ErrorLog "You are attempting to enter a value that" & _
               " is a different data type than declared in the DB."
```

```
      Case Else
         ErrorLog Err.Number & Err.Description

   End Select

End Sub
```

The code in the error handler above illustrates how we continue running the application after an error has been raised, using the Resume statement. The code uses the Resume statement in two different places, and with slightly different syntax. In the first case, we use the statement Resume Next, which tells the procedure to continue with the line of code immediately after the line of code that caused the error. The second occurrence is in the format Resume NextLine, which tells the program to continue the procedure at the marker specified – in this case NextLine.

Create a new procedure, and call it ErrorLog. It should be configured to receive one parameter, msg, which is a string. In this procedure, we'll open a file, and write the contents of msg to it. In addition, we throw a message box to the user with the same message.

> It's a good idea to place any error and audit log procedures in a module (or, better, in a class module). This allows any procedures in the project to use them. However, for simplicity's sake, we have kept the procedure in the form's code window.

```
Public Sub ErrorLog(strMsg As String)

   ' Retrieve a reference id for the file
   Dim intErrorLog As Integer
   intErrorLog = FreeFile

   ' Open the log for append
   Open App.Path & "\error.log" For Append As intErrorLog

   ' Print to the error log
   Print #intErrorLog, Now() & " : " & strMsg

   'Close the error log
   Close intErrorLog

   ' Let the user know about the error
   MsgBox "Error: " & strMsg

End Sub
```

This procedure opens a file called error.log in the same directory as the application, creating the file if it does not already exist. We are going to add data onto the end of this file, so we use the For Append keyword when we open it. We also assign a file handle to the file – a unique integer label that Windows uses to identify the file, and by which we can subsequently refer to it. This is held in the variable intErrorLog. These file handles are frequently preceded by the pound sign (#). We can assign a specific integer to our file handle, but a better solution is to use the FreeFile function. This returns the first integer value not currently in use as a file handle.

Having opened the file, we write to it the current date and time, which are returned by the Now() function, and the error message, which was passed into the procedure as the parameter strMsg. We then close the log file, and finally display the error message to the user in a message box.

To test the program, create a directory on the your hard disk (if you have not already done so), and save your project here.

Run the project. Click on each of the buttons in turn to cause the appropriate error and view the message box with the respective error message:

Each of the errors is logged in the application's path with the name error.log. Open this file in Notepad to see how the project saved each error. Error logs can be a critical part of ensuring all data is processed correctly. However, remember that error logs are only useful if checked frequently and if the cause of each error is investigated.

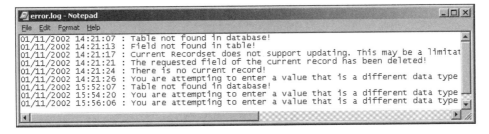

As well as a failure in the middle of a transaction caused by a system error, other data errors are made possible by conflicts when multiple users are accessing the data concurrently. It's important to identify any possible scenarios where multiple users will be accessing your database and test accordingly. You'll save yourself a great deal of unnecessary re-compiles after the system has been distributed.

Summary

In this chapter, we've covered data validation, transactions and error trapping. While some applications can survive without any consideration of these, a professional application should utilize such techniques to maximise efficiency, and user friendliness.

The question is when, or where, to implement which. There are very few, if any, applications that do not require some form of error trapping. With regard to transactions, consider what data will be lost if your application should crash before completion. Finally, consider how great the possibility is that invalid data will reach your database tables. For a field that is drawn directly from a list box, little to no validation will be required. Fields that allow freeform entry will require more validation.

p2p.wrox.com
The programmer's resource centre

ASP Today

wrox.com

wroxdirect

7

Advanced ADO

Not only has the technology for data access changed over the past decade, but our requirements and the ways in which we need to use that technology have also changed. We no longer live in a world where simple table-based data access is the answer to every problem. These days we need to bring that data back to the client and massage it. We often need to move the data across the network from one machine to another.

In the early days, computing was done on single standalone machines – mainframes, mini-computers, or the various flavors of personal or home computers used by the avant-garde. All data storage, access, and manipulation occurred on one machine. Not that things were trivial, but the problems faced were quite different from those we face today.

In the mid-90s, client-server programming came of age, with clients connected to databases and processing shared over multiple machines. Now we have the rise of the web server – effectively a hybrid of the standalone model, with a single application running on the web server, and the distributed, with each client running a browser of varying sophistication.

Internet and intranet applications are now a major focus for developers. Visual Basic 6, together with the Universal Data Access concept that dates from ADO 1.5, offers a library that can facilitate developers' work in a typical three-tier solution. With these tools in place, the Windows DNA architecture allows us to implement secure, robust, and scalable Internet and intranet applications for Windows operating systems. Windows DNA is based on the premise that the best solution for these challenges is to divide the application into three tiers comprising of:

❑ **Presentation tier**: HTML, DHTML, JavaScript, and so on presents data and information to the final user using Internet Explorer (as only IE supports advanced DHTML features such as RDS).

❑ **Business Logic tier**: using a Microsoft server tool such as Internet Information Services (IIS) or COM+, all business rules are included within this tier.

❑ **Data tier**: using ADO, ODBC, and OLE DB, this tier handles the managing of records and data.

Note that one or more of the above tiers may be further divided, to create an n-tier architecture. Windows DNA is heavily based on COM+ (COM and Microsoft Transaction Server on Windows NT), meaning it suffers from the issue of DLL Hell, as well as being dependent on the Microsoft operating system. The Microsoft .NET Framework goes along way to resolving DLL Hell, but Visual Basic 6 developers will have to produce and maintain Windows DNA applications for a long time yet. Many Windows DNA applications are already up and running on the Internet and companies are naturally reluctant to throw such investments away.

So this chapter is really aimed at those developers who wish to learn how to apply advanced ADO techniques in the Windows DNA architecture. We will cover:

❑ The ADO disconnected recordset – useful in n-tier applications as it allows developers to use server resources just for the time necessary to retrieve data from a database.

❑ Remote Data Services – a collection of COM objects that let developers add HTTP support to ADO objects.

❑ ADO and XML – XML is mainly used to exchange information between different processes and operating systems. ADO has the ability to persist recordsets as XML.

The ADO Disconnected Recordset

In the previous ADO chapters, we briefly introduced disconnected recordsets, and we have seen that to implement the disconnected recordset, we have to follow two simple steps:

1. Set the CursorLocation property of the Recordset object to adUseClient

2. Set the ActiveConnection property of the Recordset object to Nothing as soon as the SQL statement to retrieve records has been executed

Look at the following simple code snippet which retrieves all of the records from the Region table of the Northwind database:

```
' Create a new instance of an ADODB.Recordset
Dim rsRegion As New ADODB.Recordset

' First step
rsRegion.CursorLocation = adUseClient

' Retrieve all of the records from the Region table
rsRegion.Open "SELECT * FROM Region", _
            "Provider=SQLOLEDB;Initial Catalog=Northwind; " _
        & "Data Source=.;User ID=sa;Password=;", _
            adOpenStatic, adLockBatchOptimistic

' Second step
Set rsRegion.ActiveConnection = Nothing
```

```
        .
        .
        .

' Release our local reference to the rsRegion
Set rsRegion = Nothing
```

Understanding what ADO is doing under the hood is invaluable at this point. By default, when we open a connection to a data source, we use the adUseServer value of the CursorLocation property implicitly. When we execute a SQL statement to retrieve data, ADO contacts the OLE DB data provider (that is, SQLOLEDB) that communicates with the data source (which here would be SQL Server) and executes the query generating the OLE DB Rowset that contains the query's results. ADO offers the Recordset object which provides properties and methods to manage data from the OLE DB Rowset. In an n-tier application, adUseServer causes frequent memory allocation, network traffic, and makes it impossible to scale the application because all subsequent operations involve the OLE DB data provider and the data source. A connection has to be opened each time we retrieve records, insert new records, and so on, wasting server resources and compromising application scalability and performance.

On the other hand, specifying the adUseClient value of the CursorLocation property tells ADO to use the OLE DB Cursor Service that caches the OLE DB Rowset in memory but provides the same interface for ADO to manipulate data. Each subsequent operation will be redirected to local memory instead of the OLE DB data provider and data source, improving application performances, scalability, network traffic, and so on.

The caching process is performed by the OLE DB Cursor Service in the following three stages:

1. Analysis of fundamental column information such as name, data type and length, starting to build the cached OLE DB Rowset with this information.

2. The source records are all copied into the cached OLE DB Rowset using either a synchronous or asynchronous process.

3. If adBatchOptimistic has been specified as the LockType parameter, the Cursor Service appends extended information to the cached OLE DB Rowset. This extra information is essential to implement the Synchronized Service that maintains source data synchronized with cached data.

The last step allows us to reactivate the connection against the database updating the information from the modified disconnected recordset. Let's see an example:

```
' Create a new instance of an ADODB.Recordset
Dim rsRegion As New ADODB.Recordset

' First step
rsRegion.CursorLocation = adUseClient

' Retrieve all of the records from the Region table
rsRegion.Open "SELECT * FROM Region", _
              "Provider=SQLOLEDB;Initial Catalog=Northwind; " _
```

```
                     & "Data Source=DBSERVER;User ID=dev;Password=dev;", _
                       adOpenStatic, adLockBatchOptimistic

    ' Second step
    Set rsRegion.ActiveConnection = Nothing

    ' Modify the cached recordset. No access to the database is done
    rsRegion("RegionDescription") = "Eastern2"

    ' Reconnect to the database
    rsRegion.ActiveConnection = "Provider=SQLOLEDB;Initial Catalog=" _
                              & "Northwind;Data Source=.;User ID=sa;Password="

    ' Update the database
    rsRegion.UpdateBatch

    ' Release our local reference to the rsRegion
    Set rsRegion = Nothing
```

As you can see, updating the database is a piece of cake; after modifying records, we specify the connection string to the `ActiveConnection` property and call the `UpdateBatch` method. When this method is called, the Synchronization Service implicitly:

❑   Builds the necessary SQL statements to manage pending records

❑   Executes the SQL statements

❑   Refreshes the disconnected recordset

Advanced Features of Disconnected Recordsets

As we have seen, disconnected recordsets are really useful and powerful tools for n-tier solutions. The Cursor Service also offers useful functionalities such as sorting and filtering that are performed on a memory recordset without the need for database access. Let's see this functionality in detail.

Sorting

The `Recordset` object provides the `Sort` property that performs sorting functionalities on the disconnected recordset. We can specify a field on which to apply the sorting algorithm, or more than one field, separating them with a comma. Moreover, using either the `ASC` or `DESC` SQL statements, we can sort records in ascending or descending order, respectively. We can restore the records' original order by setting an empty string value to the `Sort` property.

Let's see a code snippet that implements a descending sort on the `Region` table of the Northwind database:

```
    ' Create a new instance of an ADODB.Recordset
    Dim rsRegion As New ADODB.Recordset

    ' First step
    rsRegion.CursorLocation = adUseClient
```

```
' Retrieve all of the records from the Region table
rsRegion.Open "SELECT * FROM Region", _
              "Provider=SQLOLEDB;Initial Catalog=Northwind;" _
          & "Data Source=.;User ID=sa;Password=;", _
              adOpenStatic, adLockBatchOptimistic

' Second step
Set rsRegion.ActiveConnection = Nothing

rsRegion.Sort = "RegionID DESC"

' Release our local reference to the rsRegion
Set rsRegion = Nothing
```

Of course, in production code, we'd normally only return those fields that we need, rather than all of them through the * syntax, and we'd probably assign our connection string to a variable rather than specifying it as a parameter of the Open method.

Filtering

The Recordset object's Filter property allows developers to filter a disconnected recordset to hide records that don't match the specified criteria. We can specify more than one filtering criterion using both AND and OR operators, and we can use characters such as asterisks together with the LIKE clause.

Let's see an example of filtering with the Customers table in the Northwind database:

```
' Create a new instance of an ADODB.Recordset
Dim rsRegion As New ADODB.Recordset

' First step
rsRegion.CursorLocation = adUseClient

' Retrieve all of the records from the Region table
rsRegion.Open "SELECT CustomerID,CompanyName FROM Customers", _
          & "Provider=SQLOLEDB;Initial Catalog=Northwind; " _
              "Data Source=.;User ID=sa;Password=;", _
              adOpenStatic, adLockBatchOptimistic

' Second step
Set rsRegion.ActiveConnection = Nothing

' Filtering the recordset for records starting with A
rsRegion.Filter = "CompanyName LIKE #a*#"

' Release our local reference to the rsRegion
Set rsRegion = Nothing
```

Note that if the original recordset contains 100 records, after the Filter operation it will still contain 100 records. The Cursor Service will simply hide records that don't match the filtering criteria, although new values are set for the RecordCount and PageCount properties. The MoveNext method can be used within a loop to cycle through filtered records.

Finally, to go back to displaying the full recordset, set the Filter property to adFilterNone.

Finding a Record

The Recordset object's Find method allows developers to find a record within a disconnected recordset. It is different from the Filter property as Find retrieves only the first occurrence of the matched record and it doesn't accept more than one condition (AND and OR operators aren't allowed).

Here's an example of the Find method:

```
' Create a new instance of an ADODB.Recordset
Dim rsRegion As New ADODB.Recordset

' First step
rsRegion.CursorLocation = adUseClient

' Retrieve all of the records from the Region table
rsRegion.Open "SELECT * FROM Region", _
              "Provider=SQLOLEDB;Initial Catalog=Northwind; " _
           & "Data Source=.;User ID=sa;Password=;", _
              adOpenStatic, adLockBatchOptimistic

' Second step
Set rsRegion.ActiveConnection = Nothing

rsRegion.Find "RegionDescription=#Eastern#"

' Release our local reference to the rsRegion
Set rsRegion = Nothing
```

In this method you can use characters such as asterisks and percent signs to find more than one record. However, since the Find method returns just the first occurrence you have to use the other two parameters of the method in order to go through the other occurrences. Let's see its syntax:

```
Find (Criteria As String, [SkipRows as Long], _
      [SearchDirection as SearchDirectionEnum], [Start as Variant])
```

The SearchDirection and Start parameters allow us to indicate the direction (either forwards or backwards) and the position of the start record. However the SkipRows parameter is the really important one, which allows us to reach records other than the first that match the specified searching criteria. Let's see an example:

```
' Create a new instance of an ADODB.Recordset
Dim rsRegion As New ADODB.Recordset

' First step
rsRegion.CursorLocation = adUseClient

' Retrieve all of the records from the Region table
rsRegion.Open "SELECT CustomerID,CompanyName FROM Customers", _
              "Provider=SQLOLEDB;Initial Catalog=Northwind; " & _
              "Data Source=.;User ID=sa;Password=;", _
              adOpenStatic, adLockBatchOptimistic
```

```
' Second step
Set rsRegion.ActiveConnection = Nothing

' Filtering the recordset for records starting with A
rsRegion.Find "CompanyName LIKE #a*#"

' Cycle through records
Do While rsRegion.EOF = False

    ' Process the first occurrence here

    ' Skip one record using the SkipRows parameter
    rsRegion.Find "CompanyName LIKE #a*#", 1

Loop

' Release our local reference to rsRegion
Set rsRegion = Nothing
```

Setting the `SkipRows` parameter to 1 means we'll go to the next record, achieving a similar effect to the `MoveNext` method.

Remote Data Service

Disconnected recordsets are the main way of transporting records over the network. Thanks to disconnected recordsets and the Remote Data Service (RDS) library, making use of TCP/IP to transport records from a remote server to the client is simple.

RDS has a simple object model that consists of three objects:

❑ The `DataSpace` object – invokes an ActiveX server, remotely creating a client-side proxy of the object specified by the parameter. Usually it is used to create a client-side proxy for the `DataFactory` object launching remote SQL instructions and retrieving disconnected recordsets.

❑ The `DataFactory` object – an ActiveX server component that is able to create a disconnected recordset using the specified connection string and the SQL statement.

❑ The `DataControl` object – provides methods to retrieve disconnected recordsets from a remote server. In fact, it offers methods that call the `DataSpace` and `DataFactory` objects automatically. This object is used by Internet Explorer to implement a powerful data binding mechanism.

This is the RDS object model:

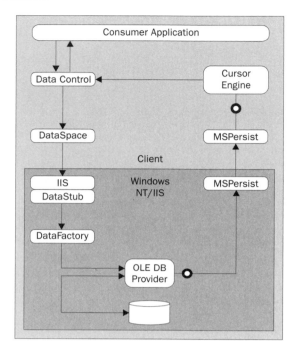

In this figure, a consumer application is seeking a disconnected recordset using the `DataControl` object's methods. This object creates an instance of the `DataSpace` class where you can indicate the remote server against which to execute the query. The `DataSpace` object locates the server invoking the `DataFactory` ActiveX server object's methods to create and retrieve a disconnected recordset. Finally, the disconnected recordset is persisted using the Advanced Data TableGram Microsoft proprietary format and transported over the network using the HTTP protocol.

> **In order to use RDS functionalities with the HTTP protocol, your operating system must have IIS 4 or later installed.**

Let's take a look at a practical example. Create a new a Visual Basic Standard EXE project and add a reference to the two Microsoft Remote Data Services libraries as shown overleaf:

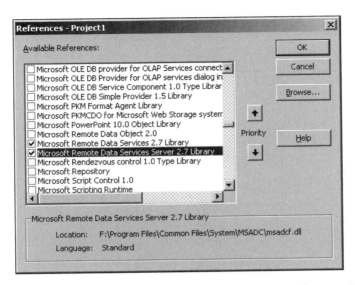

The first reference contains the `DataSpace` and `DataControl` objects; the second contains the ActiveX `DataFactory` server object. Now we can start to write some code in the `Form_Load` event handler of the **Form1** form:

```
Dim dsServer As New DataSpace
Dim dfServer As Object
Set dfServer = dsServer.CreateObject("RDSServer.DataFactory", _
                                     "http://localhost")

Dim dsClient As Object
Set dsClient = dfServer.Query("Provider=SQLOLEDB.1;Persist Security Info=" _
                      & "False;User ID=sa;Initial Catalog=Northwind", _
                        ";Data Source=.SELECT * FROM Region")

MsgBox dsClient.RecordCount

Set dsServer = Nothing
```

First of all, we create an instance of the `DataSpace` object, on which we then call the `CreateObject` method, retrieving a reference to the `DataFactory` object specified as the first parameter. The second parameter indicates the remote server where we are directing each proxy client class operation. In this example we have created the `DataFactory` object, but you can also use this method to create other objects including custom objects.

> We have to use a generic **Object** data type as the return value of the **CreateObject** method. If we try to use the **DataFactory** object we will receive a 'Type Mismatch' error.

The code continues with a call to the `Query` method, which takes two parameters. The former is the connection string to the target database and the latter is the SQL statement to execute against the database.

RDS Security Issues

So, this simple piece of code connects to a remote server and launches a query against a database. You may be thinking that this code does not seem secure. A malicious user can connect to a remote server and launch specific queries in order to retrieve private information. Moreover, remember that you can create other objects besides `DataFactory` – our server security is compromised. Fortunately, beginning with MDAC 2.0, Microsoft improved RDS security by introducing a special COM interface called `IDataFactoryHandler`. Each object that implements that interface can be used by the `DataFactory` object, and that in turn is created remotely by the `CreateObject` method of the `DataSpace` object.

In fact, in improving RDS security, Microsoft even changed some Windows system registry keys. Because RDS could be really dangerous for data and server security, Microsoft people made it so that it is not possible to unintentionally enable RDS functionality on your server. So, if you try to launch this simple program you should receive the following error:

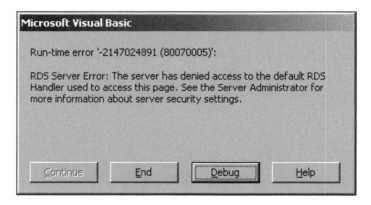

> **If you don't receive this error you either have an older version of MDAC (that is 1.5 or 2.0) or you have upgraded your operating system from an older version that used older version of MDAC (for example, you have upgraded a Windows NT operating system to Windows 2000).**

Since the release of MDAC 2.1, Microsoft decided to use the RDS safe security mode, which is set by setting the HandlerRequired registry key value to 1.

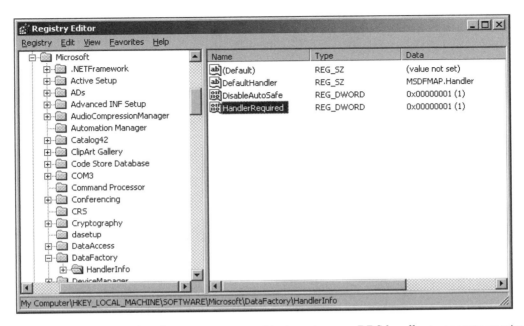

This value informs RDS that the `DataFactory` object must use an RDS handler to execute queries against the specified database. Microsoft provides a default RDS handler that is specified by the **DefaultHandler** registry key value. The **MSDFMAP.Handler** registry key value identifies the *ProgID* of the class that implements the `IDataFactoryHandler` interface. This class, created by Microsoft, resides within the `MSDFMAP.DLL` file in the **Program Files\Common Files\System\msadc** directory.

> **You can change the RDS safe mode to unsafe mode by launching the `handunsf.reg` registry file that you find in the Program Files\Common Files\System\msadc directory. Once you change the registry keys' values and restart, your server is no longer secure.**

The RDS handler is a software layer positioned between the `DataFactory` object and the database, and it prevents malicious users launching queries using the `DataFactory` object's `Query` method as this method now relies on the **MSDFMAP.Handler** default handler for database access. This reads information stored in the `msdfmap.ini` file including vital information such as connection strings, authorized users, allowed SQL statements, and so on. This file is in the Windows directory and initially contains the following:

```
;[connect name] will modify the connection if ADC.connect="name"
;[connect default] will modify the connection if name is not found
;[sql name] will modify the Sql if ADC.sql="name(args)"
;[sql default] will modify the Sql if name is not found
;Override strings: Connect, UserId, Password, Sql.
;Only the Sql strings support parameters using "?"
;The override strings must not equal "" or they are ignored
;A Sql entry must exist in each sql section or the section is ignored
;An Access entry must exist in each connect section or the section is ignored
```

```
;Access=NoAccess
;Access=ReadOnly
;Access=ReadWrite
;[userlist name] allows specific users to have special access
;The Access is computed as follows:
;   (1) First take the access of the connect section.
;   (2) If a user entry is found, it will override.

[connect default]
;If we want to disable unknown connect values, we set Access to NoAccess
Access=NoAccess

[sql default]
;If we want to disable unknown sql values, we set Sql to an invalid query.
Sql=" "

[connect CustomerDatabase]
Access=ReadWrite
Connect="DSN=AdvWorks"

[sql CustomerById]
Sql="SELECT * FROM Customers WHERE CustomerID = ?"

[connect AuthorDatabase]
Access=ReadOnly
Connect="DSN=MyLibraryInfo;UID=MyUserID;PWD=MyPassword"

[userlist AuthorDatabase]
Administrator=ReadWrite

[sql AuthorById]
Sql="SELECT * FROM Authors WHERE au_id = ?"
```

The connect sections specify the access mode as either NoAccess, which disables access to the database, ReadOnly, which allows read-only operations, or ReadWrite for full access. The sql sections specify the SQL statement that can be executed against the database. You can use the question mark placeholder character in order to specify WHERE condition values programmatically, as seen below. Finally, the userlist sections list every user that has special access.

Back up the above file, and we'll replace it with the following to allow our simple program to execute:

```
;[connect name] will modify the connection if ADC.connect="name"
;[connect default] will modify the connection if name is not found
;[sql name] will modify the Sql if ADC.sql="name(args)"
;[sql default] will modify the Sql if name is not found
;Override strings: Connect, UserId, Password, Sql.
;Only the Sql strings support parameters using "?"
;The override strings must not equal "" or they are ignored
;A Sql entry must exist in each sql section or the section is ignored
;An Access entry must exist in each connect section or the section is ignored
;Access=NoAccess
;Access=ReadOnly
;Access=ReadWrite
```

```
;[userlist name] allows specific users to have special access
;The Access is computed as follows:
;   (1) First take the access of the connect section.
;   (2) If a user entry is found, it will override.


[connect Northwind]
Access=ReadWrite
Connect="Provider=SQLOLEDB.1;Persist Security Info=False;User
ID=sa;Password=xxx;Initial Catalog=Northwind;Data Source=."


[sql Northwind]
Sql="SELECT * FROM REGION"


[userlist Northwind]
Administrator=ReadWrite
```

This new INI file authorizes just `DataFactory` objects that use a reference to the Northwind data source together with the specified SQL statement. Let's see how we have to change the Visual Basic code:

```
Dim dsServer As New DataSpace
Dim dfServer As Object
Set dfServer = dsServer.CreateObject("RDSServer.DataFactory", _
                                   "http://localhost")


Dim dsClient As Object
Set dsClient = dfServer.Query("Handler=MSDFMAP.Handler;" _
                           & " Data Source=Northwind", _
                             "SELECT * FROM REGION")


MsgBox dsClient.RecordCount

Set dsServer = Nothing
```

As you can see, we have to specify the RDS handler that has to be used to execute the query and the data source name. The last value must correspond to the section name specified in the `msdfmap.ini` file.

Let's see an example of passing parameters to use in place of the question mark character in the INI file. The query in the INI file changes in this way:

```
[sql Northwind]
Sql="SELECT * FROM REGION WHERE RegionID=?"
```

In the Visual Basic code, the second parameter of the `Query` method changes in this way:

```
Set dsClient = dfServer.Query("Handler=MSDFMAP.Handler;" _
                           & "Data Source=Northwind", _
                             "Northwind('2')")
```

189

We replace the SQL command with the section name followed by a parameter value for each question mark in the INI file. In this case we will retrieve a record with the RegionID equal to 2. However, try to launch the application and, again, an error occurs:

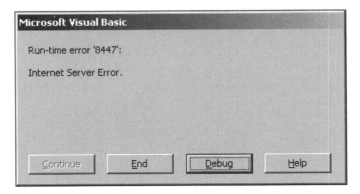

Like I said, Microsoft has to be sure that we want to enable RDS functionality on our server. To do this, launch the IIS management console, expand the Default Web Sites node and locate the MSADC virtual directory:

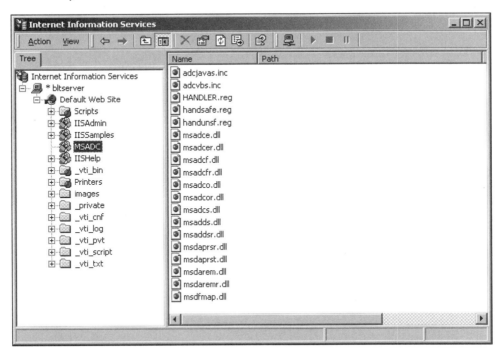

Right-click on it, and select Properties. The following dialog will appear:

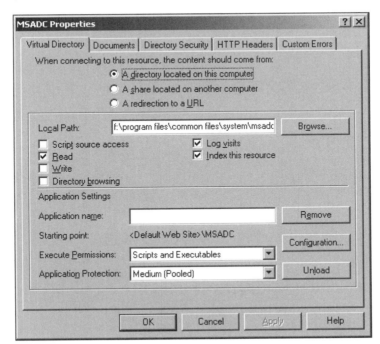

Change Execute Permissions from Scripts only to Scripts and Executables (if you use IIS 4.0 then change to Execute (Including Script)).

It's time to launch the application, but, oh no, another error!

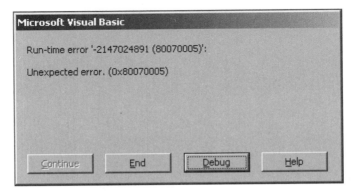

If you're still receiving the previous error, possible causes include IP limitations set on your server and interactive settings. Take a look at the *Q251122: Troubleshooting Common Problems with Remote Data Services* knowledge base article on Microsoft's site.

This error is caused by missing keys in the Windows system registry in the HKEY_LOCAL_MACHINE\ SYSTEM\CurrentControlSet\Services\W3SVC\Parameters folder. Add the following keys:

- ❏ ADCLaunch under Parameters
- ❏ RDSServer.DataFactory under ADCLaunch

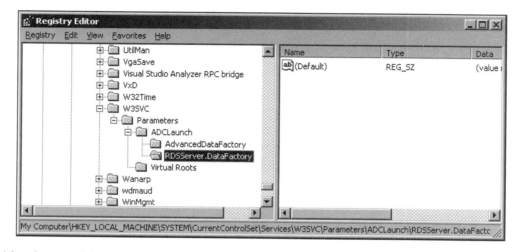

After these modifications, restart IIS and try again. Bingo! It works:

A message box should appear showing the record count value of the disconnected recordset retrieved.

Recordset Persistence

ADO's disconnected recordsets allow us to manage a recordset without having to maintain an open connection to the database, thus freeing server resources and improving application scalability. The RDS classes make it possible to transport disconnected recordsets over HTTP. Now, I'm going to explain the missing piece of this powerful mosaic: recordset persistence.

From MDAC version 2.0, a new provider was added to ADO's providers collection: the Persistence provider (MSPersist) contained in the msdaprst.dll file. This provider allows developers to save a disconnected recordset using either a proprietary format such as Advanced Data TableGram (ADTG) or using XML. We can persist data into a file, into another object, to a Microsoft Message queue for asynchronous processes (see Chapter 11), or across a network using either DCOM or HTTP.

Saving a Recordset

The `Recordset` object offers two methods for saving records in a recordset to a file. We can easily implement a procedure that stores data into a file, thus allowing users access to that data without an open connection to the database. For example, a user can load a file containing records with the `Open` method. They can then add, modify, or delete certain records, reconnect to the database, and save the data in the modified recordset.

Let's see an example of this procedure:

```
' Create a new instance of an ADODB.Recordset
Dim rsRegion As New ADODB.Recordset

' First step
rsRegion.CursorLocation = adUseClient

' Retrieve all of the records from the Region table
rsRegion.Open "SELECT CustomerID,CompanyName FROM Customers", _
              "Provider=SQLOLEDB;Initial Catalog=Northwind; " & _
              "Data Source=.;User ID=sa;Password=;", _
              adOpenStatic, adLockBatchOptimistic

' Second step
Set rsRegion.ActiveConnection = Nothing

' Save to a local file using the XML format
rsRegion.Save "C:\Customers.xml", adPersistXML

' Release our local reference to the rsRegion
Set rsRegion = Nothing
```

We have already seen the rest of the code, so let's concentrate on the `Save` method. It accepts one mandatory parameter specifying the path and the filename where you want to store the records. An optional second parameter details the format for storing the recordset. By default it is `adPersistADTG` which stores the recordset using a binary format. In the code above, we've used the constant that indicates the XML format. Choose the ADTG format to save disk space and enhance performance, or XML for its multi-platform, firewall-friendly features.

Let's see an extract of the saved file containing records from the `Customers` table of the Northwind database:

```
<xml xmlns:s='uuid:BDC6E3F0-6DA3-11d1-A2A3-00AA00C14882'
     xmlns:dt='uuid:C2F41010-65B3-11d1-A29F-00AA00C14882'
     xmlns:rs='urn:schemas-microsoft-com:rowset'
     xmlns:z='#RowsetSchema'>
<s:Schema id='RowsetSchema'>
  <s:ElementType name='row' content='eltOnly' rs:updatable='true'>
    <s:AttributeType name='CustomerID' rs:number='1' rs:writeunknown='true'
        rs:basecatalog='Northwind' rs:basetable='Customers'
        rs:basecolumn='CustomerID' rs:keycolumn='true'>
      <s:datatype dt:type='string' dt:maxLength='5' rs:fixedlength='true'
          rs:maybenull='false'/>
    </s:AttributeType>
```

```
      <s:AttributeType name='CompanyName' rs:number='2' rs:writeunknown='true'
          rs:basecatalog='Northwind' rs:basetable='Customers'
          rs:basecolumn='CompanyName'>
        <s:datatype dt:type='string' dt:maxLength='40' rs:maybenull='false'/>
      </s:AttributeType>
      <s:extends type='rs:rowbase'/>
    </s:ElementType>
  </s:Schema>
  <rs:data>
    <z:row CustomerID='ALFKI' CompanyName='Alfreds Futterkiste'/>
    <z:row CustomerID='ANATR' CompanyName='Ana Trujillo Emparedados y helados'/>
    .
    .
    .
  </rs:data>
</xml>
```

As you can see, before the `<rs:data>` section that contains every record's information, there is a header section that describes each column with information such as the column name, length, and whether the column is a primary key. The header information is essential for the `Open` method to build a fully qualified recordset from the file. Let's see how we can use this method:

```
' Create a new instance of an ADODB.Recordset
Dim rsRegion As New ADODB.Recordset

' Use client cursor location
rsRegion.CursorLocation = adUseClient

' Open the local file
rsRegion.Open "C:\Customers.xml", _
            "Provider=MSPersist", adOpenStatic, adLockBatchOptimistic

    .
    .
    .

' Release our local reference to the rsRegion
Set rsRegion = Nothing
```

After having created a new recordset, you have to use the client cursor location and open the file that contains records. The first parameter indicates the path and the filename of the file containing records. The second parameter indicates the active connection; in our case we won't connect to a database so we inform the `Open` method to use the `MSPersist` provider. This provider will help the `Open` method to regenerate recordset from information in the file.

Now we have a recordset that can be modified and stored back to the database in the usual way:

```
rsRegion("CompanyName") = "Blteam"

rsRegion.ActiveConnection= "Provider=SQLOLEDB;Initial Catalog=Northwind;" _
                         & "Data Source=.;User ID=sa;Password=;"

rsRegion.UpdateBatch
```

Persisting a Recordset to a Stream Object

From MDAC version 2.5, two new objects were added to the ADO library: `Record` and `Stream`. The `Stream` object can be used to save a disconnected recordset to a text or binary stream. This lets us store records to a string or an array rather than to a file. Using the `Stream` object's `ReadText` method returns a string containing the content of the disconnected recordset, as shown in the following example:

```
' Create a new instance of an ADODB.Recordset
Dim rsRegion As New ADODB.Recordset

' First step
rsRegion.CursorLocation = adUseClient

' Retrieve all of the records from the Region table
rsRegion.Open "SELECT CustomerID,CompanyName FROM Customers", _
              "Provider=SQLOLEDB;Initial Catalog=Northwind; " & _
              "Data Source=.;User ID=sa;Password=;", _
              adOpenStatic, adLockBatchOptimistic

' Second step
Set rsRegion.ActiveConnection = Nothing

' Save to a Stream object using the XML format
Dim stRecordset As New ADODB.Stream
rsRegion.Save stRecordset, adPersistXML

' Display the recordset content as XML
MsgBox stRecordset.ReadText

' Release our local reference to the rsRegion
Set rsRegion = Nothing
```

To store a recordset within the `Stream` object, we have to specify a reference to the object as the first parameter instead of the file name. Then, using the `ReadText` method, we can retrieve a string containing the recordset content in XML format:

Naturally, you can recreate a recordset starting from a `Stream` in the same way as we have seen for files. Using the `Open` method of the `Recordset` object you have to specify a reference to the `Stream` object as the first parameter:

```
' Recreate the recordset
rsRegion.Open stRecordset, "Provider=MSPersist", adOpenStatic, _
            adLockBatchOptimistic
```

XML versus RDS

We have seen how a program that uses RDS functionality is difficult to install due to security issues. Creating a secure RDS program is not so easy; you should avoid using the `DataFactory` object to access your database and create an ad-hoc object that implements the handler interface and checks data flow between clients and server, allowing it to retrieve very particular records using predefined queries.

On the other hand, we have seen how easy it is to store a recordset and recreate it. Moreover, XML allows you to send data to various operating systems, including non-Microsoft ones. XML is essentially a text file describing data, and data types, lengths, and so on through XML Schema, as we'll see in Chapter 13, and as text, it is quite happy to travel through the default firewall HTTP port (usually 80 or 8080).

Essentially, the big difference between the two solutions is system security, but remember that RDS is fully integrated with the ADO library and uses Microsoft's proprietary ADTG format to store information to a binary stream. Passing big recordsets over HTTP will often perform better with the ADTG format when compared to XML because of its compact size.

We have seen how to persist a recordset using XML so it's not so difficult to write a program that stores required information using XML on a web server. Now we will see how a client can easily retrieve a stored XML recordset using HTTP:

```
Dim rsCustomers As New ADODB.Recordset

rsCustomers.Open "http://localhost/Customers.xml", "Provider=MSPersist", _
            adOpenStatic, adLockBatchOptimistic

    .
    .
    .

Set rsCustomers = Nothing
```

Easy, isn't it? You simply specify the URL of the XML file as the first parameter for the `Open` method and the `MSPersist` provider will do the rest.

ADO and XML

XML is the first real universal language that allows different operating systems and hardware platforms to communicate with each other, and its importance is growing every day.

We have seen how ADO lets us to create XML files starting from a generic OLE DB database; however when we have to manage Windows DNA systems or we have to create scalable and secure n-tier applications, we shouldn't use desktop databases such as Microsoft Access or Microsoft FoxPro. These have lower performance for n-tier solutions, they don't support the advanced security features of RDBMS systems, and they are limited in the number of simultaneous users allowed and the maximum record storage, among many other things. Moreover, any application that uses persistence to retrieve its XML data is going to be slower than retrieving that XML data directly from a database. This is the main reason why Microsoft has implemented XML support in its latest version of SQL Server, Microsoft SQL Server 2000.

In this section we will analyze the most important aspects of Microsoft SQL Server 2000 related to XML and ADO:

❑　The FOR XML T-SQL extension

❑　The SQL namespace that maps XML tags to SQL Server tables and columns

❑　Advanced use of ADO Command to execute XPath queries

SQL Server 2000 and XML

Microsoft SQL Server 2000 is the first release of the Microsoft database that supports XML. Since it came out, customer demands and standard changes have caused Microsoft to release upgrades. The first was XML for SQL Server 2000 Web Release 1, which adds two new functions to the SQL Server 2000 standard release: Updategrams and **bulk load**. The former allows the XML document to specify which records are changed, which are to be deleted, and so on, triggering automatic SQL INSERT, UPDATE and DELETE commands. Bulk load allows developers to load large XML files (it's a sort of BCP command for XML files).

The second update added XSD (XML Schema Definition) mapping schemas, and improved overall performance. As we will see later in this section, XSD mapping schemas allow us to specify in the XML schema which SQL tables and columns to map to which XML tags allowing us to retrieve a XML document that respects XML schema directives.

The third and last update was SQLXML 3.0 SP1. It was released mainly for .NET Framework support with a new managed data provider. However, it allows developers to expose stored procedures and XML Templates as SOAP web services.

Each of those releases depends on the Microsoft XML Parser library (MSXML 3.0 or 4.0), ADO 2.6, or greater and, for the last release, SOAP Toolkit 2.0.

The FOR XML Clause

Retrieving records in XML format is really easy. We simply append the FOR XML clause to the end of a query, and SQL Server 2000 formats records using XML:

```
SELECT statement ::=
  < query_expression >
  [ FOR XML { RAW | AUTO | EXPLICIT } ]
```

We can query the SQL Server 2000 database retrieving three different XML format, specified by either RAW, AUTO, or EXPLICIT.

The RAW Attribute

The RAW attribute means we receive an XML tag called <ROW> for each record found.

As an example, let's retrieve an employee's first name, last name, and job description from the pubs database for each record where the ID starts with the letter 'A':

```
SELECT employee.fname, employee.lname, jobs.job_desc
FROM employee INNER JOIN jobs on employee.job_id = jobs.job_id
Where emp_id LIKE 'A%'
FOR XML RAW
```

This query will retrieve four records, as below:

```
<row fname="Aria" lname="Cruz" job_desc="Productions Manager"/>
<row fname="Annette" lname="Roulet" job_desc="Managing Editor"/>
<row fname="Ann" lname="Devon" job_desc="Business Operations Manager"/>
<row fname="Anabela" lname="Domingues" job_desc="Public Relations Manager"/>
```

Note that as this is not a well-formed XML document (it lacks a single document element), it is not as readily readable as regular XML.

The AUTO Attribute

With the AUTO attribute, we retrieve automatically nested XML tags. Let's see the same example, changing only this attribute:

```
SELECT employee.fname, employee.lname, jobs.job_desc
FROM employee INNER JOIN jobs on employee.job_id = jobs.job_id
WHERE emp_id LIKE 'A%'
FOR XML AUTO
```

This query now retrieves the records formatted as shown:

```
<employee fname="Aria" lname="Cruz">
  <jobs job_desc="Productions Manager"/>
</employee>
<employee fname="Annette" lname="Roulet">
```

```
  <jobs job_desc="Managing Editor"/>
</employee>
<employee fname="Ann" lname="Devon">
  <jobs job_desc="Business Operations Manager"/>
</employee>
<employee fname="Anabela" lname="Domingues">
  <jobs job_desc="Public Relations Manager"/>
</employee>
```

This still lacks a document element, but is better looking than the RAW output. Sometimes, though, it won't be what we need, especially if we have to retrieve an XML document that adheres to a specific XML Schema.

The EXPLICIT Attribute

The EXPLICIT attribute allows us to declare final XML tags explicitly. This is the most powerful attribute of the FOR XML clause but it is also the most complex. Let's see how our query has to be written to use the EXPLICIT attribute:

```
SELECT 1 AS TAG, 0 AS parent,
    fname AS [Employee!1!FirstName!element],
    lname AS [Employee!1!LastName!element],
    null AS [Jobs!2!Description!element]
FROM employee
WHERE emp_id = 'PMA42628M'
UNION ALL
SELECT 2, 1, null, null, job_desc
FROM jobs, employee WHERE jobs.job_id = employee.job_id and emp_id = 'PMA42628M'
FOR XML EXPLICIT
```

The first two parameters of the SELECT statement have to be the XML tag and parent position in the hierarchy of the final XML document. In the query above, the first SELECT will produce XML tags that are parents of the root level. Next, the AS clause specifies the tag characteristic following this syntax:

```
[Parent Tag Name!Level!TagName or AttributeName!element or attribute]
```

Finally, you have to use the UNION statement in order to merge different queries to produce the final XML document.

Executing the query now retrieves the following results:

```
<Employee>
  <FirstName>Paolo</FirstName>
  <LastName>Accorti</LastName>
  <Jobs>
    <Description>Sales Representative</Description>
  </Jobs>
</Employee>
```

199

XSD Mapping Schema

The EXPLICIT method is really powerful but when you have to deal with complex queries you will have to create a great number of SQL statements, making it a very difficult to maintain object. There is a better solution: XSD Mapping Schema.

> **In order to use the following code and try those examples you have to install SQLXML 2.0 or greater, along with SQL Server 2000 of course.**

Imagine we have to run a query that produces an XML document that uses this XML Schema (refer to Chapter 13 for a rundown on the ins and outs of XML Schema notation):

```xml
<?xml version="1.0" ?>
<xs:schema xmlns:xs="http://www.w3.org/2001/XMLSchema">
  <xs:element name="EmployeeRecord">
    <xs:complexType>
      <xs:sequence>
        <xs:element name="FirstName" type="xs:string" />
        <xs:element name="LastName" type="xs:string" />
      </xs:sequence>
      <xs:attribute name="ID" type="xs:string" />
    </xs:complexType>
  </xs:element>
  <xs:element name="Job">
    <xs:complexType>
      <xs:sequence>
        <xs:element name="Description" type="xs:string" />
        <xs:element ref="EmployeeRecord" />
      </xs:sequence>
      <xs:attribute name="ID" type="xs:short" />
    </xs:complexType>
  </xs:element>
</xs:schema>
```

Using the schema above, we have to produce an XML document that lists every employee that belongs to the specified job identifier.

SQL Server has an XML Schema that maps XML tags to SQL Server tables and columns, and it is intended for use within our own schemas such as the above. The xmlns:sql="urn:schemas-microsoft-com:mapping-schema" schema contains a lot of useful XML attributes that we can use in our schema to specify which tables and columns map to which XML tags:

```xml
<xs:schema xmlns:xs="http://www.w3.org/2001/XMLSchema"
    xmlns:sql="urn:schemas-microsoft-com:mapping-schema">
  <xs:element name="EmployeeRecord" sql:relation="Employee">
    <xs:complexType>
      <xs:sequence>
        <xs:element name="FirstName" sql:field="fname"
                    type="xs:string" />
        <xs:element name="LastName" sql:field="lname"
```

```
                    type="xs:string" />
        </xs:sequence>
        <xs:attribute name="ID" sql:field="emp_id"
                        type="xs:string" />
    </xs:complexType>
  </xs:element>
  <xs:element name="Job" sql:relation="Jobs">
    <xs:complexType>
      <xs:sequence>
        <xs:element name="Description" sql:field="job_desc"
                        type="xs:string" />
        <xs:element ref="EmployeeRecord"
              sql:relationship="EmployeeJob" />
      </xs:sequence>
      <xs:attribute name="ID" sql:field="job_id" type="xs:short" />
    </xs:complexType>
  </xs:element>
  <xs:annotation>
    <xs:appinfo>
      <sql:relationship name="EmployeeJob" parent="Jobs"
              child="Employee" parent-key="job_id"
                  child-key="job_id" />
    </xs:appinfo>
  </xs:annotation>
</xs:schema>
```

Let's see the meaning of each SQL schema attribute:

❑   The sql:relation attribute indicates the source SQL table from which we are getting records to map to XML elements.

❑   The sql:field attribute maps the source column name with the specified XML element.

❑   The sql:relationship attribute indicates the name of the relationship between tables. It has to be specified in the annotation section of the XML schema stating which are the parent and child tables and the primary and foreign keys.

If you carefully examine the XML schema you will see that the <Job> element contains a reference to the employee record element. This is done to include the employee description within the <Job> XML tags and it is the place to specify the relationship name between the two tables.

Executing XPath Queries with ADO Command

Now that we have created a valid XSD mapping schema we'll look at how to use it in our ADO applications. The SQLXML provider adds great functionality to the ADO Command object in order to let us to implement XML management. The most interesting functionality is the Dialect property. Specifying the {EC2A4293-E898-11D2-B1B7-00C04F680C56} GUID informs the ADO Command object that the text in the CommandText property is an XPath query and not a classic SQL statement.

Next, a lot of new properties have been added to the `Properties` collection of the ADO `Command` object. In the code below, we will use the `Mapping Schema` attribute to specify the XSD file that contains our XSD mapping schema. We will also use the `Output` object's `Stream` property to indicate a reference to the `Stream` object that will retrieve the result of the query. The rest of the code is the normal ADO preparatory when retrieving records from a data source:

```
    Dim dbConn As New ADODB.Connection
    Dim dbCom As New ADODB.Command
    Dim stRecordset As New ADODB.Stream

On Error GoTo Error_Handler

    dbConn.Open "Provider=SQLXMLOLEDB;data " _
            & "provider=sqloledb;Server=.;Database=pubs;UID=sa;PWD=;"

    dbCom.ActiveConnection = dbConn
    dbCom.CommandType = adCmdText
    dbCom.Dialect = "{EC2A4293-E898-11D2-B1B7-00C04F680C56}"
    dbCom.Properties("Mapping Schema") = "map.xsd"
    dbCom.CommandText = "/Job[@ID=11]"

    stRecordset.Open
    dbCom.Properties("Output Stream").Value = stRecordset
    dbCom.Execute , , adExecuteStream

    MsgBox stRecordset.ReadText

FreeRes:
    Set stRecordset = Nothing
    Set dbCom = Nothing
    Set dbConn = Nothing

    Exit Sub

Error_Handler:

    MsgBox Err.Description
    GoTo FreeRes
```

Since we are now dealing with XML data, we use XPath commands to retrieve specific records instead of classic SQL `SELECT` statements. The XPath language is a W3C specification that can locate one or more nodes in a XML document. XPath runs through an XML document returning a **node set** that contains all records that satisfy the query. The query pattern syntax is really quite simple, and uses the slash / character to specify XML hierarchical levels in the same way that you would specify higher directory levels in a URL address or file path.

In this situation, the XPath `/Job` would retrieve all records contained in the `Jobs` table. On the other hand, `/Job/Description` would return just the descriptions of all the records in the `Jobs` table. Finally, square brackets let us specify additional conditions, as used in the code where we have `/Job[@ID=11]`. This retrieves all jobs that have an identifier equal to 11.

Summary

In this chapter, we have examined advanced ADO features orientated towards n-tier solutions such as Windows DNA. We have seen how important it is for an n-tier application to be scalable, secure and offer high performance, something that can be greatly helped by ADO disconnected recordsets. These reduce the duration of live connections to the database to the minimum time necessary to retrieve the required records.

Next, we saw how ADO lets us to store data both to a file and to the Stream object. Using the Remote Data Service, we can then use HTTP to transport this data over the network, and even for the exchange of data between different platforms.

Finally, we have seen how SQL Server 2000, ADO, and XML allow us to generate powerful XML data sets that can be searched with XPath queries.

p2p.wrox.com

The programmer's resource centre

ASP Today

wrox.com

8

COM+

At the time, the introduction of fairly complete **COM** (**Component Object Model**) support in VB4 was a breath of fresh air. Fresh, that is, until we started building more complex applications and realized just how complex COM could be – even with VB simplifying it radically.

For all its quirks, VB shields us from almost all those issues that all too often bog down C++ COM+ developers, and allowed us to focus on business problems. VB may bring new problems with its simplicity, such as circular references, binary compatibility issues, and the fact that you can devastate your entire app by accidentally recompiling a lower-level DLL, but overall, COM+ is better in the VB world.

Many modern businesses have discovered the value of connecting and distributing not only information, but also applications themselves over multiple servers. There is no doubt that the demand for business solutions deployed across multiple servers will continue to increase, especially since the sophistication of web applications can transform the humble browser into a front-end for processing data, greatly simplifying deployment and maintenance issues. This all sounds wonderful, but distributed applications bring with them completely new issues to contend with, such as authorization, and communication between a variety of programming languages.

In 1999, Microsoft introduced its COM (Component Object Model) technology, which offered a solution for many distributed programming problems. After a couple of years following the release of COM, it had become apparent that while COM had done a decent job in achieving its design goals, it lacked advanced features critical in creating enterprise-level applications. Large-scale application development requires not only component interoperability, but also object lifecycle management. The latter is especially important for applications that serve a large number of users and support heavy transaction processing.

Microsoft responded to such demand by releasing **Microsoft Transaction Server** (**MTS**) which provides object pooling, just-in-time object activation and deactivation, and distributed transaction support. By using MTS and COM, developers could create scalable and high performance applications. MTS sits on top of COM, acting as a host – that is, a place to store COM components. This host provides a place for COM components to live and provides them with a set of services to work with. The downside to this was that, although MTS is logically sitting on top of COM, the two technologies are not very well integrated.

With the release of Windows 2000, Microsoft addresses this issue with COM+. COM+ is a fully integrated technology incorporating COM and MTS, while maintaining full backward compatibility to existing COM and MTS applications and components. Essentially, COM+ takes baseline COM and integrates the services from MTS into it (as well as several new services), instead of on top of it to form a single seamless product. This not only makes things run faster, but as you will see later, it also simplifies many of the tasks that seemed cumbersome in MTS. It's important to realize that COM+ doesn't change any of the COM theory you may already be acquainted with; all it does is integrate some more services into the bargain, enabling you to better manage your COM applications by doing some of the work for you.

This chapter discusses the COM technology and the role it has in robust and scaleable high-performance applications. COM solutions can be elegant and much simpler than previous approaches, and thus it successfully carved itself an important niche in the world of enterprise application development that it maintains to this day. We will look at COM generally for the large part of the chapter, but will also take a look at the services offered by COM+.

After completing this chapter, you will understand:

❏   What COM is all about

❏   The difference between a class, a component, an object, and an instance

❏   COM interfaces and how they work

❏   GUIDs and CLSIDs and how they are used

❏   How objects are instantiated

❏   The difference between in-process and out-of-process components

❏   How to configure COM settings for your application

What is COM?

The COM specification is a detailed plan on how COM works and how it is implemented. It comprises a few hundred pages, and can be downloaded in its entirety from the following address:

http://www.microsoft.com/COM/resources/COM1598B.zip

As we'll see in this chapter, the component object model is an outgrowth of the object-oriented paradigm. COM is a specification that is based on a binary standard for reuse through interfaces. This means that components (pre-compiled blocks of code) written for COM can be reused without any dependencies on the language in which they were written. It does not matter if an application contains components written in Visual Basic, C++, Java, or even COBOL. What is important is that the components follow the COM specification.

The COM Library

It is important to realize that the COM specification goes much further than the few hundred pages of its written version. COM actually involves system-level code that is implemented through what is known as the **COM library** in the form of **dynamic link libraries** (**DLLs**).

The COM library consists of several **application programming interface** (**API**) functions that are necessary for COM components to do their "magic". In more technical terms, the COM library is responsible for locating and activating server applications. For example, with client applications, COM APIs will bring about the necessary functions for creating objects that the client requests. Also, the COM library provides locator services through the use of the **System Control Manager** (**SCM**). The SCM is a mechanism that makes it possible for COM to find the location of a particular COM class as well as providing transparent remote procedure calls when an object is executing out-of-process in a local or remote server. If this does not appear to make much sense at the moment, have no fear – all this will be clear by the time you complete this chapter. For now, the important thing to understand is that COM provides a system of low-level programming that provides the necessary functions for the creation of objects, regardless of where the COM classes reside.

Advantages of COM

One way to help understand COM is to look at the major advantages it offers:

❑   **COM promotes component-based development**: before component-based development hit the scene, programs tended to be written in a linear form that typically executed from the first line of code and completed when the last line of code was reached. This method of programming is referred to as **procedural programming**. Both C and many VB programs today are still written this way. Component-based development has numerous advantages over linear programming. One major benefit is the ability to use pre-packaged components and tools from other vendors. In other words, a component created by a third party source can easily be incorporated into an application.

❑   **COM promotes code reuse**: even with the use of class-based development, using standard classes, classes tend not to be easily reused in other applications. In other words, classes tend to be compiled within a program and any code reuse in another program often involves the need to cut and paste portions of code to other projects. COM components, on the other hand, are designed to separate themselves from single applications. Instead, COM components can be accessed and shared by numerous different applications without any problems.

❑   **COM promotes object-oriented programming (OOP)**: COM was designed with OOP in mind. There are three major characteristics that OOP provides: **encapsulation**, which allows the implementation details of an object to be hidden; **polymorphism**, which is the ability to exhibit multiple behaviors; and **inheritance**, which allows existing classes to be reused in the creation of new and more specialized objects. Among these three characteristics, perhaps encapsulation (often referred to as COM's black box) is one of COM's most important characteristics. Encapsulation provides the ability to hide details of an object, such as data and the implementation of logic. In other words, how an object implements a procedure internally is kept hidden (it's a secret!) An analogy is turning on a lamp. All you do is flip a switch and a light goes on. Behind the scenes, there are a lot of processes going on in order for the light to shine, but we don't need to concern ourselves with the hidden details, such as voltage, alternating current, and closed circuits.

❑ **COM provides the necessary mechanics for COM components to communicate with each other**: software components (non-COM) typically do not communicate well with components written in other programming languages. Think about this: would you be able to take Visual Basic source code and expect it to work within a program written in C++? You should have answered no, as the two languages don't understand each other. This is where COM provides a solution to the language problem. As previously mentioned, COM is language-independent. As a result, COM components can be mixed and matched using different programming languages.

❑ **COM provides the means to access components across different machines on the network**: COM components are location-independent. What this means is a COM component can reside anywhere on your computer, or even on another computer connected to a network. In other words, applications using COM can access and share COM components regardless of where the components reside. The important thing to realize is that the client does not have to concern itself with the details of where the server component resides, as COM takes care of it. This is referred to as **location transparency**.

Objects & Classes

Before we delve further into the aspects of COM, let's quickly take a look at two items we've already mentioned that are essential to understanding the component object model: **classes** and **objects**.

Objects

Objects are code-based abstractions that represent real world items or real world relationships. Each object has three basic characteristics: **identity**, **behavior**, and **state**. An identity is simply a unique name assigned to an object in order for it to be distinguished from other objects. The behavior of an object is based on the set of properties and methods that can be called to query or manipulate an object's state. State is simply data that is associated with a particular object.

Classes

Every object is defined by a class. A class is simply a template (call it a blueprint or a plan if you like) from which an object is created. Because a class is a template, it stands to reason that many objects based on a single class can be created. The classic analogy is that a class is like a cookie cutter. We can make numerous cookie copies (objects) based on the cookie template. When an object is created, it is said to be **instantiated** from a class. Simply put, an object is an **instance** of a class.

The word 'class' is pretty descriptive, since we're basically *classifying* our objects. For instance, say we have a couple of objects, Invoice and SalesOrder, they could both be instances of a Document class. Each actual invoice or sales order would have its own object, which is represented by a single instance of the Document class, but all the objects would be created from the same template, the Document class.

In Visual Basic, we define classes using **class modules**. We can then create objects based on the class module, with each object being an instance of the class.

Class modules are like form or standard modules in that they have a declaration section followed by a series of Sub, Function, and Property subroutines. The difference is that the variables and code in a class module can only be used by creating an instance of the class.

A Simple Illustration

Let's see how this all fits together. Suppose we want to create a software model that represents customers who purchased books about VB. First we could design a class called VBCustomer with a method called PurchaseVBBook, and a property called NumOfBooksPurchased, keeping a tally of how many books a customer has purchased. We could then use this class to instantiate objects for each customer who purchases a book about VB. Thus we could create an object for each of the customer names such as Natalia, Dori, and Jeff. In other words, each object would represent one customer. Each object's PurchaseVBBook method maps to a particular behavior of such customers, with the NumOfBooksPurchased property tracking the number of books purchased.

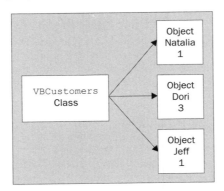

Objects exhibit identity, behavior, and state. The customer names for each object (Natalia, Dori, and Jeff) are examples of object identity. The behavior of each object is to purchase a book about VB and the number of books purchased by each customer represents their state. In this diagram, Natalia and Jeff purchased one book while the object Dori purchased three books.

So how would this appear in an executing program? When an object is instantiated during run time from a class, a contiguous block of memory is assigned for the member variables (the number of books purchased by each customer in our example). The identity of the object is simply the address in memory. The behavior is controlled by the methods (PurchaseVBBook for this example) that can be called to query or manipulate an object's state. Finally, the state is the actual contents of the block of memory.

COM Components

An important concept in software engineering is that software should be reusable. The simplest way to achieve this is through reuse at the source code level. Developers typically deal with similar or even identical situations in a range of applications, and so it makes sense to create or buy a library of code that they can use for all related situations. For instance, socket communications are essential to any applications that perform networking activities, so when a developer has built a socket library, many other developers could use the same socket library in applications that require such functionality.

This approach works, but it has its limitations, the most notable of which is that libraries can generally only be used by applications written in the same language. For instance, a Visual Basic application can't use a C++ library directly. In other words, cross-language code reuse is largely impossible. This means that if you want to make a socket library originally written in C++ available to Visual Basic applications, you would need to convert it into a Visual Basic library.

Components build on object technologies to provide a better way of achieving reuse of libraries and objects contained in them. The term **component** is one of those overused words with a different meaning to just about anyone you ask. Even within the OO community, there's a great deal of disagreement about the meaning of the term. Many people would argue that a component is nothing more than a large or complex business object.

In fact, the terms 'object' and 'component' are often used interchangeably, but there's a distinct and important difference between objects as described above and COM components:

❑ Objects are created from classes. Classes are made up of source code that defines the object's data and the routines that are needed to manipulate that data. As such, they have an associated language – you can have a VB object and a C++ object, for example.

❑ Components are created from precompiled *binary* code. Since this code (known as the **server** for the component) is precompiled, it (and the components created from it) is independent of the language in which it was created. By the time a component *becomes* a component (when it's created using a compiled server), it doesn't make sense to call it a VB (or C++) component.

One use of the word component that might catch you out is its use when refering to sections of a large application. For example, an enterprise application might include a 'mailing component', or a 'data access component. Here a single component may actually consist of a functional grouping of several objects, or indeed COM components.

In Microsoft's view, components are precompiled units of code that expose one or more interfaces for use by client programs. Typically these will be ActiveX controls made available through ActiveX servers. However, even within the Microsoft world you'll find some confusion. To many people, ActiveX controls and COM components are synonymous. In reality, however, the term "ActiveX control" refers to COM components that exhibit certain functionality.

With binary components, we can achieve a whole new level of reuse in our applications. Going back to our VBCustomer object, the diagram below depicts the scenario we had where the code from the Customer class module was in each of our applications.

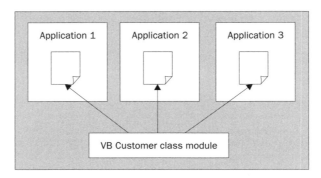

Using components, we could place the code into a component rather than into each individual application. The applications can then use the object directly from the component:

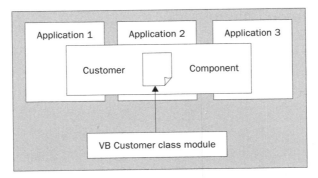

We get the same functionality as when we copied the source code into each application, but now we only need to maintain that code in a single place – the component.

There are generally hundreds of COM components within the very Windows-based system you use at work and at home. These components can potentially be used among hundreds and even thousands of different applications. Furthermore, a different software vendor can create COM components using different programming languages without any integration problems. The sky really is the limit when it comes to COM components.

Client versus Server

A COM component can be considered as either a client or a server component. Generally speaking, a client component requests some type of services from one or more server components. Thus a server component's job is to perform some type of task on the client's behalf. On a large scale, this can be as simple as a common database application where the client represents a user interface component that makes requests to the database (server) for various tasks such as information storage, manipulation of data, and data retrieval.

Assuming the client/server database application just described is built with COM technology, we can break things down into smaller pieces – COM components. COM components themselves follow the same client/server principle just described. However, determining whether a COM component is a client or a server can become confusing, because it can be both!

When a client application makes a request to a COM component, the COM component acts as a server (to the client). But when that same COM component makes a request to *another* COM component, the calling COM component is considered the client, while the COM component receiving the request is the server. In simpler terms, the reason a COM component can be both client and server is because each COM component can have multiple roles in an application. Client components request services from server components by invoking methods defined in the server component's **interface**.

Later in this chapter you will learn about interfaces and this will become clearer to you. For now, the thing to keep in mind is that a client makes requests and the server performs tasks based on client requests.

Processes, Threads, and Apartments

Now that you can properly distinguish between COM components and objects, and how COM components can act as both client and server, let's move on and look at COM components in general and see how they behave in different environments.

The COM environment provides us two options when we go to create a component. These are:

❑   Out-of-process Server

❑   In-process Server

In order to understand the distincion we need to know what is meant by a **process**. While we're at it, we'll also define a couple of other important concepts, **threads** and **apartments**.

Processes

A process is a term applied to a standalone unit that is maintained by an operating system. In practice, this means that a single process may contain code, virtual memory, system resources, and other data. For example, when you open an application like Minesweeper the application itself is contained in a single process.

The Windows operating system is capable of maintaining many processes simultaneously, which has a number of benefits. It enables you to do more than one thing at once, but also offers **process isolation**. In theory this means that if you are running two independent processes they shouldn't be able to interfere with each other, so if one of the processes crashes the other should be unaffected. In practice things are a little more complicated, since situations can arise when two processes are both using a third process so that their functionality is linked at a fundamental level, plus there are system-level functions that can completely ignore process boundaries.

Threads

Threads are blocks of code that are executed serially, that is, from start to finish. Every process contains at least one thread, and it is these threads that are processed by the operating system.

In professional application development it is extremely important that you understand threads and the various threading models that are available. For example, a simple application with a single thread requires one action to complete before another can be started. Suppose part of the operation of an application is sending out e-mails to a few thousand customers. If this application only made use of a single thread we would have to wait a long time before continuing. Alternatively, if we assign a separate thread to that activity we can continue without waiting for the mailing operation to complete.

Things become even more complicated when you write code that can be accessed from several threads simultaneously. This may sound like a ludicrous thing to do, but is actually a very powerful technique. Having a COM component capable of being accessed from several threads simultaneously means that we only need to use a single instance of that component, rather than requiring separate instances on multiple threads. Providing we design such a component in a robust way that won't cause the threads to interfere with each other, this can have far-reaching benefits, including resource saving.

Apartments

COM components that exist in a process are contained in apartments. A single process may contain several apartments, each with a separate set of COM components inside, and apartments come in different types. The type of apartment that a COM component exists in affects how the threading is handled. Without wanting to go into too much detail at this stage, it is possible for apartments to contain, for example, only a single thread. Alternatively, an apartment could contain multiple threads. Some COM components can only exist in certain types of apartment, at least if they are expected to function properly!

Out-of-process Servers

An out-of-process server is a module that is effectively a separate program containing components. This type of server will always run in its own process, and will thus be largely independent from any client programs.

Out-of-process servers are often standalone applications that happen to also provide access to their internal objects through COM, though they can be designed to only expose their objects to other applications.

These servers are often large applications in themselves, and provide access to their objects to make it easy for other programs to create macros or otherwise make use of existing functionality. Examples of out-of-process servers include Microsoft Word, Excel, and SAP.

> *A while back, Microsoft began licensing the VBA toolset to software vendors so they could use VBA as a macro language. For this to work, the software vendor has to expose their application's functionality via COM objects so a VBA programmer can write macros. The beneficial side effect of this is that we can also use those COM objects from VB or any other language that can be a COM client.*

The following diagram shows several clients interacting with objects running in the same out-of-process server:

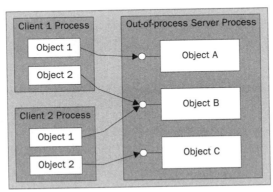

This can be very beneficial, because it means that we, as the component author, can choose our own threading models and do pretty much whatever we feel is required to make our component work.

The drawback to this is that we *have* to handle our own threading and do a lot of other work. Most of that work, however, can be handled by COM+.

There is also a performance issue. Because our client application is communicating with objects in an entirely different process, there is quite a bit of overhead. COM steps in between the client and the server in this case, and handles all the communication between them. While this is nice, because it keeps things simple and easy to program, it tends to slow things down since there is extra work involved in cross-process communication (see *Marshalling*).

In general, out-of-process servers are useful if we need to do something truly out of the ordinary, or if we are trying to make use of the objects in a pre-existing application. Otherwise more mainstream in-process servers are the way to go.

In-process Servers

An in-process server is a component where our objects run inside the *client's* process. Each client essentially gets its own private copy of our component – and therefore a copy of all our objects.

> **In-process servers are often called COM DLLs or ActiveX DLLs.**

When people talk about COM servers or COM components, they are probably talking about an in-process server.

In-process servers don't have a process of their own – they always run within the context of another process. Often this other process is the client application itself, but it may be run within the context of a different process entirely.

If the component is part of a COM+ application, it is typically hosted by the COM+ environment – running in a separate process from the client application and allowing COM+ to create a process to host the DLL.

In the case where a component is directly hosted by the client application, we get a performance boost. There is very little overhead involved when having client code interact with an object that is running in the same process (even when components are in separate apartments). When the 'in-process' component is hosted by some other process, such as a COM+ application, things are a bit different. In this case, the client has to communicate across processes to interact with the object. In fact, this is quite similar to the out-of-process server scenario.

The advantages to running such a component in a COM+ application include stability and increased manageability. We gain some theoretical stability because if a COM object crashes its process it won't bring down the client application. It *would* bring down the COM+ host process, however, including all the other objects running in that host process. We also gain some manageability. When ASP hosts an in-process server component directly in its own process, and that component goes wrong, that DLL will be locked until the IIS server is shut down and restarted. This can be impractical in a 24-7 environment.

If we run the in-process server in another process, though, such as a COM+ application, we can unlock the DLL by shutting down and restarting the COM+ application – leaving IIS running. While this still means that we have to shut down our application to update a DLL, we do avoid shutting down the entire web server.

Marshalling

In both the above sections, reference was made to the fact that COM components may not reside in the same process (or the same apartment within a process) as clients. If this is the case, then calls to and from the component must be **marshalled**. What this means is that the client doesn't call the component's method directly; instead it uses a **proxy**. A proxy is an object that looks identical to the COM component in terms of what methods, and so on, are available, but sits within the client's process (or the client's apartment). When the client calls methods on the proxy, the proxy communicates with a **stub**, which is an object that exists in the same process (or apartment) as the component. The proxy then calls methods on the component, and returns any results back to the client via the proxy.

This arrangement means that no changes to client code are necessary when dealing with in-process or out-of-process components. The only difference is that the client will be dealing with a proxy rather than the component itself, but this behavior is transparent to the client. The client doesn't care where the COM component it is using is located, since the techniques used to access the component are the same in both situations. However, we may notice the difference when it comes to performance!

Threading Models

There are two different apartment **threading models** that are supported by Visual Basic, these are:

❑   Single threaded

❑   Apartment threaded

Single-Threaded Apartments (STA)

When a component is associated with a single-threaded apartment, only that particular thread may execute calls on the object. When another thread wishes to execute a call on the single-threaded object, the call is marshalled to the apartment that contains the object and that thread executes the call. If a result is required, it is then marshalled back to the original caller.

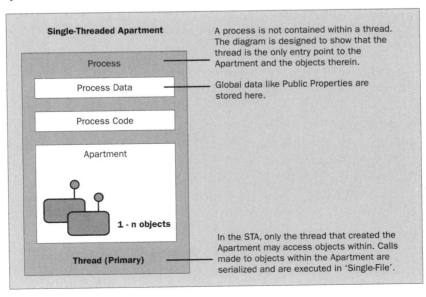

Single-Threaded Apartment

Process

Process Data

Process Code

Apartment

1 - n objects

Thread (Primary)

A process is not contained within a thread. The diagram is designed to show that the thread is the only entry point to the Apartment and the objects therein.

Global data like Public Properties are stored here.

In the STA, only the thread that created the Apartment may access objects within. Calls made to objects within the Apartment are serialized and are executed in 'Single-File'.

Since there is only one thread, calls made to the object all execute in 'single-file', meaning that calls to the object are executed in sequence. When one call is being executed, other calls must wait for the execution to complete. This is not a particularly useful scenario when you consider this model with a large amount of clients.

The following diagram shows the marshalling scenario across apartments using the proxy/stub combination. This marshalling also occurs across processes and machine boundaries.

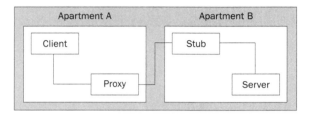

The above figure shows two apartments and the proxy/stub combination that marshals calls across apartment boundaries.

Apartment Threaded

The **Apartment Threaded** option is basically the same as the **Single Threaded** option except for the fact that there are many threads involved. An apartment can have many threads of executable code, which can all execute simultaneously. This makes it a better option for a server component, as clients do not have to wait for calls to complete while it waits in a queue as in the single-threaded option.

Although this is a better option, there is the issue of global data. Public variables declared in BAS modules in Visual Basic are considered to be global data.

When a public variable is declared, each class instance instantiates a copy of the data on its own thread. This is the way that Visual Basic deals with the potential conflicts that could occur if multiple objects were to read and write randomly to the same global data.

The negative, though, of each thread having its own copy of global data is that you can never be sure that the data is consistent between all the instances. For these reasons, it is not good practice to use non-constant public variables. Also, due to the fact that copies of the global data are made for every instance, there are also resources to consider.

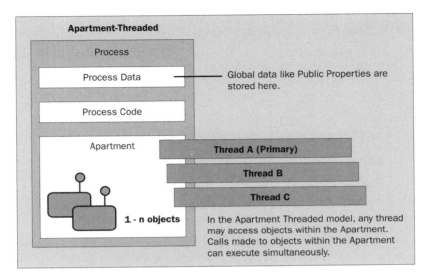

The threading models within Visual Basic are limited – other models such as neutral and free threaded apartment (which we won't look at here) are not supported, which means that it cannot take part in object pooling (see the section on *COM+ Services* later in this chapter).

Interfaces – COM's Binary Standard

The advantages that COM provides for distributed application development are provided through the use of **interfaces**. COM interfaces are the mechanisms by which a client or consumer interacts with a component.

Previously, we saw that COM components could be written in any languages that are capable of building binaries compliant to the published COM standard. If all COM components were written exclusively in only one language, then communication among objects would not be difficult. However, when we use components written in various programming languages, we need a way for these different components to communicate. For example, suppose I want to talk to my wife about how my day at work was. Because she speaks the same language as I do, there is no language problem. Communication between my wife and me is easy. But what if I wanted to address my day's events to everyone at the United Nations? Certainly I would encounter numerous language barriers. I would need someone to intervene who could communicate for me. This is similar to what an interface does. When it comes to communication with different programming languages, COM's interfaces provide a universal mechanism so each COM component can communicate in a language understood by all.

COM interfaces are nothing more than a group or collection of public functions that allows COM components to interact with each other. In other words, an interface is simply a list of methods a COM component supports. Furthermore, it's important to understand that an interface is neither a class nor an object. While a class can be instantiated to create a COM object, a COM interface cannot.

COM's Contract

Every interface constitutes a binding contract between a COM object and an object offering an interface. Interfaces must never be changed. In other words, COM interfaces are said to be **immutable** as they are never versioned (although see the next section entitled *Version Control* to see what happens in real life). This means that once an interface has been published, it must never be modified. By published, I mean that your COM component has been released into the real world production environment.

However, don't misunderstand this rule; this does not mean you cannot ever make any changes to a COM component. On the contrary, you can change business logic as much as you want as long as you don't interfere with the original properties and methods. For example, in a growing business, it is normal for business rules (business logic) to change. Being able to change business logic such as mathematical and accounting formulae in a single COM component is an important advantage to COM applications. It is much easier to change business logic within a few COM components as opposed to having to recompile every client in a monolithic environment.

In addition, COM makes life easier by being able to support more than one interface at a time. New interfaces can be added to support new features while keeping the original interfaces intact. This means older applications will continue to work by using the original interfaces of the component, while updated applications can take advantage of added functionality by working with the new interfaces.

Version Control

As previously mentioned, once a COM interface is published, it is considered immutable. Altering an existing interface is likely to cause the applications relying on the component to fail. If you want to extend the functionality of a COM component by adding new methods, the correct procedure is to introduce a new interface and append it with a version number. In other words, because COM interfaces are immutable, they must not be altered in any way. When you version a COM component, you create a new interface while leaving the original interfaces intact. For example, suppose I have a COM component that can add the sum of two numbers, with an interface called ICanAdd. Now I have a need to be able to add more than two numbers. Instead of altering the original interface, a new interface should be added. I should increment the version number for the new interface and call it something like ICanAdd2. A class module then would need to be implemented for both interfaces (ICanAdd and ICanAdd2) in order to support both old clients that rely on the interface ICanAdd and new clients that can take advantage of the new interface (ICanAdd2) functionality for adding more than two numbers.

IDL/MIDL

You may be wondering how it is possible to create a component in different languages and still be able to define an interface that can be called from any other programming language. After all, if we are programming in one language such as VB, how is it possible for an interface that is a part of one component to be able to communicate with an interface on another component that is written in C++? The answer lies with the **Interface Definition Language** (IDL).

The syntax for IDL looks very similar to C++ yet IDL goes beyond what C++ can offer by being able to define functions that extend process boundaries. IDL provides numerous extensions that allow attributes such as type libraries, interfaces, methods, and parameters to be specified; again something C++ is not able to do adequately. However, it is important to understand that IDL is not an actual programming language. Instead, IDL is used specifically for defining interfaces and nothing more.

Do you have to use IDL to define your interfaces? The answer is no. Interfaces are essential to COM yet it does not matter how they are implemented as long as there is an agreement between the caller and the implementer regarding the interface definition.

If you use Visual Basic to program, the interfaces are generated for you during compilation. Indeed VB does take care of a lot of low-level programming for the developer. However, regardless of what language you use to program it is always to the programmer's benefit to understand how interfaces are defined. Furthermore, even with Visual Basic, you do have the option to create your own interfaces and it is often beneficial to do so. Because VB tries to take matters into its own hands, version control (see previous section) can become a real headache.

If you're curious about what IDL looks like, you can use `OleView.exe` to view IDL. If you have installed Visual Studio 6.0 including Visual C++, OLE View is automatically installed for you. You can access it in your Microsoft Visual Studio 6.0 program group, under **Microsoft Visual Studio 6.0 Tools | OLE View**, from the Start menu. If you installed Visual Basic only, OLE View is not included in the installation. You can find it on your Visual Basic 6.0 installation CD, in the \Common\Tools\vb\OleTools directory. You just need to copy it to your hard disk and, if you prefer, create a shortcut to it.

❑ Fire up the OLE Object Viewer, following the instructions appropriate to you as indicated above

❑ Open the **Type Libraries** folder in the left hand pane and select the required COM object

❑ Right-click an object and select **View Type Information** to display the **ITypeLib Viewer**, where you can see the IDL file

By convention, interface names begin with the letter "I". By looking at the name `ICalcSum`, you can identify that this is an interface.

IUnknown

Due to COM's specifications, every COM object must have an interface called `IUnknown`. This is the most fundamental interface a COM object has. What makes `IUnknown` so special is it can be used to obtain a pointer to any other interface. As a matter of fact, `IUnknown` enables interfaces to be used without actually knowing anything about them.

`IUnknown` has three methods that a client can invoke: `QueryInterface`, `AddRef`, and `Release`. However, VB does all this behind the scenes; in other words, with VB you cannot directly invoke these three methods.

AddRef and Release

The methods `AddRef` and `Release` manage reference counting. This reference count is an internal count of the number of clients using a particular COM object. It is possible that several clients will invoke the services of an object at the same time. When a client actually begins a session with an object, it calls the `AddRef` method. Once `AddRef` is called, a count of one is added to the tally. As soon as the session is over, the `Release` method is invoked thus removing a count of one from the tally. As long as a client holds a single reference to the object, the object will remain in existence. However, when the reference count reaches zero, the object destroys itself.

QueryInterface

The QueryInterface method is the mechanism that a client uses to discover and navigate to the interfaces of a component dynamically. QueryInterface is probably the most significant method of all COM interfaces because it allows run-time inspection of all the interfaces that a component supports. When the QueryInterface method provides an interface pointer to a consumer, the QueryInterface calls AddRef. As we have previously seen, AddRef will increment a count by one.

GUIDs and the Windows Registry

In order for client objects to invoke methods defined in an interface, we need a way to uniquely identify every COM interface. A **globally unique identifier** (**GUID**) is a 128-bit value that uniquely identifies a COM component or a COM interface, without duplication, anywhere in the world – guaranteed. This guarantee is beneficial and mandatory to the application developer as well as the application user because it ensures that COM components will never connect to a wrong component due to duplicate GUIDs.

Take a close look at the GUID shown below. You should notice that they are typically seen as a string of hexadecimal digits. Hyphens are used to make these strings more readable.

```
{00000010-0000-0010-8000-00AA006D2EA4}
```

How is a GUID generated? An algorithm is used to generate GUID numbers by taking the unique value from the network card on the programmer's PC and the current system date and time. If the programmer's machine does not have a network card, then a random number is used with the system date and time. The chances of two GUIDs ever being the same are astronomically improbable.

You will come across strings of numbers that look like GUIDs but that are referred to as CLSIDs and IIDs. Actually CLSIDs and IIDs are *all* GUIDs. When referring to GUIDs that identify COM classes, we refer to them as **Class IDs** (**CLSIDs**). On the other hand, GUIDs that are used to name an interface are called **interface identifiers** (**IIDs**).

> **Object instances of COM classes are not identified by GUIDs or CLSIDs.**

Now that you know what a GUID is, let's continue with the next section and learn why GUIDs play such an important role within COM.

System Registry

Earlier in this chapter we learned that COM was location-independent, which means that a COM component can reside anywhere on your computer or even another computer connected to a network. Before an object can be created, the COM runtime must first locate the COM components. The COM runtime is able to locate COM components through the use of the Windows registry.

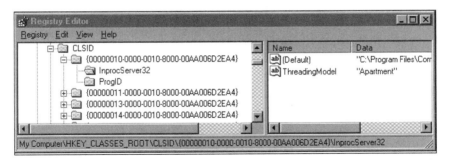

This screenshot of the registry provides a lot of information. We can see that we are looking at a CLSID, so we know that it is a COM class from which a COM object can be instantiated. Underneath the CLSID we can tell that this COM class is an in-process server (a DLL). Jumping to the right-hand pane, we can see the location path where this object is installed. The type of threading model is also identified. In this case, the object is using Apartment threading.

Back to the left-hand pane, a folder called ProgID can be opened. To further identify the object, the programmer can provide a text string that is easily read by humans. Usually, a company name and the name of the class is used for easy identification, such as:

```
MyCompanyName.CalcSUM
```

Building our own COM Component

It's time to start putting some of this knowledge into practice. A fictitious company called MyCompany has decided to write a program that will take two numbers and add them together. Off the record, I think the owners of the company plan to use this calculator to add bonuses to their regular paychecks.

Let's start by building a COM server component that adds two numbers and returns the total. We also need to build a simple Windows client application to play with the server component.

1. Start Visual Basic, and create a new ActiveX DLL project. Once the project is created, change the name of the project to SumCalculator and the name of the automatically created class to CCalcSum. Next, open the Project | Properties dialog box and enter a description for the project as illustrated in the diagram below.

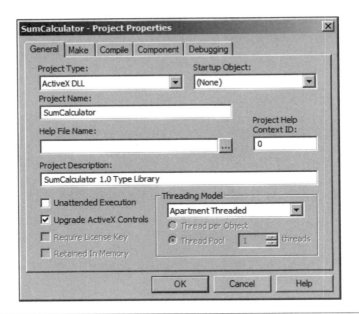

We'll look at the settings available on this tab in the next chapter.

2. The dancing floor is now ready, here comes the show. Open the `CCalcSum` class code window and create a function as listed below.

```
Option Explicit

Public Function SumOfNumbers(ByVal Num1 As Long, ByVal Num2 As Long) As Long
    SumOfNumbers = Num1 + Num2
End Function
```

3. Finally, go to File | Make SumCalculator.dll and click OK.

Congratulations – you have just built a COM component using Visual Basic. Be sure to save your project! We still need to build the client application.

4. Select a new Standard EXE project. Before we go any further, click Project from the main menu and select References from the drop-down menu. Locate SumCalculator 1.0 Type Library and select it.

You should recognize the name SumCalculator. This reference was created when we successfully built the `SumCalculator.dll` earlier. This reference is known as a type library. Type libraries are the mechanisms by which components within a COM server are described to the consumers of that server. A type library is a catalog that lists what components, interfaces, enumerations, and structures are available inside a COM server.

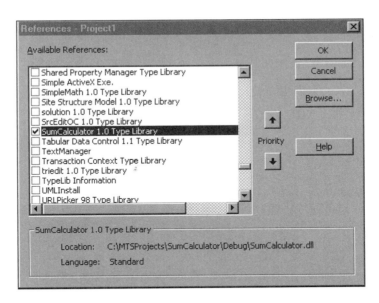

5. Let's name the project `SumCalcClient`. Name the form `frmCalc` and set the caption to I Can Add!

6. Add two command buttons to the form. Make one button larger than the other. Name the large command button `cmdCalcSum` with the caption CalcSum and name the small command button `cmdExit` with the caption Exit.

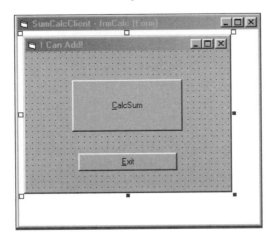

7. Open the code window by double-clicking the command button CalcSum and enter the following code:

```
Private Sub cmdCalcSum_Click()
    Dim Num1    As Long
    Dim Num2    As Long
    Dim Calc    As SumCalculator.CCalcSum

    Set Calc = New SumCalculator.CCalcSum
    Num1 = CLng(InputBox("Enter a number:"))
    Num2 = CLng(InputBox("Enter another number:"))

    MsgBox "The total = " & Calc.SumOfNumbers(Num1, Num2)

    Set Calc = Nothing
End Sub
```

Pay close attention to the code you just entered. We can deduce that the total is derived from two numbers entered by the user. However, we don't know how these numbers are being added as the formula has been encapsulated into our COM component. Although this demonstration is not a distributed (n-tier) application, you can get an idea of how business logic can be separated from the client.

Again, think in terms of a distributed client server application. This client application is not coded in a monolithic manner. If we decided that we want to change the business rule from adding two numbers to adding two numbers and then multiplying the total by two, all we need to do is adjust the formula on the server component. The client(s) accessing this component do not need to be changed or updated.

There you have it – COM in action. We can encapsulate, separate, and distribute COM components all over the world and this client application will run just as if everything was installed on the same machine.

8. Let's go ahead and put the following code in for the Exit command button:

```
Private Sub cmdExit_Click()
    Unload Me
End Sub
```

9. Save your project and then try executing it. Don't forget to add your bonus to your paycheck!

Now we've built up a little experience with COM in general, let's now start to concentrate on the features offered by COM+.

COM+ Services

As noted earlier, COM+ was the logical progression of COM and MTS fused into one seamless suite of services integrated into the Windows 2000 operating system. COM+ contains all of the services MTS did, along with some improvements and new services of its own. Let's take a look at what those are:

Automatic Transactions

Transactions are a way to group several tasks into one single unit of work which either fails or succeeds as a whole (remember back to Chapter 5?). If a transaction encounters an error while in process, it fails as a whole. That is, all changes are undone or *rolled back*. This is useful in a whole range of cases, for example on an e-commerce site. Here you'd want to check the validity of the credit card number, and if successful, log a shipping request, adjust the inventory, and send a confirmation e-mail, among other things. You'd obviously either want all of these things to happen, or none of them, so you'd group them into a single transaction. In COM+, a grouping of work into a single unit is also often referred to as an *activity*.

COM+ provides a setting to allow the *automatic* committal or rollback of a transaction based on whether the code encounters an error or not. If the routine throws an exception, COM+ will automatically roll back the transaction, otherwise the transaction is allowed to continue as normal.

Method-level Role-based Security

COM+ provides security to COM components through roles. This system is known as **role-based** security and is done by defining various roles or groups that can access components. An example of a role would be a teller or a loan officer for a banking application.

COM+ provides a very easy to use COM API to check an incoming caller, get their username, and determine if they are part of a defined role. COM+ roles are very similar to user groups in Windows NT and Windows 2000. They both can be assigned various rights, and contain a list of members and users. Role-based security also provides security settings that will automatically deny or grant users access to the component, based upon these same roles. Roles can also be used to grant or deny access to individual interfaces of a COM component, or even individual methods (note that MTS only allowed interface-level security to be defined – doing this for methods is new to COM+).

This enables developers to design their interfaces around the business requirements instead of their security requirements, which leads to a better structured and easier to follow object model.

Synchronization

Synchronization is a huge benefit for developers. It allows them to forget the fact that there is more than one concurrent user on the system and they can focus on the business logic instead. Synchronization isolates all of the tasks carried out by a COM+ activity and places locks on them. Although this may seem like it would be a performance bottleneck, it actually works quite well.

Synchronization also promotes the development of stateless components since resources are locked. It is best to lock the resources as late as possible and free them up as soon as possible. Note that the locking and unlocking of resources is done at a lower level than most developers code at, so to minimize the time the resources are locked, updates should be kept close together and database connections should be closed as soon as possible. With connection pooling, closed connections are returned to a pool of connections that can be reused by the other clients.

Synchronization within COM+ is greatly improved when compared to MTS. Where MTS simply places locks on resources that the components are utilizing, COM+ will also lock the component to stop other users from using the same instance at the same time. However, this is not very useful in components with the apartment-threading model (thread affinity), like the ones built in VB. It is very useful for free-threaded components that have the potential of being accessed by two threads at the same time, but unfortunately we don't have this option in VB.

Resource Dispenser and Notification Services

Another popular feature offered by COM+ is a resource dispenser. A resource dispenser provides a mechanism for accessing shared information. This provides an excellent way for components to persist information while still remaining stateless.

COM+ also provides hooks, or event sinks, for clients to receive notifications from COM+. This is a great feature that is often used to create monitor and logging utilities for COM+.

Improved Object Instantiation

Once of the biggest improvements when programming with COM+, as opposed to MTS, is the lack of having to use a special syntax when calling between objects. In MTS, a developer had to make a call to MTS and ask it to create an instance of the component for it. Now with COM+ all we have to do is simply create an object just like any other object and COM+ will look up its requirements for us and provide it with the proper runtime.

Object Pooling

Object pooling enables developers of free-threaded COM components to develop objects that can be recycled and used again by other consumers (clients), instead of immediately being destroyed.

Although it may seem that all objects in COM+ should be pooled, it is not always very efficient. Maintaining a pool of objects consumes resources that are usually free to be used on other tasks. The best place to utilize COM+'s object pooling functionality is when the initialization of an object is expensive (processor intensive). For instance, look at database connection pooling. ODBC and OLEDB both provide the ability to *pool* connections, but why? They pool connections because they are expensive to make. If you had to establish a database connection every time you needed a new one the application would drastically degrade in performance. For this same exact reason Microsoft has built in the ability to pool your business objects.

When a request is made to COM+ for a component that is to enable object pooling, COM+ will first look at its pool and determine if it has one to give to the component. If it does, the server passes a reference to the consumer. If all of the objects in the pool are currently in use, COM+ will analyze its maximum pool size configuration and if it has not reached it, COM+ will create a new object and pass a reference of it to the consumer. This typically only happens when the server goes from low utilization to high utilization. As consumers release their reference to the object, COM+ will take the objects and place them back into the pool, instead of destroying them.

Unfortunately for VB programmers, unless you move into VB.NET, poolable objects can only be built in VC++ because of the threading requirements. Objects that are going to be pooled must be built with the multi-threaded neutral apartment-threading model. This is rather unfortunate for Visual Basic programmers. Because Visual Basic does not provide the ability to build COM+ components with this threading model, you can't pool objects developed in Visual Basic.

Queued Components

COM+ Queued Components (QC) is a very useful feature of COM+ that allows developers to build COM components that communicate with each other asynchronously. Behind the scenes QC sits on top of Microsoft Message Queue (MSMQ). This not only allows asynchronous communication, but it also provides the ability to make a call on a component that is not even available due to network communication issues or restrictions.

The best way to visualize QC is to think of it as COM components e-mailing each other instead of opening a direct synchronous connection (RPC) to one another. This style of communication is also known as loosely coupled; the interaction between the client and the server is not direct or tight. In fact when the client creates an instance of the server object, it actually has a reference to an object within QC that is imitating the server component.

Within the architecture of QC there are four section: the recorder, MSMQ, the listener, and the player. The recorder resides on the client and logs all of the method calls invoked by the consumer. The recorder is the piece of QC that has the ability to imitate the requested server component, this way the consumer thinks they are working with the server component, when actually they haven't even communicated with the server. Once the consumer releases the reference to what it thinks is the server object, the listener builds an MSMQ message holding all of the log information from the consumer's interaction and sends it off to MSMQ.

With the utilization of MSMQ, QC inherits a lot of attributes, such as the ability to utilize server components even if the server is unavailable. MSMQ also provides the breaking point between the server and the client. MSMQ gives QC the ability to utilize loosely coupled communications as opposed to tightly coupled, which we have in the traditional COM environment.

The listener section of QC resides on the server and responds to the messages sent to MSMQ from the recorder. As the listener responds to a new message, it forwards it to the last section of the QC, the player. The player is the part of QC that actually invokes the real server object. The player analyzes the log information from the recorder and invokes the methods in the same exact order that the client invoked the recorder.

COM+ Events

COM+ event services provide a mechanism for COM components to publish and/or subscribe to events. The biggest benefit of COM+ events is that the COM classes are not directly tied to one another – everything is configured through the COM+ component manager (Microsoft Management Console (MMC) snap-in) or at run time depending on the type of subscription.

Within COM+ Events there are three parts – the publisher, the event system, and the subscriber. Before we can talk about the publisher, we need to discuss the parts it calls upon in the event class. The event class resides within the event system and is really just an interface. For the VB developers this is a normal class within an ActiveX DLL with the methods defined with no code in them, just the declaration. The event class just provides a way to define and group events and make them available for the subscribers.

Now with an understanding of an event class and its role within COM+ events we can get into the publisher. The publisher can be a consumer that understands COM: VBScript, VB, and VC++, just to name a few. The publisher creates an instance of the event class and invokes the desired methods on it. As the publisher invokes a method, COM+ notices that the class is actually an event class and looks up all of its subscribers to the event class. Once it has the list, COM+ will turn around and invoke the same method on all of its subscribers, raising events on them. You may be wondering how COM+ can invoke the method on the client. One requirement of all subscribers is that they must implement the same interface they are subscribing to. As the subscriber implements an interface it defines a routine for them to place code into.

The greatest part of COM+ Events is that once the interface is defined and configured as an event class, multiple consumers of the event class can publish events to multiple subscribers without any of them knowing about one another. Since this interaction between the publisher and the subscribers is not direct, COM+ Events are often referred to as a loosely coupled event system.

COM+ Catalog

The COM+ catalog is a database that is used to store all of the configuration settings we'll discuss shortly. The COM+ catalog is a huge improvement to COM and MTS and still enables a smooth integration of standard COM classes and configured COM+ components. This is due to the simple fact that the COM+ catalog is really one API that is used to access two data stores. One of these data stores you can probably guess: the registry. This is what allows all of the existing standard COM components to continue to work in Windows 2000, despite the introduction of COM+.

The other data store used by COM+ is known as the RegDB. The RegDB was a new data store to Windows 2000 and COM+. Microsoft decided to break off from the registry and go with a different data store. This was probably a wise decision, otherwise the registry would become even more cluttered.

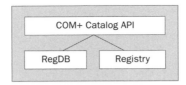

The COM+ catalog is utilized when setting normal properties like JIT and various security settings (both of which we'll look at in a moment), either through the MMC or by programming the settings through the COMAdmin API.

COM+ Applications

The configuration settings for COM+ classes are stored in COM+ beneath a structured hierarchy. At the top of the hierarchy is the computer (usually a server) running, for example, Windows 2000. Within each computer, COM+ will have multiple **applications**. These applications group multiple COM classes together and are synonymous with packages in MTS. Besides holding COM classes, COM+ applications also hold security settings known as **roles**. These are closely related to the roles from MTS and security groups in Windows NT and 2000.

The following screenshot displays the Component Services MMC snap-in. This tool is the central point for administrating COM+ and the components registered within it. To open this tool select the Component Services shortcut under the Administrative Tools folder located in the Control Panel or under the Programs folder from the Start menu.

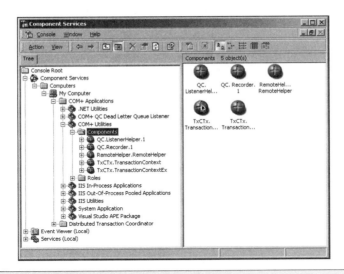

> **Within COM+ and Windows 2000, just like in MTS and Windows NT 4.0, there are two types of COM components, ones that are registered in COM+ (or MTS in Windows NT), and those that are not. Components that are registered are often referred to as configured components.**

As noted above, configured COM classes are stored within COM+ applications. We'll have a detailed look at setting up COM+ application to host COM+ components in the *Configuring Our COM+ Application* section of Chapter 11. Each class has a set of properties that informs COM+ how to accommodate the class and the requirements. COM+ settings can actually be assigned down to the interfaces and the methods on each interface. This allows COM+ administrators to have a fine-grained level of control over components.

COM+ applications provide a way to group multiple configured COM components together. So why do we have COM+ applications, and what is the need to group components together? One of the main reasons is for performance and cross-component calls. Each COM+ application can be hosted with an instance of `dllhost.exe`, therefore allowing objects to be pooled and made available for different client components. Components that are in the same application can communicate with one another without the overhead of cross-process communication, while components that are in separate applications must utilize marshalling to safely communicate with each other.

Let's take a look at some of the other reasons why configured components are grouped into COM+ applications and the settings they can be assigned. All of the settings introduced in the following sections can be configured through the Component Services MMC Snap-in or through the COM+ administration API library, `comadmin.dll` (COM+ 1.0 Admin Type Library). If you wish to set these settings programmatically, the COM+ API resides in `comadmin.dll`, located in the COM directory under the `system32` directory. For more information on configuring these settings programmatically, consult Microsoft's online documentation at

http://msdn.microsoft.com/library/en-us/cossdk/htm/pgautomatingadmin_9a26.asp

The settings we'll look at first are the application-level settings. Later on, we'll also look at the settings you can make at the component and method levels.

Security

Security in applications really comes in two forms: **authentication** and **authorization**. Authentication is the process of identifying whether or not a user is really who they say they are. This is usually done by the operating system. This would include a user logging into their workstation, or a web site requiring the user to enter a valid network username and password. However, within some applications, the process of authentication is done through code instead of relying on the operating system. But whichever process is used to verify users, it is usually done with a username and password.

Within COM+, application authentication can be configured at various levels. The most common is the packet level. At the packet level COM+ will analyze the user of the COM object on every packet that is sent back from the user to the server. This level provides a fair amount of security without dramatically degrading performance. COM+ has five other settings for authentication. It can weaken security to the point where it does not verify the client (no authentication at all), or it can also go to the other extreme and inspect each packet to make sure that no one has tampered with it while at the same time encrypting the packets as they are sent back and forth across the network. The figure below shows the Security settings tab in COM+ application properties dialog, which you can bring up by right-clicking a COM+ application in the Component Services MMC Snap-in and select Properties. Please note that this dialog box may look different if you use Windows XP, which comes with COM+ 1.5. The extra settings are beyond the scope of this book. For a good explanation of COM+ 1.5 new features, please read the MSDN Library article, What's New in COM+ 1.5, at the following URL.

http://msdn.microsoft.com/library/en-us/cossdk/htm/whatsnewcomplus_350z.asp

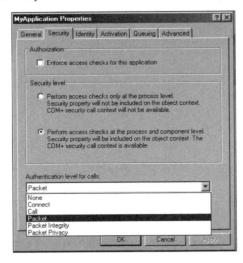

As you can imagine, the higher the security setting for authentication, the slower the applications will run. This only makes sense as the level of checking moves from none to per connection to per packet.

Once a user has been authenticated, they now have to be **authorized** to perform certain tasks throughout the system. Most of the time this is done through custom code within the application, however COM+ provides an infrastructure that developers can use if desired (which will possibly eliminate some development costs). This is where COM+'s role-based security comes in. Role-based security, as mentioned earlier, can be configured from the component level down to specific methods on an interface. We will talk more about role-based security later in the chapter.

New to COM+ is the ability for components to utilize **impersonation**. Impersonation allows the server to take on the security attributes (identity) of the caller. For example, the server will utilize a resource on the client's behalf. To this resource it will appear as if the client actually made the call. Impersonation in COM+ can be tailored for each application at four different levels: **anonymous**, **identity**, **impersonate**, and **delegate**.

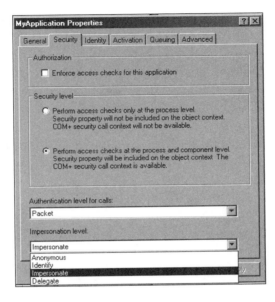

Anonymous

With the impersonation level set at Anonymous, the server cannot see and does not care who the caller is. This is basically a way to disable impersonation, which will cause COM+ to run all of the components with the security settings defined on the Identity tab on the COM+ application settings.

Identity

The Identity level setting allows the server to access the access control list (ACL) from the client, and perform checks against it. However, the server is not able to make calls on behalf of the client. Remember, in a web-based solution, the client to the COM+ configured components is IIS and not the browser.

> **The ACL is a list defining what permissions various user accounts have on a given object. An object can be anything from a file to a mailbox, or anything else that supports NT authentication (Windows-based security). In this case the object is a component.**

Impersonate

The Impersonate level allows the server to not only have the rights to identify the user, but also to make calls on the client's behalf. Even though this setting provides a great deal of functionality, there are still restrictions. The component can only access resources that are local on the server or local to the client. For example, a component could access a printer or files that are local to the web server on behalf of the client.

Delegate

Delegate is the highest level of impersonation available. It provides the same attributes of the Impersonate level without all the restrictions. The server is able to call upon resources acting as the client. It's basically like the user is sitting directly at the application server.

Considerations

When working with impersonation there are a few things to keep in mind. One showstopper that stumps some developers is that it is not supported in Queued Components. Another consideration to be aware of is the reason for all four different settings: performance. The stronger the impersonation level, the more processing that needs to be done, and therefore the more it will have a negative impact on performance. However, relying on the operating system to perform these tasks is usually faster and more cost-efficient than developing the functionality by hand.

The process of authorization is not performed at the COM+ application level; instead it is carried out at the component, interface, and method level. We'll discuss it in the section below entitled *COM+ Components, Interfaces, and Methods*.

Roles

Another type of security that is configured at the application level is roles. Roles, which are similar to groups in Windows 2000 and Windows NT security, are a way to define a set of user-specific rights to the component, its interfaces, and the methods within its interface. Roles can be very useful to grant and deny access to various parts of the business logic. The following screenshot displays a COM+ application that has two roles defined below it. Also note that each of these roles has a series of users (or members) within them. Also note that under the Public role the entire users group has been added. This provides an easy way to utilize existing Windows groups; in fact it is even possible to add the Everyone group.

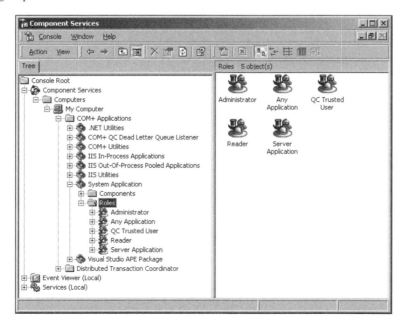

Although the defining of roles is done at the application level, the assignment of rights to these roles is done at the component, interface, and method level, which will be discussed in the *Security* section of the *Configuring COM+ Components, Interfaces, and Methods* area below.

Identity

The next tab on the Properties dialog is Identity. The identity of the COM+ application determines what user account the components within the COM+ application will run under. This enables the developer to consistently rely on a set of permissions to code with.

The following screenshot displays the Identity tab of a COM+ application's properties dialog:

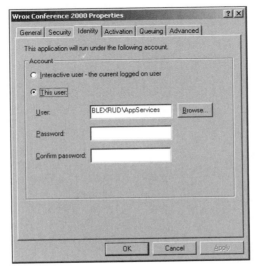

Notice that in the above screenshot there are two options, Interactive user and This user. Within a normal production environment it is always better to specify a user with the This user setting. This enables the components within the COM+ application to be available even when no one is logged into the active console (at the actual computer).

The Interactive user setting is great within a development environment. This enables developers to interact with the component for debugging.

Activation

Within COM+ there are two activation types for applications: **library** and **server**. Library applications run within the process space of the client, which can really speed up communications between the consumer and the components. A good example of where a lot of developers utilize library web applications is with IIS front-ends.

One drawback to configuring a COM+ application as a library is that since the consumer of the components and the components themselves are in the same process space, process isolation is lost. If a COM object were to encounter an error and spin out of control, it would bring down the IIS process, since this is really where the object resides.

Another drawback of utilizing library applications is security. When an application is set to be a library application, COM+ will run the components under the caller's identity. In the case of web applications in IIS this is usually IUSR_<ComputerName>, if anonymous access is permitted. Within COM+ and Windows 2000, there is one way to get around this, called **cloaking**. Although cloaking is not very easy to implement, it does provide the ability for components to run under a different user identity than the consumer's. For more information on cloaking and how to implement it reference Microsoft's documentation at http://msdn.microsoft.com/library/en-us/com/security_71lz.asp.

The following screenshot displays the Activation type setting within COM+. The tag setting is located on the Activation tab with the properties of a COM+ application.

Usually, though, COM+ applications are configured as server applications. This provides process isolation for the consumer and also allows the processing to reside on a different machine from the client. The server where the COM objects reside for this type of configuration is known as an application server. The drawback to using a Server application in COM+ is performance. Since each method call has to be marshalled across processes (sometimes to another machine depending on the architecture), performance can be impacted. However, as the number of users within a system increases, this loss in performance is usually regained since the load is being distributed across various processes and computers.

Queuing

The queuing configurations in the COM+ application settings enable the components within the application to utilize COM+ queued component services, which were discussed earlier in the chapter. The following screenshot displays the queuing configurations that can be set on a COM+ application. This screen, like the others within this section, is the properties dialog in the Components Service MMC snap-in. Below we see the Queuing tab.

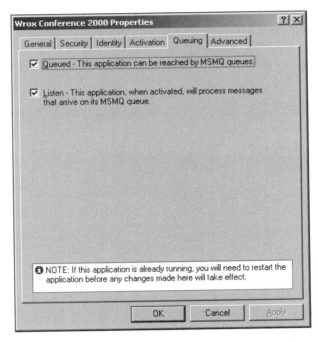

As you can see above, there are two settings within the Queuing section: Queued and Listen. The Queued setting enables the components within the application to utilize the services provided by queued components. The Listen setting informs COM+ to automatically watch MSMQ for incoming messages to be processed.

There are two important things to note when setting these configuration values. The first is the one that Microsoft placed on the bottom of the tab; that the application must be restarted before any changes will be seen. The other important note is that this is not the only setting that must be set to utilize COM+ Queued Components. There are other settings that must be set within the Interface properties in each Component. This setting will be discussed in *Configuration Class Requirements* below.

Now with an understanding of the settings and resources available at the COM+ application level, let's take a look into the classes within these applications and the settings available.

Component Activation

The most common way to instantiate COM objects is through the `CreateObject` function for VB developers. COM+ can determine the run-time requirements of the requested class.

As requests are made for objects, COM+ uses a technique called **interception** to step in between the consumer of the component and the component itself. As COM+ intercepts the requests for instances of COM classes, it can take a brief moment to determine the requirements of the class and create the proper run-time environment.

COM+ has also altered the context wrappers from MTS and created a new form of them called Contexts. Contexts are actually the objects that sit between the consumer and the object and perform the interception. We will be discussing these in more detail later on in the chapter, but for now note that the context object sits in front of the COM object and also acts as the stub for communication with the client's proxy.

COM+ Object Communication

Let's look at how COM+ communicates between objects. The consumer creates a proxy and sends calls to the server via a Remote Procedure Call (RPC) channel. On the server side, things have changed. The stub has been moved into the COM+ runtime and is processed with the same object as the interceptor and the COM+ context.

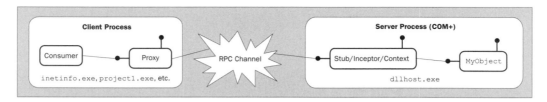

COM+ Components, Interfaces, and Methods

The run-time requirements for a COM+ class, its interfaces, and the methods on those interfaces, can all be configured one of two ways, just like the COM+ applications settings above; either through the Component Services MMC snap-in, or programmatically using the COM+ API. This chapter will cover setting the requirements or properties through the MMC snap-in.

Let's take a look at the configuration option within the class level and the layers below it (interface and method). To access any of the following screens, open the Properties dialog box on the specified level (component, interface, or method). The dialog is similar, but not identical, to the application-level properties dialog.

Transactions

We have already covered the definitions of a transaction while discussing the services provided by COM+, now let's take a look at the various configuration settings that can be applied at the component level within COM+.

First of all, recall from earlier that a transaction is a group of tasks that either succeeds or fails as a whole. With COM+, these tasks can span from a single method within a single component to multiple methods from multiple components, which can even be configured from different COM+ applications. In many situations, developers need all of the components to be in a single transaction together, but there are times when we might not. The following diagram shows the Transactions tab of a COM+ component's properties.

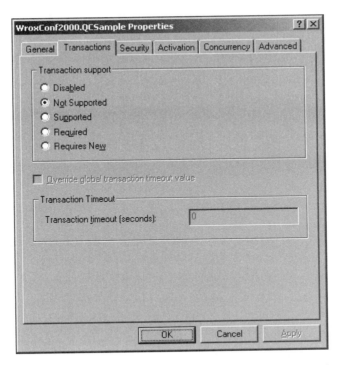

Since this is such a major part of COM+, we have devoted a whole chapter to this very topic – Chapter 9, *Transactions*. Because of this we won't cover the various settings here.

Security

As discussed above, COM+ utilizes roles to grant or deny access to functionality provided from a component, down to the method level. Let's take a look at securing a component at its various levels, and how the impact of other security settings at the application level affect it.

The following screenshot displays the options that COM+ provides at the component level. Since the component level is the highest level roles can be assigned to, you will notice some differences compared to the role settings that are set at the interface and method level.

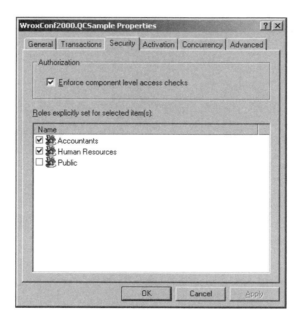

Notice above that two of the three roles (**Accountants** and **Human Resources**) have been assigned access at the component level. Any users that are not members of these roles will receive an access denied error when trying to utilize the component, unless other settings at the interface or method level override these settings. Actually this overriding of the security settings at the component level is displayed in the following screenshot, which is at the method level (under the interface, which is under the component).

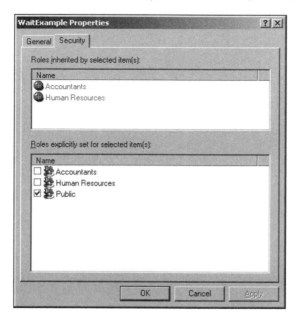

At the top of the Security tab are the settings that are inherited from the levels above. In this case they are inherited from the settings at the component level. Next, notice the overriding of these settings at the bottom of the screenshot where the Public role is granted access. This property box is for the WaitExample method, so any members of the Public role will only be able to utilize the functionality provided by that method and nothing else throughout this component.

COM+ security provides the ability for developers to write code that interacts with its security model. This can be very useful when more granular control is needed to solve a business need. For instance, you may want to grant two or more roles access to a method, but you may need the method to behave differently depending on the role the user is in. Checking security through code is easily done by checking the IsCallerInRole function from the ISecurityCallContext interface (see COM+ Context later in this chapter).

```
Dim objContextSecurity as COMSVCLib.SecurityCallContext
Set objContextSecurity = GetSecurityCallContext

If objContextSecurity.IsCallerInRole("Teller") Then
...
Else
...
End If
```

Activation

The Activation tab provides the ability to change the run-time behavior that a component takes when it is initialized. The first part of the Activation tab allows for the enabling of object pooling, if the object utilizes a multi-threaded apartment or the neutral apartment, is stateless, and implements the IObjectControl interface. The following screenshot displays how the Activation tab looks for most developers. Notice that the object pooling settings are disabled, due to the fact that the WroxConf2000.QCSample component was built in VB 6.0, which does not utilize multi-threaded or neutral apartments.

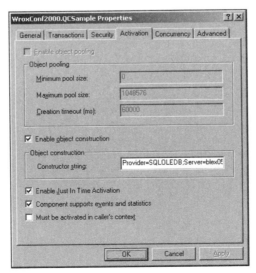

Another group of settings located on the **Activation** tab is the **Constructor string**. The **Constructor string** provides an administrative location to place information to be used at run time by a method within the component. A connection string is a common value that is assigned to the constructor string, although if there are components within the application the registry is a much better place.

The following code displays how to access the constructor string from VB. Notice that we first implement the `IObjectConstruct` interface and then wait for the `Construct` routine to fire from COM+. Once the routine is called the value is cached to a private string where it can be called upon from other routines in the class module.

```
Option Explicit

Implements COMSVCSLib.IObjectConstruct

Private m_strMyConstructorString As String

Private Sub IObjectConstruct_Construct(ByVal pCtorObj As Object)
  m_strMyConstructorString = pCtorObj.ConstructString
End Sub
```

Another configuration setting on the **Activation** tab is the **Just In Time** (JIT) activation. JIT allows the server to conserve system resources. Instead of creating an instance of the class when the client requests it, COM+ waits for the client to invoke the method. Once this happens COM+ creates an instance of the COM+ class, invokes the method call from the client, returns any result to the client, and then destroys the object.

COM+ will not always use JIT with all COM+ classes. The only time it does is if the component is configured to utilize it or if the component uses transactions. If a component is in a COM+ transaction, JIT is always used.

JIT also promotes the use of stateless components. However, just because it promotes stateless programming doesn't mean that stateful classes cannot be installed. COM+ will work happily with almost any type of COM+ class as long as they are contained within a DLL. However, if components are built as stateless, it only makes sense to use JIT, which can dramatically increase the scalability of an application. The idea behind it is fairly simple: why maintain an object when the consumer is not utilizing it? This may not seem like a big deal with 10 to 100 clients, but move this to a system with thousands of users and the difference is very noticeable.

There are two other settings that are available when configuring the activation setting within a component; the support for events and the caller's context requirements. By enabling the component to support events and statistics, the component services MMC snap-in will provide information about it such as how many objects are active and the average call time in milliseconds, just to name a couple.

The last setting, caller's context, informs COM+ to only let the component be activated within the context of the initial caller. By default this setting is unchecked, and for good reason, since it is normally not used. However, if the component does not support cross-context marshalling, or performance requirements are very high, checking this will cause the call to fail if the consumer is not the initial caller (ASP for example).

Concurrency

COM+ has another service that works very closely with the neutral apartment type, which is **call concurrency**. This provide developers who write components that can be accessed by multiple threads concurrently (neutral and multi-threaded components) with the ability to forget about the dangers of multiple threads stepping on one another, and allows them to concentrate on the task of solving business needs. The concurrency service provides this by implementing an idea **called activity-based synchronization**. Activity-based synchronization does just what it says; it stops threads from interfering with each other by blocking ones that are trying to access an object that is currently participating in another activity.

As you might guess, activity-based synchronization is not really needed for apartment-threaded components because the apartment enforces this, but you might be wondering what is the point of multi-threaded and neutral threaded components? One reason is for object pooling and the ability for different threads to access the same component at different times. If you recall, single-threaded components can only run on one thread. This isn't always bad, because you can rely on resources like thread-local storage. However, it is sometimes unacceptable to limit each object to a single thread. This is known as thread affinity. When a call is made to a component that requires synchronization and is currently involved in an activity, any new call will be blocked until the first activity is complete.

COM+ provides five settings for synchronization that can be configured through the MMC snap-in. Each one of these settings provides a different level of synchronization support from COM+ and Windows 2000 or later. The following screenshot displays the settings available for synchronization support on the Concurrency tab. Notice that most of the options are unavailable. This is because the component WroxConf2000.QCSample was built in VB 6 and uses the single-threaded apartment model.

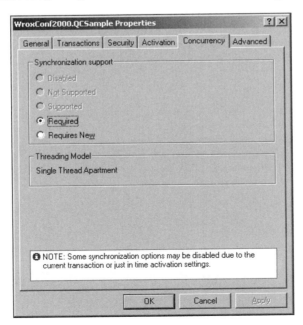

Let's look at the ones we're able to use.

Required

The Required setting is a very friendly setting because it will join with the consumer's activity and take advantage of the synchronization support. If the consumer is not taking advantage of the support, it will start its own.

Requires New

The Requires New setting is similar to Required, however it will always enter its own activity and therefore will be separate from the consumer.

There are a few considerations to be aware of when working with the synchronization support in COM+. First of all it is closely related to the transactional requirements of components. In fact, depending on the transactional requirements, certain concurrency settings are not available.

Now that we have a grasp on the majority of the configuration settings available in COM+ and where they are stored, let's take a look into COM+'s Context and how it is used to provide a source of information for developes on the run-time COM+ environment that is surrounding their components.

COM+ Context

Earlier in this chapter we saw how COM components exist in an apartment within a process. With COM+, however, we have an additional layer to contend with, **context**. Context fits into the above scheme by the fact that every COM+ object is associated with a context, and each apartment can contain several contexts. This means that components are divided up not just by apartment, but by context too.

A context includes configuration information that is essential for COM+ components to work with COM+ services. This information includes information such as the identity of the component client and what role they are in, transaction details if the component is participating in a transaction, and so on. Code within a COM+ component has access to this information, and can make changes to it where required.

Components can get access to their context via a context object **object** (an instance of the `ObjectContext` class), and this is where most developers interact with COM+. The context object provides anything and everything a developer needs to know about the current component and the run-time environment surrounding it that COM+ provides. Although most of the information within the context object is read-only, it does expose various interfaces and methods on these interfaces to interact with the COM+ runtime.

Context Interfaces

The context object that accompanies every COM+ component has a variety of interfaces that allow developers to gain access to context information. Each one of these interfaces provides the developers with different information from the same context object. Most of these interfaces will be used through the remaining chapters in this book (in fact we've already used `IObjectContext` in this chapter), so for now let's take a quick look at the different interfaces available, and a summary of the functionality they provide.

IObjectContext

The `IObjectContext` interface is the most common interface. It provides a single interface that will enable developers to have access to the most common properties from the other interfaces. The information available from the `IObjectContext` interface can be broken down into three categories: object creation, transaction, and security. To obtain a reference to the `IObjectContext` simply make a call to the `GetObjectContext` method.

The `GetObjectContext` function is global to the `COMSVCSLib` library and is available once a reference is made to `comsvcs.dll`.

```
Dim objContext As COMSVCSLib.ObjectContext
Set objContext = GetObjectContext()

If objContext.IsCallerInRole("User") Then
    ...
End If

objContext.SetComplete
```

IObjectContextInfo

`IObjectContextInfo` is one of the interfaces that are new to COM+. It provides various IDs that surround the current object, such as the transaction ID, context ID, and the activity ID. The transaction ID is a unique identifier that ties all of the participating objects of a single transaction together. The context ID provides an ID that identifies the context that is associated with the current COM+ object. Remember that since each instance of a COM class has its own context this ID will always be unique. The activity ID is used by COM+ to tie together all of the objects that have been invoked from the same task. COM+ uses this ID to know when to block another call or to allow it to pass through when synchronization support is required.

The `IObjectContextInfo` can be referenced by accessing the `ContextInfo` object from the `GetObjectContext` method, mentioned above.

```
Dim objContextInfo As COMSVCSLib.ContextInfo
Dim strActivityID As String

    Set objContextInfo = GetObjectContext.ContextInfo
    strActivityID = objContextInfo.GetTransaction
```

IContextState

This interface is used by COM+ to allow the developer to vote (play a role in determining the outcome) on the current transaction and set flag stating that their part is completed to inform COM+ that the transaction is complete. This is the same functionality that is accessed when utilizing the `SetAbort`, `SetCommit`, `DisableCommit`, and `EnableCommit` methods from the `IObjectContext` interface.

The `IContextState` allows developers to set the flag by invoking `SetDeactivateOnReturn`, and set the transaction vote (also known as the happy bit) by invoking `SetMyTransactionVote`. There are also two methods that allow the developer to look up the current status of these bits, `GetDeactivateOnReturn` and `GetMyTransactionVote`.

A pointer to this interface can be obtained by querying the return value of the `GetObjectContext` function for the `IContextState` interface.

```
Dim objContextState As COMSVCSLib.IContextState
Set objContextState = GetObjectContext()

SetMyTransactionVote TxCommit
objContextState.SetDeactivateOnReturn True
```

ISecurityCallContext

This interface provides the developer with a mechanism to retrieve security for the current call. This can be very useful when the basic role-based security checks don't give the developers enough flexibility. With this interface the developer can check the roles of the caller of the current call at runtime and take appropriate action.

Most of the functionality exposed through this interface can be accessed through the `IObjectContext` interface via the `IsSecurityEnabled` and `IsCallerInRole` methods. However, the `ISecurityCallContext` exposes a collection of roles the caller is a part of.

Getting a reference to the `ISecurityCallContext` interface is a little different than the others. It is the return value of the `GetSecurityCallContext` method, which is available when making a reference to the `COMSVCSLib` library, just like the `GetObjectContext` routine. The `GetSecurityCallContext` method will return `Nothing` if the current object does not utilize COM+'s role-based security.

```
Dim objContextSecurity As COMSVCSLib.SecurityCallContext
Set objContextSecurity = GetSecurityCallContext

If objContextSecurity.IsSecurityEnabled Then
  If objContextSecurity.IsCallerInRole("Accounting") Then
    ...
  End If
End If
```

IObjectControl

This is not an interface used to provide information or functionality like the others. Instead the `IObjectControl` interface provides an interface for developers to implement within their classes. By implementing this interface, developers can respond to various events that COM+ will invoke during the activation and deactivation of a configured COM+ object.

The `IObjectControl` interface is comprised of three methods; `Activate`, `Deactivate`, and `CanBePooled`. This interface is mostly used by objects that support object pooling. As a single object (class instance) can be utilized by more than one consumer, developers sometimes need an event to respond to, to clean up the object and make it ready for the next user. The `Activate` and `Deactivate` methods on the `IObjectControl` interface provide this functionality. The `Activate` event fires just before COM+ passes a reference to the object to the requester. The `Deactivate` event is fired off when the COM+ consumer is done with the object, just before the object is placed back into the pool.

The last part of the interface is really COM+ asking a question; `CanBePooled`. By returning the appropriate value to COM+ (`True` or `False`) COM+ will know whether or not to place the current object into a pool or to destroy it.

Summary

This chapter covered one of the most fundamental building blocks for *n*-tier development with VB6, namely the Component Object Model (COM). We started off by explaining COM's written specification as well as introducing COM's system-level code called the COM library.

We learned how COM:

- ❑   Promotes component-based development and OOP
- ❑   Promotes code reuse
- ❑   Provides the necessary mechanics for COM components to communicate with each other

We also learned the differences between COM components and COM objects and then moved on to learning about how COM components behave in different environments.

Next we toured COM's interfaces. We learned about COM's binary standard and a little about Interface Definition Language (IDL). We also learned about COM's most fundamental interface, `IUnknown`, and its three fundamental methods, `QueryInterface`, `AddRef`, and `Release`.

At the end of the vanilla COM section, we brought together all the concepts covered so far and saw how an object is instantiated from a COM component. To wrap things up, we had a hands-on exercise where we built a simple COM application using VB components.

Throughout the second half of this chapter we delved into COM+, the services it provides, and the various settings at the application level, component level, and deeper. We looked into how COM+ stores these configuration settings within its catalog. Lastly we looked at how developers can communicate with COM+ to fully take advantage of the run-time environment it provides.

COM+ (and its predecessor, MTS) can make our lives either a lot simpler or a lot more complex depending on how well its transactional support is used. It can be invaluable for transactionally updating multiple databases, or to allow us to release the locks on DLLs without stopping IIS entirely, but it does bring performance penalties, and transactional support should not be enabled blindly.

There is a zen to COM+. Once you understand its consequences (both positive and negative) you can weigh the benefits against the costs. This gets complex fast, because it isn't just a choice of COM+ or no COM+. We need to weigh the use of Library Applications versus Server Applications and ADO transactions versus COM+ transactions. Once you understand the ramifications of each choice you'll reach a state of true comprehension and productivity with COM+.

As a parting note, don't believe that .NET will make our COM and COM+ knowledge redundant, as in many ways, .NET builds on COM. It is true that .NET doesn't use COM per se, except for backwards compatibility, but the concepts of COM in terms of components, interfaces, properties, and events carry forward. Whether you learn these concepts in COM or in .NET – eventually you'll have to learn them. The same applies with the advanced features of COM+. In .NET they are part of what is called Enterprise Services, and although many of the reasons for using COM+ in VB6 don't apply to VB.NET (such as avoiding locked DLLs or simplifying deployment), the concepts behind 2-phase transactions, queued components, and the other COM+ features carry forward intact.

p2p.wrox.com
The programmer's resource centre

ASP Today

wrox.com

9

Component Development

In this chapter we will discuss issues relating to the design and development of COM+ components, both from the logic point of view, and from the angle of actually creating your components in code. This will involve considering issues of performance, compatibility, reusability, and scalability, as we build our own component-based application. The chapter will also offer tips and advice to help component developers to avoid some common pitfalls.

Introducing Business Objects

The idea behind using business objects is that we can create an abstract model of our business entities and concepts in an application. If these business objects enforce the rules and behaviors of our business processes, then we will have created a software model of our business. Having such a model makes it very easy to build applications that satisfy the business requirements, since new applications can simply interact with these objects – with complete assurance that the objects will only allow us to perform valid processes or behaviors.

So what exactly is a business object? Essentially it's an object just like any other we might create, except that it is written in such a way as to model an aspect of our business. So we might have an object called `SalesOrder` that would represent just that – each instance of a `SalesOrder` object would represent a different physical sales order, with all the properties and methods that a real sales order could have.

Business objects help us to conceptualize our logic and think of it in terms we're already familiar with. If your sales team tell you that each client can have multiple sales orders, and that each sales order has one and only one salesperson, then you would find it easier to understand if you created `SalesOrder`, `Client`, and `Salesperson` objects and adjusted their behavior accordingly. Also, if you found that salespeople and clients featured elsewhere in your code, you could easily reuse your existing objects there too.

Business Logic

If business objects encapsulate **business logic** (and related data), then it makes sense that we should have a good grasp of the concept of business logic itself.

Types of Business Logic

Business logic is a fairly broad term, and it is not always clear just what is or is not business logic within an application. Unfortunately, if we don't encapsulate all the right business logic into our objects we will largely defeat the purpose of using objects at all.

Another risk is that we could start overloading our objects with logic that *isn't* business logic – often this will be UI or presentation logic that accidentally slips into our objects.

> **The single biggest mistake made when using business objects is to blur the line between business logic and user interface (UI) logic.**

Three types of logic that we can identify are:

- ❏ **Calculations** – Most calculations performed in an application are business logic. Typically the calculations are required by the business, and the way in which they are performed is dictated by the rules of our business. However, *some* calculations exist solely for the benefit of the user's presentation. We may choose to sort a list of values to make them appear nicely for the user – even though the business itself doesn't dictate such a sort. In other cases a sort might be part of the business rules – such as choosing the correct inventory bucket from which to sell some parts.

- ❏ **Rules** – Rules are another fairly obvious type of business logic. Many of these will appear as conditional checks within our code, for example, 'If the customer's debt rating is below x then don't issue the loan.' In some cases rules and calculations will blur, since the results of calculations are often used as the basis for conditional rules checks. Rules often dictate relationships or requirements of data. A sales order line item can't exist without an actual sales order. A sales order can't exist without a customer.

- ❏ **Validation** – One type of business logic that's often overlooked is validation of data. For example, a specified field must be a date – or perhaps it must specifically be a date in the past. For whatever reason, validation is often considered to be a user interface artifact rather than 'real' business logic. Yet this logic is as 'real' as any other. Consider for a moment what would happen if the validation rules *weren't* enforced. Our application would either cease to function, or more likely would allow the user to perform actions that are invalid for our business. That's the real litmus test – does non-compliance mean that the application could do something that is invalid for our business? If so, then we're dealing with business logic.

UI Logic versus Business Logic

Note that the litmus test mentioned in the preceding bullet point does not concern whether non-compliance is inconvenient for a particular application. For instance, let's take the formatting of data. Our business logic may calculate a price for a sales order by summing up all the line items and applying tax. That process is governed by a set of business rules – and so it's pretty obviously business logic. However, the result is just a numeric value with no specific display format.

Before displaying the value to the user, we need to change its format to make it aesthetically pleasing. The logic to handle this formatting is *not* business logic – it's UI logic. A different UI might need a different format: while another application might not want it formatted at all. In short, the display format of a value is irrelevant when we're compiling our business rules.

Other common examples include the code to format a list as an HTML table, sorting some values alphabetically for user convenience, or code to populate an ActiveX grid control in a certain way.

> **In the final analysis, business logic includes all calculations, rules, and validation that must occur to ensure our application behaves properly and prohibits any actions that would be invalid for our business. Any such logic should be contained within our business objects. Everything outside of that sphere is not business logic, and doesn't belong in business objects – belonging instead in other parts of our application.**

We've looked a little at what business objects are and how we can use them, and we've considered the design strategies for dividing objects into logical units. Now let's take a look at specific code-based issues that affect how a component is written.

Building Components in Visual Basic

Visual Basic is a language well known for hiding complexities. The language has clearly entered a new phase in this respect with many of the complexities that were previously hidden from the developer now being opened up in the .NET Framework. This development in the life of VB will appeal to those who have believed that it has hidden too much. But for our current needs, some complexities may hinder our progress when designing applications that do not need it. So, how well does VB6 hide the complexities of COM+?

Building COM+ components in Visual Basic is by no means difficult, but do not be complacent – COM+ is an intelligent system that needs intelligence in the developer. VB *does* hide many complexities, but as a consequence, it also loses a bit of the power that C++ would grant you.

If there were a theme to this chapter it would be 'Simplicity over Complexity – a better choice!' The word 'Simplicity' here does not mean that you will *not* write complex code, or shouldn't have to, it means that the developer using your components should *feel* that it is a simple component, which most of the time means that you have to *encapsulate* more, and code even harder. This is underlined by the fact that VB has become one of the most popular languages today by being simpler than most other languages, even though this does not make VB itself simple to code well.

Simplicity is a powerful aspect of VB that suits many implementations. VB grants us power by letting us keep our code simple and clean. It can also provide more time as its simplicity can lead to shorter development time. Less time is wasted on the complexities, which grants us the ability to enhance our applications rather than iron out technicalities of implementation.

Creating a COM+ Component in VB

In this chapter we'll be looking at a variety of issues which need to be considered when designing and building a COM+ component. Since the arrival of the 2-tier approach to developing applications, more commonly known as the client-server model, many advances in the way that applications are developed have been made. These advances have helped both the design process as well as the implementation of the next generation of scaleable applications. The two-tier approach with its business logic, presentation code, and data accessing code all compiled into one executable offered little towards easy maintenance. The 3-tier and n-tier approaches are a more sophisticated alternative that has brought in a new wave of application design issues, together with the new technologies that have been developed for it. As one of these new technologies, COM+ offers tremendous features for this n-tier approach.

> **The component that you build in this chapter will be used to access a SQL Server database. The database, and the UI code are available to download from the Wrox web site at www.wrox.com.**

The Contacts Sample

This application will allow us to access a database of contacts and enable us to create, read, update, and delete records in it. Most of our business logic will be taken care of by Visual Basic code. Components built with Visual Basic are compiled, so they're a bit more difficult to update than simple script code. On the other hand, VB code has access to a wide range of data types, is compiled for better performance, and employs `vtable` binding for talking to COM objects – all contributing to fast, scalable, and easily maintained applications.

The overall architecture and design of this application will follow good Windows DNA principles. The presentation is browser neutral, providing for the widest possible audience for the application. Our user interface code will run within IIS, and was built using the Active Server Pages environment and VBScript. All business logic, including validation, rule enforcement, and business processing, will be encapsulated within the set of COM objects created in this chapter, using Visual Basic. Those same business objects will encapsulate our data access code as well. Finally, all of the data processing is handled separately, away from the business logic, in stored procedures.

Because our sample application's scope is small, we'll be only creating two business objects:

- ❑   `Contact` – provides an abstract representation of a contact, allowing us to add, edit, and remove a contact

- ❑   `ContactList` – provides access to a list of contacts for display and selection

The Contact Object

This object will encapsulate all the business logic and data access code for a contact – meaning that the ASP UI code can rely entirely on this object for all business validation, rules, and processing. The following UML (Unified Modeling Language – a way of describing systems and objects – class diagram illustrates the makeup of this class:

If you'd like more information about UML, check out the resources on the book's CD. The Contact object is a fine-grained object, meaning that it has many properties and methods rather than a few that do a lot of work each. This type of object provides a powerful set of services to the UI developer, since it's pretty obvious how to set or retrieve data from the object, and there is a great deal of flexibility in how it can be used.

There are two data types worth mentioning – PhoneType and EMailType. These will be implemented as Enums – user-defined numeric types. This object will allow us to maintain a list of phone numbers and e-mail addresses for each contact. The index into each of these lists is a numeric value – made more readable by creating a human-readable data type via an Enum.

Notice that the object also has two private methods, Fetch and Update. Not only will the Contact object encapsulate data access, hiding those details from the ASP code, but these two methods further encapsulate the data access code from the rest of the Contact object itself.

This model gives us two benefits. First, it shields as much code as possible from the underlying database and data access technology. If either SQL Server or ADO need to be replaced at some point, we've severely limited the amount of code affected. Second, this model makes it very easy to scale our solution up to the next level.

> **Applications should be designed, whenever possible, to make it easy to adapt to future scalability requirements.**

The ContactList Object

The second object will follow a different model, simply providing a set of data to the ASP developer via an ADO `Recordset`. This object's job is to allow the UI developer to retrieve a list of contact data for display to the user. The object provides read-only data, and basically encapsulates the underlying data access from the ASP code, so the UI developer can focus entirely on building a presentation based on the supplied data. The object's design is illustrated by the following UML diagram:

This object is much simpler, since it merely encapsulates the process of retrieving an ADO `Recordset` object for use within ASP. However, we still have the public `GetContacts` method separate from the `Fetch` method where we'll implement the actual data access. This provides much of the same abstraction from the database as we had with the `Contact` object – and makes it very easy for the application to be enhanced to be more scalable later.

There is a tradeoff between scalability and complexity, as well as between scalability and performance. The model we're using in this chapter is quite simple and easy to implement. To increase scalability, we may choose to move the `Fetch` and `Update` methods to another object running on an application server separate from the web server, but this is a more complex way of organizing our code.

This model has very high *performance*, even if it sacrifices some scalability. Performance is the measure of response time for a user. Scalability is a measure of response time as we add load to the system – either more users or more transactions per user. In many cases we sacrifice a single user's performance to gain scalability. This is almost always true when we add extra physical tiers to an architecture.

For example, old-fashioned single-tier FoxPro applications are much faster than n-tier SQL Server-based applications – for a small number of users. This is because of the minimal overhead involved in dealing with xBase databases as compared to something more complex like SQL Server. However, as we scale up by adding more and more users, the FoxPro application would rapidly decrease in response time, while the SQL Server solution keeps a decent response time.

The Database

The database for our application was created in SQL Server 2000 and can be built by executing the script provided. First, you must create the Contact database in SQL Server. To do this, open the Enterprise Manager, expand the Microsoft SQL Server tree until you can see **Databases**. Right-click and select **New Database**. Call this database **Contact**. You'll also need to set up your login for the application. Open Enterprise Manager, and drill down to **Security**, then **Logins**. Right-click and select **New Login**. Set **Name** to **contactapp** and **Password** to **contact**, ensuring that the **Database** field is set to **Contact**.

The SQL script must be executed inside the **Query Analyzer**. With SQL Server 2000 installed you can run the **Query Analyzer** by selecting the **Microsoft SQL Server I Query Analyzer** off the **Start** button. Inside the **Query Analyzer** select **File I Open** on the toolbar and point the dialog to the SQL script. The ID fields in the **Contact**, **Phone** and **Email** fields are designated as primary keys for the table. They're marked as `uniqueidentifier` data types, which means that ID can store a GUID (Globally Unique Identifier) value. We need to set it so that the GUID value is automatically generated as a new row is added to the table by checking the **IsRowGuid** box in the bottom table of the Design Table screen. (To find this, right-click on the table you want to set this in).

> *The SQL Script, and all the code in this chapter, can be downloaded from the Wrox web site at http://www.wrox.com.*

The above diagram of the database shows the layout of the tables and the relationships between the tables that the script will create inside of SQL Server.

Design Issues

Deciding what methods, properties, and events should appear on which interface is important in creating a great finished product. As you will see in the next section, COM+ offers services that will make certain tasks easier when writing scaleable applications, but you must understand the basic concepts first. This section will discuss what considerations you will want to keep in mind as you develop your COM+ components.

Designing in Layers

The n-tier approach to servers allows us to split our application so that it resides in a number of different tiers, comprising of the presentation, business logic, and data layers.

Data layer – concerned with data.

Creates easier debugging of data as it provides you with one entry point for all other objects accessing the data which means that no other object needs to access the database directly. This is important for database efficiency. This layer encapsulates the functionality of actually speaking to the database. It's best to keep our application relatively database-independent. How many applications started out talking to Jet (Access) databases and then had to be rewritten to work well with SQL Server or Oracle? In many cases these applications were written with data access code spread throughout the application – meaning that changing the database engine affected virtually every part of the program.

In addition, it's preferable to shield our application from *data access* technology. Microsoft has continually updated its data access technologies. First we had dblib, then DAO, then DAO with ODBC, then RDO, then ADO, and of course, now ADO.NET. Each time a new data access technology comes out, we end up going through our entire application, changing the code to accommodate, and hopefully take advantage of, the new services. In some cases, this type of change can be even more difficult to implement than simply changing the type of database with which we're interacting.

To make this truly successful we need to design our objects to restrict the use of data access technology here as well. Rather than spreading data access logic through all the routines within our objects, we should create two methods – one to retrieve data and one to save it.

Business layer – concerned with applying business logic.

When componentized into its own layer, it is easier to replace or update business rules without touching the UI or how the data access logic.

Presentation layer – concerned with presenting information and accepting input from the user.

Separating this into its own layer is very useful in today's fast paced world of e-commerce, where regular changes are required to keep the look and feel up to date, letting us snap on a new interface to an application without needing to touch the underlying business rules. It also makes it much easier to create entirely new interfaces for existing applications.

> **All in all the separation of the layers allows for easier maintenance from all angles, from data access to presentation layer and so on.**

The Contacts sample is split into a data access layer and a business logic layer. Building two separate layers does have a number of advantages. The sample lends itself easily to the fact that we could have two different servers: one holding the data access layer (contactList) and the database, and another holding the middle layer, which could distribute resource usage over two machines rather than one.

Designing an n-tier system requires that different components be developed and compiled for each of the layers. Since they are separate, information must be passed from one component to another. Passing information sounds easy enough, but there are issues to address in transporting this data.

Transport Data

Creating a component that passes data from one layer to another requires some form of container, a carrier if you will, such as the ADO recordset object. An ADO recordset is commonly used by developers to pass information from one piece of code to another. It is used in the `contactList` component for various reasons, one of which is to keep the sample code uncomplicated by not dealing with another abstract (even if it is better) solution. Arrays are probably the fastest of all the transport *carriers* but leave a lot to be desired when it comes to sorting the data or deleting entries within the array. Also, we need to handle data received from the client with deleted or added records, as in the case of a batch update, and the recordset has facilities for this. The `Collection` object in VB is a little friendlier, but unfortunately is a lot slower when accessing items and moving them around within it. The fatal problem with the VB `Collection` object, and other VB objects for that matter, is that COM+ always marshals them by reference. This may cause a huge performance problem when they are passed across process or machine boundaries. Every call to the object needs to be marshalled across those boundaries back to the process where the object is instantiated.

XML (discussed in Chapter 13) is more powerful than a traditional string or array if we want to query the data within the XML document. The fact that SQL Server 2000 offers many XML capabilities makes XML a better option still. Furthermore, as XML documents can be serialized into strings that can be passed around by value, it overcomes the shortcomings of passing VB objects.

However, even though data access technologies change very frequently – a tremendous drawback considering the changes that must then be made to existing code – the ADO recordset is still a very versatile mechanism thanks to the services that it provides.

The passing of objects brings us to another point. In MTS (Microsoft Transaction Server), objects could only be passed from one component to another by use of the `SafeRef` function in Visual Basic. This is not now the case with COM+. We can now pass objects safely, but that it does not mean it is necessarily the best choice. Passing objects can be extremely inefficient, as it involves a great deal of activity between client and server components.

Within this section, objects and methods within the context of a data transport mechanism have been mentioned, but no discussion on how these methods should look or where they should be found. In the next section let us look at this in more detail.

Factoring

Imagine a COM+ component server that contains over forty methods and properties on each of its twenty or so objects. Also imagine that each of the object's methods contains at least fifteen parameters. You might agree that this prospect is a little daunting, and in fact, a COM+ component server should *never* contend with such numbers.

Instead, when designing your objects, try and follow the golden rule – *simplicity*. Simplicity has been mentioned many times, and is probably the most crucial factor of building effective components, so I make no apologies for repeating it. I am not saying that creating an extremely large component is an incredibly bad thing, but a handful of components aided by a few smaller components is generally the better solution.

When dealing with a complex set of business rules for a large system, the code within a component could be extremely complex, which can cause debugging and maintenance nightmares. In many situations, getting around the fact that many objects would need to be created is a difficult task, especially in certain circumstances. The point that needs to come across, though, is that there are many situations that lend themselves to reusability. The smaller the components or objects, the more reusable they tend to be.

Any developer who uses your component should be able to do so successfully without major effort or a tremendous amount of reading on their part. You can achieve this in many ways:

❑ Try and keep your methods to a five or six parameter *maximum,* unless completely necessary. This will make for easier coding.

❑ Make sure that all of those parameters and methods have meaningful names. Try and spell the function out rather than keeping it short. As an example, it is not as easy to identify the name 'GetCnts' as it is to identify the name 'GetContacts'.

❑ Do not over-exert yourself by adding every conceivable method and functional enhancement that it can have; rather think ahead, but code later. You can easily complicate matters for your developers by granting them too much choice, and at the same time you may be adding functionality that may not ever be used.

❑ Try and keep objects within your component server down to a minimum. Enhanced reuse comes from keeping your servers smaller.

❑ Properties are extremely useful in a component, and enable it to be used more easily, but there is a tradeoff when it comes to efficiency as well as maintaining object instance state. (Read on for more on this issue.)

Multi-Use Objects

Windows DNA (Windows Distributed interNet Applications Architecture) allows Windows applications to work with the Web. Here the web client is an extremely valuable part of the entire architecture, and designing objects for use over the web as well as for the traditional form-based client creates all kinds of problems. The web client does not support all the features supported by your form-based client. Therefore the term 'Multi-Use' in this case means creating objects that can be used from both languages and scripts.

As an example, *events* within an object can be extremely useful from a form-based client, but ASP cannot receive these events. So building objects with events proves useless when deploying for the web. It would be better to replace callbacks and events with a method, which could be called from the client to interrogate the status of a routine. In other words, let the object handle any callbacks or events that are raised and make the result available via a property or a method on the interface. The client can interrogate the interface you expose for results.

Early binding is another feature that only works with a form-based (compiled executable) client, but cannot be implemented by scripts. The reason behind this goes all the way down to what makes an object a COM object. COM objects have to implement an interface known as IUnknown and optionally also inherit from IDispatch. These two interfaces are responsible for how the objects are used and called. When a COM object supports both IUnknown and IDispatch is it is known as having a **dual interface**. Visual Basic objects only support dual interfaces and cannot inherit from only IUnknown. The reason behind this is probably largely due to the fact that scripts can only create an instance of a class that supports IDispatch, which is known as **late binding**, and Visual Basic, to save on complexity, opted to support both. In Visual Basic you can create an instance of a class by means of early binding as well as late binding. Let's see how we implement each of these in VB now.

Early Binding

- ❏ Explicitly referencing a COM Server by selecting it in the References window. (Project | References menu item.)

- ❏ By explicitly declaring a variable (placeholder) as the appropriate type:

```
Dim MyObj as Recordset
```

- ❏ By creating an instance of the class with the New keyword or using the CreateObject function:

```
Set MyObj = New Recordset
```

Late Binding

- ❏ With no reference made to the COM Server.

- ❏ Declaring a variable (placeholder) as Object (Object is the fundamental interface for all objects).

```
Dim MyObj as Object
```

- ❏ Using the CreateObject method to create an instance of the desired class.

```
Set MyObj = CreateObject("ADODB.Recordset")
```

ASP only supports the latter – late binding – because VBScript and JavaScript are type-less. Defining a variable in VBScript is the equivalent of defining it As Object in VB. ASP instantiates objects using either the CreateObject() or the Server.CreateObject() method.

Also, scripts such as ASP do not support **typecasting,** and thus depend on the variant data type for everything. This means that passing parameters as reference to any other type than variants will not work. This plays a role in how you code your objects.

The Business Objects

In a Windows DNA environment, business objects are typically contained in COM+ component servers, or ActiveX DLLs. These can be created using any language that has the ability to create a COM+ DLL. In this chapter we'll use Visual Basic, as it's arguably the most widely used COM development language in the world.

Now we will code the component server, and examine the topics that you have to bear in mind when creating components.

Unattended Execution

You should never use message boxes or other UI functions within a DLL, which typically runs without any user interface. For this reason, make sure that Unattended Execution is checked and the Retained In Memory option is checked as well. Both can be seen on the Properties window as shown in the screenshot below. When you add a form or other user-interface objects, this setting is disabled.

When the unattended execution property is set to True, Visual Basic logs any user interface calls to the event log. Therefore the MsgBox function writes to the log and does not appear on screen. This is a necessary and important option, as you do not want anything stopping the execution of your object and its methods. Remember that a message box is modal and will not let anything else in the object occur until the message box has been dealt with.

The Retained In Memory option will cause our DLL to be retained in memory even if there are no objects currently in use. Loading a DLL into memory takes precious time, and if this operation had to happen each time a user came to our site that could be a problem. Turning on this option will help improve performance by keeping the DLL loaded in memory and ready for use.

Open Visual Basic and create a new ActiveX DLL project. Choose the Project | Properties menu option, and change the project's name to ContactObjects. Also make sure to check the Unattended Execution and Retained In Memory boxes:

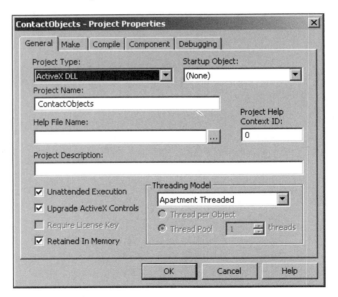

Click OK to accept these settings.

Once you've set a reference to Microsoft ActiveX Data Objects 2.7 Library in your project, we're ready to cut some code!

The ContactMain Module

In this component server, we'll end up with two class modules: `ContactList` and `Contact`. Both of these will contain code to access the database – meaning both will need a database connection string for use with ADO. This connection string is just a simple string value:

```
"Provider=SQLOLEDB.1;Password=contact;User ID=contactapp;" _
& "Initial Catalog=contact;Data Source=dbserver"
```

You may remember from Chapter 3 that the `Provider` entry specifies the type of database – in this case a SQL Server database.

The `User ID` and `Password` entries contain the database login information. By always using the same login name throughout our application, we will take full advantage of database connection pooling.

Database connections are pooled by connection string. If we need a new connection, the pooling mechanism will look for connections with the exact same connection string as ours. The more connections based on the same connection string, the more efficient the pooling will be.

The `Initial Catalog` specifies the name of the database to be used – in our case the `Contact` database.

The `Data Source` sets the database server to *dbserver* (this will need to be changed to reflect the actual server name in your environment).

There are many ways of making a connection string available to our code. It may be stored in the registry, be provided to our component via the COM+ constructor string, be stored in an INI file, or be coded directly into the component server.

For simplicity, we'll code it directly into the component server by storing it in a globally available constant. This can easily be adapted to one of the other techniques if that's more appropriate for a given environment.

In Visual Basic, choose the **Project | Add Module** menu option to add a code module. In the **Properties** window (typically on the right-hand side) change the **(Name)** property to `ContactMain`.

Add the following code:

```
Option Explicit

Public Const DB_CONN As String = "Provider=SQLOLEDB.1;Password=contact;" & _
    "User ID=contactapp;Initial Catalog=Contact;Data Source=dbserver"
```

Remember to change *dbserver* to reflect the real database server name.

The constant DB_CONN is now available throughout our component server – centralizing the management of the database connection string.

The ContactList Class

When we opened the new project, Visual Basic started us out with the default `Class1` module. Double-click on this entry in the **Project** window to bring up the code window. In the **Properties** window change the **(Name)** property to `ContactList`.

This class will be fairly simple, since we'll use it primarily to encapsulate the process of retrieving an ADO `Recordset` object and converting it to a `Variant` array. The `Variant` array containing the data will then be provided directly to the ASP code, so it can create whatever display is appropriate for the data.

The use of a `Variant` array is a nod toward the capabilities of scripting languages. Scripting languages deal with data types like a `Variant` array much faster than they do with objects such as a `Recordset`. One of the key performance tips for ASP developers is to use the `GetRows` method to convert a `Recordset` to a `Variant` array before working with the data. In our case, we'll bypass this step by simply providing a `Variant` array right up front – the ASP code will never see a `Recordset`.

The Fetch Method

In the `Contact.sql` code (available from the download), there is a `getContacts` stored procedure. This stored procedure returns all the basic contact information for all contacts in the database, and it was designed to support the `ContactList` object. The `Fetch` method will invoke that stored procedure and will return the resulting `Recordset` containing the data.

Add the following code to the module:

```
Option Explicit

Private Function Fetch() As ADODB.Recordset
    Dim cn As ADODB.Connection
    Dim cm As ADODB.Command
    Dim rs As ADODB.Recordset

    Set cn = New Connection
    cn.CursorLocation = adUseClient
    cn.Open DB_CONN

    Set cm = New Command
    With cm
        .ActiveConnection = cn
        .CommandText = "getContacts"
        .CommandType = adCmdStoredProc
        Set rs = .Execute
    End With
    Set rs.ActiveConnection = Nothing
    Set Fetch = rs

    Set rs = Nothing
    Set cm = Nothing
    cn.Close
    Set cn = Nothing
End Function
```

This code opens an ADO Connection object to gain access to the database, using the DB_CONN constant we declared earlier. It's also set to use a client-side cursor. This is important, as we want to retrieve the data from the database and provide it to the ADO code as a disconnected Recordset to minimize the impact on the database. We then create a Command object that will be used to call the stored procedure. The Command object is set to use the Connection object we just opened, and it then calls the getContacts stored procedure, returning a Recordset object containing the data. The next line is important, as it disconnects the Recordset object from the database – meaning that the Recordset can be used without tying up valuable database server resources. Then, the Fetch function is set to return the Recordset, and all the various objects are closed and de-referenced to clean up. The Fetch method is now set up to retrieve all the data returned by the getContacts stored procedure.

The GetContacts Method

Unlike the Fetch method, the GetContacts method will be Public in scope – making it available to be called from outside the class module itself. It's the GetContacts method that will be called by the ASP code when we build the user interface.

In this case, all the hard work is being done in the Fetch method, so the GetContacts method is pretty straightforward. It merely converts the Recordset into a Variant array by calling the GetRows method, and then returns the array as a result.

Add the following code:

```
Public Function GetContacts() As Variant
   GetContacts = Fetch.GetRows
End Function
```

In both the ContactList and Contact objects we will keep all the code that interacts with the database contained in Private methods. The reason for doing this is to make it as easy as possible to alter our code in the future if we need more scalability. By keeping the data access code separate from the bulk of the other code in our class modules, we make it relatively easy to move that data access code out to other objects – possibly running on an application server instead of the web server.

Though this leads to a bit more coding now, it is worth the effort since it keeps our options open in the future.

That wraps up the ContactList class. It can now be used to retrieve a Variant array with a simple method call like this:

```
Dim objContactList
Dim arData
Set objContactList = Server.CreateObject("ContactObjects.ContactList")
arData = objContactList.GetContacts
```

All the ADO code, database connection strings, and other details are nicely encapsulated within the object itself, making the ASP code very streamlined and focused on UI creation.

The Contact Class

The Contact class will be quite a bit more sophisticated than the class we just created. This class will do more than simply provide data to the UI – it will actually encapsulate business logic as well as data access.

In Visual Basic, choose the **Project | Add Class Module** menu option, and change the **(Name)** property of the new module to Contact.

Declarations

To get started, let's declare the variables and types that will be used within the class. First off, to make our code as readable as possible, let's create a couple of enumerated types to indicate the type of phone and e-mail values we're dealing with:

```
Option Explicit

Public Enum PhoneType
   HomePhone
   WorkPhone
   CellPhone
End Enum

Public Enum EMailType
   HomeEMail
   WorkEMail
End Enum
```

Each entry corresponds to a numeric value (starting with zero and counting up). Enums work much like constant values, but they have the advantage of being clearly related to each other, and they work with Visual Basic's IntelliSense technology where appropriate.

Next we'll declare a set of variables to store the contact data itself. While it is possible to keep this data in a Recordset object, it's faster and easier to work with the data if it is stored in a set of local variables within the object:

```
Private mstrID As String
Private mstrLastName As String
Private mstrFirstName As String
Private mstrAddress1 As String
Private mstrAddress2 As String
Private mstrCity As String
Private mstrState As String
Private mstrZipCode As String
Private mstrPhoneWork As String
Private mstrPhoneHome As String
Private mstrPhoneCell As String
Private mstrEMailWork As String
Private mstrEMailHome As String
```

As we'll see in the code, storing the data in local variables means that only two methods within the entire class will need to interact with ADO.

Finally we'll need some variables to keep track of our object's status. In particular we need to keep track of whether the user wants to delete our object, any data in the object has been changed, and if our object is new:

```
Private mblnIsDeleted As Boolean
Private mblnIsDirty As Boolean
Private mblnIsNew As Boolean
```

These are all the module-level variables we'll need for the class.

We'll also need a `Class_Initialize()` method:

```
Private Sub Class_Initialize()
  mblnIsNew = True
End Sub
```

Next let's build the basic set of properties that will allow client code to view or change the data for a contact.

Basic Properties

Visual Basic allows us to expose properties to client code through the use of `Get` methods. We can also allow the client code to change property values by implementing `Let` methods. Of course, neither of these methods needs to actually allow direct access to a private attribute value – we write code to control the access.

For instance, the `ID` attribute is read-only, since it reflects the primary key for the contact in the database. Therefore, we'll implement only a `Get` method. Add the following code:

```
Public Property Get ID() As String
  ID = mstrID
End Property
```

The `LastName` property will be read/write, so it will have both a `Get` and `Let` property. Add the following code:

```
Public Property Get LastName() As String
  LastName = mstrLastName
End Property

Public Property Let LastName(ByVal Value As String)

  If Len(Value) <= 50 Then
    mstrLastName = Value
  Else
    Err.Raise vbObjectError + 1001, , "String too long"
  End If
  mblnIsDirty = True

End Property
```

The `Let` accessor is a bit more complex, since this is a primary location for the enforcement of business rules. In this case, we're simply checking to make sure that the new value doesn't exceed the maximum length of 50 characters. However, we could implement more complex business logic and validation code here if needed.

Also note that we set the `mblnIsDirty` variable to `True` if the value is changed. This variable is used to identify whether the object's internal data has been changed.

The property routines for the remainder of the basic contact information are very similar:

```
Public Property Get FirstName() As String
  FirstName = mstrFirstName
End Property

Public Property Let FirstName(ByVal Value As String)

  If Len(Value) <= 50 Then
    mstrFirstName = Value
  Else
    Err.Raise vbObjectError + 1001, , "String too long"
  End If
  mblnIsDirty = True

End Property

Public Property Get Address1() As String
  Address1 = mstrAddress1
End Property

Public Property Let Address1(ByVal Value As String)

  If Len(Value) <= 50 Then
    mstrAddress1 = Value
  Else
    Err.Raise vbObjectError + 1001, , "String too long"
  End If
  mblnIsDirty = True

End Property

Public Property Get Address2() As String
  Address2 = mstrAddress2
End Property

Public Property Let Address2(ByVal Value As String)

  If Len(Value) <= 50 Then
    mstrAddress2 = Value
  Else
    Err.Raise vbObjectError + 1001, , "String too long"
  End If
  mblnIsDirty = True

End Property
```

```
Public Property Get City() As String
  City = mstrCity
End Property

Public Property Let City(ByVal Value As String)

  If Len(Value) <= 30 Then
    mstrCity = Value
  Else
    Err.Raise vbObjectError + 1001, , "String too long"
  End If
  mblnIsDirty = True

End Property

Public Property Get State() As String
  State = mstrState
End Property

Public Property Let State(ByVal Value As String)

  If Len(Value) <= 20 Then
    mstrState = Value
  Else
    Err.Raise vbObjectError + 1001, , "String too long"
  End If
  mblnIsDirty = True

End Property

Public Property Get ZipCode() As String
  ZipCode = mstrZipCode
End Property

Public Property Let ZipCode(ByVal Value As String)

  If Len(Value) <= 20 Then
    mstrZipCode = Value
  Else
    Err.Raise vbObjectError + 1001, , "String too long"
  End If
  mblnIsDirty = True

End Property
```

The basic properties for this class are fairly simplistic, but it should be pretty obvious that we could implement substantially more complex logic as needed. The advantage to this is that the logic is encapsulated in an object that will be compiled into a COM component. The resulting component can be used across many different ASP pages, as well as by other possible clients of our application, such as Microsoft Office applications.

The Phone and EMail Properties

The Phone and EMail properties are a bit different from the properties we've seen so far. This is because our Contact object will allow the user to provide a number of different phone numbers and e-mail addresses.

The type of property we'll use in this case is called a **named property**. A named property has more than one value – each value being differentiated by a parameter value. A named property is essentially an array of property values.

Add the following code to implement the Get property for the phone numbers:

```
Public Property Get Phone(ByVal PhoneType As PhoneType) As String

  If PhoneType = WorkPhone Then
    Phone = mstrPhoneWork
  ElseIf PhoneType = HomePhone Then
    Phone = mstrPhoneHome
  ElseIf PhoneType = CellPhone Then
    Phone = mstrPhoneCell
  Else
    Phone = ""
  End If

End Property
```

Notice that the method accepts a parameter. This parameter is used to determine which phone number is to be returned – based on the PhoneType enumerated value. To call this property we'd use code similar to the following:

```
Debug.Print objContact.Phone(WorkPhone)
```

Note that we will not have Debug.Print statements in our real code: this just illustrates how the property would be called.

The Let accessor is similar, in that it also uses the PhoneType enumerated type to determine which phone number to update. Enter the following code:

```
Public Property Let Phone(ByVal PhoneType As PhoneType, _
                   ByVal Value As String)

  If Len(Value) > 20 Then
    Err.Raise vbObjectError + 1001, , "String too long"
  Else
    If PhoneType = WorkPhone Then
      mstrPhoneWork = Value
    ElseIf PhoneType = HomePhone Then
      mstrPhoneHome = Value
    ElseIf PhoneType = CellPhone Then
      mstrPhoneCell = Value
    End If
```

```
      mblnIsDirty = True
   End If

End Property
```

Before the object's internal variable is updated, the business rules are checked – in this case to make sure that we don't exceed the maximum length.

When we raise an error we're using the vbObjectError *constant. This constant is provided for our convenience to ensure that the error numbers raised by our program don't conflict with those raised by Microsoft-supplied components. Any error numbers raised by our VB code should start at* vbObjectError *+ 513, as* vbObjectError *reserves error numbers from its own offset to offset + 512, and climb from there.*

The methods to handle the e-mail addresses work in the same manner. Enter the following code:

```
Public Property Get EMail(ByVal EMailType As EMailType) As String

   If EMailType = WorkEMail Then
      EMail = mstrEMailWork
   ElseIf EMailType = HomeEMail Then
      EMail = mstrEMailHome
   Else
      EMail = ""
   End If

End Property
```

```
Public Property Let EMail(ByVal EMailType As EMailType, _
                          ByVal Value As String)

   If Len(Value) > 100 Then
      Err.Raise vbObjectError + 1001, , "String too long"
   Else
      If EMailType = WorkEMail Then
         mstrEMailWork = Value
      ElseIf EMailType = HomeEMail Then
         mstrEMailHome = Value
      End If
      mblnIsDirty = True
   End If

End Property
```

At this point we've added properties to handle all the basic contact data, as well as the phone and e-mail addresses. Of course our object isn't set up to interact with the database yet. Let's add code to retrieve data first.

Retrieving Data

Following the practice of keeping the data access code isolated from the rest of the class – including the public interface used to request data from the database – we'll first implement a `Fetch` method that contains all the code needed to read our data.

The `Fetch` method will make use of a stored procedure, `getContact` (in `Contact.sql`), as shown below:

```
CREATE PROCEDURE getContact @id uniqueidentifier
AS
SELECT * FROM Contact WHERE ID = @id;
SELECT * FROM Phone WHERE ContactID= @id;
SELECT * FROM EMail WHERE ContactID= @id
RETURN
```

This stored procedure is interesting in that it returns three data sets as a result – the basic contact data, the phone numbers, and the e-mail addresses. Fortunately, ADO supports this concept, making it quite easy to work with this set of results.

Enter the following code:

```
Private Sub Fetch(ByVal ID As String)

  Dim objCN As ADODB.Connection
  Dim objCM As ADODB.Command
  Dim objRS As ADODB.Recordset

  Set objCN = New Connection
  objCN.Open DB_CONN

  Set objCM = New Command
  With objCM
    .ActiveConnection = objCN
    .CommandText = "getContact"
    .CommandType = adCmdStoredProc
    .Parameters.Append .CreateParameter("id", adGUID, _
                       adParamInput, -1, ID)
    Set objRS = .Execute
  End With

  With objRS
    mstrID = objRS("ID")
    mstrLastName = objRS("LastName")
    mstrFirstName = objRS("FirstName")
    mstrAddress1 = objRS("Address1")
    mstrAddress2 = objRS("Address2")
    mstrCity = objRS("City")
    mstrState = objRS("State")
    mstrZipCode = objRS("ZipCode")
  End With
```

```
Set objRS = objRS.NextRecordset
With objRS
  Do While Not .EOF
    If objRS("PhoneType") = PhoneType.WorkPhone Then
        mstrPhoneWork = objRS("Phone")
    ElseIf objRS("PhoneType") = PhoneType.HomePhone Then
        mstrPhoneHome = objRS("Phone")
    ElseIf objRS("PhoneType") = PhoneType.CellPhone Then
        mstrPhoneCell = objRS("Phone")
    End If
    .MoveNext
  Loop
End With

Set objRS = objRS.NextRecordset
With objRS
  Do While Not .EOF
    If objRS("EMailType") = EMailType.WorkEMail Then
      mstrEMailWork = objRS("EMail")
    ElseIf objRS("EMailType") = EMailType.HomeEMail Then
      mstrEMailHome = objRS("EMail")
    End If
      .MoveNext
  Loop
End With

Set objRS = Nothing
Set objCM = Nothing
objCN.Close
Set objCN = Nothing

mblnIsNew = False
mblnIsDeleted = False
mblnIsDirty = False

End Sub
```

This routine opens a Connection object to the database. That connection is then used when running a Command object to execute the getContact stored procedure:

```
Set objCM = New Command
With objCM
  .ActiveConnection = objCN
  .CommandText = "getContact"
  .CommandType = adCmdStoredProc
  .Parameters.Append .CreateParameter("id", adGUID, _
                      adParamInput, -1, ID)
  Set objRS = .Execute
End With
```

This stored procedure accepts a single parameter – the primary key value of the contact to be retrieved. This is provided to the stored procedure via the `Parameters` collection of the `Command` object. The `CreateParameter` method creates the parameter, setting the value to the `Fetch` method's parameter – `ID`. As we'll see shortly, the `Fetch` method is called from the `Load` method. The client code is expected to have already retrieved the contact's unique `ID` number – presumably through the use of the `ContactList` object.

Once the procedure has been executed we'll have a `Recordset` object that contains three data sets. ADO handles this by having the `Recordset` object start out by reflecting the first data set returned – in this case, the data from the `Contact` table. Later, we'll use the `NextRecordset` method to move through the remaining data sets.

For now we can use the data from the `Contact` table to load our object's variables:

```
With objRS
  mstrID = objRS("ID")
  mstrLastName = objRS("LastName")
  mstrFirstName = objRS("FirstName")
  mstrAddress1 = objRS("Address1")
  mstrAddress2 = objRS("Address2")
  mstrCity = objRS("City")
  mstrState = objRS("State")
  mstrZipCode = objRS("ZipCode")
End With
```

With that done, we're ready to move on to the `Phone` table's data. This is as simple as calling the `NextRecordset` method of the `Recordset` object. This method can be used to set either a new `Recordset` variable, or the one we already have. Since we no longer need the `Contact` table's data, we can simply reuse the same variable:

```
Set objRS = objRS.NextRecordset
With objRS
  Do While Not .EOF
    If objRS("PhoneType") = PhoneType.WorkPhone Then
      mstrPhoneWork = objRS("Phone")
    ElseIf objRS("PhoneType") = PhoneType.HomePhone Then
      mstrPhoneHome = objRS("Phone")
    ElseIf objRS("PhoneType") = PhoneType.CellPhone Then
      mstrPhoneCell = objRS("Phone")
    End If
    .MoveNext
  Loop
End With
```

From there, we simply work with the `Recordset` object, which now reflects the data from the `Phone` table. The process is repeated to get the `EMail` table's data.

The `Fetch` method is `Private` in scope. To allow our object's client code to request that a contact be retrieved from the database, we'll need to add a `Public` method – `Load`. Enter the following code:

```
Public Sub Load(ByVal ID As String)
  Fetch ID
End Sub
```

This simple method accepts the ID value from the client code, and uses it to call the Fetch method we built earlier. That Fetch method retrieves the data from the database and places it in our object's local variables for use by the rest of our object's code.

At this point, we've built routines to retrieve the data for the contact that's required to set up the object's internal variables. Now our object's client code can view, print, or edit the data as needed. Next the object needs to be able to store those changed values into the database.

Adding and Updating Data

Adding a contact to the database is handled through the addContact stored procedure, while updating the data is handled via the updateContact procedure. (Look at the Contact.sql in the code download if you would like to view this code.)

With the exception of the ID parameter (the first one), the parameter lists of each stored procedure are identical. This makes it very easy to write the code for an Update method in the class, since we can reuse most of the code that sets up the call to each stored procedure.

To keep our object's functionality as simple as possible, the Update method will also take care of deleting the object. We'll know if the object is to be deleted because the mblnIsDeleted variable will be set to True. We'll cover the code to manage this flag shortly.

For now, enter the following code to create the Update method itself:

```
Private Sub Update()

  Dim objCN As ADODB.Connection
  Dim objCM As ADODB.Command

  Set objCN = New Connection
  objCN.Open DB_CONN

  Set objCM = New Command
  With objCM
    .ActiveConnection = objCN
    .CommandType = adCmdStoredProc
  End With

  If mblnIsDeleted Then
    With objCM
      .CommandText = "deleteContact"
      .Parameters.Append .CreateParameter("id", adGUID, adParamInput, _
                                          4, mstrID)
      .Execute
    End With
    mblnIsNew = True
  Else
    If mblnIsNew Then
```

```
            With objCM
              .CommandText = "addContact"
              .Parameters.Append .CreateParameter("@id", adGUID, _
                                                  adParamOutput)
          End With
        Else
          With objCM
            .CommandText = "updateContact"
            .Parameters.Append .CreateParameter("@id", adGUID, _
                                                adParamInput, 4, mstrID)
          End With
        End If
        With objCM
          .Parameters.Append .CreateParameter("@lname", adVarChar, _
                                              adParamInput, 50, mstrLastName)
          .Parameters.Append .CreateParameter("@fname", adVarChar, _
                                              adParamInput, 50, mstrFirstName)
          .Parameters.Append .CreateParameter("@add1", adVarChar, _
                                              adParamInput, 50, mstrAddress1)
          .Parameters.Append .CreateParameter("@add2", adVarChar, _
                                              adParamInput, 50, mstrAddress2)
          .Parameters.Append .CreateParameter("@city", adVarChar, _
                                              adParamInput, 30, mstrCity)
          .Parameters.Append .CreateParameter("@state", adVarChar, _
                                              adParamInput, 20, mstrState)
          .Parameters.Append .CreateParameter("@zip", adVarChar, _
                                              adParamInput, 20, mstrZipCode)
          .Parameters.Append .CreateParameter("@phome", adVarChar, _
                                              adParamInput, 30, mstrPhoneHome)
          .Parameters.Append .CreateParameter("@pwork", adVarChar, _
                                              adParamInput, 30, mstrPhoneWork)
          .Parameters.Append .CreateParameter("@pcell", adVarChar, _
                                              adParamInput, 30, mstrPhoneCell)
          .Parameters.Append .CreateParameter("@emhome", adVarChar, _
                                              adParamInput, 100, mstrEMailHome)
          .Parameters.Append .CreateParameter("@emwork", adVarChar, _
                                              adParamInput, 100, mstrEMailWork)
          .Execute
          Set .ActiveConnection = Nothing
          If mblnIsNew Then
            mstrID = objCM.Parameters("@id").Value
            mblnIsNew = False
          End If
        End With
      End If

      Set objCM = Nothing
      Set objCN = Nothing
      mblnIsDeleted = False
      mblnIsDirty = False

  End Sub
```

As with our other database methods, this routine opens a `Connection` object to access the database, and then uses it to initialize a `Command` object. In this case, we'll choose the particular stored procedure to invoke, based on the state of the object. To begin with, if the `mblnIsDeleted` variable is `True` then the object is to be deleted, so we'll call the `deleteContact` procedure:

```
If mblnIsDeleted Then
   With objCM
      .CommandText = "deleteContact"
      .Parameters.Append .CreateParameter("id", adGUID, adParamInput, _
                                          4, mstrID)
      .Execute
   End With
   mblnIsNew = True
```

If, on the other hand, the object is not marked for deletion then it will either be a new object that we're adding, or an existing object that needs to be updated. The `mblnIsNew` variable designates whether the object is new. If this value is `True` then the `addContact` procedure will be called:

```
If mblnIsNew Then
   With objCM
      .CommandText = "addContact"
      .Parameters.Append .CreateParameter("@id", adGUID, _
                                          adParamOutput)
   End With
```

If the object isn't marked as new then the `updateContact` procedure will be called:

```
With objCM
   .CommandText = "updateContact"
   .Parameters.Append .CreateParameter("@id", adGUID, _
                                       adParamInput, 4, mstrID)
End With
```

Again, the first `Parameter` object is created, though this time it is marked as an input parameter – it is being passed from our VB code into the procedure.

Once the stored procedure and first parameter have been set up, the code to call either stored procedure is identical. In both cases we simply set up all the remaining parameters and call the `Command` object's `Execute` method:

```
.Execute
Set .ActiveConnection = Nothing
If mblnIsNew Then
   mstrID = objCM.Parameters("@id").Value
   mblnIsNew = False
End If
```

Once the `Execute` method has been called, the `Command` object is disconnected from the database by setting the `ActiveConnection` property to `Nothing`. If the object was marked as being new, we get the new primary key value from the `@id` parameter, and mark the object as no longer being new. After all, now that it's stored in the database it is no longer new.

Note that the `ActiveConnection` *property* **must** *be set to* `Nothing` *before the* `@id` *parameter value can be retrieved. This is because the stored procedure doesn't return a* `Recordset` *object as a result and this step is required to force ADO to update the local values. This behavior doesn't occur with client-side cursors, but is the case with server-side cursors like this one.*

To wrap things up we set a couple of variables:

```
mblnIsDeleted = False
mblnIsDirty = False
```

Since we've now updated the database, the data we have in the object is no longer considered marked for deletion. Likewise, since we now know that the data in our object exactly matches the database (since we just updated it), the data is no longer considered to be dirty, so the `mblnIsDirty` flag can be set to `False`.

The `Update` method is `Private` in scope. To allow client code to request that the `Contact` object be saved, we'll add a `Public` method called `Save`:

```
Public Sub Save()

  If Not mblnIsDeleted Then
    If Len(mstrLastName) = 0 Then
      Err.Raise vbObjectError + 1002, , "Last name required"
    End If
    If Len(mstrFirstName) = 0 Then
      Err.Raise vbObjectError + 1003, , "First name required"
    End If
    If Len(mstrCity) = 0 Then
      Err.Raise vbObjectError + 1004, , "City required"
    End If
    If Len(mstrState) = 0 Then
      Err.Raise vbObjectError + 1005, , "State required"
    End If
  End If

  If mblnIsDirty Then Update

End Sub
```

This method is interesting. It first checks some business rules – in this case to make sure some required fields are filled in. The `Save` method is the final checkpoint before the database is updated, so it's an ideal location for this type of validation.

Assuming the business rules are met, the database can be updated. The `Update` method itself is only called if the data in the `Contact` object has been changed – a condition marked by the `mblnIsDirty` variable being set to `True`.

Deleting Data

The `Contact` object is marked for deletion by setting the `mblnIsDeleted` variable to `True`. This is handled by the `Delete` method. Enter the following code:

```
Public Sub Delete()

  mblnIsDirty = True
  mblnIsDeleted = True
  Save

End Sub
```

To keep the object's behavior simple, this method not only sets the flag to mark the object as deleted, but it also calls the `Save` method to cause an immediate database update.

Since we know that a primary client of the `Contact` object will be ASP pages, it would also be nice to allow a client to directly remove a contact from the database without first having to load the `Contact` object. This makes sense for performance – it's a waste to load the data from the database if all we're going to do is turn around and delete it.

Enter the following `DeleteContact` method to support this functionality:

```
Public Sub DeleteContact(ByVal ID As String)

  mstrID = ID
  Delete

End Sub
```

Instead of marking an already loaded `Contact` object for deletion, this method accepts the primary key value as a parameter, sets it into the object's internal state, and then calls the `Delete` method. This will cause the specified contact to be removed cleanly and simply.

Building the Component Server

At this point our `ContactList` and `Contact` objects are complete. However, before we can use them we need to compile the ActiveX DLL, by choosing File | Make ContactObjects.dll and confirming the path in the subsequent dialog. We can't build the component server straight away – there are a few settings that we will want to discuss and then set.

Compiling a COM+ Object Under VB

When compiling a Visual Basic project that uses COM+ services and/or runs on a server, or indeed, only runs locally, you should be aware of the property options available to you. Some are self-explanatory, others you can find more on from MSDN or from other resources. Earlier in this chapter, we explained what Unattended Execution and Retained in Memory settings mean to our components. In the following sections we will be discussing the following main Project | Properties options:

❑ Compatibility Issues

❑ Threading Model

❑ Base Address

Compatibility Issues

Since OOP, COM, and all related technologies aim for reusability, scalability, and performance, it is very important to maintain **compatibility**. Compatibility is important for deployment, and it is not always necessarily done successfully on your behalf. When you deploy an application and later want to enhance a feature, COM+ components are meant to make that process easier by allowing you to simply change a DLL and 'upgrade' your existing installation by only supplying the new DLL.

This is all fine, provided that the existing application can see your new DLL, and can use it successfully. When you compile an EXE that references a DLL, the EXE is bound to the interfaces of the DLL. Changes to the DLL's interfaces, or more importantly the GUIDs that represent them, will result in errors from the EXE. Compatibility will then be broken.

COM+ objects consist of interfaces that are defined in IDL. Within the declaration language, each interface and method is assigned a valid GUID, a CLSID (class identifier) and IID (interface identifier). The type library also has a GUID associated with it known as LIBID.

The assignments of those IDs are for the purpose of distinguishing the interfaces from one another and to provide uniqueness where textual naming cannot. When your component server is compiled, the type library that has been generated for it is compiled into the DLL as well, thus embedding these GUIDs. Any changes to this type library will make your component server incompatible with previous compilations of it. The trick is to make sure that the interfaces of the DLL do not change.

Visual Basic does provide some assistance by providing you with the Compatibility settings in the Options dialog. Visual Basic offers three types of settings for the purpose of remaining compatible between builds. These settings are used when VB negotiates the IDL declarations for you:

❑ No Compatibility – Visual Basic will recompile the type library and will not care about the GUIDs involved, thus generating new GUIDs for the LIBID or CLSID as well as IIDs.

❑ Project Compatibility – for when you are designing your application and have not yet compiled or released it. Visual Basic will then preserve the LIBID and CLSIDs but will not reserve the IIDs, as it generated new GUIDs for them.

❑ Binary Compatibility – a little closer to the aim of making DLLs compatible with previous builds. Setting this option will inform VB that you wish to keep compatibility for your DLL against a particular interface. When you set the option, you must also specify with which DLL you wish to be compatible. Usually this is a copy of the DLL you have just compiled. VB will then make sure that builds have the same LIBID, CLSID, and IIDs.

We will concentrate on binary compatibility, as it is the most relevant to our concerns.

As mentioned above, when the binary compatibility option is set, Visual Basic makes sure that all GUIDs are the same as the type library it has been made to try and be compatible with. What happens though if you had to change a method name, parameter, or even add something new?

If you do change anything in the declarations, that is the Get, Let, Set, Sub, or Function lines or any user-defined types, VB will be forced to break compatibility as the interface is no longer the same as the interface it is trying to be compatible with. When this occurs Visual Basic prompts you with a form asking for permission to do one or the other actions. It is strongly recommended however that you never get this far. Maintaining compatibility is important for versioning, upgrading, and keeping older systems in good working order.

In conclusion, be aware of these issues and always try to avoid changing an interface once it has been released into the world. Saying that, there are ways to improve the compatibility situation, which involve implementing interfaces and perhaps even building your interfaces in IDL rather than just with VB. These should always be considered, depending on the type of components that you are developing.

Now that we have discussed compatibility, we can come back to the setting in the dialog. In the Project | Properties window, click on the Component tab. Change the Version Compatibility setting to Binary Compatibility. Then click on the ellipsis (...) button to bring up a file dialog.

Click on the ContactObjects.dll file, press *Ctrl-C* and *Ctrl-V*. This will make a copy of the DLL in the same directory as the original. Click on the copy, click Open, and then OK:

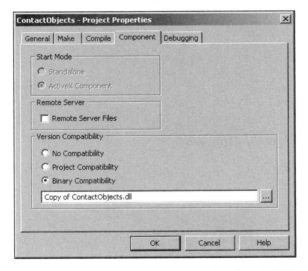

I generally prefer to set compatibility to a copy of the DLL rather than the DLL itself as firstly, this is recommended by Microsoft themselves, but also because it protects us from 'accidental' changes to the component, in that we'll be constantly reminded that we've broken an interface until we take the extra step of updating the copy of the DLL with any updated version.

The Threading Model

Understanding this section depends on the concepts of:

❑ A **process** (to keep it simple), which is a combination of data and code.

❑ An **apartment**, which is where instances of classes (objects) are created.

❑ A **thread**, which is a block of code to be executed.

These terms are all low level abstractions and are not physical elements, but an analogy to a building could be beneficial. The building is the Process; the Apartments are the apartments within the building, which are of different types just like in the physical world where a penthouse is different to, say, a one bed apartment on the first floor.

As discussed in Chapter 8, there are two different **threading models** supported by Visual Basic, namely single threaded and apartment threaded. Refer back to that chapter for a full discussion of these concepts if you wish.

Base Address

Too many developers ignore the **base address** on their components, much to their own downfall. Managing the base address of your component is a good thing and doesn't require much effort on your part. The following screenshot shows the Visual Basic Project I Properties window with the DLL Base Address at its default value:

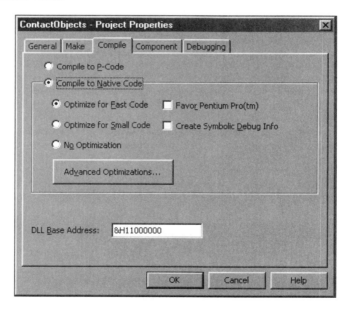

Firstly, the base address is simply the address where your component is loaded into memory. This becomes a potential issue when one or more components are already in memory when your component is loaded. If another active component is already occupying the address your component requires, the operating system must dynamically change the address into which it your component loads. This process, known as **rebasing**, will increase the load time slightly, and it becomes possible that your component's code could then be loaded more than once, unnecessarily consuming resources.

> **If the DLL Base Address value is &H11000000 as in the above figure, then it is still at the default, and it may be worth altering the value.**

You can never be certain of avoiding rebasing as you can't know at compile time what other components may already be on a particular system, it is possible to at least make sure that all of your own components do not fall over each other.

A great many developers compile without changing the base address, so many components out there are configured to load at the default address of &H11000000. Note that when you change this value, the new value must lie in the address range &10000000 to &80000000 (16,777,216 or 16 Mb to 2,147,483,648 or 2 Gb) and be a multiple of 64k (65536). For example, good values are &H10000000, &H10100000, &H10200000, and so on.

The way to get the base address of your next component is to add the size of your DLL or OCX to the base address of that component and round that number to the nearest multiple of 64k (65536). It is good practice to keep track of your components and their base addresses in a database or specification document.

Things to Watch For

When we use COM+ objects within a Windows DNA application, there are a few issues that we need to be aware of. Some of these, if ignored, can cause serious problems with our applications – fortunately most are easily dealt with once understood.

Though there are many factors that go into building a successful application based on COM objects, there are some common areas of concern. These fall into three main areas – **usability**, **performance/scalability** and **maintainability**.

Object and Component Usability

COM+ is a very powerful technology. While COM+ components are the building blocks to the Windows DNA architecture, they extend into other types of applications as well. Because of this, they provide some capabilities that don't fit well (or at all) into the Windows DNA environment.

Multiple interfaces

COM objects can be accessed in two main ways – via IDispatch (late binding) or via a v-table (early binding). IDispatch is a general technique for accessing COM objects by which the calling code asks the object a series of questions to determine whether it has a specific method, how to call that method, and finally to actually invoke that method. It is powerful in that it allows the calling code to know very little about the object with which it is interacting. It is also the technique used by scripting languages such as VBScript and JavaScript – hence it's critical to ASP programmers.

> **To be used from ASP, an object *must* implement an IDispatch interface. All objects built in Visual Basic implement this interface.**

The problem with IDispatch is that it is quite slow, and doesn't provide access to all the features provided by COM+. Most objects implement a v-table interface, which allows calling code to directly call the methods exposed through the object's interface.

Even more powerful is the ability of an object to expose more than one interface. This allows us to create, say, a SalesOrder object, and have that object also expose a more generic IDocument interface. If our Invoice objects also expose the IDocument interface, we can write code that treats both types of object just as generic documents:

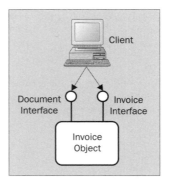

This capability is not available to ASP coders – so it's very important that our COM objects always provide any needed functionality via the default IDispatch interface.

In Visual Basic the default IDispatch interface is composed of all properties and methods that are declared with Public scope in our class module.

There are two solutions to allow ASP developers to use objects with multiple interfaces:

❑ The easiest is to simply add all the methods and properties from any secondary interfaces to the object's main interface. This is not always good object design, since the object's main interface can become quite large and complex, but it does make the object very easy to work with from an ASP perspective.

❑ The second approach is to create a set of façade objects that expose the alternate interfaces as their native interface. The only code behind each method in such an object will be code that delegates the method call to the actual business object – using the appropriate interface on that object:

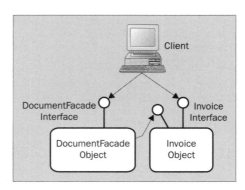

Now our client code can interact with the Invoice object through its regular interface, or if we need the Document interface, it can interact with a DocumentFacade object. The DocumentFacade object merely relays each method call to the same method on the Invoice object's Document interface.

This second approach is more complex, but is particularly useful when dealing with pre-existing objects that already implement multiple interfaces.

Events

A COM+ object can raise events to the code that holds a reference to the object. This is handled through a type of callback mechanism, so when the object raises the event a method is called within the original code:

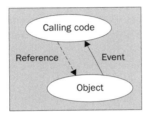

The exception is error events, since they are handled via HRESULT, not via COM+ callbacks.

This technology originated with ActiveX controls, since controls are constantly raising events into the dialog in which they are contained. Subsequently it has been extended throughout COM, so it works between objects and most calling code.

However, it is not a universal capability. In particular, this capability is useless for scripting languages such as those available within ASP pages.

> **This means that, while a COM+ object can raise an event, code in an ASP page can't receive it.**

This is an important usability concern as we design our objects. While raising events is a powerful and useful technique, we need to provide alternate means for the script coder to get the functionality if our objects will be used by scripting languages. In short, if our object will be used by scripting languages, avoid the use of events.

Parameter Data Types

COM+ objects support many data types – some quite complex. Scripting languages, on the other hand, are typeless – only supporting the concept of a Variant.

The Variant 'data type' is powerful, since it can hold many different types of data:

Byte	Date
Integer	String
Long	Boolean
Single	Empty
Double	Null
Currency	Object
Decimal	Nothing

Notice the `Object` entry in the list. A variable of type `Variant` (such as all those in a scripting language) can hold a reference to an object. The unfortunate thing is that this is a reference to the object's default `IDispatch` interface rather than any specific interface.

Performance/Scalability

Performance and scalability are two different, though closely related, concepts. Performance is typically viewed as the speed of an application for one user. Scalability is what happens to performance as we add more load to the system – typically by adding more simultaneous users.

In many cases, things that increase performance will increase scalability. This is not always the case however, so it's worth considering the larger ramifications of any change made to increase performance.

The two main areas of concern when using business objects in a Windows DNA application affect both scalability and performance.

Using COM+ Objects in ASP

ASP makes it very easy to interact with COM+ objects. We can simply create an object and begin working with it with very little code:

```
<%
  Dim objObject
  Set objObject = Server.CreateObject("MyDLL.MyClass")
  objObject.DoSomething
  Set objObject = Nothing
%>
```

What isn't obvious from this code is that there is a performance issue lurking under the surface. COM allows us to interact with objects in various ways – some more efficient, others more flexible.

ASP uses a technique known as **late binding** to interact with COM+ objects. This is the most flexible approach, allowing languages (such as VBScript and JavaScript) that have no formal concept of data types to interact with objects. Unfortunately, it is also the slowest mechanism available for communicating with objects.

Late binding is handled via the `IDispatch` COM interface implemented by many objects. Not all COM+ objects implement this interface – and those that don't are unavailable for use by ASP. However, most COM+ objects for Windows DNA applications are written using Visual Basic, which always provides the `IDispatch` interface for our use.

What this means to us is that we need to design our business objects with efficient, easily used interfaces. The fewer properties and methods called by ASP code, the faster our application will run.

This is one major benefit of handling data access within a COM+ object rather than directly from ASP. ASP communicates with ADO `Recordset` objects via late binding as well, while C++ and Visual Basic use the very fast v-table binding approach – thus often providing substantial performance benefits over ASP.

Direct Access or COM+ App – Performance versus Reliability

Another important issue is the question of whether to run our business objects in the same process as ASP, or to have the objects run in their own process.

Code running within a single process tends to be quite fast. All method and property calls, though late-bound, happen within the same memory and context – making them pretty efficient:

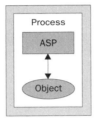

If our objects are running in their own process, separate from ASP, then things get a bit more complex. In order to ensure safe and proper interaction between the code in two processes, COM+ steps in the middle and provides a set of services for us. On the upside, this makes communicating between processes very easy, but the downside is that the extra processing tends to slow things down.

The performance hit means that it is at least 60 times slower to go across processes as opposed to working within the same process. For a single method call this doesn't matter much, but if our ASP code is making dozens of property and method calls to our objects, this can become a serious issue for performance.

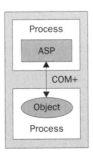

However, there are a couple of benefits to running our objects in their own process that may offset the performance impact. By running the objects in their own process, we may increase the overall stability of our application. Additionally, if the objects are running in a COM+ application, we will gain some important management capabilities.

Our application's overall stability may be improved by running the business objects in a separate process from ASP. The primary scenario where this comes into play is if our objects are unstable and crash. When they crash they'll bring down the process in which they are running. By being in a separate process from ASP, we can avoid crashing the ASP process itself – minimizing the impact.

In reality, most COM+ business objects tend to be quite stable. It's relatively unlikely that such objects will destabilize our process – especially if we apply some decent testing to the components before running them live on the server. Additionally, if our application makes heavy use of business objects (which it should), then there would still be substantial impact on users were our objects to crash – regardless of whether they are in the ASP process or a separate process.

The management benefits are more tangible. If our COM components are running in the same process as ASP, the only way to update them is to restart the entire IIS process. This is because IIS loads the DLL into memory and never releases it – increasing performance, but making it very difficult to update the site with changes.

If we choose to run our DLL in some other process (using COM+ applications or other techniques), we can leave IIS running and just restart the process hosting our DLL when we need to apply an update.

In the end, running our component in the ASP process is *much* faster, but has potential stability and management drawbacks. Running our component outside of ASP increases stability and management, but the price tag comes in the form of slightly slower performance.

Maintainability

One of the major goals behind the use of objects is to increase the maintainability of our applications. It sounds nice – encapsulate business data and logic in objects, then use those objects from any user interface as needed, reusing the logic over and over.

And, with care, use of objects can dramatically increase the maintainability of our applications. Unfortunately, there are some key areas where many object-based projects fall short, leading to serious maintenance problems over time. As we said earlier, the most common mistake is to blur the line between the user interface logic and business logic.

Another challenging area is deciding what logic to put in objects and what logic to put into the database, using stored procedures and triggers. Let's cover the use of stored procedures and triggers first.

Stored procedures are perhaps the easiest topic to cover. Stored procedures allow us to write part of our application's logic directly within the database itself.

This is powerful, since we can set up our database security so that users *must* use our stored procedures to interact with the data. Essentially we can ensure that there's no way to bypass our logic and interact directly with the data. On the surface this seems like the perfect place to put all our business logic – centralized and inescapable.

There are a couple of drawbacks, however. First, this means we'd be writing our business logic in SQL rather than in a conventional programming language. As compared to Visual C++ or Visual Basic, SQL and its related debugging environments are pretty primitive and limiting.

Heavy use of PL-SQL in Oracle or Transact-SQL for SQL Server will limit portability of our application as well. Given the continual mergers and acquisitions in business today, we can't assume our application will always use the same database forever.

Perhaps more importantly, putting logic in the database means that we can't find out if any business rules or validation rules have been broken until we are physically trying to store the data. This means we can't tell the user if they've entered good data until long after they've clicked the **Save** button. This is kind of the ultimate in terms of providing the user with a batch-oriented experience.

Finally, if we put business logic into the database when we're constructing an application based around business objects, there will be substantial complexity introduced – leading to complicated design and maintenance difficulties.

The primary reason for putting business logic (not data manipulation, but *business* logic) in stored procedures is to centralize all the business logic to control and protect both it and the data. The primary reason for using business objects is exactly the same! Having two tiers in our architecture with the exact same goal is problematic.

How do we decide which logic goes where? By moving any logic out of the database we've negated the benefit of totally protecting our data, so then why put *any* logic there? The reason is performance.

Stored procedures can utilize services within the database to interact with data much faster than our business objects can. Using stored procedures to retrieve data – especially when joins are involved, and to insert or update data, will often improve an application's performance substantially.

Rather than moving *business logic* into stored procedures, we should look at stored procedures as places to store *data logic*. Data logic is entirely concerned with highly efficient access to data for retrieval or update:

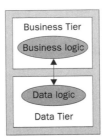

This is exactly where stored procedures shine – increasing our application's performance while retaining the clarity of our architecture.

Designing for COM+ Services

This next section will deal with some issues specifically surrounding COM+. Other COM+ services, such as making your component transactional, will be described later, in Chapter 10. COM+, as described again and again, is in essence the encapsulation of COM and MTS (Microsoft Transaction Server) with extended services such as security.

If you are familiar with coding for MTS, you will remember a reference to a DLL named `mtxas.dll` that had to be made with each and every MTS project. The file might have changed but the principle is the same. This time, the COM Services DLL (`comsvcs.dll`) is responsible for COM+ functionality. The following diagram shows the file in the `References` window.

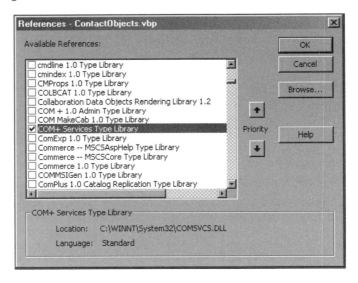

As opposed to the relatively simple model of the MTS version, the COM+ Services model is packed with COM+ niceties. The COM+ services DLL is by default provided by all the Windows 2000 and XP operating systems, so with one installed you will have no problem in referencing it from VB. Once referenced, you can gain a peek at its contents by viewing the type library information in your **Object Browser**.

Supporting Transactions

Components may link to a database of some form or another and when doing so, risk the chance of being affected by an inadequate database design. A good design involves a great number of variables that can be discussed in volumes of books, so it would be foolish to think that it could be conveyed in its entirety here, although we can mention some factors that may be useful. As an example, querying data on primary keys or indexes and using stored procedures are all important to help speed up queries. It is important that you make sure that you are aware of the best SQL practices. Tips and tricks on database design can be found from many resources, including online web sites as well as books and magazines.

> **For more information on COM+ Transactional Services, see Chapter 10.**

Coding: Properties, Objects, Parameters, and More

When creating a Windows COM+ component, you are faced with issues regarding the actual building of the interfaces and will need to decide what the interface will look like. Traditionally, a developer would go straight ahead and start creating properties on a class, which may represent certain fields in the database. Properties, though, under COM+, are not always very efficient, as accessing them may require a trip to the server, which may reside in another process or even on another machine.

Although the Contacts sample makes use of properties (*a.* to show you the normal property approach and *b.* to get you as an informal exercise to change it so it uses a method instead), the 'no properties' approach would be a speedier option if the client objects of the Contact component were in another process. The larger the amount of parameters required generally means the faster it will execute as a method, as it will decrease the amounts of trips that the same amount of properties would incur. If the client objects are in the same process, however, dealing with properties is far more appealing than long-winded parameters on methods.

For similar reasons, in order to also reduce trips across process or machine boundaries, you should not use object hierarchies in your objects or objects that return other objects if you expect the component to live in a separate process than its client components. Each call has to be marshalled back and forth between processes and thread boundaries.

A recordset should be disconnected when given to the client because otherwise you will be holding a connection open unnecessarily. Another aspect, in terms of efficient coding for COM+, is making sure that objects are released from memory as soon as possible as is the case with the following code snippet:

```
Dim myObj As Object
'Other code

Set myObj = New Object  'Acquire Late
MyObj.SomeMethod        'Just before this method
Set myObj = Nothing     'Release Early

'Other code
```

> It is good practice to release your objects once you are finished with them. In other words, acquire late, release early.

The issues described in this section all have two aims in common, to save resources and to make COM+ objects more efficient. The techniques to accomplish this often require you to code against a term known as *instance state*. Each instance of a class is required to know its purpose and the data it requires at any given time. Unfortunately, issuing property values in quick succession is not foolproof. Consider the following:

```
MyObj.Gallons = 10 ' a call is made to the COM+ SetComplete() method
                     in this property.
MyObj.Pump = 1       ' can you be sure that the Gallons property is still 10
MyObj.BuyGallons     ' if network traffic delayed the execution of this line?
```

For this reason, your objects cannot expect to know the values that were being held after they were recreated. If you think of this as not having state, then you are on track. You handle state, and COM+ does not care either way. The issues described here continue with a slightly different angle as we look at the next related COM+ service.

Just-In-Time (JIT) Activation

Just-in-time activation is a service that COM+ provides, and which achieves a high level of resource efficiency for objects on the server. The objects that you create with Visual Basic will automatically draw on these benefits provided that they support transactions one way or the other. JIT takes care of your objects' activation and deactivation for you.

Resource Friendly

Resources such as CPU and memory are extremely valuable to a server, as they affect the performance of any running applications or server components, and JIT's main purpose is to enhance the efficiency of those resources. Usually, the client application would control the resources used by objects created on the server by keeping track of instances and setting them back to Nothing when complete. Making a public variable in Visual Basic and setting it when the form loads will require resources of the server until it is set back to Nothing.

This is an expensive method of coding, and scaling the example up 100-fold could have disastrous results on server performance.

There is also a performance hit when many objects are constantly loaded and reloaded into memory, because initializing an object often takes longer than the average execution time for a method. To help this situation, COM+ activates and deactivates objects when needed and not needed respectively.

Leaving a Trace

When you call a method or property on your transactional object and COM+ is told that it can deactivate your object, it releases the object from memory on your behalf. When you access another property on that object, COM+ creates the object once again on your behalf and executes it, releasing it again when done.

So COM+ activates and deactivates instances of your objects for you. But isn't that what you are told to do?

As you have seen, the registry is important to COM+. It manages the GUIDs associated with your components' objects and this is what COM+ uses for instantiating those objects. COM+ searches the registry for the GUID and creates a proxy on the client. The proxy is created based on the type library information, and when a method is called it sends the call to the stub on the server. The stub also has to be created based on the GUID provided, and is responsible for actually executing the called method on the server. This involves time-consuming searching within the registry, time for proxy-stub creation, the creation of additional structures like context, and then the time for the called method to execute. When you release the object, all of these activities are then made void and the reference freed when released from memory.

In the case of JIT activation, the server knows the connection is valid and although it releases the object from memory, it caches the information about the object. The proxy, stub, and context structures are left intact, leaving a trace of itself.

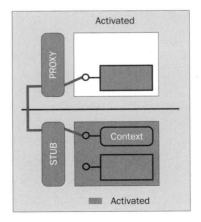

Therefore registry lookups are not needed, proxy-stub and context structures do not have to be recreated, and thus recreating the object is much simpler and faster.

JIT activation occurs when you access another method on the cached object as it activates the object just in time. As it gets the new call, it recreates the object and calls the method. This is a faster solution than any "instantiating and releasing" code you may use.

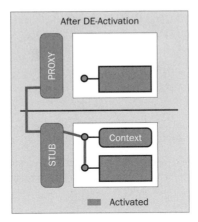

As was said before, JIT works hand in hand with transactions. If your object supports transactions, then it also supports JIT.

Although COM+ documentation advises you to take advantage of JIT within COM+ and not care about when and why you release your objects, I must urge you to still maintain your coding practice by acquiring late and releasing early. The reason is clear. Not all of your objects are going to be transactional, thus not all of your objects are going to be JIT-enabled. To simply keep track of which objects are benefiting from JIT and those that are not is not good enough for me. Also, many web clients are written in server-side ASP and, since it is usually on the same server as the objects, the proxy-stub situation overhead is decreased due to the fact that no network travel is needed.

Hooking into JIT

The activation and deactivation features of JIT on your object can be hooked into by means of **interface inheritance**. Inheriting interfaces is not a new thing and is a powerful method of using the interfaces of other COM objects.

In order to hook into JIT, you must implement IObjectControl, an interface provided by the COM+ Services object model. When implementing interfaces you must implement all methods on the interface. The IObjectControl interface contains the following methods:

- ❑ Activate()
- ❑ CanBePooled()
- ❑ Deactivate()

To implement the IObjectControl interface, a reference to comsvcs.dll must be made and the following code inserted:

```
Option Explicit

    Implements ObjectControl

Private Sub ObjectControl_Activate()

End Sub

Private Function ObjectControl_CanBePooled() As Boolean

End Function

Private Sub ObjectControl_Deactivate()

End Sub
```

The methods seen here have to be implemented, as those are the methods that IObjectControl exposes.

Activate() and Deactivate() correspond to the activities that the JIT service provides and fires for you to write code behind that activity. Object initialization code and deactivation code can be inserted into these methods. A common practice is to instantiate class-level objects in Activate() and destroy them in Deactivate(), so that each method doesn't have to expressly manage those objects.

AVOID coding in the Class_Initialize event, especially when hooking into IObjectControl. The Class_Initialize event occurs before the Activate event and could cause problems for your object. This event may not even be fired if the object is pooled. While objects written in Visual Basic can't be pooled, it's bad practice to take advantage of this limitation.

Consider the following code within a transaction object implementing the IObjectControl interface:

```
Dim myObject As Class1

Private Sub Class_Initialize()
  Set myObject = New Class1
End Sub
```

A COM+ transactional object is an object that has a context, which is itself an object that stores information on the enclosed object. The information that the context contains is encapsulated inside of properties, some of which you can Get and Set. (See IContextState, IObjectContextInfo in your COM+ documentation.)

Since the Class_Initialize event fires before the Activate method on IObjectControl, objects created within the class' event will not be included in the context of the object. Also do not use SetComplete or SetAbort within any of the IObjectControl methods.

With our coding complete and the DLL compiled, the component is ready to be used by the user interface. Once the database has been built (using the instructions earlier in the chapter), place the code from the **Chapter08UI** download in the root directory for your web site (this is **C:\inetpub\wwwroot** by default). Now, all you need to do is point your browser at this directory and the default.htm file.

Running the VB project before attempting to view the web page avoids the necessity to go through the routine of registering components on our machine before trying to access them. When the project is run, VB instantly registers entries for all the classes that make up the project and references them back to a file called Vb6debug.dll that gets installed along with the rest of VB.

This then acts as a proxy back into the Visual basic process. So, when Active Scripting creates an instance of an object implemented inside the project VB is running, the COM subsystem (the part of Windows that actually implements the core COM functionality) actually asks Vb6debug to create the object. Vb6debug intercepts this call and routes it all the way into Visual Basic, which basically runs the code that makes up the object in an interpreted fashion. Essentially, this creates an object in the Visual Basic process, a reference to which is passed back to the original caller. When you stop running the project, VB undoes the changes it made to the registry.

Now, you should be able to view and modify the database, via our user interface, using the business tier to access the data tier!

Summary

In this chapter we have defined business objects and business logic. We explored the key benefits of business objects:

- ❑ Encapsulation
- ❑ Abstraction
- ❑ Maintainability
- ❑ Code reuse

We also discussed the recommended use of business objects within the Windows DNA architecture, which is to encapsulate business logic and data. When using objects in this scenario, our ASP code should handle all user interface and presentation logic, relying entirely on our business objects to handle business processing and data access. This approach maximizes our flexibility, as well as increasing the performance and scalability of our application.

There are three incredibly important factors to pay attention to when designing and developing a COM+ component in VB. Firstly you must pay special care in how you design your interfaces, in terms of naming conventions, instance state, and trips over the wire as well as what techniques you use for carrying data across layers and more. Secondly, when applying COM+ services like transactions, you must be aware of how JIT works and how to utilize it, which will give you better performance. Lastly, develop in tiers so that you create a climate for better scalability.

A last point to leave you with regards testing. Always test performance and design issues. Never accept the first solution as law; there just may be a better way. When you test be on the lookout for bottlenecks, most used methods, and queries.

p2p.wrox.com
The programmer's resource centre

ASP Today

wrox.com

wroxdirect

10

Transactions

As we've seen in previous chapters, COM+ enhanced COM to include built-in support for the features of **Microsoft Transaction Server** (**MTS**), allowing the developer to specify the transactional support required for individual components of an application. COM+ also adds other services such as object pooling. There is more to MTS, and, by extension, COM+, than transactional support, but this is undoubtedly one of its core offerings, and one that developers will be primarily interested in.

In this chapter, we're going to concentrate on the concepts behind transactional programming, and see how COM+ makes our job easier. In particular, this chapter includes:

❑   A basic introduction to transactions

❑   How resource managers and transaction managers work

❑   Transactional support in COM+

❑   How to build transactional components, and in particular, how to create a Compensating Resource Manager

So let's start by recapping exactly what a transaction is.

Basics of Transactions

A **transaction** is a discrete unit of work that represents a particular activity or function within a system. The activity is generally made up of a series of steps that must be treated as a single unit of work. In other words, it's all or nothing – either all of the steps successfully complete, or none of them do.

Providing transactional support within your applications may sound deceptively easy. However, transactional programming is very difficult to implement without a supporting infrastructure, especially across heterogeneous data sources.

Requirements for a Transactional System

All participants in a transaction must satisfy the so-called **ACID properties**. In order to pass the ACID test, all components must be:

❏ **Atomic** – all actions in a single transaction will either commit together or abort together. If a transaction **commits**, all of the actions of the transaction successfully complete. If a transaction **aborts**, then all of the effects of the steps that have completed up to the point of failure will be undone, or **rolled back**. As an example, say you ask to transfer five hundred dollars from your checking account to your savings account. Such a transaction is atomic, because either the money both leaves your checking account and is added to your savings, or neither happens.

❏ **Consistent** – a transaction is a *correct* transformation of the state of a system. Individual steps within a transaction may alter the state of the system so that it is temporarily invalid, but before a transaction completes, it must ensure that the system is returned to a valid state. In the funds transfer example, one of the steps is to deduct five hundred dollars from your checking account. But if those funds are not deposited into your savings account, the system state is invalid. Regardless of the success or failure of any of the steps, you should not be one hundred dollars poorer: your checking account balance should be reset, or five hundred dollars should be added to your savings account.

❏ **Isolated** – uncommitted changes are hidden from other concurrent transactions. This is often accomplished by controlling access to data used by a transaction through **locks**. For instance, say the step to withdraw money out of your checking account has completed, but the step to deposit the money into your savings account has not. If a transaction responsible for creating your monthly statement is executed concurrently, the withdrawal should not appear on your statement until the transaction has been committed.

❏ **Durable** – once a transaction commits, changes made to the system state will persist even if there are system failures. For example, say I deposit my paycheck into my account. If a power outage occurs just after the transaction commits, my deposit should still be on record after the system comes back online.

Why Do We Need Transactions?

So what's the big deal about built-in support for transactions?

First and foremost it makes the programmer's life much easier. Writing your own transactional logic in applications, and manually ensuring that the ACID properties of a transaction are maintained, can be very difficult.

For example, say we write an accounting component that implements a transactional `Withdraw` method:

```
Private Sub Withdraw (lAcctID as Long, curAmount as Currency)

    Dim objCN As ADODB.Connection
    Dim objRS As ADODB.RecordSet
    Dim strSQL As String
    Dim strConnection As String
    Dim curBalance As Currency
```

```
' Initialize
strConnection = "Provider=SQLOLEDB;server=ServerName;" _
                & "Database=DBName;User ID=sa;Password=;"


' Open the database connection
Set objCN = New ADODB.Connection
objCN.Open strConnection


' **** BEGINNING OF TRANSACTION ****

' Step 1:  Account balances can never fall below 0, so we must check
'          that sufficient funds are available
strSQL = "SELECT sum(DebitCredit) Balance FROM Ledger WHERE " _
         & "AccountID = " & lAcctID
Set objRS = New Recordset
objRS.Open strSQL, objCN, adOpenKeyset, adLockOptimistic, adCmdText
curBalance = objRS("Balance")

If (objRS("Balance") < curAmount) Then _
    Err.Raise vbObjectError + 1, "TransferFunds", "Insufficient funds!"
objRS.Close


' Step 2:  Deduct the amount from the account
strSQL = "SELECT DebitCredit FROM Ledger WHERE AccountID = " & lAcctID
objRS.Open strSQL, objCN, adOpenKeyset, adLockOptimistic, adCmdText
objRS.AddNew
objRS("AccountID") = lAcctID
objRS("DebitCredit") = curAmount * (-1)
objRS.Update

' Ignore errors once change has been committed to DB
On Error Resume Next

objRS.Close
' **** END OF TRANSACTION ****

' Close the database connection
objCN.Close
Set objRS = Nothing
Set objCN = Nothing

End Sub
```

This simple routine obtains the account balance from the database and checks to see if there are sufficient funds to make the withdrawal. If there are, the withdrawal amount is added to the account's ledger. However, even code as simple as this violates the ACID properties. Can you spot which one?

Since the above transaction is only performing one action that modifies system state, all steps within the transaction will either fully commit or abort. Therefore, the transaction is *atomic*. Since the modification to the database will only be visible to concurrent transactions once the transaction completes, it is *isolated*. Also, since the new ledger entry is recorded persistently in the database, the transaction is *durable*.

However the code sample violates the *consistency* rule. In order to understand why, let's look at the following scenario. Say the starting balance is one hundred dollars, and we call the Withdraw method to withdraw all one hundred dollars. If the account balance were modified by a separate concurrent Withdraw transaction in-between steps 1 and 2 of our transaction, the one hundred dollar deduction in step 2 would drop our account balance below zero, violating our rule imposed by step 1.

We can correct this by having the Withdraw method call a stored procedure, which performs the validation and withdrawal all within the context of a transaction. The stored procedure checks to see if the account has sufficient funds. If it does, then we insert a record to withdraw the requested amount:

```
CREATE PROCEDURE sp_withdraw @nAcctID AS INT, @curAmount AS MONEY AS

BEGIN TRANSACTION

IF (SELECT SUM(DebitCredit) Balance FROM Ledger
    WHERE AccountID = @nAcctID) > @curAmount
BEGIN
    INSERT INTO Ledger (AccountID, DebitCredit)
                values(@nAcctID, @curAmount * (-1))
    COMMIT TRANSACTION
END
ELSE
BEGIN
    RAISERROR ('Insufficient funds.', 16, 1)
    ROLLBACK TRANSACTION
END
```

SQL Server ensures that the range of rows in the Ledger table is locked for the specified account. Therefore, concurrent transactions would not be allowed to add, modify, or delete records containing the account ID. As we'll see later in the chapter, COM+ can handle these details (and many more) for us.

What if the Withdraw method was just one of a series of steps within a transaction? What if the transaction spanned multiple method calls? What if those multiple method calls were contained in many different objects? What if, over the course of the transaction, multiple persistent resources were modified? What if those resources existed on multiple servers? If we had to write all this transactional code, it would get very complicated, very quickly. That's the beauty of a transactional processing system – it provides an infrastructure for managing transactions onto which we can build our applications.

Transaction Processing Systems

A transaction processing system is one that provides an infrastructure for handling and coordinating transactions. A transaction processing system consists of:

❑ An application

❑ Transaction managers

❑ Resource managers

The application contains business logic. If the implementation of the business logic requires support from the transaction processing system, a transaction manager is enlisted. The transaction manager is responsible for coordinating with resource managers enlisted in the transaction on the local machine, and it is the resource managers that bear the responsibility for coordinating updates to persistent data.

A typical transaction processing architecture is shown in the following figure:

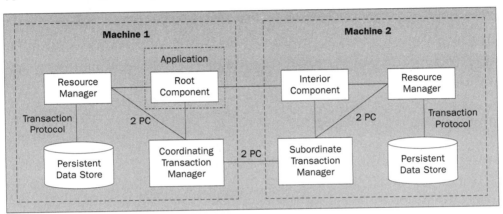

2PC stands for "two-phase commit". We'll cover this in more detail later in the chapter, but essentially, it's a protocol that helps ensure ACID properties are not violated.

In this figure, the root component of the application enlists another component located on another machine (an **interior component** – we'll see why shortly) to perform some work on its behalf. The interior object must perform its work within the root component's transaction. Therefore, the transaction manager on machine 1 enlists the transaction manager on machine 2 to coordinate the resource managers enlisted in the transaction on machine 2.

Let's clarify this by discussing the three major constituents of a transaction processing system in more detail.

Resource Managers

> **Resource managers ensure that modifications made to persistent resources in a transaction are made in a consistent, isolated, and durable manner.**

The resource manager assists the transaction manager by ensuring that all changes are either fully committed upon successful completion of the transaction, or completely rolled back should the transaction be aborted. The resource manager is responsible for notifying the persistent resource of the isolation level that needs to be maintained throughout the life of the transaction, as well as whether or not it should abort or commit the changes.

A persistent resource must have an associated resource manager (or a Compensating Resource Manager for COM+ initiated transactions) in order to participate in a distributed transaction. We'll discuss Compensating Resource Managers later in the chapter.

For example, Microsoft Active Directory does not have a resource manager, meaning that it cannot participate in distributed transactions. Any changes made to Active Directory during a transaction would be committed to the directory data store whether the transaction commits or aborts.

The most commonly used resource managers are those that ship with relational databases such as SQL Server and Oracle. Additional resource managers are available through third party vendors, and if a resource manager is unavailable for a particular persistent resource, you could of course write your own. However, writing a resource manager is not trivial and is beyond the scope of this book.

Compensating Resource Managers

A **Compensating Resource Manager** (**CRM**) provides an alternative way to integrate a persistent resource with a Distributed Transaction Coordinator (DTC) managed transaction. We will explain DTC in more detail shortly. A CRM should be created when a persistent resource needs to be updated within the context of a COM+ transaction, and a resource manager is not available from either the vendor of the persistent resource or a third party.

The CRM is able to vote on the outcome of a transaction, and will receive notification as to whether or not the transaction was committed or aborted. The CRM also provides a durable log that it uses for recovery when the system crashes.

In order to create a CRM, we must write two components – the **CRM Worker** and the **CRM Compensator** – both of which support standard interfaces. The CRM Worker is responsible for accessing and manipulating resources, and the CRM Compensator is responsible for voting on the outcome of the transaction, and for committing or aborting the operations performed against a resource by the CRM Worker. We'll look at these in more detail in the *Compensating Resource Manager* section later in the chapter.

Compensating Transactions

A **compensating transaction** is one that violates the *isolated* requirement. During the course of a compensating transaction, changes made to a persistent resource are visible to other transactions. This is usually done for the sake of better concurrency, or when the persistent resource lacks support for locking mechanisms necessary to implement a fully ACID-compliant transaction. However, compensating transactions can wreak havoc if used within transaction processing systems.

For example, say a compensating transaction to create a new employee involves creating a record in the employee table, then creating a record in the address table, and then creating records in various other tables, including creating a record in the contact information table for each phone number. In the midst of creating the records for the new employee, another transaction to set up the employee's payroll completes successfully. However, the first transaction fails because an invalid phone number was given. Since the setting up of the payroll record was in a separate transaction, even though the employee record is deleted, the individual will start receiving paychecks. Obviously this is not the most ideal situation!

The CRM ensures consistency and durability, and the transaction manager ensures atomicity. However, the CRM does not inherently ensure isolation, and it is up to the CRM developer to ensure that changes made during the course of a transaction are not visible to any other transaction until it is complete. In a later section, we'll examine an example implementation of a CRM that ensures isolation.

Transaction Managers

When multiple resource managers are deployed for a given transaction, something has to be responsible for the overall transaction.

> **A transaction manager oversees and coordinates resource managers on the local machine, and enlists other transaction managers when required.**

When a transaction manager enlists a remote transaction manager on a different machine, the local transaction manager is referred to as the **coordinating transaction manager**, and the remote one as a **subordinate transaction manager**. If the application fails, the coordinating transaction manager is responsible for informing each enlisted resource manager and any subordinate transaction manager to rollback any changes that were made.

The Distributed Transaction Coordinator

The Microsoft **Distributed Transaction Coordinator** (**DTC**) is Microsoft's transaction manager. The DTC runs as a multi-threaded service, and guarantees atomicity when transactions span across multiple resource managers.

The DTC was first introduced with SQL Server 6.5, and is now installed by default with Windows 2000, XP, and .NET Server. It ensures that distributed transactions do not violate the ACID properties by enlisting the resource managers for each machine involved in the transaction, communicating through the use of a two-phase commit protocol.

Two-Phase Commit Protocol

The **two-phase commit protocol** mentioned earlier is used when managing distributed transactions. The transaction manager communicates with the resource managers enlisted in a transaction via the two-phase commit protocol. This communication usually occurs over a separate communication channel and, as the name implies, is composed of two phases: the **prepare** phase and the **commit/abort** phase.

The prepare phase is entered when the root and its interior objects have all voted to commit the transaction. In the prepare phase, the transaction manager asks each of the enlisted resource managers to prepare to commit the transaction. Each resource manager attempts to save its state to a durable store without actually committing the changes, and votes on whether or not to commit the transaction. Once the resource manager completes the prepare phase, it must honor the outcome of the transaction.

In the commit/abort phase, a commit or abort is sent to each resource manager. If the transaction manager receives a vote to commit the transaction from every enlisted resource manager within the transaction timeout period, a commit is sent to each resource manager. If the transaction manager receives a vote to abort the transaction by the root object, its interior components, or the enlisted resource manager, or does not receive all of the votes within the transaction timeout period, an abort is sent to each of the resource managers.

The transactional communication between the resource manager and the persistent resource usually occurs over a separate communication channel using any one of a number of transaction protocols. Typical transactional protocols utilized within Windows DNA applications include:

- ❑ OLE Transactions – the native protocol used by the DTC to communicate with the resource managers.

- ❑ X/Open XA – a standard transaction protocol defined by the X/Open Distributed Transaction Processing (X/Open DTP) group, which defines the API used by the resource manager to communicate with the transaction manager. For relational databases that support the XA protocol, the ODBC driver typically acts as a bridge between the DTC and the XA compliant resource manager.

- ❑ Transaction Internet Protocol (TIP) – a standard transaction protocol defined by the Internet Engineering Task Force (IETF). The DTC provides direct support for communicating with resource managers via TIP.

The Application's Role

The **application** is responsible for enlisting the resource manager to coordinate its distributed transactions, and each of the resource managers needed. On the Microsoft platform, the application must:

- ❑ Establish a connection with the coordinating DTC by calling the `DtcGetTransactionManager` function to receive a reference to the `ITransactionDispenser` interface

- ❑ Create a new transaction by calling the `BeginTransaction` member function, which returns a reference to the new transaction through its `ITransaction` interface

- ❑ Obtain connections to persistent resources, and then manually enlist their transaction managers to participate in the transaction

Clearly, there are quite a few error prone areas that require special attention when writing transactional applications. Wouldn't it be nice if these details were already taken care of?

Well, that's exactly what COM+ does. COM+ Component Services are responsible for enlisting the DTC, creating the root component, enlisting the root component within the transaction, and finally enlisting the resource managers for persistent resources on behalf of the application.

As we'll see in the next section, COM+ provides a rich declarative environment that greatly simplifies the creation and control of transactional component-based applications.

Transactional Support in COM+

COM+ provides a declarative environment for managing transactions within component-based applications. Very minor changes, if any, are required to the component in order to support transactions.

COM+ lets us declare which components require transactional support via an administrative interface (the Component Services GUI). When a component requiring transactional support is created, it's automatically enlisted in the transaction. When the transactional component acquires a connection to a persistent resource, COM+ automatically enlists the resource manager in the component's transaction.

Root and Interior Objects

The declarative model lets us combine various methods exposed by many different objects to compose a single transaction.

The **root object** is the first COM+ object that is included in the context of a new transaction. The root object may instantiate additional COM+ objects in order to accomplish its tasks – these objects are referred to as **interior objects**. Depending on its configuration, an interior object may or may not participate in the transaction.

The diagram below shows two transactions. The first transaction contains a root object and two interior objects. The object created by the second interior object requires its own transaction: therefore, it becomes the root of a new transaction and creates its own interior object:

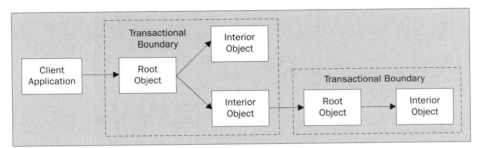

The root object and each of the interior objects participating in its transaction get an opportunity to vote on the outcome of the transaction. When the root object is deactivated, the transaction completes, at which point the votes of the root and all of its participating interior objects are tallied, and the transaction is either committed or aborted. For a transaction to be committed, all objects must vote to commit the transaction. If any object participating in the transaction votes to abort, the transaction is aborted, and all changes made to persistent resources managed by resource managers are rolled back to their original state.

So how do we specify whether the interior objects we create will enlist in the current transaction or become the root object of a new transaction? And how can we ensure that a particular object will always be the root of a new transaction? We can specify the transactional behavior of any component using the transactional support property.

The Transactional Support Property

Each class has its own transactional support property that specifies the type of transactional support objects of this class require.

As we saw in Chapter 8, we can view the transactional support property for a particular class by selecting that class in the Component Services MMC, and opening the Transactions tab of the Properties dialog box:

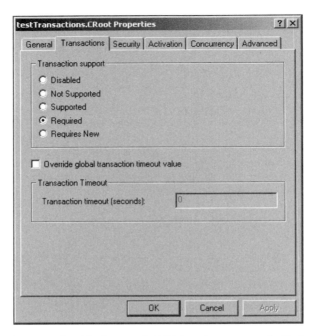

This property can be manipulated both using the MMC, and programmatically from within our components. We return to the programmatic approach later in the chapter.

The options for transaction support are:

❑ **Disabled** – the object still exists within a context and is a part of an activity stream. However, COM+ will simulate the transactional behavior of an unconfigured COM component. In general, this option is selected if the object does not manipulate any persistent resources managed by a resource manager, and is not required to be the root of a transaction. We can select this if we don't want to incur transaction-related overheads.

❑ **Not Supported** – the default setting for all COM+ components. The object will not participate in a transaction regardless of the transactional state of its caller. The object will not be able to vote within the caller's transaction, or start a transaction of its own. Any changes made to persistent resources in this class will be committed, regardless of whether the resources are managed by resource managers or if they depend on the outcome of the caller's transaction.

❑ **Supported** – objects created from such classes can participate in a transaction, but don't require one. The object will participate in the caller's transaction, if one exists. However, the object will not be allowed to initiate its own transaction. This setting is frequently used when an object updates a single persistent resource that is managed by a resource manager. In order to leave the system in a valid state, the component may be required to participate in a larger transaction.

❑ **Required** – objects created from this class require a transaction. If the caller is enlisted in a transaction, the object will participate in the caller's transaction. Otherwise, COM+ will create a new transaction with the object serving as the root. This is the most common setting for objects that must update, either directly or indirectly, multiple persistent resources in a consistent manner, because it guarantees COM+ will provide transactional support for the object.

❑   Requires New – an object created from this class will always serve as the root object of a transaction, regardless of whether or not the object was created within the context of a transaction. Since a new transaction is created for the object, the outcome of the caller's transaction will not affect the outcome of the new transaction, and visa versa. Objects that need to update persistent data managed by resource managers, independent of the outcome of other existing transactions, require a new transaction. For example, an audit of all attempted transactions may be desired, regardless of whether the transaction was committed or aborted. In this scenario, an auditing component that needs to ensure that the auditing database is left in a valid state may require a new transaction.

So we can specify the level of transactional support our components have. The next thing we need to understand is how COM+ helps to ensure that the ACID properties are not violated. The Object Context is fundamental to how COM+ does its job.

Object Context

As we noted in Chapter 9, every COM+ object has an **object context**. The object context serves a variety of functions, but the following are the most important in transaction processing:

❑   Transaction management

❑   Concurrency

❑   Just-In-Time (JIT) activation

We've already come across these in previous chapters, but let's take a closer look at each from the perspective of transactional applications.

The IObjectContext Interface

COM+ provides an interface to some of the Object Context's properties and methods via the appropriately named `ObjectContext` object.

A reference to the `ObjectContext` can be obtained via the VB `GetObjectContext` function. The function returns the default interface for the `ObjectContext`, in other words `IObjectContext`.

The `IObjectContext` interface was introduced with MTS 1.0 and is still supported in COM+. It has the following methods that allow us to programmatically control the outcome of a transaction and query the state of the context:

Methods	Description
CreateInstance	Deprecated method for creating an instance of an object. Now simply use `CreateObject` in VB. Included for backward compatibility with MTS.
DisableCommit	Called just before an object is about to modify state in an inconsistent manner.
EnableCommit	Called when an object has modified state in a consistent manner, but the object should not be deactivated unless the transaction has completed.

Table continued on following page

Methods	Description
IsCallerInRole	Returns a Boolean indicating whether the object's direct caller is in a specified role (either directly or as part of a group).
IsInTransaction	Returns a Boolean indicating whether the object is participating in a transaction.
IsSecurityEnabled	Returns whether or not security is enabled for the object.
SetAbort	Called when an object can be deactivated and has modified its state in an inconsistent manner, or an unrecoverable error has occurred.
SetComplete	Called when an object has modified state in a consistent manner and the object can be deactivated.

There is very little overhead involved in obtaining a reference to the object context through GetObjectContext, therefore the performance gains by retaining a reference for later use are minimal.

For example, the following code snippet shows a completely acceptable way to call the SetComplete method in VB:

```
GetObjectContext.SetComplete
```

The ObjectContext class exposes the following properties:

Property	Description
Count	Returns the number of properties available to the object.
Item	Retrieves a particular property.
Security	Returns the security object.
ContextInfo	Returns a reference to the ContextInfo object, and hence to the transaction, activity, and context information on the current context object.

Casting Your Vote

Each object that participates within a transaction gets an opportunity to vote on its outcome.

Participants in a transaction cast their vote on the outcome of a transaction through its ObjectContext. There are two bits that control the outcome of a transaction: DeactivateOnReturn and MyTransactionVote. These bits are often referred to as the **Done** and **Consistency** bits:

❑ COM+ uses the DeactivateOnReturn or Done bit to determine whether or not to deactivate the object once the method call completes

❑ COM+ uses the MyTransactionVote or Consistency bit to determine whether to commit or abort the transaction

The state of these bits is exposed via the `ObjectContext`'s `IContextState` interface, through the methods shown in the following table:

Method	Description
SetDeactivateOnReturn	Sets the value of the `DeactivateOnReturn` bit.
GetDeactivateOnReturn	Returns the value of the `DeactivateOnReturn` bit.
SetMyTransactionVote	Sets the value of the `MyTransactionVote` bit.
GetMyTransactionVote	Returns the value of the `MyTransactionVote` bit.

In order to obtain the state of a context, you retrieve the context using the `GetObjectContext` function and cast the returned context object to its `IContextState` interface. Here is a short example:

```
Dim objOC As COMSVCSLib.ObjectContext
Dim objCS As COMSVCSLib.IContextState

Set objOC = GetObjectContext
Set objCS = objOC
```

Note that if we do not need the object context object for other purposes, we can dispense with the `objOC` intermediate variable, and set `objCS` directly like so:

```
Set objCS = GetObjectContext
```

We could use these methods as shown in the following code, which displays the state of the two transactional bits in the Visual Basic IDE's Immediate Window:

```
Dim objCS             As COMSVCSLib.IContextState
Dim bDeactivateOnReturn As Boolean
Dim myTransactionVote  As COMSVCSLib.tagTransactionVote

' Obtain a reference to the IContextState interface of the ObjectContext.
Set objCS = GetObjectContext()

' Obtain the state of the transaction bits.
objCS.GetDeactivateOnReturn bDeactivateOnReturn
objCS.GetMyTransactionVote myTransactionVote

' Display the current state of the transaction bits.
Debug.Print "DeactivateOnReturn = " & bDeactivateOnReturn

If (myTransactionVote = TxCommit) Then
    Debug.Print "MyTransactionVote = TxCommit"
ElseIf (myTransactionVote = TxAbort) Then
    Debug.Print "MyTransactionVote = TxAbort"
End If
```

The code sets up a couple of variables to tell us the current state of our transaction bits:

- ❑ MyTransactionVote (the Consistency bit) contains the state of the object's vote to either commit or abort the transaction
- ❑ bDeactivateOnReturn contains the value of the DeactivateOnReturn (or Done) bit

The code retrieves the values of these variables using the GetDeactivateOnReturn and GetMyTransactionVote methods respectively.

Setting the Transaction Parts

COM+ uses the DeactivateOnReturn bit to determine whether or not to deactivate the object once the method call has completed: if DeactivateOnReturn is set to True, then COM+ will deactivate the object. Unless the object supports pooling (which we discussed in Chapter 8), the object is deactivated by destroying it. The default state of the DeactivateOnReturn bit is False, and we can use the SetDeactivateOnReturn method to change it if required.

MyTransactionVote contains the state of the object's vote to either commit or abort the transaction, and we can use the SetMyTransactionVote method to change the value of this bit. This method accepts one of two values in the tagTransactionVote enumeration – TxAbort and TxCommit – where the initial state of the MyTransactionVote bit is TxCommit. When the transaction completes, COM+ will tally all of the votes, and either commit or abort the transactions based upon all of the votes received.

We can also use the methods provided by the IObjectContext interface to set the MyTransactionVote and DeactivateOnReturn bits. The methods we're most interested in are SetAbort, SetComplete, EnableCommit, and DisableCommit. These methods allow us to alter both bits with a single method call.

The following table shows how the methods for modifying the transactional bits relate to the IObjectContext and IContextState interfaces:

	DisableCommit	EnableCommit	SetAbort	SetComplete
MyTransaction Vote	TxAbort	TxCommit	TxAbort	TxCommit
DeactivateOn Return	False	False	True	True

For example, in its initial state an object has MyTransactionVote set to TxCommit and DeactivateOnReturn set to False – which is equivalent to calling the EnableCommit method. Calling SetAbort indicates that something has gone wrong, so we want COM+ to deactivate the object, abort the transaction, and so forth.

Using Transaction Bits to Ensure the ACID Properties

It's important to realize that if the transaction bits are not altered from the initial state through the course of a method call, and no other step in the transaction voted to abort the transaction, any changes made during the course of the method call will be committed. This could be a problem if your error handling has a code path where the MyTransactionVote bit is not changed to TxAbort. Therefore, it's good practice to call DisableCommit or its equivalent at the beginning of the method call, alter persistent state, and then call SetAbort or EnableCommit when complete.

At the very least, you should call DisableCommit or its equivalent before updating persistent data in such a way as to leave the system in an invalid state. For example, say a particular method call is responsible for creating a customer record. When a customer record is created, it must be added to both the sales force automation (SFA) system and the billing system. DisableCommit or its equivalent should be called before attempting to add the new customer record to the SFA application and billing system. Doing so would help ensure that the transaction was properly aborted in the event that an error occurred updating one of the two systems. Say DisableCommit was not called, and the SFA application was successfully updated, but there was an error updating the billing system. If a code path exists in the error handling code where the MyTransactionVote bit is not set to TxAbort, then the transaction may commit, leaving the system in an invalid state.

Concurrency

In a multi-user, component-based COM+ application there is going to be concurrent processing on behalf of your users. If it's not managed, concurrency can be the death of transaction processing systems.

As we've already seen, resource managers often use locks to ensure that transactions are isolated (the 'I' in ACID). Two potential side effects of locking are reduced throughput of the system, and a condition known as deadlocks. In this section, we'll see how COM+ manages concurrency issues through an abstraction called activities and the just-in-time (JIT) activation feature.

Activities

> **An activity is a single logical thread of execution that flows through a collection of distributed COM+ objects.**

A **single** thread of execution implies that only one object in an activity is running at a time. A collection of **distributed** COM+ objects implies that an activity can flow across machine or process boundaries. The activity starts when a client creates a COM+ object that requires synchronization and then flows through any child objects created by the original object.

To demonstrate activities, we'll use the following VB code to implement the class CTestProj.CTest. We'll write a couple of clients that utilize the CTest class to illustrate an activity, and we'll modify CTest's transaction support property to test the resulting behavior.

In order to use COM+ concurrency management, we need to configure the CTest class to require transaction support. We can either set its MTSTransactionMode property to 2 – RequiresTransaction in the Visual Basic IDE, or we can set its Transaction Support property to Required using the COM+ Component Services MMC Snap-in. The code for our CTest module is as follows:

```
Option Explicit

'*********************************************
'*              Class: CTest                 *
'*********************************************

Private m_objChild As CTest

Public Property Get contextID() As String
    contextID = GetObjectContext().ContextInfo.GetContextId
End Property

Public Property Get activityID() As String
    activityID = GetObjectContext().ContextInfo.GetActivityId
End Property

Public Property Get transactionID() As String
    If (GetObjectContext().isInTransaction) Then
        transactionID = GetObjectContext().ContextInfo.GetTransactionId
    Else
        transactionID = "Object not in transaction."
    End If
End Property

Public Sub CreateChild(Optional strMachineName As String = "")
    If (strMachineName <> "") Then
        Set m_objChild = CreateObject ("CTestProj.CTest", _
                                       strMachineName)
    Else
        Set m_objChild = CreateObject("CTestProj.CTest")
    End If
End Sub

Public Property Get child() As CTest
    Set child = m_objChild
End Property
```

This code simply uses methods of the ContextInfo object to get identifiers for the current object's context, activity, and transaction. It also encapsulates the functionality to create a child object of the root object (we'll come back to the various ways we can create interior objects later in this chapter). Make sure you've added a reference to COM+ Services Type Library, and build the DLL.

Host the component using the Component Services manager, and then we can create a client for it. The client application will create a root object and an interior object, and display each object's context information:

```
Dim objTest As Object

Set objTest = CreateObject("CTestProj.CTest")

Debug.Print "Root Object:"
Debug.Print vbTab & "Context ID    = " & objTest.contextID
Debug.Print vbTab & "Activity ID   = " & objTest.activityID
```

```
Debug.Print vbTab & "Transaction ID = " & objTest.transactionID
Debug.Print

objTest.CreateChild
Debug.Print "Child Object:"
Debug.Print vbTab & "Context ID   = " & objTest.child.contextID
Debug.Print vbTab & "Activity ID  = " & objTest.child.activityID
Debug.Print vbTab & "Transaction ID = " & objTest.child.transactionID
```

With CTest's transaction support property set to Required, the client code produces something like the following output in the Immediate Window:

```
Root Object:
    Context ID      = {A54C4BBE-8361-479E-AE86-99D65F294E98}
    Activity ID     = {156882FC-7B54-414E-8EE7-90E1A8FDB89A}
    Transaction ID = {7A535BE1-E3A4-41AB-ADCB-48129F80948B}

Child Object:
    Context ID      = {12D4F591-C436-4564-BCE7-F75308A624EA}
    Activity ID     = {156882FC-7B54-414E-8EE7-90E1A8FDB89A}
    Transaction ID = {7A535BE1-E3A4-41AB-ADCB-48129F80948B}
```

As you might have expected, the root and the child objects reside within their own context, and they both reside within the same activity and transaction.

Now if we adjust the transaction property to Requires New using the Component Services manager, and rerun the client code, we'll see something like the following output in the Immediate Window:

```
Root Object:
    Context ID      = {A7488D30-D0BA-439D-B8ED-3E25098819C0}
    Activity ID     = {1267FFEF-493D-4FFF-BBD4-48226D0C817F}
    Transaction ID = {59955773-C75D-4412-A002-AA83075D0E71}

Child Object:
    Context ID      = {71C027F1-448A-4DA7-A5ED-703180517C6D}
    Activity ID     = {1267FFEF-493D-4FFF-BBD4-48226D0C817F}
    Transaction ID = {3C643012-A7AA-4C54-926E-577E3F713183}
```

Notice that each object not only has its own context, but it also has its own transaction. However, both objects still reside in the same activity.

Next we'll modify the transaction property back to Required, and then change the line in the client code so that the child object is created on another machine. Obviously you will need to install the CTestProj.dll on another machine using its COM+ Component Services manager. The client code changes to give the name of the machine where the child object is to be created as highlighted below:

```
Dim objTest As Object

Set objTest = CreateObject("CTestProj.CTest")
```

```
Debug.Print "Root Object:"
Debug.Print vbTab & "Context ID    = " & objTest.contextID
Debug.Print vbTab & "Activity ID   = " & objTest.activityID
Debug.Print vbTab & "Transaction ID = " & objTest.transactionID
Debug.Print

ObjTest.CreateChild "LABSERVER2"
Debug.Print "Child Object:"
Debug.Print vbTab & "Context ID    = " & objTest.child.contextID
Debug.Print vbTab & "Activity ID   = " & objTest.child.activityID
Debug.Print vbTab & "Transaction ID = " & objTest.child.transactionID
```

The new client code produces the following output in the Immediate Window:

```
Root Object:
    Context ID   = {289C0A45-3499-4C76-ADAF-AD56E1CFED04}
    Activity ID  = {A3C79A20-5C03-41D5-9BE6-2FB87C7108DB}
    Transaction ID = {B171FCA3-1661-4EDF-8585-3110F7684990}

Child Object:
    Context ID   = {67C334A7-3D26-4448-AA48-5492A98F0DE6}
    Activity ID  = {A3C79A20-5C03-41D5-9BE6-2FB87C7108DB}
    Transaction ID = {B171FCA3-1661-4EDF-8585-3110F7684990}
```

Notice that both the transaction and the activity flowed to the second machine, LABSERVER2 above. This is evident from the fact that the root and the child share the same activity and transaction ID. The logical thread of execution and the transaction boundaries now span across two machines.

Deadlocking

Deadlocking can occur when a single thread of execution attempts to acquire a resource that it already has locked. Recall that most resource managers utilize locking as a means to achieve isolation. Let's take a look at a potential single thread deadlocking scenario, shown in the figure below:

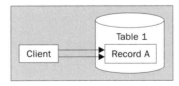

A transactional thread of execution modifies Record A in Table 1, and places a read/write lock on that record until the transaction completes, to enforce the isolation property. It then attempts to obtain all of the records in Table 1: but the thread cannot obtain all of the records in Table 1, since it must wait until the read/write lock is released for the modified record (Record A). This lock will not be released until the transaction completes, and since the transaction won't complete until all of the records are obtained, the thread deadlocks as a result.

Most modern databases can recognize and resolve deadlock situations that occur within the context of a single database connection (most databases will rollback one transaction after a certain period of time has passed in a deadlock situation). However, what if the root object modifies the record in Table 1, and an interior object attempts to obtain all of the records in Table 1 using a separate database connection?

Activities play an important role in avoiding this type of deadlock. The DTC is responsible for recognizing when the same activity tries to acquire resources from the same resource manager, and will request that the resource manager compensate accordingly, usually by allowing one of the connections to override the locks established by the other connection. Note that this doesn't violate the isolated property, since both connections are within the context of the same transaction.

A second type of deadlock occurs when two transactional threads of execution stall because they are competing for the same resources. An example of this is shown in the figure below. Client 1 creates a lock on Table 1, and Client 2 creates a lock on Table 2. Then they both try to obtain resources that the other already has locked in the same thread that placed a lock:

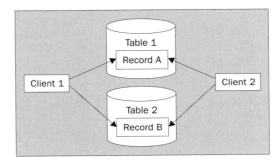

In this scenario, client 1 locks record A in table 1 and attempts to read records in table 2, which has been locked by client 2. At the same time, client 2 also tries to read records in table 1 while holding the lock on record A in table 2. Both are holding the locks in one table and waiting for the other to release the lock in another table. Such deadlock situations, where none can complete their required operations, are usually resolved by one or both transactions timing out, and therefore aborting.

The default timeout for a transaction is 60 seconds, but this value can be altered in the Component Services MMC. Right-click on the computer icon, select **Properties**, and then select the **Options** tab. The timeout value can also be overridden at the class level by right-clicking on a particular class, and then selecting the **Transactions** tab.

Isolation

As we have learned, the isolation property of a transaction ensures that uncommitted changes to the state of a system are hidden from other concurrent transactions. Isolation is typically achieved by using locks to serialize access to the data.

Serialization guarantees data integrity within the system, but on the down side, serialization can reduce the overall throughput of the system. For example, as the number of concurrent transactions requiring serialized access the same data increases, the throughput of the system decreases.

The ANSI SQL 2 standard published by the ANSI SQL Committee defines four isolation levels, and each of these levels is defined according to which of three violations of serialization they permit. The three phenomena in which serialization can be violated are:

❑ **P1 – Dirty Read** – Say transaction 1 (T1) modifies a row. Transaction 2 (T2) then reads the row before T1 completes. If T1 performs a rollback, then T2 has seen a row that never really existed.

❑ **P2 – Non-repeatable Read** – Say T1 retrieves a row, and then T2 updates that row. If T1 retrieves the same row again, then T1 has retrieved the same row twice, but has seen two different values for it.

❑ **P3 – Phantoms** – Say T1 reads a set of rows that satisfy certain search conditions. T2 then inserts one or more rows that satisfy the same search conditions. If T1 repeats the read, it will see rows that did not exist previously – "phantoms".

The four isolation levels are then defined as follows:

❑ **READ_UNCOMMITTED** – Permits P1, P2, and P3: the lowest level of isolation, where transactions are isolated just enough to ensure that physically corrupt data is not read. Transactions of this type are typically read-only.

❑ **READ_COMMITTED** – Permits P2 and P3, but does not permit P1. This is usually the default isolation level for databases like SQL Server.

❑ **REPEATABLE_READ** – Permits P3, but does not permit P1 and P2.

❑ **SERIALIZABLE** – Does not permit P1, P2, or P3: the highest level of isolation, where transactions are completely isolated from one another. This is the default isolation level for COM+ 1.0.

OLE transactions, the default transaction protocol of the DTC, has always supported different isolation levels. However, COM+ 1.0 shipped with Windows 2000 only supports serializable, the most conservative isolation level. COM+ 1.5, shipped with Windows XP, on the other hand, allows us to set the isolation level to any of the four listed above. The root object will determine the isolation level required for the transaction, and interior objects must support the same isolation level or lower. COM+ will deny requests to create interior objects that require a higher isolation level than the root object.

Allowing certain transactions to run under a lower isolation level can help improve the overall scalability of the application. However, the lower the isolation level, the higher the potential is for incorrect data. When determining the isolation level of a transaction, it's better to err on the safe side, and select a high level of isolation. Setting the isolation level to anything other than serializable should be a very deliberate and conscious decision.

You should also avoid modifying the isolation level within the implementation of the COM+ object. For example, avoid modifying the isolation level for a SQL Server connection by calling the T-SQL command SET TRANSACTION ISOLATION LEVEL. Instead, place the code that requires different isolation levels in separate classes, and configure the isolation level in COM+ for each class. If you need to create a class where its methods support various isolation levels, consider creating an interface class. The interface class itself would be configured to not support transactions: the actual implementation of the methods would be deferred to classes configured for the required isolation level.

Just-In-Time Activation

Since the root object has ultimate control over the lifetime of the transaction, it is important that COM+ deactivates the root object as soon and as often as possible throughout the object's lifetime, ideally at the end of each method call. Otherwise, the transaction may live longer than intended, potentially decreasing the throughput of your application and increasing the probability of deadlock situations. This is the reasoning behind just-in-time (JIT) activation, which we've already met in the earlier COM+ chapters.

Building Transactional Applications in VB 6

In this section, we'll explore how to build transactional component-based applications using Visual Basic 6. Specifically, we'll learn how to set the default transactional attribute for a VB class. We'll also examine one of the idiosyncrasies of VB, and its potential effect on the outcome of a transaction. Finally, we'll learn how to create a Compensating Resource Manager component.

Transactional Support for VB 6 Classes

VB 6 offers integrated support for transactional MTS/COM+ components. You can use this built-in transaction support by setting one of the properties of classes created in ActiveX DLL projects, namely `MTSTransactionMode`, through the **Properties** window. This property allows us to declare whether the component is COM+ aware and, if so, whether or not the component requires transactional support:

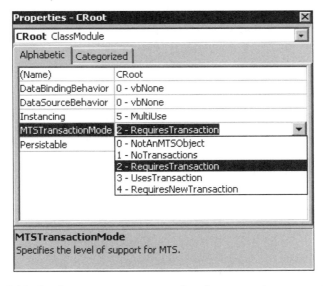

The five values available for this property correspond to the transaction support that should be set for the given VB class, and equate to the COM+ properties we saw earlier:

MTSTransactionMode	COM+ Transaction Support
0 – NotAnMTSObject	Disabled
1 – NoTransactions	Not Supported
2 – RequiresTransaction	Required
3 – UsesTransaction	Supported
4 – RequiresNewTransaction	Requires New

This property is stored in the component's type library, and is only referenced by COM+ to set the transaction support property when the component is installed into a COM+ application. Below is the IDL – the textual representation of the type library – for the CRoot class that was reverse-engineered using the OLE/COM Object Viewer:

```
[
  uuid(2993189E-98AE-4B54-B46A-2312C174D325),
  version(1.0),
    custom({17093CC5-9BD2-11CF-AA4F-304BF89C0001}, "0")
]
coclass CRoot {
    [default] interface _CRoot;
};
```

Chapter 8 introduced the basic concepts of type library and IDL, so refer back to it if you wish. As we can see in the code above, there is a custom property associated with the class. When a new COM+ component is being installed, COM+ will read the type library and set the transactional support property based on the custom property. We can then look up the transactional support type for the specified custom property in MTXATTR.H, or use the following table:

IDL Transactional Support Type Definition	Custom IDL Property
TRANSACTION_REQUIRED	17093CC5-9BD2-11CF-AA4F-304BF89C0001
TRANSACTION_NOT_SUPPORTED	17093CC6-9BD2-11CF-AA4F-304BF89C0001
TRANSACTION_REQUIRES_NEW	17093CC7-9BD2-11CF-AA4F-304BF89C0001
TRANSACTION_SUPPORTED	17093CC8-9BD2-11CF-AA4F-304BF89C0001

When the component is installed, COM+ will examine the component's type library and set the initial transaction setting accordingly. Note that in order for COM+ to act upon the transactional support properties defined in a component's type library, you must choose the Install new component(s) button in the COM+ Component Install Wizard:

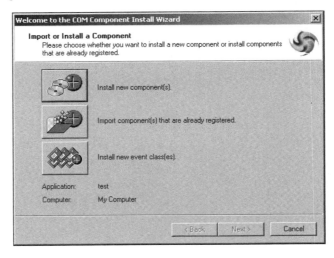

The second option, Import component(s) that are already registered, will install the component with default COM+ options. That is, it will set the transaction support property to Not Supported.

Creating Interior COM+ Objects in VB

VB programmers have the ability to create interior COM+ objects in a variety of different ways:

❑ Using the `CreateObject` method

❑ Using the `New` operator

❑ Using the `ObjectContext.CreateInstance` method

Prior to COM+, the preferred method for creating interior MTS objects was via the `ObjectContext.CreateInstance` method. This was the only way to create objects within the same activity as the root object. Now that MTS and COM have been integrated into COM+ that's no longer the case, and `CreateObject` is the preferred method.

The VB `New` operator reacts differently depending on how it is used. When the `New` operator is used to create an object from another DLL, it instantiates the object in a similar fashion to `CreateObject`. However, if the class for the requested object resides within the same DLL as the client, the implementation of the `New` operator bypasses COM+ altogether. The problem is that the child object resides within the same Object Context as the parent object.

To demonstrate this, we'll add a method to the `CTest` class we used earlier in the Activities section. The new method will be called `CreateChildUsingNew`, and as the name suggests, it creates a child using the `New` keyword rather than by calling `CreateObject`:

```
Public Sub CreateChildUsingNew()
    Set m_objChild = New CTest
End Sub
```

We'll now create a client to test the difference between using the `New` operator and calling `CreateObject`. The following code generates two message boxes that display the context ID for the root object and its interior object:

```
Dim objTest As Object

' Initialize
Set objTest = CreateObject("CTestProj.CTest")

' Create child using CreateObject.
objTest.CreateChild
MsgBox "Root object context ID = " & objTest.contextID & vbCrLf _
    & "Interior object context ID = " & objTest.child.contextID, vbOKOnly, _
        "CreateObject"

' Create child using the New operator.
objTest.CreateChildUsingNew
MsgBox "Root object context ID = " & objTest.contextID & vbCrLf _
    & "Interior object context ID = " & objTest.child.contextID, vbOKOnly, _
        "CreateObject"
```

The first message box displays the context ID for an interior object created with `CreateObject`, and the second message box displays the context ID for an interior object created with the `New` operator.

The first message box produced by the code above will be similar to that shown below:

Notice that the root and its interior object each have their own Object Context, as shown by the different context IDs.

The second message box detailing the objects created with `New` will be something like this:

As you can see, the context IDs are the same for both the root and child object. Since the root and interior object share the same Object Context, they also share the same transaction bits. This can be a problem because COM+ only accepts one vote per object context. Therefore one object has the ability to override the other's vote without its knowledge.

Take a look at the following VB code:

```
'*********************************************
'*              Client Code                  *
'*********************************************
Dim objRoot As New CRoot

objRoot.DoSomething


'*********************************************
'*              Class: Croot                 *
'*********************************************
Public Function DoSomething()
    Dim objInterior As New CInterior

    objInterior.DoSomethingElse

    GetObjectContext.SetComplete
End Function
```

```
'*********************************************
'*              Class: Cinterior            *
'*********************************************
Public Function DoSomethingElse()
    GetObjectContext.SetAbort
End Function
```

Here, the problem is that even though the DoSomethingElse method in objInterior votes to abort the transaction, the transaction will still commit – objRoot overrides the vote since they share the same object context. It's the equivalent of having a voting booth with one ballot and a pencil. The last person to vote determines the outcome of the election... not what you want to have happen.

The solution is to rewrite CRoot so that it creates objInterior by using either IObjectContext.CreateInstance or CreateObject like so:

```
'*********************************************
'*              Client Code                 *
'*********************************************
Public Function DoSomething()
    Dim objInterior as CInterior

    Set objInterior = CreateObject("CTestProj.CInterior")

    objInterior.DoSomethingElse

    GetObjectContext.SetComplete
End Function
```

Now the transaction will abort because COM+ gets the abort request from objInterior via its own object context.

> *Remember, since* IObjectContext.CreateInstance *is deprecated,* CreateObject *is the preferred method.*

The Compensating Resource Manager

As we mentioned earlier, the Compensating Resource Manager (CRM) provides a framework that allows us to integrate a persistent resource within the context of a transaction. We're going to walk through the steps required to create a CRM in VB. Our sample CRM will be used to create and delete directories within the context of a transaction.

Recall that in order to implement a CRM, we need to create two classes:

❑ The **CRM Worker** is responsible for performing the actual work on behalf of the user

❑ The **CRM Compensator** is responsible for ensuring that the changes made to the persistent resource were properly committed or aborted

CRM Worker

Our worker is a VB class responsible for creating and deleting the directories within the file system, so it will need two methods: `Create` and `Delete`. This sample project uses the `FileSystemObject` class provided in the Microsoft Scripting Runtime library, so add a reference to this library in addition to the now familiar COM+ Services Type Library.

Let's step through the `Create` method. We start with some declarations:

```
Public Sub Create(ByVal strDirPath As String)

    On Error GoTo ErrorHandler

    Dim objFS               As Scripting.FileSystemObject
    Dim strDirName          As String
    Dim objCRMLogCtl        As COMSVCSLib.ICrmLogControl
    Dim aRecord(2)          As Variant
    Dim lErrNumber          As Long
    Dim strMyActivityID     As String
    Dim strLocksActivityID  As String
    Dim bAquiredLock        As Boolean
    Dim strCompProgID       As String
    Dim strCompDesc         As String
```

Then in the initialize section, we obtain a `CRMClerk` object and cast it to the `ICrmLogControl` interface which will let us call its `RegisterCompensator` method:

```
' Initialize
Set objFS = New Scripting.FileSystemObject
Set objCRMLogCtl = New COMSVCSLib.CRMClerk
strDirName = objFS.GetFolder(strDirPath).Name
strCompProgID = "FileSystemCRM.CDirectoryCompensator"
strCompDesc = "The compensator for CDirectory."
strMyActivityID = GetObjectContext().ContextInfo.GetActivityId
bAquiredLock = False

' Strip the trailing backslash off the directory path.
If (Right(strDirPath, 1) = "\") Then _
    strDirPath = Left(strDirPath, Len(strDirPath) - 1)
```

The next thing to do is to register the compensator that will be used during the two-phase commit portion of the transaction via the `RegisterCompensator` method of the `ICrmLogControl` interface for the `CRMClerk` object. The `RegisterCompensator` method will return an error if there is a recovery currently in progress. When this occurs, the SDK documentation advises you to retry until the Compensator is registered. Unfortunately, the CRM framework does not provide a way for the method call to block while the recovery is in progress, so we have little choice but to enter into a spin lock instead. You can improve this by suspending execution for a short moment, say 1 second, before retrying, but we will ignore such details here:

```
    ' Register compensator
    On Error Resume Next
    Do
        objCRMLogCtl.RegisterCompensator strCompProgID, strCompDesc,_
                                COMSVCSLib.CRMREGFLAG_ALLPHASES
        lErrNumber = Err.Number
    Loop While (lErrNumber = XACT_E_RECOVERYINPROGRESS)
```

Note that we need to define the XACT_E_RECOVERYINPROGRESS error number as a private Const with the value -2147799170# in the declarations section of our class. If you prefer to deal with hexadecimal numbers, this error number is &H7FFB2F7E.

```
    On Error GoTo ErrorHandler

    If (lErrNumber <> 0) Then _
        Err.Raise vbObjectError + 1, "RegisterCompensator", _
        "Could not register the compensator component " & _
        "(err=" & lErrNumber & ")."
```

Next, we need to enforce serialized access to resources participating in a transaction. We do this by implementing a lock file for the directory – a text file that resides within the subdirectory's parent directory. The naming convention we use for the file is the name of the subdirectory followed by _lock.txt.

The file contains one line of text, which stores the activity ID that owns the lock. It's important to note that the lock is owned by the activity, and not by any one process. This is to help avoid an activity deadlocking on itself. In order to obtain the lock, we implement a simple spin lock, and we'll remain in the spin lock until our activity acquires the lock or the transaction times out:

```
    ' Obtain lock for folder
    On Error Resume Next
    Do While (bAquiredLock)
        ' Loop until lock is freed
        Do
            If (objFS.FileExists(strDirPath & "\..\" & strDirName & _
                "_lock.txt")) Then _
                    strLocksActivityID = objFS.GetFile(strDirPath & "\..\" & _
                    strDirName & "_lock.txt").OpenAsTextStream.ReadLine
        Loop While (strLocksActivityID = "" Or _
                strMyActivityID <> Trim(strLocksActivityID))

        ' If not locked by my activity, attempt to obtain lock
        If (strLocksActivityID = "") Then
            objFS.CreateTextFile(strDirPath & "\..\" & strDirName & _
                "_lock.txt", False)._
                WriteLine GetObjectContext.ContextInfo.GetActivityId
            If (Err = 0) Then bAquiredLock = True
        Else
            bAquiredLock = True
        End If
    Loop
```

Once we've registered the compensator and have obtained a lock on the required resource, we can write records to the CRM persistent log by calling the `WriteLogRecordVariants` method. The persistent log is used to document what actions were performed over the course of a transaction, and the Worker must write to the logs before performing an action. This is necessary in case a crash occurs while the action is being performed, because the Compensator would require this information to bring the system back to a consistent state.

We must represent the record as a variant array of simple variant data types. In our case, the first element represents the command being executed, and the second contains the path for the final destination of the directory. Finally, we call the `ForceLog` method to force the record to be written to disk. For efficiency, the `WriteLogRecordVariants` method performs a lazy write to the log, and is not flushed to disk until the `ForceLog` method is called:

```
' Write event information to the CRM log
aRecord(0) = tagDirCommands.DIRDELETE
aRecord(1) = strDirPath
objCRMLogCtl.WriteLogRecordVariants aRecord
objCRMLogCtl.ForceLog
```

Finally, we perform the action on the persistent resource. In this case, we add the requested directory:

```
' Perform the action and attempt to isolate the new directory from
' other clients
objFS.CreateFolder strDirPath
objFS.GetFolder(strDirPath).Attributes = objFS.GetFolder(strDirPath) _
                                         .Attributes + Hidden

' Clean up
Set objFS = Nothing
Set objCRMLogCtl = Nothing

Exit Sub

ErrorHandler:
    Err.Raise vbObjectError + 1, "Delete", "Error deleting directory: " & _
            Err.Source & " (err=" & Err.Number & "): " & Err.Description

End Sub
```

Note that we lock the directory before we create it to prevent a potential race condition. We also hide the directory after it has been created in an attempt to isolate this change from other clients.

Another important point is that our locking mechanism is only valid for clients manipulating directories via our CRM. Clients accessing the directory directly can easily bypass our locking mechanism. One solution would be to secure the directory and its contents by modifying the permissions on the directory.

The `Delete` method of our class is very similar. The first major difference is that we need an extra section of initialization, to ensure that the directory we're trying to delete actually exists:

```
Public Sub Delete(ByVal strDirPath As String)

    On Error GoTo ErrorHandler

    Dim objFS               As Scripting.FileSystemObject

    .
    .
    .


    Dim strCompDesc         As String

    ' Initial validation.
    If (Not objFS.FolderExists(strDirPath)) Then _
        Err.Raise vbObjectError + 1, "FolderExists", _
        "Directory does not exist."

    .
    .
    .
```

And we also don't need any code to perform the action, as we're going to defer the actual delete to the Compensator:

```
    .
    .
    .


    ' Write event information to the CRM log.
    aRecord(0) = tagDirCommands.DIRDELETE
    aRecord(1) = strDirPath
    objCRMLogCtl.WriteLogRecordVariants aRecord
    objCRMLogCtl.ForceLog

    ' no action to perform

    ' Clean up.
    Set objFS = Nothing
    Set objCRMLogCtl = Nothing

    .
    .
    .
```

The complete code for this class is available for download from the Wrox web site at http://www.wrox.com.

CRM Compensator

The compensator for `CDirectory` is `CDirectoryCompensator`. It's responsible for committing or aborting the actions performed by the `CDirectory` methods, `Create` and `Delete`.

```
Option Explicit

' Class:    CDirectoryCompensator
Implements COMSVCSLib.ICrmCompensatorVariants

Public Enum tagDirCommands
    DIRCREATE = 0
    DIRDELETE = 1
End Enum

Private m_bCommitTX          As Boolean
Private m_objDirsToBeUnlocked  As Scripting.Dictionary

Private Sub ICrmCompensatorVariants_SetLogControlVariants _
        (ByVal pLogControl As COMSVCSLib.ICrmLogControl)

    ' First method called when compensator is created
    ' Used to obtain the ICrmLogControl interface, if needed

End Sub
```

```
Private Sub ICrmCompensatorVariants_BeginPrepareVariants()

    ' Used to receive notification when prepare phase is beginning
    ' Note that prepare phase is skipped during recovery
    m_bCommitTX = True

End Sub
```

During the prepare phase, the Compensator is responsible for ensuring that changes made to the persistent store can be committed. In order to facilitate this, it is passed each log entry written by the Worker, and its `PrepareRecordVariants` method is called for each of these log entries. Our implementation validates each record to ensure that we can commit the transaction. Also notice that the CRM framework appends the CRM flags and the sequence number at the end of the array. The CRM flags provide information about when the record was written and whether this record was forgotten at some point. Finally, we indicate that we don't want this record to be forgotten and effectively removed from the log, by setting the return parameter to true:

```
Private Function ICrmCompensatorVariants_PrepareRecordVariants _
            (pLogRecord As Variant) As Boolean

    Dim lCommand    As Long
    Dim strDirPath  As String

    ' Initialize
    lCommand = pLogRecord(0)
    strDirPath = pLogRecord(1)
```

```
' If in debug mode, display the CRM flags and sequence number
' appended to the end of the array
#If DEBUGGING Then
    Debug.Print "CRM flags  = " & pLogRecord(UBound(pLogRecord) - 1)
    Debug.Print "Sequence # = " & pLogRecord(UBound(pLogRecord))
#End If


' See if we received a valid record
If (m_bCommitTX = False) Then
    ' Do nothing. No need to continue validating if we are not going
    ' to commit the transaction
ElseIf (lCommand = tagDirCommands.DIRCREATE And strDirPath <> "") Then
    ' Do nothing
ElseIf (lCommand = tagDirCommands.DIRDELETE And strDirPath <> "") Then
    ' Do nothing
Else
    m_bCommitTX = False
End If


' We don't want to forget this record...
ICrmCompensatorVariants_PrepareRecordVariants = False

End Function
```

The Compensator informs the DTC whether or not it is prepared to commit the transaction via the return value of its EndPrepare method. In our case, we'll return the value of m_bCommitTX. If the Compensator returns True, it is obligated to commit the changes made by the Worker when asked to do so:

```
Private Function ICrmCompensatorVariants_EndPrepareVariants() As Boolean

    ' Return whether or not prepare phase completed successfully
    ' and it is OK to commit transaction
    ICrmCompensatorVariants_EndPrepareVariants = m_bCommitTX

End Function
```

The commit phase starts when the BeginCommit method is called. The method is passed the bRecovery parameter, which indicates whether or not a recovery is in progress:

```
Private Sub ICrmCompensatorVariants_BeginCommitVariants _
        (ByVal bRecovery As Boolean)

    ' Don't need to perform any initialization nor care whether this
    ' is a recovery

End Sub
```

327

Next, the `CommitRecordVariants` method is called to commit each action logged by the Worker or the Compensator itself. Notice that once the action is performed, we don't immediately release the lock on the resource. The reason is that we don't want to release any locks until all actions are performed, since more than one action in the activity may have required a lock on the resource:

```
Private Function ICrmCompensatorVariants_CommitRecordVariants _
                (pLogRecord As Variant) As Boolean

    Dim objFS          As Scripting.FileSystemObject
    Dim lCommand       As Long
    Dim strDirPath     As String

    ' Initialize.
    Set objFS = New Scripting.FileSystemObject
    lCommand = pLogRecord(0)
    strDirPath = pLogRecord(1)

    Select Case lCommand
        Case tagDirCommands.DIRCREATE

            ' Unhide directory and then add it to the list of locks
            ' to be removed
            If (objFS.FolderExists(strDirPath)) Then
                objFS.GetFolder(strDirPath).Attributes = _
                    objFS.GetFolder(strDirPath).Attributes - Hidden
                If (Not m_objDirsToBeUnlocked.Exists(strDirPath)) Then _
                    m_objDirsToBeUnlocked.Add strDirPath, "unlock"
            End If
        Case tagDirCommands.DIRDELETE
            If (objFS.FolderExists(strDirPath)) Then
                ' Delete folder and then add it to the list of locks
                ' to be removed
                objFS.DeleteFolder strDirPath
                If (Not m_objDirsToBeUnlocked.Exists(strDirPath)) Then _
                    m_objDirsToBeUnlocked.Add strDirPath, "unlock"
            End If
    End Select

    ' We don't want to forget this record
    ICrmCompensatorVariants_CommitRecordVariants = False

End Function
```

Once all actions are performed by the resource manager, `EndCommitVariants` is called signaling the end of the commit phase. Since all updates on the persistent resource in the context of the transaction have been completed, we then release all of the open locks:

```
Private Sub ICrmCompensatorVariants_EndCommitVariants()

    Dim varLock     As Variant
    Dim objFS       As Scripting.FileSystemObject
    Dim strDirName  As String
```

```
        ' Remove lock(s) from directory(s)
    For Each varLock In m_objDirsToBeUnlocked
        strDirName = objFS.GetFolder(varLock).Name
        objFS.DeleteFile varLock & "\..\" & strDirName & "_lock.txt"
    Next

End Sub
```

The implementation for the abort phase is similar to the commit phase. BeginAbortVariants is called when the abort phase starts:

```
Private Sub ICrmCompensatorVariants_BeginAbortVariants(ByVal bRecovery As Boolean)

    ' Don't need to perform any initialization nor care whether
    ' this is a recovery

End Sub
```

Then AbortRecordVariants is called for each log where each action is rolled back:

```
Private Function ICrmCompensatorVariants_AbortRecordVariants _
            (pLogRecord As Variant) As Boolean

    Dim objFS           As Scripting.FileSystemObject
    Dim lCommand        As Long
    Dim strDirPath      As String

    ' Initialize
    Set objFS = New Scripting.FileSystemObject
    lCommand = pLogRecord(0)
    strDirPath = pLogRecord(1)

    Select Case lCommand
        Case tagDirCommands.DIRCREATE
            If (objFS.FolderExists(strDirPath)) Then
                ' Delete folder and then add it to the list of locks
                ' to be removed
                objFS.DeleteFolder strDirPath
                If (Not m_objDirsToBeUnlocked.Exists(strDirPath)) Then _
                    m_objDirsToBeUnlocked.Add strDirPath, "unlock"
            End If
        Case tagDirCommands.DIRDELETE
            If (objFS.FolderExists(strDirPath)) Then
                ' Add directory to the list of locks to be removed
                objFS.DeleteFolder strDirPath
                If (Not m_objDirsToBeUnlocked.Exists(strDirPath)) Then _
                    m_objDirsToBeUnlocked.Add strDirPath, "unlock"
            End If
    End Select

End Function
```

Finally, `EndAbortVariants` is called at the end of the abort phase, where all locks are released:

```
Private Sub ICrmCompensatorVariants_EndAbortVariants()

    Dim varLock     As Variant
    Dim objFS       As Scripting.FileSystemObject
    Dim strDirName  As String

    ' Remove lock(s) from directory(s).
    For Each varLock In m_objDirsToBeUnlocked
        strDirName = objFS.GetFolder(varLock).Name
        objFS.DeleteFile varLock & "\..\" & strDirName & "_lock.txt"
    Next

End Sub
```

Configuring and Using the FileSystemCRM

A CRM can only be used within a COM+ Server application. If the CRM will only be used by one COM+ application, then you can install it in the application where it will be used. However, the CRM will only be available for use within that application. If the CRM will be used by more than one application, you may install it within its own COM+ Library application and call it from a Server application. However, the Worker and Compensator should always be installed in the same application.

The Worker and Compensator classes' settings should be configured as follows:

	Transaction Support	**JIT**	**Threading Model**
Worker	Required	Checked	Apartment or Both
Comensator	Disabled	Unchecked	Apartment or Both

In order to use a CRM, the server application must have the Enable Compensating Resource Managers option checked. To do so, open the Component Services MMC and navigate to the COM+ application that will use the CRM. Open the application properties dialog box by right-clicking on the COM+ application, and select Properties. Finally, check the Enable Compensating Resource Managers checkbox:

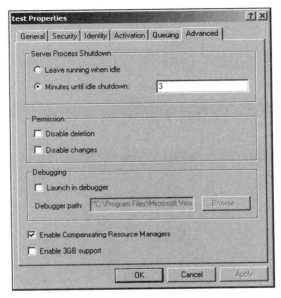

Once the CRM is configured, components within the application can use the CRM by creating a worker object, and then calling its methods to manipulate a persistent resource.

Summary

In this chapter we learned the fundamental properties of a transaction, summed up as:

- ❑ Atomic
- ❑ Consistent
- ❑ Isolated
- ❑ Durable

We moved on to learn about the major components within a transaction processing system, and the role they play in ensuring that the ACID properties are met throughout the lifetime of a transaction. Resource managers are deployed to ensure that a transaction is consistent, isolated, and durable, whereas the transaction manager ensures atomicity for distributed transactions.

COM+ provides a robust infrastructure that provides transactional support for component-based applications. We learned how to create and configure transactional COM+ components, and how to use the Object Context to vote on the outcome of a transaction.

COM+ uses a declarative model and leverages auto-enlisting resource managers to make transactional programming as easy for the developer as possible. However, we have also learned that a good solid understanding of the underlying architecture is important to ensure that the application behaves as expected. For example, we learned that any persistent resources modified within the context of a transaction should have a corresponding resource manager or should be modified through a correctly written CRM.

p2p.wrox.com
The programmer's resource centre

ASP Today

wrox.com

11

COM+ Distributed and Queued Components

As you may expect, the earliest distributed computing technologies were not centered on an object-oriented metaphor. However, you may be a little more surprised to discover that, depending on where you draw the line between the communications infrastructure and distributed computing technology, these early distributed technologies still lurk underneath more recent arrivals such as **Distributed COM**, or **DCOM**. DCOM is based on a system of remote procedure calls (RPC), which in turn are built on the primeval Windows sockets technology.

Distributed Processing with COM+

Distributed COM (DCOM) was introduced at the time of Windows NT 4.0, and it is in essence an extension for COM – quite literally in fact: DCOM is often referred to as "COM with a longer wire". The challenges of network applications are handled by COM runtime services as quietly as possible, but the addition of DCOM's various scalability features changed the equation a little as we shall see. COM+ integrated COM and DCOM, as well as MTS as explained in previous chapters.

To use in-process server components for distributed COM+ calls, the component must be installed as a configured COM+ application and the COM+ runtime acts as a proxy for the application. COM+ components execute in the COM+ Component Services process space, and applications call across to the COM+ Component Services, which hands off calls to the relevant components. Calls are invoked through marshalling, meaning that when a pointer is passed as a parameter to a call, the data it refers to must be copied over to the other machine's memory space in order for the pointer to remain valid, and when the called method completes, the data must be copied back to the caller's memory space. As you might imagine, this copying can chalk up a substantial overhead.

When you use COM+ in its distributed form to make method calls to a remote server, issues that aren't apparent in the local case arise. Distributed COM may be "COM with a longer wire", but that wire has a few twists in it.

Marshalling

Once you cross machine, process, or even apartment boundaries, you run into the issue of **marshalling**. Marshalling in COM+ with in-process servers is very much like what we've already seen on out-of-process servers in the local case, in Chapter 7, because parameters to be passed lie in a different memory space to that of the called component. The parameters are transmitted to the remote machine together as a block, and the values are then copied, or marshalled, into the process space of the server component.

On the server, the COM+ runtime libraries in the operating system handle this marshalling for you. The client machine, however, must have information about the called component's interface and must have a component to perform the marshalling. In the case of the IDispatch interface, which you might use from a scripted client, the operating system again comes to your rescue. Dispatch interfaces require no early knowledge of the interface. The names of methods and the names and types of method parameters are not checked until the method invocation takes place on the server. So far, this is pretty easy; you point the client machine to the server and everything works.

If you are using a compiled client, for example a C++ application for performance, you need a proxy for the component, as well as a type library on the client. The proxy may be provided by the Universal Marshaller in the presence of a standalone type library. The type library describes the interface to the client machine, while the proxy handles marshalling on the client.

Security and Authentication

When you are making calls to a local component, the local security subsystem checks your permissions when you instantiate a component. In Windows 2000 and XP, this involves checking Active Directory. Once you have the component running, you are assumed to have access to its methods and properties.

The distributed case is a bit different. The local machine checks to see if it has access to the proxy, but the server must check to see if that machine may instantiate the component and have access to its methods. Since calls traverse a network, checks need to be more meticulous. The component services in COM+ can be configured to check security rights at various levels. First, the identity of the caller can be the caller's user ID or the caller can impersonate a user on the server. Security will be enforced when the component is launched, and COM+ components can be configured to check access at every method call and even down to the level of individual packets. Whereas a local component can assume all packets for a method call come from the same client, in the distributed case it must defend against attacks where a malicious user spoofs valid packets in an attempt to take control of the component.

Resource Collection

A locally hosted in-process server reclaims resources for any components that have been forgotten, or if the application crashes. We can invoke resource collection manually by setting the object variable's value to nothing, which implicitly calls the component's Release method (part of the IUnknown interface common to all COM+ components).

When making distributed calls, though, there are more ways that resources can become orphaned. Both the client machine and the server can be up and running with all software intact, but the server-side component will become orphaned if the network path between them is broken. COM+ uses a **machine-level ping** to ensure such orphans are freed. So long as a client requires components instantiated on a remote server, it will periodically send a small message to the COM+ system on that server to indicate that it is still interested in the components. The server reclaims any components for which it does not detect this message for some configurable interval, thus conserving resources and reducing memory leaks.

Application Issues

When an in-process component is executing locally, the overhead of COM+ calls is small. You can make as many property Sets and Gets as you wish, and call methods as often as you wish without undue penalty. In that case, it makes sense to expose a lot of properties and set them individually before calling a method. This keeps the parameter list for methods simple. Anything that can be considered to be the state of the component should be exposed as a property. Only information specific to the method to be invoked should be passed as parameters of the method.

On the other hand, distributed COM+ components should expose COM+ interfaces that are designed to minimize network round trips and enhance scalability, because of the considerable overhead of marshalling and network latency imposed on calls. Instead of accessing memory via the bus that is physically inches from the processor with high-speed connection, COM+ accesses memory on another machine via the network with limited bandwidth that is no closer than a few feet and could even be in another country. Therefore, it makes sense to compromise the logical purity of the interface and pack as much as we can into each method call. All those property calls that suit the local case are now best included in the parameter list, perhaps as a user-defined type. If multiple related methods are usually called in sequence, they may be best combined into a single method in a class.

This guideline fits neatly with our other concern, scalability. Recall that MTS, and by succession, COM+, works best with stateless components. Ideally, state is not held across method invocations, and everything the component needs is sent as part of the method call. Once the call completes, COM+ is free to release or reuse the component, depending on what the component communicates to COM+ and how the component is configured.

A Julian Dates Component

Let's now put these ideas in practice. We'll take a COM+ in-process component and install it under Windows 2000 or XP as a configured component, giving an excellent opportunity to see how COM+ manages calls to remote components.

The component in question allows you to calculate calendar dates using the Julian numbering system. This component can take a date and return the Julian number, as well as tell you what day of the week this date represents. The Julian number is a real number whose integral part is a count of days since a start date and whose fractional part denotes the time as a fraction of a whole day. The Gregorian reform wasn't adopted all at once. Most countries in Europe made the switch in 1582, while Great Britain and her colonies held out until 1752. Nations such as Greece and Russia even waited until the twentieth century to follow suit.

Anyway, the component exposes properties that will specify when we're making the Gregorian switch, as well as other technical details related to calendar conversions. If you supply a Julian number, the component will helpfully tell you the day, month, and year of the date.

The component defaults to the civil calendar in use in the UK and the United States, so for those countries, we can forget the other properties. In fact, as we are dealing with modern dates and won't use the component for astronomical calculations, we can forget about the properties entirely. There are three methods that interest us:

❑ `MakeJulianNumber` – compute the Julian number given the year, month, and day

❑ `DateFromJulian` – compute the year, month, and day for a given Julian number

❑ `DayOfWeek` – determine the number of the day of the week for a given Julian number

In the code download for this chapter, there is an Excel spreadsheet that provides a user-friendly UI for this component. The component itself provides no conversion from the human-friendly form of a date, for example, 16 September 1974, and the parameters passed to and from the component. That's why Excel has been used to put together a rough user interface, as it has such capabilities. VBA code matches the interface to the component. Here's what it looks like:

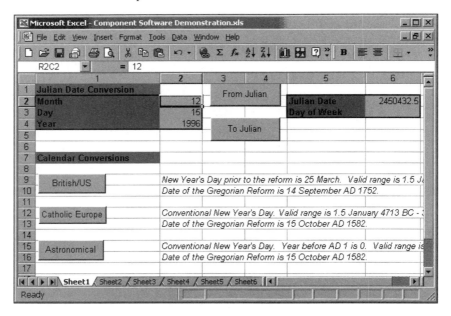

Here's an extract of the VBA code that illustrates how the component is used to compute Julian numbers. VBA a subset of Visual Basic that is built into many Microsoft and third party applications such as Microsoft Office:

```
Sub ToJulian_OnClick()
    'Button click handler for the To Julian Button
    Dim month As Long
    Dim year As Long
```

```
Dim day As Double
Dim jnum As Double
Dim index As Long
Dim week As String

' Set error handler

On Error GoTo ErrorHandlerToJulian

month = CLng(form.Cells(2, 2).Value)
year = CLng(form.Cells(4, 2).Value)
day = CDbl(form.Cells(3, 2).Value)
```

At this point, the subroutine has done some housekeeping. It establishes an error handler and retrieves the month, year, and day from known cells in the spreadsheet. The user would have input 6, 6, 1944 in three different cells to represent the date 6 June 1944, for example. The cell at R2C2 holds the number of the month, while R4C2 holds the year and R3C2 holds the day. Elsewhere in the VBA script code we've instantiated an instance of the component in a variable named `dtg` (for "date-time group"). Let's put it to work:

```
jnum = dtg.MakeJulianNumber(year, month, day)
index = dtg.DayOfWeek(jnum)
```

In two lines we've got the Julian number and the number (0 – 6) of the day of the week for good measure. Now it is up to Excel and VBA to stuff the values back into the spreadsheet for the user to see. We use the built-in VBA `WeekDay` utility to turn the index returned from the component into a string, such as Sunday, Monday, and so on, for display:

```
form.Cells(2, 6).Value = jnum
form.Cells(3, 6).Value = WeekDay(index)
Exit Sub
```

The error handler needs a bit of explanation:

```
ErrorHandlerToJulian:
  week = Error(Err)
  If Err = 91 Then
    Auto_Open
    Resume Next
  Else
    MsgBox ("Error: " & week)
  End If

End Sub
```

Error 91 indicates that the component has not been instantiated. The `Auto_Open` routine, invoked when the page is opened, instantiates the component. We call that routine in an attempt to fix things, then call the VBA `Resume Next` instruction to keep processing the script. For any other error, we convert the error to string format and display it to the user.

The component as you see provides a fairly simple yet robust capability for handling dates in the Western calendar. Since the implementation is centralized in a well-tested COM component, all applications that use it can be assured of proper date calculations. Application programmers don't have to worry about calendar algorithms, which is a bigger benefit than you might think.

Implementation

The following lines declare the long integer property `OldNewYearMonth`:

```
Public Property Let OldNewYearMonth(ByVal Value As Long)
    If Value >= 1 And Value <= 12 Then
        mOldNewYearMonth = Value
    End If
End Property
```

The remainder of the component source is similar to this. Our immediate purpose is to discuss the issues that arise when a local component is made distributed, so there is little value in wading through the algorithms for implementing Julian date calculations. The interested reader can download the entire source from the Wrox web site at http://www.wrox.com.

Deploying Components with COM+

Remember that one of our goals was to show how an existing component could integrate with COM+. Further consider that in a distributed setting we will need to install and configure support for our server component on multiple client machines. It is therefore desirable to see how to configure our sample component on the server using COM+ management tools. We'll also show how to create a file that will let you configure client computers with minimal fuss.

There are three steps to be performed:

❑ First, you must create a COM+ application on your server and add the sample component to it.

❑ Next, you export a proxy to that application to a Windows install file. Install files are covered in Appendix B.

❑ Finally, you use the install file to configure client computers.

When you are done, you can use the sample spreadsheet to invoke the component on the server computer from a client.

Configuring Our COM+ Application

The first thing to do is create a COM+ application on the server using the **Component Services snap-in** for the Windows MMC, accessed from the Administrative Tools menu or the folder of the same name in Control Panel.

Before configuring the server component, you must create a new application. This is done by expanding the desired server computer under the Component Services branch, right-clicking on the COM+ Applications node, and selecting New | Application. You will see the first window of the COM Application Install wizard. Clicking the Next button brings you to a window asking you to make the choice between installing a pre-built application and creating an empty application. Select the latter choice. This brings you to a window in which you need to provide a name for the application and indicate how the application will run:

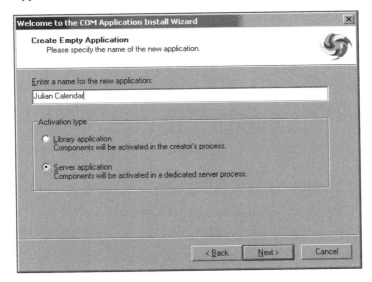

Since we intend to call this component from a remote client, we need to create a server application. The other option, of library application, is like an in-process server. It is faster to load but does not provide process isolation, hence a fault in the application or the component will cause both to fail.

The next window prompts you to indicate the application identity for the COM+ application. This is the account under which the application executes. You may select the interactive user, in which case the component will run with whatever permissions are accorded the user currently logged into the server. If you intend to run the server unattended, create a user account for the application (or designate an existing one with suitable permissions) and specify that account here. After finishing with the application identity information, click the button labeled Finish on the final window. The wizard will then create a new application. A node for the application will appear under the COM+ Applications branch in the Component Services tool. You may wish to fine-tune the security settings here, including when authentication is performed. For the purposes of our demonstration, we'll stick with the default.

Now that we have an application, we need to add the component and its proxy through the COM Component Installation wizard. This tool is invoked by expanding the application node added in the previous step, right clicking on the Components node, and selecting New | Component.

339

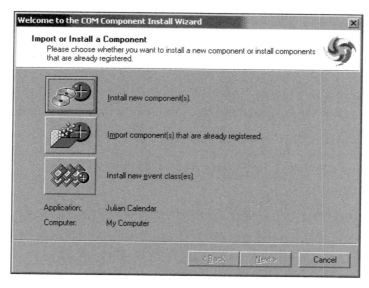

If you have built the component by building the Visual Basic project, the component will be registered on the build machine. Once you have finished with the Component Installation wizard, you will see a node for the new component. You can right-click and inspect its properties, or expand the node and view its interfaces and methods. For the purposes of this demonstration, you have finished configuring the server.

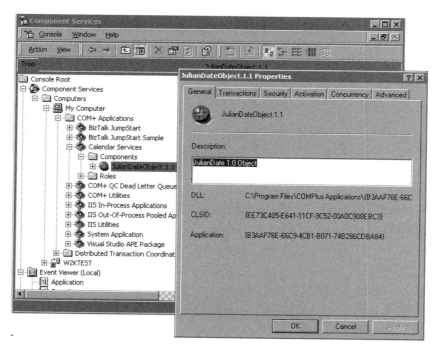

Packaging a Component for Export

The simplest way to get the required files to the client is to package the COM+ application for export using the COM Application Export wizard. The Export wizard produces a Windows installation file with an .MSI extension, and a CAB file containing the same installation file and the INF file needed to install it. Start the wizard by selecting the application node in the Component Services tool, right-click, and select Export.

If the machine on which you are performing the export operation is not the intended server, select the My Computer node in the Component Services tool prior to invoking the wizard, right-click, and select Properties. On the Options tab of the resulting dialog, enter the name of the server machine in the edit field labeled Export Application proxy RSN. This causes the export package to configure the client for the desired machine.

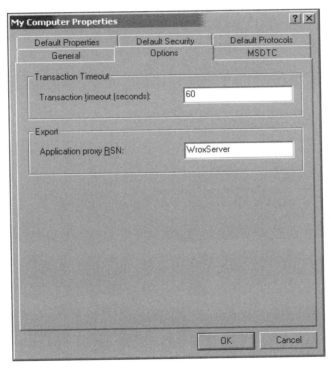

Once you invoke the Export wizard, you must decide what type of install file to create. If you simply want to install copies of the component on other machines for local use, you can select the Server Application option. This option generates an install file that would result in copying the component to the client and registering it for local use. The second option, Application Proxy, is intended to install the type library and the proxy stub DLL and configure the client to invoke the component on the server from which the export package was created. This is the option to select for our example.

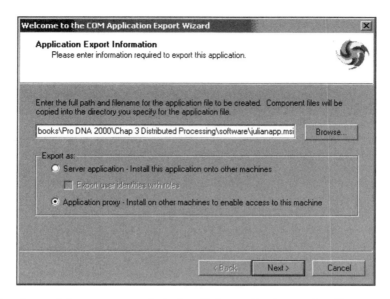

When the wizard completes, you are ready to install the application on the client computer.

Configuring the Remote Client

The installation file you created in the preceding step makes configuring the client very easy. Prior to MTS and COM+, you had to register the proper DLLs manually, then invoke the configuration utility DCOMCNFG to specify the remote server. This still works, but the installation file is much simpler.

The easiest way to install the application is to double-click on the installation file from Windows Explorer. You may also drag and drop the file into the Component Services tool when the **COM+ Applications** node is expanded. Once the installer completes, you will see a new COM+ application that is indistinguishable from the server except that the configuration options are disabled. If you use a tool like OLE View (from Visual Studio), you will not see the component under the **All Objects** node. Instead, look under **AppIds**. At this point, you may run the Excel spreadsheet or any other client that invokes this component and it will run on the server.

Implications for Real World Applications

By now you may be getting the feeling that this example was contrived solely to show you what *not* to do. There is a lot of effort involved in getting a proxy stub DLL, and the interface we presented makes a lot of round trips to configure and use the component. That is indeed the case. There are some problems here that show that distributed COM+ is not simply "COM with a longer wire". The component runs effectively in the distributed case, but it will not scale well and there are concerns regarding multiple users. The problems are these:

- ❑   The component maintains state across method calls
- ❑   The interface requires too many round trips between the client and the server
- ❑   The component requires a proxy stub DLL and type library on the client machine

Let's dissect these problems in turn and see what you might do about them to improve the performance of this component and make it a better candidate for distributed processing. Logically, it makes sense to distribute this component. We'd like everyone in our organization to use the same calendar. Practically, though, this component would need some work.

Stateful Components and Network Round Trips

At first glance, our component's `IJulianDate` interface looks like a good candidate for distribution. The principal methods are basically functions: we pass some parameters and receive values in return. So long as we can accept the default values established upon the creation of the component, this is the case.

The properties are the problem. Simply selecting the civil over the astronomical calendar takes a round trip, assuming you are not simply staying with the default value. If you wish to change from the default British Gregorian changeover date, you may need to set as many as seven properties. Not only do these entail expensive round trips to the server, but the state of the component is being held until you finish with your method calls. A French user wishing to calculate the Julian date for a day falling within the period between the time France accepted the Gregorian calendar reform and the time Britain accepted the reform would need to instantiate the component, make those seven round trips, and then – only then – call the method that gives him the value he really wants.

A better solution would be to incorporate the reform-related values in the parameter list for each method. Another alternative would be to incorporate all the reform values into a single method, say, `SetReformDate`, that would configure the component. Assuming the user wishes to make multiple calls for multiple dates, he would only have to pass the reform date parameters once. State would still be held, but at least the number of round trips would be reduced.

Proxies and Stubs

Unlike the local case, we had to worry about proxy stub components. For the purposes of our example, we simply deployed the component itself and redirected the COM+ application to the remote server. Of course, this defeats much of the purpose of resorting to distributed computing. In production we would want to build a separate type library and proxy stub DLL for the component. Without some sort of marshalling assistance, we cannot use DCOM. The problem is especially acute with early binding, in other words a library reference in a Visual Basic project. At that point we can no longer rely on dispatch marshalling and we absolutely have to have a type library local to the client machine. In production, we must be careful to keep the proxy stub and type library up to date with the server-side component.

> *An interesting comparison can be drawn with SOAP. SOAP is inherently late-bound insofar as the client has to discover the available methods of a server. The server may or may not use late binding. While the equivalent of the type library must still exist, it is downloaded from the hosting server when needed.*

Platform Incompatibilities

The key to the success of the Web is **ubiquity**. You can connect to the Internet from anywhere using any browser available. So far as connectivity goes, all the physical differences between the various hardware and software platforms disappeared with the HTTP protocol. The whole industry embraced it as the standard protocol for connecting machines, and companies developed their platform-specific code on *top* of it.

Today when you connect to a web site, you don't know – and more importantly, you don't care – what the web server and the underlying platform are. As a *user*, you only care about the *content* the page actually delivers. As a *programmer*, you only care about the *functions* the page actually exposes. When it comes to connecting, the characteristics of the platform are simply a non-issue, as long as you choose HTTP as the networking protocol.

If you decide to go for other approaches – including **COM+** or **Internet InterORB Protocol (IIOP)** – it's not long before the platform hardware/software configuration once again becomes a serious issue. Both of these protocols seem to be great for server-to-server communications, but they're not so effective for a client-to-server interaction. The reason is that in server-to-server situations, you usually have more control over the environment and the products involved. Both protocols, in fact, perform best when used within a single vendor's implementation.

COM+ and its ancestor DCOM, for example, are mostly Windows NT/2000/XP protocols (even though DCOM implementations do exist for other platforms). If you want to get the best out of COM+, you should definitely choose a configuration based on Windows 2000/XP. As for IIOP and CORBA, to get the most out of them you should consider working with a single Object Request Broker (ORB) to make sure you get a really interoperable environment.

In a client-to-server scenario – especially when the Internet is in the middle – both protocols have to comply with the possible presence of firewalls or proxy servers that usually block all but a few ports. The HTTP port 80 is one of the few exceptions.

In summary, the best available solution to our platform compatibility issues for client-server Internet applications is to use HTTP as our standard protocol.

SOAP and COM+

As we're discussing a protocol to invoke methods on remote components, you might wonder how SOAP compares to COM+. In a certain sense, SOAP was developed due to the difficulty that both COM+/DCOM and CORBA's IIOP encountered in becoming a de-facto standard for Internet-based communications.

While SOAP and COM+ share the same basic idea, they are opposite in terms of practical implementation. In particular, COM+ turns out to be rather complex in its configuration and administrative aspects. More importantly, it relies on dynamically assigned ports that make it pretty difficult for it to jump over firewalls.

COM+ has a far richer and extensible object model that provides some features that SOAP does not. In particular, SOAP doesn't manage and require object identity – it uses only URLs to identify objects, and needs stateless objects. With COM+, on the other hand, CLSIDs and ProgIDs allow you to identify precisely the object to call. The COM+ object's lifetime is manipulated by the client through IUnknown interface methods, whereas no particular measure is mandated by SOAP, other than timing-out the call or requiring stateless components.

There's also a performance aspect – since XML is a relatively verbose way of describing data, SOAP is not as efficient as COM+.

All of these disadvantages, though, are partly a result of the way that SOAP has been designed – the principal aim is simplicity and platform independence, in place of non-essential features and slightly enhanced performance.

In summary, SOAP and COM+ have the following respective benefits – and bear in mind that what is a pro for one is a con for the other:

SOAP pros include:

❑ Platform and language neutrality

❑ Simplicity and ease of use

❑ Jumps through firewalls

COM+ pros include:

❑ Object identification

❑ Object lifetime

❑ Transmission of binary data

❑ Performance

Today, we design client applications to communicate with specific server applications, taking into careful account the target platform. In most cases, especially when different hardware and software platforms are involved, we end up using proprietary text-based protocols. Sometimes we use XML to get more flexibility and ease of description. If you've already done this in the past, then you have implemented your own SOAP protocol – SOAP simply codifies existing practices.

> There's one more benefit of SOAP that's frequently overlooked – the load balancing implementation that's immediately solved for you once you implement SOAP. Technology for load balancing the HTTP protocol has already been successfully implemented in several different ways: for example, Microsoft offers Network Load Balancing Services. This still works with various back-end implementations of component based software, and eliminates the need to use Microsoft's Component Load Balancing Service (CLBS), which forces you to use COM+ based implementation of component development

COM Internet Services

Firewalls and proxy servers are a common presence between corporate networks and the Internet. Firewalls usually block all ports but a few, one of those few being the HTTP port 80. This means that if we want to run applications that reside outside the firewall, we should obtain an additional range of ports from the system administrator, in order for a client and a server to talk to each other. However, since SOAP is based on HTTP, we can solve this big issue without lifting a finger.

If you can't resort to using some of the DCOM typical services that SOAP doesn't provide, then **COM Internet Services** (**CIS**) might help to force DCOM and COM+ to operate over TCP port 80. CIS introduces support for a new DCOM and COM+ transport protocol known as **Tunneling Transmission Control Protocol** (**TTCP**). TTCP works around firewall limitations by introducing a special HTTP handshake at the beginning of each DCOM connection. After this, the wire protocol is simply DCOM and COM+ over TCP. Using CIS, neither the client code nor the server code needs updating, and you have all of the DCOM and COM+ advantages, including security and lifetime management.

TTCP, though, is a platform-specific solution. In fact, it requires IIS 4.0 or higher to be on the server machine, since most of the CIS functionality is implemented through an ISAPI filter. While this is not the only limitation of CIS, it is enough to highlight that it can't help to get *real* interoperability over the Internet.

Microsoft Message Queue

MSMQ is a service that runs on the Windows NT family of operating systems, including NT 4.0 Server, 2000 Server, XP Professional, and the soon to be released .NET Servers. It provides loosely coupled, asynchronous communication between applications. Consumer and service provider do not communicate directly and do not have to be online at the same time. MSMQ 1.0 is available for Windows NT 4.0 Server in the NT 4.0 Option Pack. MSMQ 2.0, which this chapter will focus on, comes with the standard Windows 2000 Server installation.

MSMQ 3.0 was released as a part of Windows XP Professional, which is the only non-server Windows operating system that supports independent MSMQ clients without a MSMQ server. We will discuss MSMQ servers and clients later in this section.

The basic concept of MSMQ is simple: it's a message forwarding system. It allows for messages – arbitrary blocks of data that can contain almost anything – to be bundled up and sent to a destination across a network for another application or service to process. Think of it as "e-mail for applications". Like e-mail, queues are **asynchronous**, and this is the chief virtue of MSMQ (and indeed, all other messaging middleware applications like it). Asynchronous processing allows non-linear execution of code, and in effect this means that applications need only be capable of processing the average load. If demand spikes, messages will be held in a queue and dealt with in turn. This allows our applications to consume less server resources than would be required in the synchronous case, as synchronous communications require servers that can handle the maximum expected load.

Where clients make requests that the server will be able to fulfill within an acceptable time frame, or clients require immediate feedback, synchronous processing is the better choice. Asynchronous processing such as queuing is appropriate where requests take more time, and it is acceptable to simply let clients know that their requests have been received, and that the results will be available soon.

MSMQ implicitly understands COM+ objects. Any component that implements the `IPersistStream` interface, such as the ADO recordset or instances of the Microsoft XML parser, MSXML, can be assigned to a message body, and placed in a queue.

Queues can be configured to be *reliable*, in which cases messages added to queues are written to disk, allowing recovery in the event of a crash. MSMQ queues can guarantee delivery of messages (**store-and-forward** messaging), regardless of the state and reliability of a network connection. Another aspect of availability is the ability to deal with detect network outages, and in such cases, MSMQ servers can be set up to try another path rather than waiting for connectivity to resume.

The receiver of a message in MSMQ is defined by who has "receive access" to the queue. This enables multiple receivers to respond to a single message in a single queue. For example, in most web applications that use MSMQ, the sender of the message is the web server (either through ASP or a COM component) and the receiver (responder) to the message is a custom application that resides on a different machine. The custom application doesn't have to be on a different machine, but it allows for greater scalability and flexibility.

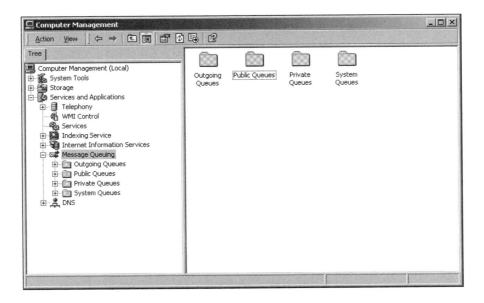

MSMQ Servers

MSMQ networks are organized around the concepts of **enterprise** and **site**. The enterprise is the entire business organization. A site is a bit more abstract, but generally corresponds to a single physical site or LAN. Each enterprise has a single **Primary Enterprise Controller** (**PEC**), and each site has a **Primary Site Controller** (**PSC**). All sites, including that hosting the PEC, have a **Backup Site Controller** (**BSC**) that steps in should the primary controller fail.

These messaging servers host the **Message Queue Information Store** (**MQIS**): a database that describes the MSMQ network, the structure of the network, the names of the servers, queue information, and so on. Clients query the MQIS to discover queue details. Servers use the MQIS to perform **smart routing**. Smart routing allows servers to forward messages along the shortest path under normal circumstances, and to route around outages when the network is degraded. Primary controllers – the PEC and PSCs – hold read/write copies of the MQIS and replicate changes between themselves. BSCs hold read-only copies of the MQIS.

MSMQ Clients

Any computer that has the software for accessing the MSMQ COM API is considered a client. MSMQ provides for two forms of clients: **independent** and **dependent**. Independent clients are capable of managing local queues for the storage of messages awaiting transmission, allowing applications to send messages while disconnected from the network, useful for mobile users for example. When connectivity is reestablished, the local queue is cleared and the messages sent.

Dependent clients, by contrast, require access to a server at all times. Dependent clients are good for users – fewer local resources – but bad for availability as they require more storage capacity on the server. They can even impact scalability as there is a four gigabyte limit on the amount of queue storage on servers that all dependent clients must share.

347

The Nature of MSMQ Queues

Queues are a place for requests to sit and wait until a process is ready to handle them. A message will stay in a queue until it expires, is read, or until the queue is purged (cleaned out). Each queue belongs to a single server, but one server can have multiple queues. Note that the queue does not *process* anything; its sole purpose is to *store* requests.

The main attributes of a queue are a **unique name** and two **globally unique identifiers** (**GUIDs**). The unique name is a simple string that is commonly used to refer to the queue. The first GUID, known as the ID, also defines the queue uniquely. The second GUID is a TypeID, which defines a group or type of queue. The TypeID can and will most likely be duplicated across multiple queues that perform a common task to group them together.

MSMQ is administered via the Microsoft Management Console (MMC) snap-in called Computer Management, also found in the **Administrative Tools** folder of **Control Panel**. The following screenshot displays the new MSMQ administrator in Windows 2000, which is located under the **Services and Applications** node. The following screenshot displays what an MSMQ message looks like from the MMC snap-in administrator. This can be accessed by selecting to view the properties of any message in a queue. Notice the GUIDs and other attributes of the message which were discussed above:

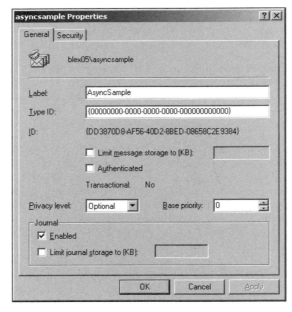

There are four types of queues within MSMQ 2.0 – each type and the queues beneath them can be accessed through the Computer Management MMC snap-in, under the **Message Queues** node:

- ❑ Outgoing
- ❑ System
- ❑ Public
- ❑ Private

Outgoing Queues

Outgoing queues are used to persist messages when a remote MSMQ server is unavailable. Outgoing queues are what provide MSMQ with the flexibility to operate even when another server is down. Applications cannot be programmed to use outgoing queues; they are only used internally by MSMQ when a queue is opened, by specifying the `FormatName` with the `DirectOS` identifier.

When the `FormatName` name is utilized, MSMQ will not directly communicate with the destination server. Instead, it allows the code to send a message to a queue that could be offline. The message is placed in an outgoing queue until the destination server is available or the message expires.

If a queue is opened by specifying the `PathName` property, it will only work when all resources are available. Unlike when the `FormatName` name is utilized, using the `PathName` requires that the destination server be available. If not, the opening of the queue will fail.

System Queues

System queues are also used internally by MSMQ, but are not available to custom applications. Examples of system queues are dead-letter queues, report queues and journal queues.

The dead-letter queues are used to store messages that could not be delivered. Report queues are used when tracing is enabled. A report queue will receive messages as a message is moved from the sender to its final destination. The journal queues are used to track the messages that have been read from a queue. Journaling is great for storing historical information.

Public Queues

Public queues are the most common queues in MSMQ. They are the queues that can be used by custom applications to fulfill business needs. Public queues are stored in the Active Directory service, and therefore are known to all other MSMQ servers throughout the enterprise. An example of a public queue would be an order queue for an order processing system.

Private Queues

Private queues are similar to public queues in that they can be accessed from custom applications, however they are not published in the Active Directory, so they are not available to applications outside of the local computer. These are not only faster to work with, but they are very secure, since they are not available from other computers.

Now let's look into the messages that are stored within these queues and the attributes associated with them.

MSMQ Messages

Messages in MSMQ are similar to e-mail messages, however, they are not sent to a single user or even a group of users. Instead they are sent from one single application to a single queue on a single computer. However, a message may be sent through a series of servers before it reaches its destination queue.

MSMQ messages are mainly comprised of three parts:

❑ The label

❑ The body

❑ The destination queue

The **label** is similar to the subject of an e-mail message. Most of the time a label is used to group various types of messages together, so a custom server-side application can distinguish what the message contains.

The **body** of an MSMQ message is very extensible. It is designed to hold anything from a string, to an array, to a COM+ object that supports the IPersist interface. For example, it is possible to create an instance of an ADO recordset, retrieve a result set, disconnect it from the data source and set it to the body of an MSMQ message. Then when the message is read, the instance of the ADO recordset object is pulled out of it!

The **destination queue** property of a message can be compared to the recipient of an e-mail message, especially since the introduction of MSMQ 3.0, which allows messages to be sent to multiple queues. Don't forget however that one message in a single queue may be read by multiple applications, a little unlike the e-mail analogy perhaps.

Let's take a look at an MSMQ message from the administrator point of view, through the MMC snap-in. The component for controlling MSMQ is within the Computer Management snap-in under the Services and Applications node. The following screenshot displays what the properties of an MSMQ message look like through the administrator. This dialog box can be displayed by right-clicking on a message and selecting Properties:

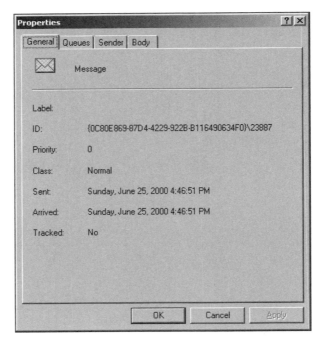

Although MSMQ queues are basically first-in, first-out mechanisms, MSMQ allows priorities to be assigned so that higher priority messages can be delivered sooner.

Messages may also be declared **public** or **private**. Private messages are encrypted for the user by MSMQ when they are sent, and decrypted upon receipt, which can be useful for some situations, such as virtual private networks over the Internet, although such links are usually encrypted at packet level.

Now that we have a general overview of MSMQ and the high-level parts it is comprised of, let's take a detailed look at its object model.

The MSMQ Object Model

Like most services, MSMQ has a COM API, which provides an interface for developers to code against. MSMQ's object model is comprised of a series of objects, although most applications only need to utilize four of them:

- ❑   MSMQQueueInfo
- ❑   MSMQQueue
- ❑   MSMQMessage
- ❑   MSMQEvent

The following diagram shows all of the MSMQ objects and how they relate to one another. Although we will give an overview of all of the objects and their purpose, we will only concentrate on the four objects mentioned above.

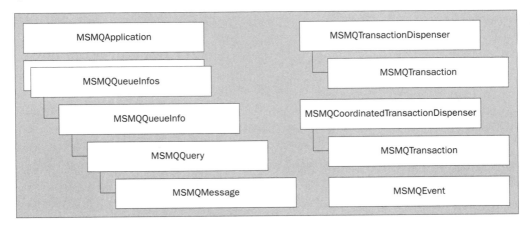

MSMQApplication

MSMQApplication is a small object that is normally not used when developing solutions with MSMQ. It has two methods: MachineIdOfMachineName and RegisterCertificate. MachineIdOfMachineName is used to look up the GUID (unique identifier) for the server name passed to it. This GUID can be used to specify the server instead of coding to the common NETBIOS name. The RegisterCertificate method is used by the clients to register a certificate. This verifies the identity of themselves and the server.

MSMQQueueInfo

The `MSMQQueueInfo` object provides the functionality to add, delete, and open queues within MSMQ on a given server. This object is often the starting point when working with the MSMQ object model.

In order to work with a queue the `PathName` or the `FormatName` is usually set. The `PathName` and `FormatName` properties inform MSMQ what queue is desired and also tell it which machine the queue is located on. The `PathName` is used when the server where the queue resides is known to be available. An example of this, although it is not recommended, is when the code is running on the MSMQ server itself. The `FormatName` is more commonly used, because it does not require the server to be available.

The following code is an example of opening a queue named `MyQueue` located on the local computer:

```
<%
Dim objQueueInfo
Dim objQueue

Set objQueueInfo = Server.CreateObject("MSMQ.MSMQQueueInfo")
objQueueInfo.FormatName = "DIRECT=OS:MyServer\MyQueue"

Set objQueue = objQueueInfo.Open(MQ_SEND_ACCESS, MQ_DENY_NONE)
%>
```

First, we dimension a variable (optional, but good practice). Next, we create an instance of the `MSMQQueueInfo` object. The next line sets the name and location of a queue and the last line opens the queue. When opening a queue, two parameters must be specified: `Access` and `ShareMode`. `Access` determines what can be done with the queue. The possible values for this parameter can be found within the `MQACCESS` enumerator, which has three values:

❑ `MQ_RECEIVE_ACCESS` (1) – Messages within the queue can be removed as they are read

❑ `MQ_SEND_ACCESS` (2) – Used when sending messages to the queue

❑ `MQ_PEEK_ACCESS` (32) – Used to look (peek) at messages, but does not remove them

The `Open` method returns a reference to an `MSMQQueue` object that is to send and receive messages. The `MSMQQueue` object is discussed below.

Creating and deleting message queues is performed much like opening a queue, by setting the `PathName` and then calling the `Create` or `Delete` method. Although this is usually done through the MMC snap-in, the following shows how it can be done through code:

```
<%
  Dim objQueue
  Set objQueue = Server.CreateObject("MSMQ.MSMQQueueInfo")
  objQueue.PathName = ".\MyQueue"
  objQueue.Create
%>
```

```
<%
  Dim objQueue
  Set objQueue = Server.CreateObject("MSMQ.MSMQQueueInfo")
  objQueue.PathName = ".\MyQueue"
  objQueue.Delete
%>
```

MSMQQueue

The MSMQQueue object provides the functionality to work with a queue that has been opened through the MSMQQueueInfo object. Although most web applications that use MSMQ are usually *sending* messages, there are times when web applications need to open a queue and *display* the messages, such as administrative pages. Also, all MSMQ-enabled applications need a server-side service or application to respond to the messages as they are received.

MSMQ messages can be read asynchronously or synchronously from a queue. Reading messages asynchronously allows a process to respond to a message though the use of events. MSMQ will get a reference to the code within the process and raise an event when a message arrives. Reading messages synchronously requires a process to occasionally open the queue and look for messages on its own. This can not only take up unnecessary system resources, but can be much more difficult to program. An example of responding to messages asynchronously is covered below. The following code shows how to open a queue synchronously and display the messages within the queue in a standard message box:

```
Public Sub DisplayMessages()

  Dim objQueueInfo As MSMQQueueInfo
  Dim objQueue As MSMQQueue
  Dim objMessage As MSMQMessage

' Create the queue, ignoring the error if it's already there
  Set objQueueInfo = New MSMQQueueInfo
  objQueueInfo.PathName = ".\MyQueue"
  objQueueInfo.Label = "My Sample Queue"

' If queue already exists ignore it
  On Error Resume Next

  objQueueInfo.Create
  On Error GoTo 0

' Open the queue
  Set objQueue = objQueueInfo.Open(MQ_RECEIVE_ACCESS, MQ_DENY_NONE)

' Loop through all the messages in the queue
  Do While True
      Set objMessage = objQueue.Peek(, , 1000)
      If objMessage Is Nothing Then Exit Do
      MsgBox "Message: " & objMessage.Label
  Loop
  MsgBox "No more new messages."
```

```
' Clean up
  objQueue.Close
  Set objMessage = Nothing
  Set objQueue = Nothing
  Set objQueueInfo = Nothing

End Sub
```

The above code starts off by using the `MSMQQueue` object and enters a `Do While ... Loop` until the `Peek` method returns `Nothing`. When this routine returns `Nothing`, it means that the time-out expires. In this case the time-out is set to 1000 milliseconds. Although we have not covered the `MSMQMessage` object yet (below), the main part to note is that the code is setting a reference to an MSMQ message through the use of the `Peek` method on the queue.

MSMQMessage

The `MSMQMessage` object is the heart of MSMQ and provides a piece of functionality that all MSMQ-enabled applications take advantage of – sending and reading messages. An `MSMQMessage` object is very extensible because it is designed to hold a wide variety of information. For example, the `Body` of the message can hold a string, byte array, any numeric types, or even an instance of a persistable COM object! The `Label` of a message is a string that simply describes what the message is. It is comparable to the title of an e-mail message.

Messages can be retrieved in one of two ways, by opening or peeking. When a message is opened, it is removed from the queue once it is read and placed in the journal folder, if journaling is enabled. When a message is peeked, it remains in the queue until the message expires or until it is read by another process. The opening and peeking of a message is performed in the `MSMQQueue` object through the `Open` and `Peek` routines, which then return back a reference to the instance of an `MSMQMessage` object.

The following code displays how to open a message and display the `Body` and `Label`:

```
Private Sub LookForMessage()

  Dim objQInfo As MSMQQueueInfo
  Dim objQReceive As MSMQQueue
  Dim objMessage As MSMQMessage

' Open the queue
  Set objQInfo = New MSMQQueueInfo
  objQInfo.PathName = ".\MyQueue"
  Set objQReceive = objQInfo.Open(MQ_RECEIVE_ACCESS, MQ_DENY_NONE)

' Look for a message with a time-out of 100 ms
  Set objMessage = objQReceive.Receive(, , , 100)

' Was there a message?
  If Not objMessage Is Nothing Then
    'Display the contents of the message
    MsgBox objMessage.Label & " - " & objMessage.Body
  Else
    'No message
    Msgbox "Nothing in the queue"
```

```
      End If

   ' Clean up
      objQReceive.Close
      Set objQInfo = Nothing
      Set objQReceive = Nothing
      Set objMessage = Nothing

   End Sub
```

The code sample above starts by opening a queue, then looks for a message within the queue, by invoking the Receive routine with a time-out of 100 milliseconds. A time-out is used to tell MSMQ when to stop waiting for a message. To see if there was a message, we test the MSMQMessage object returned by the Receive function to see if it is Nothing. If the Receive method returned a valid message the code then displays the Label and the Body properties.

Sending a message is the most common task performed with MSMQ in web applications. To send a message, a queue is opened with send access (MQ_SEND_ACCESS), a message is built, and the Send method on an MSMQMessage object is invoked.

```
<%
'Dim some variables
Dim objQInfo
Dim objQSend
Dim objMessage

'Open the queue
Set objQInfo = Server.CreateObject("MSMQ.MSMQQueueInfo")
objQInfo.PathName = ".\test"

Set objQSend = objQInfo.Open(MQ_SEND_ACCESS, MQ_DENY_NONE)

'Build/send the message
Set objMessage = Server.CreateObject("MSMQ.MSMQMessage")
objMessage.Label = "This is the label."
objMessage.Body = "This is the body."
objMessage.Send objQSend
objQSend.Close

'Clean up
Set objQInfo = Nothing
Set objQSend = Nothing
Set objMessage = Nothing
%>
```

The code example above starts out like the other sample and opens a queue, but this queue is opened with send access. Next a message is built by creating an instance of the MSMQMessage class and setting the Label and Body properties. Finally, the message is sent by calling the Send method on the message, passing a reference of the queue in as a parameter.

MSMQQuery

The MSMQQuery object is used to provide a way to search for a queue given a wide variety of information. This object has just a single method, LookupQueue, which returns a collection of MSMQQueueInfo objects within a single MSMQQueueInfos object.

MSMQQueueInfos

MSMQQueueInfos is returned from the LookupQueue method on the MSMQQuery object. This object is a limited collection of MSMQQueueInfo objects (missing the Add, Remove, Count, and so on.) only has two methods.

MSMQEvent

The MSMQEvent object is a very useful class when building server-side applications built in languages like VB and VC++, because it provides a mechanism for MSMQ to call into the code and fire events when messages are received in a queue (asynchronously). The MSMQEvent object is a small object, in fact, it has no properties or methods; it only consists of two events, Arrived and ArrivedError.

The following code example shows how to open a local queue and respond to messages asynchronously through the use of the MSMQQueue and MSMQEvent objects:

```
Option Explicit

Private m_objQueueInfo As MSMQQueueInfo
Private m_objQueue As MSMQQueue
Private WithEvents m_objMSMQEvent As MSMQEvent

Private Sub Form_Load()

' Create the queue, ignoring the error if it's already there
  Set m_objQueueInfo = New MSMQQueueInfo
  m_objQueueInfo.PathName = ".\MyQueue"
  m_objQueueInfo.Label = "My Sample Queue"

' If queue already exists ignore it
  On Error Resume Next
  m_objQueueInfo.Create
  On Error GoTo 0

' Open the queue
  Set m_objQueue = m_objQueueInfo.Open(MQ_RECEIVE_ACCESS, MQ_DENY_NONE)

' Link the events
  Set m_objMSMQEvent = New MSMQEvent
  m_objQueue.EnableNotification m_objMSMQEvent, MQMSG_CURRENT, 1000

End Sub

Private Sub m_objMSMQEvent_Arrived(ByVal Queue As Object, _
                                   ByVal Cursor As Long)
```

```
' Process the message
  Dim objMessage As MSMQMessage
  Set objMessage = Queue.PeekCurrent

  MsgBox "Message Received: " & m_objMessage.Label

' Link the event for the next message
  m_objQueue.EnableNotification m_objMSMQEvent, MQMSG_NEXT, 10000

End Sub

Private Sub m_objMSMQEvent_ArrivedError(ByVal Queue As Object, _
                                        ByVal ErrorCode As Long, _
                                        ByVal Cursor As Long)
' Something went wrong!
  MsgBox "Error recorded: " & ErrorCode

End Sub
```

The above code starts with the Form_Load event and opens a queue named MyQueue. Then the m_objMSMQEvent object is linked to the queue. This is done by calling the EnableNotification method on the MSMQQueue object and passing a reference to the m_objMSMQEvent object. Once the MSMQEvent object is linked, the only thing left to do is fulfill the Arrived and Arrived_Error (optional) events. The Arrived event fires every time a new message is received in the queue. However, any time a notification is received of a message arrival or error, the EnableNotification method must be called again to tell MSMQ to inform the code when the next message is received. If the code fails to call EnableNotification, the next message will never be seen. When the Arrived event is raised by MSMQ it returns a reference to the queue where the message can be read from and also returns a reference to the cursor. If an error occurs, the ArrivedError event will fire with a reference to the Queue object, a long variable holding the error number, and a reference to the cursor.

MSMQTransaction

The MSMQTransaction object is used to tell MSMQ to abort or commit a transaction that has been started by either the MSMQTransactionDispenser or the MSMQCoordinatedTransactionDispenser object. An instance of the MSMQTransaction object can not created by using the New keyword or CreateObject function. It can only be created through the use of the BeginTransaction method on the MSMQTransactionDispenser and MSMQCoordinatedTransactionDispenser objects.

MSMQCoordinatedTransactionDispenser

The MSMQCoordinatedTransactionDispenser object provides one way to hook into the power of the Distributed Transaction Coordinator (DTC) within MSMQ. This object is quite small and only contains a single method called BeginTransaction. By using the DTC, transactions are not only able to encompass reads and writes to message queues, but they are also able to contain any other service that supports DTC. This enables developers to write routines that modify data in databases like SQL Server (6.5, 7.0, or 2000) and send/read messages from a queue, all within one single transaction.

Transactions that span across multiple DTC-compliant services can also be held within a transaction under COM+ (or MTS in Windows NT). This enables developers to encapsulate code into COM+ DLLs and place them under the control of COM+ Component Services.

357

MSMQTransactionDispenser

The MSMQTransactionDispenser object provides the functionality to wrap multiple messages, send to and receive from multiple queues in MSMQ in a transaction. Using this object is very useful for internal MSMQ transactions, but it cannot contain anything else like SQL Server database updates or inserts. When a transaction is needed and will only contain operations with MSMQ, use the MSMQTransactionDispenser object transaction. It is much faster than the MSMQCoordinatedTransactionDispenser transaction because it does not have to deal with the overhead of the DTC.

An MSMQ Application

Now it's time to utilize what we've learned about MSMQ and develop an application that uses MSMQ to implement asynchronous communication.

We'll start by defining the queue where requests will be sent. To do this, open the Computer Management MMC snap-in located in the Administrative Tools folder, and expand the Message Queuing node under Services and Applications. Add a new queue called AsyncSample in the Public Queue node:

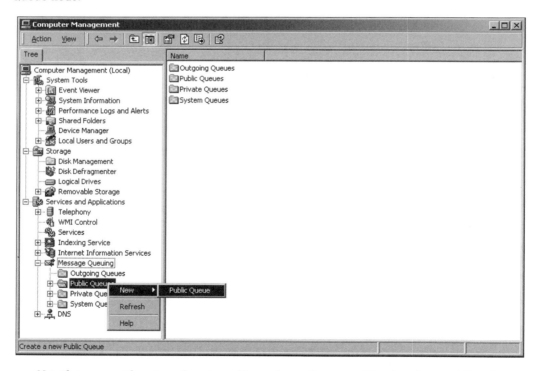

Note that you must be using a domain machine, not a workgroup machine, in order to get this code to work. Check out MSDN for more information on how to determine this.

API to Queue

Now that we have a queue to send requests or messages to, we can turn to the code. Create a new project called MSMQSample. Next make a new reference to the **MSMQ 2.0 Object Library**. Our code first creates an instance of the MSMQQueueInfo object that provides functionality to create, delete, and open various queues. We use this object to open the queue we already created with send rights:

```
Public Sub SubmitRequest(ByVal strConnectionString As String, _
                   ByVal strSQL As String, ByRef strError As Variant)

   Dim objQueueInfo As MSMQ.MSMQQueueInfo
   Dim objQueue As MSMQ.MSMQQueue
   Dim objMessage As MSMQ.MSMQMessage


   On Error GoTo Error_Handler

   ' open the queue with send access
     Set objQueueInfo = New MSMQ.MSMQQueueInfo
     objQueueInfo.FormatName = "DIRECT=OS:blex05\AsyncSample"
     Set objQueue = objQueueInfo.Open(MQACCESS.MQ_SEND_ACCESS, _
                 MQSHARE.MQ_DENY_NONE)

   '   set the message
     Set objMessage = New MSMQ.MSMQMessage
     With objMessage
        .Label = strConnectionString
        .Body = strSQL
        .Send objQueue
     End With

   Exit_Handler:
   Set objMessage = Nothing
   If Not objQueue Is Nothing Then If objQueue.IsOpen = 1 Then _
           objQueue.Close
   Set objQueue = Nothing
   Set objQueueInfo = Nothing
   Exit Sub

   Error_Handler:
     strError = Err.Description & " (" & Err.Number & " - " & _
             Err.Source & " )"
     Resume Exit_Handler

End Sub
```

The code above starts off with the same interface as the database example, but instead utilizes MSMQ. Note how it first attaches to the queue by using the FormatName and invoking the Open method on the objQueueInfo object. Next the code creates a message and stores the connection string in the label of the message, and the SQL string in the body. It sends the message by invoking the Send routine on the message itself and passes a reference to the queue. Lastly the code cleans up by setting all of the object references to nothing, and closes the queue.

Let's take a more detailed look at how we opened the queue. A call is made to the Open method on the MSMQQueueInfo object once the desired queue is specified. Notice that the example above sets the desired queue by specifying the FormatName property with DIRECT=OS:. Queues can also be opened by specifying the machine and queue name through the PathName property, objQueueInfo.PathName = "MyComputer\MyQueue". When using the PathName property, the opening of the queue is very fast; however, if the desired queue is unavailable then the Open routine will fail. With the FormatName property, the opening of the queue takes a little longer, but it will not fail when the queue is opened, even if the specified queue is unavailable. Unless you can guarantee the queue will always be available it is best to use the FormatName with Direct=OS:.

Request Processor

Create a new project called MSMQProcessor In this solution we will listen for messages that are sent to the queue. This means the program doesn't need to continually check the queue for requests, yet it will be able to respond almost immediately when a request is received.

Start by adding a reference to the **MSMQ Object Library 2.0**. We still need a reference to ADO as we need to execute the SQL statement sent from the client. Next declare two private objects at form level, one called m_objQueue, which will be a reference to the desired queue, and the other m_objMsmqEvents which is declared with WithEvents and is of type MSMQEvent. The instance of the MSMQEvent class declared with WithEvents provides an event sink in which MSMQ can raise events informing us when a new message has arrived in the queue (m_objQueue).

```
Dim m_objQueue As MSMQ.MSMQQueue
Dim WithEvents m_objMsmqEvents As MSMQ.MSMQEvent
```

> *Declaring objects with* WithEvents *provides a mechanism to alert the object's consumer by raising events. Responding to these events is very similar to responding to the click event of a button; the only difference is the action that prompted the event.*

On form load, we need to open the AsyncSample queue for read access, and hook up the m_objMsmqEvents object. This is done by opening the queue, as in the MSMQSample project, but with the MQ_RECEIVE_ACCESS flag instead of the MQ_SEND_ACCESS flag. Once the queue is opened the code creates a new instance of the MSMQEvent class and passes a reference of it to MSMQ through the EnableNotification method on the m_objQueue object:

```
Private Sub Form_Load()

    Dim objQueueInfo As MSMQ.MSMQQueueInfo

    On Error GoTo Error_Handler

    '    open the queue
        Set objQueueInfo = New MSMQ.MSMQQueueInfo
        objQueueInfo.FormatName = "DIRECT=OS:blex05\AsyncSample"
        Set m_objQueue = objQueueInfo.Open(MQACCESS.MQ_RECEIVE_ACCESS, _
                    MQSHARE.MQ_DENY_NONE)
```

```
'    hook in the events
      Set m_objMsmqEvents = New MSMQ.MSMQEvent
      m_objQueue.EnableNotification m_objMsmqEvents, , 1000

   Exit_Handler:
    'clean up
    Set objQueueInfo = Nothing
  Exit Sub

   Error_Handler:
     MsgBox Err.Description & " (" & Err.Number & ")", vbCritical, Err.Source
     Resume Exit_Handler

End Sub
```

Now the only code left to write is to respond to the events from the m_objMsmqEvents and execute the SQL statement request from the client:

```
Private Sub m_objMsmqEvents_Arrived(ByVal Queue As Object, _
          ByVal Cursor As Long)

  Dim objConn As ADODB.Connection
  Dim objMessage As MSMQ.MSMQMessage

  On Error GoTo Error_Handler

    'get the current message
     Set objMessage = Queue.ReceiveCurrent

    'connect to the db and execute the string
    Set objConn = New ADODB.Connection
    objConn.Open objMessage.Label
    objConn.Execute CStr(objMessage.Body), , adExecuteNoRecords

    'everything worked!
    txtInfo.Text = "Processed: " & objMessage.Body

  Exit_Handler:
    'hook in the next event
    Set m_objMsmqEvents = New MSMQ.MSMQEvent
    m_objQueue.EnableNotification m_objMsmqEvents

    'clean up
    Set objMessage = Nothing
    If objConn.State = adStateOpen Then objConn.Close
    Set objConn = Nothing
  Exit Sub

  Error_Handler:
    txtInfo.Text = Err.Description & " (" & Err.Number & ")"
    Resume Exit_Handler

End Sub
```

361

The code above will be fired every time a message is received by MSMQ within the `AsyncSample` queue. The code starts off by reading the current message. Once it has the message, the code reads the `Label` that contains the connection string and the `Body` that contains the SQL statement and performs the desired execution on the desired database.

Notice that as the method is finishing it reconnects the `m_objMsmqEvents` object. This needs to be done every time a message is read from MSMQ; in fact it is even needed in the other event that can be raised by MSMQ, the `ArrivedError` event.

Depending on the requirements of each application, different things can be done when MSMQ raises the `ArrivedError` event. This example displays a message box stating the message label. In a production environment you wouldn't want to display a message box, but for testing it is useful.

```
Private Sub m_objMsmqEvents_ArrivedError(ByVal Queue As Object, _
                        ByVal ErrorCode As Long, ByVal Cursor As Long)

  Dim objMessage As MSMQ.MSMQMessage

  On Error GoTo Error_Handler

    'see what happened
    Set objMessage = Queue.ReceiveCurrent
    MsgBox "Investigating message: " + objMessage.Label
    m_objQueue.EnableNotification m_objMsmqEvents, , 10000

    Exit_Handler:
    Set objMessage = Nothing
  Exit Sub

  Error_Handler:
    MsgBox Err.Description + " in Arrived event"

End Sub
```

Client

Now that all of the pieces to submit a request and process the request through MSMQ have been developed, let's revisit the ASP code for the UI and make one small modification. Since the class name, `Request`, and the method signature have remained unchanged, the only code that needs to be modified is the `ProdID` within the `AsyncSample2.asp` page:

```
<%@ Language=VBScript %>
<HTML>
<HEAD>
<META NAME="GENERATOR" Content="Microsoft Visual Studio 6.0">
</HEAD>
<BODY>

<%

  Dim objRequest
  Dim strError
```

```
    Set objRequest = Server.CreateObject("MSMQSample.Request")
    objRequest.SubmitRequest Request.Form("txtConnectionString"), _
            Request.Form("txtSQL"), strError

    If len(strError & "") = 0 then
      Response.Write "Request was successfully sent."
    Else
      Response.Write "Error sending request: " & strError
    End If

    Set objRequest = Nothing

%>

<BR>
<BR>

<A href="javascript:history.back(1)">Back</A>

</BODY>
</HTML>
```

Let's try it out! Open the AsyncSample1.asp page in a browser and submit a request:

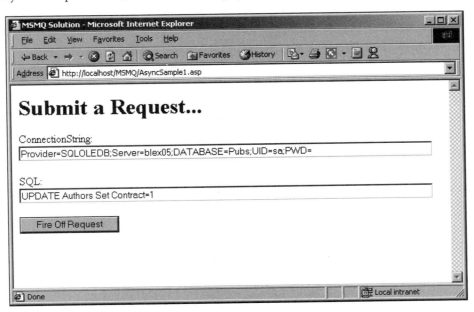

As requests are made to the MSMQSample COM component, messages are sent to the AsyncSample queue within MSMQ. If the MSMQProcessor executable is not running, you can open the MSMQ administrator (Computer Management MMC snap-in) and view the messages (the messages are not processed until the MSMQProcessor is running).

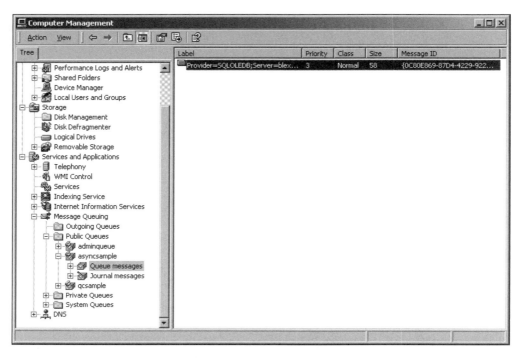

You can also view the properties of the message by right-clicking on it and selecting **Properties**. This shows a wide variety of attributes, as well as the body of the message and how it is stored:

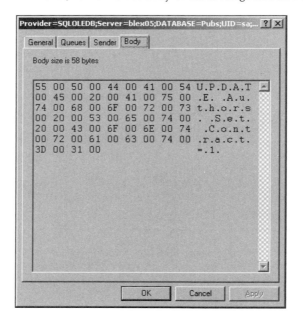

Now, if you haven't already fired up the MSMQProcessor executable, do so and it will process any messages within the queue. Also, as noted above, the messages will be processed right away as long as the MSMQProcessor executable is running:

Other Possibilities

As you can see, MSMQ provides a very powerful and flexible way to implement asynchronous communication. Since the body of a message is a variant, it can hold a wide variety of information, including objects, as long as they support the IPersist interface. Another great benefit of MSMQ is that the communication is loosely coupled and you can easily add more servers into the mix to counteract an increase in users.

Another possible way to use MSMQ is for an ordering system. There can be various queues for each step within the order process, from placing an order to its fulfillment. As each message is processed, within each step a new message is created and placed in the next queue, with the required information. The information or state for each message can even be stored within a COM+ object that supports IPersist and can be placed in the body of the message.

MSMQ might also be used in a dispatching system that invokes a COM object on behalf of the client. This can be very useful when web clients need to invoke a routine that is very processor-intensive. Instead of the client invoking the method directly, a request can be made through MSMQ where a listener of the queue can invoke the process. This type of architecture is very useful; in fact it is so useful Microsoft developed a service within COM+ called Queued Components, which is the subject of the next section in this chapter.

MSMQ Queued COM+ Components

MSMQ uses the IPersistStream interface built into COM/COM+ interfaces to allow programmers to rapidly pass component state to another application. The hard work of serializing the component to a data message and reconstituting it on the receiving end is performed within the MSMQ object model and COM+. IPersistStream extends the data passing metaphor slightly so that we have an object-passing model. The applications on both ends of the exchange are able to use component software, while the communications between application tiers benefit from asynchronous communications and the simplicity of the data passing metaphor.

A pair of components mediates between a queued COM+ server component and a client invoking methods on it:

❑ When a client makes a call to a queued component, the COM+ Recorder component accepts the call and writes the parameters to an MSMQ queue along with the security context of the client.

❑ This message is taken off the queue by the COM+ Listener component on the server. The listener acts as a proxy for the client, making the call using the client security context.

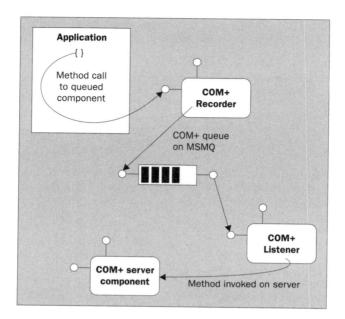

The method the application calls shown in this diagram are one-way, that is you cannot have methods with return values or which pass parameters by reference as the calling process might not be around by the time the server actually executes the method call. Indeed, the COM+ component may not even be active at the time the client makes the method call, so the application can expect no more than an acknowledgment indicating successful acceptance and commitment to the queue.

To receive information from the server component, you need to set up a separate queued component on the client for that purpose.

Queued COM+ components merge the logical integrity of the component model with the scalability and availability of the data passing, messaging model.

COM+ Queued Components

Queued Components (QC) is a service within COM+ that is built upon MSMQ. QC provides an advanced architecture for the interaction with a component (method calls) to be recorded and packed into an MSMQ message, and then read by another process where the actual method call performed by the client is carried out.

Queued Components Architecture

Even though it may sound like a lot of magic is happening here, the architecture behind QC is actually quite straightforward and closely relates to the MSMQ sample developed above.

QC can really be broken up into three sections: the **recorder**, **listener**, and **player**. The recorder is similar to our MSMQSample component in the fact that it hides all of the underlying MSMQ instructions inside of it. However, the recorder section of QC is quite flexible. Instead of simply taking a connection string and a SQL string, the recorder records or logs the interaction (method calls) between the consumer (ASP in this case) and the object. Once the consumer is finished with the object and the reference is dropped, the recorder takes all of the interaction it logged and sends it to a queue within MSMQ where it sits and waits for the listener to pick it up.

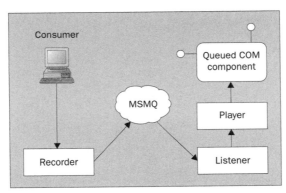

If you think about it, the recorder within QC is actually a very powerful component. It has to be very intelligent to understand how each method performs and to condense all of that information into a single MSMQ message. However, there are a few restrictions with QC that you should be aware of while developing components. The two main restrictions are very similar: there can be no parameters passed in ByRef (pointers) and there can be no return values. These restrictions are not dependent upon a language – they are a limitation of QC and COM+. This makes sense because the caller (ASP in this case) is not actually interacting with the component, it's really talking to the recorder object within COM+'s QC.

The next piece of the QC architecture is the listener. The listener does just what its name suggests: it listens for MSMQ messages and passes them on to the player. When a component is registered in COM+ as a queued component, a series of queues are made, one public and five private. The main queue is the public queue and it is given the same name as the COM+ application in which the component resides. QC uses the five other queues in case it encounters communication issues processing the MSMQ message and sending the message to its final destination.

To make a COM+ application available through QC, all that is needed is to check the Queued selection on the Queuing tab of the Properties page of the desired COM+ application:

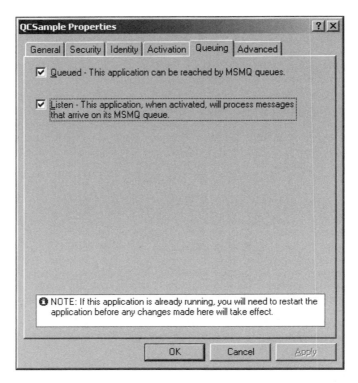

Notice the Listen section on this tab: this specifies how to inform COM+ to watch the queue and inform the next section of QC, the player, to carry out the interaction recorded from the client.

The player is the section of QC that takes the message from the listener section, creates an instance of the desired class, and invokes the method calls the recorder logged from the user's interaction.

One important note within this whole process of QC is that it is broken up into three transactions. The first is the recording of the message. This is all done within the process of the client and can easily be transactional with other tasks the client is performing. The next transaction is solely within MSMQ and that is the sending of the message from the client to the server. There is nothing that we need to do; it is a benefit of MSMQ's guaranteed delivery of messages. The last transaction is the reading of the message. Since the listener and player components of QC are contained within a COM+ application and are configured to require a transaction, they and the component that is queued will all be contained within the same transaction.

QC Sample Solution

Let's again take the same sample we have been working with and rework it to utilize the asynchronous aspects of COM+ Queued Components. As we convert the code you will notice that most of the layers we wrote in the database and MSMQ samples above will be ripped out. This is because we are simply building upon the architecture of QC instead of writing it ourselves.

Start by opening the MSMQSample or DBSample project and renaming it QCSample. Now it's time to rework the SubmitRequest method. Since we can now rely on QC to package the interaction from the client into an MSMQ message, the code within this routine can simply execute the SQL statement on the connection string that is passed from the client. There are a couple of other changes to this routine. First the error string parameter has been taken out. Since the code within this routine will actually be run by the player component within QC, there is no benefit from passing an error string. In fact, since it was passed by reference, it would violate one of QC's restrictions.

```
Public Sub SubmitRequest(ByVal strConnectionString As String, _
                         ByVal strSQL As String)

  Dim objConn As ADODB.Connection

  On Error GoTo Error_Handler

      'connect to the db and execute the string
      Set objConn = New ADODB.Connection
      objConn.Open strConnectionString
      objConn.Execute strSQL, , adExecuteNoRecords

  Exit_Handler:
    'clean up
    If Not objConn Is Nothing Then If objConn.State Then objConn.Close
    Set objConn = Nothing
  Exit Sub

  Error_Handler:
    'log to the event log
    App.LogEvent Err.Description & " (" & Err.Number & ")", _
                 LogEventTypeConstants.vbLogEventTypeError
  End Sub
```

The other change is within the error handler, which is changed because of the loss of the error string. Since a BackOffice process is actually invoking the method, an entry is logged to the event viewer. Another possibility here would be to submit an e-mail message to submit an MSMQ message to an error queue.

Since the code above provides an interface for the client to call upon and QC will execute the code within it back on the server, the MSMQProcessor and DBProcessor sections are not needed in this example. We will instead pull the functionality from QC.

The last change to the code is for the user interface. The ASP code within the AsyncSample.asp page needs to create an instance of the QCSample.Request class instead of the DBSample.Request or the MSMQSample.Request classes. However, the simple CreateObject method on the Server object cannot be used. This is because of QC and the way that the record is instantiated. Notice in the code, shown below, that the GetObject routine is used with the queue: and new: monikers. By creating the object with GetObject instead of the normal CreateObject the recorder within QC is able to step in and act as the ProgID specified. This is very similar to the proxy within normal DCOM calls.

> A moniker is nothing more than another COM object that knows how to create other COM objects based on a string provided from the consumer. Monikers have actually been around since the early days of OLE when they were used for compound document linking.

369

This change in creating objects is the only change that is required on the client. Also note that the error string is also removed from this page and now relies on QC to raise an error if the listener object were to fail.

```
<%@ Language=VBScript %>
<HTML>
<HEAD>
<META NAME="GENERATOR" Content="Microsoft Visual Studio 6.0">
</HEAD>
<BODY>

<%
  Dim objRequest

  Set objRequest = GetObject("queue:/new:QCSample.Request")
  objRequest.SubmitRequest Request.Form("txtConnectionString"), _
                           Request.Form("txtSQL")

  Response.Write "Request was successfully sent."

  Set objRequest = Nothing
%>

<BR>
<BR>

<A href="javascript:history.back(1)">Back</A>

</BODY>
</HTML>
```

The last part to make this work is it to configure the QCSample.Request component as a configured COM+ queued component:

❑ First compile the new component.

❑ Next open the **Component Services MMC** snap-in located within the **Administrative Tools** folder. Drill down in the **COM+ Applications** folder and create a new application called **QCSample** (right-click on the COM+ application node and select **New**).

❑ Now expand the node for the new application and add the **QCSample.Request** component.

❑ Next configure the new COM+ application as a queued application. This is done by selecting the **Queuing** tab within the application's **Properties** and checking the **Queued** and **Listen** boxes.

❑ The last step is to specify the interface or interfaces that are queued within the COM+ application. This is done by selecting the **Properties** on the desired interface and marking the **Queued** checkbox on the **Queuing** tab. In this case select the interface called **_Request**, located under the **Interfaces** folder, which can be found in the **QCSample** COM+ application.

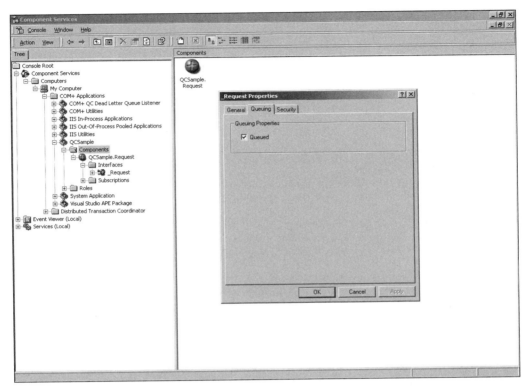

Since this example uses a web client with anonymous access turned on, the COM+ application must also be configured to ignore authentication-level security, since all requests will be assigned to the IUSR_<Computer Name> account. To disable authentication within COM+, open the Properties window on a COM+ application and select the Security tab. Next set the Authentication level for calls to None. Just to make sure that the change takes place immediately, shut down the application, by right-clicking on the COM+ application and selecting Shut down. Although this type of security setting may be useful in some circumstances (as it is for this demonstration), remember that it opens a security hole. A better solution for a production environment would be to leave the authentication level at Packet and require the browser users to authenticate themselves.

Now fire up the browser to the AsyncSample1.asp page and submit a request. Instead of our code comprising MSMQ messages, COM+'s Queued Components architecture is building the message on our behalf, while another process (the listener and player) will carry out the execute on the database for us. The best part about the whole process is that the client is not waiting for the processing of the SQL statement to complete, instead the interaction from the ASP page has been queued and will process somewhere else. Another great benefit of QC is that the actual processing of the MSMQ messages can actually be postponed and queued until more server resources are available. This can be very useful for accounting and billing tasks.

As you can see, there is a wide variety of asynchronous processing that can be done by utilizing queues in one form or another. Now, let's take a look at another way to implement an asynchronous process by using events and callbacks.

Events and Callbacks

At this point, we'll digress a little to discuss events and callbacks. These provide a way for another process to hook in and notify the consumer (client) that something has happened. One example of this that was used earlier is the MSMQEvent object. This object was declared with events and was passed by reference to MSMQ, which raised events within the code when a message arrived or an error occurred. Utilizing events and callbacks eliminates a lot of unnecessary code that sits in a loop or a timer, periodically checking the status of something.

How Do Events and Callbacks Work?

So how does an event or callback really work? Well, it starts when the client invokes a method on the object. Within this method call or a previous method call, the consumer must pass a reference of itself or an object it is using. This provides a hook for the process to call back to the client, and invokes a method that actually fires on the client. Although you may not be aware of it, this is the same type of communication which happens when a user client clicks on a button in a normal form-based application, where Windows and the VB runtime capture the user's interaction and raising the Click event in your code.

There are a wide variety of object models that support asynchronous processing by implementing events and callbacks, and you can also utilize events in your own objects. For example, many technologies and tools developed by Microsoft, such as ActiveX Data Objects (ADO), Remote Scripting, and XMLDOM, support events and callbacks. We'll look at each of these next.

ActiveX Data Objects

Many of the objects within **ActiveX Data Objects** (**ADO**) support asynchronous processing by providing events for the consumer to listen to. One of most widely used ones is the Connection object. For example, instead of waiting for a connection to be made to the data source, a flag can be set on the Open routine stating to make this call asynchronous. This call would look like the following statement:

```
m_objMyConn.Open txtMyConnectionString, , adAsyncConnect
```

Now that ADO knows to make the call asynchronous, it will need an event to respond to and raise once the connection is made, ConnectionComplete. This is done by declaring the objMyConn at the form, module, or class level and using the WithEvents keyword:

```
Dim WithEvents m_objMyConn As ADODB.Connection
```

Once a variable is declared using WithEvents, a series of methods are available to code to. This list is available by looking at the **Object Browser** within VB, or by selecting the variable in the combo box at the top left of the code panel and then looking at the list of events in the combo box to the right. Once the event is defined, all that is left is to place code within it:

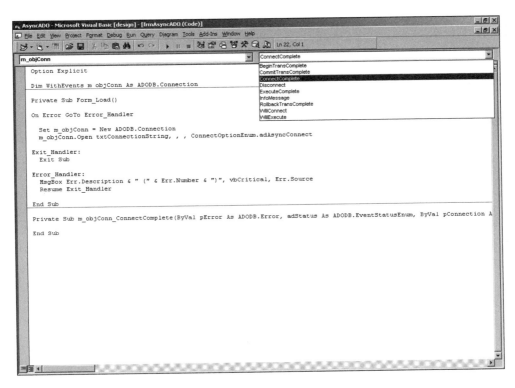

ADO Sample Solution

Let's build a sample VB application that executes a SQL statement asynchronously, just like our other example did, but instead use the asynchronous ability of ADO.

First start out by opening a new standard EXE VB project. Next add a reference to Microsoft **ActiveX Data Objects** and place three textboxes and one button on the form. Within the code below, one textbox is named `txtInfo`, another is named `txtConnectionString`, and the last one is named `txtSQL`. The command button on the form has been named `cmdExecute`.

Now that the form is set up, we can add the code to asynchronously execute the SQL statement input by the user. First declare a variable called `m_objConn` at the form level using `WithEvents`:

```
Dim WithEvents m_objConn As ADODB.Connection
```

Next add the code to connect to the data source defined in the `txtConnectionString` textbox on loading of the form:

```
Private Sub Form_Load()

On Error GoTo Error_Handler
```

```
    Set m_objConn = New ADODB.Connection
    m_objConn.Open txtConnectionString

    Exit_Handler:
    Exit Sub

    Error_Handler:
      MsgBox Err.Description & " (" & Err.Number & ")", vbCritical, _
            Err.Source
      Resume Exit_Handler

End Sub
```

Now that a connection has been made to the data source, it is time to make the asynchronous call to ADO. This is done on the `Click` event of the `cmdExecute` button, which makes a call to the `Execute` routine on the `m_objConn` object:

```
Private Sub cmdExecute_Click()

  On Error GoTo Error_Handler

    m_objConn.Execute txtSQL.Text, , ExecuteOptionEnum.adAsyncExecute

    Exit_Handler:
  Exit Sub

  Error_Handler:
    MsgBox Err.Description & " (" & Err.Number & ")", vbCritical, Err.Source
    Resume Exit_Handler

End Sub
```

Notice that with the method call to execute the SQL statement, the flag `adAsyncExecute` from the `ExecuteOptionEnum` enumeration is specified. This is a flag that informs ADO to create another thread behind the scenes and execute the SQL statement on that, letting the client's thread continue processing other tasks such as painting the VB form.

The last piece of code that needs to be implemented is to respond to ADO when the execution of the SQL statement completes. Once this happens ADO will raise an event by calling the `ExecuteComplete` routine:

```
Private Sub m_objConn_ExecuteComplete(ByVal RecordsAffected As Long, _
    ByVal pError As ADODB.Error, _
    adStatus As ADODB.EventStatusEnum, _
    ByVal pCommand As ADODB.Command, _
    ByVal pRecordset As ADODB.Recordset, _
    ByVal pConnection As ADODB.Connection)

  txtInfo.Text = "Execute complete!"

End Sub
```

As you can see, for this example we will simply inform the user that the SQL statement has been executed. This example also has added code to respond to another event from ADO, the `WillExecute` event, which is fired right before a command is executed. This way the user can see that something is happening while the SQL statement is executed:

```
Private Sub m_objConn_WillExecute(Source As String, _
    CursorType As ADODB.CursorTypeEnum, _
    LockType As ADODB.LockTypeEnum, _
    Options As Long, _
    adStatus As ADODB.EventStatusEnum, _
    ByVal pCommand As ADODB.Command, _
    ByVal pRecordset As ADODB.Recordset, _
    ByVal pConnection As ADODB.Connection)

    txtInfo.Text = "Executing SQL."

End Sub
```

Try it out! Fire up the VB application and enter a valid connection string and SQL statement. Notice that the `txtInfo` textbox displays Executing SQL when the button is clicked and then Execute complete when it finishes:

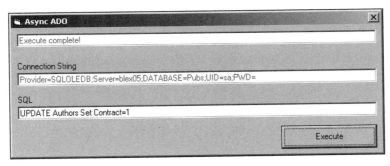

If the execute completed too quickly and you're using SQL Server, copy and paste the SQL statement a few times, placing semicolons between each statement. If you add enough to the SQL statement to slow it down sufficiently, you will notice that the form can be moved around while the SQL statement is still executing and the VB form still paints. Normally if this was done without asynchronous processing, the VB form would not paint until the SQL statement completed executing.

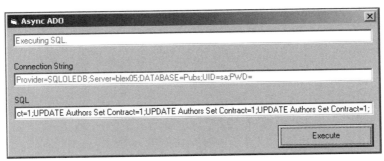

This example of asynchronous processing with ADO is just one of many events that ADO supports. For a list of other events to code to, reference the object browser within VB, by pressing *F2* after referencing the Microsoft **ActiveX Data Object** library. Another common utility that developers use is the OLE View, which can be found in the **Visual Studio 6 Tools** in the **Start** menu.

Summary

The challenges of network applications became apparent in this chapter as we considered the technologies available for implementing communication between the tiers of a distributed, n-tier application. To demonstrate this, we took an existing COM component, developed for local use, and use it in a distributed setting. COM+ takes the best parts of MTS, and utilities like DCOMCNFG, and pulls them into the operating system. Looking at the example, we saw how the act of distributing resources should force changes in the interface of a component.

Distributed processing is integral to the applications of the future. The advent of the Web and business-to-business integration has irretrievably brought distributed technologies into the mainstream of application development. Windows DNA fully embraces distributed processing to the extent that distributed technologies are available throughout the architecture. Programmers, particularly those who design application architectures, must understand both the challenges of network applications and the ramifications of the technologies used to meet those challenges.

Although out of the scope of this chapter, it is pertinent to mention SOAP and .NET at this stage. SOAP is a cross-platform protocol that is increasingly gaining acceptance as an open standard, and is discussed further in Chapter 14. It follows the function call model of RPCs, but allows programmers to use functional or component-based technologies for the implementation. Its implementation on Windows .NET promises to allow programmers to extend the benefits of their internal systems, notably COM+ components, to outside users through web services. Although .NET is still unfolding, it is arguably one of the most important developments in the platform in recent years. The features enjoyed by Windows programmers for years will now be available to rapidly construct web applications and services.

Finally, in our chapter we also considered the refinements MSMQ brings to the data passing metaphor. The simplicity of sockets is joined to the reliability and scalability of message queuing middleware. In Windows DNA, COM+ joins MSMQ with components to offer the best of both. Programmers enjoy the component interface metaphor, while also gaining the benefits of queuing. The integration of IStream-based component persistence in MSMQ is seldom noted, but is an excellent example of the productivity gained by subscribing to a single platform's architecture.

Whether you implement your own queued solution, use MSMQ, or build Queued Components, remember to keep in mind the pros and cons of asynchronous processing when deciding how or if to utilize it. If you do not require immediate feedback, a queued solution is a great choice, but if you need the immediate feedback, and still want to break up the processing, consider using events and callbacks.

p2p.wrox.com
The programmer's resource centre

ASP Today

wrox.com

VBScript and ASP

So far we've been focusing mainly on application development using Visual Basic. While a fine language in itself, its younger sibling, VBScript, is also powerful in its own right. VBScript is a subset of Visual Basic that can be used for tasks ranging from the mundane copying of files to the dynamic display of complex data on a web page using Microsoft's server-side programming platform: Active Server Pages, or ASP. Therefore, to start the chapter, we'll look at VBScript and cover how it differs from standard Visual Basic.

We'll then move on to ASP. Server-side programming such as ASP offers many advantages. You are able to draw upon the wealth of data available on the server that can be spread throughout the enterprise in various databases. Pages can be customized to the needs of each visitor to your web site. Best of all, server-side script makes it easier to move web sites to multi-tier or distributed web applications.

It can be used to create anything from simple, static web pages to database-aware dynamic sites, using HTML and scripting. Its other important use is as a programming "glue" for holding together various server-side components, facilitating the use of these components on the Web.

Finally, we'll look at some real-world examples of ASP to give some idea of the power and versatility of server-side scripting with ASP.

VB Lite

Microsoft Visual Basic Scripting Edition, **VBScript**, is a trimmed down version of Visual Basic for Applications, which is in turn a simplified version of Visual Basic. VBScript was created to allow scripting within Internet Explorer (version 3.0 and up) on the client side, and within Internet Information Server (version 3.0 and up) on the server side. This scripting language differs from Visual Basic in that there is no integrated development environment, or IDE. One creates script files, which usually end with a .vbs extension, using Notepad or a similar text editor.

As with most server-side scripting languages, server-side VBScript is processed on the server before being transmitted to the client. It provides a simple way to have your web pages retrieve data from a database, do calculations, validate forms, and much more. We'll discuss this more when we talk about Active Server Pages.

The major difference between Visual Basic and VBScript is that VBScript is typeless. There is no way in VBScript to declare a variable of a specific type. All VBScript variables are of the type `Variant`. VBScript however, does provide functionality to convert your data to specific types as you need them. This is both a blessing and a curse. It's great to not have to type your data for quick and dirty programming. But when you're writing mission-critical applications, a misinterpreted variable type (such as a `Double` instead of a `Long`) can be a difficult bug to find. Be mindful of this in your coding and type casting when using VBScript.

Windows Scripting Host

VBScript, in conjunction with the Windows Scripting Host, represents a very useful tool for writing quick and dirty batch files, and provides an excellent replacement for tired old DOS command batch files. The code below is the VBScript version of the consummate Hello World:

```
Dim sMessage

sMessage = "Hello World!"

MsgBox sMessage, vbOkOnly, "Hello!"
```

First we declare a variable (and it's a `Variant`) called `sMessage` to hold our message. We then populate our variable with the string "Hello World!". Finally we call the Visual Basic function `MsgBox` to display our message. VBScript has no default form or window so we must call the `MsgBox` function to display information at this point.

> **You can actually edit your VBScript files in the Visual Basic environment. This gives you the benefit of the color-coding and error checking that the IDE provides. Once you're done editing, copy your code into Notepad and save!**

We store this in a file called `HelloWorld.vbs` and simply double-click on this stored file to run it. If your system has the Microsoft Scripting Runtime installed, the `.vbs` extension will be automatically associated with the appropriate script runtime engine.

> **If you find that your system will not run .vbs files or you do not have the scripting runtime installed, it is easily downloaded and installed from the Microsoft web site at http://msdn.microsoft.com/scripting.**

Here are the results of our little script:

The real power of VBScript is that the entire Visual Basic runtime is available to your script. In our example above we used the `MsgBox` function to pop up a window displaying our message. Being familiar with the wealth of functionality built into the VB runtime you can do pretty much anything you want with your VBScript scripts.

Let's try something a little more practical. If you run a web site it's a good bet that you're producing log files of some sort. Well, these log files can pile up in a single directory. Perhaps you'd like them to be moved automatically for you each day? Furthermore, you might like for them to be archived and moved offline. These types of routine tasks are what VBScript does best!

The Log Mover

For this example we'll use an imaginary server that stores daily log files for our web site. Every day at a specified time we need to move yesterday's log files to an archive directory. Our script looks like this:

```
Dim dtDate, sMask, fso

'Create our file object
Set fso = CreateObject("Scripting.FileSystemObject")

'Get yesterday's date
dtDate = DateAdd("d", -1, Date)

'Create date mask... YYYYMM
sMask = Right("0000" & DatePart("yyyy", dtDate), 4) _
        & Right("00" & DatePart("m", dtDate), 2) _
        & Right("00" & DatePart("d", dtDate), 2)

'Move log files...
fso.MoveFile "C:\LogFiles\Current\" & sMask & "*.log", _
             "C:\LogFiles\Archive"

Set fso = Nothing
```

As in most of your scripts, you'll declare your variables first, as we've done in the above example. Next we instantiate an instance of the `FileSystemObject`. This is Microsoft's file system manipulation object. It is part of the Microsoft Scripting Runtime and is an extremely useful object. With it you can create and modify files, manipulate folders, and change file attributes. It can be used from your Windows scripts and even in your server-side scripts. Complete documentation on the `FileSystemObject` can be found at http://msdn.microsoft.com/scripting.

Since we want to move yesterday's log files, we need to get yesterday's date. This is done by using the `DateAdd` function and is stored in the `dtDate` variable. Next we create a string that contains yesterday's date in the YYYYMMDD format (which is the format of our log file names). This is done by pulling out the portion of the date needed (using `DatePart`) then padding it with zeros and trimming it off with the `Right` function. This is a handy trick for zero-padding your numbers.

> Because all variables are variants in VBScript, the type-specific functions of the Visual Basic Runtime are not available. These are mainly the string functions like `Right$`, `Left$`, `Mid$`, and so on. However, the variant version of each of these functions is available (`Right`, `Left`, `Mid`) in VBScript.

The next line of code calls the `MoveFile` method of the `FileSystemObject` to move a file name pattern, in this case C:\LogFiles\Current\YYYYMMDD*.log to a directory named C:\LogFiles\Archive. Finally, we release the `FileSystemObject` that we instantiated.

This script has no user interface component and will be scheduled to run unattended, therefore it does not use the `MsgBox` function like our Hello World example. Using the Windows Task Scheduler, this script can be scheduled to run at 6:00 AM each morning.

Hopefully you can see that using VBScript for scripting Windows batch files and functions offers you all the flexibility and power of Visual Basic. As you explore and learn more about VBScript you'll discover more and more things that can be done with this powerful tool.

In the next section we're going to discuss Active Server Pages. This is important as it allows you to use VBScript in your web application programming. In fact, VBScript is the default language of Active Server Pages.

Introducing Active Server Pages

The World Wide Web is based on very simple concepts. A web browser makes a request to the web site, and the site provides the requested data. While this may occur dozens of times on a single web page, the base transaction is the request/response. What you're looking at here is really the foundations of client/server computing. A client makes a request from a server and the server fulfils that request. We see this pattern of behavior throughout the programming world today, not only in web programming.

Microsoft recognized this pattern and developed a new technology that rendered web programming a much more accessible technique. This technology is **Active Server Pages** or **ASP** for short. ASP is a server-side scripting environment that comes with Microsoft's Internet Information Services. ASP allows you to embed scripting commands inside your HTML documents. The scripting commands are interpreted by the server and translated into the corresponding HTML, then sent back to the server. This enables the web developer to create content that is dynamic and fresh. The beauty of this is that it does not matter which browser your web visitor is using, because the server returns only pure HTML. Sure you can extend your returned HTML with browser-specific programming, but that is your prerogative. By no means is this all that ASP can do, but we'll cover more of its capabilities like form validation and data manipulation later on in this chapter.

By default, the ASP scripting language is VBScript. You can choose other languages such as JavaScript or even Perl, but as a Visual Basic programmer, it is to your advantage to leverage your knowledge of VB and be creating dynamic web pages in less than 20 minutes!

ASP Basics

ASP files are really just HTML files with scripting embedded within them. When a browser requests an ASP file from the server, it is passed on to the ASP processing DLL for execution. After processing, the resulting file is then sent on to the requesting browser. Any scripting commands embedded from the original HTML file are executed and then removed from the results. This is excellent in that all of your scripting code is hidden from the person viewing your web pages. That is why it is so important that files that contain ASP scripts have an .asp extension.

ASP Tags

To distinguish the ASP code from the HTML inside your files, ASP code is placed between <% and %> tags. This convention should be familiar to you if you have ever worked with any kind of server-side commands before in HTML. The tag combination implies to the ASP processor that the code within should be executed by the server and removed from the results. Depending on the default scripting language of your web site, this code may be VBScript, JScript, or any other language you've installed. Since this book is for the Visual Basic programmer, all of our ASP scripts will be in VBScript.

The following snippet of HTML shows some ASP code between <% and %> tags:

```
<TABLE>
<TR>
<TD>
<%
  dim x
  x = 1
  x = x + 1
%>
</TD>
</TR>
</TABLE>
```

<SCRIPT> Blocks

You may also place your ASP code between <SCRIPT> </SCRIPT> blocks. However, unless you direct the script to run at the server level, code placed between these tags will be executed at the client as normal client-side scripts. To direct your script block to execute on the server, use the RUNAT attribute on the opening <SCRIPT> tag:

```
<SCRIPT Language="VBScript" RUNAT="Server">
... Your Script ...
</SCRIPT>
```

The Default Scripting Language

As stated previously, the default scripting language used by ASP is VBScript. However, you may change it for your entire site, or just a single web page. Placing a special scripting tag at the beginning of your web page does this. This tag specifies the scripting language to use for this page only.

```
<%@ LANGUAGE=ScriptingLanguage %>
```

ScriptingLanguage can be any language for which you have the scripting engine installed. ASP comes with VBScript and JScript.

You can set the default scripting language for the entire application by changing the Default ASP Language field in the Internet Service Manager on the App Options tab. This is shown in the following screenshot:

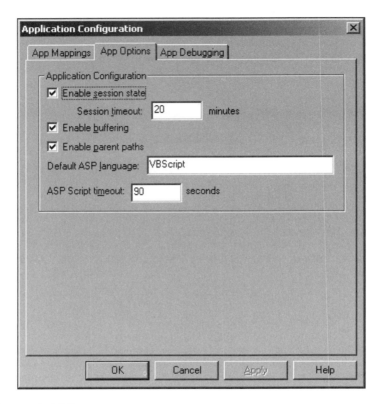

Mixing HTML and ASP

So ASP allows us to mix server-side VB into our HTML code. VBScript has all of the control flow mechanisms like If...Then, For...Next, and Do While... loops. But with ASP you can selectively include HTML code based on the results of these operators. Let's look at an example.

Suppose you are creating a web page that greets the viewer with a "Good Morning", "Good Afternoon", or "Good Evening" depending on the time of day. This can be done as follows:

```
<HTML>
<BODY>
<P>The time is now <%=Time()%></P>
<%
  Dim iHour

  iHour = Hour(Time())

  If (iHour >= 0 And iHour < 12 ) Then
%>
Good Morning!
<%
  ElseIf (iHour > 12 And iHour < 17 ) Then
%>
```

```
Good Afternoon!
<%
   Else
%>
Good Evening!
<%
End If
%>
</BODY>
</HTML>
```

First we print out the current time. The `<%=` notation is shorthand to print out the value of an ASP variable or the result of a function call. We then move the hour of the current time into a variable called `iHour`. Based on the value of this variable we write our normal HTML text.

Notice how the HTML code is outside of the ASP script tags. When the ASP processor executes this page, the HTML that lies between control flow blocks that aren't executed is discarded, leaving you with only the correct code. Here is the source of what is returned from our web server after processing this page:

```
<HTML>
<BODY>
<P>The time is now 7:48:37 PM</P>

Good Evening!

</BODY>
</HTML>
```

As you can see, the scripting is completely removed leaving only the HTML and text.

The other way to output data to your web page viewer is using one of ASP's built-in objects called `Response`. We'll cover this approach in the next section as you learn about the ASP object model.

Commenting Your ASP Code

As with any programming language, it is a good long-term strategy to adequately comment your ASP code as much as possible.

Comments in ASP are identical to comments in VB. When ASP comes across the single quote character, it will ignore the rest of that line:

```
<%
Dim iLumberJack

'I'm a comment and I'm O.K.
iLumberJack = iLumberJack + 1
%>
```

The Active Server Pages Object Model

ASP, like most Microsoft technologies, utilizes the Component Object Model, or COM, to expose functionality to consumer applications. ASP is actually an extension to your web server that allows server-side scripting. At the same it also provides a compendium of objects and components, which manage interaction between the web server and the browser. These objects form the **Active Server Pages Object Model** and can be manipulated by scripting languages. Take a look at the following diagram:

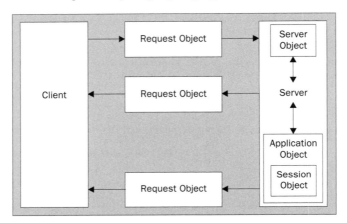

ASP neatly divides up into six objects, which manage their own part of the interaction between client and server. As you can see in the diagram, at the heart of the interaction between client and server are the Request and Response objects, which deal with the HTTP request and response; but we will be taking a quick tour through all of the different objects and components that are part of ASP. For a more detailed examination of all the ASP objects, take a look at Wrox Press's *Professional ASP 3.0* (ISBN 1-86100-261-0).

The object model consists of six core objects, each one with distinct properties and methods. The objects are:

❑   Request

❑   Response

❑   Application

❑   Session

❑   Server

❑   ObjectContext

Each of the objects, barring the Server and ObjectContext object, can use collections to store data. Before we look at each object in turn we need to take a quick overview of collections.

Collections

Collections in ASP are very similar to their VB namesakes. They act as data containers that store their data in a manner close to that of an array. The information is stored in the form of name/value pairs.

The `Application` and the `Session` object have a collection property called `Contents`. This collection of variants can hold any information you wish to place in it. Using these collections allows you to share information between web pages.

To place a value into the collection, simply assign it a key and then assign the value:

```
Application.Contents("Name") = "Evil Kneivel"
```

or:

```
Session.Contents("Age") = 25
```

Fortunately for us, Microsoft has made the `Contents` collection the default property for these two objects. Therefore the following shorthand usage is perfectly acceptable:

```
Application("Name") = "Evil Kneivel"
Session("Age") = 25
```

To read values from the `Contents` collections, just reverse the call:

```
sName = Application("Name")
sAge = Session("Age")
```

Iterating the Contents Collection

Because the `Contents` collections work like regular Visual Basic collections, they are easily iterated. You can use the collection's `Count` property, or use the `For Each` iteration method:

```
For x = 1 To Application.Contents.Count
  ...
Next

For Each Item In Application.Contents
  ...
Next
```

> Please note that the **Contents** collection is 1-based. That is to say that the first element in the collection is at position 1, not 0.

To illustrate this, the following ASP script will dump the current contents of the `Application` and `Session` object's `Contents` collections:

```
<HTML>
<BODY>
<P>The Application.Contents</P>
<%
   Dim Item

   For Each Item In Application.Contents
      Response.Write Item & " = [" & Application(Item) & "]<BR>"
   Next
%>
<P>The Session.Contents</P>
<%
   For Each Item In Session.Contents
      Response.Write Item & " = [" & Session(Item) & "]<BR>"
   Next
%>
</BODY>
</HTML>
```

Removing an Item from the Contents Collection

The `Application` object's `Contents` collection contains two methods, `Remove` and `RemoveAll`. These allow you to remove one or all of the items stored in the `Application` object's `Contents` collection. At the time of this writing, there is no method to remove an item from the `Session`'s `Contents` collection.

Let's add an item to the `Application` object's `Contents` collection, and then remove it.

```
<%
   Application("MySign") = "Pisces"
   Application.Contents.Remove("MySign")
%>
```

Or we can just get rid of everything...

```
<%
   Application.Contents.RemoveAll
%>
```

Not all of the collections of each object work in this way, but the principles remain the same and we will explain how each differs when we discuss each object.

The Request Object

When your web page is requested, much information is passed along with the HTTP request, such as the URL of the web page request and format of the data being passed. It can also contain feedback from the user such as the input from a text box or drop-down list box. The `Request` object allows you to get at information passed along as part of the HTTP request. The corresponding output from the server is returned as part of the `Response`. The `Request` object has several collections to store information that warrant discussion.

The Request Object's Collections

The `Request` object has five collections. Interestingly, they all act as the default property for the object. That is to say, you may retrieve information from any of the five collections by using the abbreviated syntax:

```
ClientIPAddress = Request("REMOTE_ADDR")
```

The `REMOTE_ADDR` value lies in the `ServerVariables` collection. However, through the use of the collection cascade, it can be retrieved with the above notation. Please note that for ASP to dig through each collection, especially if they have many values, to retrieve a value from the last collection is inefficient. It is always recommended to use the fully qualified collection name in your code. Not only is this faster, but it improves your code in that it is more specific, and less cryptic.

ASP searches through the collections in the following order:

❑   QueryString

❑   Form

❑   Cookies

❑   ClientCertificate

❑   ServerVariables

If there are variables with the same name, only the first is returned when you allow ASP to search. This is another good reason for you to fully qualify your collection.

QueryString

Contains a collection of all the information attached to the end of a URL. When you make a URL request, the additional information is passed along with the URL to the web page appended with a question mark. This information takes the following form:

```
URL?item=data[&item=data][...]
```

The clue to the server is the question mark. When the server sees this, it knows that the URL has ended, and variables are starting. So an example of a URL with a query string might look like this:

http://www.buythisbook.com/book.asp?bookname=VB6Resource

We stated earlier that the collections store information in name/value pairs. Despite this slightly unusual method of creating the name/value pair, the principle remains the same. `Bookname` is the name and `ProfessionalWebProgramming` is the value. When ASP gets hold of this URL request, it breaks apart all of the name/value pairs and places them into this collection for easy access. This is another excellent feature of ASP. Query strings are built up using ampersands to delimit each name/value pair so if you wished to pass the user information along with the book information, you could pass the following:

http://www.buythisbook.com/book.asp?bookname=VB6Resource&buyer=JerryAblan

Query strings can be generated in one of three ways. The first is, as discussed, by a user-typed URL. The second is as part of a URL specified in an anchor tag.

```
<A HREF="book.asp?bookname=ProfessionalWebProgramming">Go to book buying page</A>
```

So when you click on the link, the name/value pair is passed along with the URL. The third and final method is via a form sent to the server with the GET method:

```
<FORM ACTION="book.asp" METHOD="GET">
Type your name: <INPUT TYPE="TEXT" NAME="buyer"><BR>
Type your requested book:  <INPUT TYPE="TEXT" NAME="bookname" SIZE=40><BR>
<INPUT TYPE=SUBMIT VALUE=Submit>
</FORM>
```

You input the information onto the text boxes on the form and the text is submitted when you click on Submit and two query strings are generated.

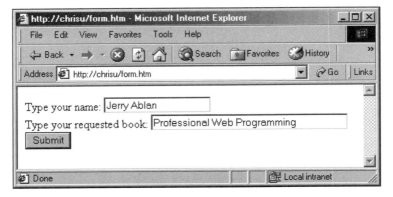

Next you need to be able to retrieve information, and you use this technique to retrieve it from each of the three methods used to generate a query string.

```
Request.QueryString("buyer")
Request.QueryString("bookname")
```

Please note that these lines won't display anything by themselves. You need to add either the shorthand notation (equality operator) to display functions in front of a single statement, or when a number of values need displaying then use Response.Write *to separately display each value in the collection.*

For example,. <%=Request.QueryString("buyer")%> *or*
Response.Write(Request.QueryString("bookname"))

The first of the two Request object calls should return the name of Jerry Ablan on the page and the second of the two should return Professional Web Programming. Of course you could always store this information in a variable for later access.

```
sBookName = Request.QueryString("bookname")
```

Form

Contains a collection of all the form variables posted to the HTTP request by an HTML form. Query strings aren't very private as they transmit information via a very visible method, the URL. If you want to transmit information from the form more privately then you can use the form collection to do so which sends its information as part of the HTTP Request body. The easy access to form variables is one of ASP's best features.

If we go back to our previous example, the only alteration we need to make to our HTML form code is to change the METHOD attribute. Forms using this collection must be sent with the POST method and not the GET method. It is actually this attribute that determines how the information is sent by the form. So if we change the method of the form as follows:

```
<FORM ACTION="book.asp" METHOD="POST">
Type your name: <INPUT TYPE="TEXT" NAME="buyer"><BR>
Type your requested book:  <INPUT TYPE="TEXT" NAME="bookname" SIZE=40><BR>
<INPUT TYPE=SUBMIT VALUE=Submit>
</FORM>
```

Once the form has been submitted in this style, then we can retrieve and display the information using the following:

```
Request.Form("buyer")
```

Cookies

Contains a read-only collection of cookies sent by the client browser along with the request. Because the cookies were sent from the client, they cannot be changed here. You must change them using the Response.Cookies collection. A discussion of cookies can be found in the next topic.

ClientCertificate

When a client makes a connection with a server requiring a high degree of security, either party can confirm who the sender/receiver is by inspecting their **digital certificate**. A digital certificate contains a number of items of information about the sender, such as the holder's name, address, and length of time the certificate is valid for. A third party, known as the Certificate Authority or CA, will have previously verified these details.

The ClientCertificate collection is used to access details held in a client-side digital certificate sent by the browser. This collection is only populated if you are running a secure server, and the request was via an https:// call instead of an http:// call. This is the preferred method to invoke a secure connection.

ServerVariables

When the client sends a request and information is passed across to the server, it's not just the page that is passed across, but information such as who created the page, the server name, and the port that the request was sent to. The HTTP header that is sent across together with the HTTP request also contains information of this nature such as the type of browser, and the type of connection. This information is combined into a list of variables that are predefined by the server as environment variables. Most of them are static and never really change unless you change the configuration of your web server. The rest are based on the client browser.

These server variables can be accessed in the normal method. For instance, the server variable HTTP_USER_AGENT, which returns information about the type of browser being used to view the page, can be displayed as follows:

```
<%=Request.ServerVariables("HTTP_USER_AGENT")%>
```

Alternatively you can print out the whole list of Server Variables and their values with the following code:

```
For Each key in Request.ServerVariables
   Response.Write "<B>" & (Key) &"</B> "
   Response.Write (Request.ServerVariables(key)) & "<BR>"
Next
```

This displays each of the ServerVariables collection in bold, and the contents of the key (if any) after it. The final product looks like this:

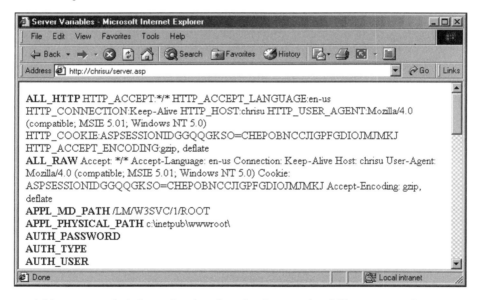

Server variables are merely informative, but they do give you the ability to customize page content for specific browsers, or to avoid script errors that might be generated.

Request Object Properties and Methods

The Request object contains a single property and a single method. They are used together to transfer files from the client to the server. Uploading is accomplished using HTML forms.

TotalBytes Property

When the request is processed, this property will hold the total number of bytes in the client browser request. Most likely you'd use it to return the number of bytes in the file you wish to transfer. This information is important to the BinaryRead method.

BinaryRead Method

This method retrieves the information sent to the web server by the client browser in a POST operation. When the browser issues a POST, the data is encoded and sent to the server. When the browser issues a GET, there is no data other than the URL. The BinaryRead method takes one parameter, the number of bytes to read. So if you want it to read a whole file, you pass it the total number of bytes in the file, generated by the TotalBytes property.

It's very rarely applied because Request.QueryString and Request.Form are much easier to use. That's because BinaryRead wraps its answer in a safe array of bytes. For a scripting language that essentially only handles variants, that makes life a little complicated. However this format is essential for file uploading. You can find full details on how to upload files and then decode a safe array of bytes in this excellent article at 15seconds.com, http://www.15seconds.com/Issue/981121.htm.

The Response Object

After you've processed the request information from the client browser, you'll need to be able to send information back. The Response object is just the ticket. It provides you with the tools necessary to send anything you need back to the client.

The Response Object's Collections

The Response object contains only one collection: Cookies. This is the version of the Request object's Cookies collection that can be written to.

If you've not come across them before, **cookies** are small (limited to 4kb of data) text files stored on the hard drive of the client that contain information about the user, such as whether they have visited the site before and what date they last visited the site on. There are lots of misapprehensions about cookies being intrusive as they allow servers to store information on the user's drive. However you need to remember that the user has to voluntarily accept cookies or activate an Accept Cookies mechanism on the browser for them to work, and that this information is completely benign and cannot be used to determine the user's e-mail address or such like. They are used to personalize pages that the user might have visited before. Examples of things to store in cookies are unique user IDs, or user names; then, when the user returns to your web site, a quick check of his cookies will let you know if he is a return visitor or not.

You can create a cookie on the user's machine as follows:

```
Response.Cookies("BookBought") = "Professional Web Programming"
```

You can also store multiple values in one cookie using an index value key. The cookie effectively contains a VBScript Dictionary object and using the key can retrieve individual items. Its function is very close to that of an array.

```
Response.Cookies("BookBought")("1") = "Professional Web Programming"
Response.Cookies("BookBought")("2") = "Instant HTML"
```

A cookie will automatically expire (that is, disappear from the user's machine) the moment a user ends their session. To extend the cookie beyond this natural lifetime, you can specify a date with the Expires property. The date takes the following format WEEKDAY DD-MON-YY HH:MM:SS

```
Response.Cookies("BookBought").Expires = #31-Dec-99#
```

The # sign can be used to delimit dates in VBScript or ASP.

Other properties that can be used in conjunction with this collection are:

❑ Domain: A Cookie is only sent to page requested within the domain from which it was created.

❑ Path : A Cookie is only sent to pages requested within this path.

❑ HasKeys: specifies whether the Cookie uses an index/Dictionary object or not.

❑ Secure: specifies whether the cookie is secure. A cookie is only deemed secure if sent via the HTTPS protocol.

You can retrieve the cookies information using the Request object cookies collection, mentioned earlier. To do this you could do the following:

```
You purchased <%=Request.Cookies("BookBought")%> last time you visited the site.
```

If there were several cookies in the collection you could iterate through each cookie and display the content as follows:

```
For Each cookie in Request.Cookies
   Response.Write (Request.Cookies(cookie))
Next
```

The Response Object's Methods

To understand what the Response object's methods and properties do, we need to examine the workings of how ASP sends a response in more detail. When an ASP script is run, an **HTML output stream** is created. This stream is a receptacle for the web server to store details and create the dynamic/interactive web page in. As mentioned before the page has to be created entirely in HTML for the browser to understand it (excluding client-side scripting, which is ignored by the server).

The stream is initially empty when created. New information is added to the end. If any custom HTML headers are required then they have to be added at the beginning. Then the HTML contained in the ASP page is added next to the script, so anything not encompassed by <% %> tags is added. The Response object provides two ways of writing directly to the output stream, either using the Write method or its shorthand technique.

Write

Probably the most used method of all the built-in objects, Write allows you to send information back to the client browser. You can write text directly to a web page by encasing the text in quotation marks:

```
Response.Write "Hello World!"
```

Or to display the contents of a variant you just drop the quotation marks:

```
sText = "Hello World!"
Response.Write sText
```

For single portions of dynamic information that only require adding into large portions of HTML, you can use the equality sign as a shorthand for this method, as specified earlier, for example:

```
My message is <% =sText %>
```

This technique reduces the amount of code needed, but at the expense of readability. There is nothing to choose between the techniques in terms of performance.

AddHeader

This method allows you to add custom headers to the HTTP response. For example, if you were to write a custom browser application that examined the headers of your HTTP requests for a certain value, you'd use this method to set that value. Usage is as follows:

```
Response.AddHeader "CustomServerApp", "BogiePicker/1.0"
```

This would add the header `CustomServerApp` to the response with the value of `BogiePicker/1.0`. There are no restrictions regarding headers and header value.

AppendToLog

Calling this method allows you to append a string to the web server log file entry for this particular request. This allows you to add custom log messages to the log file.

BinaryWrite

This method allows you to bypass the normal character conversion that takes place when data is sent back to the client. Usually, only text is returned, so the web server cleans it up. By calling `BinaryWrite` to send your data, the actual binary data is sent back, bypassing that cleaning process.

Clear

This method allows you to delete any data that has been buffered for this page so far. See discussion of the `Buffer` property for more details.

End

This method stops processing the ASP file and returns any currently buffered data to the client browser.

Flush

This method returns any currently buffered data to the client browser and then clears the buffer. See discussion of the `Buffer` property for more details.

Redirect

This method allows you to relinquish control of the current page to another web page entirely. For example, you can use this method to redirect users to a login page if they have not yet logged on to your web site:

```
<%
If (Not Session("LoggedOn") ) Then
  Response.Redirect "login.asp"
End If
%>
```

The Response Object's Properties

Buffer

You may optionally have ASP buffer your output for you. This property tells ASP whether or not to buffer output. Usually, output is sent to the client as it is generated. If you turn buffering on (by setting this property to `True`), output will not be sent until all scripts have been executed for the current page, or the `Flush` or `End` methods are called.

`Response.Buffer` has to be inserted after the language declaration, but before any HTML is used. If you insert it outside this scope you will most likely generate an error. A correct use of this method would look like:

```
<@ LANGUAGE = "VBSCRIPT">
<% Response.Buffer = True %>
<HTML>
    .
    .
    .
```

The `Flush` method is used in conjunction with the `Buffer` property. To use it correctly you must set the `Buffer` property first and then at places within the script you can flush the buffer to the output stream, while continuing processing. This is useful for long queries, which might otherwise worry the user that nothing was being returned.

The `Clear` method erases everything in the buffer that has been added since the last `Response.Flush` call. It erases only the response body however and leaves intact the response header.

CacheControl

Generally when a proxy server retrieves an ASP web page, it does not place a copy of it into its cache. That is because by its very nature, ASP pages are dynamic, and most likely will be stale the next time they are requested. You may override this feature by changing the value of this property to `Public`.

Charset

This property will append its contents to the HTTP content-type header that is sent back to the browser. Every HTTP response has a content-type header that defines the content of the response. Usually the content-type is `text/html`. Setting this property will modify the type sent back to the browser.

ContentType

This property allows you to set the value of the content-type that is sent back to the client browser.

Expires

Most web browsers keep web pages in a local cache. The cache is usually fine for as long as you keep your browser running. Setting this property allows you to limit the time the page stays in the local cache. The value of the `Expires` property specifies the length of time in minutes before the page will expire from the local cache. If you set this to zero, the page will not be cached.

ExpiresAbsolute

Just like the `Expires` property, this property allows you to specify the exact time and date on which the page will expire.

IsClientConnected

This read-only property indicates whether or not the client is still connected to the server. Remember that the client browser makes a request then waits for a response? Well, imagine you're running a lengthy script and during the middle of processing, the client disconnects because he was waiting too long. Reading this property will tell you if the client is still connected or not.

Status

This property allows you to set the value returned on the status header with the HTTP response.

The Application and Session Objects

The `Application` and `Session` objects, like `Request` and `Response`, work very closely together. `Application` is used to tie all of the pages together into one consistent application, while the `Session` object is used to track and present a user's series of requests to the web site as a continuous action, rather than an arbitrary set of requests.

Scope Springs Eternal

Normally, you will declare a variable for use within your web page. You'll use it, manipulate it, then perhaps print out its value, or whatever. But when your page is reloaded, or the viewer moves to another page, the variable, with its value, is gone forever. By placing your variable within the `Contents` collection of the `Application` or `Session` objects, you can extend the life span of your variable!

Any variable or object that you declare has two potential scopes: procedure and page. When you declare a variable within a procedure, its lifespan is limited to that procedure. Once the procedure has executed, your variable is gone. You may also declare a variable at the web page level but like the procedure-defined variable, once the page is reloaded, the value is reset.

Enter the `Application` and `Session` objects. The `Contents` collections of these two objects allow you to extend the scope of your variables to session-wide, and application-wide. If you place a value in the `Session` object, it will be available to all web pages in your site for the life span of the current session (more on sessions later). Good session scope variables are user IDs, user names, login time, and so on; things that pertain only to the session. Likewise, if you place your value into the `Application` object, it will exist until the web site is restarted. This allows you to place application-wide settings into a conveniently accessible place. Good application scope variables are font names and sizes, table colors, system constants, and so on; things that pertain to the application as a whole.

The global.asa File

Every ASP application may utilize a special script file. This file is named `global.asa` and it must reside in the root directory of your web application. It can contain script code that pertains to the application as a whole, or each session. You may also create ActiveX objects for later use in this scripting file.

The Application Object

ASP works on the concept that an entire web site is a single web application. Therefore, there is only one instance of the Application object available for your use in your scripting at all times. Please note that it is possible to divide up your web site into separate application, but for the purposes of this discussion we'll assume there is only one application per web site.

Collections

The Application object contains two collections: Contents and StaticObjects. The Contents collection we discussed above. The StaticObjects collection is similar to Contents, but only contains the objects that were created with the <OBJECT> tag in the scope of your application. This collection can be iterated just like the Contents collection.

> **You cannot store references to ASP's built-in objects in Application's collections.**

Methods

The Application object contains two methods as detailed below.

Lock

The Lock method is used to lock-down the Contents collection so that it cannot be modified by other clients. This is useful if you are updating a counter, or perhaps grabbing a transaction number stored in the Application's Contents collection.

Unlock

The Unlock method unlocks the Application object thus allowing others to modify the Contents collection.

Events

The Application object generates two events: Application_OnStart and Application_OnEnd. The Application_OnStart event is fired when the first view of your web page occurs. The Application_OnEnd event is fired when the web server is shut down. If you choose to write scripts for these events they must be placed in your global.asa file.

The most common use of these events is to initialize application-wide variables. The following is an example global.asa file with script for these events:

```
<SCRIPT LANGUAGE=VBScript RUNAT=Server>
Sub Application_OnStart
  'Globals...
  Application("ErrorPage") = "handleError.asp"
  Application("SiteBanAttemptLimit") = 10
  Application("AccessErrorPage") = "handleError.asp"
  Application("RestrictAccess") = False
```

```
   'Keep track of visitors...
   Application("NumVisits") = Application("NumVisits") + 1
End Sub
</SCRIPT>
```

The Session Object

Each time a visitor comes to your web site, a `Session` object is created for him if he does not already have one. Therefore there is an instance of the `Session` object available to you in your scripting as well. The `Session` object is similar to the `Application` object in that it can contain values. However, the `Session` object's values are lost when your visitor leaves the site. The `Session` object is most useful for transferring information from web page to web page. Using the `Session` object, there is no need to pass information in the URL.

The most common use of the `Session` object is to store information in its `Contents` collection. This information would be session-specific in that it would pertain only to the current user.

Many web sites today offer a "user personalization" service. That is, they can customize a web page to the user's preference. This is easily done with ASP and the `Session` object. The user variables are stored in the client browser for retrieval by the server later. Simply load the user's preferences at the start of the session and then, as he browses your site, utilize the information regarding his preferences to display information.

Suppose your web site displays stock quotes for users. You could allow a user to customize the start page to display his favorite stock quotes when he visits the site. By storing the stock symbols in your `Session` object, you can easily display the correct quotes when you render your web page.

This session management system relies on the use of browser cookies. The cookies allow the user information to be persisted even after a client leaves the site. Unfortunately, if a visitor to your web site does not allow cookies to be stored, you will be unable to pass information between web pages within the `Session` object.

Collections

The `Session` object contains two collections: `Contents` and `StaticObjects`. The `Contents` collection we discussed above. The `StaticObjects` collection is similar to `Contents`, but only contains the objects that were created with the `<OBJECT>` tag in your HTML page. This collection can be iterated just like the `Contents` collection.

Properties

Below are the properties that the `Session` object exposes for your use:

CodePage

Setting this property will allow you to change the character set used by ASP when it is creating output. This property could be used if you were creating a multinational web site.

LCID

This property sets the internal locale value for the entire web application. By default, your application's locale is your server's locale. If your server is in the US, then your application will default to the US Much of the formatting functionality of ASP utilizes this locale setting to display information correctly for the country in question. For example, the date is displayed differently in Europe versus the US. So based on the locale setting, the date formatting functions will output the date in the correct format.

You can also change this property temporarily to output data in a different format. A good example is currency. Let's say your web site had a shopping cart and you wanted to display totals in US dollars for US customers, and Pounds Sterling for UK customers. To do this you'd change the LCID property to the British locale setting, and then call the currency formatting routine.

SessionID

Every session created by ASP has a unique identifier. This identifier is called the SessionID and is accessible through this property. It can be used for debugging ASP scripts.

Timeout

By default, an ASP session will timeout after 20 minutes of inactivity. Every time a web page is requested or refreshed by a user, his internal ASP time clock starts ticking. When the time clock reaches the value set in this property, his session is automatically destroyed. You can set this property to reduce the timeout period if you wish.

Methods

The Session object contains a single method, Abandon. This instructs ASP to destroy the current Session object for this user. This method is what you would call when a user logs off your web site.

Events

The Session object generates two events: Session_OnStart and Session_OnEnd. The Session_OnStart event is fired when the first view of your web page occurs. The Session_OnEnd event is fired when the web server is shut down. If you choose to write scripts for these events they must be placed in your global.asa file.

The most common use of these events is to initialize session-wide variables, such as items like usage counts, login names, real names, user preferences, and so on. The following is an example global.asa file with script for these events:

```
<SCRIPT LANGUAGE=VBScript RUNAT=Server>
Sub Session_OnStart
    Session("LoginAttempts") = 0
    Session("LoggedOn") = False
End Sub

Sub Session_OnEnd
    Session("LoggedOn") = False
End Sub
</SCRIPT>
```

The Server Object

The next object in the ASP object model is the `Server` object. The `Server` object enables you to create and work with ActiveX controls in your web pages. In addition, the `Server` object exposes methods that help in the encoding of URLs and HTML text.

Properties

ScriptTimeout

This property sets the time in seconds that a script will be allowed to run. The default value for all scripts on the system is 90 seconds. That is to say that if a script has run for longer than 90 seconds, the web server will intervene and let the client browser know something is wrong. If you expect your scripts to run for a long time, you will want to use this property.

Methods

CreateObject

This method is the equivalent to Visual Basic's `CreateObject`, or using the `New` keyword - it instantiates a new instance of an object. The result can be placed into the `Application` or `Session` `Contents` collection to lengthen its life span.

Generally you'll create an object at the time the session is created and place it into the `Session` `Contents` collection. For example, let's say you've created a killer ActiveX DLL with a really cool class that converts Fahrenheit to Celsius and vice versa. You could create an instance of this class with the `CreateObject` method and store it in the `Session Contents` collection like this:

```
Set Session("MyConverter") = Server.CreateObject("KillerDLL.CDegreeConverter")
```

This object would be around as long as the session is and will be available for you to call. As you'll see in later chapters, this method is invaluable when working with database connections.

ASP comes with its own built in set of components that you can create instances of using the `CreateObject` method. These are:

❑ **Ad Rotator** – used to display a one of a selection of images with a link every time a user connects to the page.

❑ **Browser Capabilities** – manipulates a file `browscap.ini` contained on the server computer to determine the capabilities of a particular client's browser.

❑ **Content Linker** – provides a central repository file from where you manage a series of links and their URLs, and provide appropriate descriptions about them.

❑ **Content Rotator** – a cut down version of the `Ad Rotator` that provides the same function but without optional redirection.

❑ **Counters** – counts any value on an ASP page from anywhere within an ASP application

❏ **IIS Log** – allows you to create an object that allows your applications to write to and otherwise access the IIS log.

❏ **MyInfo** – can be used to store personal information about a user within an XML file.

❏ **Page Counter** – Counts the number of times a page has been hit.

❏ **Permission Checker** – checks to see if a user has permissions before allowing them to access a given page.

❏ **Status** – used to collect server profile information.

❏ **Tools** – a set of miscellaneous methods that are grouped under the generic heading of Tools.

Execute

This method executes an ASP file and inserts the results into the response. You can use this call to include snippets of ASP code, like subroutines.

GetLastError

This method returns an ASPError object that contains all of the information about the last error that has occurred.

HTMLEncode

This method encodes a string for proper HTML usage. This is useful if you want to actually display HTML code on your web pages.

MapPath

This method returns a string that contains the actual physical path to the file in question. Subdirectories of your web site can be virtual. That is to say that they don't physically exist in the hierarchy of your web site. To find out the true whereabouts of a file, you can call this method.

Transfer

The Transfer method allows you to immediately transfer control of the executing page to another page. This is similar to the Response.Redirect method except for the fact that the Transfer method makes all variables and the Request collections available to the called page.

URLEncode

This method, as its title suggests, encodes a URL for transmission. This encoding includes replacing spaces with a plus sign (+) and replacing unprintable characters with hexadecimal values. You should always run your URLs through this method when redirecting.

The ObjectContext Object

The final object we shall consider is the `ObjectContext` object, which comes into play when you use transactions in your web page. When an ASP script has initiated a transaction, it can either be committed or aborted by this object. It has two methods to do this with.

SetAbort

`SetAbort` is called when the transaction has not been completed and you don't want resources updated.

SetComplete

`SetComplete` is called when there is no reason for the transaction to fail. If all of the components that form part of the transaction call `SetComplete`, then the transaction will complete.

Using Active Server Pages Effectively

For the final part of this chapter we're going to build a web site to showcase some of the features of ASP. This sample site will demonstrate many of the ASP features and principles described earlier in this chapter.

Designing the Site

Before we start creating our new web site, we should discuss the design. For your first ASP application, we'll keep it quite simple. What we want to create is an HTML form that accepts for input a search string. The page will then search through a text database of book titles and display any matches that are found.

The following screenshot illustrates what the screen should look like:

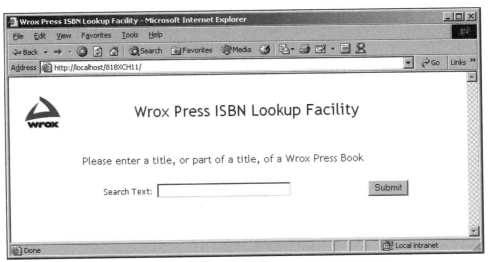

After we enter a search string and press the Submit button, the results are displayed:

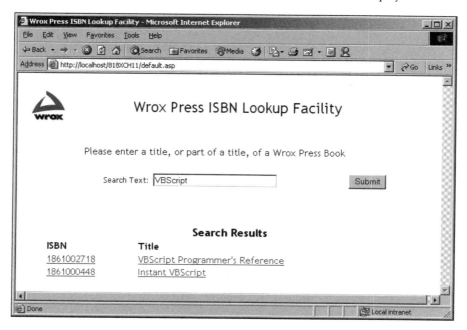

Note that the search string is still displayed in the search text field and the search results are displayed below the form. If there was nothing found the following error message would display:

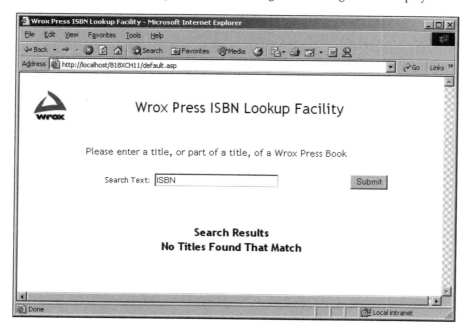

Creating the global.asa File

The first step in creating a new ASP application is to create your `global.asa` file. This is the file that houses your event handlers for the `Application` and `Session` objects. In addition, in this file you may set application, and session-wide variables to their default values. To create this file, in the root of your web server directory create a file called `global.asa` with the text editor of your choice.

Here is the content of our sample `global.asa`:

```
<SCRIPT LANGUAGE=VBScript RUNAT=Server>
Sub Application_OnStart
  'Nothing to do here...
End Sub

Sub Session_OnStart
  'Nothing to do here...
End Sub

Sub Session_OnEnd
  'Nothing to do here...
End Sub

Sub Application_OnEnd
  'Nothing to do here...
End Sub
</SCRIPT>
```

Our file has handlers defined for `Application_OnStart`, `Application_OnEnd`, `Session_OnStart`, and `Session_OnEnd`. These events are not used in this example, but are shown above for completeness.

Creating our Main Page

Now that we've got the groundwork laid for our ASP application, it's time to build the main page. Since this is a simple example, we will only utilize a single web page. Let's begin by creating this single page.

Create a new web page on your site and rename it to `default.asp`. This is the file name used by IIS as the default web page. The default web page is the page that is returned by a web server when no web page is specified. For example, when you call up `http://www.wrox.com/`, you aren't specifying a web page. The server looks through its list of default file names and finds the first match in the web site's root directory.

The following shows the contents of our sample `default.asp` page:

```
<%@ Language=VBScript %>
<%
Dim iDisplayed
Dim txtSearchText

'Set our counter to 0
iDisplayed = 0
```

```
'*************************************************************************
'* Main
'*
'* The main subroutine for this page...
'*************************************************************************

Sub Main()
  Dim txtTitle
  Dim txtISBN
  Dim fso
  Dim f
  Dim aStr
  Dim sLine

  'Was this page submitted?
  If (Request("cmdSubmit") = "Submit") Then
    'Pull the requested title from the request
    txtSearchText = Request("txtSearchText")

    If ( txtSearchText <> "" ) Then
      'Open our data file
      Set fso = Server.CreateObject("Scripting.FileSystemObject")
      Set f = fso.OpenTextFile(Server.MapPath("data/wroxdata.txt"))
      If (Not f Is Nothing) Then
        Do While Not f.AtEndOfStream
          'Read the next line of text
          sLine = f.ReadLine

          'If we've hit the end of the file then bail...
          If (f.AtEndOfStream) Then Exit Do

            'if this line of text is not blank, parse it
            If (sLine <> "") Then
            'Is this a match?
              If (InStr(1, sLine, txtSearchText, vbTextCompare) > 0) Then
                aStr = Split(sLine, ",")
                txtISBN = Replace(aStr(0), Chr(34), "")
                txtTitle = Replace(aStr(1), Chr(34), "")
                If ( iDisplayed = 0 ) Then
                  Response.Write "<tr><td><font face='Trebuchet MS'>" & _
                                 "<b>ISBN</b></font></td>"
                  Response.Write "<td><font face='Trebuchet MS'>" & _
                                 "<b>Title</b></font></td></tr>"
                End if
                Response.Write "<tr><td><font face='Trebuchet MS'>" & _
                               "<a target=_blank " & _
                               "href=http://www.wrox.com/books/" & txtISBN _
                               & ".htm>" & txtISBN & "</a></font></td>"
                Response.Write "<td><font face='Trebuchet MS'>" & _
                               "<a target=_blank " & _
                               "href=http://www.wrox.com/books/" & txtISBN _
                               & ".htm>" & txtTitle & "</a></font></td></tr>"
                iDisplayed = iDisplayed + 1
              End If
```

```
              End If
         Loop
       End If

       'Close our file and release objects
       f.Close
       Set f = Nothing
       Set fso = Nothing
     End if
   End If
End Sub
%>
<html>
<head>
  <title>Wrox Press ISBN Lookup Facility</title>
</head>

<body>

<table border="0" cellPadding="0" cellSpacing="0" width="600">
  <tr>
    <td width="100"><a href="http://www.wrox.com" target="_blank"
        border=0 alt><img border=0
        title="Check out the Wrox Press Web Site!"
        src="http://www.wrox.com/images/wxmainlogowhitespace.gif"></a></td>
    <td width="500"><center><font size="5"
        face="Trebuchet MS">Wrox Press ISBN Lookup Facility
        </font></center></td>
  </tr>

  <tr>
    <td width="100"> </td>
    <td width="500" align="left"><font face="Trebuchet MS"><br>
    Please enter a title, or part of a title, of a Wrox Press Book</font>
      <form action="default.asp" id="FORM1" method="post" name="frmMain">
        <table border="0" cellPadding="1" cellSpacing="5" width="100%">
          <tr>
            <td width="100" nowrap align="right"><font size="2"
                face="Trebuchet MS">
                Search Text:</font></td>
            <td width="350"><font size="2" face="Trebuchet MS">
            <input title="Enter your search text here" name="txtSearchText"
                size="30"
                value="<%=Request("txtSearchText")%>"
                tabindex="1"></font></td>
            <td width="50"><div align="right"><font size="2"
                face="Trebuchet MS">
            <input type="submit" title="Submit this data for processing..."
                value="Submit"
                name="cmdSubmit" tabindex="4"></font></td>
          </tr>
        </table>
      </form>
```

```
      <p> </td>
    </tr>
  </table>

<%if ( Request("cmdSubmit") = "Submit" ) then%>
<blockquote>
<table border="0" cellPadding="0" cellSpacing="0" width="600">
<tr>
  <td colspan=2 align=center width="100%">
    <font face="Trebuchet MS" size=4><b>Search Results</b></font>
  </td>
<tr>
<%end if%>

<%
'**********************************************************************
'* Call our main subroutine
'**********************************************************************

Call Main()
%>

<%if ( Request("cmdSubmit") = "Submit" ) then%>
<%if ( iDisplayed = 0 ) then%>
<tr>
  <td colspan=2 align=center width="100%">
    <font face="Trebuchet MS" size=4><b>No Titles Found That Match</b></font>
  </td>
<tr>
<%end if%>
</table>
</blockquote>
<%end if%>

</body>
</html>
```

As you can see, the page is quite long. But it breaks logically into two distinct sections: the ASP/VBScript portion, and the HTML portion. Let's examine each section individually.

The ASP/VBScript Section

To separate your code for clarity and the benefit of others, it's a good thing to keep your ASP routines either at the top or the bottom of your ASP pages. Just make sure you stick with your selection. We've chosen the top for this sample. So the first thing we see at the top of our page is our ASP routine Main. This is the code that is executed by the server before the page is returned to the browser that requested it. Any code, as you've seen, that is to be executed on the server before returning is enclosed in the special <% and %> tags.

For clarity (and sanity!), the ASP code has been divided into subroutines. This not only makes the code more readable, but also will aid in its reuse. This particular ASP page has a single subroutine: Main.

Before we do anything however, we declare some variables:

```
Dim iDisplayed
Dim txtSearchText
```

When variables are declared outside of a subroutine in an ASP page, they are considered global variables to the page. That is to say that the variables retain their data until the page is completely processed. This allows you to pass information from your ASP code to your HTML code, as you'll see.

After our variables have been declared, we have the code for our Main subroutine. This is what is called by our ASP code every time a browser retrieves the page. Please note that unlike Visual Basic, the Main subroutine is not called automatically. We must explicitly call it ourselves.

```
'*******************************************************************
'* Main
'*
'* The main subroutine for this page...
'*******************************************************************

Sub Main()
  Dim txtTitle
  Dim txtISBN
  Dim fso
  Dim f
  Dim aStr
  Dim sLine

  'Was this page submitted?
  If (Request("cmdSubmit") = "Submit") Then
    'Pull the requested title from the request
    txtSearchText = Request("txtSearchText")

    If ( txtSearchText <> "" ) Then
      'Open our data file
      Set fso = Server.CreateObject("Scripting.FileSystemObject")
      Set f = fso.OpenTextFile(Server.MapPath("data/wroxdata.txt"))
      If (Not f Is Nothing) Then
        Do While Not f.AtEndOfStream
          'Read the next line of text
          sLine = f.ReadLine

          'If we've hit the end of the file then bail...
          If (f.AtEndOfStream) Then Exit Do

            'if this line of text is not blank, parse it
            If (sLine <> "") Then
              'Is this a match?
              If (InStr(1, sLine, txtSearchText, vbTextCompare) > 0) Then
                aStr = Split(sLine, ",")
                txtISBN = Replace(aStr(0), Chr(34), "")
                txtTitle = Replace(aStr(1), Chr(34), "")
                If ( iDisplayed = 0 ) Then
```

```
                        Response.Write "<tr><td><font face='Trebuchet MS'>" & _
                                "<b>ISBN</b></font></td>"
                    Response.Write "<td><font face='Trebuchet MS'>" & _
                                "<b>Title</b></font></td></tr>"
                End if
                Response.Write "<tr><td><font face='Trebuchet MS'>" & _
                            "<a target=_blank " & _
                            "href=http://www.wrox.com/books/" & txtISBN _
                            & ".htm>" & txtISBN & "</a></font></td>"
                Response.Write "<td><font face='Trebuchet MS'>" & _
                            "<a target=_blank " & _
                            "href=http://www.wrox.com/books/" & txtISBN _
                            & ".htm>" & txtTitle & "</a></font></td></tr>"
                iDisplayed = iDisplayed + 1
            End If
          End If
        Loop
      End If

      'Close our file and release objects
      f.Close
      Set f = Nothing
      Set fso = Nothing
    End if
  End If
End Sub
```

First we see if the form was actually submitted by the user. To determine if the page has been submitted, we check the value of the cmdSubmit Request variable. This is the button on our form. When pressed, the form calls this page and sets the value of the cmdSubmit button to Submit. If a user just loads the page without pressing the button, the value of cmdSubmit is blank (""). There are other ways to determine if a web page was submitted, but this method is the simplest.

After we have determined that the page was in fact submitted, the search text is moved into our global variable txtSearchText. If this is not blank we proceed into the meat of this function.

We need to open up our data file and look for this search string. To do this, we instantiate an instance of the FileSystemObject and store the reference in the variable fso. We then call the OpenTextFile method of the FileSystemObject to open our data file.

Our data file is stored on our web site in the **/data** directory and is called wroxdata.txt. It is a comma-delimited file that contains ISBN numbers and titles. Here is a sample of that file:

```
"1861000065", "Instant PowerBuilder Objects"
"1861000081", "Beginning Visual C++ 5"
"1861000111", "Beginning ATL COM Programming"
"186100012X", "Ivor Horton's Beginning C++ - The Complete Language"
"1861000146", "Professional MFC with VC++ 5 Programming"
"1861002718", "VBScript Programmer's Reference"
"1861000448", "Instant VBScript"
```

We use the `Server` object's `MapPath` method to determine the location of our file for the `OpenTextFile` method. This is a handy way to reference parts of your site without having to hard-code drive letters and physical paths. The `MapPath` method converts logical web placements to physical file names.

Once opened, we loop through the file one line at a time using the `ReadLine` method. If the line read is not blank we check to see if it contains our search string. If it does, we use the VBScript method `Split` to split the line into an array. Now that we've got the parsed data, we can display it to the user. This is done using the `Response.Write` method. We output rows in a table, which is built in our HTML section below.

A neat trick here is that once we find a match we check to see if we've displayed any data yet. We can tell this by looking at the value of the `iDisplayed` variable. For each item that is displayed, we increment this counter. If there is a match and the `iDisplayed` variable is equal to 0, then we know that this is the first row we are going to display. This gives us a chance to insert a header for our data. Also, once completed, if `iDisplayed` is still equal to 0 we know that no data was displayed and we can display an appropriate message.

The HTML Section

This section is a regular HTML form with a smattering of ASP thrown in for good measure. The ASP that we've embedded in the HTML sets default values for the input fields, and displays any messages that our server side code has generated.

The most important part of the HTML is where the ASP code is embedded. The following snippet illustrates this:

```
<input title="Enter your search text here" name="txtSearchText" size="30"
 value="<%=Request("txtSearchText")%>" tabindex="1">
```

Here we see a normal text input box. However, to set the value of the text box we use the `Response.Write` shortcut (`<%=`) to insert the value of the variable `txtSearchText`. Remember that we dimensioned this outside of our ASP functions so that it would have page scope. Now we utilize its value by inserting it into our HTML.

After our form HTML comes the results display section:

```
<%if ( Request("cmdSubmit") = "Submit" ) then%>
<blockquote>
<table border="0" cellPadding="0" cellSpacing="0" width="600">
<tr>
  <td colspan=2 align=center width="100%">
    <font face="Trebuchet MS" size=4><b>Search Results</b></font>
  </td>
<tr>
<%end if%>

<%
'****************************************************************************
'* Call our main subroutine
'****************************************************************************
```

```
        Call Main()
        %>

        <%if ( Request("cmdSubmit") = "Submit" ) then%>
        <%if ( iDisplayed = 0 ) then%>
        <tr>
          <td colspan=2 align=center width="100%">
            <font face="Trebuchet MS" size=4>
              <b>No Titles Found That Match</b></font>
          </td>
        <tr>
        <%end if%>
        </table>
        </blockquote>
        <%end if%>
```

To build our results section we create an HTML table. We open this table before we call our `Main` subroutine. We do this because the subroutine outputs HTML table rows expecting an HTML table to be open. An alternative way to write this would be to have your `Main` routine create the table in its entirety.

So if this is the result of the user pressing the **Submit** button, we write out the `<TABLE>` tags and a header row that says "Search Results". We then call our `Main` subroutine above. Finally we close our HTML table. If there were no data rows displayed (`iDisplayed` equals 0) we display our appropriate error message.

Summary

You should have learned much in this chapter. We first learned about VBScript and how it differs from Visual Basic, and its importance to client- and server-side programming. We then discussed Active Server Pages, or ASP. You learned how ASP pages are created, and what special HTML tags you need to include in your files to use ASP.

We looked at the ASP object model and saw that the `Request` and `Response` objects are used to manage details of the HTTP request and responses. We saw that the `Application` object is used to group pages together into one application and we saw that the Session is used to create the illusion that the interaction between user and site is one continuous action. Finally we created a small application that demonstrates two uses for ASP: form entry and data manipulation and display.

p2p.wrox.com
The programmer's resource centre

ASP Today

wrox.com

13

Essential XML

Before the relational database concept had risen to dominance, people experimented with various data storage concepts, such as that of the hierarchical database engine. It is interesting to see that there's once again a rise in interest in hierarchical data representation – this time in the form of XML.

XML has tremendous benefits when compared to the proprietary hierarchical database engines from the past. XML is less focused on efficient data storage and retrieval and more on open data interchange. That said, as time goes on we're seeing more and more database-like features and functionality added to the suite of XML tools. XML has grown from simple text representation of data into an army of related technologies to parse, translate, query, link, and otherwise interact with the data.

There can be few developers remaining who've not yet heard of the Extensible Markup Language (XML) and its suite of associated standards (XSL, DOM, XML Namespaces, XML Schema, and friends). We also have XHTML, which is HTML 4.0 rewritten to comply with the rules of XML.

In this short guide, we will examine XML, the so-called "ASCII of the Future", and see how to use it from within VB6. Specifically, we'll see how to:

- ❑ Create valid XML documents
- ❑ Utilize DTDs
- ❑ Manipulate the DOM to parse XML for output
- ❑ Turn results of an ADO recordset into XML using custom code, and the DOM
- ❑ Use the `ServerXMLHTTP` object to convert XML to HTML on the server, obviating the need for an XML-aware client
- ❑ Upload an XML file from client to server

For the latest information about XML and related standards, visit the W3C's homepage at www.w3.org.

XML as a Second Language

HTML describes both the content of a web page, and how this page is to be presented. XML on the other hand is concerned solely with the representation of data – how that data is to be presented is deliberately left out of the equation.

XML uses tags that are enclosed in angle brackets, similar to those of HTML. Also similar to HTML, XML start tags may contain one or more attribute-value pairs. Unlike HTML, XML requires that the value given for an attribute be surrounded in quotes (double or single). Attribute-value pairs are delimited by whitespace.

HTML has fewer than 100 different tags, each tag having a specific meaning and allowed set of attributes. The example below is a fairly simple HTML page. Notice how display information (font size, widths, and so on) is intermingled with the content of the page:

```html
<html>

<head>
<meta http-equiv="Content-Language" content="en-us">
<meta http-equiv="Content-Type" content="text/html; charset=windows-1252">
<meta name="AUTHOR" content="PGB">
<title>Markup Languages</title>
</head>

<body>

<h1>*ML Languages</h1>
<hr>
<p>Here is a table with the 3 *ML languages:</p>
<table border="1" width="100%">
  <tr>
   <td width="10%"><font size="2">SGML</font></td>
   <td width="50%"><font size="2">Standard Generalized Markup Language</font></td>
   <td width="40%"><font size="2">Used to describe other languages</font></td>
  </tr>
  <tr>
   <td width="10%"><font size="2">HTML</font></td>
   <td width="50%"><font size="2">Hypertext Markup Language</font></td>
   <td width="40%"><font size="2">Used to describe web pages</font></td>
  </tr>
  <tr>
   <td width="10%"><font size="2">XML</font></td>
   <td width="50%"><font size="2">Extensible Markup Language</font></td>
   <td width="40%"><font size="2">Used to describe structured data</font></td>
  </tr>
</table>
<p><font size="2">Note: UML stands for Universal Modeling Language and does not
fit in the above category.</font></p>

</body>

</html>
```

The screenshot below shows this HTML as it appears in Internet Explorer 6. Other browsers would show our data in a similar manner, determined by the tags and attributes around the content:

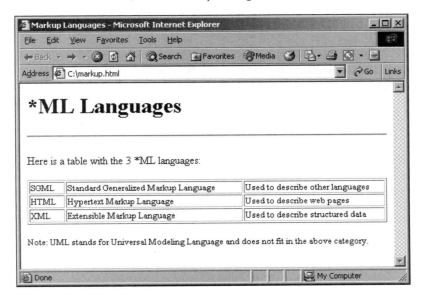

XML's primary purpose is to provide a powerful, flexible, and intuitive format for data, and so it does not contain information about how that data should be presented.

Thus, we might rewrite our sample HTML page in XML like so:

```
<?xml version="1.0" standalone="yes"?>
<Languages>
  <Title>Markup Languages</Title>
  <Heading1>*ML languages</Heading1>
  <Intro Text="Here is a table with the 3 *ML languages:"></Intro>
  <Language>
    <Abbreviation>SGML</Abbreviation>
    <FullName>Standard Generalized Markup Language</FullName>
    <Description>Used to describe other languages</Description>
  </Language>
  <Language>
    <Abbreviation>HTML</Abbreviation>
    <FullName>Hypertext Markup Language</FullName>
    <Description>Used to describe web pages</Description>
  </Language>
  <Language>
    <Abbreviation>XML</Abbreviation>
    <FullName>Extensible Markup Language</FullName>
    <Description>Used to describe structured data</Description>
  </Language>
  <FootNote Text="Note: UML stands for Universal Modeling Language and does not
                  fit in the above category."></FootNote>
</Languages>
```

Figure 2 shows you this XML document opened in Internet Explorer 6. All the XML language tokens, not just the content of the tags, are visible:

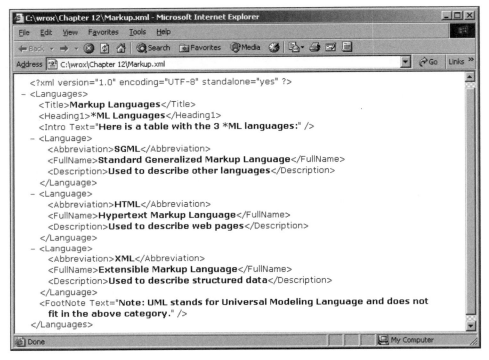

XML lets the developer create their own tag names to best describe the data in question – there are no 'reserved' XML tags with special meaning.

> Unlike HTML, XML is case-sensitive, so the tags `<language>`, `<Language>`, and `<LANGUAGE>` would be treated as different names for three distinct elements.

Note that XML has a shorthand notation for tags without content (empty tags). In the above example, rather than showing:

```
<Intro Text="Here is a table with the 3 *ML languages:"></Intro>
```

IE displays this tag using its shorthand form:

```
<Intro Text="Here is a table with the 3 *ML languages:" />
```

In XHTML, this is how one writes standalone tags, like `<hr />` – whitespace before the closing `/>` is optional. In XML, empty tags are commonly used in conjunction with attributes.

Finally, XML comments are delimited by `<!--` and `-->` and, unlike HTML comments, may not contain the sequence "--".

Putting XML in Perspective

XML's user-defined tags and attributes give it great power for describing structured data. By linking an XML document to a DTD or XML Schema, we can define rules to govern the XML structure of a document with a very fine degree of control, as we'll see later.

This is analogous to a database with tables containing columns and rows. Here, a language "row" is delimited by <Language> tags. The "columns" are <Abbreviation>, <FullName> and <Description>. XML provides enough flexibility to include several "tables" in a document, and enough power to express parent-child relationships with a variable number of children. XML, the "ASCII of the Future", provides a standardized data format which we can manipulate in a number of ways, as we'll see in the examples below. The icing on the cake is that XML data is stored in a format relatively easy to read by humans.

Of course, all this does not mean that you should rush out and start converting all your proprietary data formats to XML. The downside is that XML is not efficient enough to store data for heavy-duty processing purposes. XML is primarily designed for data communication between applications, particularly when running on different platforms or with different technologies.

Well-Formed XML

An XML document is said to be **well-formed** if it meets the requirements set out by the W3C's XML Recommendation, and are summed up in the bullet points below. Some of these requirements have already been covered in the preceding sections.

❑ The W3C specification recommends that XML documents start with the XML declaration <?xml version="1.0"?>, although it is not required.

❑ There must be a single document element, containing all the other XML elements in the document.

❑ All elements must be closed.

❑ Elements must be nested properly, and cannot overlap, so <X> ... <Y> ... </X> ... </Y> is not well formed, but <X> ... <Y> ... </Y> ... </X> is.

❑ Element names are case-sensitive, and must start with a letter or an underscore, but letters, digits, underscores, hyphens, and periods may be used for the remaining characters.

❑ Element names may not contain the string 'xml' (in any combination of casing).

❑ No element may have two attributes with the same name.

❑ Attribute values must be enclosed in single or double quotes.

As in HTML, escape sequences are used in place of certain characters that would otherwise interfere with the intended structure of the XML document:

Character	Escape Sequence
<	<
>	>
&	&
'	'
"	"

Valid XML

As we've seen, ensuring that an XML document is well-formed is a simple matter of applying the simple rules discussed previously. However, we can also ensure that a given XML document is valid, that is, that it strictly follows our agreed structure and business rules. There are two ways of specifying rules that elements in an XML document must adhere to in order to be valid.

The **Document Type Definition** (**DTD**) is an existing standard that can be applied to XML, however it is quite restrictive in the rules that it can describe. DTDs do not allow data types or legal ranges to be specified, so they are best for XML formats that only contain strings, rather than numbers. In addition, they are not extensible, they only allow limited validation of the sequence and frequency that elements appear in a document, and they do not themselves follow XML syntax. To overcome these shortcomings, the W3C devised the XML Schema Definition language (also known as XML Schema, or XSD).

> **A valid XML document is well-formed and conforms to its DTD or XML Schema.**

DTDs

A **Document Type Definition** (**DTD**) lays out rules for an XML document's data structure, such as the cardinality (order) of elements, how many of them may appear in a single document, the attributes allowed and/or required for each element, the data type that an element will contain, and so on. There are two main constructs:

> `<!ELEMENT` *elementname rule*`>`
>
> `<!ATTLIST` *elementname attributedef*`>`

`<!ELEMENT>` lets us describe what children an element may contain, as either a comma-separated list of elements, or PCDATA if it may only contain text data. We then have an `<!ATTLIST>` for each element that may have attributes.

The DTD can be embedded just before the XML declaration of the XML file to which it applies, or it can be held in a separate file. Below is an inline DTD for the XML document shown above:

```
<!DOCTYPE Languages [
<!ELEMENT Languages (Title , Heading1, Intro?, Language+, FootNote?)>
<!ELEMENT Title (#PCDATA)>
<!ELEMENT Heading1 (#PCDATA)>
<!ELEMENT Intro (#PCDATA)>
<!ATTLIST Intro Text CDATA #REQUIRED>
<!ELEMENT Language (Abbreviation, FullName, Description)>
<!ELEMENT Abbreviation (#PCDATA)>
<!ELEMENT FullName (#PCDATA)>
<!ELEMENT Description (#PCDATA)>
<!ELEMENT FootNote (#PCDATA)>
<!ATTLIST FootNote Text CDATA #REQUIRED>
]>
```

If this DTD were to be placed in a separate file, called say `Markup.dtd`, it would contain just those items which appear between square brackets ([]) above:

```
<!ELEMENT Languages (Title , Header1, Intro?, Language+, FootNote?)>
<!ELEMENT Title (#PCDATA)>
<!ELEMENT Header1 (#PCDATA)>
<!ELEMENT Intro (#PCDATA)>
<!ATTLIST Intro Text CDATA #REQUIRED>
<!ELEMENT Language (Abbreviation, FullName, Description)>
<!ELEMENT Abbreviation (#PCDATA)>
<!ELEMENT FullName (#PCDATA)>
<!ELEMENT Description (#PCDATA)>
<!ELEMENT FootNote (#PCDATA)>
<!ATTLIST FootNote Text CDATA #REQUIRED>
```

The XML document then references the DTD by the following line immediately before the XML declaration:

```
<!DOCTYPE Languages SYSTEM "Markup.dtd" >
```

As with a table and its DDL, it's possible for a DTD to affect the XML data, most commonly through the use of default values. If you don't need to load the DTD to populate certain XML data, then the XML file is called a **standalone** XML file. One can indicate this using the `standalone` attribute on the XML declaration (the attribute can be either `"yes"` or `"no"`). It is worth emphasizing that the `standalone` attribute does **not** indicate whether the DTD is internal or external.

XML Schema

The W3C XML Schema Recommendation was approved in May of 2001. XML Schemas (or more correctly, XML Schemata) are themselves an XML format, and they enhance the validation offered by DTDs by allowing more sophisticated data types, more precise specification of the elements' cardinality, support for XML namespaces, and more.

XSD is a very complex and comprehensive standard, and we have neither the space nor the need to go into it in great detail. Because of their precision, an XML Schema is generally more verbose than its equivalent DTD.

As we've mentioned, a schema document must meet the requirements of well-formed XML that we've already covered. The opening document element is <xs:schema>, inside which we place <xs:element> elements describing the types of all legal elements in XML documents that it is to apply to.

If you examine the XML Schema below, which validates our XML file, note that elements that represent simple types (such as strings, decimals, and so on) can be defined in a single line. The <xs:complexType> element is used to define more sophisticated elements, including any that have attributes, or that contain child elements. Sequences of child elements are enclosed in <xs:sequence> elements, and such elements must occur in the same order in the XML as they appear. Where the sequence is not important, use an <xs:all> element in place of <xs:sequence>. The <xs:choice> element is similar, but only one of the elements it contains may appear.

Also note the use of the minOccurs and maxOccurs attributes, for specifying how many occurrences of a specified element are allowed:

```xml
<?xml version="1.0"?>
<xs:schema xmlns:xs="http://www.w3.org/2001/XMLSchema">

  <xs:element name="Title" type="xs:string" />
  <xs:element name="Heading1" type="xs:string" />

  <xs:element name="Intro">
    <xs:complexType>
      <xs:attribute name="Text" type="xs:string" use="required" />
    </xs:complexType>
  </xs:element>

  <xs:element name="Abbreviation" type="xs:string" />
  <xs:element name="FullName" type="xs:string" />
  <xs:element name="Description" type="xs:string" />

  <xs:element name="Language">
    <xs:complexType>
      <xs:sequence>
        <xs:element ref="Abbreviation" />
        <xs:element ref="FullName" />
        <xs:element ref="Description" />
      </xs:sequence>
    </xs:complexType>
  </xs:element>

  <xs:element name="FootNote">
    <xs:complexType>
      <xs:attribute name="Text" type="xs:string" use="required" />
    </xs:complexType>
  </xs:element>

  <xs:element name="Languages">
    <xs:complexType>
      <xs:sequence>
        <xs:element ref="Title" />
        <xs:element ref="Heading1" />
```

```
            <xs:element ref="Intro" />
            <xs:element ref="Language" minOccurs="0" maxOccurs="unbounded" />
            <xs:element ref="FootNote" />
        </xs:sequence>
      </xs:complexType>
    </xs:element>

</xs:schema>
```

For more on XML, DTD, and XML Schemas (as well as XSL, XPath, and DOM covered in the next sections), I recommend "Professional VB6 XML", ISBN 1-86100-332-3, and "Professional XML Schemas", ISBN 1-86100-547-4; both published by Wrox Press.

Related Standards

One of XML's key strengths is that there is a bevy of companion standards, such as DOM, XSL, and XLink, which greatly enhance its capabilities. For instance, we can manipulate XML data through the Document Object Model (**DOM**), then present it as HTML using the Extensible Style Language (**XSL**), and link it to other documents through the Extensible Linking Language (**XLink**). We'll look at DOM and XSL in some detail over the course of the chapter.

Another important standard that enhances XML's power and versatility is XML **namespaces**, which facilitates mixing different sets of XML tags in a single document. Namespaces are a familiar concept for C++, Java, or .NET programmers, and they group related items ('names') together in a single place, or space, hence the name. Any item can then be uniquely identified by specifying the namespace to which it belongs, thus avoiding name collisions. For instance, a set of XML tags for describing music may include a tag called <track>, but another set of tags, say for railway engineers, uses <track> to describe something quite different. If we know the namespace for the music tags is www.mymusicplayer.com, we can refer to elements in that set rather than any other by specifying this namespace, or more likely the shorthand **namespace prefix**. Notice how XML namespaces use unique resource identifiers (**URI**), as firstly they are guaranteed unique, and also ownership is not a problem, as most companies will already have their own URL to use.

Manipulating XML Data

Two of XML's fundamental rules – not allowing tags to overlap, and the requirement that all data in an XML document (that is, everything apart from the XML declaration, the DTD, and any instructions for the XML parser) be enclosed in a tag – ensure that XML documents follow a robust structure. This data structure allows us to navigate a document without any knowledge of the data or tags it may contain. This allows us to create applications that read XML and yet still be able to change the format or content of the XML without breaking the applications.

A Tree Grows in XML

Well-formed XML has a clear hierarchical structure that can be viewed as a tree. There is a single **root node**, with a variable number of child nodes contained directly within it. Each of those children can have any number of their own children, and so on ad nauseam. XML attributes and elements are each represented by a node in the tree, as are text data (called text nodes), comments, and processing instructions.

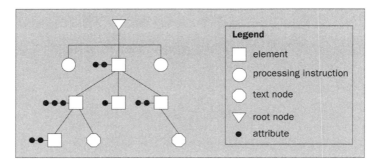

XPath, which we'll look at in a moment, is a way of identifying any particular node in an XML document using this tree model. For simplicity, comment nodes and namespace nodes have been left out of the above figure. Comment nodes are as you would expect, but XML elements qualified by a namespace have an appropriate child **namespace node**.

Also, remember that the root node is an implicit element which provides a known starting point for navigating any XML document. Do not confuse it with the **document element**, or **root element**, of which there can also be only one, but which is an explicit element which contains all the XML elements that represent the document's content.

The Document Object Model (DOM), a browser-independent API for manipulating XML documents, also traverses nodes using this tree model. As with other standards, not all browsers support the DOM in the same way and some add their own non-standard extensions. Microsoft exposes DOM objects through COM interfaces. The next three tables show the main methods and properties of Microsoft's DOM, and we'll put them into practice in the following sections.

Document Partial Interface		
`async`	Property	A read/write Boolean property that indicates whether asynchronous download should be enabled. `True` by default.
`createElement(tagName)`	Method	Creates an element with the name of `tagName`.
`load(url)`	Method	Loads an XML document from the location specified by the URL. If the URL cannot be resolved or accessed, or it does not refer to an XML document, the `documentElement` is set to `Nothing`. Returns a Boolean indicating success or failure.

Document Partial Interface		
save(destination)	Method	Serializes the XML. The parameter can be a filename, an ASP response, an XML document, or any other COM object that supports IPersistStream, IStream, or IPersistStreamInit.

Node Partial Interface		
appendChild(newChild)	Method	Appends newChild as the last child of this node.
transformNode(stylesheetNode)	Method	Returns the result of processing the sourceDOMNode (the root node) and its children with the stylesheet indicated by stylesheetDOMNode.
xml	Property	A read-only property that returns the XML representation of the node and all its descendants as a string.

ParseError Interface		
errorCode	Property	The error code number.
filepos	Property	The absolute file position where the error occurred.
line	Property	The number of the line containing the error.
linepos	Property	The character position where the error occurred.
reason	Property	The reason for the error.
srcText	Property	The full text of the line containing the error.
url	Property	The URL of the XML file containing the error.

Extensible Style Language (XSL)

XSL is an XML language for describing how given XML documents should be transformed and styled. In this chapter, we'll investigate the most commonly used part of XSL, XSL-Transformations, or XSLT. The other part, XSL-Formatting Objects, or XSL-FO, can describe how an XML document should be laid out with great precision and is compatible with a wide range of global languages. It is only really used in very specialist areas, and is not supported by the widely available browsers, so we won't worry about it here.

An XSLT stylesheet specifies rules that should be applied to an XML document in a particular dialect in order to transform it into a new XML, or plain text, format. Perhaps the most common use of XSLT is to create HTML for displaying the information in a given XML file.

XPath

XPath is a W3C standard for specifying nodes in an XML document using a path format very similar to that used in command-line environments such as MS-DOS and Unix. Just as we would denote the root directory of a file system by a single slash, we also specify the root node of an XML document with a single slash. Note however that XPath uses the forward slash, as does Unix, rather than the backslash favored by MS-DOS. It is most commonly used in XSL, but it is a specification in its own right, and is also used in XPointer.

We indicate nodes using XPath in much the same way that we specify directories on the command line, so, in our sample XML document, we could refer to the `/Languages`, `/Languages/Language`, and `/Languages/Language/Abbreviation` nodes. These are all called **absolute location paths** because they provide an unambiguous route to the desired node, regardless of where we may be currently – they all start from the root node. Often however, we wish to locate nodes in relation our current position in the document. For instance, if the current node (more properly called the **context node**) is `/Languages/Language`, then a path of `Abbreviation` would indicate the `/Languages/Language/Abbreviation` node.

In addition, the `.` character is used to indicate the context node itself, just as it indicates the current directory in file paths.

> *The XPath standard is a fairly complex beast, which we don't have space to describe in full here. More sophisticated features, such as axes and XPath functions, have been left out of this discussion for simplicity.*

Transforming XML for Display Using XSL

In this section, we'll create a stylesheet, `Markup.xsl`, that transforms our sample XML document into an HTML document that will produce the same output as that of the HTML file we saw at the beginning of the chapter. Since an XSL stylesheet is an XML document, we start off with the XML declaration:

```
<?xml version="1.0"?>
```

The document element of any XSLT stylesheet is `<xsl:stylesheet>`, which specifies the namespaces that are in use in the stylesheet:

```
<xsl:stylesheet xmlns:xsl="http://www.w3.org/TR/WD-xsl"
                xmlns="http://www.w3.org/TR/REC-html40"
            result-ns="">
```

The attribute `xmlns:xsl="http://www.w3.org/TR/WD-xsl"` sets the namespace prefix `xsl` to the XSL namespace, and so we'll use this prefix in front of all stylesheet element names (including the `<stylesheet>` element itself). We also reference the HTML 4.0 namespace with the attribute `xmlns="http://www.w3.org/TR/REC-html40"` since we are generating HTML. Note that we don't actually specify a prefix for this namespace – it is the **default namespace** – which means that any unqualified tag names in the stylesheet are to be taken as HTML tags.

Now we start adding our transformation rules, which are defined by `<xsl:template>` elements. These elements use their `match` attribute to specify which element in the source XML they should be applied to.

We start with a template that matches all text nodes in the source XML, by setting its `match` attribute to `"text()"`. Any source nodes that satisfy this rule are then replaced in the target document with the contents of the `<template>` element. Thus, all text nodes will be replaced by the result of the `<xsl:value-of>` element, which in this case will be the text itself:

```
<xsl:template match="text()">
   <xsl:value-of select="." />
</xsl:template>
```

Next, we start a template that will match the root node – that is, the document itself – by specifying a `match` attribute of `"/"`. As this template will match the implicit root node that contains all the XML in the source, and of which there is always one and only one, it is the ideal place for specifying the overall structure of our target document. In our case, it is where we can specify the HTML tags that start and close all XHTML documents:

```
<xsl:template match="/">
<HTML>

<HEAD>
<META http-equiv="Content-Language" content="en-us" />
<META http-equiv="Content-Type" content="text/html; charset=windows-1252" />
<META name="AUTHOR" content="PGB" />
```

The code we've had so far does not contain any XSL instructions (that is, tags that have the `xsl` prefix) and so will be copied verbatim to the resulting document, which is what we want, as these elements will be valid for all HTML documents we create.

However, we'll create a title for our HTML dynamically, using `<xsl:value-of>`. This time, we set the `select` attribute to specify the XPath that will lead us from our current position (which in this template will be the root node as that is what the `match` attribute specifies) to the source XML we want to use:

```
<TITLE>
 <xsl:value-of select="Languages/Title" />
</TITLE>

</HEAD>
```

The next section of this template creates the `<BODY>` element, which is created by a sequence of `<xsl:for-each>` loop elements. The contents of this element are inserted in the output document for every occurrence of the node specified by its `select` attribute. The first elements we'll deal with are the `<Heading1>` elements, which we'll turn into `<H1>` elements:

```
<BODY>

<xsl:for-each select="Languages/Heading1">
  <H1>
```

427

```
    <xsl:value-of select="." />
  </H1>
</xsl:for-each>

<HR />
```

Now we proceed, turning the remaining elements that we wish to display into HTML:

```
<xsl:for-each select="Languages/Intro">
  <P>
  <xsl:value-of select="@Text" />
  </P>
</xsl:for-each>

<TABLE border="1" width="500">

<xsl:for-each select="Languages/Language">

  <TR>
   <TD width="10%">
     <FONT size="2">
      <B>
        <xsl:for-each select="Abbreviation">
         <xsl:value-of select="." />
        </xsl:for-each>
      </B>
     </FONT>
   </TD>
   <TD width="50%">
   <FONT size="2">
      <xsl:for-each select="FullName">
        <xsl:value-of select="." />
      </xsl:for-each>
   </FONT>
   </TD>
   <TD width="40%">
   <FONT size="2">
      <xsl:for-each select="Description">
        <xsl:value-of select="." />
      </xsl:for-each>
   </FONT>
   </TD>
  </TR>
</xsl:for-each>
</TABLE>

<xsl:for-each select="Languages/FootNote">
  <P>
   <FONT size="2">
     <xsl:value-of select="@Text" />
   </FONT>
  </P>
</xsl:for-each>
```

```
    </BODY>

  </HTML>
```

Lastly, we close the `<xsl:template>` and `<xsl:stylesheet>` elements:

```
  </xsl:template>

</xsl:stylesheet>
```

To view what the output this transformation produces in Internet Explorer, we can simply add a link to it from the source XML document like so:

```
<?xml version="1.0" encoding="UTF-8" standalone="yes"?>
<?xml-stylesheet type="text/xsl" href="Markup.xsl"?>
<!DOCTYPE Languages [
...
```

When we now open this in IE6, it appears like so:

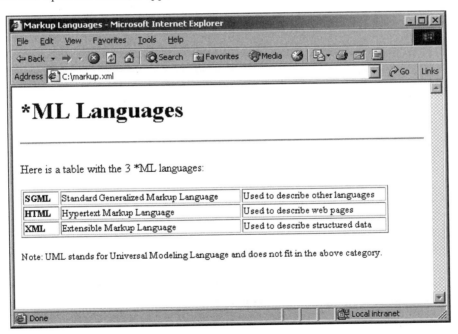

Client-side XML

As with many web technologies, we must decide whether processing is to occur on the client or on the server. Processing on the server may free you from requiring a specific technology to be available on the client, but will increase the heavy workload on the server. Processing on the client frees the server, but may require a specific browser.

Generating XML Using Visual Basic 6

There are a multitude of data sources which could provide XML data, but in this section, we concentrate on extracting data from a database, the most common requirement. Rather than getting bogged down with specific database features, we'll instead use Active Data Objects (ADO) as a universal data access tool. It would be easy enough to adapt the code presented here to use another data source (such as an Excel spreadsheet) by replacing the data navigation code (MoveFirst, MoveNext, and EOF) with code appropriate for the other data source.

We'll examine three methods of creating XML from an ADO recordset. The first method, using an ADO native method, is easy to use, but has some limitations. The two other methods are custom implementations that are more flexible, and they return the XML data as a string, which can sometimes save the overhead of reading from a file. Our custom implementations are also capable of handling hierarchical recordsets.

Hierarchical recordsets can represent complex relationships in a hierarchical fashion, and they are made available through a special OLE DB provider called MSDataShape. Hierarchical recordsets present an alternative to SQL JOIN syntax when accessing parent-child data. They differ from a JOIN in that with a JOIN, both the parent table fields and child table fields are represented in the same recordset. With a hierarchical recordset, the recordset contains only fields from the parent table. In addition, the recordset contains an extra field that represents the related child data, which you can assign to a second recordset variable and traverse. A new clause, SHAPE, is provided to relate SELECT statements in a hierarchical fashion. The syntax is summarized below:

```
SHAPE {parent-command} [[AS] name]
APPEND ({child-command} [[AS] name] RELATE parent-field TO child-field)
[,({child2-command} ...)]
```

For more about this sophisticated feature of ADO, take a look at David Sussman's "ADO 2.6 Programmer's Reference", ISBN 1-86100-463-X, by Wrox Press.

Using the ADO Save Method to Save a Recordset as XML

In this section, we will look at the easiest way to save an ADO recordset to a file: using the ADO recordset's Save method. This method can persist recordsets to an XML file in a single line of code:

```
rsResult.Save strXMLFilename, adPersistXML
```

Let's implement this in a project, using the SQL Server pubs sample database as our data provider. Start a new **Standard EXE** Visual Basic project. Select **Project | References**, and check **Microsoft ActiveX Data Objects 2.7 Library**.

Remove the standard form from the project and add a module instead (not a class module). We'll create an XML file called Authors.xml in the same directory as the project, which we find using the App.Path property. Finally, we call the CreateAuthorsXML method that we'll implement shortly:

```
Public Sub Main()
    Dim strPath            As String

    ' Normalize Path
    strPath = App.Path
    If Right$(strPath, 1) <> "/" Then
        strPath = strPath & "/"
    End If

    CreateAuthorsXML strPath & "Authors.xml"
End Sub
```

We create our XML file in the CreateAuthorsXML method. The code is straightforward. First, we declare and instantiate a recordset object:

```
Sub CreateAuthorsXML(strXMLFile As String)
    Dim rsAuthors         As ADODB.Recordset

    Set rsAuthors = New ADODB.Recordset
```

Then, we open the recordset object after setting the query string and data source parameters:

```
    ' SQL to populate recordset with a few columns from Authors table
    rsAuthors.Source = "SELECT au_id, au_fname, au_lname FROM Authors"

    ' Change localhost below to your SQL Server name if necessary
    rsAuthors.ActiveConnection = "Provider=sqloledb;Data Source=localhost;" _
                        & "Initial Catalog=pubs;User Id=sa;Password="

    ' All set to open the recordset...
    rsAuthors.Open
```

Since the recordset Save method throws a run-time error if the target file already exists, we should check its existence and delete the target file if needed:

```
    If FileExists(strXMLFile) Then Kill strXMLFile
```

Then we call the Save method:

```
    rsAuthors.Save strXMLFile, adPersistXML
```

Finally, we close and destroy the recordset object:

```
    rsAuthors.Close
    Set rsAuthors = Nothing
End Sub
```

431

We need the following helper function to check whether a file exists:

```
Function FileExists(ByVal strFileName As String) As Boolean

    FileExists = CBool(Len(Dir$(strFileName, vbNormal _
                                 + vbHidden _
                                 + vbSystem _
                                 + vbVolume _
                                 + vbDirectory)))

End Function
```

Running the project creates an XML file containing the author details as taken from the pubs database. As you'll see if you open this file, it includes an inline schema describing the elements used to hold the recordset information:

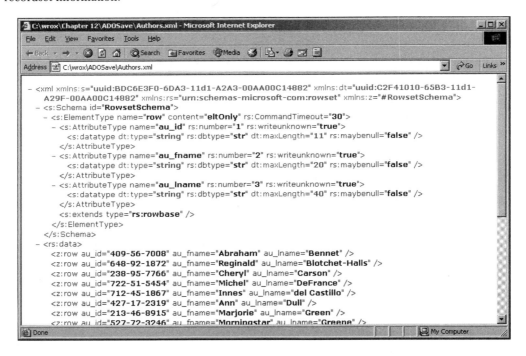

Saving a Recordset as XML Using Custom Code

When you want maximum flexibility, you have to be prepared to do more coding. The most flexible way to create XML (either as a string or as a file) is by coding everything yourself. In this section, we'll create a recursive function called strRS2XML. Our implementation uses tags to hold field values, but it would be easy to modify this code so the field values are attributes of a "row" tag, as is the case when the recordset Save method is used. Also note that it works correctly with hierarchical recordsets.

Again, we'll demonstrate this on the SQL Server pubs database. Create a new **Standard EXE** project, with a reference to the ADO 2.7 library as before. Remove the standard form from the project and add a module in its place.

Add the following constants to the General Declarations section:

```
' Set to 0 for Production Mode
#Const DEMO_MODE = 1

#If DEMO_MODE = 1 Then
Private Const MAX_RECORDS = 5
#End If

Private Const DOUBLE_QUOTE = """"
Private Const CHAR_SMALLER = "<"
Private Const CHAR_GREATER = ">"
Private Const CHAR_OBLIQUE_SMALLER = "</"
Private Const CHAR_OBLIQUE_GREATER = " />"

Private Const DEFAULT_INDENTATION = 2
```

We need a couple of helper functions to create valid tag names and to handle special characters within the text nodes. The code is self-explanatory:

```
Private Function strValidXMLTag(strTagCandidate As String) As String
    ' This function only handles occurrences of "xml" and
    ' replaces white space with "_".
    ' The implementation of the remaining rules is left as
    ' an exercise for the reader. ;)

    ' Get rid of occurrences of 'xml'
    strTagCandidate = Replace(strTagCandidate, "xml", "x_m_l")
    ' Get rid of spaces
    strValidXMLTag = Replace(strTagCandidate, " ", "_")
End Function

Private Function strValidXMLContent(strContenCandidate As String) As String
    ' Get rid of occurrences of '<'
    strContenCandidate = Replace(strContenCandidate, "<", "&lt;")
    ' Get rid of occurrences of '>'
    strContenCandidate = Replace(strContenCandidate, ">", "&gt;")
    ' Get rid of occurrences of '&'
    strContenCandidate = Replace(strContenCandidate, "&", "&amp;")
    ' Get rid of occurrences of '"'
    strContenCandidate = Replace(strContenCandidate, """", "&quot;")
    ' Get rid of occurrences of "'"
    strValidXMLContent = Replace(strContenCandidate, "'", "&apos;")
End Function
```

Now we come to the `strRS2XML` subroutine. In order to save on stack space and allocation time, we declare all variables and objects that do not need to be maintained during recursive function calls as static:

```
Public Function strRS2XML(rs As ADODB.Recordset, strName As String, _
                          Optional vntIndentation As Variant) As String
    Static objField       As ADODB.Field
    Static strSpaces      As String
    Static strFieldName   As String
    Static intLevel       As Integer
    Static intIndentation As Integer
```

The variables that maintain state during recursive function calls cannot be made static:

```
    Dim rsChapter         As ADODB.Recordset
    Dim strXML            As String
    Dim strDocName        As String
    Dim lngRecCount       As Long
```

We pass the number of spaces to use for indentation as an optional parameter. Note that we use a variant for proper functioning of the IsMissing function. Using this function allows us to distinguish between a zero (meaning do not indent) and an unspecified indentation level:

```
    If IsMissing(vntIndentation) Then
        intIndentation = DEFAULT_INDENTATION
    Else
        intIndentation = vntIndentation
        If intIndentation < 0 Then intIndentation = DEFAULT_INDENTATION
    End If
```

Since this function is recursive, we need to take care to only write the XML declaration once. We use the static variable intLevel for this: it has an initial value of zero, and is subsequently incremented as you traverse the recordset, making it suitable for testing whether this is the first call for the document. By the time we have processed the whole recordset, intLevel will again have the value of 0, the correct value to process another recordset in a subsequent call. We use this variable to determine how many spaces to indent:

```
    If intLevel = 0 Then    ' Only on top-level call.
        strXML = "<?xml version=" _
                & DOUBLE_QUOTE & "1.0" & DOUBLE_QUOTE _
                & " ?>" & vbCr
    End If

    strSpaces = Space$(intLevel * intIndentation)
```

Since the actual choice of tag names is not really relevant to understanding XML generation in VB, we'll use a simple algorithm to determine these. We use the same noun, passed as a parameter, in the singular and plural and assume adding an 's' to the singular will produce the plural (or subtracting the 's' from the plural will give us the singular). This is not a perfect solution, but is acceptable in this situation:

```
    strName = strValidXMLTag(strName)
    If Right$(strName, 1) = "s" Then
        strDocName = strName
        strName = Left$(strName, Len(strName) - 1)
```

```
    Else
        strDocName = strName & "s"
    End If
```

We first create the start document tag, and increase the indentation level.

```
    ' Start of Document TAG
    strXML = strXML & CHAR_SMALLER & strDocName & CHAR_GREATER & vbCr

    intLevel = intLevel + 1
    strSpaces = Space$(intLevel * intIndentation)
```

Then we move to the first record in the recordset, initializing our count of how many records have been processed so far:

```
    rs.MoveFirst
    lngRecCount = 1
```

We then create the loop that will iterate through all records. In demo mode, we limit the number of records that will be processed to a programmer-defined constant:

```
#If DEMO_MODE = 1 Then
    While Not rs.EOF And lngRecCount < MAX_RECORDS
#Else
    While Not rs.EOF
#End If
```

We then create the start tag for this record:

```
    strXML = strXML & strSpaces & CHAR_SMALLER & strName & CHAR_GREATER & vbCr
```

Now we iterate through all the fields in this record:

```
    For Each objField In rs.Fields
```

To determine whether we have a hierarchical recordset, we look at the Type property:

```
        If objField.Type = adChapter Then
```

If we have a hierarchical recordset, our field Value is actually another recordset, recognizable by the adChapter field Type. So if this recordset is not empty, we increase the level and make a recursive call to strRS2XML, with the desired indentation level passed along. (The current indentation level is maintained through a static variable.) We add a prefix to the field name to avoid creating duplicate tag names. We could alternatively use namespaces, as in the recordset's Save method.

```
            Set rsChapter = objField.Value
            If Not rsChapter.EOF Then
                intLevel = intLevel + 1
```

435

```
            strXML = strXML & strRS2XML(rsChapter, strName & "." _
                                    & objField.Name, intIndentation)
            intLevel = intLevel - 1
        End If
```

If we don't have a hierarchical recordset, we create a field tag. We create empty tags for NULL values. We call `strValidXMLTag` to ensure the field name is created according to the XML rules, while `strValidXMLContent` ensures that the field values conform to the rules:

```
        Else
            ' Ensure we have a correctly formed tag name
            strFieldName = strValidXMLTag(strName & "." & objField.Name)

            If IsNull(objField.Value) Then
                ' Empty Field tag
                strXML = strXML & strSpaces & Space$(intIndentation) _
                    & CHAR_SMALLER & strFieldName & CHAR_OBLIQUE_GREATER & vbCr
            Else
                ' Start of Field tag
                strXML = strXML & strSpaces & Space$(intIndentation) _
                    & CHAR_SMALLER & strFieldName & CHAR_GREATER
                ' Field tag Content
                strXML = strXML & strValidXMLContent(objField.Value)
                ' End of Field tag
                strXML = strXML & CHAR_OBLIQUE_SMALLER _
                    & strFieldName & CHAR_GREATER & vbCr
            End If
        End If
```

We can now move on to the next field:

```
        Next objField
```

When we leave that loop, we'll have processed all the fields, and are done with the record. We'll put in a `DoEvents` call to keep the application responsive when processing large recordsets:

```
        strXML = strXML & strSpaces & CHAR_OBLIQUE_SMALLER & strName _
            & CHAR_GREATER & vbCr
        DoEvents
```

Since we have processed the record, we fetch the next one:

```
        rs.MoveNext
        lngRecCount = lngRecCount + 1
    Wend
```

After we leave the `While` loop, we are done with our recordset. We need to get the `intLevel` variable back to 0 for the next call to `strRS2XML`:

```
    intLevel = intLevel - 1
    strSpaces = Space$(intLevel * intIndentation)
```

All that remains is to close our document tag and return the result of our processing to the caller:

```
    strXML = strXML & strSpaces & CHAR_OBLIQUE_SMALLER & strDocName _
             & CHAR_GREATER & vbCr
    strRS2XML = strXML
End Function
```

Using the `strRS2XML` function is straightforward. In the following example, we create an XML file (as opposed to creating a string with XML data). The key line in the code below is simply the print to file line using the sub you just wrote: `Print #intFileNumber, strRS2XML(rsAuthors, "Author")`

```
Public Sub Main()
    Dim strPath          As String

    ' Normalize Path
    strPath = App.Path
    If Right$(strPath, 1) <> "/" Then
        strPath = strPath & "/"
    End If

    CreateAuthorsXML strPath & "Authors.xml"
End Sub

Public Sub CreateAuthorsXML(strXMLFile As String)
    Dim intFileNumber    As Integer
    Dim rsAuthors        As ADODB.Recordset

    Set rsAuthors = New ADODB.Recordset
    rsAuthors.Source = "SELECT au_id, au_fname, au_lname FROM Authors "

    rsAuthors.ActiveConnection = "Provider=sqloledb;Data Source=localhost;" _
                              & "Initial Catalog=pubs;User Id=sa;Password="

    ' All set to open recordset...
    rsAuthors.Open

    ' Get unused file number create file
    intFileNumber = FreeFile
    Open strXMLFile For Output As #intFileNumber

    ' Output text
    Print #intFileNumber, strRS2XML(rsAuthors, "Author")

    ' Clean Up
    Close #intFileNumber
    rsAuthors.Close
    Set rsAuthors = Nothing

End Sub
```

Running the project will create the following XML file:

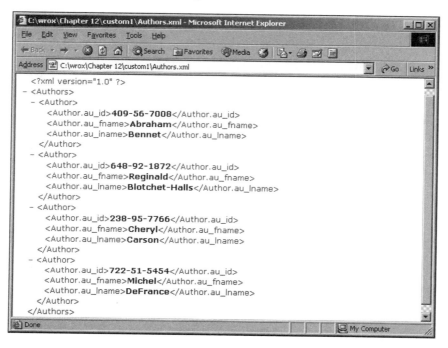

Saving a Recordset as XML Using The DOM

An alternative to coding a regular VB function like the one above is to use Microsoft's XML parser, MSXML. We'll now rewrite our RS2XML function to use the DOM. As before, it will be recursive and will support hierarchical recordsets. Again, we'll use tags to hold field values, but it wouldn't be hard to modify the code to write field values as attributes of <row> elements, as is the case with the XML generated by ADO's Save method.

We'll use the project from the previous example. To use the MSMXL library, we need a reference to Microsoft XML from our standard EXE project, as well as one to the ADO 2.7 library. The latest version is 4.0.

Now add the DOM function, objRS2XML_DOM:

```
Public Function objRS2XML_DOM(rs As ADODB.Recordset, strName As String) _
        As MSXML2.IXMLDOMElement
```

Again, we declare as static all variables and objects that do not need to be maintained during recursive function calls to save on stack space and reduce allocation time:

```
Static objField         As ADODB.Field
Static intLevel         As Integer
Static objXMLDocument   As MSXML2.DOMDocument
Static objChild         As MSXML2.IXMLDOMElement
```

Other variables cannot be made static:

```
Dim objRoot          As MSXML2.IXMLDOMElement
Dim objElement       As MSXML2.IXMLDOMElement
Dim rsChapter        As ADODB.Recordset
Dim strDocName       As String
Dim lngRecCount      As Long
```

We choose tag names using the simplistic algorithm we've already seen, and determine whether this is the first call to the method by looking at `intLevel`:

```
strName = strValidXMLTag(strName)
If Right$(strName, 1) = "s" Then
    strDocName = strName
    strName = Left$(strName, Len(strName) - 1)
Else
    strDocName = strName & "s"
End If
If intLevel = 0 Then    ' Only on top-level call
    Set objXMLDocument = New MSXML2.DOMDocument
End If

intLevel = intLevel + 1
```

We first need an element with the document name. This element is either the document element itself, in which case it does not have a parent, or it is the top-level element of a child recordset, in which case it will be appended after the recursive call, below:

```
' Start of Document TAG
Set objRoot = objXMLDocument.createElement(strDocName)
```

Now we move to the first record in the recordset, initializing our count of how many records we have processed so far:

```
rs.MoveFirst
lngRecCount = 1
```

We then start the loop that will iterate through the records:

```
#If DEMO_MODE = 1 Then
    While Not rs.EOF And lngRecCount < MAX_RECORDS
#Else
    While Not rs.EOF
#End If
```

For each record, we create a new element and append it to the root object using DOM methods:

```
Set objElement = objXMLDocument.createElement(strName)
objRoot.appendChild objElement
```

Now we iterate through all the fields in this record:

```
        For Each objField In rs.Fields
            ' Is this a hierarchical recordset?
          If objField.Type = adChapter Then
              Set rsChapter = objField.Value
              If Not rsChapter.EOF Then
                  objElement.appendChild objRS2XML_DOM(rsChapter, strName & "." _
                                                    & objField.Name)
              End If
          Else
              Set objChild = objXMLDocument.createElement( _
                          strValidXMLTag(strName & "." & objField.Name))
              If Not IsNull(objField.Value) Then
                  objChild.Text = strValidXMLContent(objField.Value)
              End If
              objElement.appendChild objChild
          End If
        Next objField
      DoEvents
      rs.MoveNext
      lngRecCount = lngRecCount + 1
    Wend
```

Outside of the `While` loop, we again need to start winding the `intLevel` variable back down to zero:

```
    ' The (child) recordset has been processed so decrease the level
    intLevel = intLevel - 1
```

If this is the top-level call, we need to destroy the `Document` object we created:

```
    If intLevel = 0 Then    ' this is only true in top-level call
        Set objXMLDocument = Nothing
    End If
```

We return the result of our processing to the caller:

```
    ' Finally, return root node
    Set objRS2XML_DOM = objRoot
End Function
```

Using the DOM function is very similar to using `strRS2XML` function. The changes to `CreateAuthorsXML` are highlighted below, and consist of creating an XML document element to receive the result, since the functions differ in return types. We also need to use the new return variable when we output to file:

```
    CreateAuthorsXML strPath & "Authors.xml"
End Sub

Public Sub CreateAuthorsXML(strXMLFile As String)
    Dim intFileNumber    As Integer
```

```
Dim rsAuthors          As ADODB.Recordset
Dim objRoot            As MSXML2.IXMLDOMElement

Set rsAuthors = New ADODB.Recordset

' Open recordset with a few columns
' Limit to just a few records with WHERE clause
rsAuthors.Source = "SELECT au_id, au_fname, au_lname " _
                 & "FROM Authors WHERE au_id < 5"

' In the following, you need to change "srvr" to the
' name of your SQL Server
rsAuthors.ActiveConnection = "Provider=sqloledb;" & _
    "Data Source=srvr;Initial Catalog=pubs;User Id=sa;Password=; "

' All set to open recordset...
rsAuthors.Open    ' Open recordset (limit to just a few records with WHERE
                  ' clause)

' Call objRS2XML_DOM which returns the root node
Set objRoot = objRS2XML_DOM(rsAuthors, "Author")

' Get unused file number
intFileNumber = FreeFile
' Create file name
Open strXMLFile For Output As #intFileNumber
' Output text
Print #intFileNumber, objRoot.xml
' Close file
Close #intFileNumber

' Clean Up
rsAuthors.Close
Set rsAuthors = Nothing
End Sub
```

The XML file produced by this new method is identical to that produced by the previous code.

Server-Side XML

XML techniques such as these can be employed in web solutions without requiring XML-capable browsers, thanks to IIS. If we install Microsoft XML v4.0 on the server, we can use the XML parser in an IIS application to transform XML into HTML on the server, or another format such as WML. In this section, we'll create some Visual Basic code for such an IIS application.

Generating HTML from XML Server-Side

In this sample we'll use an XSL stylesheet to transform an XML document into an HTML page using an IIS application. As in the previous project, we need a reference to the Microsoft XML parser in order to use the DOM objects.

Start a new Visual Basic IIS Application project. Double-click on WebClass1 in the Project window to bring up the Web Class designer. In the Properties window, change the class name to XML2HTMLonServer and its `NameInURL` property to XML2HTML. Right-click on the Custom WebItems folder, and select Add Custom WebItem. Name the WebItem XML2HTML. Double-click it and add the following helper sub:

```
Private Sub ShowParseError(objParseError As MSXML2.IXMLDOMParseError)

    With Response
        .Write "<B>Invalid XML/XSL file!</B><HR/>"

        .Write "<B>Please report the following error info to your nearest" _
            & " helpful Systems geek:<BR/><BR/>"

        .Write "File URL :</B>" & objParseError.URL & "<BR/>"
        .Write "<B>Line No :</B>" & objParseError.Line & "<BR/>"
        .Write "<B>Character :</B>" & objParseError.linepos & "<BR/>"
        .Write "<B>File Position :</B>" & objParseError.filepos & "<BR/>"
        .Write "<B>Source Text :</B>" & objParseError.srcText & "<BR/>"
        .Write "<B>Error Code :</B>" & objParseError.errorCode & "<BR/>"
        .Write "<B>Description :</B>" & objParseError.reason & "<BR/>"
    End With
End Sub
```

Next remove all the default code from the `WebClass_Start()` event handler, and replace it with the following. We declare a string variable and two XML document objects: one for the XML document and one for its stylesheet:

```
Private Sub WebClass_Start()
    Dim strPath         As String
    Dim objXMLDocument  As MSXML2.DOMDocument
    Dim objXMLStyle     As MSXML2.DOMDocument
```

We make sure our path ends with a / so we can append a filename to get a full path:

```
    strPath = App.Path
    If Right$(strPath, 1) <> "/" Then
        strPath = strPath & "/"
    End If
```

Then we parse the XML document. Before calling the `load` method, we set the `async` property to `False` to get synchronous parsing:

```
    Set objXMLDocument = New MSXML2.DOMDocument
    objXMLDocument.async = False
    objXMLDocument.load strPath & "Markup.xml"
```

Then we query the `parseError` object to ensure no errors occurred. If no errors occurred, we repeat the loading process on the stylesheet:

```
If (objXMLDocument.parseError.errorCode = 0) Then
    ' No parsing errors!
    ' Load the associated XSL document
    Set objXMLStyle = New MSXML2.DOMDocument
    objXMLStyle.async = False
    objXMLStyle.load strPath & "Markup.xsl"
```

Again we query the `parseError` object to ensure no errors occurred.

```
If (objXMLStyle.parseError.errorCode = 0) Then
    ' No parsing errors!
```

We have now successfully loaded both the XML document and its stylesheet, so we can call the `transformNode` method to obtain the transformed XML as a string. We can then show this in the browser with `Response.Write`:

```
Response.Write objXMLDocument.transformNode(objXMLStyle)
```

We use the `Else` blocks to pass the `parseError` object of the document where an error occurred to the helper function that will display the error information. Along the way, we also release the XML documents:

```
    Else
        ' Show parsing errors occurring while
        ' loading the associated XSL document
        ShowParseError objXMLStyle.parseError
    End If

    ' Clean up
    Set objXMLStyle = Nothing
Else
    ' Show parsing errors occurring while loading the XML document
    ShowParseError objXMLDocument.parseError
End If

Set objXMLDocument = Nothing
End Sub
```

Copy the `Markup.xml` file and the `Markup.xsl` stylesheet we created earlier to the project directory. Add the reference to MSXML if you haven't already, and run the project. When Visual Studio displays the Project Properties dialog, click OK, and choose a suitable virtual root name if asked. Shortly thereafter you should see the following page displayed in your browser:

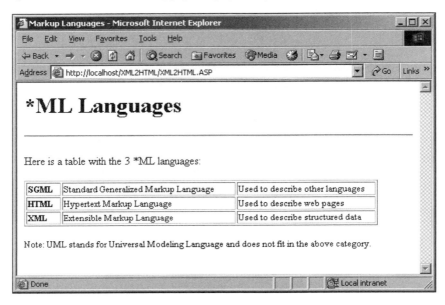

Right click on the page and select **View source**. As you can see below, the only hint of XML is the notation used for standalone tags, such as `<HR />`:

Uploading XML to the Server

How you choose to send XML to the server will depend on the application's specific requirements. In this section, we'll see two methods for sending XML to the server. The first uses the Microsoft-specific DOM extension `ServerXMLHTTP` and is especially appropriate when you want the XML data processed as it is received. As its name indicates, a `ServerXMLHTTP` object uses the HTTP protocol to send requests to the web server. We will also implement the server component to receive this data, using both an ASP script and a Visual Basic IIS application.

Another option is to use FTP. This, and similar methods such as `HTTP POST`, are appropriate when you simply want to place the XML document on the server, without performing any further server-side processing.

Using the ServerXMLHTTP Object

This solution requires the Microsoft XML Parser on the client machine and relies on the server component described in the *Receiving XML on the Server* section. Using the `ServerXMLHTTP` object isn't hard. Once we've established a connection to our web server through its `Open` method, we send our XML as a string parameter of the `send` method.

That's really all there is to sending. The server component sends response information back, which we can get through the object's `responseXML` property.

Let's see a complete sample using this idea. Create a new standard EXE project, and add references to both ADO and MSXML. Place a label, a button (named `cmdSend`), and a textbox (named `txtAU_ID`) on the default form. Lay them out and label them as shown in the following screenshot:

All the work is done in the `Click` event of the `cmdSend` button. We first declare a few variables:

```
Private Sub cmdSend_Click()
    Dim strPath         As String
    Dim strXMLFile      As String
    Dim strQuery        As String
    Dim strXML          As String
    Dim rsAuthors       As ADODB.Recordset
    Dim objXMLDocument  As MSXML2.DOMDocument
    Dim objXMLHttp      As MSXML2.ServerXMLHTTP40
    Dim objXSLDocument  As MSXML2.DOMDocument
```

Then we populate a recordset using the ID given in the textbox:

```
    Set rsAuthors = New ADODB.Recordset
```

```
        rsAuthors.Source = "SELECT au_id, au_fname, au_lname " _
                        & "FROM Authors WHERE au_id = '" _
                        & DoQuotes(txtAU_ID.Text) & "'"

        rsAuthors.ActiveConnection = "Provider=sqloledb;Data Source=localhost;" _
                        & "Initial Catalog=pubs;User Id=sa;Password="

        ' All set to open recordset...
        rsAuthors.Open
```

Then we use the ADO `Recordset.Save` method to make a temporary client-side copy of the data:

```
        ' Normalize Path
        strPath = App.Path
        If Right$(strPath, 1) <> "\" Then
            strPath = strPath & "\"
        End If

        'Persist Recordset to file as XML
        strXMLFile = strPath & "recordset.xml"
        If FileExists(strXMLFile) Then Kill strXMLFile
        rsAuthors.Save strXMLFile, adPersistXML
```

Now we are done with the recordset, so we can close it:

```
        ' Clean up ADO objects
        rsAuthors.Close
        Set rsAuthors = Nothing
```

Before we send the XML to the server, we'll simplify it a little with an XSL transform called `standard.xsl`. We'll come back to write this stylesheet later:

```
        ' Load the XML document we just created
        Set objXMLDocument = New MSXML2.DOMDocument
        objXMLDocument.async = False
        objXMLDocument.load strXMLFile

        ' Load the stylesheet to standardize the XML
        Set objXSLDocument = New MSXML2.DOMDocument
        objXSLDocument.async = False
        objXSLDocument.load strPath & "standard.xsl"

        'Standardize the XML
        strXML = objXMLDocument.transformNode(objXSLDocument)
        Set objXSLDocument = Nothing
        Set objXMLDocument = Nothing
```

To make sure everything is fine, we'll display the transformed XML in a message box:

```
        MsgBox strXML, vbOKOnly, "XML"
```

Finally, we're ready to send this XML to the server using an XMLHttpRequest object:

```
' Create a XMLHttpRequest object
  Set objXMLHttp = New MSXML2.ServerXMLHTTP40

    ' Here we omit the optional bstrUser and bstrPassword of the objXMLHttp.Open
    ' method. They may be required to access a production web server.

    ' Send the file using HTTP POST
    objXMLHttp.Open "POST", "http://localhost/receiveXML.asp", False
    objXMLHttp.send strXML
```

We display the server response in a message box and clean up.

```
    ' Get the response from the Server
    MsgBox objXMLHttp.responseXML.xml, vbInformation, "Response from Server"

    ' Clean Up
    Set objXMLHttp = Nothing
  End Sub
```

We now need two helper functions. We could perhaps do without the helper function that handles quotes within quotes in this case, but we'll include it as it's generally required when using string parameters in a query string:

```
Private Function DoQuotes(ByVal strToken As String) As String
    DoQuotes = Replace(strToken, "'", "''")
End Function
```

```
Private Function FileExists(ByVal strFileName As String) As Boolean
    FileExists = CBool(Len(Dir$(strFileName, vbNormal _
                    + vbHidden _
                    + vbSystem _
                    + vbVolume _
                    + vbDirectory)))
End Function
```

Finally, we create the XSL stylesheet that simplifies the XML file, since, as we saw earlier, the content generated by the ADO Save method is somewhat verbose. The stylesheet is called standard.xsl, and it simply turns attributes into elements within an <author> tag. Notice the use of the @ character in the select attribute, indicating that we're selecting an attribute from the source document:

```
<xsl:stylesheet xmlns:xsl="http://www.w3.org/TR/WD-xsl">

  <xsl:template match="//">
    <xsl:apply-templates/>
  </xsl:template>
  <xsl:template match="//z:row">
  <Author>
    <xsl:element name="au_id"><xsl:value-of select="@au_id"/></xsl:element>
```

```
    <xsl:element name="au_fname"><xsl:value-of select="@au_fname"/></xsl:element>
    <xsl:element name="au_lname"><xsl:value-of select="@au_lname"/></xsl:element>
  </Author>
  </xsl:template>

</xsl:stylesheet>
```

Receiving an XML File on the Server

Before we run the project, we need to create the server component. There are several ways to handle the receipt of the XML once the client has uploaded it, and we'll look at the best of these in this section.

Receiving XML Using an ASP Script

The simplest solution is to create an ASP page to save the received file with the `ServerXMLHTTP` object. Even if you're going to implement another approach in the final production version, a script such as this is still useful for testing purposes. Rather than creating a separate virtual directory for this example, we'll simply place the ASP file in the `wwwroot` directory.

The ASP file `receiveXML.asp` is very simple:

```
<% @LANGUAGE=VBScript%>
<%
  Set xmlCust = Server.CreateObject("MSXML2.DomDocument")
  xmlCust.async = False
  xmlCust.load (Request)
  If xmlCust.parseError.reason = "" Then
    xmlCust.Save (Server.MapPath("customer.xml"))
    Response.ContentType = "text/xml"
    Response.Write ("<result>Processed Successfully</result>")
  Else
    Response.Write ("<error/>")
  End If
%>
```

Receiving XML Using a Visual Basic IIS Application

If you wish to accomplish more complex tasks upon receiving your XML data on the server, you could write a receiving application in Visual Basic. The key idea is to create a `DOMDocument` in the `BeginRequest` event of a custom `WebItem`. Then, we load the XML data sent to the server using the `load` method, using the `Request` object as the input stream, like so:

```
objXMLDocument.load Request
```

Once we have loaded the XML document, we can manipulate it as we wish. In the example, we'll simply save the XML to a file.

Below is the complete listing for a custom WebItem that receives and saves an XML document sent by a `ServerXMLHTTP` object. As usual, our IIS application needs a reference to MSXML.

```
Private Sub WebClass_BeginRequest()
    Dim objXMLDocument      As MSXML2.DOMDocument
    Dim objXMLStyle         As MSXML2.DOMDocument

    ' First we load the XML document received in the Request
    Set objXMLDocument = New MSXML2.DOMDocument
    objXMLDocument.async = False
    objXMLDocument.load Request

    ' Parsing errors while loading the XML document?
    If (objXMLDocument.parseError.errorCode = 0) Then
        ' No parsing errors!
        ' Save the XML document on the Server
        objXMLDocument.save (Server.MapPath("author.xml"))

        ' Say "OK!"
        Response.ContentType = "text/xml"
        Response.Write "<result>Processed Successfully</result>"
    Else
        ' Show parsing errors occurring while loading the XML document
        ShowParseError objXMLDocument.parseError
    End If

    ' Clean up
    Set objXMLDocument = Nothing
End Sub

Private Sub ShowParseError(objParseError As MSXML2.IXMLDOMParseError)
    Dim strParseError       As String

    Response.ContentType = "text/xml"

    strParseError = "<Error><B>Invalid XML!</B><HR/>" & vbCr
    strParseError = strParseError & _
        "<B>File URL :</B>" & objParseError.URL & "<BR/>" & vbCr
    strParseError = strParseError & _
        "<B>Line No :</B>" & objParseError.Line & "<BR/>" & vbCr
    strParseError = strParseError & _
        "<B>Character :</B>" & objParseError.linepos & "<BR/>" & vbCr
    strParseError = strParseError & _
        "<B>File Position :</B>" & objParseError.filepos & "<BR/>" & vbCr
    strParseError = strParseError & _
        "<B>Source Text :</B>" & objParseError.srcText & "<BR/>" & vbCr
    strParseError = strParseError & _
        "<B>Error Code :</B>" & objParseError.errorCode & "<BR/>" & vbCr
    strParseError = strParseError & _
        "<B>Description :</B>" & objParseError.reason & "<BR/></Error>"

    Response.Write strParseError
End Sub
```

Running the Code

Once the receiving component is in place on the server, go ahead and run the client project. Note that the code we've added already is for the ASP solution. If you wish to try the IIS application, change click handler as highlighted below:

```
...
' Create a XMLHttpRequest object
Set objXMLHttp = New MSXML2.ServerXMLHTTP40

' Here we omit the optional bstrUser and bstrPassword of the objXMLHttp.Open
' method. They may be required to access a production Web Server.

' Send the file using HTTP POST
objXMLHttp.Open "POST", "http://localhost/VBReceiveXML.ASP", False
objXMLHttp.send strXML
...
```

When we click the Send button, we'll see the following message box showing that the XML has been successfully generated from the SQL query:

The following message box indicates the server received the file:

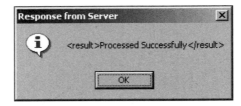

On the server, the following XML will have been created in the customer.xml file:

```
<Author>
  <au_id>172-32-1176</au_id>
  <au_fname>Johnson</au_fname>
  <au_lname>White</au_lname>
</Author>
```

Summary

This chapter has covered the essentials of using XML in VB6 applications. We looked at the basics of well-formed XML documents, and some of the companion standards of XML: DTD, XML Schemas, and namespaces. We saw how XSL can transform XML into HTML (or XHTML to be precise) for display in a browser, and also looked at how the Document Object Model (DOM) can be used to achieve similar results programmatically.

In the long run, XML skills may well diminish in importance. Not that XML will go away, but it is quite likely to become hidden. How many people today know Postscript? Yet in the late 80's as it emerged it was a relatively common skill. With the advent of Web Forms in .NET, how long will it be before most web developers never see HTML? How many people know the structure of TCP packets?

The same thing will most probably happen with XML over time but the tools and technologies are far from mature enough for XML to become invisible yet, so for the next several years at least, a solid understanding of XML and its related technologies will be very important. To this end, in this chapter, we created a handful of Visual Basic applications that generated XML from a recordset using a variety of methods: native ADO, plain Visual Basic, and the DOM. Finally, we wrote the code to upload XML from the client to a server.

14

SOAP and XML Web Services

I like to compare SOAP and web services to ODBC. SOAP is to objects what ODBC was to databases.

What do I mean by that? Let's turn back the clock to the early 90s. PC developers who wanted to use Oracle would write their applications using Oracle's proprietary database libraries. PC developers who wanted to use Sybase would likewise use proprietary Sybase libraries. Changing from one database to another was prohibitively difficult, because your code was tightly linked to a specific database vendor.

Along came Microsoft with this ODBC idea. The proposal was that we developers should be able to write our code to talk to ODBC and ODBC would figure out how to talk to specific databases. Though the database vendors kicked and screamed, ultimately ODBC changed the world. Who today thinks about proprietary APIs for any database? At most we deal with finding the right ODBC (or OLEDB or JDBC) driver for the database in question.

The end result is that we choose our database based on price, performance. Only three databases remain vibrant in the world – SQL Server, Oracle, and DB2. While others exist, they've been largely unable to compete on a level playing field and they are minor players.

Flash forward to the year 2000. Developers who want to talk to COM objects use DCOM. Developers who want to talk to CORBA objects use IIOP and those who want to talk to Java objects use RMI. All of these are effectively proprietary libraries. Even though IIOP is technically an 'open' technology, it doesn't interoperate with DCOM or RMI, so it locks you into CORBA through its use. Objects are stuck in the same rut that databases were in a decade ago.

Along this SOAP idea, which proposes that developers write code to talk to SOAP, and SOAP handles the details of how to talk to specific objects. Some middle-tier vendors have been kicking and screaming, but ultimately SOAP will change the world. In a few years from now, no one will ever think about using DCOM, IIOP or RMI. The playing field for middle-tier object vendors is changing as we watch.

This chapter aims to introduce VB6 developers to the new and exciting world of SOAP and XML Web Services. In the first section, we learn the concepts and standards that web services are built on. We then move on to get a practical taste of things as we implement and consume web services in VB6 using the Microsoft SOAP Toolkit, rounding things off with a short discussion of the future of web services and .NET.

The World Wide Web is now truly a worldwide phenomenon but its main concern currently is interactions between people and machine. Web services aim to enable programs and computers to talk to each other using the Internet's existing infrastructure.

XML Web Services

In essence, a web service is simply a web-based interface to a programmable component making its services available to remote software. **XML Web Services** provide this application-to-application communication through the Internet-friendly standard of XML, making the technology accessible to a wide range of systems. A web service can be used privately, on an intranet, by a single application, or it can be made public and published over the Internet for use by any number of applications. Web services' standard interface also makes them ideal for enabling disparate systems to work together on a single distributed application.

> XML Web Services do not require the use of any particular programming language. The standard simply describes the interface that provides access to the underlying logic. Just as the standard way for providing access to components in Windows is through API calls, you can think of web services as providing the standard API for the web.

Instead of using a portable code strategy, such as Java, to provide interoperability between heterogeneous systems, XML provides a way to enable transportation of data between such systems. This allows systems with completely different application models, operating systems, and even different programming languages to work together and exchange data. These can even include legacy systems or applications as long as they support XML, giving far more choice in the way that distributed web applications are built. The biggest advantage is that existing code can be made accessible as a web service by simply providing an interface to the parts that are to be published. XML Web Services allow us to use our system and programming language of choice: something that is lost when using proprietary systems.

One core attribute of an XML Web Service is the high level of abstraction of the interface to a component. Since the component is created and accessed by XML-based messages alone, the web service consumer needs only know the inputs, outputs, and location. No details of the component's internal workings need be known.

Founding Principles

When the standards that XML Web Services are built on were being devised, there were certain key objectives that were deemed essential in order to achieve maximum interoperability:

- ❑ **Loosely Coupled** – A loosely coupled system is made up of components that communicate through well-defined interfaces thus reducing the interdependencies of one component on any other.

- ❑ **Ubiquitous Communication** – The Internet has gained such wide acceptance that it is integrated into all major operating systems, and even operating systems for devices such as mobile phones.

- ❑ **Universal Data Format** – By transferring data as XML, web services can communicate over just about any electronic barrier without difficulty. It is not only a text-based and widely accepted data format, but it is also self-describing. In other words, XML not only transports data but also metadata about the data it is transporting.

In addition to these three requirements, web services have been designed to support automatic discovery, enabling the programmatic location of web services that provide certain functionality.

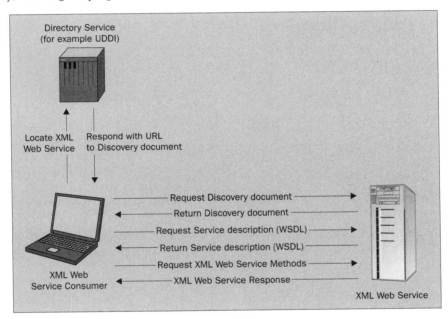

Web Services Directories

Much like a telephone directory enquiry service, web services directories such as UDDI (**Universal Description, Discovery and Integration**) provide a resource that one can query in order to locate web services provided by other organizations. However, it is not a requirement for a web service consumer to query such a directory. Again, using the phone directory analogy, if you already know the number, you do not need to use the phone directory and you can just dial direct.

A web service directory in fact supplies the web service **discovery document** that provides all the information the consuming application requires to gain access to the web service.

Web Service Discovery

Discovery is the process of locating one or more related documents that describe a web service using the **Web Services Description Language** (**WSDL**). What is commonly known as the DISCO specification lets us locate the service description. This process can be bypassed if the URL of the service description is already known.

Web Service Description

The WSDL file defines what operations a web service supports. The WSDL file tells the client what parameters are required when calling a web service and what return values to expect, as well as some other details such as endpoint information.

Web Service Wire Format

The protocol used for requests to and get responses from web services on a network is an XML protocol called **Simple Object Access Protocol (SOAP)**.

Introduction to SOAP

DCOM, covered in Chapter 11, is Microsoft's proprietary binary communication protocol for distributed applications. The propriety nature of such a protocol makes it ill-suited for universally accessible web services – it is too dependent on the details of the underlying architecture. SOAP was invented to provide a communication protocol that is completely independent of the platform on which it operates.

SOAP is what makes web service communication possible. It is an XML format for data exchange in a peer-to-peer, distributed environment, and it offers the following benefits:

❑ **Lightweight** – the overhead from using SOAP communication is small.

❑ **Decentralized** – SOAP communication is not dependent on a central server, making implementing SOAP easier and also enhancing system robustness.

❑ **Existing Transport Infrastructure** – Because XML's text format is compatible with existing Internet infrastructure, SOAP can be used to communicate with any system with access to the Internet.

❑ **Exchange of Structured Data** – As part of its support for remote procedure calls (RPC), SOAP can transmit complex structured data such as an invoice, a purchase order, or an employee record to or from a web service.

SOAP defines a messaging framework that is independent of any application layer or transport semantics. As a result SOAP is modular and extensible.

The SOAP protocol defines four distinctive parts for messages:

1. **SOAP envelope** – a mandatory extensible envelope for encapsulating data. The envelope forms the basic unit of exchange between SOAP consumers. This is the only mandatory part of SOAP, the rest define optional additional properties.

2. **Protocol Specification** – defines data-encoding rules for representing user-defined data types. It provides a uniform model for converting non-syntactic data models to text, in other words for **serializing** the model.

3. **Request/Response pattern** – defines an RPC-style message exchange pattern (request/response). Because SOAP is not limited to RPC-style messaging, this part is optional.

4. **HTTP Binding** – defines a binding between SOAP and HTTP. This part is also optional and you can use any other transport layer or mechanism to transport the SOAP envelope including SMTP, FTP, or disk-based transfer (SOAP messages can be transported by floppy disk or CD should you wish).

For more details on SOAP, see the W3C site at http://www.w3.org/TR/soap

The Microsoft SOAP Toolkit

The SOAP toolkit brings web services to the VB6 world, and it is freely downloadable from the Microsoft web site. (Go to http://msdn.microsoft.com/library/default.asp?url=/nhp/Default.asp?contentid=28000523 – at the time of writing, the latest version is 3.0.)

After you have downloaded the setup file `SoapToolkit30.EXE`, run it and follow the on-screen installation instructions. You can also download the samples file `SoapToolkit30Samples.EXE`, which has some interesting samples that demonstrate various features of the SOAP toolkit.

The Microsoft SOAP toolkit 3.0 includes the following components:

1. **Client-side Component** – allows client applications to connect to and consume web services described by a WSDL file.

2. **Server-side Component** – allows you to build and expose COM object methods as web service methods. The COM methods are described by the WSDL and **Web Services Meta Language (WSML)** files. (WSML is required when implementing web services with Microsoft's SOAP Toolkit.)

3. **Marshalling Components** – the components required for communication with SOAP. They are responsible for constructing, transmitting, reading, and processing SOAP messages. Collectively, these processes are called **marshalling** when connecting, and **unmarshalling** when disconnecting.

The toolkit also includes a **WSDL/WSML Generator Tool** that can generate WSDL and WSML files automatically, by examining the code that is to be exposed.

Component Objects

The client-side component consists of a high-level API object, the `SoapClient30` object, which internally uses a set of low-level API objects such as `WSDLReader30`, `WSDLOperation30`, `SoapSerializer30`, `SoapReader30`, and `SoapConnector30`. The server-side component consists of a high-level API object `SoapServer30` that uses the same low-level API as `SoapClient30`.

❑ `SoapClient30` – processes client requests to consume a web service, transmitting the request to the web service server. When the server responds, `SoapClient30` interprets the SOAP message and passes the result back to the application. This object is part of the high-level API.

❑ `SoapServer30` – process client requests for a web service. Requests are decoded and passed to the underlying COM object. The result from the COM object is processed, packaged in a SOAP message, and sent back to the requesting client. This object is part of the high-level API.

❑ `WSDLReader30` – Responsible for reading and analyzing the WSDL and WSML files. This object is part of the low-level API.

❑ `WSDLOperation30` – responsible for programmatically providing specific methods and properties as defined by the WSDL and also generating or processing the SOAP request. This object is part of the low-level API.

❑ `SoapSerializer30` – Builds the SOAP message. This object is part of the low-level API.

❑ `SoapReader30` – Reads incoming SOAP messages. This object is part of the low-level API.

❑ `SoapConnector30` – Establishes communication and transport links between the client and server.

COM and the SOAP Toolkit

The web service paradigm uses a stateless programming model, meaning that each request has no knowledge of prior requests. For the SOAP toolkit, this means that each request creates a new COM object to evaluate the requested method, and the COM object is then destroyed. If the method changes a variable in the COM object, the value is lost after the call completes and is not available for the next request.

For this reason, it is important to use COM objects that are fast to instantiate and are happy to work in a stateless mode.

SOAP Toolkit Basics

Now let's have a go at building a web service to get an idea of what is actually involved. The samples will cover a range of topics and issues that you will likely encounter in your work.

For the samples, we'll use Microsoft's **Internet Information Server** (**IIS**) as the web server, along with VB6 and the SOAP toolkit of course.

For Windows 2000 or XP (Professional level), IIS is installed as a Windows Component using the Add/Remove Programs tool in Control Panel.

The SOAP server requires a web server API (ISAPI) such as ASP hosted by IIS on Microsoft Windows XP, Windows 2000, or Windows NT 4.0 Service Pack 6. IIS hosts ASP natively, but other web servers such as Apache generally require additional modules to host ASP pages.

The SOAP client is supported on Microsoft Windows XP, Windows 2000 Service Pack 1, Windows NT 4.0 Service Pack 6, Windows 98, or Windows ME.

Setting Up IIS

To install IIS on Windows 2000/XP, open the Add/Remove Program tool in Control Panel, and click the Add/Remove Windows Component button. This will open the Windows Components Wizard window, shown in the following screenshot. Make sure Internet Information Services (IIS) is selected:

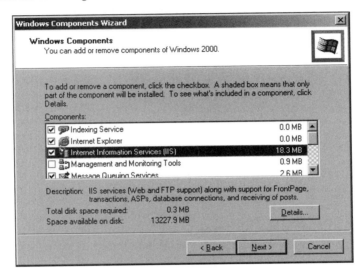

Click on the Details button to see the various options for IIS:

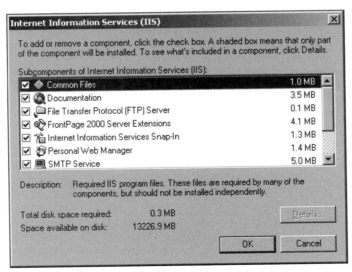

Make sure that Common Files, Documentation (the Help files), Internet Information Services Snap-In (the snap-in for managing IIS), and World Wide Web Server are selected. Click OK and then Next to begin the installation. When it is done, click on Finish.

Before we can create the web service, we need to set up an IIS **virtual directory** to host it.

> A virtual directory is a web directory on a web server that points to an actual
> directory on the disk. For example if the local server has a web directory
> `http://localhost/MSSoapSample30` then `MSSoapSample30` is a virtual
> directory. In actual fact MSSoapSample30 may refer to the actual directory such as
> `C:\Program Files\MSSOAP\Samples30`.

To set up a virtual directory on IIS, we can use the IIS admin snap-in tool, or the `soapvdir.cmd` utility provided with the Toolkit.

To use `soapvdir.cmd` on the command prompt, navigate to the `Binaries` subdirectory off the folder containing the toolkit installation, and enter the following command:

```
SOAPVDIR.CMD [Command VdirName [DirectoryPath]] [-s:server][-w:root]
```

There are three possible values for `Command`:

❑ CREATE – Creates a new Virtual Directory with the name `VdirName` and with the physical directory path specified by `DirectoryPath`. Maps the `.wsdl` file to the `SOAPIS30.dll` (the ISAPI handler of the SOAP toolkit).

❑ UPDATE – Updates the mapping of a `.wsdl` extension for an existing virtual directory.

❑ HELP – Provides detailed help about `SOAPVDIR.CMD`.

`VdirName` indicates the name of the virtual directory that will be used in URLs of web pages, `DirectoryPath` specifies the physical path for the virtual directory. This is required when you create a new virtual directory.

The optional `-s` switch specifies a web server instance if you have more than one running on the same machine. The default is 1. The `-w` switch specifies the root of the virtual directory. The default is `root`.

So, to set up a virtual directory called `VB6ProWebServiceSample`, you could enter the following:

> **> SOAPVDIR.CMD CREATE VB6ProWebServiceSample**
> **C:\Development\VB6ProWebServiceSample**

The output should be something like this:

```
Registered virtual DIR:
IIS://localhost/w3svc/1/Root/VB6ProWebServiceSample
with addition scriptmap entry:
.wsdl,C:\Program Files\Common Files\MSSoap\Binaries\SOAPIS30.dll,1,GET,POST
```

If the physical path doesn't actually exist, the virtual directory will still be created, but will be marked as invalid in IIS.

You can alternatively use the IIS admin snap-in. Under **Administrative Tools**, start the Internet Information Services management console (MMC). Navigate to the **Default Web Site**, right-click it, and choose **New | Virtual Directory**:

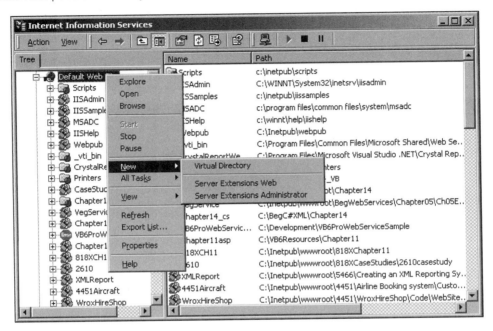

On the **Welcome** screen, click **Next**. On the **Virtual Directory Alias** window, type `VB6ProWebServiceSample` (this is the name of the virtual directory that will be created) and click **Next**. On the **Web Site Content Directory** window, enter the name of the actual directory that the virtual directory will point to, **C:\Localhost\Development\VB6ProWebServiceSample** in our case. (You can also click **Browse** to navigate to a directory). On the **Access Permission** window, leave the default selections in the checkboxes and click **Next**.

The wizard will create the virtual directory, but you will need to change certain properties before it can be used with the SOAP toolkit. (These properties are automatically set up if `soapdir.cmd` is used). Right-click the new virtual directory, and select **Properties**. On the **Virtual Directory** tab, click **Configuration**, opening the **Application Configuration** window shown next.

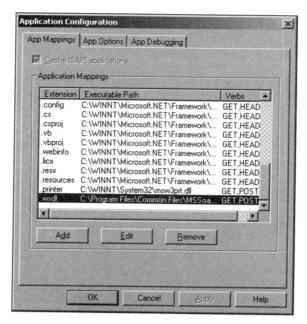

Click **Add**, and create the following application mapping:

Extension of `.wsdl`

Execution Path of C:\Program Files\Common Files\MSSoap\Binaries\SOAPIS30.dll

Verbs are `GET`, `POST`

Now we are ready to start building our web service. The samples for this chapter will all be hosted in subdirectories off the `VB6ProWebServiceSample` virtual directory.

A Simple Web Service

We'll start by creating a very simple web service that will expose three methods for testing the SOAP connection. The first is a `Ping` method that returns a message as a string from the server. The second is a `ServerDate` method that returns the server's system date demonstrates how to use data types other than strings. The last is an `Echo` method. It echoes a message from the server, but it also echoes the value passed through a reference parameter, plus the server date in another parameter. This method demonstrates how SOAP can return multiple values.

Create a VB IIS Application Project and create an ActiveX DLL class in that project called `SimpleServer`. The code for this class is shown below:

```
Option Explicit

Public Function Ping() As String
   Dim ServerDate As Date
   Dim StrRtn As String
```

```
    'Get the current system date
    ServerDate = Now()

    StrRtn = "Simple Server says: Today is "

    StrRtn = StrRtn + CStr(ServerDate)

    Ping = StrRtn
End Function

Public Function ServerDate() As Date

    'Get the current system date
    ServerDate = Now()

End Function

Public Function EchoAll(ByVal InputVal As String, _
                        ByRef Echo As String, _
                        ByRef ServerTime As Date) As String

    'Get the current system date
    Echo = InputVal
    ServerTime = Now()

    EchoAll = "Echoed back"
End Function
```

This is a fairly straightforward class that simply returns the date on the server. We now need to compile this project into a DLL (ServerSample01.dll).

> Because the DLL will run on IIS, we need to compile it with the **Retained in Memory** and **Unattended execution** options selected on the **General** tab of the Project Properties dialog box.

Once compiled, you can now move to the more interesting step of generating the WSDL files.

Generating WSDL Files

To generate our WSDL, we need to run the **WSDL Generator** included with the SOAP toolkit by following these steps:

1. Start the wsdlgen.exe WSDL Generator in C:\Program Files\MSSOAP\Binaries.

2. On the Welcome Screen, click Next, and on the Specify Configuration (Optional) screen, click Next again.

3. On the Select the COM .dll file to analyze screen, enter the name of our web service (SimpleServer in our case) and in Local Path, enter the physical path to the DLL created earlier:

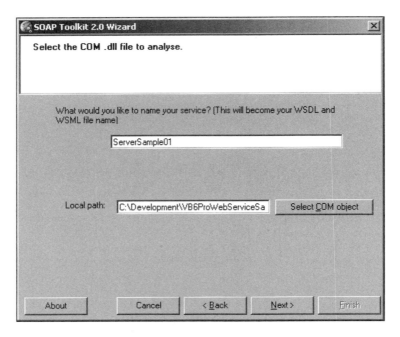

4. Click Next to go to the Select the services you would like to expose screen. Here, select which methods to expose in the web service. For SimpleServer, we want to expose all three available methods:

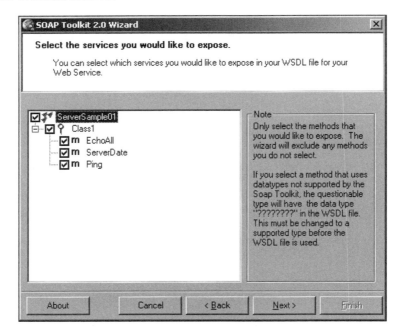

5. Click Next when you are done. On the SOAP listener information screen, enter the URL for the WSDL file. This must be a valid URL on the server (such as http://localhost/VB6ProWebServiceSample/Sample01/ServerSample01/). Make sure ISAPI is selected as the listener type, and click Next.

6. On the Specify URIs screen, click Next.

This screen is where you specify the namespace of your web service. For the purposes of the example, we'll leave this at the default.

7. On the Specify location for new WSDL and WSML files screen, select the location where you want to save the file and click Next.

8. The files are now generated. Click Finish to close the WSDL generator.

Once generated, make sure that the files are located in virtual directory we created earlier, or in a subfolder off it. You can test that the WSDL is available by typing its URL into your browser:

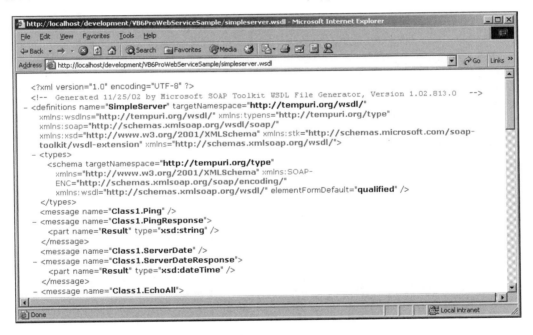

A Simple Consumer

Now we can move on to consuming our little web service. The simplest way is to use the SOAP toolkit high-level API in a simple Windows form. Create a Windows form with 3 buttons (one for each of the exposed methods of our web service) and two text controls (one for inputting the web service parameter, and the other to show the web service's output):

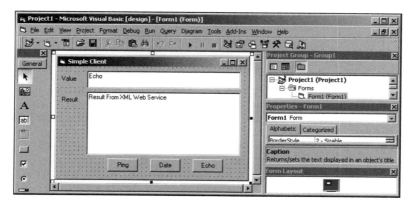

In the `Declaration` section of the form, define a variable to hold the high-level API object. It is through this object that we will interact with the web service:

```
Option Explicit

'Location of the WSDL file
Private Const CONST_WSDL_URL As String = _
    "http://localhost/Development/VB6ProWebServiceSample/" + _
    "SimpleServer.WSDL"

'Declare object to allow interaction with web service
Dim SoapClient3 As Object
```

Notice that we also define a constant `CONST_WSDL_URL` to hold the location of the WSDL file. This can be a URL or a file path if the file is available locally.

Now, let's look at the initialization of `SoapClient3` in the `Form_Load` method:

```
Private Sub Form_Load()

    'Initialize the Object
    Set SoapClient3 = CreateObject("MSSOAP.SoapClient30")

    On Error Resume Next
    'Create the SOAP object
    Call SoapClient3.mssoapinit( _
      CONST_WSDL_URL, _
      "SimpleServer", _
      " Class1SoapPort")

    'Error Handling
If Err <> 0 Then
    ResultText.Text = _
      "Unable to create SOAP object, error: " + _
      Err.Description
End If

End Sub
```

SoapClient3 is created as an `MSSOAP.SoapClient30` object, and initialized to our `SimpleServer` using the `mssoapinit` method. We display any error that may appear.

The `Class1SoapPort` value must be the same as that defined under the service section of the WSDL file:

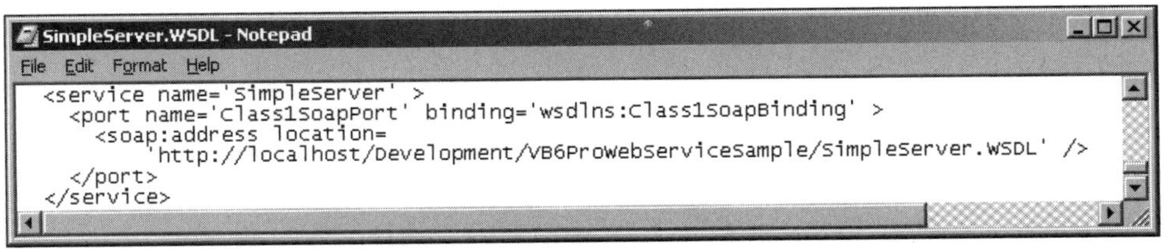

It can be any text value, but it must be defined in the WSDL file. The SOAP toolkit uses this port to listen to client connections.

SoapClient3 provides our means of consuming the web service's methods. We'll start with the `Ping` and `ServerDate` methods. The code for the **Ping** button is shown below:

```
Private Sub PingCommand_Click()
  On Error Resume Next

  'Call the ping method of the service
  ResultText.Text = SoapClient3.Ping()
  'Error Handling
  If Err <> 0 Then
   ResultText.Text = ResultText.Text + " faultcode=" + _
     SoapClient3.faultcode
   ResultText.Text = ResultText.Text + " faultstring=" + _
     SoapClient3.faultstring
   ResultText.Text = ResultText.Text + " faultactor=" + _
     SoapClient3.faultactor
   ResultText.Text = ResultText.Text + " detail=" + _
     SoapClient3.detail
  End If


End Sub
```

The code for the **Date** button follows next:

```
Private Sub DateCommand_Click()

  'Call the ServerDate method of the service
  ResultText.Text = "Service date is " + CStr(SoapClient3.ServerDate())
  If Err <> 0 Then
    ResultText.Text = "Error in Ping : " + Err.Description
    ResultText.Text = ResultText.Text + " faultcode=" + _
      SoapClient3.faultcode
    ResultText.Text = ResultText.Text + " faultstring=" + _
      SoapClient3.faultstring
```

```
            ResultText.Text = ResultText.Text + " faultactor=" + _
                SoapClient3.faultactor
            ResultText.Text = ResultText.Text + " detail=" + _
                SoapClient3.detail
        End If

    End Sub
```

The result of the `Ping` and `ServerDate` methods will be displayed in the text control. We also make sure that we catch any error that the `SoapClient30` object throws. In a production environment, we may wish to take further action in the event of error, beyond merely displaying a message.

Now, let's look at the slightly more complicated `EchoAll` method:

```
Private Sub EchoCommand_Click()

    'Declare Variable to pass and retrieve data from web service
    Dim strEchoBack As String
    Dim rtn As String
    Dim SrvDate As Date

    'Call the EchoAll method of the service
    rtn = SoapClient3.EchoAll(EchoText.Text, strEchoBack, SrvDate)
    ResultText.Text = "Echoed back " + strEchoBack + _
        " - date " + CStr(SrvDate)

    'Error Handling
    If Err <> 0 Then
        ResultText.Text = "Error in EchoAll: " + _
            Err.Description
        ResultText.Text = ResultText.Text + " faultcode=" + _
            SoapClient3.faultcode
        ResultText.Text = ResultText.Text + " faultstring=" + _
            SoapClient3.faultstring
        ResultText.Text = ResultText.Text + " faultactor=" + _
            SoapClient3.faultactor
        ResultText.Text = ResultText.Text + " detail=" + _
            SoapClient3.detail
    End If
End Sub
```

The beauty of the SOAP toolkit and the high-level API is that you do not have to worry about the underlying plumbing. Once you have initialized the object, you can call web methods just as if they were regular local methods.

Consuming a .NET Web Service with SoapClient30

We'll have a little taste of the interoperability of web services now as we investigate how we would consume SimpleServer if it were implemented in .NET (or any other technology for that matter). All we need to change are the connection and initialization of the SoapClient30 object in the client. The specific connection string will be dependent on the platform.

```
Private Const CONST_WSDL_URL As String = _
    "http://localhost/DotNETWebService/SimpleServerDOTNet.asmx?WSDL"
```

where http://localhost/DotNETWebService/SimpleServerDOTNet.asmx is the location of the .NET version of SimpleServer. Note that the .NET version is found in the code for this chapter on the CD-ROM. We also need to change the mssoapinit call to match the service name and port name of the new web service:

```
Call SoapClient3.mssoapinit(CONST_WSDL_URL, "SimpleServerDOTNet", _
    "SimpleServerDOTNetSoap")
```

To find the name of the service and of the port you need to examine the WSDL file of the service. With .NET you can do this online if you know the location of the service's .asmx page by opening SimpleServerDOTNet.asmx?WSDL in a browser.

The rest of the code is unchanged. As far as the client is concerned, all it needs to understand is SOAP; the language it was written in or what platform it runs on are not important.

This platform independence is valid as long as the data being transported can be rendered using the built-in SOAP types. If you are using complex data types, for instance if you're passing COM objects or data types not natively supported on the platform you are using, you will need to create your own data-mapper.

Handling Errors

Since SOAP lives in a distributed environment, error handling can be daunting. The SOAP specification caters for application errors through the <Fault> element, which can contain a child <detail> element to describe the error. When an error occurs at the web service server, an <errorInfo> element inside the <detail> element holds detailed error information.

Errors with SoapClient30

When an error is generated, the server will return a SOAP message containing a `<Fault>` element. The `SoapClient30` object automatically generates an `ErrorInfo` object that can be used by the standard `Err` object in your application. A `SoapClient30` object also contains certain properties. Two useful ones are:

❑ `Faultstring` – Provides the value of the `<faultstring>` element of the SOAP `<Fault>` element.

❑ `Faultdetail` – Provides the value of the `<detail>` element in the `<Fault>` element. This gives a more detailed error message for the error.

Handling User-Defined Data Types

The SOAP toolkit can automatically handle any of the standard types that have direct mapping to data types in the **Schema Definition language (XSD)**. However, XSD, as discussed in Chapter 13, can also handle any non-standard data types and user-defined data types. If the data type is an array of standard types, then SOAP can also handle it automatically, but for more complex user defined types, we need to use a type mapper or the `IXMLDOMNodeList` parameter. The `IXMLDOMNodeList` parameter loads the data into a DOM object (for more details, refer back to Chapter 13) that your application can parse for the relevant data.

The SOAP toolkit includes its own generic type mapper that can be used in most instances. The generic type mapper can, however, be replaced with a custom type mapper if you have more specific data type mapping requirement.

The SOAP toolkit contains several good examples of how to create and use your own data type mapper, but what it does not show is how to consume a data type that is not natively supported in VB6. Microsoft is actively pushing .NET, where the primary data access technology is ADO.NET. Unlike ADO and its `Recordsets`, ADO.NET has the `DataSet` class.

`DataSets` do not, however, map directly to `Recordsets` and as .NET can directly serialize `DataSet`, the chances of you encountering a web service method that returns a `DataSet` is very high. Let's learn a little about `DataSets` and look at how you will be able to get at the data you need even if a web service only provides methods that deal with the `DataSet`.

A Little Help From DataSet

You can think of `DataSet` as an in-memory representation of part of a database. It can include multiple tables (`DataTables`), relations, and constraints. `DataTables` include within them rows (`DataRows`). In .NET, the `DataSet` can be serialized and can be automatically transferred to XML. Below is a typical example:

```
<?xml version="1.0" encoding="utf-8" ?>
<DataSet xmlns="http://tempuri.org/">
  <xs:schema id="EmployeeDS" xmlns=""
    xmlns:xs="http://www.w3.org/2001/XMLSchema" xmlns:msdata="urn:schemas-
```

```
          microsoft-com:xml-msdata">
            <xs:element name="EmployeeDS" msdata:IsDataSet="true">
              <xs:complexType>
                <xs:choice maxOccurs="unbounded">
                  <xs:element name="Employee">
                    <xs:complexType>
                      <xs:sequence>
                        <xs:element name="ID" type="xs:int" minOccurs="0" />
                        <xs:element name="CountryID" type="xs:int"
                                    minOccurs="0" />
                        <xs:element name="Names" type="xs:string" minOccurs="0" />
                        <xs:element name="Surname" type="xs:string"
                                    minOccurs="0" />
                        <xs:element name="JobTitle" type="xs:string"
                                    minOccurs="0" />
                      </xs:sequence>
                    </xs:complexType>
                  </xs:element>
                  <xs:element name="Country">
                    <xs:complexType>
                      <xs:sequence>
                        <xs:element name="ID" type="xs:int" minOccurs="0" />
                        <xs:element name="Name" type="xs:string" minOccurs="0" />
                      </xs:sequence>
                    </xs:complexType>
                  </xs:element>
                </xs:choice>
              </xs:complexType>
            <xs:unique name="Constraint1">
                <xs:selector xpath=".//Country" />
              <xs:field xpath="ID" />
            </xs:unique>
            <xs:keyref name="FK_Country" refer="Constraint1">
              <xs:selector xpath=".//Employee" />
              <xs:field xpath="CountryID" />
            </xs:keyref>
          </xs:element>
        </xs:schema>


        <diffgr:diffgram xmlns:msdata="urn:schemas-microsoft-com:xml-msdata"
                 xmlns:diffgr="urn:schemas-microsoft-com:xml-diffgram-v1">
          <EmployeeDS xmlns="">
            <Employee diffgr:id="Employee1" msdata:rowOrder="0">
              <ID>1</ID>
              <CountryID>1</CountryID>
              <Names>Ryan Neil</Names>
              <Surname>Payet</Surname>
              <JobTitle>Developer</JobTitle>
            </Employee>
            <Employee diffgr:id="Employee2" msdata:rowOrder="1">
              <ID>2</ID>
              <CountryID>1</CountryID>
              <Names>Jon</Names>
```

```
            <Surname>Dow</Surname>
            <JobTitle>Not Much</JobTitle>
        </Employee>
        <Country diffgr:id="Country1" msdata:rowOrder="0">
            <ID>1</ID>
            <Name>Seychelles</Name>
        </Country>
        <Country diffgr:id="Country2" msdata:rowOrder="1">
            <ID>2</ID>
            <Name>England</Name>
        </Country>
    </EmployeeDS>
  </diffgr:diffgram>
</DataSet>
```

The first section is the schema definition and the second is the actual data. The question here is: how can we get this data into VB6?

A .NET Web Service

To follow this sample, you will need the .NET Framework to run the .NET web service. The Framework will be installed as part of the .NET SDK (freely downloadable from MSDN). You'll need the SDK to compile and host the web service, unless you happen to already have a suitable version of Visual Studio .NET installed.

Here, I will show you the code for the web method that we will use throughout this sample. Do not worry too much about the syntax – it's close enough to VB, and very intuitive:

```
<WebMethod()> Public Function Get_Employee() As DataSet

    Dim EmployeeDS As New DataSet()
    Dim EmployeeDT As New DataTable()
    Dim CountryDT As New DataTable()

    Dim RowRef As DataRow
    Dim DataRel As DataRelation

    EmployeeDS.Tables.Add(EmployeeDT)
    EmployeeDS.Tables.Add(CountryDT)

    EmployeeDS.DataSetName = "EmployeeDS"

    EmployeeDT.TableName = "Employee"
    CountryDT.TableName = "Country"

    'Define Employee
    EmployeeDT.Columns.Add("ID", Type.GetType("System.Int32"))
    EmployeeDT.Columns.Add("CountryID", Type.GetType("System.Int32"))
    EmployeeDT.Columns.Add("Names", Type.GetType("System.String"))
    EmployeeDT.Columns.Add("Surname", Type.GetType("System.String"))
    EmployeeDT.Columns.Add("JobTitle", Type.GetType("System.String"))
```

```
'Define country
CountryDT.Columns.Add("ID", Type.GetType("System.Int32"))
CountryDT.Columns.Add("Name", Type.GetType("System.String"))

DataRel = New DataRelation("FK_Country", _
                              CountryDT.Columns("ID"), _
EmployeeDT.Columns("CountryID"))
EmployeeDS.Relations.Add(DataRel)

'Create Seychelles
RowRef = CountryDT.NewRow()
RowRef.Item("ID") = 1
RowRef.Item("Name") = "Seychelles"
CountryDT.Rows.Add(RowRef)

'Create England
RowRef = CountryDT.NewRow()
RowRef.Item("ID") = 2
RowRef.Item("Name") = "England"
CountryDT.Rows.Add(RowRef)

'Create Ryan
RowRef = EmployeeDT.NewRow()
RowRef.Item("ID") = 1
RowRef.Item("CountryID") = 1
RowRef.Item("Names") = "Ryan Neil"
RowRef.Item("Surname") = "Payet"
RowRef.Item("JobTitle") = "Developer"
EmployeeDT.Rows.Add(RowRef)

'Create Jon
RowRef = EmployeeDT.NewRow()
RowRef.Item("ID") = 2
RowRef.Item("CountryID") = 1
RowRef.Item("Names") = "Jon"
RowRef.Item("Surname") = "Dow"
RowRef.Item("JobTitle") = "Not Much"
EmployeeDT.Rows.Add(RowRef)

EmployeeDS.AcceptChanges()
Get_Employee = EmployeeDS
End Function
```

This method simply creates a `DataSet` with two tables: `Country` and `Employee`. It also defines a relation between the tables:

```
DataRel = New DataRelation("FK_Country", _
                              CountryDT.Columns("ID"), _
EmployeeDT.Columns("CountryID"))
EmployeeDS.Relations.Add(DataRel)
```

This is serialized into XML by the web service as:

```
<xs:unique name="Constraint1">
  <xs:selector xpath=".//Country" />
  <xs:field xpath="ID" />
</xs:unique>
<xs:keyref name="FK_Country" refer="Constraint1">
  <xs:selector xpath=".//Employee" />
  <xs:field xpath="CountryID" />
</xs:keyref>
```

Normally you would populate a `DataSet` with data from an external data source such as a database or an XML file. To keep this example simple, however, I have hard-coded the data, which will be represented in XML as the following:

```
<Employee diffgr:id="Employee1" msdata:rowOrder="0">
  <ID>1</ID>
  <CountryID>1</CountryID>
  <Names>Ryan Neil</Names>
  <Surname>Payet</Surname>
  <JobTitle>Developer</JobTitle>
</Employee>
<Employee diffgr:id="Employee2" msdata:rowOrder="1">
  <ID>2</ID>
  <CountryID>2</CountryID>
  <Names>Jon</Names>
  <Surname>Dow</Surname>
  <JobTitle>Not Much</JobTitle>
</Employee>
<Country diffgr:id="Country1" msdata:rowOrder="0">
  <ID>1</ID>
  <Name>Seychelles</Name>
</Country>
<Country diffgr:id="Country2" msdata:rowOrder="1">
  <ID>2</ID>
  <Name>England</Name>
</Country>
```

The challenge now is getting this XML data into an `ADODB.Recordset`.

XML DataSet to ADODB.Recordset

Since the `DataSet` is now in XML, you could use XSLT to convert the XML `DataSet` to a format that VB6 can easily use. However, this would require a reasonably solid understanding of XML and XSLT. A simpler solution, especially if you only need to read the data in the `DataSet`, would be to implement a function that parses the `DataSet` XML.

We will use the MSXML parser for our XML parsing and manipulation.

The first thing our conversion routine needs to do is convert XML XSD data types to `ADODB.Recordset` data types. Create a module containing the following function:

```
Private Function GetDataType (ByVal vsType As String) As ADODB.DataTypeEnum
    'Maps the XSD datatype to a ADO datatype
    Select Case vsType
        Case "xs:string"
            GetDataType = adVarChar
        Case "xs:int"
            GetDataType = adInteger
        Case "xs:dateTime"
            GetDataType = adDate
        Case "xs:decimal"
            GetDataType = adDouble
        Case "xs:short"
            GetDataType = adBoolean
        Case "0"
            GetDataType = adVarChar

    'Anything we do not know we keep as string
        Case Else
            GetDataType = adVarChar
    End Select
End Function
```

This function converts the common XSD data types. You can extend the function to include more types as and when required.

We now have all the parts in place for us to start writing our conversion routine. Since `ADODB.Recordset` can only hold one table at a time, we need to extract one table from the XML `DataSet` at a time.

Declare the function signature as follows:

```
Option Explicit

Public Function XMLDataSettoRecordset( _
    ByVal XMLDOM_DOC As DOMDocument40, _
    ByVal vsTableName As String) As ADODB.Recordset

End Function
```

The `XMLDataSettoRecordset` function requires a `DOMDocument40` object and a `String` variable as parameters, and it will return an `ADODB.Recordset`. The `DOMDocument40` contains the XML `DataSet` and the `String` variable specifies the table name that we wish to extract.

Now, extend `XMLDataSettoRecordset` to include the variables that we will need. We also create the `RecordSet` that we will return from the function:

```
Public Function XMLDataSettoRecordset( _
    ByVal XMLDOM_DOC As DOMDocument40, _
    ByVal vsTableName As String) As ADODB.Recordset
```

```
'Object to help parse XML Doc
Dim XML_TableNode As IXMLDOMNode
Dim XML_RecordNode As IXMLDOMNode
Dim XML_FieldsNode As IXMLDOMNode
Dim XML_DataList As IXMLDOMNodeList

'Recordset object to build
Dim RSFromDS As ADODB.Recordset

'Control Variable
Dim strXPath As String
Dim dataLength As Long

'Create record set object
Set RSFromDS = New ADODB.Recordset
```

The `IXMLDOMNode` variables will access nodes in the `DOMDocument40` object.

> **Nodes in a DOM can include several child nodes. A DOM can be thought of as a tree of nodes and child nodes.**

The `XML_DataList` is an `IXMLDOMNodeList` because we will use it to access data and data from a table. Data in a table is represented by a set of nodes at the same level in the DOM tree:

```
<Employee diffgr:id="Employee1" msdata:rowOrder="0">
  <ID>1</ID>
  <CountryID>1</CountryID>
  <Names>Ryan Neil</Names>
  <Surname>Payet</Surname>
  <JobTitle>Developer</JobTitle>
</Employee>
```

`<ID>`, `<CountryID>`, `<Names>`, `<Surname>`, `<JobTitle>` will all form nodes at the same level in a DOM tree.

Before we can load the data into the `RecordSet`, we first need to build the table structure, using the XML to get the schema of the table we want:

```
'Set the Xpath parse string
strXPath = "//xs:element[@name=""" & _
  vsTableName & _
  """]/xs:complexType/xs:sequence"

'Get XML Table Node
Set XML_TableNode = XMLDOM_DOC.selectSingleNode(strXPath)
```

For the `Employee` table, `strXPath` would be:

```
//xs:element[@name="Employee"]/xs:complexType/xs:sequence.
```

This XPath would locate the element highlighted overleaf:

```
<xs:element name="Employee">
  <xs:complexType>
    <xs:sequence>
      <xs:element name="ID" type="xs:int" minOccurs="0" />
      <xs:element name="CountryID" type="xs:int" minOccurs="0" />
      <xs:element name="Names" type="xs:string" minOccurs="0" />
      <xs:element name="Surname" type="xs:string" minOccurs="0" />
      <xs:element name="JobTitle" type="xs:string" minOccurs="0" />
    </xs:sequence>
  </xs:complexType>
</xs:element>
```

This element holds the XSD definition of the Employee table. We can now run through each child `<xs:element>` element and build the table structure:

```
'Get all fields in Node
For Each XML_FieldsNode In XML_TableNode.childNodes

  'Process only those with attributes
  If Not XML_FieldsNode.Attributes Is Nothing Then
    'Initialize Maximum Length
    dataLength = 0

    'We only need to specify a length for string or char data
    'Note Second attribute (1) specifies Data type
    If XML_FieldsNode.Attributes(1).Text = "xs:string" Then
      'Find all records of current field

      'Use first attribute (0), which should be Name of field
      strXPath = "//" & vsTableName & "/" & _
      XML_FieldsNode.Attributes(0).Text

      'Get data from DOM object
      Set XML_DataList = XMLDOM_DOC.selectNodes(strXPath)

      'Go through all records to find maximum length
      For Each XML_RecordNode In XML_DataList
        If Len(XML_RecordNode.Text) > dataLength Then
          dataLength = Len(XML_RecordNode.Text)
        End If
      Next
    End If

    On Error Resume Next

    'Add field, including data type and field name
    Call RSFromDS.Fields.Append( _
         XML_FieldsNode.Attributes(0).Text, _
         GetDataType(XML_FieldsNode.Attributes(1).Text), _
         dataLength)

  End If
Next
```

First, we use a For Each loop to step though each of the child nodes:

```
For Each XML_FieldsNode In XML_TableNode.childNodes
```

The loop will process only <xs:element> nodes that have attributes. In particular, we are interested in the name and type attributes, attribute(0) and attribute(1) respectively. However, before we can create the field in the record set, we need to know the maximum length of the xs:string columns.

We could either set a value that would hold any string if we know the maximum allowed or we can loop through the data and check each one's length. I will defer the explanation for this section of code until we reach the section on populating the RecordSet with actual data as they follow similar logic:

```
'We only need to specify a length for string or char data
'Note Second attribute (1) specify Data type
If XML_FieldsNode.Attributes(1).Text = "xs:string" Then
  'Find all records of current field

  'Use first attribute (0), which should be Name of field
  strXPath = "//" & vsTableName & "/" & _
            XML_FieldsNode.Attributes(0).Text

  'Get data from DOM object
  Set XML_DataList = XMLDOM_DOC.selectNodes(strXPath)

  'Go through all records to find maximum length
  For Each XML_RecordNode In XML_DataList
    If Len(XML_RecordNode.Text) > dataLength Then
      dataLength = Len(XML_RecordNode.Text)
    End If
  Next
End If
```

If the field is a string, we need to get the maximum data length (for all other types, we use a length of zero). We can then create the field in the RecordSet.

```
On Error Resume Next

'Add field, including data type and field name
Call RSFromDS.Fields.Append( _
    XML_FieldsNode.Attributes(0).Text, _
    GetDataType(XML_FieldsNode.Attributes(1).Text), _
    dataLength)

End If
```

XML_FieldsNode.Attributes(0).Text will hold the field type.

GetDataType(XML_FieldsNode.Attributes(1).Text) will get the XSD type and convert it to ADODB.DataTypeEnum.

Once we are done looping through the XSD, we can move to the next section where we actually populate the RecordSet:

```
'-----------------------------------------------
'            Now populate the RecordSet
'-----------------------------------------------

'Add the data to the empty Recordset
strXPath = "//" & vsTableName
Set XML_DataList = XMLDOM_DOC.selectNodes(strXPath)

Call RSFromDS.Open

'Cycle through all records
For Each XML_RecordNode In XML_DataList

  'Add Record
  Call RSFromDS.AddNew

  'Go through all fields of current record
  For Each XML_FieldsNode In XML_RecordNode.childNodes
    If Len(XML_FieldsNode.baseName) > 0 Then
      'Set value
      'MsgBox XML_FieldsNode.baseName & ":" & XML_FieldsNode.Text
      RSFromDS.Fields(XML_FieldsNode.baseName) = XML_FieldsNode.Text
    End If
  Next
Next
```

strXPath gets hold of the elements that contain the data. For example, for the Employee table, we get the following two <Employee> elements, with child nodes <ID>, <CountryID>, <Names>, <Surname>, and <JobTitleL>:

```
<Employee diffgr:id="Employee1" msdata:rowOrder="0">
  <ID>1</ID>
  <CountryID>1</CountryID>
  <Names>Ryan Neil</Names>
  <Surname>Payet</Surname>
  <JobTitle>Developer</JobTitle>
</Employee>
<Employee diffgr:id="Employee2" msdata:rowOrder="1">
  <ID>2</ID>
  <CountryID>1</CountryID>
  <Names>Jon</Names>
  <Surname>Dow</Surname>
  <JobTitle>Not Much</JobTitle>
</Employee>
```

We then loop through each element, which in this case represents a row:

```
For Each XML_RecordNode In XML_DataList
```

For each of these, we need to loop through each of the child nodes so that we parse data for each column:

```
'Go through all fields of current record
For Each XML_FieldsNode In XML_RecordNode.childNodes
  If Len(XML_FieldsNode.baseName) > 0 Then
    'Set value
    RSFromDS.Fields(XML_FieldsNode.baseName) = XML_FieldsNode.Text
  End If
Next
```

We only process columns that have a name, which we determine by checking whether the length of XML_FieldsNode.baseName is greater than zero.

Now, we are done parsing and all that remains is to return the RecordSet:

```
'Set the position to first row
If Not (RSFromDS.BOF And RSFromDS.EOF) Then Call RSFromDS.MoveFirst

'Return the Recordset
Set XMLDataSettoRecordset = RSFromDS

End Function
```

Testing the Conversion

We have coded the main logic for the conversion, so now comes the time to test it. Before you can do so you need to have access to the .NET web service we described earlier or you can simulate the service with an XML file like the one I described earlier.

Create a form that contains a text control (XMLDataSet), two DataGrids (DBGridEmployee and DBGridCountry), and a button (DSCommand), laid out as shown in the following screenshot:

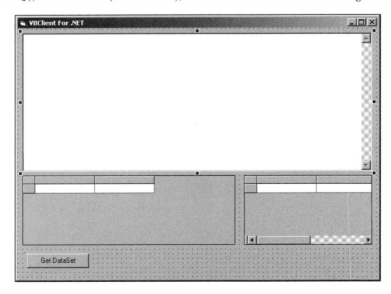

In the declarations section of the Form, enter the following:

```
Option Explicit

'Soap client to consume service
Dim objSOAPClient As New SoapClient30

'Variable to store returned XML DataSet
Dim objXMLResultNodes As IXMLDOMNodeList

'Dom document for parsing XML
Dim DS_DOM As New DOMDocument40

Dim RSSetEmployee As ADODB.Recordset
Dim RSSetCountry As ADODB.Recordset

'Location of WSDL.
'Change to match your environment
Const DOTNETWEBSRV As String = _
   "http://localhost/DotNETWebService/SimpleServerDOTNet.asmx?wsdl"
```

We will use the SoapClient30 object, objSOAPClient, to query the .NET web service. The value returned is a complex type, and we will return it in an IXMLDOMNodeList object. We will also use a DOMDocument40 to parse the XML data. We use a constant to point to the WSDL of our web service. You will need to change yours to match your particular environment.

Now add the following line to Form_Load:

```
Private Sub Form_Load()

    'Initialize the SOAP object and Client
    objSOAPClient.MSSoapInit DOTNETWEBSRV

End Sub
```

This code simply initializes the SoapClient30 object, objSOAPClient. Next, add the following as the Click event handler for the button:

```
Private Sub DSCommand_Click()

    Dim str As String

    'Because of complex and unknown data we get the
    '.NET DataSet as an objXMLResultNodes
    Set objXMLResultNodes = objSOAPClient.Get_Employee()

    'Because the objXMLResultNodes separates the DataSet XML into two nodes we
    'need to recombine then so that we can create a DOM object
    str = "<DataSet>" & _
          objXMLResultNodes.Item(0).xml & _
          objXMLResultNodes.Item(1).xml & _
                       "</DataSet>"
```

```
'Display the combined XML to user
  XMLDataSet.Text = str

  'Generate a DOM document from the XML
  DS_DOM.LoadXml (str)

  'Make sure we set the SelectionLanguage and
  'schems for xs so that we can parse DOM
  DS_DOM.SetProperty "SelectionLanguage", "XPath"
  DS_DOM.SetProperty "SelectionNamespaces", _
                     "xmlns:xs='http://www.w3.org/2001/XMLSchema'"

  'Get employee record
  Set RSSetEmployee = XMLDataSettoRecordset(DS_DOM, "Employee")

  'Get Country record
  Set RSSetCountry = XMLDataSettoRecordset(DS_DOM, "Country")

  'Bind to data Grid to view
  Set DBGridEmployee.DataSource = RSSetEmployee
  Set DBGridCountry.DataSource = RSSetCountry
```

```
End Sub
```

The first part of the code gets the `DataSet` from the web service:

```
Set objXMLResultNodes = objSOAPClient.Get_Employee()
```

The data returned in `objXMLResultNodes` actually contains two nodes. The first holds the XSD schema and the next the XML data of the `DataSet`. We need to combine the XML value of the two nodes and load the XML in to `DS_DOM`.

```
'Because the objXMLResultNodes separates the DataSet XML into two nodes we
'need to recombine them so that we can create a DOM object
str = "<DataSet>" & objXMLResultNodes.Item(0).xml _
    & objXMLResultNodes.Item(1).xml & "</DataSet>"

'Display the combined XML to user
XMLDataSet.Text = str

'Generate a DOM document from the XML
DS_DOM.LoadXml (str)
```

At this stage, you could load an external XML file instead of accessing a real .NET web service: the effect would be the same.

Next, we must prepare the DS_DOM object for parsing:

```
'Make sure we set the SelectionLanguage and
' xs namespaces so that we can parse DOM
DS_DOM.SetProperty "SelectionLanguage", "XPath"
DS_DOM.SetProperty "SelectionNamespaces", _
                "xmlns:xs='http://www.w3.org/2001/XMLSchema'"
```

If we do not define the SelectionNamespaces we will get a run-time error, **Reference to undeclared prefix: 'xs'**.

We can now go on to retrieve our tables and populate the DataGrids:

```
'Get employee record
Set RSSetEmployee = XMLDataSettoRecordset(DS_DOM, "Employee")

'Get Country record
Set RSSetCountry = XMLDataSettoRecordset(DS_DOM, "Country")

'Bind to data Grid to view
Set DBGridEmployee.DataSource = RSSetEmployee
Set DBGridCountry.DataSource = RSSetCountry

End Sub
```

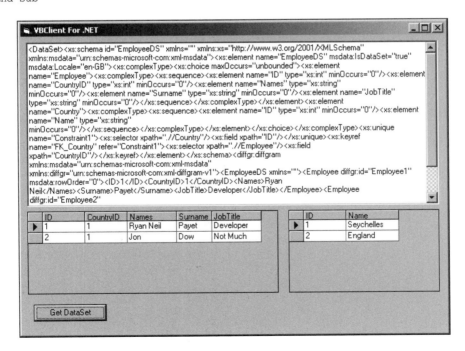

Limitations of the Conversion Routine

The conversion function works well when the dataset is simple, and you only need to read data sent from a web service. To convert a `RecordSet` to a `DataSet`, you would be best to use an alternative method such as XSLT.

Due to the way the parsing is performed, the function will also generate extra blank rows if the name of a column in the table is the same as the name of the table.

Summary

As you have seen, the SOAP toolkit and SOAP in general is really quite straightforward. Microsoft's SOAP toolkit allows current VB6 professionals to leverage their existing knowledge and experience and apply it to distributed systems. Hopefully this chapter has demonstrated that building and consuming web services isn't nearly as difficult as it may seem. In fact, the hardest part of working with SOAP and web services is not creating or calling web services, but transforming the returned data to a format that your system can understand.

p2p.wrox.com
The programmer's resource centre

ASP Today

wrox.com

wroxdirect

15

Looking Forward to .NET

The aim of this book is to give a greater understanding of how to implement VB in an enterprise environment. However, in any enterprise you will work with a number of systems that will be writing in different languages and running on different platforms. You must understand not only what exists today, but equally importantly where the enterprise will be tomorrow and what kind of languages and platforms may be required to interact with the VB 6 applications you are building today. The next generation of application development on a Microsoft platform will be based on the .NET Framework, which at the time of writing has been released as a product for almost a year and is gaining support in the enterprise.

Of course, as a new environment, most enterprises are approaching .NET with caution, developing most applications using current languages such as VB 6 while prototyping some less business-critical applications using the .NET Framework. What you have learned throughout this book is extremely important in today's corporate application developments, because it will be a while before .NET is the framework of choice for all developments and a long time before we see no VB 6 development required (enhancements, fixes, support, and so on).

The aim of this chapter is not to give you a detailed look at the .NET Framework, but to help you build an understanding of what you need to know so that past, current and future VB 6 developments can easily work with and eventually migrate to .NET.

What is .NET?

.NET is the next evolution of the Microsoft development platform and advances on the lessons learned from COM and COM+ to create a new general framework supporting multiple languages, but allowing them to seamlessly work with each other via common standards. One of these standards is the Common Language Runtime (CLR) which provides a set of services common to all applications such as code access security, cross language integration, garbage collection, debugging, and more. Furthermore, the Common Type System (CTS) provides a standard set of types that are adhered to by all languages conforming to the framework standards, which allow applications to talk to each other without fear of data type nuances. (For languages that are currently supported by the .NET Framework, see http://msdn.microsoft.com/vstudio/partners/language). This avoids many of the problems that have been encountered in the past with technologies such as COM. A powerful versioning system is also part of the framework to avoid the DLL collision problems of the past. In fact, installing a .NET application can be as simple as copying the files to a directory – no registration in the registry required.

So how are objects in VB 6 different from objects created using VB.NET? Well, when working with Visual Basic 6, the classes you create are independent and inherit only the features of the language. You build COM components and these components interact through interfaces.

However, when working with .NET, although the core concept of interfaces still exists, they are not required for objects to talk to each other. Instead, communication is via the Common Language Runtime (or CLR). Additionally, all classes automatically inherit from the System.Object base class that provides many of the core language features that are used in all of your classes.

One of the consequences of this is that powerful object-oriented capabilities have been introduced to the language (we look at these later) and VB.NET has changed much of how we work with VB. There are some who debate some of the changes, but overall VB.NET is a far more feature-rich language that any of its VB predecessors and certainly a language suited to multi-tier distributed applications.

So if .NET is the future for VB, what does it mean for VB 6 and all of the current and future applications that are developed using it? Remember .NET is still relatively young and it will be a long time before everyone converts applications!

The Implications for Visual Basic

Visual Basic 6 has, in fact, been upgraded to VB.NET, and from an average programmer's point of view, this will bring the power and flexibility of VB into the same league as C++ and its .NET partner language, C#. However, with this power and flexibility, the language has become more complex and although current VB 6 programmers will find many similarities in .NET to how they program today, there are some distinct differences that will affect how you architect your code. .NET is entirely object-oriented and VB.NET allows powerful object-oriented techniques such as inheritance and overriding, overloading, overloaded constructors, and many other features.

Why Move From VB 6 to .NET?

There are many reasons why you may be tempted to move your application development from VB 6 to VB.NET. Here are some of the key reasons:

- ❑ Powerful object-oriented techniques allowing code reuse across other applications.

- ❑ Simpler to deploy applications and avoid the problem of component versioning (DLL Hell). Components are simply copied to a directory.

- ❑ Coding is easier and an increased number of components can be dropped onto the interface whether you are developing a Windows application or web application.

- ❑ ADO.NET is an integral part of the .NET Framework, bringing together the worlds of relational databases with XML. This allows for caching of data, serialization for network transport.

- ❑ Creating Windows Services is now very easy, even for Visual Basic developers. A wizard gets you started and creating the logic. Also installing the service is a lot simpler than it has been in the past.

- ❑ ASP Pages can now be written in VB rather than VBScript, allowing early binding and much more powerful and scalable web applications.

> Note that using Interop, you can use existing COM+ components in your new .NET application. It even allows you to use .NET components within new or existing COM+ components.

Architecting VB 6 Applications with a View to .NET

VB.NET continues the idea of multi-tier DNA architecture with clear logical boundaries between, and even within, each tier. For example, the presentation layer is composed of the user interface and logic, which are two separate layers. This approach has been the recommended method of creating applications, especially web applications for the last few years. When moving to .NET you want to have as clear a separation between presentation and logic as is possible to enable a more straightforward upgrade process in the future.

DHTML applications and ActiveX documents are no longer supported by the VB.NET language and you would want to either leave existing applications in VB 6 or upgrade the business logic to VB.NET and create a new application. `WebClasses` are upgraded to ASP.NET, however, and provide a vastly more powerful architecture that combines the strengths of web classes and ASP pages into a new technology called `WebForms`.

Powerful new debugging features make it much easier to debug across layers and even across languages allowing for the faster release of multi-tier applications that was previously possible (mainly because they have been extremely difficult to debug in the past!).

N-Tier, But Different

Enterprise applications are developed according to a tiered model that separates the data, business, and presentation into separate layers, often distributed across a number of machines. When creating enterprise applications with VB 6 and COM+, this multi-tiered architecture is used to create scalable, distributed solutions. The diagram below shows a typical n-tier architecture.

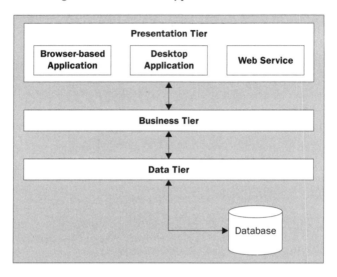

The presentation tier is where the various forms of an application are exposed, whether that is as a VB client, a web server application with browser interaction or another format. The presentation layer effectively defines how the user sees the data and interacts with the application. In the COM world the presentation layer may be a VB 6 client or a web application written using Active Server Pages; optionally there are Web Classes and DHTML Applications that can also display presentation-level information. The important point is that all of these various presentation implementations actually use the same business logic, which models the problem the application is trying to solve. This common business logic is defined in the business layer and is commonly hosted on a client or web server.

The business layer is where the business processes that must be implemented by the application are hosted and the business layer typically contains code that communicates with the data layer. The business layer may bring together diverse sources of data into a single transaction, such as updating a customer order database and removing the item from the inventory database at the same time. If either fails, the entire transaction fails and all data is restored to the original values. These components will be COM components, often written in VB 6 and hosted in COM+, which provide enterprise services such as distributed transaction management and asynchronous queuing. Also, your ADO code will be in this layer, despite being data access code. The business layer is commonly implemented on an Application Server.

The final layer is the data layer, which is typically SQL Server, although it may be another OLEDB accessible source (such as Microsoft Exchange Server). Often, this layer will also contain Stored Procedures, which minimize the data knowledge required in the business layer and brings the data components closer to the data layer.

This idea of a multi-tier architecture is not going to change with the move to .NET, but the implementation will vary slightly. In the COM+ world, the data access components are in the business layer and do the work of getting and updating the data base. This model won't change in any dramatic way, but .NET introduces the ability to cache data in a scalable and efficient manner through a technology called `DataSets`. These `DataSets` are typically cached in the presentation layer and can contain tables, relationships and constraints, along with allowing data to be read and updated. They can then be synchronized with the database to confirm any changes. However the creation of a dataset will typically go through the business layer and the data access components will return a dataset, which can then be cached, even for the lifetime of an application, on the web server. This model improves the scalability and performance capabilities of multi-tier programming – especially in read-only situations!

Web Services

The middle tier is now richer thanks to the two technologies of **web services** and **Remoting**. Web services have been around for a couple of years now and may well have already found their way into your VB 6 applications. .NET dramatically improves the ability to create web services and expose new and existing enterprise components to clients over HTTP. These clients can be from a multitude of platforms and programming languages – as long as they support HTTP and the SOAP protocol, they are able to access the web service. They pass standard XML between the client and the server and thus open the application to a much wider community in the enterprise.

As powerful as web services are for remote communication between components, the overhead of SOAP can sometimes be too inefficient for intranet or local applications that don't necessarily need to worry about conforming to standards as they are only intended to work with each other. For this, we previously used distributed COM (or DCOM) written in VB or C++, which allows you to call methods on remote objects. However, DCOM is relatively inefficient and never worked well over the Internet, mainly due to firewalls and other security issues.

Remoting

The replacement for DCOM in the .NET Framework is .NET Remoting, which also improves the capabilities offered by web services in situations where you don't have to worry about clients on other operating systems and environments. The term "Web Services Anywhere" has often been applied to Remoting as it can be used in any application to communicate over any transport protocol (HTTP, TCP, and so on) with any kind of data encoding. This, of course, means that you can also use SOAP and HTTP as the communication method for Remoting. Remoting can also be accessed over other protocols such as TCP as well as HTTP, transporting a binary format, making it faster than web services. However, this is at the expense of interoperability.

The basic architecture of Remoting is shown below:

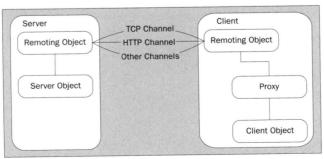

The remote object runs on the server and is never directly called on the client. Instead a proxy is created, which can then be used to call the methods of the server object. Communication between the client and server is done via a channel, which can be HTTP, TCP, or other protocols.

When a client calls a server method, a message is passed, containing details on the remote object method that was called and any parameters that are to be passed. A formatter is then used to encode the message before it is sent into the channel. This can be SOAP to work with web services that are not based on the .NET Framework, or in a binary format to improve speed and efficiency when working internally.

The configuration of such a service can be done in compiled code. The problem is that this may change often and will very likely increase in scope relatively often, requiring a recompilation each time. To improve on this, the entire configuration for remoting clients and server can be specified in an XML configuration file.

Depending on your requirements comparing interoperability with speed you may choose web services over Remoting or vice versa. It is definitely worth looking into both before you make that choice.

VB 6 Programming Recommendations

There are some useful guidelines you can follow when creating your VB 6 applications so that when the time comes to upgrade them it is as seamless as possible. This section will take you through some of the most important of these.

Explicitly Declare your Variables

When coding with VB 6 you can declare multiple variables on the same line, with only the last variable being of the specified type and all preceding variables being of variant type.

```
Dim myA, myB, myC As Integer
```

In VB 6 this in fact declares myA and myB as Variants and myC as an Integer. In VB.NET, however, myA, myB and myC will all be Integer datatypes and so could cause problems if this is not expected later in the code.

To ensure you are always working with the correct type and so that the upgrade does not convert a type when you don't expect it to, explicitly declare your variables in VB 6 as follows.

```
Dim myA As Variant
Dim myB As Variant
Dim myC As Integer
```

Take Care with Parameters

When passing parameters in VB 6 the intrinsic datatypes such as Integer, Char, and Date are passed ByRef and everything else is passed ByVal. In VB.NET the default for all datatypes is ByVal and so you should update your VB 6 methods to explicitly pass the variables ByVal or ByRef to avoid any contention.

Furthermore, the VB 6 IsMissing function is no longer supported in VB.NET and so all optional parameters should carry default values.

Use Early Binding

Convenience has often meant that VB 6 has used late binding, particularly when working with ASP web applications (where we had no real choice anyway). Late binding allows us to declare a variable of type `Object` and assign the instance of the class at run time. This is still supported in .NET (and in fact can be very useful where you don't know the type of object you will be working with). However, during the upgrade process, if your object is late bound then the upgrade process is unable to determine the type of a given object and so any interface changes (the methods, properties, and events) cannot be assigned. A great example of this is when using late binding to assign a `Label` in a VB 6 form.

```
Dim obj As Object
Set obj = Me.lblTitle
obj.Caption = "Professional Visual Basic 6"
```

The problem here is that the application will only know that it is working with a `Label` type at run time when it assigns the `Caption` property. However, in VB.NET the `Caption` property has now changed to `Text` and so the upgrade process would attempt to make these changes. In the case of late binding, the upgrade doesn't know it is working with a `Label` and so won't make the change required. This would, therefore, have to be done manually. Modifying the above code to the code shown below will ensure that the upgrade process goes much more successfully.

```
Dim obj As Label
Set obj = Me.lblTitle
obj.Caption = "Professional Visual Basic 6"
```

This time early binding is used and so the upgrade can determine that the `Caption` property must be changed to `Text`.

In cases where you have to use late binding, you need to consider explicitly converting the types using VB 6 functions such as `CStr()` and `CInt()`.

Application Upgrade

Visual Studio.NET in fact automatically upgrades your Visual Basic 6 applications to VB.NET code, but as expected this upgrade is not seamless (Microsoft say it copes with 95% of the code to upgrade) and before doing so you should prepare your VB 6 code for the upgrade.

When planning to upgrade applications in your enterprise, it is recommended that you should start by selecting a simple application and gradually move to the larger, complex applications. Start by upgrading the modules, classes, and forms, and then move to ActiveX and COM components. Then, finally tackle multi-tier and web applications.

ActiveX Documents and DHTML Applications cannot be upgraded to .NET and so you should leave them in VB 6 and navigate between them and web forms via a web browser. WebClasses, however, have been upgraded to Web Forms in .NET, which allows essentially the same functionality. Unlike WebClasses, however, which require the web server to be restarted each time a web class is deployed, web forms do not require IIS to be restarted during deployment.

So, What's Changed?

VB 6 Forms move to Windows Forms (or WinForms) in VB.NET and with them you get automatic form resizing, control docking, and visual inheritance (you can create a new control based on an existing control).

New Features

There are a number of important new features that have been added to Visual Basic; some are enhancements on features that were previously available and others are entirely new concepts that promise to evolve and improve the language itself.

Let's take a look at some of these new features.

Inheritance

Perhaps the most significant change is Visual Basic becoming a true object-oriented language, the lack of which often kept more experienced developers from using it. Inheritance allows you to create a base class from which other classes can inherit and derive to create more specific classes, but all using the sharing the same code base. VB.NET actual provides two forms of inheritance.

The first is implementation inheritance whereby you can create a new class based on an existing class implementation. This is very useful where you want to include default implementation for a set of methods or properties within your class. It is also extremely useful where you have a specific case, which requires a method to be implemented differently. You can use a new keyword in the VB.NET language, Overrides, to override the implementation of that method while not affecting the others.

The second type of inheritance in VB.NET is visual inheritance for forms, which allows you to create base controls that you can build more powerful controls on top of. This is a great idea and will allow you to create powerful graphical controls by reusing existing controls.

The final type of inheritance is called interface inheritance where your class can inherit existing interfaces and implement the functionality of those methods within the class. This is very useful when you want to create standard interfaces that will be used in multiple classes – it allows you to control the interfaces, yet allow flexibility in how they are actually implemented.

Overloading

Overloading is yet another of those object-oriented features that once you start using, you wonder why it was never there in the first place. Overloading allows you to create more than one method with the same name, which each take a different set of arguments.

In VB 6 you would have to create different methods with different names, but VB.NET allows you to use the same name and the method selected is based on the parameters that are passed to the method at runtime. Consider the case where you have a method that returns the full name of a business given either the ID of a business or the first few letters of its name.

In VB 6 you may define this as:

```
Public String GetCompanyNameByID(ID As Integer)
...
Public String GetCompanyNameByName(name As String)
...
```

Here you have two methods with different names, `GetCompanyNameByID()` and `GetCompanyNameByName()`.

In VB.NET you can rewrite this using the `Overloads` keyword and have more intuitive method names.

```
Public String GetCompanyName(ID As Integer)
....
Public Overloads String GetCompanyName(name As String)
....
```

In this case you have two methods called `GetCompanyName()` and the method that is invoked will depend on whether the parameter passed in an `Integer` or a `String`.

Parameterized Constructors

Now when creating instances of objects you can initialize them at the same time using constructors. As an example, an object containing a reference to an open database connection may be essential to any of your methods and so you may decide that whenever a new instance of this class is created, a database connection object must be passed in. This allows you to initialize a global variable for example that can then be used in all examples that you are working on.

Constructors don't return anything and are used purely for initializing class instances. Like method overloads you can have multiple constructors to initialize the constructors in different ways and the construction that is used depends on the data types passed to the constructor.

Declaration and Initialization

When coding in previous versions of VB the ability to declare and initialize variables on the same line has been something that has been in popular demand. It only saves typing a single line extra, but for some reason has been one of those things that just seems like you're forever doing it. So in VB 6 you may define a new `Integer` variable as follows:

```
Dim myInt As Integer
myInt = 100
```

VB.NET now allows you to both declare and initialize a variable on a single line as follows:

```
Dim myInt As Integer = 100
```

This is very useful when you start working with more complex data types later in the code.

Structured Exception Handling

Error handling in VB.NET is a massive improvement on what has been available in previous versions of VB. The On Error Resume statement used in VB 6 has now been replaced by structured error handling using the Try...Catch...Finally construct, although On Error Resume is still supported.

The Try statement will contain the code that you intend to execute, with the Catch statement being called if any of the code within the Try statement produces an error. The Finally statement is very useful as it runs immediately after the code within the Try or Catch statements has been evaluated and allows you to clean up objects you created earlier in the code, such as closing open database connections or files.

Free Threading

VB.NET now has the ability to spawn multiple threads, which allows for much better scalability for synchronous applications developed using VB.NET. This allows the application to create a new thread for a particular part of the application that may take a longer period of time to execute while the rest of the application continues to run.

Short Circuiting

Something I found particularly useful recently is the ability to short circuit If statements in VB.NET – something that is not possible with VB 6. Short circuiting allows you to execute an If statement, but exit the statement at the first part if the statements that is evaluated is false.

So, in the following case IsNothing() will be evaluated and then the second ToString() statement will be evaluated. However, the second statement will cause an exception and fail if the object has not been created, so ideally you would want to exit the If statement if the first statement is false. This is called short circuiting and cannot be done in VB 6 – you would probably write an embedded If statement:

```
If ((IsNothing(myObj)) Or (myObj.Value.ToString() = "")) Then
    Response.Write("No Value has been set!")
End If
```

VB.NET allows you to achieve this however using the OrElse keyword, which will exit at the first statement that returns True. This can be coded as follows:

```
If ((IsNothing(myObj)) OrElse (myObj.Value.ToString() = "")) Then
    Response.Write ("No Value has been set!")
End If
```

Shared Members

VB.NET introduces shared members, which allow a member (property or method) of a class to be shared by all instances of a given class. This allows a member to be set in one instance of a class and reused in another instance of that class, with this shared member being independent of any given instance.

Strict Typing

The `Option Strict` statement can now be used in VB.NET to help prevent data type conversion problems. You can convert many data types to other data types using VB, but the precision of the original value can be lost during this process. The `Option Strict` statement generates compilation errors when a conversion may fail at run time or cause an unexpected value to be returned.

Garbage Collection

Garbage collection is used in .NET to remove objects that are no longer in use. Unlike in VB 6, this means that even though you have destroyed an object, there will be a lag before it is actually removed from memory. Garbage Collection helps to eliminate problems such as forgetting to free an object (memory leaks) and works to allocate memory for newly created objects. It then removes them when they are no longer needed.

Feature Changes

There have been a number of feature changes, which are not necessarily language changes, but modifications or changes to Visual Basic that must be considered.

Some of the simpler, but more notable feature changes are as follows:

- ❑ The VB 6 `Caption` property has been replaced with the `Text` property in VB.NET.
- ❑ The VB 6 `Image` control has now been replaced by the .NET `PictureBox` control (this in fact replaces the `Image` and `PictureBox` controls).
- ❑ The `PrintForm` method has been replaced by a powerful printing framework in VB.NET. It also includes a facility for Print Preview.
- ❑ VB.NET introduces the `System.Drawing` namespace to draw shapes, replacing the `Shape` and `Line` controls in VB 6.
- ❑ The OLE Control Container is not supported in VB.NET and you should avoid using it.
- ❑ VB.NET also has no support for Dynamic Data Exchange (DDE) and so you should avoid using it also.

Watch Your Fonts

The font support has changed in VB.NET to now only support `TrueType` or `OpenType` fonts. This is important to know, because in VB 6 you had the ability to use any font, so when you upgrade your applications to VB.NET, any fonts that are not `TrueType` or `OpenType` will be changed to the default `WinForm` font but you will lose any formatting set on that font.

Language Changes

With the upgrade in the language, there have been the inevitable changes to the language, arguably more so than with any previous version of Visual Basic. Some of the fundamental changes are:

The `Variant` data type is no longer supported by VB.NET and has been replaced by the `Object` data type that can represent any data type. This is even more significant when creating ASP pages as you can now strongly type variables and take advantage of strict type checking and early binding.

The numeric data types have also changed. The VB 6 `Integer` data type (16-bit whole number) is now the `Short` data type in .NET. The `Integer` data type in .NET actually represents 32-bit whole numbers and replaces the VB 6 `Long` data type. Finally, the VB 6 `Long` data type now represents 64 bit whole numbers in .NET. When you upgrade your VB applications with these types, they are automatically converted to their equivalents in .NET.

Also avoid storing dates as doubles, although this is permitted by VB 6 – dates are not stored as doubles and may cause problems when converting your code to VB.NET. VB.NET does provide the `ToOADate()` and `FromOADate()` methods to convert to and from doubles when working with dates, but it is preferable, and you will avoid any possible contention, by using the `Date` data type in VB 6.

Other important changes to the language include:

❑ Parentheses are now always required around the parameters when calling procedures in VB.NET, whereas they were not required in VB 6 unless using the `Call` keyword.

❑ The default for passing parameters is now `ByVal` rather than `ByRef`.

❑ Object variables are now initialized to `Nothing` rather than `Empty`.

❑ `Type` has been replaced by `Structure`.

❑ `Debug.Print` has been replaced by `Debug.Write` and `Debug.WriteLine`.

❑ The `currency` data type is no longer supported in VB.NET and you should use the `Decimal` or `Long` data type in VB.NET.

❑ To disable the timer control set its `Enabled` property to `False` rather than the `Interval` to 0.

❑ Any code that rescales and resizes the windows should be disabled as this is done automatically in .NET.

Let's look at a few more of the important language changes in a little more detail.

Take Care with Default Properties

Default properties without parameters are no longer supported. However, unless you are using late binding and default parameters in combination you don't have to worry as the upgrade process will automatically fill in the default parameter for you in VB.NET. As an example, the `Text` property on a VB 6 Text control is a default property and so you can set the value of the `Text` default property as `Me.TextBox1`, however, VB.NET will convert this code to `Me.TextBox1.Text`, explicitly adding the `Text` property.

In contrast, default properties that take parameters are supported in VB.NET. The best example of this is the `Fields` property of the `RecordSet` class, where `Fields` is the default property and typically takes a parameter indicating the name (or index) of the column within the `RecordSet` to retrieve. So you can write:

```
myValue = objRS.Fields("myField").Value
```

An alternative way of writing this is:

```
myValue = objRS("myField")
```

However, in preparing for VB.NET we have to remember to avoid using parameterless default parameters. The default parameter of the `Fields` property is `Value`, which is in fact parameterless. So, the correct way of writing the above line is as follows:

```
myValue = objRS("myField").Value
```

As was stated earlier, where you are using early binding, these default parameters will be filled in for you, but when working with late binding they won't be and will ultimately be a source of error in your VB.NET application.

Arrays Have Changed

Visual Basic has always taken a controversial stand when working with arrays, allowing you to define the lower bound of an array to be a number greater than zero. However as of VB.NET, arrays in Visual Basic are now always zero-based, thus removing `Option Base` from the language. This allows much better operation between other .NET languages and arrays can now be easily passed to other components written in other .NET languages.

This is a fairly fundamental change and means that any logic that requires the lower bound of an array to be anything other than zero will cause you problems and will have to be manually reworked. However, in most cases the change will simply redimension the array to start from zero and will be the same size as the previously defined array. So, the following code declares a string array that can contain 100 elements:

```
Dim arr(1 to 100) As String
```

When upgraded to VB.NET, this will be redefined as follows:

```
Dim arr(100) As String
```

The result is still a string array that can contain 100 elements, but starts from 0 rather that 1. An additional point on this is that you can only use the `ReDim` keyword on a variable that was already declared as an array. So the following VB 6 code would cause a problem when upgraded to VB.NET.

```
Dim arr
ReDim arr(100) As String
```

To make the upgrade seamless, you should rewrite the code as shown below.

```
Dim arr(10) As String
ReDim arr(100) As String
```

Use Constants Rather than Values

It is always good programming practice to use named constants rather than specific values (or variables representing these values) when assigning values to controls, and to aid the upgrade process it is important that you stick with this principle. So rather than:

```
bolAllowed=-1
```

or

```
bolAllowed=0
```

which uses a specific value, use

```
bolAllowed=True
```

or

```
bolAllowed=False
```

This is required because in some cases the values represented by constants have changed and although the upgrade will attempt to resolve these for you, if you have used values and variables rather than the constants it will often not be able to make the required changes for you.

VB.NET Classes

All classes in VB.NET inherit from the System.Object base class, which provides low-level services to derived classes. Every class that is part of the .NET Framework is part of a namespace which groups classes of similar types – there are over 60 namespaces grouping the thousands of classes that are part of the .NET Framework. As an example, the System.Data namespace contains classes such as the DataSet class which represents a in-memory cache of data, or the DataTable class representing a single table of data (such as a table in relational database).

ADO moves to ADO.NET

ADO, RDO, and DAO are all supported in VB.NET along with the newer ADO.NET, which is extremely powerful. ADO.NET allows for disconnected data access, thus dramatically improving performance and scalability. Data binding, although not supported in DAO and RDO within .NET, is used in ADO.NET and has become even more powerful. XML also receives huge support in ADO.NET bringing the world of relational databases and XML together.

It is therefore recommended that all VB 6 projects use ADO so that the move to ADO.NET may be as seamless as possible.

A New IDE

We won't go through the entire IDE in this section, as it is so powerful that a whole book has been dedicated to it (see *Effective Visual Studio .NET*, from Wrox Press, ISBN 1-86100-696-9). However, it is useful to see the upgrade wizard in action so that you have an idea of how Visual Studio .NET helps upgrade your VB 6 applications to VB.NET. Like all great things we are going to start simple and that means with the mandatory "Hello World" sample.

A simple Visual Basic 6 form was created with some code added to highlight the upgrade process. The figure below shows the VB 6 code that dynamically sets the caption on the button at run time and sets the Text and Caption properties of a textbox and label when the command button is clicked.

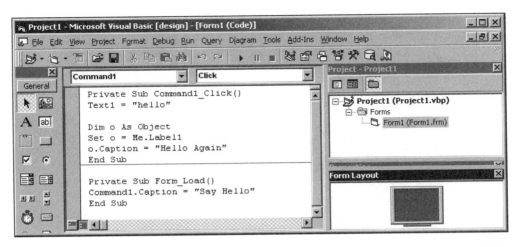

This example is also designed to illustrate some of the pitfalls when you don't take the VB.NET upgrade process into consideration. The first consideration is that the `Caption` property is used to set the text on the `Command` button at run time – the `Caption` property, as we stated earlier, is no longer supported by VB.NET and has been replaced by the `Text` property. When the command button is clicked we also set the `Text` property of the `Text1` control; `Text` is the default property for this control so we don't need to explicitly use it. VB.NET however doesn't support parameterless default properties, so it will be interesting to see how it handles this in the upgrade.

Finally, a new `Object` variable is created and a reference to the label control is assigned to it. The `Caption` property, which we know is supported by the `Label` in VB 6, is then assigned against the `Object` variable. Watch out for how this will be affected during the upgrade process.

When the above application is run in VB 6, we get the following output when the command button is clicked:

So let's now upgrade this application to VB.NET using the Visual Studio .NET IDE. When the Visual Studio .NET IDE is launched, click the File | Open | Project option and navigate to the place where the HelloWorld project file is stored (`Project1.vbp` in our case). Select this and click the Open button and the welcome screen for the Visual Basic Upgrade Wizard will start.

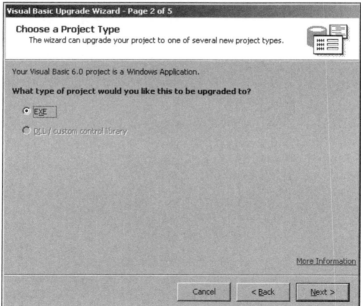

Step 3 will ask you to choose a location for the upgraded files to be placed and Step 4 tells you the upgrade is about to start. Step 5 performs the actual upgrade process as shown opposite;

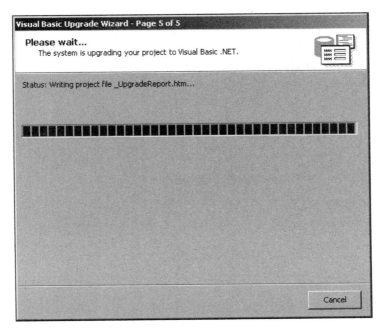

When the upgrade process has completed, the new project will be contain the upgraded files and a report that contains details on the upgrade such as warnings and errors that were encountered. On viewing the report we shouldn't be surprised to learn there was a single warning.

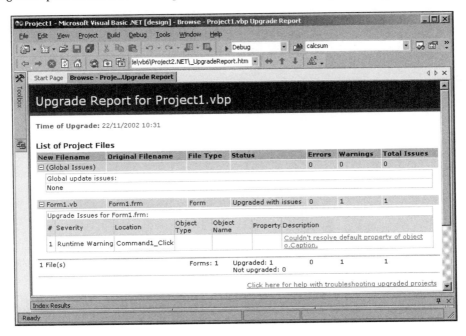

We discussed earlier in the chapter that if you create an object variable and assign an object instance to it at run time, the upgrade will be unable to determine whether any of the properties were required to be changed. This is only a warning, though, because in many cases the change won't be necessary, especially if it is your own classes you are upgrading. However, in this case we do run into a problem because the Caption property is no longer supported, so when we run the application (hit the play button or press *F5* in the Visual Studio.NET IDE) it compiles fine, but at run time when the "Say Hello" button is clicked we get the following problem:

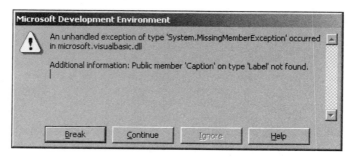

The message box is correctly indicating that the Caption property is no defined on the Label, which is what we expected because it now uses the Text property to achieve the same functionality.

The problem itself lies in the source code as shown in the screenshot below. We can see where the Caption property is used and there is even a warning indicating that the property was unable to be resolved. If you look at the other two methods in the class, you can see that the Text property was inserted during the upgrade – remember, no parameterless default properties are allowed.

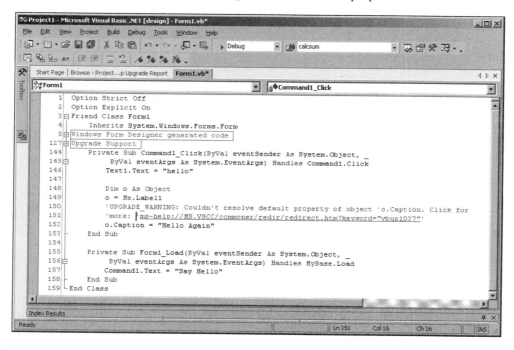

What is remarkable about this upgrade is that the form was preserved identically to that in the Visual Basic 6 version and almost all of the code was converted. The `Text` property of the `Text1` control was added and the `Caption` property of the `Command1` control was changed to `Text`.

The main problem we ran into could have been avoided had we properly read this chapter before we started the upgrade process (now let that be a lesson to you!). Applying the various pieces of knowledge we have about preparing for the upgrade to existing Visual Basic 6 applications would take out most of the conversion and leave us with a little manual conversion to complete the upgrade.

Summary

This chapter looked at what .NET is, why you may want to move to it and what considerations you should make when planning to upgrade your applications. In particular we discussed:

❑ What .NET is, including the CLR and the CTS.

❑ How the architecture is generally the same but that there are also a number of changes from the architecture used in VB 6/5 applications.

❑ Programming Recommendations that should be considered when creating VB 6 applications or modifying an existing application for an upgrade to .NET.

❑ New features that have been added to Visual Basic.

❑ Changes to existing features that may affect your applications.

❑ Changes to the VB 6 languages that you should be aware of.

❑ ADO and the move to ADO.NET.

❑ A sample of upgrading a simple VB 6 application.

p2p.wrox.com
The programmer's resource centre

ASP Today

wrox.com

wroxdirect

wrox

Visual Basic Tips and Tricks

This appendix contains some snippets of code that highlight certain particularly useful techniques for VB programmers. All code can be found in the download in the TipsAndTricks project for you to copy and paste into your own applications.

The Win32 API

Correct and appropriate use of the Win32 API can be indispensable when creating robust VB6 applications. The Win32 API is the backbone of all Windows-based applications, but normally Visual Basic hides the complexities of the syntax from us. However, there are situations where we need direct control over calls to the API. After a few cracks at it and a couple of general protection fault errors, you'll probably find it best to cut and paste examples such as those in this section, or those from Microsoft or some other web site rather than attempting to figure out all the syntax yourself.

List boxes and Combo boxes

Listboxes and combo boxes are two of the most common controls of user interfaces. Both these controls fire the Click event when the user selects an item from the list. The Click event also fires when you set the ListIndex property. However, in many situations you don't want the code in the Click event to be executed. One workaround is to dimension a form-level flag that is set to True before you set the ListIndex property and check in the Click event whether or not to execute the code. A much better way to solve the problem is to call an API function that doesn't fire the Click event.

```
Private Const LB_SETCURSEL = &H186
Private Const CB_SETCURSEL = &H14E

Private Declare Function SendMessage Lib "user32" Alias _
    "SendMessageA" (ByVal hWnd As Long, ByVal wMsg As Long, _
                    ByVal wParam As Long, lParam As Any) As Long
```

```
Private Sub SetListIndex(lst As Object, ByVal NewIndex As Long)

  If TypeOf lst Is ListBox Then

    Call SendMessage(lst.hWnd, LB_SETCURSEL, NewIndex, 0&)

  Else

    Call SendMessage(lst.hWnd, CB_SETCURSEL, NewIndex, 0&)

  End If

End Function
```

Another common UI feature is to allow the user to enter new items in a combo box on the fly by setting the Style property to Dropdown Combo. In most applications, as the user enters the text in the combo box the items that best match what they are typing are automatically selected in the combo box. This feature is not built into the standard combo box but can be accomplished with an API call.

```
Private Const CB_FINDSTRING = &H14C

Private Declare Function SendMessage Lib "user32" Alias "SendMessageA" _
        (ByVal hWnd As Long, ByVal wMsg As Long, _
        ByVal wParam As Long, lParam As Any) As Long

Public Sub FindString(ByVal Combo As ComboBox, ByRef KeyAscii As Integer)

  Dim ComboText As String
  Dim Result As Long

  ComboText = Left$(Combo.Text, Combo.SelStart) & Chr(KeyAscii)

  Result = SendMessage(Combo.hWnd, CB_FINDSTRING, -1, ByVal ComboText)

  If Result <> -1 Then

    Combo.ListIndex = Result
    Combo.Text = Combo.List(Result)
    Combo.SelStart = Len(ComboText)
    Combo.SelLength = Len(Combo.Text)

    KeyAscii = 0

  End If

End Sub
```

In the KeyPress event of the combo box you then need to call FindString and pass in the combo box and the KeyAscii variable.

Another common routine is to allow the user to select all items in a listbox by clicking a button. This can be done by looping through the items in the listbox and setting the Selected property to True but this moves the focus to the last item in the listbox. This can also be accomplished by an API call.

```
Private Const LB_SETSEL = &H185

Private Declare Function SendMessageLong Lib "user32" Alias "SendMessageA" _
        (ByVal hWnd As Long, ByVal wMsg As Integer, _
        ByVal wParam As Long, ByVal lParam As Long) As Long

Public Sub SelectItemsInListbox(ListBox As ListBox, Selected As Boolean)

  SendMessageLong ListBox.hWnd, LB_SETSEL, Selected, -1

End Sub
```

Intercepting Windows Messages – Subclassing

Visual Basic does not provide event handlers for all messages sent to a window. For example, there is no event that fires when the user clicks on a combo box to expand the list. You can intercept these messages with a technique called subclassing. Be careful here because incorrectly implementing subclassing can cause your program to hang or throw you out. The API declarations are:

```
Declare Function CallWindowProc Lib "user32" Alias _
    "CallWindowProcA" (ByVal lpPrevWndFunc As Long, _
    ByVal hwnd As Long, ByVal Msg As Long, _
    ByVal wParam As Long, ByVal lParam As Long) As Long

Declare Function SetWindowLong Lib "user32" Alias _
    "SetWindowLongA" (ByVal hwnd As Long, _
    ByVal nIndex As Long, ByVal dwNewLong As Long) As Long
```

The routines to create a hook and process the messages are:

```
Public Sub Hook(hwnd As Long)
  lpPrevWndProc = SetWindowLong(hwnd, GWL_WNDPROC, AddressOf WindowProc)
End Sub

Public Sub Unhook(hwnd As Long)
  Dim temp As Long
  temp = SetWindowLong(hwnd, GWL_WNDPROC, lpPrevWndProc)
End Sub

Function WindowProc(ByVal hw As Long, ByVal uMsg As Long, _
                    ByVal wParam As Long, ByVal lParam As Long) As Long

  Select Case uMsg
    Case CBN_DROPDOWN
      Debug.Print "Dropdown List shown"

    Case Else

  End Select

  WindowProc = CallWindowProc(lpPrevWndProc, hw, uMsg, wParam, lParam)
End Function
```

The `WindowProc` function is the routine where the messages will be processed. It prints the message to the immediate window when the drop-down list is shown and then processes the message by calling `CallWindowProc`. The `Hook` sub tells your program to process Windows messages in the `WindowProc` procedure by passing the function pointer to the `SetWindowLong` API call. The `AddressOf` keyword is used to get the pointer to a function. The `Unhook` procedure is used to detach the `WindowProc` function.

You can subclass a combo box by passing its `hwnd` property to the `Hook` routine.

```
Private Sub Command1_Click()
  If Not mbHooked Then
    Hook Combo1.hwnd
    mbHooked = True
  End If
End Sub
```

INI Files

INI files are an old school programming practice that were used to store program settings and other local settings. INI files are generally text files that are broken into **sections** using a header wrapped in brackets [ ]. Headers are followed by key-value pairs. A typical INI file looks as follows:

```
[DATABASE]
PATH=c:\Program Files\VB\test.mdb
```

The section name is DATABASE, and the key name is PATH. The value for PATH is C:\Program Files\VB\test.mdb. For VB6 applications, Microsoft advises that program settings are stored in the registry, which is more secure, although NTFS permissions can be set to secure an INI file. It's also interesting to note that .NET appears to have come full circle, preferring application settings files, although this time they are XML. However, INI files are quick and easy if you don't have to worry about security issues, and we can read, write, and delete sections and keys with a few API calls:

```
Private Declare Function GetPrivateProfileString Lib "kernel32" Alias _
  "GetPrivateProfileStringA" (ByVal SectionName As String, _
  ByVal KeyName As String, ByVal Default As String, _
  ByVal ReturnedString As String, ByVal StringSize As Long, _
  ByVal FileName As String) As Long

Private Declare Function WritePrivateProfileString Lib "kernel32" Alias _
  "WritePrivateProfileStringA" (ByVal SectionName As String, _
  ByVal KeyName As String, ByVal KeyValue As String, _
  ByVal FileName As String) As Long

Private Declare Function DeleteKeyValue Lib "kernel32" Alias _
  "WritePrivateProfileStringA" (ByVal SectionName As String, _
  ByVal KeyName As String, ByVal KeyValue As Long, _
  ByVal FileName As String) As Long

'Returns a key value from the ini file
Public Function GetKeyValue(ByVal INIFile as String, _
  ByVal Section As String, ByVal KeyName As String, _
  ByVal DefaultValue As String) As String
```

```vb
   Dim lRet As Long
   Dim sBuf As String * 128
   Dim NullPosition as Long

   lRet = GetPrivateProfileString(Section, KeyName, DefaultValue, _
             sBuf, Len(sBuf), INIFile)

   NullPosition = InStr(sBuf, vbNullChar)

   If NullPosition > 0 Then
     GetKeyValue = Left$(sBuf, NullPosition - 1)
   Else
     GetKeyValue = sBuf
   End if

End Function

'Writes a key value to the INI file
Public Sub SaveKeyValue(ByVal INIFile as String, ByVal Section As String, _
        ByVal KeyName As String, ByVal Setting As String)

   Dim lRet As Long

   lRet = WritePrivateProfileString(Section, KeyName, Setting, INIFile)

End Sub

'Deletes a key in the INI file
Public Sub DeleteKey(ByVal INIFile as String, ByVal Section As String, _
                  ByVal KeyName As String)

   Dim lRet As Long

      lRet = DeleteKeyValue(Section, KeyName, 0&, INIFile)

      If lRet = 0 Then
         'Raise Error "Cannot delete key."
      End If

End Sub

'Deletes a section in an INI file
Public Function DeleteSection(ByVal INIFile as String, _
                        ByVal Section As String) As Long

   DeleteSection = WritePrivateProfileString(Section, vbNullString, _
                                    vbNullString, INIFile)

End Function
```

ADO

Connection Strings

Figuring out the correct syntax for a connection string can be a real pain, but we can use the ADO Data Control to ease this task. Place an ADO Data Control on a form, right-click it, and select **ADODC Properties**. Select the **Use Connection String** option on the Property Pages dialog and click the **Build** button. This displays the Data Link Properties screen. Select the OLE DB Provider and click **Next**. Fill in the appropriate connection information and click **OK**. You can now copy and paste the connection string as you wish.

Stored Procedures

While using a `Command` object is a good way to pass parameters into a stored procedure, you can also execute a stored procedure by calling the `Connection` object's `Execute` method. For instance, say we have the following stored procedure which adds a record to the `Jobs` table in the `pubs` database:

```
CREATE Procedure JobsAdd
(
  @job_desc varchar(50),
  @min_lvl tinyint,
  @max_lvl tinyint
)
As
set nocount on
INSERT INTO jobs (job_desc, min_lvl, max_lvl)
VALUES (@job_desc, @min_lvl, @max_lvl)
return

GO
```

This stored procedure takes three parameters and inserts them into the `jobs` table. We can call this stored procedure with the following syntax:

```
cn.Execute "{call JobsAdd ('Test', 10, 100)}", Options:=adExecuteNoRecords
```

When calling a stored procedure, it must be in curly braces `{}`, and parameters are passed just as for regular Visual Basic functions. Notice also the `Options := adExecuteNoRecords`. This demonstrates two concepts: first, this stored procedure does not return a recordset so passing `adExecuteNoRecords` executes faster. Second, optional parameters can be specifically referenced as a named argument using `:=`.

I put this code in a loop that inserts 10,000 records. I also added 10,000 records using a `Command` object, and I found that the `Execute` method on a connection is about 20% faster. However, you cannot use this technique if the stored procedure has output parameters or returns a value.

Identity Fields

Often when adding records we need to retrieve the ID of the newly added record. There are numerous ways to accomplish this task. If we are using stored procedures, we can return the ID as an output parameter:

```
CREATE Procedure JobsAddOutputID
(
  @job_desc varchar(50),
  @min_lvl tinyint,
  @max_lvl tinyint,
  @id int output
)
As
set nocount on
INSERT INTO jobs (job_desc, min_lvl, max_lvl)
VALUES (@job_desc, @min_lvl, @max_lvl)

SELECT @id = @@IDENTITY
GO
```

Here is the VB code to call the stored procedure:

```
Dim cn As ADODB.Connection
Dim cmd As ADODB.Command
Dim id As Long

Set cn = New ADODB.Connection

cn.Open "Provider=SQLOLEDB;User ID=sa;Password=;Data " & _
        "Source=YourSQLServer;Initial Catalog=pubs"

Set cmd = New ADODB.Command

With cmd
  .CommandText = "JobsAddOutputID"
  .CommandType = adCmdStoredProc
  Set .ActiveConnection = cn
  .Parameters.Append .CreateParameter("@job_desc", adVarChar, _
                                      adParamInput, 50, "Test")
  .Parameters.Append .CreateParameter("@min_lvl", adTinyInt, _
                                      adParamInput, , 10)
  .Parameters.Append .CreateParameter("@max_lvl", adTinyInt, _
                                      adParamInput, , 100)
  .Parameters.Append .CreateParameter("@id", adInteger, adParamOutput)
  .Execute Options:=adExecuteNoRecords
  id = .Parameters("@id").Value
End With

Set cmd = Nothing

cn.Close
Set cn = Nothing

MsgBox "New ID: " & id
```

If we are not using stored procedures we can still insert the record and retrieve the ID in one statement:

```
Dim cn As ADODB.Connection
Dim id As Long
Dim rs As ADODB.Recordset
Dim SQL As String

Set cn = New ADODB.Connection

cn.Open "Provider=SQLOLEDB;User ID=sa;Password=;" & _
        "Data Source=YourSQLServer;Initial Catalog=pubs"

SQL = "SET NOCOUNT ON " & _
      "INSERT INTO jobs (job_desc, min_lvl, max_lvl) " & _
      "VALUES ('Test', 10, 100) " & _
      "SELECT @@IDENTITY SET NOCOUNT OFF"

Set rs = cn.Execute(SQL)

id = rs.Fields(0).Value

cn.Close
Set cn = Nothing

MsgBox "New ID: " & id
```

Always Close Recordsets and Connections

It is important to explicitly close any recordsets or connections that are opened. You can simply call the Close method of each object, but if an error occurs in the routing where the recordset or connection was opened, you must also make sure the object was closed in the error handler:

```
SubErr:
  If Not rs Is Nothing Then
    If rs.State = adStateOpen Then
      rs.Close
    End If
    Set rs = Nothing
  End If

  If Not cn Is Nothing Then
    If cn.State = adStateOpen Then
      Cn.Close
    End If
    Set cn = Nothing
  End If
```

Disconnected Recordsets and Firehose Cursors

The disconnected recordset and firehose cursor are the two most common recordset configurations that you will use. The disconnected recordset allows you to open a recordset and disconnect the connection from it, which throws the connection back into the connection pool so another caller can use it. You can then make changes to the data in the recordset and reconnect the connection when you are ready to save your changes.

```
Set rs = New ADODB.Recordset

rs.CursorLocation = adUseClient
rs.CursorType = adOpenStatic
rs.LockType = adLockBatchOptimistic
rs.Open "SELECT * FROM jobs", cn

'Here is where the recordset get disconnected
set rs.ActiveConnection = Nothing
```

You must use a client-side cursor to create a disconnected recordset and disconnected recordsets must use a static cursor. Even if you don't specify a static cursor, ADO will change the cursor type for you. The `LockType` property must either be `adLockBatchOptimistic` or `adLockReadOnly` depending on what you want to do with the data.

Firehose cursors are the least resource-intensive. They are server-side, forward-only, read-only recordsets that allow you to quickly pass through the data once. Moving the cursor back and forth is not supported. Firehose cursors are connected to the database for the life of the recordset, so it is always a good idea to immediately close the recordset and connection after you are finished so the connection can go back into the connection pool. The following code creates a firehose cursor:

```
Set rs = New ADODB.Recordset

rs.CursorLocation = adUseServer
rs.CursorType = adOpenForwardOnly
rs.LockType = adLockReadOnly
rs.Open "SELECT * FROM jobs", cn
```

GetRows

The `GetRows` method of a recordset returns a two-dimensional variant array of the recordset. The first subscript is the column number and the second subscript is the row number. You can optionally pass in the number of rows you want returned and the fields. In a n-tiered application, you can pass variant arrays through tiers rather than ADO recordsets and avoid having to install MDAC on each computer.

SQL Syntax

If you are embedding your SQL into your code, you need to do some special handling for single quotes and dates. If you are inserting a string that has a quote in it, you must replace the single quote with two single quotes. If you do not check for single quotes like this, you leave yourself vulnerable to injection attacks. These attacks are where people enter malicious parameters that will end up in SQL statements, such as a DROP TABLE statement. You can protect yourself with the following code:

```
sSQL = Replace(sSQL, "'", "''")
```

Dates and Date/Time fields also need to be formatted correctly. The following works for SQL Server and Oracle:

```
sSQLDate = "{d'" & Format(dteDate, "YYYY-MM-DD") & "'}"
```

```
sSQLDateTime = "{ts'" & Format(dteDate, "YYYY-MM-DD HH:nn:ss") & "'}"
```

Collection Classes

The Visual Basic intrinsic collection object is a useful object that can be used to store any type of data. The `Collection` object is similar to an array but with this, you don't have to worry about redimensioning the object when adding items, and searches can be quicker. A `Collection` class is an extension of the intrinsic `Collection` object and assures the user that the only objects in the collection are the base object.

A nice feature of the collection class is that it allows the user of your collection to enumerate through its members with a `For Each` loop. To add support for the `For Each` loop you need to add the following code to the collection class:

```
Public Function NewEnum() As IUnknown
    Set NewEnum = mCol.[_NewEnum]
End Function
```

You're not done yet. You must also go to **Tools | Procedure Attributes** from the Visual Basic menu. Select the `NewEnum` name, click the **Advanced** button, and set the `Procedure ID` to -4, check the `Hidden` checkbox, and click **OK**. A common mistake is to forget to set the procedure attributes and then when you execute a `For Each` on your collection you get an error, **Object doesn't support this property or method.**

Forms

Center a Form on the Screen Programmatically

You can easily center a form on the screen programmatically by placing the following code in the form's `Load` event:

```
Me.Move (Screen.Width - Me.Width) / 2, (Screen.Height - Me.Height) / 2
```

Memory Management

A form in Visual Basic is basically a class with a visual interface. Just as a class has an `Initialize` and `Terminate` event, so does a form. The `Initialize` event fires first, before the `Load` event. The `Terminate` event fires last, after the `Unload` event. It is very important to understand the order of these events and when they are fired. Member variables in your form will retain their values if you don't destroy the code page, which could lead to unexpected results.

Create a form called frmInitializeTerminate and add a single button. Change the button caption to Unload Me, and add the following code:

```
Private mbTest As Boolean

Private Sub Command1_Click()
   Unload Me
End Sub

Private Sub Form_Initialize()
   MsgBox "Initialize"
End Sub

Private Sub Form_Load()
   MsgBox mbTest
   mbTest = True
   MsgBox "Load"
End Sub

Private Sub Form_Terminate()
   MsgBox "Terminate"
End Sub

Private Sub Form_Unload(Cancel As Integer)
   MsgBox "Unload"
End Sub
```

Create another form with a button on it. In the button click event show the first form modally. When you click on the button you will see that the Intialize event fires first, then a message box with the message false, then the Load event. Click the Unload Me button, and you'll notice that only the Unload event fires. Click on the button to show the form again. Notice now the Initialize event did not fire, and the message box now shows true. The reason is that the form was not released from memory, only its visual interface was unloaded from the screen. The code page is still hanging around in memory. To make sure that all resources are freed when a form is unloaded you must set the form to Nothing in the Unload event:

```
Private Sub Form_Unload(Cancel As Integer)
  MsgBox "UnLoad"
  Set frmInitializeTerminate = Nothing
End Sub
```

Now try showing the form again and clicking Unload Me. The Terminate event fires and subsequent calls to show the form fire the Initialize event and display the false message.

Catching Errors on Form_Load

The Load event is a good place to put code to initialize the fields on the form. As we all know, unexpected run-time errors can occur at anytime. So if a run-time error occurs during the Load event you probably don't want to show the form to the user because they may have incorrect data being displayed. A clean solution to this problem is to create a form-level variable and expose a read-only property to this variable. In the error handler section of the Load event, set this variable to True. Now any code that loads this form can check the status of the variable and decide to show the form or not.

```
Private mFormLoadError As Boolean

Public Property Get FormLoadError() As Boolean
  FormLoadError = mFormLoadError
End Property

Private Sub Form_Load()

On Error GoTo SubErr

  'Do something that causes an error
  MsgBox 5 / 0

Exit Sub

SubErr:
  mFormLoadError = True
End Sub
```

Code to display this form:

```
Load frmFormToShow

If frmFormToShow.FormLoadError Then
  Unload frmFormToShow
Else
  frmFormToShow.Show
End If
```

Looping Through a Form's Controls

Every form has a controls collection which allows you to enumerate through each control. The following code enumerates through a form's controls:

```
Dim cnt as Control

For Each cnt in Me.Controls

  If TypeOf cnt is CommandButton Then

    Msgbox cnt.Name

  End If

Next cnt
```

The TypeOf keyword allows you to determine the object type. Note that the TypeOf keyword only works with objects, not simple data types such as Longs and Integers.

Looping Through the Forms Collection

The `Forms` collection allows you to enumerate through all open forms in an application. This is useful in a MDI application. You can loop through the `Forms` collection to determine if a form should be loaded or brought to the foreground when the user clicks on the menu item:

```
Dim frm as Form

For Each frm in Forms

   MsgBox frm.Name

Next frm
```

ZOrder Method

The `ZOrder` method sets the Z coordinate of a control or form. If the X and Y coordinates are left and right, and up and down, the Z coordinate is towards and away from the screen. Thus, `ZOrder` allows you to move a control or form to the foreground or background.

Reading and Writing Files

Importing and exporting files is a common task in many Visual Basic programs. The Microsoft Scripting Runtime supplies easy-to-use objects that allows you to read, write, and create files. You must set a reference to the Microsoft Scripting Runtime in order to use these objects.

The `FileSystemObject` is an extremely useful object that encapsulates many prior Visual Basic versions' file functions. You can use this object to check if a file, folder, or drive exists, copy files or folders, move files or folders, create and delete files or folders, and read or write files. The `TextStream` object is used to point to a file and allow you to read or write to the file. The following code opens a tab-separated file and prints it to a comma-separated file:

```
Dim fso As FileSystemObject
Dim tsIn As TextStream
Dim tsOut As TextStream
Dim Line As String
Dim aFields As Variant
Dim i as Integer

Set fso = New FileSystemObject

If fso.FileExists(sImportFile) Then

  'Open the import file
  Set tsIn = fso.OpenTextFile(sImportFile)
  Set tsOut = fso.OpenTextFile(sOutputFile, ForWriting, True)

  'Read to the end of file.
  Do Until tsIn.AtEndOfStream
    Line = tsIn.ReadLine
```

```
        'Split the line into an array
        aFields = Split(Line, vbTab)

        For i = 0 to Ubound(aFields)
          If i = Ubound(aFields) Then
            tsOut.WriteLine aFields(i)
          Else
            tsOut.Write aFields(i) & ","
          End If
        Next

    Loop

    tsIn.Close
    Set tsIn = Nothing
    tsOut.Close
    Set tsOut = Nothing
  End If
  Set fso = Nothing
```

Working with Objects

With...End With Block

The With... End With block allows you to reference an object's properties or methods without having to repeat the object name. Using the With statement executes faster than fully qualifying an object's methods or properties. The With keyword can also be used with user-defined types. It is always good practice to use the With block when referencing an object more than once.

```
Dim cm as ADODB.Command

Set cm = New ADODB.Command
With cm
  .ActiveConnection = ConnString
  .CursorLocation = adUseClient
  .CursorType = adOpenStatic
  .LockType = adLockBatchOptimistic
End With
```

Is Operator

The Is operator is used to compare an object's reference to another object's reference. You also use the Is operator to determine if an object has been initialized. When an object hasn't been initialized, the object is Nothing.

The following code will cause an error:

```
Dim a As Customer
Dim b As Customer
```

```
Set a = New Customer
Set b = New Customer

If a = b Then
  MsgBox "Equal"
Else
  MsgBox "Not Equal"
End If
```

To fix the error you would simply replace the = comparison operator with Is.

```
If a Is b Then
```

In this instance you would receive the message Not Equal.

New Keyword

There are two methods for instantiating objects using the New keyword:

```
Dim x as New MyClass
```

or

```
Dim x as MyClass
Set x = New MyClass
```

If an object is dimensioned with the New keyword, every call to that object's properties or methods must check to see if the object has already been instantiated. Therefore, it is good programming practice to dimension and instantiate an object in two separate statements.

Events

Often in a Visual Basic application you need to have one form show another form modally and the modal form needs to pass back a user response to the calling form. A simple way to accomplish this task is to have an event raised in the modal form and have it caught in the calling form.

Create a form with a textbox and a command button. Name the textbox txtMessage and the command button cmdOK. Enter the following code:

```
Public Event OKClicked(ByVal Message As String)

Private Sub cmdOK_Click()

    RaiseEvent OKClicked(txtMessage.Text)
    Unload Me

End Sub
```

Create another form with a label and a command button. Name the label lblMessage and the command button cmdGetMessage. Enter the following code:

```
Private WithEvents mfrmGetMessage As frmGetMessage

Private Sub cmdGetMessage_Click()

   Set mfrmGetMessage = New frmGetMessage
   mfrmGetMessage.Show vbModal
   Set mfrmGetMessage = Nothing

End Sub

Private Sub mfrmGetMessage_OKClicked(ByVal Message As String)
   lblMessage.Caption = Message
End Sub
```

When you run the project and click the `cmdGetMessage` button, the first form shows modally. When the OK button is clicked, `lblMessage` changes to whatever was entered in the textbox.

ByVal and ByRef

Be careful when passing objects `ByVal`. Even if you specify that an argument is `ByVal`, objects are passed by reference so any changes made by a called routine will be reflected in the calling procedure:

```
Private Sub Command1_Click()

   Dim oCustomer As Customer

   Set oCustomer = New Customer

   oCustomer.ID = 1
   oCustomer.Name = "Joe"
   oCustomer.Address = "111 First Street"

   Test oCustomer

   Debug.Print oCustomer.ID
   Debug.Print oCustomer.Name
   Debug.Print oCustomer.Address

End Sub

Private Sub Test(ByVal oCustomer As Customer)

   oCustomer.ID = 2
   oCustomer.Name = "Jack"
   oCustomer.Address = "222 Second Street"

End Sub
```

The Immediate Window will show the following text:

```
2
Jack
222 Second Street
```

General Syntax

Nulls

Trying to set the `Text` property of a textbox or the `Caption` property of a label with a null value will generate an "invalid use of null" error. A cheesy workaround is to append "" at the end of the line:

```
txtTextbox.Text = MyTable.Fields("MyField") & ""
```

Optional Parameters

Optional parameters can be declared for a function or sub using the `Optional` keyword. If you specifically type a parameter and the variable is not passed in, the parameter's value is the default value for the type. For example, if you type the parameter as an integer the value would be 0. If you type the parameter as a variant and the parameter is not passed in, the value of the parameter is `Missing`. You must then check if the parameter was passed in using the `IsMissing` function. It is good practice to specify default values for optional parameters so you don't get tripped up:

```
Private Sub Test(x As String, Optional y As Integer)

    If IsMissing(y) Then
        MsgBox "y parameter missing"
    Else
        MsgBox "y parameter was passed in"
    End If

End Sub
```

This code will never show the "y parameter missing" message, unless you change y to a variant.

ParamArrays

If you have an indefinite number of arguments that you need to pass to a routine, you need to use the `ParamArray` keyword. The arguments passed to the routine are placed in a variant array:

```
Public Sub Test(ParamArray vArguments())

    Dim v           As Variant
    Dim iIndex      As Integer

    For Each v In vArguments
        Debug.Print TypeName(vArguments(iIndex))
        iIndex = iIndex + 1
    Next

End Sub
```

When enumerating through the parameter array, the enumerator must be a variant so it is a good idea to check this. Alternatively, you can loop through the array by checking the upper bound:

```
For iIndex = 0 To UBound(vArguments)
      Debug.Print TypeName(vArguments(iIndex))
Next
```

Option Compare Text

If you always want to compare strings without case sensitivity, use `Option Compare Text` at the beginning of a code module. All text comparisons in that module will then be case insensitive.

Keyboard Shortcuts

Here are some of the most useful keyboard shortcuts that can save time as you code:

❑ *Ctrl+Spacebar* – Out of all shortcuts, this is the most important. When you type the first few letters of a variable or function name and hit *Ctrl+Spacebar*, either the word will automatically be completed for you or a drop-down list will appear if there are multiple choices that match what you have typed.

❑ *Shift+F2* – When the cursor is on a variable and you press *Shift +F2*, you will be taken to the declaration of that variable. When the cursor is on a function or subroutine name, *Shift+F2* will take you to the declaration of the function or sub.

❑ *Ctrl+Shift+F2* – If you press *Shift+F2* to go to a declaration, pressing *Ctrl+Shift+F2* will take you back to where you originally pressed *Shift+F2*.

❑ *F9* – Inserts or removes a breakpoint.

❑ *F5* – Starts your program.

❑ *Ctrl+F5* – Starts your program with a full compile. If you start with a full compile, any compile errors will be brought to your attention before the program can start.

❑ *Ctrl+Break* – Puts you in break mode so you can step through code or change existing code.

❑ *F8* – Single-steps through code in break mode.

❑ *Shift+F8* – Runs a function or sub routine without stepping into the routine.

❑ *Ctrl+F8* – Executes all code up to where your cursor is located.

❑ *Ctrl+F9* – Moves the next executable line to where your cursor is positioned.

❑ *Ctrl+L* – Brings up the call stack.

❑ *Ctrl+I* – Displays the tooltip with a variable's declaration or a function's signature.

❑ *F4* – Displays the Properties window.

❑ *Ctrl+G* – Displays the Immediate window.

❑ *F2* – Displays the Object Browser.

❑ *Ctrl+R* – Displays the Project Explorer window.

❏   *Ctrl+C* – Copies the selected text or control to the clipboard.

❏   *Ctrl+V* – Pastes the item in the clipboard.

❏   *Ctrl+X* – Cuts the selected text or control to the clipboard.

❏   *Ctrl+Z* – Undoes your last action.

❏   *Ctrl+F* – Displays the Find dialog box.

❏   *F3* – Finds the next occurrence of the last item you did a find for.

❏   *Ctrl+H* – Displays the Find and Replace dialog box.

❏   *Ctrl+A* – Selects all text in the code page.

p2p.wrox.com

The programmer's resource centre

ASP Today

wrox.com

wroxdirect

Visual Studio Installer

Microsoft Windows Installer

The release of Microsoft Windows 2000 introduced the programming world to a completely new paradigm for application deployment. In previous versions of Microsoft Windows, developers took great risks in deploying new applications. The overwhelming reality of a newly deployed application that could break another application on the same machine created so much havoc that programmers affectionately referred to the problem as "DLL Hell". With Windows 2000, Microsoft offered a new technology called Microsoft Windows Installer, which while not eliminating "DLL Hell" for Visual Basic applications, did reduce the risk of encountering it. This appendix will explain the basic concepts in creating reliable installation files using Windows Installer.

"DLL Hell" refers to the problem where installing different versions of the same component on the same machine would break one or more of the applications using the component. Sometimes components had bugs that the application treated as a feature. Then, when the bug was fixed, the applications relying on the older version of the component would break. In an attempt to keep applications from breaking, programmers attempted to maintain binary compatibility within the supporting components. However, maintaining backwards compatibility in applications is extremely difficult in this ever-changing world. Often business requirements mean making changes to components that can break backwards compatibility.

Traditionally Visual Basic programmers relied on the "Package & Deployment Wizard" to create installation files (contrary to the name, the wizard did not deploy the software). The "Package & Deployment Wizard" would analyze the Visual Basic Project to identify what supporting files or components the application used. These components were then stored in a compressed file along with the application files. Finally, the wizard would create a Setup.exe file that the user could run. The setup file would walk the user through installing the application on their local machine. Although the "Package & Deployment Wizard" simplified the process of deploying the application, the wizard was never able to handle the problem of "DLL Hell".

Microsoft Windows Installer reduces the risk associated with deploying applications. The Installer increases deployment options for the system administrator and simplifies the installation process for the end-user. Windows Installer is an application that manages installing, maintaining, and removing programs and is responsible for maintaining the integrity of the applications installed on the computer. Microsoft Windows Installer reads database files called packages, which contain all the information about the program being deployed. These packages identify what version of components the application needs, where the components can be found, registry settings, data files, and so on. Each time an application runs, the installer verifies that the application has all the required parts. If any part of the application is incorrect or missing, the installer will repair the problem so that the application can continue to work.

The following are a few of the many features introduced with Windows Installer:

❑ Simplified installation so users are required to make fewer decisions when installing applications.

❑ Components can be installed when needed or "on-demand".

❑ The installer repairs problems automatically.

❑ Applications can be deployed remotely to a specific user, group of users, machine, or group of machines.

❑ Applications can be deployed on computers without needing Administrative access.

❑ Components can be isolated to a specific application.

To find more information on the benefits of using Windows Installer and the strategies to create packages, refer to the Microsoft web site. Perform a search with the keywords "Windows Installer Benefits" for additional information.

Before applications can take advantage of the benefits Windows Installer has to offer, they must be bundled into Installer Packages. There are many products available on the market that can create the installer packages. Installer, InstallShield, and Wise are a few of the third-party products available in the market that can support the Microsoft Installer file format. Visual Studio Installer is a free Microsoft plug-in that can be used to create the packages.

The purpose of this appendix is to provide the information required to get developers up and running with Visual Studio Installer as quickly as possible. This appendix does not present an exhaustive study on the Windows Installer or Visual Studio Installer. The appendix is meant to provide an introduction on how to package applications using Windows Installer.

In this appendix we will learn:

❑ How to install Windows Installer and Visual Studio Installer

❑ How to create Installer Packages

❑ How to deploy COM Components within Installer Packages

❑ How to deploy COM Components within Merge Modules

❑ How to create an Update Package

❑ How to use Orca Editor

Installing Visual Studio Installer

Visual Studio Installer is a plug-in module that creates Microsoft Installer Packages. The Visual Studio Installer plug-in is part of the Software Development Kit (SDK). Visual Studio Installer can be downloaded free of charge from Microsoft's web site if you do not have the SDK. To find the download for Visual Studio Installer, from the Microsoft Home Page type in the phrase "Download Visual Studio Installer" in the search textbox. After locating and downloading the plug-in, the files will need to be extracted into a temporary folder. When the files have been extracted into a folder, run the `Setup.exe` application to install Visual Studio Installer. The screens are very straightforward and include the typical license agreement.

Installing the Installer Engine

The Installer Engine controls installation, maintenance, and rollback of Windows Installer Packages. Without the Installer Engine, the packages are useless. The Installer Engine comes preloaded on Windows 2000, XP, and .NET, and is available for installation on Windows 95, 98, and ME platforms.

The redistributable is the application that installs the installer engine. There are two flavors of the redistributable: `InstMsiA.exe` (ANSI version) and `InstMsiW.exe` (Unicode version). The ANSI version is available for Windows 9x and ME platforms and the Unicode version is available for Windows 2000 and later. If you have installed Visual Studio Installer, then the redistributable can be found in the folder "`%ProgramFiles%\Microsoft Visual Studio\Common\Tools\VSInst\BuildRes`". For the latest version of the redistributable, search the Microsoft web site using the text Windows Installer Redistributable.

A message stating that the service already exists will be displayed if the Installer Engine was preloaded on your machine. Otherwise, if the correct version is installed then a progress form will display until the installation is complete. When the Installer Engine has been installed successfully, you will need to reboot the computer.

Creating an Installer Package

An Installer Project contains the instructions to create an Installer Package. The Installer Package is a database that contains both the instructions and files required for the application to work. The instructions are used by the Installer Engine to install, maintain, and rollback the application. The components in the package are the files and settings that define the application. In this section, we will create a simple Installer Project, and learn about the Visual Studio Installer Integrated Development Environment (IDE).

Creating a Visual Studio Installer Project

1. In Visual Studio Installer, create a new project.

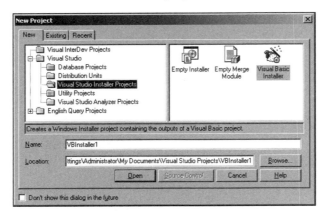

2. Select the Visual Basic Installer menu option.

3. Select a separate folder location from the one where the Visual Basic code is located.

> By default, the Package & Deployment Wizard stores the instruction files in the same folder as the application code. In Visual Studio, the Installer Project is a program in and of itself. It is best to keep the installer code separate from the application code. The installer code should be managed the same as any other programming language code base.

4. Create a name for the installer package and click on the Open button.

5. In the Visual Studio Installer Setup Wizard, click on the Browse button, and navigate to the folder where the Visual Basic Project is located.

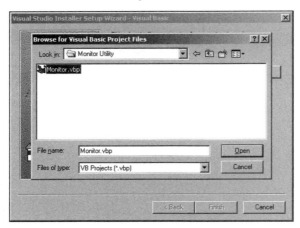

6. Select the Visual Basic Project file. Check the option Create Installer and click on the Finish button.

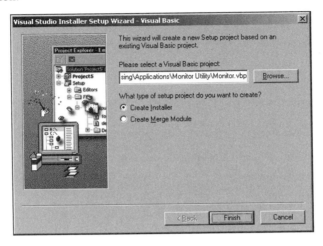

The Visual Studio IDE

The Visual Studio Integrated Development Environment (IDE) provides a centralized location to access the project features. The IDE consists of seven windows: Project Explorer, Properties, Task List, File System, User Interface, Registry, and Associations. These windows enable the developer to configure common use properties for the Installer Project.

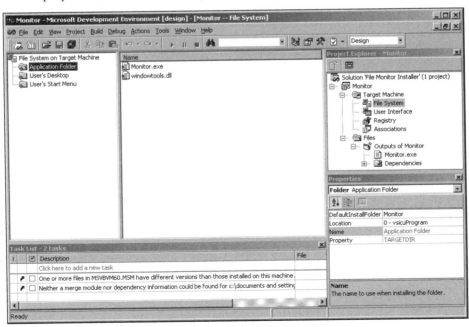

The following is a list of the windows in the IDE and what they do:

❑ The Project Explorer window displays the files used by the application that will be included in the installer package. In addition, the explorer window provides access to the target machine layout windows (File System, User Interface, Registry, and Associations). The layout windows can be opened through the Project Explorer window by double-clicking on the desired layout window.

❑ The File System window identifies where the Visual Basic Project files will be installed.

❑ The User Interface window allows the developer to identify which pre-defined screens to show the user.

❑ The Registry window identifies the keys and values to install on the target computer.

❑ The Associations window identifies the shared or registered file settings to deploy.

❑ The Properties window displays the options for the selected component. In Windows Installer, a component is an object in the package. The component could be a file, a registry key, a dialog, or any other item in the project.

❑ The Task List window contains any problems that may exist in the project are displayed in the. The Task List shows informational errors, warnings, and severe errors.

Configuring the Visual Studio Installer Project

In a perfect world, the computer would create the installer project with all of the objects and settings required for the application. Unfortunately, as applications have grown more complicated, so too has the process of deploying applications. Today programmers need to plan how to package the application for their particular deployment scenario. This section identifies how to initialize the project and modify the components in the project to meet various application deployment requirements.

The project properties form describes the package. Project properties identify how to build the project. Support information displayed to the user when an error occurs is defined in the project properties. The project properties form includes information on build options, installation options, product information, support information, file summary, merge modules folders, and launch conditions.

To access the project properties select Project from the menu bar and click on the last item in the menu. By default, the Properties... option will begin with the Visual Basic Application Title. For example, in the image below the option to select is titled "Monitor Properties..." Do not confuse the project properties form with the component properties window referred to previously.

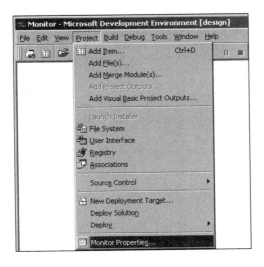

Build Options

The Build tab controls the destination and name of the installer package, and identifies how to build the package. The package name is recorded in the Output file name text box. The folder where the package will be stored is defined in the Output folder text box. Files that are part of the installer project can be compiled into the package itself, into a cabinet file, or they can be left separate from the installer file.

The options in the Build tab apply to a specific configuration. All other tabs apply to all configurations. Windows Installer is preloaded with two configurations: Debug and Release. By default, the Debug and Release build settings are initialized with the same values. Used correctly, configurations ensure that production packages are not accidentally replaced with test packages, as they can be stored in a different folder to the debug packages. Another useful option is to build debug packages without any compression. This saves time as the compression option can slow down the compilation of the project.

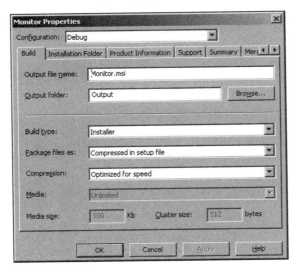

Installation Folder

The File System window has a folder titled **Application Folder**. The **Installation Folder** tab defines the location of the application folder on the target machine. To set the application folder, select the desired folder path in the **Location** drop down box. Supply a name in the **Name** text box. The default application folder path is the Program Files folder. The folder name is initialized to the Visual Basic Project title. Visual Studio Installer restricts deploying the application to one of the pre-defined location folders.

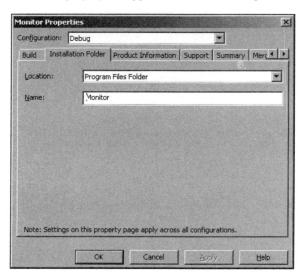

Product Information

Product Information identifies the specific package to deploy. Product Information includes the name, the version, codes, and signatures. The install package uses the product name for the title and is the caption displayed for the specific package in Add/Remove Programs. Visual Studio defaults the product name to the Visual Basic Project Title. Once installed, the version of the install package can be viewed with the support information. Finally, the package is assigned two GUIDs: a Produce Code and an Upgrade Code. These codes uniquely identify the package to the operating system. Changing these values can be compared to breaking binary compatibility in Visual Basic.

Support

The **Support** tab provides a location to record whom to contact should an error occur during the install or rollback of the installation package. The company name, support telephone number, and a web URL provide the user with the contact information needed to solve any installation problems. This information can be accessed from **Add/Remove Programs** in the **Control Panel** once the package has been installed on the target machine.

Summary

The Summary tab contains the properties for the package file when viewed from the file explorer. The Title, Subject, Author, Keywords, and a brief description of the package provide general information about the package to the user. This information can be viewed from the file explorer by right-clicking on the installer package with the right mouse button, selecting Properties, and the Summary tab.

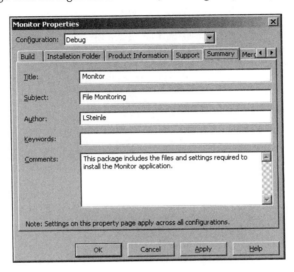

Merge Module Search Path

When compiling the application, supporting components may require complex installation rules. Merge modules provide a way to encapsulate the complexity of deploying ActiveX components. Whenever possible Visual Studio Installer will substitute merge modules in place of the ActiveX component. We will learn more about merge modules in the section *Creating a Visual Studio Merge Module Project*.

Launch Condition

Finally, launch conditions identify when an application can and cannot be installed. If any launch condition fails, the Installer Engine discontinues the installation and notifies the user of the specific problem via the error message defined with the condition. For example, a package could be created with a launch condition requiring MDAC 2.5 or greater. If the package were installed on a computer with MDAC 2.1 an error would be raised informing the user to upgrade to MDAC 2.5 before installing the application.

Organizing Component Properties

Once the package properties have been defined, review the component properties. Verify that the required components exist in the package, and check the properties for each component. In this section, we will analyze the issues surrounding deploying files, registry keys, and review screen options for the user interface.

Modifying the File System

Often programmers will build an installation package in Visual Studio expecting the wizard to understand they need initialization files, text files, help files, and other non-referenced files. Non-referenced files are the components that are linked to using commands like the `CreateObject` command. When the wizard fails to import the initialization files people wonder, "Why should I continue to use Visual Studio Installer? It doesn't do anything more than the already familiar Package & Deployment Wizard!" This analysis could not be further from the truth. Keep in mind that even in Package & Deployment Wizard these "missing files" must be added to the package. The difference is that Visual Studio Installer gives the programmer more control over how these files should be maintained once installed. However, it is true that the additional control given to the developer results in the fact that the programmer must spend more time planning how to deploy the application.

In the File System window, we can define the target install folder for each component. To add a new folder from the menu bar select "**Actions**," and click on "**Add Special Folder**" or "**Add Folder**". Files can be moved from one folder to another by dragging the file over the desired folder and dropping the file into the folder. Press the *F2* key to change the name of a file. Once the files are in the desired destination folders we are ready to record how the files should be maintained.

As most properties are self-explanatory we will only cover the properties that may generate problems or cause confusion. Component properties control how the Installer Engine will install, maintain, and remove the files from the target computer. With appropriate planning these properties can make life much easier for the developer.

The **ComponentID** is the globally unique identifier (GUID) for the file in the project. Each file has a `ComponentID`. The `ComponentID` property should remain unchanged. The Wizard creates a valid property for the files and there is no need to modify the default value. Whenever a file is manually added to the project, Visual Studio automatically generates a new GUID for the added file.

The **Register** property tells the Installer Engine how to install ActiveX Components. Never use the value `vsifrFont` for the register property. The `vsifrFont` value is reserved for True-Type Font components. By default, any ActiveX component added to the project will be initialized to **vsifrSelfReg**; all other file types are initialized to **vsifrNone**.

The **Vital** property can be a source of contention for new users of Visual Studio Installer. This has to be the most confusing property in Visual Studio Installer. Reading the documentation leads one to believe that if a file is marked as vital, and the package cannot install the file, then the Installer Engine cancels installation. In reality, identifying if a project can be installed because of a file is just part of the functionality behind the vital command. The gotcha with this property is that the file can never change. If the file is modified by the program, manually or automatically, the Installer Engine will, first, notify the operating system to stop executing the application. It will then replace the file with the version from the installer package, and notify the operating system to continue running the application. By design, the `Vital` property defaults to `True`.

Initializing the Registry

In the Registry window we define the key structure and add the parameters to each key. By default keys remain on the computer when the application is removed. Set the property `DeleteOnUninstall` to `True` to remove the keys when the application is removed from the registry. Set the `AlwaysCreate` property to `True` if the key should be created even if there are no parameters in the key. If the `AlwaysCreate` property is set to `False` and there are no parameters in the key or if the parameters have no value, then the key will not be installed.

Guiding the User through the Install Process

Each package can contain wizard dialogs to step the user through the installation process. In addition, some of the screens impact the package's behavior. For example, the "Welcome" dialog gives the user the option to repair or remove the application if the package is run more than once on the same computer. Unlike the behavior in "Package & Deployment Wizard", applications can only be installed on the same machine once. This eliminates the troublesome bug where extra occurrences of the application remained in Add/Remove Programs until the computer was rebuilt.

To add a new dialog to the install package select the Action option from the menu bar or click on the right mouse button in the User Interface window, and select Add Dialog... To remove a dialog from the package, click on the desired dialog and press the Delete button. Each dialog can be customized with a bitmap image in the background.

Compiling the Installer Project

Visual Studio Installer provides two options to create the installer package: Build and Rebuild. The Build option takes the instructions in the project at face value and creates the package with the defined instructions. The Rebuild option analyzes each component to verify that the component is the correct version, then checks to see if the file is needed at all, and looks for any missing support components. Once the project components have been verified, then the rebuild option creates the installer package. Generally, you will want to use the Build option as Rebuild resets some of the component properties back to the default values before creating the package.

Visual Studio Installer saves the compiled project into the folder identified in the project property's Build tab. The file that needs to be executed to install the application has the extension `.msi`. The `.msi` extension stands for Microsoft Installer. The file is not an actual executable but instead is a database file. The `msi` extension was assigned to the Installer Engine when the redistributable was installed on the computer.

Using the right-mouse button click on the `msi` file to view the three options specific to the package: Install, Repair, and Uninstall. Initially the repair and uninstall options are disabled. After the application has been installed on the target computer, the options will be enabled.

Deploying COM Components

In the previous section, we learned how to create an installer project. We learned that the wizard automatically identifies early-bound ActiveX Components used by our application and adds the components to the project. By default, the wizard deploys the components with the same method used by the Package & Deployment Wizard. Although there may be times when the traditional method must be implemented, most of the time it will create severe problems for both pre-existing software on the target machine and software in the installer package. In this section, we will learn how to correctly initialize and deploy ActiveX Components.

> **Failure to correctly deploy an ActiveX Component could break any application installed on the target computer. It is imperative to spend an appropriate amount of time and attention to the detail and planning of the installation of ActiveX Components. The information contained in this section will simplify the process of deploying ActiveX Components within Microsoft Installer Packages without sacrificing the reliability intended by Windows Installer.**

Registering the Component

Before the ActiveX Components may be used by the calling application, they must first be registered on the target machine. Visual Studio Installer provides two methods to register the components: the default option self-registration, and association. Each method has advantages and disadvantages that must be understood before deploying the application. Otherwise, the installation may end up breaking existing applications or vice versa.

Self-registration

Traditionally ActiveX Components are copied to the target computer, and registered on the computer using `RegSvr32.exe`. The Package & Deployment Wizard performed these steps automatically for the user. There are several potential problems with deploying components using self-registration. First, how does the operating system know when it is safe to remove the component from the computer? Shared components are especially vulnerable. In the past it was up to the user to decide when to remove shared components but the complicated error message confused and scared many users. To simplify the process of removing applications, Windows Installer does not give the user the choice to keep or remove shared components. Second, self-registration with shared components created the problem known as "DLL Hell". Why then, does Visual Studio Installer continue to support self-registration? In two words: backwards compatibility.

Currently, it would appear that Visual Studio Installer supports late binding to a Visual Basic ActiveX DLL component only when deployed using self-registration. However, Microsoft recommends that self-registration be used sparingly if not at all. Self-registration is the default setting for ActiveX Components in the Visual Studio Installer project. Once again, the default settings cannot be modified.

In the event that a component requires self-registration, rest assured that with a little effort it can be deployed safely. Whenever deploying a component with self-registration, set the `Register` property to `1-vsifrSelfReg` and set the `DoNotUninstall` property to `True`. When the package is removed from the computer, any other applications that rely on the component will continue to work. If the `DoNotUninstall` property is set to `False`, then the component is unregistered and removed from the computer. Any applications relying on the component will cease to work. Detecting and correcting unregistered components remains one of the few problems that the Installer Engine cannot handle. In the event that an application should cease to work due to missing components, open Add/Remove Programs, click on the broken application, and select the repair option.

Association

Whenever possible, ActiveX components should be registered using associations. Each time a component is installed on the target computer, if it is registered using association, the Installer Engine increments a counter identifying how many applications use the component. When the component is removed, the file and registration details remain until there are no applications using the component. If the component should somehow be removed or unregistered, the Installer Engine can detect and correct the problem automatically. Unfortunately, in the case of ActiveX DLLs, associations appear to work only with early-bound components. However, you can get the best of both worlds by deploying the component using both associations and self-registration.

To register a component using associations:

1. Disable the self-registration option by setting the `Register` property to `0-None`.

2. Find the Class ID and Type Library ID for each object in the component.

3. Assign the IDs to the component.

Find the Class ID and Type Library ID

The Class ID is a GUID for the ActiveX Component. The Type Library ID is a GUID to the object's methods and properties. Visual Basic ActiveX Components include a single type library for all objects in the compiled component. Other languages, such as C++, generally have a separate type library file for each object in the component. All of the GUIDs for components and applications are recorded in the registry editor under HKEY_CLASSES_ROOT. The component can be found in the registry by searching for the compile name.

1. Select Start from the Windows Toolbar, and click on Run...

2. Type RegEdit.exe and press the *Enter* key.

3. Click on the *HKEY_CLASSES_ROOT* key.

4. Press *Ctrl + F* and type in the file name for the ActiveX component.

5. When the component is located in the registry, record the Class ID. In the example below the Visual Basic ActiveX Component WindowTools.dll was found in the registry. The Class ID for the component is the parent folder to InprocServer32. The Class ID for WindowTools.dll is {753D8429-5FA4-4B45-BEA5-321D9A650AEE}.

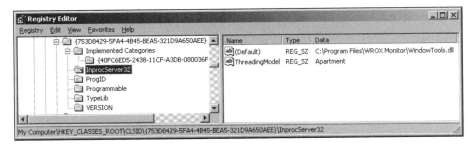

6. Next, record the Type Library ID. The Type Library ID can be found in the TypeLib folder.

7. Press *F3* to find the next object's Class ID in the ActiveX Component. Each object in the component will have its own Class ID. All objects in the component will share the same Type Library ID so this value only needs to be recorded once.

> Whenever a Visual Studio Project is compiled using the Rebuild option, late-bound components in the project reset to the default registry value `vsifrSelfReg`. The associations are disconnected from the component. To keep from losing the relationship between the GUIDs and the component, record the ProgID for each Class ID. The ProgID can then be stored in the description field for the Class ID. Don't forget to record the component name in the description field for the Type Library as well. If the link between the component and the GUID is severed then the description will make it much easier to rebuild the association from the GUID back to the parent component.

Assign the Class IDs and Type Library ID

1. Open the Associations window.

2. For each Class ID recorded in the previous steps:

a. Select Actions from the menu bar and click on Add COM Object.

b. Type in the Class ID.

c. In the description field for the component record the ProgID.

d. Set the Context property to the appropriate value based on the ActiveX Component:

Component Type	Context Property Value
ActiveX Control	vsiccInprocServer32
ActiveX DLL	vsiccInprocServer32
ActiveX EXE	vsiccLocalServer32

e. Select the Component property and click on the Browse button.

f. Click on the The following component: option and select the ActiveX component.

g. Click on the OK button.

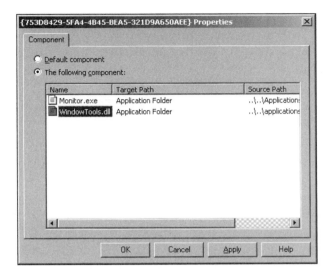

3. Select **Actions** from the menu bar and click on **Add Type Library**.

4. Type in the Type Library ID recorded in the previous steps.

5. In the description field for the Library ID record the name of the component.

6. Select the `Component` property and click on the **Browse** button.

7. Click on the **The following component:** option and select the ActiveX component.

8. Click on the **OK** button.

Isolation

An ActiveX component is isolated if the component is restricted to run for one and only one executable. Isolation allows different versions of the same component to run at the same time for different applications on the same machine without breaking any of the applications. Side-by-side deployment refers to multiple versions of components that can run simultaneously. Each application will use its own isolated component. An application that makes use of isolated components will continue to work correctly even if another application installed on the same computer has a newer version of the component that breaks binary compatibility. In essence, isolation solves the "DLL Hell" problems.

To isolate a component to an application two settings must be initialized:

1. The component must be shared. To share the component set the **Shared** property to `True`.

2. The component must be isolated to the calling application. A component may be isolated only to one executable in the package. To isolate the component select the **IsolateTo** property for the component.

3. Click on the Browse button, then click on the The following component option.

4. Select the calling application then click on the OK button to save the selection.

Before the Install Engine copies and registers any components onto the target machine, it checks to see if any components are isolated to the application. Those components that are isolated, regardless of the target folder, are copied into the application folder. Next, the Install Engine creates an empty text file with the name of the executable and the extension .local. In our example, we are packaging the application, Monitor.exe. The Install Engine will create an empty text file called Monitor.exe.local. The .local extension informs the operating system to search in the application folder for any components before looking in the folder's recorded in the system path.

Creating a Merge Module Package

As you can see, a great deal of planning must go into deploying ActiveX Components. In the event that a component will be deployed for more than one application, it would be nice to hide that complexity. Each time an application is packaged, there is the risk that the component will be deployed with invalid settings increasing the risk that when the bad package is removed from the target computer, your application will crash as well! To resolve these and many other issues, Microsoft created the Merge Module.

While installer packages are deployed for users, merge modules are deployed solely for use by applications. Whenever an installer package is created with an ActiveX Component, Visual Studio Installer searches for merge modules to use in place of the component. If a merge module can be found, then the instructions and files are imported into the installer package when the project is compiled.

Merge modules make it possible for new Visual Studio Installer developer's to easily create and deploy complicated applications. They reduce the risk of adding error(s) into a package while "recreating the wheel". Merge modules are the recommended means to deploy ActiveX Components. In this section, we will learn how to create a merge module and use the merge module in our own installer packages.

Creating a Visual Studio Merge Module Project

With a few minor differences the steps for deploying a merge module are the same as those for deploying a Visual Basic Application:

1. We begin by opening Visual Studio and creating a new project.

2. Select the Visual Basic Installer menu option.

3. Record the location to save the Installer Project. Again, select a separate folder from the one where the Visual Basic code is located.

4. Create a name for the installer package and click on the Open button.

5. In the Visual Studio Installer Setup Wizard, click on the Browse button, and navigate to the folder where the Visual Basic Project is located.

6. Select the Visual Basic Project file for the ActiveX Component and click on the **Open** button.

7. Check the **Create Merge Module** option and click on the **Finish** button.

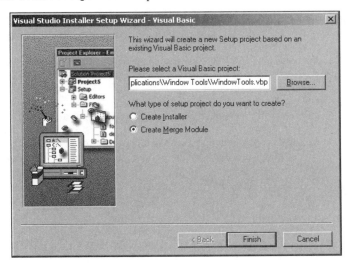

8. Configure the project properties.

9. Configure the component properties. Add any files required for the ActiveX component to function, and provide default registry settings. Add GUIDs for the type library and for all of the objects in the component into the Association Window. The User Interface window can be ignored as all of the forms are disabled when the project is compiled.

10. After configuring the project and its components, build the package.

Visual Studio Installer compiles the Merge Module Project into the folder defined in the project property's Build tab. The merge module file includes the extension .msm. Unlike the installer package, the merge module package cannot be installed by executing the file. Instead, the merge module must be "consumed" into the installer package.

Deploying and Consuming a Merge Module Package

Applications are designed, coded, tested, and implemented. In most development environments, the programs have to endure a design review and code review; they have to be promoted into testing, approved for production, and deployed into the production environment. Although merge modules are designed for programmers instead of end-users, the merge module should go through the same processes.

A change in audience does not create a change in process. As merge modules and the components inside them will be used by multiple applications, it is even more important to spend time managing the code. Remember, a single bug coded into a shared component can impact many applications. Be sure to get it right the first time! To clarify, the code referred to is both the code required to build the ActiveX component and the code to package the component.

When deploying the merge module for testing or production, define an appropriate location to store the merge module. A specific test folder and production folder should serve as a repository for all of the merge modules supported by the company. The folders provide a single place to go to load the correct version of the components.

As stated earlier, merge modules are used by installer projects. When an ActiveX component is detected in the Visual Basic Project, the Installer Project searches for the component's merge module. The location for the project to look for merge modules is defined in the **Merge Module Search Path** tab of the project properties. By default, Visual Studio Installer searches for merge modules in the folder `%ProgramFiles%\Microsoft Visual Studio\Common\Tools\VSInst\BuildRes`. Merge modules loaded into a Visual Studio Installer project are "consumed" by the project.

To consume merge modules within the Visual Studio Installer Project, add a path to the folder where the merge modules have been deployed. After adding the merge module path(s), save the changes by clicking on the **OK** button in the project properties. At this point Visual Studio Installer examines the project in an attempt to find merge modules for the ActiveX Components in the project.

Isolating a Merge Module Package

Previously we discussed the benefits of isolating ActiveX Components. Visual Studio Installer adds merge modules without isolating them. The steps to isolate a merge module are the same as those for isolating an ActiveX Component. The only catch is that when the merge module was created, every file in the merge module had to be defined as a `SharedLegacyFile`. If a single file has `False` for the value in the `SharedLegacyFile` then the merge module cannot be isolated.

To isolate a merge module:

1. Find the module in the dependencies list in the Project Explorer window.

2. Select the `IsolateTo` property and click on the **Browse** button.

3. Click on the **The following component** option and select the application to isolate the merge module to.

4. Click on the **OK** button.

Testing and Deploying Installer Packages

There are three steps to deploying applications:

1. Package the application and the components used by the application.

2. Test the deployment of the package created in Step 2.

3. Install the application manually or automatically using a deployment tool like Active Directory or SMS.

Testing Installer Packages and Merge Modules

Every package should be thoroughly tested before deploying for installation onto production machines. Create test scripts for each merge module and installer package. This includes thoroughly testing the installation, maintenance, and removal of the package.

Ensure that each package deploys the files to the correct folder. Verify that the required registry keys are created and initialized with the correct information. Simplify the installation for the end-users by using as few user interfaces as possible. Don't use an interface simply because it is available. There should be a valid business reason for displaying the interface to the user.

Identify that your application will continue to work if another application that uses the same merge modules is removed from the computer. If a component is removed or unregistered, can the Installer Engine repair the problem? If the application is removed from the computer, will other applications that use the same merge modules continue to work?

Spend the time fixing the problems before deploying the package. The more problems resolved up front, the less frustration for the users, and the system administrators. Remember, an application packaged with the incorrect settings can create severe problems for other programs in production!

Deploying Installer Packages

After the install packages are created, the only task that remains is to install the software on the target machines. Software can be installed manually, of course, by executing the Windows Installer (.msi) file. Often software needs to be installed on hundreds of machines that are often in different buildings, towns, states, or even countries. In order to save on the time to travel to each site, sit at each computer, and manually install the software, there are tools available to automate the process. Generally, these automation tools take advantage of existing Intranet and Internet connections to distribute the software. The more commonly used automated deployment utilities include: Active Directory Groups, NetSupport, SMS, Track-It! Deploy, and Update Expert.

Advanced Packaging Concepts

Although Visual Studio Installer offers many benefits over the Package & Deployment Wizard, it contains a few frustrating restrictions. The Software Development Kit (SDK) includes additional tools designed specifically for managing Windows Installer Packages. In this section, we learn how to use the Orca Editor, one of the many useful tools from the SDK, to overcome some of the limitations in Visual Studio Installer.

Orca Editor

Orca Editor is an application that allows developers to view the inner workings of an Installer or Merge Module Package. The editor displays the various tables, parameters, and values in the package. Each Installer Package consists of at least 40 tables. To learn more, search the Microsoft web site using the keywords "Orca Editor".

Before Orca Editor can be installed, the Software Development Kit must be installed, which is available online from Microsoft's web site. Use the keyword "Orca Editor SDK" to find the correct path. Most articles referring to the Orca Editor provide a link to the site where the editor can be downloaded. I would recommend using the SDK CD provided with the MSDN License as the entire SDK must be downloaded and installed to get access to Orca Editor. Once the SDK is installed, search for the file Orca.msi. It is advisable to use typical options when installing the editor.

Creating a Package with a Custom Application Path

Visual Studio Installer does not allow program paths that include special characters such as the backslash key but the process of updating an installer package to use a custom path is extremely simple with Orca Editor.

1. From Orca Editor, select File, and Open.

2. Navigate to the installer package to update and click on the Open button.

3. Select the table CustomAction.

4. Search the Action column for the value DIR_CA_TARGETDIR.

5. Edit the Target column on the same row by double clicking on the Target cell.

6. Modify the path to reflect the desired destination path and press *Enter*.

7. Select File from the menu bar and click on Save to save the changes.

In the example below, the target installation path has been changed from C:\Program Files\Monitor to C:\Program Files\WROX\Monitor.

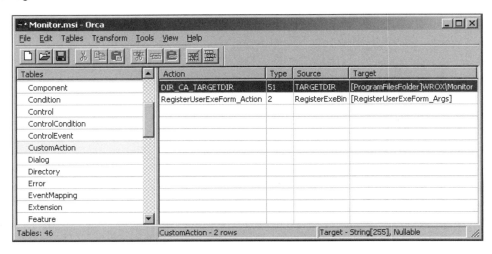

Creating Per-Machine Install Packages

By default, all Windows Installer packages created by Visual Studio Installer are per-user installs. The per-user install can be changed to a per-machine installs by using a command line option when running `MSIEXEC.exe`. However, this adds complexity to the install and we want to keep the install process as simple as possible for the user. The package can be modified using Orca Editor to support a per-machine install.

1. From Orca Editor, select File, and Open.

2. Navigate to the installer package to update and click on the Open button.

3. Select the Property table.

4. Select Tables from the menu bar and click on Add Row.

5. Select the Property row and type in the value ALLUSERS. The property is case-sensitive so be sure to type in upper case.

6. Select the Value row and type in one of the following values:

Value	Description of Action
0	Default. Per-user install: Installs the application into the user's profile that is currently logged into the computer. If a value of 0 is used then the ALLUSERS property may be omitted from the package.
1	Per-machine install: Installs the application into the All Users profile. Installs the application on a per-machine basis if the user has permissions. If the user does not have permissions to run a per-machine install, the package fails.
2	Per-machine default, per-user backup: The package will install on a per-machine basis if the user has permissions. If the user does not have adequate permissions, the package will install on a per-user basis.

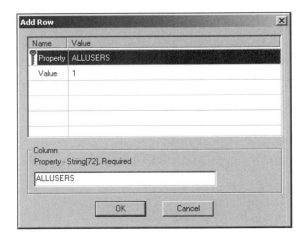

7. Click on the OK button to add the row.

8. Select File from the menu bar and click on Save to save the changes.

Conclusion

Visual Studio Installer provides Visual Basic programmers with the power and flexibility to ensure that their applications will not crash when another program is installed. The technology allows the developer to maintain control of the deployed application. For the user, the install packages are much easier to use and less confusing than previous install programs and, with the aid of modern deployment tools, system administrators can save time installing the applications onto multiple users machine.

With the experience gained through this appendix, applications can be deployed without the need to worry about "DLL Hell". Microsoft Windows Installer has finally simplified life for the developers entrusted with the responsibility to maintain applications. With the correct settings, the technology in Windows Installer makes the deployment process simple and reliable.

p2p.wrox.com

The programmer's resource centre

ASP Today

wrox.com

wrox

wroxdirect

Deployment Techniques – Wise Installation System

The installation program is the first interaction that your customer has with your software, so it is important that you make a good first impression. This appendix contains an overview of the **Wise Installation System – Professional Edition 9.02**, which can be used as an alternative to the Visual Studio Package and Deployment Wizard. The Wise Installation System tool creates Windows-based installations using a proprietary language call **WiseScript**, and you can choose to write purely in this or you can use the **Installation Expert**, which is a graphical user interface that generates WiseScript automatically.

Wise is a popular choice among developers as it is an intuitive installation tool that hasn't compromised on power and flexibility for all types of installations. Some of its major advantages over competitive installation packages are the options it offers to improve the quality and overall professionalism of the installation. Examples of this include the ease of creating dialog boxes, billboards, or web-based installations. It is even possible to create just one installation EXE that can intelligently install the correct components based on the operation system being deployed to. Such functionality sets Wise apart from competitors in these areas.

An entire book could be written about all of the advanced features of the Wise Installation System, but this appendix will only discuss the most commonly used features and point out some of the additional functionality that is not included in the Visual Studio Package and Deployment Wizard.

Installation Expert

The Installation Expert is a graphical interface, similar to a wizard, which can be used to quickly and easily build an installation program without having any knowledge of WiseScript. We will create a simple installation for the `HelloWorld.exe` program using the Installation Expert, and then review the WiseScript using the **Script Editor**. (If you would like to build this, the code is in the download for this book).

Launch the Wise Installation System and select the **Empty Project** template. The following screenshot is the interface for the Installation Expert.

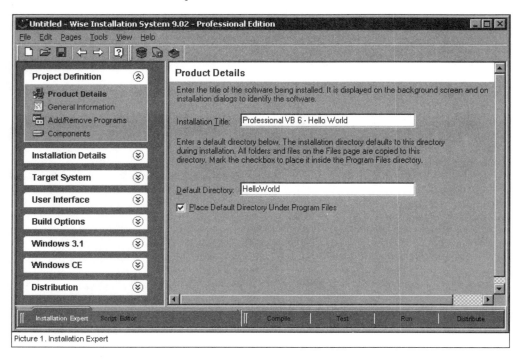

Picture 1. Installation Expert

The left-hand pane contains **Page Groups** and the **Pages** within each group. In the above screenshot, Project Definition is the Page Group and Product Details, General Information, Add/Remove Programs, and Components are the Pages. You can navigate through the Installation Expert as if it were a wizard by clicking on the left and right arrows on the toolbar or you can click directly on a page. Clicking on the Page Group name will expand or contract the pages in the group.

Project Definition Group

Product Details

The Product Details page allows you to specify the installation title that will appear in the background while your program is being installed. You also specify the default folder where your program files will be installed. Windows programs are typically installed in a folder under the Program Files folder.

In our HelloWorld example, the Product Details are as follows:

❑ Installation Title = Professional VB 6 – Hello World

❑ Default Directory = HelloWorld

General Information

The General Information page allows you to specify the file properties for the setup program executable. This is what the user sees when they right-click on the setup program executable and select Properties.

In our HelloWorld example, the General Information is as follows:

- ❏ Installation Version = Version 1.0
- ❏ Description = HelloWorld Sample Setup
- ❏ Copyright = Copyright 2002. All rights reserved.
- ❏ Company Name = Wrox Press

Add Remove Programs

The Add/Remove Programs page allows you to customize the appearance of your program entry in the Control Panel for Windows 2000/XP. The Add/Remove Programs control panel in Windows 2000/XP can display a hyperlink for support information which can display custom information to the user about your company and products. This feature is not implemented in the Visual Studio Package and Deployment Wizard.

In our HelloWorld example, the Add/Remove Programs information is as follows:

- ❏ Publisher = Wrox Press
- ❏ Contact Person = John Smith
- ❏ Phone Number = (111) 555-1212
- ❏ Online support URL = http://www.wrox.com
- ❏ Software Version = Version 1.0
- ❏ Help URL = http://www.wrox.com
- ❏ Comments = This is the HelloWorld program.

Components

The Components page allows you to separate files into components such as client components, server components, help files, reports, database scripts, and so on. A component screen is displayed during installation that allows the user to choose which components they want to install. This is useful when building distributed applications that need to be have components installed on a client and a server. This is a nice feature that is not implemented in the Visual Studio Package and Deployment Wizard.

In our HelloWorld example, there will be one component named "Reports".

Installation Details Group

Files

The Files page allows you to specify the executable, dll, ocx, and all other program files that make up your application. Do not specify required runtime files for Visual Basic. This is done in a later step. The following screenshot shows the Files screen:

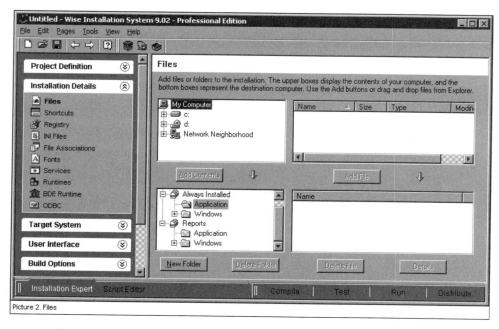

Picture 2. Files

The top two boxes display the folder and file name for the source files. The bottom two boxes display the destination for these files when they are installed on the client's computer. Under each component there are two folders, Application and Windows and under the Windows folder there are three folders, Fonts, System, and System32. You can also create your own folders for items such as help files or reports.

In the above screenshot, there are two top-level items, Always Installed and Reports. Reports is a top-level item because we defined it as a component. If the user chooses to install the Reports component, then the files in the Reports Application and Windows folder will be installed.

In our HelloWorld example, add the HelloWorld.exe file to the AlwaysInstalled Application folder. Add the Sample.rpt file to the Reports Application folder.

Shortcuts

The Shortcuts page allows you to customize the location for your program's shortcut on the user's Start menu or Desktop. You specify the program group name and then add the shortcuts contained in that group. After specifying the name for your shortcut and target file you can optionally specify command line arguments, the shortcut location, and also specify whether all users or only the local user has access to the shortcut.

In our HelloWorld example, the Shortcut properties are as follows:

❑   Default Folder Name = HelloWorld Group

❑   Shortcut Name = HelloWorld Program

To get to the Shortcut Details dialog box, you will need to click the Add button, then select the file and click OK. The following screenshot shows the Shortcut details screen:

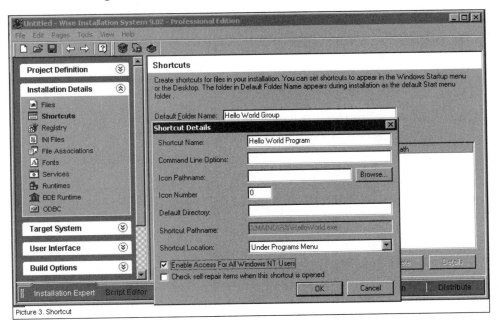

Picture 3. Shortcut

Registry

The Registry page allows the user to create, read, and delete registry keys. The Registry page is quite simple to use; you simple click on the parent key, HKEY_CLASSES_ROOT, HKEY_CURRENT_USER, HKEY_LOCAL_MACHINE, HKEY_USERS, or HKEY_CURRENT_CONFIG and specify the key you want to create or delete. The user must have permissions to the key that you are writing to or they will get an error and they're out of luck.

INI Files

The INI Files page allows you to create new INI files or read and update existing INI files. INI files are supposed to be a thing of the past because application settings are supposed to be stored in the registry, but if you're like me, you still use them to avoid permission errors.

File Associations

The File Associations page allows you to associate a three-character file extension to your application. For example, doc is the file association for Microsoft Word files. When the user opens a file with an extension of doc, Microsoft Word is launched. The File Associations page is a nice feature that is not supported in the Visual Studio Package and Deployment Wizard.

Fonts

The Fonts page allows you to install fonts that are used in your application. If a user opens a screen in your application where a label has an unrecognized font, they will get an error.

Services

The Services page is used to install a Windows Service. If you are writing Visual Basic programs you are probably not installing your own services.

Runtimes

The Runtimes page is the one page that will save you more time than any other page. If you've ever gone through the process of manually trying to figure out what runtime files are needed by Visual Basic, MDAC, or Crystal Reports, you will surely appreciate the time and effort saved by this one little page.

The Runtimes page allows you to check off the references and components included in your application. The install script will then reference an include file that contains the required runtime files for that component. The choices for components are:

- MDAC 2.7, MDAC 2.6 Service Pack 1, MDAC 2.6, MDAC 2.5 Service Pack 1 & 2, and MDAC 2.1.
- DAO 3.6, DAO 3.5, MSDE, MSJet 4.0 Service Packs 3 & 5, and Apollo Database Drivers.
- Visual Basic 6 Service Pack 4 & 5, Visual Basic 5, Visual Basic 4 WIN 32 & WIN16, Visual FoxPro (Service Packs 4 & 5), Visual FoxPro 7, and Visual C++ (MFC 4.2).
- DirectX, VShare, OLE2, and Win32s Support.
- Crystal Reports 8.5, Crystal Reports 8.0, and Crystal Reports 7.

I cannot stress the importance of this page. By simply checking the component you are using, you get all of the required runtime files along with the correct setting for which files need to be registered, where they are to be installed, and how to replace the files based on version number or date/time stamp. There is a Download Runtimes menu item that will go to the Wise web site and download the latest version of the required runtime files.

In our Hello World example, check the Visual Basic 6, Service Pack 5 component.

BDE Runtime

The BDE Runtime page allows you to include support for Complete BDE 16 and 32, Partial BDE 32, and BDE 16 and 32 Alias support.

ODBC

The ODBC page allows you to create and configure ODBC datasources. You can specify the Data Source Name, the driver name, data source attributes, and whether it should be a system DSN.

Target System Group

System Requirements

The System Requirements page allows the user to specify minimum values for the Windows version, Windows NT version, the screen resolution, the screen colors, and sound support. The Visual Basic 6 include file contains script to determine if the correct operating system is installed, so you can skip this unless you are specifically targeting an operating system.

System Search

The System Search page allows you to search for a file, an INI value, or a registry value. You have the option to search local drives or network drives, and a specific number of folder levels to search down in each drive. During installation, the installation program displays a status screen with the phrase "Checking for previously installed components..." This can be useful if you want to install into the same directory as the previous installation or are upgrading the application.

Installation Log

The Installation Log page allows you to include a log file that keeps track of all of the files copied and replaced during the installation. The installation log is a useful tool for debugging a failed installation.

In our HelloWorld example, select the option to create the installation log.

Uninstall Support

The Uninstall Support page allows you to include uninstall support for your application. This is a standard requirement for most applications and can be included in your installation by simply checking the option that you want to support uninstall.

In our HelloWorld example, select the option to support uninstall.

User Interface Group

Dialogs

The Dialogs page allows you to customize the screens for the wizard displayed during installation. A typical installation program guides the user through the install with a wizard. The choices for the dialog screens are:

❑ Welcome – Displays a friendly welcome message for the user.

❑ Read Me – Displays a readme file.

❑ Branding/Registration – Displays a page to enter the name and company of the user installing the application.

❑ Destination Directory – Allows the user to select a destination folder where the program files will be installed.

❑ Backup Replaced Files – Allows the user to choose whether or not to back-up any replaced files during the installation. It is a good idea to not include this page, but back-up the files by default. This way, if you incorrectly copied a wrong file, you can rollback the installation.

❑ Select Components – Allows the user to select the components that were defined in the Components page.

❑ Select Icon Group Name – Allows the user to change the default program manager group.

❑ Start Installation – Starts the copying of the files to the computer.

❑ Finished – Displays a finished message.

Each dialog screen can be customized by clicking on the Edit button. The Custom Dialog Editor is displayed, similar to the Visual Basic design environment. You can then customize the labels or add new controls to the form. You can also add new dialogs to the wizard by click on the Add button. This displays the custom dialog editor with a blank form. The screenshot below shows the Custom Dialog Editor.

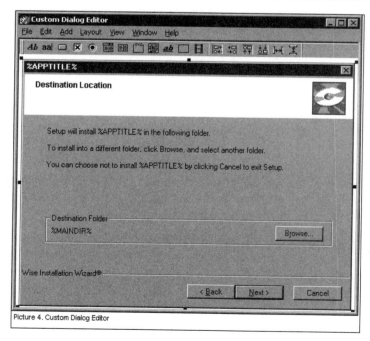

Picture 4. Custom Dialog Editor

In our HelloWorld example, we will include the Welcome, Destination Directory, Select Components, Start Installation, and Finished dialogs.

Screen

The Screen page allows you to customize the background gradient screen that is displayed during installation. By default, the background color is blue, but you can customize it to any color. You can also change the font and choose to display or not display a title bar.

Billboards

The Billboards page allows you to display billboards during the installation. If you've ever installed Visual Basic, you notice that new feature billboards are displayed during installation. This is a nice marketing feature that allows you to point out new features of your program or advertise other products. You can customize the effects of how the billboard is displayed in much the same way as a PowerPoint slide. This is another advanced feature that is not incorporated in the Visual Studio Package and Deployment Wizard.

Progress Bar

The Progress Bar page allows you to specify how the progress bar is displayed as the files are being copied to the computer. You can specify the progress as being the percentage of selected files, the position in the installation exe, or the position in the installation script. You can also prevent users from canceling the installation.

Build Options

Build Settings

The Build Settings page allows you to customize the activity of the installation program that you create. You can specify to replace files that are in use, beep on new disk prompt, specify a destination platform, as well as a handful of other settings. You probably will not change these settings.

Compiler Variables

Compiler Variables are similar variables to those you would use in Visual Basic. You can declare a compiler variable that refers to a folder and then use the variable name in the WiseScript rather than the real path. This way, if you need to change the path, you only need to change the compiler variable. Compiler variables start and end with an underscore, (_). By default the script has variables for the System32 and Windows folders.

CAB Files

The CAB Files page allows you to create CAB files that can be automatically downloaded using the Internet.

Languages

The Languages page allows you to support French, German, Italian, or Spanish for installer messages.

Password

The Password page allows you to designate a single password for all installations or create individual serial numbers for each installation. This can be helpful, but it doesn't do much if users know each other's passwords or serial numbers!

Media

The Media page allows you to specify if the installation file will be a single file or multiple files. You can specify multiple files and then copy the installation to floppy disks. If you have a CD burner, you can copy the single file to the CD, provided it does not exceed the size of the CD.

Distribution Group

Wise Update

The WiseUpdate page allows you to include automatic update support. The WiseUpdate client is installed and periodically checks for an update of software on your web site. This feature can give your application a polished and professional look as well as saving you time on distributing service packs.

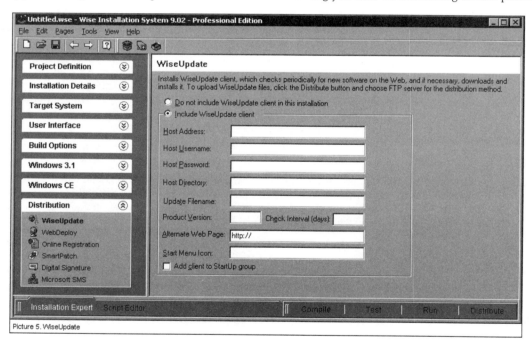

Picture 5. WiseUpdate

Installation Expert Summary

There are a few other advanced deployment options that we will not go into in depth, but as you can see, the Installation Expert provides an easy to use interface to build a complex application. The next section will discuss the Script Editor where you can see the WiseScript that was automatically generated by the Installation Expert.

WiseScript

WiseScript is the proprietary scripting languages used to create an installation program. The Installation Expert makes it easy to generate an installation program, but it is in your best interest to learn the scripting language that is working behind the scenes.

Script Editor

The Script Editor is the alternative view to the Installation Expert. Once you have completed the Installation Expert process, click on the Script Editor text in the lower left corner of the screen. The screenshot below shows the Script Editor screen.

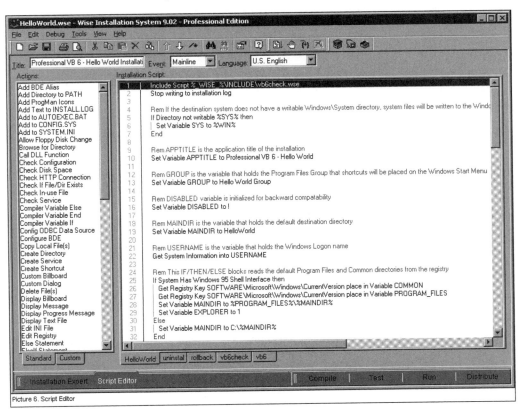

Picture 6. Script Editor

The WiseScript Actions are listed in the left pane and the WiseScript file is listed in the right pane. When you want to add an action to your script, you simply double click on the action and a dialog box prompts you for the details of the action to perform. It is good practice to create four sections in your script; initialization, user input, file copy, and system configuration. The Installation Expert already guided you through this process and created these four sections for you. Let's take a look at the script that was created for our HelloWorld example. I won't go over each and every line, but I will discuss the areas, which I feel are most important.

```
Include Script %_WISE_%\INCLUDE\vb6check.wse

Stop writing to installation log
```

Include Files

The first line is `Include Script %_WISE_%\INCLUDE\vb6check.wse`. This is an include action which allows you to include other WiseScripts. This is similar to an `Include` in an ASP page or C++. If you double click on the line, the **Include File** dialog is displayed, which prompts you for the location of the WiseScript to include. Notice the %_WISE_%? This indicates that there is a compiler variable called _WISE_. By default, this is the location where the Wise Installation program was installed. If you want to view the setting for this variable, you can click on the Compiler Variable page in the Installation Expert. The \INCLUDE\vb6check.wse is the relative path to the vb6check.wse script. The vb6check.wse script checks to make sure the client is running the correct operation system to run a Visual Basic 6 program. The vb6check.wse is displayed on another tab at the bottom of the screen.

Remark

Remark actions are used to insert comments into your WiseScript. The word `Rem` appears at the beginning of a Remark action.

```
Rem If the destination system does not have a writable Windows\System directory,
system files will be written to the Windows\ directory
```

Check If File/Dir Exists

The `Check If File/Dir Exists` action is used to determine if a file or directory exists, does not exist, if the directory is not writable, or if the module is loaded in memory. This code above is checking if the System32 folder is writable. `If` actions must have a corresponding `End` action.

```
If Directory not writable %SYS% then

  Set Variable SYS to %WIN%

End
```

Set Variable

The following lines, from the main body of the code, were generated by the **Product Details** page in the Installation Expert:

```
Set Variable APPTITLE to Professional VB 6 - HelloWorld

Set Variable MAINDIR to HelloWorld
```

This is an example of a `Set Variable` action that creates a **Runtime Variable**. Runtime variables differ from compiler variables in that they are resolved during the installation and compiler variables are resolved when the script is compiled into an executable. Compiler variables must start and end with an underscore, and runtime variables cannot.

The variable name `APPTITLE` is being set to `Professional VB 6 – HelloWorld`. The variable `MAINDIR` is being set to `HelloWorld`. Throughout the script you will see `MAINDIR` being referenced. This is the folder where the application is to be installed.

Get Registry Key Value

```
Get Registry Key SOFTWARE\Microsoft\Windows\CurrentVersion place in Variable
PROGRAM_FILES

Set Variable MAINDIR to %PROGRAM_FILES%\%MAINDIR%
```

The install program will read the value `ProgramFilesDir` from the registry key `SOFTWARE\Microsoft\Windows\CurrentVersion` and place it into a runtime variable called `PROGRAM_FILES`. The variable `MAINDIR` is being reset to hold the program files folder and its original value, `HelloWorld`. Now `MAINDIR` has the complete path to the application folder.

Install File(s)

```
Install File c:\HelloWorld\HelloWorld.exe to %MAINDIR%\HelloWorld.exe (Version)
```

The `Install File` action will include a file that is to be copied to the user's computer. If you double click on the line, the Install File Settings dialog box is displayed.

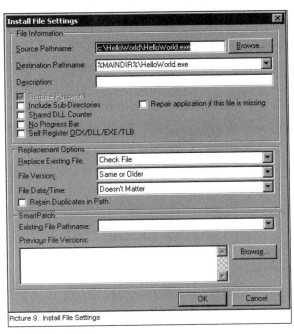

Picture 9. Install File Settings

This is a dialog box that you will need to be familiar with. The source path is the name of the file that is to be included in the installation program. The destination path is the folder where the file will be installed. If you wanted to install a DLL that needs to be registered, you would check **Self Register OCX/DLL/EXE/TLB**. This passes the file name to `regsvr32.exe`, which writes the correct entries into the registry.

The **Replacement Options** frame allows you to overwrite existing files based on the file version or the file date/time. It is extremely important to get the replacement options correct or you might replace a newer file with an older one and cause other applications to break. A nice feature about the prewritten include files is that they already have the correct replacement option settings. From experience I can tell you that it is not an easy task to figure out which files should be replaced based on version and which should be replaced by the date/timestamp.

Custom Dialog

```
Custom Dialog "Welcome"
```

The `Custom Dialog` action refers to the screen in the wizard. If you double-click on the custom dialog action, the **Custom Dialog Editor** screen is displayed and you can add controls to the screen or change the wording. The default dialogs are sufficient for most installations.

Create Shortcut

```
Create Shortcut from %MAINDIR%\HelloWorld.exe to
%CGROUPDIR%\%CGROUP_SAVE%\HelloWorld Program.lnk
```

The `Create Shortcut` action allows you to customize the shortcut for your application. This was set in the **Shortcut** page in the Installation Expert. Notice that the target is the path to the `HelloWorld.exe` file and the location is set to the program group. The `%CGROUPDIR%` is the location for common application files. This was read from the registry using the `Get Registry Key Value` action.

Self-Register OCXs/DLLs/EXEs

The `Self-Register OCXs/DLLs/EXEs` action is the point in the installation where all of the `.dlls` and `.ocxs` marked to be registered are actually registered. A message box is displayed to the user while is occurring because it may take a while. The default message is **Updating System Configuration, Please Wait...**, but you can change the message by double clicking on the action.

It is extremely important that you include this action in your script. The dreaded "Error 429ActiveX component can't create object" will occur in your program if the DLLS and OCXS are not registered.

WiseScript Summary

There are dozens of actions that you should become familiar with and I've just tried to illustrate some of the most important ones here. For the most part though, you can use the Installation Expert to build the majority of your installation and use the Script Editor to add files as your program grows.

Import VB Project

Another useful wizard provided by the Wise Installation System is the **Import VB Project** wizard. This wizard is similar to the Visual Studio Package and Deployment Wizard in that you specify the location of the Visual Basic Project file and the wizard will read the file and determine which support files are needed.

To start the Import VB Project wizard, create a new installation script by choosing File | New from the main menu. Select the Import VB Project template.

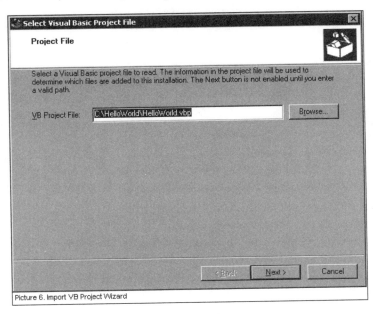

Picture 6. Import VB Project Wizard

The first screen asks for the location of the Visual Basic Project File. The next screen asks for the location where Visual Basic was installed. This is usually under your Program Files folder. The wizard then reads the project files and lists the files it has determined should be included in the installation script. If you have any extra files, such as reports, you can add them to the list by clicking the Add button and selecting the file. The next screen prompts you for the install title, install directory, icon name, and start menu name. This is similar to the Product Details page in the Installation Expert. Then all you have to do is click Finish. The script is automatically generated for you with all of the required runtime files. You can then use the Script Editor or the Installation Expert to customize the installation program.

ApplicationWatch Wizard

The ApplicationWatch wizard is a tool that can be used to monitor the DLLS and OCXS that are loaded into memory while a program is being executed. The WiseScript is automatically generated for you as you navigate through your program. This is a tremendous time saver when trying to figure out the file dependences for third party controls.

To start the ApplicationWatch wizard, create a new installation script by choosing File | New from the main menu. Select the ApplicationWatch template.

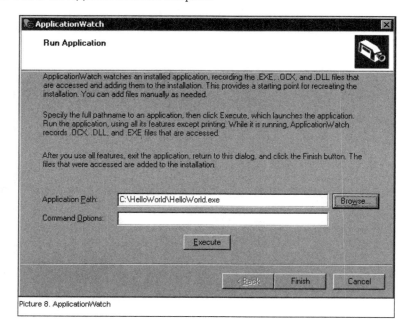

Picture 8. ApplicationWatch

Enter the path to the program you want to distribute in the Application Path textbox. You can optionally specify command line parameters in the Command Options text box. Next, click the Execute button. Your program will then be launched in the foreground. It is a good idea to navigate to every module of the program so all third party OCXS and supporting files will be loaded into memory. As you navigate through your program, the ApplicationWatch program writes the installation script for you. Once you exit your application, you use the Script Editor or the Installation Expert to customize the installation program. I can't tell you how many hours I've spent searching for dependent dlls before I knew about the ApplicationWatch wizard.

Compiling the WiseScript

Once you have created the script, you need to compile it into an executable file. You simply need to click on the Compile button in the lower right hand corner of the screen. This will compress all of the files into a self-installing executable file. The name of the executable defaults to the same name as the script and is created in the same folder where the script has been saved. You can change the name of the executable to Setup.exe after it has been compiled. Setup.exe is a standard naming convention for a setup program. All you need to do now is distribute the executable to your clients and collect the money!

You can run the Setup.exe program that is included with this book to see the installation program in action.

Conclusion

The Wise Installation System is a powerful tool that can help you create professional looking installations in a matter of minutes. Let's face it, you want to spend your time developing your application, not wasting time on figuring out how to install it. The Installation Expert is a great tool to get you up and going, and you can create more sophisticated installs once you learn the ins and outs of the WiseScript language. Remember, the installation program is the first interaction that your customer has with your application, and you never get a second chance to make a first impression.

p2p.wrox.com
The programmer's resource centre

ASP Today

wrox.com

wroxdirect

wrox

ADO Object Summary

Note that all properties of objects featured in this appendix are read/write unless otherwise stated.

The Objects

The Main Objects	Description
Command	A Command object is a definition of a specific command that you intend to execute against a data source.
Connection	A Connection object represents an open connection to a data store.
Recordset	A Recordset object represents the entire set of records from: a base table; the results of an executed command; or a fabricated recordset. At any given time, the 'current record' of a Recordset object refers to a single record within the recordset.
Record	A Record object represents a single resource (file or directory) made available from a Document Source Provider, or a single row from a singleton query.
Stream	A Stream object is an implementation of the IStream COM interface, allowing reading and writing to blocks of memory. In conjunction with the OLE DB Provider for Internet Publishing it allows access to the contents of resources (files) made available from a Document Source Provider. It can also be used to accept the output from executed Commands.

The Other Objects	Description
Error	An Error object contains the details of a data access error pertaining to a single operation involving the provider.
Field	A Field object represents a single column of data within a common data type (Recordset or Record).
Parameter	A Parameter object represents a single parameter or argument associated with a Command object based on a parameterized query or stored procedure.
Property	A Property object represents a single dynamic characteristic of an ADO object that is defined by the provider.

The Collections	Description
Errors	The Errors collection contains all of the Error objects created in response to a single failure involving the provider.
Fields	A Fields collection contains all of the Field objects for a Recordset or Record object.
Parameters	A Parameters collection contains all the Parameter objects for a Command object.
Properties	A Properties collection contains all the Property objects for a specific instance of an ADO object.

The Command Object

Methods of the Command Object	Return Type	Description
Cancel		Cancels execution of a pending Execute or Open call.
CreateParameter	Parameter	Creates a new Parameter object.
Execute	Recordset	Executes the query, SQL statement, or stored procedure specified in the CommandText property.

Properties of the Command Object	Return Type	Description
ActiveConnection	Variant	Indicates to which Connection object the command currently belongs.
CommandStream	Variant	Identifies the Stream object that contains the commands to be issued against a data provider.
CommandText	String	Contains the text of a command to be issued against a data provider.
CommandTimeout	Long	Indicates how long to wait, in seconds, while executing a command before terminating the command and generating an error. Default is 30.
CommandType	CommandType Enum	Indicates the type of command specified by the Command object.
Dialect	String	A Globally Unique IDentifier (GUID) that identifies the command dialect to be used by a particular command.
Name	String	Indicates the name of the Command object.
NamedParameters	Boolean	Indicates whether or not the parameter names are sent to the provider or whether parameters are identified by their position in the collection.
Prepared	Boolean	Indicates whether or not to save a compiled version of a command before execution.
State	Long	Describes whether the Command object is open or closed. Read-only.

Collections of the Command Object	Return Type	Description
Parameters	Parameters	Contains all of the Parameter objects for a Command object.
Properties	Properties	Contains all of the Property objects for a Command object.

The Connection Object

Methods of the Connection Object	Return Type	Description
BeginTrans	Integer	Begins a new transaction.
Cancel		Cancels the execution of a pending, asynchronous Execute or Open operation.
Close		Closes an open connection and any dependent objects.
CommitTrans		Saves any changes and ends the current transaction.
Execute	Recordset	Executes the query, SQL statement, stored procedure, or provider-specific text.
Open		Opens a connection to a data store, so that provider-specific statements (such as SQL statements) can be executed against it.
OpenSchema	Recordset	Obtains database schema information from the provider.
RollbackTrans		Cancels any changes made during the current transaction and ends the transaction.

Properties of the Connection Object	Return Type	Description
Attributes	Long	Indicates one or more characteristics of a Connection object. Default is 0.
CommandTimeout	Long	Indicates how long, in seconds, to wait while executing a command before terminating the command and generating an error. The default is 30.
ConnectionString	String	Contains the information used to establish a connection to a data source.
ConnectionTimeout	Long	Indicates how long, in seconds, to wait while establishing a connection before terminating the attempt and generating an error. Default is 15.
CursorLocation	CursorLocation Enum	Sets or returns the location of the cursor engine.
DefaultDatabase	String	Indicates the default database for a Connection object.

Properties of the Connection Object	Return Type	Description
IsolationLevel	IsolationLevel Enum	Indicates the level of transaction isolation for a Connection object.
Mode	ConnectMode Enum	Indicates the available permissions for modifying data in a Connection.
Provider	String	Indicates the name of the provider for a Connection object.
State	ObjectStateEnum	Describes whether the Connection object is open, closed, or currently executing a statement. Read-only.
Version	String	Indicates the ADO version number. Read-only.

Collections of the Connection Object	Return Type	Description
Errors	Errors	Contains all of the Error objects created in response to a single failure involving the provider.
Properties	Properties	Contains all of the Property objects for a Connection object.

Events of the Connection Object	Description
BeginTransComplete	Fired after a BeginTrans operation finishes executing.
CommitTransComplete	Fired after a CommitTrans operation finishes executing.
ConnectComplete	Fired after a connection opens.
Disconnect	Fired after a connection closes.
ExecuteComplete	Fired after a command has finished executing.
InfoMessage	Fired whenever a ConnectionEvent operation completes successfully and additional information is returned by the provider.
RollbackTransComplete	Fired after a RollbackTrans operation finished executing.
WillConnect	Fired before a connection starts.
WillExecute	Fired before a pending command executes on the connection.

The Error Object

Properties of the Error Object	Return Type	Description
Description	String	A description string associated with the error. Read-only.
HelpContext	Integer	Indicates the ContextID in the help file for the associated error. Read-only.
HelpFile	String	Indicates the name of the help file. Read-only.
NativeError	Long	Indicates the provider-specific error code for the associated error. Read-only.
Number	Long	Indicates the number that uniquely identifies an Error object. Read-only.
Source	String	Indicates the name of the object or application that originally generated the error. Read-only.
SQLState	String	Indicates the SQL state for a given Error object. It is a five-character string that follows the ANSI SQL standard. Read-only.

The Errors Collection

Methods of the Errors Collection	Return Type	Description
Clear		Removes all of the Error objects from the Errors collection.
Refresh		Updates the Error objects with information from the provider.

Properties of the Errors Collection	Return Type	Description
Count	Long	Indicates the number of Error objects in the Errors collection. Read-only.
Item	Error	Allows indexing into the Errors collection to reference a specific Error object. Read-only.

The Field Object

Methods of the Field Object	Return Type	Description
AppendChunk		Appends data to a large or binary Field object (such as an image or text field in SQL Server).
GetChunk	Variant	Returns all or a portion of the contents of a large or binary Field object (such as an image or text field in SQL Server).

Properties of the Field Object	Return Type	Description
ActualSize	Long	Indicates the actual length of a field's value. Read-only.
Attributes	Long	Indicates one or more characteristics of a Field object.
DataFormat	Variant	Identifies the format in which data should be displayed.
DefinedSize	Long	Indicates the defined size of the Field object.
Name	String	Indicates the name of the Field object.
NumericScale	Byte	Indicates the scale of numeric values for the Field object.
OriginalValue	Variant	Indicates the value of a Field object that existed in the record before any changes were made. Read-only.
Precision	Byte	Indicates the degree of precision for numeric values in the Field object. Read-only.
Status	Field Status Enum	Identifies the current state of the field. Read-only.
Type	DataType Enum	Indicates the data type of the Field object.
Underlying Value	Variant	Indicates a Field object's current value in the database. Read-only.
Value	Variant	Indicates the value assigned to the Field object.

Collections of the Field Object	Return Type	Description
Properties	Properties	Contains all of the Property objects for a Field object.

The Fields Collection

Methods of the Fields Collection	Return Type	Description
Append		Appends a `Field` object to the `Fields` collection.
CancelUpdate		Cancels any changes made to the `Fields` collection of a `Record` object.
Delete		Deletes a `Field` object from the `Fields` collection.
Refresh		Updates the `Field` objects in the `Fields` collection.
Resync		Resynchronizes the values of the `Fields` collection of a `Record` object, with values from the data provider.
Update		Confirms any changes made to `Field` objects in the `Fields` collection of a `Record` object.

Properties of the Fields Collection	Return Type	Description
Count	Long	Indicates the number of `Field` objects in the `Fields` collection. Read-only.
Item	Field	Allows indexing into the `Fields` collection to reference a specific `Field` object. Read-only.

The Parameter Object

Methods of the Parameter Object	Return Type	Description
AppendChunk		Appends data to a large or binary `Parameter` object (such as an image or text field in SQL Server).

Properties of the Parameter Object	Return Type	Description
Attributes	Long	Indicates one or more characteristics of a `Parameter` object.
Direction	Parameter Direction Enum	Indicates whether the `Parameter` object represents an input parameter, an output parameter, or an input/output parameter, or if the parameter is a return value from a statement.
Name	String	Indicates the name of the `Parameter` object.

Properties of the Parameter Object	Return Type	Description
NumericScale	Byte	Indicates the scale of numeric values for the Parameter object.
Precision	Byte	Indicates the degree of precision for numeric values in the Parameter object.
Size	Long	Indicates the maximum size (in bytes or characters) of a Parameter object.
Type	DataType Enum	Indicates the data type of the Parameter object.
Value	Variant	Indicates the value assigned to the Parameter object.

Collections of the Parameter Object	Return Type	Description
Properties	Properties	Contains all of the Property objects for a Parameter object.

The Parameters Collection

Methods of the Parameters Collection	Return Type	Description
Append		Appends a Parameter object to the Parameters collection.
Delete		Deletes a Parameter object from the Parameters collection.
Refresh		Updates the Parameter objects in the Parameters collection.

Properties of the Parameters Collection	Return Type	Description
Count	Long	Indicates the number of Parameter objects in the Parameters collection. Read-only.
Item	Parameter	Allows indexing into the Parameters collection to reference a specific Parameter object. Read-only.

The Properties Collection

Methods of the Properties Collection	Return Type	Description
Refresh		Updates the `Property` objects in the `Properties` collection with the details from the provider.

Properties of the Properties Collection	Return Type	Description
Count	Long	Indicates the number of `Property` objects in the `Properties` collection. Read-only.
Item	Property	Allows indexing into the `Properties` collection to reference a specific `Property` object. Read-only.

The Property Object

Properties of the Property Object	Return Type	Description
Attributes	Long	Indicates one or more characteristics of a `Property` object.
Name	String	Indicates the name of the `Property` object. Read-only.
Type	DataType Enum	Indicates the data type of the `Property` object.
Value	Variant	Indicates the value assigned to the `Property` object.

The Record Object

Methods of the Record Object	Return Type	Description
Cancel		Cancels any pending, asynchronous method call.
Close		Closes the currently open `Record`.
CopyRecord	String	Copies a file, or a directory and its contents, to a new location.
DeleteRecord		Deletes a file, or a directory and its contents.
GetChildren	Recordset	Returns a `Recordset` containing the child resources of the `Record`'s underlying resource.

Methods of the Record Object	Return Type	Description
MoveRecord	String	Moves a resource and its contents, to a new location.
Open		Opens an existing resource, or creates a new resource.

Properties of the Record Object	Return Type	Description
ActiveConnection	Variant	Identifies the connection details for the resource. Can be a connection string or a Connection object.
Mode	Connect ModeEnum	Indicates the permissions used when opening a Record.
ParentURL	String	Identifies the absolute URL of the parent of the current Record.
RecordType	Record TypeEnum	Indicates the type of the record, whether it's a directory, a simple file, or a complex file.
Source	Variant	Identifies the source of the Record. This will either be a URL or a reference to a Recordset object.
State	Object StateEnum	Indicates whether the Record is open, closed, or a statement is currently executing.

Collections of the Record Object	Return Type	Description
Fields	Fields	Contains a Field object for each property of the resource.
Properties		Contains all of the Property objects for the current Record object.

The Recordset Object

Methods of the Recordset Object	Return Type	Description
AddNew		Creates a new record for an updateable Recordset object.
Cancel		Cancels execution of a pending asynchronous Open operation.
CancelBatch		Cancels a pending batch update.

Table continued on following page

Methods of the Recordset Object	Return Type	Description
CancelUpdate		Cancels any changes made to the current record, or to a new record, prior to calling the Update method.
Clone	Recordset	Creates a duplicate Recordset object from an existing Recordset object.
Close		Closes the Recordset object and any dependent objects, including clones.
CompareBookmarks	Compare Enum	Compares two bookmarks and returns an indication of the relative values.
Delete		Deletes the current record or group of records.
Find		Searches the Recordset for a record that matches the specified criteria.
GetRows	Variant	Retrieves multiple records of a Recordset object into an array.
GetString	String	Returns a Recordset as a string.
Move		Moves the position of the current record in a Recordset.
MoveFirst		Moves the position of the current record to the first record in the Recordset.
MoveLast		Moves the position of the current record to the last record in the Recordset.
MoveNext		Moves the position of the current record to the next record in the Recordset.
MovePrevious		Moves the position of the current record to the previous record in the Recordset.
NextRecordset	Recordset	Clears the current Recordset object and returns the next Recordset by advancing to the next in a series of commands.
Open		Opens a Recordset.
Requery		Updates the data in a Recordset object by re-executing the query on which the object is based.
Resync		Refreshes the data in the Recordset object with the current data from the underlying data store.
Save		Saves the Recordset to a file, a Stream, or any object that supports the standard COM IStream interface (such as the ASP Response object).

Methods of the Recordset Object	Return Type	Description
Seek		Searches the recordset index to locate a value.
Supports	Boolean	Determines whether a specified Recordset object supports particular functionality.
Update		Saves any changes made to the current Recordset object.
UpdateBatch		Writes all pending batch modifications (updates, inserts and deletes) to the underlying data store.

Properties of the Recordset Object	Return Type	Description
AbsolutePage	PositionEnum	Specifies the page in which the current record resides.
AbsolutePosition	PositionEnum	Specifies the ordinal position of the Recordset object's current record.
ActiveCommand	Object	Indicates the Command object that created the associated Recordset object. Read-only.
ActiveConnection	Variant	Indicates the Connection object to which the Recordset object currently belongs.
BOF	Boolean	Indicates whether the record pointer is pointing before the first record in the Recordset object. Read-only.
Bookmark	Variant	Returns a bookmark that uniquely identifies the current record in the Recordset object, or sets the record pointer to point to the record identified by a valid bookmark.
CacheSize	Long	Indicates the number of records from the Recordset object that are cached locally in memory.
CursorLocation	Cursor LocationEnum	Sets or returns the location of the cursor engine.
CursorType	CursorType Enum	Indicates the type of cursor used in the Recordset object.
DataMember	String	Specifies the name of the data member to be retrieved from the object referenced by the DataSource property.
DataSource	Object	Specifies an object containing data, to be represented by the Recordset object.

Properties of the Recordset Object	Return Type	Description
EditMode	EditModeEnum	Indicates the editing status of the current record. Read-only.
EOF	Boolean	Indicates whether the record pointer is pointing beyond the last record in the Recordset object. Read-only.
Filter	Variant	Indicates a filter for data in the Recordset.
Index	String	Identifies the name of the index currently being used.
LockType	LockTypeEnum	Indicates the type of locks placed on records during editing.
MarshalOptions	Marshal OptionsEnum	Indicates which records are to be marshaled back to the server, or across thread or process boundaries.
MaxRecords	Long	Indicates the maximum number of records that can be returned to the Recordset object from a query. Default is zero (no limit).
PageCount	Long	Indicates how many pages of data are contained in the Recordset object (and is thus dependent on the values of PageSize and RecordCount). Read-only.
PageSize	Long	Indicates how many records constitute one page in the Recordset.
RecordCount	Long	Indicates the current number of records in the Recordset object. Read-only.
Sort	String	Specifies one or more field names the Recordset is sorted on, and the direction of the sort.
Source	String	Indicates the statement used to populate the data in the Recordset object.
State	Long	Indicates whether the recordset is open, closed, or whether it is executing an asynchronous operation. Read-only.
Status	Integer	Indicates the status of the current record with respect to match updates or other bulk operations. Read-only.
StayInSync	Boolean	Indicates, in a hierarchical Recordset object, whether the parent row should change when the set of underlying child records changes. Read-only.

Collections of the Recordset Object	Return Type	Description
Fields	Fields	Contains all of the Field objects for the Recordset object.
Properties	Properties	Contains all of the Property objects for the current Recordset object.

Events of the Recordset Object	Description
EndOfRecordset	Fired when there is an attempt to move to a row past the end of the Recordset.
FetchComplete	Fired after a Recordset has been populated with all of the rows from an asynchronous operation.
FetchProgress	Fired periodically during a lengthy asynchronous operation, to report how many rows have currently been retrieved.
FieldChangeComplete	Fired after the value of one or more Field objects has been changed.
MoveComplete	Fired after the current position in the Recordset changes.
RecordChangeComplete	Fired after one or more records change.
RecordsetChangeComplete	Fired after the Recordset has changed.
WillChangeField	Fired before a pending operation changes the value of one or more Field objects.
WillChangeRecord	Fired before one or more rows in the Recordset change.
WillChangeRecordset	Fired before a pending operation changes the Recordset.
WillMove	Fired before a pending operation changes the current position in the Recordset.

The Stream Object

Methods of the Stream Object	Return Type	Description
Cancel		Cancels any pending, asynchronous commands.
Close		Closes the current Stream.

Table continued on following page

Methods of the Stream Object	Return Type	Description
CopyTo		Copies a number of characters or bytes into another Stream object.
Flush		Forces the contents of the buffer into the underlying object.
LoadFromFile		Loads the contents of a file into the Stream object.
Open		Opens a Stream object from a URL or a Record object.
Read	Variant	Reads a number of bytes from the Stream.
ReadText	String	Reads a number of characters from the Stream.
SaveToFile		Saves the contents of a Stream to a file.
SetEOS		Sets the position that identifies the end of the stream.
SkipLine		Skips a line when reading in a text stream. Uses the LineSeparator property to identify the end of line character.
Write		Writes binary data to the stream.
WriteText		Writes text data to the stream.

Properties of the Stream Object	Return Type	Description
Charset	String	Indicates the character set to translate the Stream contents into.
EOS	Boolean	Indicates whether or not the end of the Stream has been reached.
LineSeparator	Line Separator Enum	Identifies the binary character that separates lines.
Mode	Connect ModeEnum	Identifies the permissions used when opening the Stream.
Position	Long	Identifies the current position with the Stream.
Size	Long	Indicates, in bytes, the size of the Stream.
State	Object StateEnum	Indicates whether the Stream is open or closed.
Type	Stream TypeEnum	Indicates whether the Stream contains binary or text data.

ADO Method Calls – Quick Reference

Command Object Methods

```
Command.Cancel
Parameter = Command.CreateParameter([Name As String], [Type As DataTypeEnum], _
            [Direction As ParameterDirectionEnum], [Size As Integer], _
            [Value As Variant])
Recordset = Command.Execute([RecordsAffected As Variant], _
            [Parameters As Variant], [Options As Long])
```

Connection Object Methods

```
Long = Connection.BeginTrans
Connection.Cancel
Connection.Close
Connection.CommitTrans
Recordset = Connection.Execute(CommandText As String, _
            [RecordsAffected As Variant], [Options As Long])
Connection.Open([ConnectionString As String], [UserID As String], _
            [Password As String], [Options As Long])
Recordset = Connection.OpenSchema(Schema As SchemaEnum, _
            [Restrictions As Variant], [SchemaID As Variant])
Connection.RollbackTrans
```

Errors Collection Methods

```
Errors.Clear
Errors.Refresh
```

Field Object Methods

```
Field.AppendChunk(Data As Variant)
Variant = Field.GetChunk(Length As Long)
```

Fields Collection Methods

```
Fields.Append(Name As String, Type As DataTypeEnum, [DefinedSize As Long], _
            [Attrib As FieldAttributeEnum], [FieldValue As Variant])
Fields.CancelUpdate
Fields.Delete(Index As Variant)
Fields.Refresh
Fields.Resync([ResyncValues As ResyncEnum])
Fields.Update
```

Parameter Object Methods

```
Parameter.AppendChunk(Val As Variant)
```

Parameters Collection Methods

```
Parameters.Append(Object As Object)
Parameters.Delete(Index As Variant)
Parameters.Refresh
```

Properties Collection Methods

```
Properties.Refresh
```

Record Object Methods

```
Record.Cancel
Record.Close
String = Record.CopyRecord([Source As String], [Destination As String], _
            [UserName As String], [Password As String], _
            [Options As CopyRecordOptionsEnum], [Async As Boolean])
Record.DeleteRecord([Source As String], [Async As Boolean])
Recordset = Record.GetChildren
String = Record.MoveRecord([Source As String], [Destination As String], _
            [UserName As String], [Password As String], _
            [Options As MoveRecordOptionsEnum], [Async As Boolean])
Record.Open([Source As Variant], [ActiveConnection As Variant], _
            [Mode As ConnectModeEnum], _
            [CreateOptions As RecordCreateOptionsEnum], _
            [Options as RecordOpenOptionsEnum], [UserName As String], _
            [Password As String])
```

Recordset Object Methods

```
Recordset.AddNew([FieldList As Variant], [Values As Variant])
Recordset.Cancel
Recordset.CancelBatch([AffectRecords As AffectEnum])
Recordset.CancelUpdate
Recordset = Recordset.Clone([LockType As LockTypeEnum])
Recordset.Close
CompareEnum = Recordset.CompareBookmarks(Bookmark1 As Variant, _
            Bookmark2 As Variant)
Recordset.Delete([AffectRecords As AffectEnum])
Recordset.Find(Criteria As String, [SkipRecords As Long], _
            [SearchDirection As SearchDirectionEnum], [Start As Variant])
Variant = Recordset.GetRows([Rows As Long], [Start As Variant], _
            [Fields As Variant])
String = Recordset.GetString(StringFormat As StringFormatEnum, _
            [NumRows As Long], [ColumnDelimeter As String], _
            [RowDelimeter As String], [NullExpr As String])
Recordset.Move(NumRecords As Long, [Start As Variant])
Recordset.MoveFirst
Recordset.MoveLast
Recordset.MoveNext
Recordset.MovePrevious
Recordset = Recordset.NextRecordset([RecordsAffected As Variant])
Recordset.Open([Source As Variant], [ActiveConnection As Variant], _
```

```
                   [CursorType As CursorTypeEnum], [LockType As LockTypeEnum], _
                   [Options As Long])
Recordset.Requery([Options As Long])
Recordset.Resync([AffectRecords As AffectEnum], [ResyncValues As ResyncEnum])
Recordset.Save([FileName As String], [PersistFormat As PersistFormatEnum])
Recordset.Seek(KeyValues As Variant, SeekOption As SeekEnum)
Boolean = Recordset.Supports(CursorOptions As CursorOptionEnum)
Recordset.Update([Fields As Variant], [Values As Variant])
Recordset.UpdateBatch([AffectRecords As AffectEnum])
```

Stream Object Methods

```
Stream.Cancel
Stream.Close
Stream.CopyTo(DestStream As Stream, [CharNumber As Long])
Stream.Flush
Stream.LoadFromFile(FileName As String)
Stream.Open([Source As Variant], [Mode As ConnectModeEnum], _
            [Options As StreamOpenOptionsEnum], [UserName As String], _
            [Password As String])
Variant = Stream.Read([NumBytes As Long])
String = Stream.ReadText([NumChars As Long])
Stream.SaveToFile(FileName As String, [Options As SaveOptionsEnum])
Stream.SetEOS
Stream.SkipLine
Stream.Write(Buffer As Variant)
Stream.WriteText(Data As String, [Options As StreamWriteEnum])
```

p2p.wrox.com

The programmer's resource centre

ASP Today

wrox.com

wrox

SQL Reference

SQL (Structured Query Language) lets us manipulate and retrieve data from a relational database: we can update information in database tables, create or change the structure of the database, and query the database to retrieve information. ANSI SQL-92 is the most widely implemented release of the industry standard that formally defines the core elements of SQL, although a later version is available (SQL-99).

Although the ANSI standard represents a baseline for the implementation of many contemporary database features, different vendors implement it to varying degrees. In the second part of this appendix, we'll look at the support for SQL-92 offered by Microsoft's T-SQL and Jet engines.

Three levels of ANSI SQL-92 conformance have been established. They are:

- ❑ **Entry SQL** – representing essentially a full implementation of the previous ANSI SQL standard, SQL-89.
- ❑ **Intermediate SQL** – indicates Entry SQL conformance, plus implementation of a specific subset of the new capabilities of ANSI SQL-92
- ❑ **Full SQL** – indicates Intermediate SQL conformance, plus nearly a dozen additional features.

Rather than attempt a full discussion of the SQL standard, this appendix provides a quick overview of the most common SQL commands and is intended as a basic command reference rather than a comprehensive technical manual.

Notation

This appendix uses the following conventions when presenting SQL command syntax:

> < > – element names are enclosed in angle brackets, for example `<table name>`. The angle brackets are not to be included in the actual SQL command.

{ } – required portions of the command are enclosed in braces. The entire portion contained in the braces must be entered, except for the braces themselves.

[ ] – optional syntax is enclosed in square brackets. The square brackets are not to be included in the SQL command.

| – when a choice of parameters or elements is offered, the pipe character will separate the choices. The pipe is not part of the actual SQL command.

: : = – certain important commands (such as CREATE TABLE, SELECT) are investigated in some detail. When defining a portion of the syntax separate from the command, this definition operator will be used.

. . . – when a particular portion of a command can be repeated, this will be indicated by the use of ellipses.

KEYWORD – SQL keywords appear in uppercase, but SQL itself is not case-sensitive, so you may enter them in either upper or lower case.

SQL Data Types

SQL provides a series of data types that can be used to define columns in the database, and they fall into three categories: **character**, **numeric**, and **date/time**.

Character Data Types

Character data types are either fixed-length or variable-length strings.

CHAR(n) (or CHARACTER(n)) represents a fixed-length string of n characters, where n must be greater than zero.

VARCHAR(n) (or CHARACTER VARYING(n)) represents a string which can vary in length from one to n characters. Again, n must be greater than zero.

The primary reason for these two different types is that variable-length strings are more efficient in general, but they carry a processing overhead. If a column will always contain a given number of characters and the column will almost always be populated, fixed-length strings (CHAR) are best. If a column will contain varying lengths of strings or will often be empty, use variable strings (VARCHAR).

Here is an example of a table creation command using these character types:

```
CREATE TABLE MyTable
(MyFixedString CHAR(10),
 MyVariableString VARCHAR(10) )
```

Numeric Types

An important goal of database development is the storage and manipulation of data in as efficient a manner as possible. This goal has led to the definition of several different numeric types to provide a good fit to the type of numbers that are to be stored.

Mirroring fixed and variable-length strings, numeric data types can be either **exact** or **approximate**.

Exact Numerics

NUMERIC (precision, scale) – can have fractional and integer components. Precision and scale (number of digits in fractional component) exactly as specified.

DECIMAL (precision, scale) – as NUMERIC except that precision may be equal to or greater than that specified.

INTEGER – no fractional component. Precision (maximum allowed number of digits) depends on specific implementation (for example 16-bit or 32-bit)

SMALLINT – as INTEGER. Precision cannot be greater than INTEGER, for a specific implementation.

Approximate Numerics

REAL – a single-precision floating-point value (precision depends on implementation)

DOUBLE PRECISION – double-precision floating-point number (precision depends on implementation)

FLOAT [(precision)] – a floating-point number for which the precision may be specified.

For example:

```
CREATE TABLE MyNumericTable
(MyInteger INTEGER,
MyNumeric NUMERIC(8,2),
MyFloat FLOAT )
```

Date/Time Data Types

The ANSI-92 standard defines DATE, TIME and TIMESTAMP data types. Although all SQL implementations offer DATE data types and most also have TIME and TIMESTAMP (combination of date and time) data types, it is important to check your specific vendor's type list.

Now that we have discussed our syntax conventions and understand what types of data we can deal with, we are ready to begin reviewing the actual SQL commands. Before we do that, however, let's discuss how SQL commands can be arranged by their function. This will provide us a logical sequence for discussing the specific commands.

SQL Sublanguages

SQL can be divided into three sublanguages, each providing a specific set of functions: Data Definition Language (DDL), Data Manipulation Language (DML) and Data Control Language (DCL).

Data Definition Language (DDL)

Data Definition Language allows the creation, modification, and deletion of objects in the database structure. DDL is the starting point for the database creation and maintenance processes, it does not concern the addition or retrieval of data in the database – it's strictly for building and maintaining the structure.

Sample commands: CREATE, ALTER, DELETE

Data Manipulation Language (DML)

Data Manipulation Language enables retrieval as well as addition, deletion, and updating of information in the database. The vast majority of the average developer's time is spent using the data retrieval capabilities of DML. Note that DML cannot be used to change the structure of the underlying database.

Sample commands: SELECT, INSERT, UPDATE, DELETE

Data Control Language (DCL)

Data Control Language enables control over the security of objects in the database. Each user can be granted rights to specific objects in the database such as tables, views, and procedures. DCL can also be used to control database-level rights, such as who has permission to assign access rights to other users.

Sample commands: GRANT, REVOKE

ANSI SQL-92

This section covers some of the most common commands and functions of ANSI SQL-92, focusing on those commands that are most commonly used.

Explicit Transaction Commands

ANSI-92 supports certain commands dealing with transactions, although it does not specify any command for starting a transaction.

COMMIT (or COMMIT WORK)

Writes the changes from the transaction to the database and marks the transaction as completed.

ROLLBACK (or ROLLBACK WORK)

Any changes made are undone and the database is restored to its original state.

ANSI SQL-92 Commands

The following commands are all part of the ANSI SQL-92 specification and are dealt with in alphabetical order.

ALTER DOMAIN

The domain of a table column defines the finite range of values that can be stored in that column.

```
ALTER DOMAIN <domain name>
ADD <domain constraint definition> |
DROP CONSTRAINT <constraint name> |
SET DEFAULT <default value> |
DROP DEFAULT
```

ALTER TABLE

```
ALTER TABLE <table name> <action>
```

<action> ::= <add table constraint> | <drop table constraint> | <add column> | <alter column> | <drop column>

❑   <add table constraint> ::= ADD <table constraint definition>

❑   <drop table constraint> ::= DROP CONSTRAINT <constraint name> [RESTRICT | CASCADE].

The RESTRICT and CASCADE qualifiers are referred to as drop behaviors. They control the manner in which a drop is executed if table relationships are being used. Technically they are required elements, however most database vendors either do not implement them or implement them as optional elements. Check your vendor's documentation to find out the support for these qualifiers.

❑   <add column> ::= ADD [COLUMN] <column definition>. The new column will be added after the last column in the table. The new column must obey all rules defined in the table.

❑   <alter column> ::= ALTER [COLUMN] <column name> { SET <default specifier> | DROP DEFAULT }

The SET <default specifier> command will change the existing default condition applied to a column (see CREATE TABLE). The DROP DEFAULT command will remove an existing default condition on a column.

> *You cannot change the data type of a column using ALTER TABLE. Each vendor uses their own methods of storing database columns based on the data type, the hardware implementation, and their own experience of what works best. Thus, to change a column's data type, the table must be recreated from scratch (preserving the existing data to be copied across if applicable).*

❑   <drop column> ::= DROP [COLUMN] <column name> [RESTRICT | CASCADE]

For example:

```
ALTER TABLE Customers DROP COLUMN Region
```

CLOSE

```
CLOSE <cursor name>
```

CONNECT

Connects to a database.

CREATE ASSERTION

Creates an assertion (a constraint not associated with a specific table).

CREATE CHARACTER SET

CREATE DOMAIN

```
CREATE DOMAIN <domain name> [AS] < data type>[DEFAULT <default value>]
CHECK <check predicate>[INITIALLY DEFERRED | INITIALLY IMMEDIATE | DEFERRABLE |
NOT DEFERRABLE]
```

CREATE SCHEMA

A schema is a complete description of the structure of the entire database, including the database data, rules governing the structure of this data, operators, and any other defined rules.

```
CREATE SCHEMA <schema name> | AUTHORIZATION <authorization ID>
```

CREATE TABLE

```
CREATE TABLE [[GLOBAL|LOCAL] TEMPORARY]<table name>
            ({ <column definition> [ <column constraint> ] } [,…])
            [ON COMMIT DELETE|PRESERVE ROWS]
```

<column definition> ::= <column name> (<data type>| <domain name>) [<default specifier>]

You cannot define a column without also specifying the type of data it will hold (the designation of a domain – an expression of permissible values for the column – is also supported):

```
CREATE TABLE MyTable
            (Column1 INTEGER,
             Column2 CHARACTER(3),
             Column4 REAL)
```

<default specifier> ::= DEFAULT <value> | <system value> | NULL

The optional <default specifier> is used to assign standard, or default, values to particular columns. Three options are available for the <default specifier>:

❑ <value> : literal value, such as "99.99" or "USA"

❑ <system value> : such as the current date and time, server name, or other system-provided value

❑ NULL : a null value is assigned (this is the default if <default specifier> is not included in the statement.

`<column constraint>` ::= NOT NULL | `<uniqueness>` | `<references>` | `<check constraint>`

A constraint is applied to a column and represents a rule that will be applied to values entered into that column. There are four types of constraints that can be applied to a column. One or more can be can be used together with NOT NULL:

- ❑ NOT NULL – prevents a row from being added if no value is provided for that specific field. Note that if a default is specified for the field, that value will be used automatically and the NOT NULL constraint will be satisfied even if you don't provide a value.

- ❑ `<uniqueness>` ::= UNIQUE | PRIMARY KEY. Each of these keywords instructs the database server not to allow duplicate values in a specified column. The PRIMARY KEY keyword indicates that the column should be used as the primary key for that table. Only one primary key column per table is permitted whereas several columns may have the UNIQUE constraint applied. The primary key determines in what default order records are to be retrieved. When declaring a primary key, the NOT NULL constraint is applied automatically. The UNIQUE constraint does not automatically invoke the NOT NULL condition. One or more null-valued rows for a column are allowed with the UNIQUE constraint, unless NOT NULL is also specified.

- ❑ `<references>` ::= REFERENCES `<referenced table name>` [(referenced table column name)]. This constraint does not specifically control the value to be inserted in a column, but rather establishes a relationship between the column and another column of a referenced table. This means that a value inserted into a column in one table must also exist in a particular column of the referenced table:

```
CREATE TABLE Orders
      (...(other columns),
       CustomerID INTEGER NOT NULL REFERENCES Customers(CustomerID))
```

- ❑ `<check constraint>` ::= CHECK (`<logical expression>`). This allows the application of a test (or condition), based on a logical expression, to each row that inserted. If the expression evaluates to FALSE or UNKNOWN, then the insert will fail. The `<logical expression>` can be any condition that is a valid SQL logical expression (such as ordervalue > 500). Powerful rules can be established linking various columns (from multiple tables) using this constraint.

CREATE TRANSLATION

CREATE VIEW

```
CREATE VIEW <virtual table name> [(<column list>)]
AS <query expression> [WITH [CASCADED | LOCAL]CHECK OPTION]
```

`<column list>` is optional and allows you to control the name of the columns referenced through the view.

`<query expression>` can be any valid SELECT statement.

```
CREATE VIEW MyOrderView AS
      (SELECT C.Name, CO.Quantity, E.Name
       FROM Customers AS C, CustomerOrders AS CO, Employees AS E
       WHERE C.CustomerID = CO.CustomerID
       AND E.EmployeeID = CO.EmployeeID)
```

DECLARE CURSOR

Cursors convert result sets from SQL queries into records whereby the application program can access each row individually. DECLARE CURSOR defines the name of the cursor and its scope.

```
DECLARE <cursor name> [INSENSITIVE] [SCROLL]
CURSOR FOR <cursor specification>
```

- ❑ <cursor specification> ::= <query expression> [ORDER BY <sort specification list>] [<updatability clause>]

- ❑ <updatability clause> ::= FOR {READ ONLY | UPDATE [OF <column name list>]}

- ❑ <sort specification list> ::= <sort specification> [(<comma><sort specification>)...]

- ❑ <sort specification> ::= <sort key> [<collate clause>] [ASC | DESC]

- ❑ <sort key> ::= <column name> | <unsigned integer>

DECLARE LOCAL TEMPORARY TABLE

DELETE

```
DELETE FROM <table name> [ WHERE <search condition> ]
```

The following statement would remove every row from the Orders table:

```
DELETE FROM Orders
```

DISCONNECT

DROP ASSERTION

Removes an assertion from a schema.

DROP CHARACTER SET

DROP COLLATION

DROP DOMAIN

```
DROP DOMAIN <domain name> [RESTRICT | CASCADE]
```

DROP SCHEMA

```
DROP SCHEMA <schema name> [RESTRICT | CASCADE]
```

DROP TABLE

This statement deletes the table definition and all the data from the table. Thus, unless there exists script for the table creation and/or a backup of the data, the table would need to be rebuilt from scratch, should it be needed again.

```
DROP TABLE <table name> [RESTRICT | CASCADE]
```

DROP TRANSLATION

DROP VIEW

```
DROP VIEW <table name> [RESTRICT | CASCADE]
```

FETCH

The FETCH statement retrieves data using a cursor.

```
FETCH [<fetch orientation>]
FROM <cursor name>
INTO <fetch target list>
```

❏ <fetch orientation> ::= NEXT |PRIOR | FIRST | LAST | {ABSOLUTE | RELATIVE} <ROW NUMBER>

❏ <fetch target list> ::= <target specification> [{<comma><target specification>...]

Variables in the <fetch target list> are host variables, so values from the SQL database must be converted into their data types. The ANSI-92 standard defines rules for matching SQL and host language data types.

GET DIAGNOSTICS

GRANT

The GRANT statement will assign privileges to users on particular objects in the database.

```
GRANT <access rights>
ON <object name>
TO {PUBLIC | <user identifier>}
[WITH GRANT OPTION]
```

`<access rights>` ::= ALL PRIVILEGES | SELECT | DELETE | INSERT |UPDATE | |REFERENCES | USAGE

> *The use of the GRANT statement assumes that a* `<user identifier>` *record exists in the database. Consult your vendor's manuals for details regarding how to maintain user records.*

INSERT

```
INSERT INTO <table name> [(<column list>)] <data source>
```

The optional `<column list>` tells the database what columns will have data inserted, and in what order they will be populated. If `<column list>` is not specified, then columns will be populated in the order they were created in the table. It is not necessary to provide values for all columns when inserting a row, providing that the columns for which you do not wish to insert data have been assigned a valid default value. All existing column constraints will be applied to the inserted data.

`<data source>` ::= VALUES (`<value list>`) | DEFAULT VALUES | `<query expression>`

❑ VALUES(`<value list>`) : An explicit list of values that will be inserted a single row at a time. Values in the `<value list>` must be listed in the same order as the columns they will populate (the order of which can be implicitly or explicitly implied, as described above). Also the data type must match that specified for a particular column. Consult your specific vendor manual for details about specifying data types.

❑ DEFAULT VALUES: Fills each column with its specified default value. Bear in mind that certain columns (like primary key columns) do not have default values (since each entry must be unique)

❑ `<query expression>`: A complete SELECT statement that retrieves (multiple) rows and columns from one table for insertion into another table. All rules concerning column constraints, column order, data types, and so on, apply here also. An example of use of the `<query expression>` is given below.

```
INSERT INTO CustomerOrders (CustomerID, OrderID, Terms, Comments)
SELECT CustomerID, OrderID, Terms, AgentComments + CustomerComments
FROM ImportTable
```

> *Beware that if, for example, the length of the character strings in the two comment fields in the ImportTable, when combined, exceeds the length of the CustomerOrders Comments field in the CustomerOrders table, then an error will result.*

OPEN

The OPEN statement collects the table rows selected by the DECLARE CURSOR expression.

```
OPEN <cursor name>
```

REVOKE

The REVOKE statement will remove privileges from users on particular objects in the database. See the GRANT command for details of component parts.

```
REVOKE [GRANT OPTION FOR] <access rights> ON <object name> FROM {PUBLIC | <user
identifier>,…} {RESTRICT | CASCADE}
```

SELECT

The SELECT statement can contain numerous clauses and predicates. Only the most commonly used ones will be covered in any detail. For the sake of clarity, the explanation has been divided into several sections. Each section deals with the SELECT statement with regard to single table queries. Only the final section covers multiple table queries.

```
SELECT [DISTINCT | ALL] {<column expression> | *}
FROM {<table name> [AS <correlation name>]} | {<table name> [<complete join table
statement>]}
[WHERE <search condition>]
[GROUP BY <column list>]
     [HAVING <group selection predicate>]
[{UNION | INTERSECT | EXCEPT} [CORRESPONDING BY <column list>] <complete SELECT
statement>]
[ORDER BY <sort expression>]
```

<column expression> Essentially a list of column names, but which can also include literal values, and logical expressions:

Example 1 – column names only:

```
SELECT CustomerID, OrderID FROM CustomerOrders
```

Example 2 – column names and literal values (with examples of use of correlation names):

```
SELECT CustomerID, OrderID, 12 AS Quantity,
'These are comments.' AS Comments
FROM CustomerOrders
```

Example 3 – column names and logical expressions:

```
Select CustomerID, OrderID, Comments + Terms, Quantity * UnitPrice
From CustomerOrders
```

`<complete join table statement>` ::= {`<join statement>` `<table name>`[`<join specification>`]}

- ❏ `<join statement>` : For example, INNER JOIN, LEFT OUTER JOIN, RIGHT OUTER JOIN

- ❏ `<join specification>` ::= ON`< join condition>`.

`<search condition>` ::= {`<logical expression>` [{`<Boolean operator>` `<logical expression>`}...] | `<complete comparison predicate>` | `<complete SELECT statement>`}

If the result of this search expression is TRUE, the row is displayed in the result set. If the result is FALSE or UNKNOWN, the row is dropped from the result set.

`< logical expression>`: for example Quantity>10.

`<complete comparison predicate>`:

- ❏ `<IN predicate>` ::= {`<expression>` [NOT] IN (`<value1>`,...)}

- ❏ `<LIKE predicate>`::= {`<expression>` [NOT] LIKE `<pattern>`}

  Two wildcard characters are used to specify the `<pattern>` string. The '%' character represents multiple characters and the '_' represents a single character

- ❏ `<BETWEEN predicate>`::= `<expression>` [NOT] BETWEEN `<low value expression>` AND `<high value expression>`

`<sort expression>` ::= {{`<column name>` [ASC | DESC]} , ...}

SET CATALOG

```
SET CATALOG <catalog name>
```

SET CONNECTION

SET CONSTRAINTS MODE

```
SET CONSTRAINTS MODE {<constraint name>, … | ALL}
DEFERRED|INTERMADIATE
```

SET SCHEMA

```
SET SCHEMA <schema name>
```

SET SESSION AUTHORISATION

SET TIME ZONE

SET TRANSACTION

Specify the characteristics of a transaction.

UPDATE

The UPDATE statement enables changes to be made to the data after the rows have been inserted into the table.

```
UPDATE <table name> SET <set list> [WHERE <search condition> ]
```

<set list> ::= {<column name> = {<value expression> | NULL | DEFAULT}}, ...}

ANSI SQL-92 Aggregate Functions

The following functions provide aggregate calculations in ANSI SQL-92. These aggregate functions cannot be nested and the <value expression> cannot be a subquery.

COUNT

```
COUNT (* | [ALL | DISTINCT] <value expression>)
```

COUNT(*) will return a count of all the rows in a table including those with null values. The use of COUNT with a <value expression> will return the count of the members in the <value expression>.

SUM

```
SUM( [ALL | DISTINCT] <value expression> )
```

The SUM function will return the total of all values in the <value expression>.

AVG

```
AVG( [ALL | DISTINCT] <value expression> )
```

The AVG function returns the average of all members of the <value expression>.

MAX

```
MAX( [ALL | DISTINCT] <value expression> )
```

The MAX function returns the largest value from the <value expression>

MIN

```
MIN( [ALL | DISTINCT] <value expression> )
```

The MIN function returns the smallest value from the <value expression>.

SQL Server and Transact-SQL

In this section, we cover the primary enhancements to, and departures from, the ANSI SQL-92 standard for Microsoft SQL Server's Transact-SQL.

For full details of the implementation of particular extensions, consult your DBMS documentation.

General ANSI SQL-92 Compatibility

SQL Server compliance with SQL-92 can be established for the duration of a running trigger or stored procedure by setting the ANSI_DEFAULTS option ON via the SET statement:

```
SET ANSI_DEFAULTS ON
SET ANSI_NULLS
SET ANSI_NULL_DFLT_ON
SET ANSI_PADDING
SET ANSI_WARNINGS
SET CONCURRENCY LOCKCC
SET CURSORTYPE CUR_STANDARD
SET CURSOR_CLOSE_ON_COMMIT ON
SET FETCHBUFFER 1
SET IMPLICIT_TRANSACTIONS
SET QUOTED_IDENTIFIER
SET SCROLLOPTION FORWARD
```

It should be noted that SET ANSI_DEFAULTS OFF is not supported. Reverting to normal SQL Server behavior requires individual resetting of affected options to their original value.

Distributed Queries

ANSI SQL-92 distributed query behavior is supported. However, any connection which must execute distributed queries must first set the ANSI_NULLS and ANSI_WARNINGS options for the connection via the SET statement:

```
SET ANSI_NULLS ON
SET ANSI_WARNINGS ON
```

Entity Naming Scheme

The SQL-92 standard specifies a three-part naming convention regarding entities that contain system metadata. The actual names of these entities within SQL Server do not match those called out in the standard. However, a view exists for each table that maps the SQL Server entity name with the correct corresponding SQL-92 name. The mapping is as follows:

SQL Server	SQL 92
DATABASE	CATALOG
OWNER	SCHEMA
OBJECT	OBJECT
User-defined data type	DOMAIN

Explicit Transaction Commands

SQL Server 7.0 supports commands to explicitly define the start and end points of a transaction:

BEGIN TRAN[SACTION] [name]

Indicates the beginning of a transaction.

COMMIT TRAN[SACTION]

Writes the changes from the transaction to the database and marks the transaction as completed.

ROLLBACK TRAN[SACTION] [name | savept_name]

When an abnormal condition is encountered, requiring an in-process transaction to be aborted, this command rolls back all pending changes to affected database tables and restores them to their pre-transaction state. If savept_name is supplied, only those elements of the transaction up to the declaration of the savepoint are rolled back.

SAVE TRAN[SACTION] savept_name

This statement establishes a savepoint to which a transaction may be partially rolled back. To accomplish a partial rollback, issue the ROLLBACK TRAN command, supplying the name of the savepoint established in this statement.

ANSI SQL-92 Commands in Transact-SQL

The following commands are all part of the ANSI SQL-92 specification. This section indicates the degree to which the database supports the command along with special syntax enhancements that may be implemented.

ALTER DOMAIN

Not implemented.

ALTER TABLE

The basic SQL-92 syntax is implemented, with the following exceptions or enhancements:

❑ When adding columns, a ROWGUIDCOL can be added or dropped.

❑ When altering columns, defaults cannot be dropped.

❑ Constraints can be added with the optional WITH CHECK / WITH NOCHECK clause. This allows checking against a foreign key or check constraint.

❑ The NOT FOR REPLICATION clause is used to inhibit column replication.

CLOSE

The CLOSE command supports the GLOBAL qualifier to determine the namespace to be searched to find the target cursor.

COMMIT [WORK]

Identical to COMMIT TRANSACTION, except that it does not accept a user-defined transaction name.

CONNECT TO

Supported in SQL 2000, but not in version 7.0.

CREATE ASSERTION

Not supported.

CREATE CHARACTER SET

Not supported.

CREATE COLLATION

Not supported.

CREATE DOMAIN

Not supported.

CREATE SCHEMA

This statement is supported, with the following differences:

❑ Schemas cannot be named.

❑ The AUTHORIZATION clause is mandatory, and must represent a valid security account.

❑ The CREATE ASSERTION, CREATE CHARACTER SET, CREATE COLLATION, CREATE DOMAIN, CREATE TRANSLATION, and DEFAULT CHARACTER SET clauses are not supported.

CREATE TABLE

This statement is supported, with the following differences:

❑ The ANSI-optional [{GLOBAL|LOCAL} TEMPORARY] qualifier is not supported.

❑ The ON COMMIT {DELETE|PRESERVE ROWS} clause is not supported.

❑ For column names, the COLLATION clause is not supported.

❏ For table creation, the ON {filegroup | DEFAULT} clause allows specification of the storage location of the table.

❏ For column definitions with the table, the [ROWGUIDCOL] qualifier is allowed to define a column as a holder of a globally unique identifier.

❏ The {CLUSTERED | NONCLUSTERED} qualifier is supported for PRIMARY KEY and UNIQUE constraints.

❏ ANSI SQL-92 supports the designation of a domain for a column; this is not supported.

CREATE TRANSLATION

Not supported.

CREATE VIEW

This statement is supported, with the following differences:

❏ The ANSI-optional [CASCADED | LOCAL] qualifier of the WITH CHECK OPTION clause is not supported.

❏ An optional WITH ENCRYPTION clause is supported that causes the text of the view within the <syscomments> table to be encrypted.

DECLARE CURSOR

Two distinct forms of this command are supported: one is the exact SQL-92 syntax; the other is specific to Transact-SQL. The two forms cannot be intermixed. The extended Transact-SQL syntax follows:

```
DECLARE <cursor_name> CURSOR
[LOCAL | GLOBAL]
[FORWARD_ONLY | SCROLL]
[STATIC | KEYSET | DYNAMIC | FAST_FORWARD]
[READ_ONLY | SCROLL_LOCKS | OPTIMISTIC]
[TYPE_WARNING]
FOR <select statement>
[FOR UPDATE [OF <column name> [,…n]]]
```

[LOCAL | GLOBAL] defines the scope of the cursor, whether local to the entity in which the cursor was created, or global to the connection.

[FORWARD_ONLY] specifies that the cursor can only be scrolled from the first record to the last, and not back.

[SCROLL] specifies the cursor can be scrolled in any direction

[STATIC | KEYSET | DYNAMIC | FAST_FORWARD] defines how storage of records is handled within the cursor. STATIC causes a temporary copy of the actual data to be used. KEYSET causes the keys of the underlying data to be copied, thus causing cursor membership to be fixed upon creation. DYNAMIC causes the cursor to reflect the current status of the underlying data; records may be added or removed between each fetch. FAST_FORWARD is a FORWARD_ONLY, READ_ONLY cursor with performance optimizations.

[READ_ONLY] disallows updates through the cursor.

[SCROLL_LOCKS] guarantees successful cursor updates by locking rows in underlying tables.

[OPTIMISTIC] does not guarantee successful cursor updates; underlying table rows are not locked.

[TYPE_WARNING] causes a message to be sent to the client if an implicit data type conversion has taken place.

[FOR UPDATE] causes the cursor to allow updates on all columns unless the [OF <column name>] clause is also specified.

DECLARE LOCAL TEMPORARY TABLE

Not supported.

DELETE

The full SQL-92 syntax is supported, with the following extensions:

❑   The FROM clause can specify a <rowset_function_limited> qualifier that maps either to the OPENQUERY or OPENROWSET function. This is specific to OLEDB data providers.

❑   WITH (<table_hint_limited>) allows certain locking characteristics to be defined.

❑   An optional OPTION (<query_hint>) qualifier can be specified.

DISCONNECT

Supported in SQL 2000, but not in version 7.0.

DROP ASSERTION

Not supported.

DROP CHARACTER SET

Not supported.

DROP COLLATION

Not supported.

DROP DOMAIN

Not supported.

DROP SCHEMA

Not supported.

DROP TABLE

The [CASCADE | RESTRICT] clauses are not supported.

DROP TRANSLATION

Not supported.

DROP VIEW

The statement is supported, with the following exceptions:

❑ The [CASCADE | RESTRICT] clauses are not supported.

❑ Multiple views can be dropped in the same statement via a comma-delimited list of view names.

FETCH

The statement is supported, with the following exceptions:

❑ The [GLOBAL] qualifier is allowed to specify the namespace to be searched for the specified cursor.

❑ With the ABSOLUTE and RELATIVE qualifiers, an integer literal or Transact-SQL variable name can be specified.

GET DIAGNOSTICS

Not supported.

GRANT

The statement is supported, with the following differences:

❑ Transact-SQL allows assignment of privileges to specific Transact-SQL statements via the following syntax:

```
GRANT {ALL | <statement_list>} TO <security_account_list>
```

❑ The DOMAIN, COLLATION, CHARACTER SET, and TRANSLATION qualifiers are not supported.

❑ The USAGE qualifier is not supported.

❑ An additional [WITH GRANT OPTION] clause is supported to give individual users the ability to grant a particular privilege.

❑ An additional [AS {group | role}] is supported to indicate the identity of the grantor.

❑ SQL-92 specifies an optional column list with the permission to be granted; however, Transact-SQL places the column list after the target table or view:

SQL-92 sample: GRANT INSERT (<column list>) ON TABLE

Transact-SQL sample: GRANT INSERT ON TABLE (<column list>)

Transact-SQL also allows assignment of permissions to stored procedures and extended stored procedures.

INSERT

This statement is supported with the following differences:

❑   The WITH (<table_hint_limited>) clause specifies locking characteristics of the insert.

❑   The target can be a <rowset_function>, which is specific to OLE DB data providers.

❑   The source data can be derived from an EXECUTE statement that returns data with a SELECT.

❑   Single-record inserts can be performed via the VALUES (<value list>) clause.

OPEN

This statement is supported, with the following exception:

❑   The optional [USING <values source>] clause is not supported.

REVOKE

This statement is supported, with the following differences:

❑   Permissions can be granted to specific statements.

❑   The target of the revoke can be a stored procedure or extended stored procedure.

❑   The target of the revoke can be restricted to a specific column within a table or view.

❑   The RESTRICT clause is not supported.

❑   An additional [AS {group | role}] clause is provided to specify the security context of the REVOKE.

ROLLBACK [WORK]

Fully supported. The WORK keyword is optional.

SELECT

This statement is supported, with the following differences and extensions:

❑   An additional [{TOP INTEGER} | {TOP INTEGER PERCENT} [WITH TIES]] clause is allowed to specify only those records that fall into the first INTEGER records of the entire result set, or that percentage of all records in the record. SET [WITH TIES] specifies whether duplicate records are included in the criteria

❑   The INTERSECT and EXCEPT qualifiers are not supported.

❑   The CORRESPONDING clause is not supported.

❑   An optional [INTO] clause allows for record insertion into a separate table.

❑ An optional [WITH {CUBE | ROLLUP}] clause is supported in conjunction with GROUP BY for summary statistical information.

❑ An optional COMPUTE BY clause allows for breaks and subtotals based on various aggregate functions.

❑ An optional FOR BROWSE clause is used for applications communicating with SQL Sever via DB-Library.

❑ An optional OPTION clause specifies a query hint that should be used for the query.

❑ JOINS across a named list of columns is not supported.

❑ An optional [join_hint] can be specified for optimization purposes.

❑ The source of a table can be a table, a view, or a rowset function, or a table derived from a nested SELECT statement. A rowset function is specific to OLEDB data providers.

❑ Aliases can be provided for source tables and columns.

❑ All ANSI SQL-92 standard JOIN types are supported.

❑ Search conditions using LIKE may include an [ESCAPE <esc_char>] clause.

❑ The UNIQUE clause, and the MATCH and OVERLAPS predicates are not supported.

Because the SELECT statement is fundamental to the operation of SQL and by its nature can be extremely complex, the reader is strongly encouraged to study the vendor-specific documentation to become conversant in the subtleties of the SELECT statement for their particular product and application.

SET CATALOG

Not supported.

SET CONNECTION

Supported in SQL 2000, but not in version 7.0.

SET CONSTRAINTS MODE

Not supported.

SET SESSION AUTHORIZATION

Not supported.

SET TIME ZONE

Not supported.

SET TRANSACTION

Supported with the following exception:

- ❏ The {READ ONLY | READ WRITE} qualifier is not supported.
- ❏ The {DIAGNOSTICS SIZE} qualifier is not supported.

UPDATE

This statement is supported with the following extensions:

- ❏ When used in stored procedures, the SET qualifier can include a variable name.
- ❏ The source for update can be a table, view, rowset function, or derived table (table derived from a SELECT statement). Rowset functions are specific to OLEDB data providers.
- ❏ An optional [OPTION <query_hint>] qualifier is supported.
- ❏ An optional [WITH <table_hint>] is supported as a qualifier against the <table name> parameter.

ANSI SQL-92 Functions in Transact-SQL

The following describes various implementation specifics of SQL-92 standard functions in Transact-SQL.

Aggregate Functions

For all aggregate functions, the DISTINCT | ALL qualifier is supported.

AVG

Supported.

COUNT

Supported.

MAX

Supported.

MIN

Supported.

SUM

Supported.

Non-ANSI SQL-92 Mathematical Functions

FUNCTION	DESCRIPTION
ABS	Absolute value
ACOS	Arccosine
ASIN	Arcsine
ATAN	Arctangent – one argument
ATN2	Arctangent – two arguments
CEILING	Ceiling function for numerics
COS	Cosine
COT	Cotangent
DEGREES	Converts radian angle measurement
EXP	Exponential
FLOOR	Floor
LOG	Natural Logarithm
LOG10	Logarithm (base 10)
PI	Constant value of PI
POWER	Carries x to y power
RADIANS	Converts degree angle measurement
RAND	Generates random number
ROUND	Performs rounding to n decimal places
SIGN	Returns sign of number
SIN	Sine
SQUARE	Returns square of argument
SQRT	Returns square root of argument
TAN	Tangent

String-related functions

FUNCTION	DESCRIPTION
ASCII	Returns integer representing numeric value of character
CHAR	Returns character corresponding to integer value
CHARINDEX	Returns location of substring within string
DIFFERENCE	Returns difference between SOUNDEX values of strings
LEFT	Returns left *n* characters of string
LEN	Returns length of string
LOWER	Converts all characters to lower case
LTRIM	Removes leading blanks
NCHAR	Returns Unicode character of given integer code
PATINDEX	Returns starting position of pattern in an expression
REPLACE	Replace substring with new string
QUOTENAME	Adds quotes to Unicode string to create valid SQL Server identifier
REPLICATE	Repeat a character *n* times
REVERSE	Reverse the order of characters in a string
RIGHT	Return rightmost *n* characters of string
RTRIM	Strip trailing blanks
SOUNDEX	Return value corresponding to phonetic equivalent of string
SPACE	Return *n* spaces
STR	Convert argument to string
STUFF	Deletes a number of characters and inserts another set of characters
SUBSTRING	Returns a substring of a string
UNICODE	Returns value corresponding to first character of a Unicode string
UPPER	Converts all characters to uppercase

Date and Time Functions

FUNCTION	DESCRIPTION
DATEADD	Adds a unit of time to a date
DATEDIFF	Returns the number of date units (days) between two dates
DATENAME	Returns name corresponding to portion of date variable
DATEPART	Returns a portion of a date value
DAY	Returns integer portion of date value, representing day of month
GETDATE	Returns current system date
MONTH	Returns month of specified date
YEAR	Returns year of specified date

Conversion Functions

FUNCTION	DESCRIPTION
CAST	Explicitly converts expression of one type to another
CONVERT	Explicitly converts expression of one type to another

Other Unlisted Functions

Transact-SQL supports numerous other functions to interrogate SQL Server about system status, system configuration, system table information, security, users, and file systems related to a particular database. However, these functions arise from the implementation specifics of SQL Server, and as such are beyond the scope of this document.

Commands Not Part of ANSI SQL-92

SQL Server's implementation of ANSI SQL-92 includes non ANSI-standard extensions, or alternative formats to existing commands. A brief description of many commands is provided; however, if the command is specific to features significantly departed from ANSI SQL-92 or is obvious by its name, a description may be omitted. Statements marked with an asterisk are not part of ANSI SQL-92. Those without indicate a command that may be defined in ANSI SQL-92, but only with a specialized syntax or in a context that is not consistent with ANSI SQL-92.

ALTER DATABASE*

Modify structure of a database.

ALTER PROCEDURE*

Updates a stored procedure.

ALTER TRIGGER*

Updates a table trigger.

ALTER VIEW*

Updates a view.

BEGIN DISTRIBUTED TRANSACTION*

Establishes the starting point of a transaction. The transaction may be distributed to multiple remote systems.

BEGIN TRANSACTION*

Establishes the starting point of a transaction.

COMMIT TRANSACTION*

Establishes the end point of a transaction.

CREATE DATABASE*

Creates a new database.

CREATE DEFAULT*

Creates a named default.

CREATE INDEX*

Creates an index on one or more columns of a table.

CREATE PROCEDURE*

Defines a new stored procedure.

CREATE STATISTICS*

Creates histogram for specified columns.

CREATE TRIGGER*

Defines a new table trigger.

DROP DATABASE*

Removes a database and its tables.

DROP DEFAULT*

Removes a named default.

DROP INDEX*

Removes a table index.

DROP PROCEDURE*

Removes a stored procedure.

DROP RULE*

Removes a rule.

DROP STATISTICS*

Removes statistical information generated by CREATE STATISTICS.

DROP TRIGGER*

Removes a table trigger.

ROLLBACK TRANSACTION*

Rolls a transaction back, optionally to a named savepoint.

Data Types

Some SQL Server data type names differ from those established in SQL-92 for the same physical data. The correspondences are as follows:

SQL Server	SQL 92
varbinary	binary varying
char	character
varchar	char varying or character varying

Other SQL Server Data Types

DATA TYPE	DESCRIPTION
Bit	32-bit integer with a value of 1 or 0
Int	32-bit signed integer
Smallint	16-bit signed integer
Tinyint	8-bit unsigned integer

Table continued on following page

DATA TYPE	DESCRIPTION
Decimal	Fixed precision and scale numeric data from $-10\char`^38-1$ to $10\char`^38-1$
Numeric	Synonym for decimal
Money	64-bit signed value
Smallmoney	Monetary values from -214,748.3648 to 214,748.3647
float	Floating precision value from -1.79E+308 to 1.79E+308
real	Floating precision value from -3.40E+38 to 3.40E+38
datetime	Date and time data from Jan 1, 1753 to Dec 31, 9999, accurate to 3.33 milliseconds
smalldatetime	Date and time data from Jan 1, 1900 to June 6, 2079, accuracy of one minute
Cursor	Reference to a cursor
TimeStamp	Database-wide unique number
Uniqueidentifier	Globally unique identifier (GUID)
char	Fixed-length non-Unicode data $<=8,000$ characters
Varchar	Variable-length non-Unicode data $<=8,000$ characters
Text	Variable-length non-Unicode data $<= 2\char`^31-1$ characters
Nchar	Fixed-length Unicode data $<=4,000$ characters
Nvarchar	Variable-length Unicode data $<=4,000$ characters
Ntext	Variable-length Unicode data $<=2\char`^30-1$ characters
Binary	Fixed-length binary data $<=8,000$ bytes
Varbinary	Variable-length binary data $<=8,000$ bytes
Image	Variable-length binary data $<=2\char`^31-1$ bytes

Microsoft Access Database Engine (Jet)

Microsoft Access was originally designed as a single-user database system. As the PC became pervasive in business environments, more and more "part-time" developers began to leverage the Access environment for increasingly complex tasks. Unfortunately, as the demands upon Access grew, so did the cracks in its proverbial armor. In its defense, Access was never designed or intended to handle large-scale multi-user applications; that it leveraged at all could be viewed as surprising. Yet ask any Access veteran a naïve question about writing a multi-user Access database application, resolving Access locking disputes, or Access "you name it" problems, and you're likely to get a bruise on the head from the Access manual, thrown at you for your trouble.

This "personal database" heritage of Access makes it fundamentally different from its larger cousins, SQL Server and Oracle8. Where the latter strive to meet or exceed the goals of ANSI SQL-92, offer client-server performance (in whatever way that might be defined this week) and provide differentiation in the marketplace with vendor-specific extensions and scalability, the former sought to serve as an increasingly competent relational database. Moreover, Access sought to hide the technical complexities of queries and databases through a graphical user interface; most Access users have little or no formal SQL training or exposure. This is in sharp contrast to the Enterprise Manager (SQL Server) or SQL*Plus (Oracle) applications that provide a direct, interactive query interface to the database itself.

Mixed with this offering was tight integration into the Office suite of productivity applications. Most of that integration is achieved through Visual Basic for Applications, the common programming language among all Office products. Less important in the Access world is rigid adherence to conventional SQL; in fact, a significant portion of ANSI SQL-92, such as cursors GRANT-type database security, isn't even remotely supported.

Access by itself is really the name of a front end to the actual database "engine" itself, known as the "Jet Database Engine." Its legacy dates back to the oft-treacherous days of Windows 3.x, when the letters "ODBC" looked like a typographical error and Bill Gates wasn't worth more than the gross national product of most third world countries. With this brief bit of Jet history behind us, let's dive into its SQL-92 compatibility issues.

One important note: This section covers the Jet engine as implemented for Access97. Documentation for Access2000, as a part of the Office 2000 suite of productivity applications, was not available at the time of writing. Further, this version of the Jet engine was compared with ANSI SQL-89; however, most of the relevant information carries forward to this document.

General SQL-92 Compatibility Issues

The BETWEEN condition has the following form:

> <expression> [NOT] BETWEEN <value1> and <value2>

In Jet SQL, <value1> can be greater than <value2>. This is a departure from the ANSI standard.

❑   Grouping on expressions is allowed

❑   '?' and '*' are used for wildcard character and string matching instead of the ANSI '_' and '%'

ANSI SQL-92 Commands

The following commands are all part of the ANSI SQL-92 specification. This section indicates the degree to which the database supports the command along with special syntax enhancements that may be implemented.

ALTER DOMAIN

Not supported.

ALTER TABLE

This command is supported, with the following differences:

- ❑ The ALTER COLUMN clause is not supported
- ❑ The RESTRICT | CASCADE clause of the DROP clause is not supported
- ❑ Column constraints can be added via the ADD CONSTRAINT clause
- ❑ Constraints can be dropped via the DROP CONSTRAINT clause

CLOSE

Not supported.

COMMIT [WORK]

Not supported.

CREATE ASSERTION

Not supported.

CREATE CHARACTER SET

Not supported.

CREATE COLLATION

Not supported.

CREATE DOMAIN

Not supported.

CREATE SCHEMA

Not supported.

CREATE TABLE

This statement is supported, with the following differences:

- ❑ The ANSI-optional [{GLOBAL|LOCAL} TEMPORARY] qualifier is not supported.
- ❑ The ON COMMIT {DELETE|PRESERVE ROWS} clause is not supported.
- ❑ For column names, the COLLATION clause is not supported.
- ❑ A multi-column index can be defined using the CONSTRAINT clause.

CREATE VIEW

Not supported.

DECLARE CURSOR

Not supported.

DECLARE LOCAL TEMPORARY TABLE

Not supported.

DELETE

The statement is supported, with the following difference:

❑ The WHERE CURRENT OF <cursor name> clause is not supported.

DROP ASSERTION

Not supported.

DROP CHARACTER SET

Not supported.

DROP COLLATION

Not supported.

DROP DOMAIN

Not supported.

DROP SCHEMA

Not supported.

DROP TABLE

The statement is supported, with the following differences:

❑ The [CASCADE | RESTRICT] clauses are not supported.

DROP TRANSLATION

Not supported.

DROP VIEW

Not supported.

FETCH

Not supported.

GET DIAGNOSTICS

Not supported.

GRANT

Not supported.

INSERT

The statement is supported, with the following differences:

- ❏ The DEFAULT VALUES clause is not supported.
- ❏ Inserts can be performed into an external database via the IN <externaldb> clause.
- ❏ Single-record inserts can be performed via the VALUES <(value list)> clause.

OPEN

Not supported.

REVOKE

Not supported.

ROLLBACK [WORK]

Not supported.

SELECT

The statement is supported, with the following differences:

- ❏ The UNION, INTERSECT, and EXCEPT qualifiers are not supported.
- ❏ The CORRESPONDING BY <column list> is not supported.
- ❏ An additional DISTINCTROW and TOP predicates restrict the number of records returned.
- ❏ The records forming the FROM source of the query can be an external database via the IN <external database name> clause.
- ❏ The WITH OWNERACCESS OPTION allows a query to be executed by someone other than its owner.

SET CATALOG

Not supported.

SET CONNECTION

Not supported.

SET CONSTRAINTS MODE

Not supported.

SET SESSION AUTHORIZATION

Not supported.

SET TIME ZONE

Not supported.

SET TRANSACTION

Not supported

UPDATE

The statement is supported, with the following differences:

❑ The WHERE CURRENT OF <cursor name> clause is not supported.

ANSI SQL-92 Functions in Microsoft Access

Aggregate Functions

Note that for all aggregate functions, the DISTINCT qualifier is not supported.

AVG

Supported.

COUNT

Supported.

MAX

Supported.

MIN

Supported.

SUM

Supported.

Non ANSI SQL-92 Mathematical Functions

Most extended functions, such as those seen in Oracle8 and SQL Server, are provided by the Visual Basic for Applications environment within Access, or within Visual Basic itself.

FIRST (field)

Returns value of *field* in the first row of a query.

LAST (field)

Returns value of *field* in the last row of a query.

STDEV (expr)

Returns standard deviation of a population sample.

STDEVP (expr)

Returns standard deviation of a population.

VAR (expr)

Returns variance of a population sample.

VARP (expr)

Returns variance of a population.

String-related Functions

Most extended functions, such as those seen in Oracle8 and SQL Server, are provided by the Visual Basic for Applications environment within Access, or within Visual Basic itself.

Date and Time Functions

Most extended functions, such as those seen in Oracle8 and SQL Server, are provided by the Visual Basic for Applications environment within Access, or within Visual Basic itself.

Conversion Functions

Most extended functions, such as those seen in Oracle8 and SQL Server, are provided by the Visual Basic for Applications environment within Access, or within Visual Basic itself.

Commands Not Part of ANSI SQL-92

The Jet Database Engine supports several specialized commands that are not part of SQL-92. A brief summary of these commands is provided here.

PARAMETERS

Defines one or more parameters to a parameterized query.

PROCEDURE

Declares a stored query.

TRANSFORM

Creates a crosstab query to display summary data. For example:

```
TRANSFORM Count([OrderID]) AS [The Value]
SELECT CustomerID, Count([OrderID]) AS [TotalCount]
FROM Orders
GROUP BY [CustomerID]
PIVOT Format([OrderDate], "yyyy")
```

Data Types

Jet	SQL-92
BINARY	BIT, BIT VARYING
TEXT	CHARACTER, CHARACTER VARYING
DOUBLE	DOUBLE PRECISION, FLOAT
SINGLE	REAL

Other Jet data types

DATA TYPE	DESCRIPTION
BIT	8-bit unsigned integer
BYTE	8-bit unsigned integer
COUNTER	32-bit unsigned integer
CURRENCY	Scaled integer between -922,337,203,685,477.5808 and 922,337,203,685,477.5807
GUID	128-bit Globally Unique Identifier
LONGBINARY	As needed
LONGTEXT VALUE	byte per character

p2p.wrox.com

The programmer's resource centre

ASP Today

wrox.com

Index

Important entries have numbers in **bold** type.

Field objects, ADO, 82, 570, **575**
  ActualSize property, 82, 575
  AppendChunk method, 575
  Attributes property, 82, 575
  DataFormat property, 575
  DefinedSize property, 82, 575
  GetChunk method, 575
  Name property, 575
  NumericScale property, 575
  OriginalValue property, 76, 77, 575
  Precision property, 575
  Properties collection, 575
  Status property, 575
  Type property, 82, 575
  UnderlyingValue property, 76, 77, 575
  Value property, 66, 74, 76, 575
FieldAttributeEnum constants, ADO, 81, 82
FieldChangeComplete event, ADO Recordset
  objects, 583
Fields collection, ADO Recordset objects, 66,
  80-82, 583
  Append method, 81-82, 576
  CancelUpdate method, 576
  Count property, 81, 576
  Delete method, 82, 576
  Item property, 80-81, 576
  Refresh method, 81, 576
  Resync method, 576
  Update method, 576
Fields collections, ADO, 570, 576
  Record objects, 579
File Associations page, Installation Expert interface,
  556
File System window, Visual Studio Installer, 532, 534,
  536
filepos property, XML DOM **ParseError**
  interface, 425
files, 519-20
Files page, Installation Expert interface, **554**
FileSystemObject objects, 381-82, 410, 519
  MoveFile method, 382
  OpenTextFile method, 410-11
Filter property, ADO Recordset objects, 70, 71,
  75, 181, **582**
FilterGroupEnum constants, ADO, 71
Find method, ADO Recordset objects, 70, 182-83,
  580
firehose cursors, ADO recordsets, **515**
FIRST function, SQL, **622**
FlexGrid controls, **123**
FLOAT data type, SQL, **591**
float data type, SQL Server, 616
FLOOR function, SQL, **611**
Flush method, ADO Stream objects, **584**
Flush method, ASP Response object, **395**, 396
fonts, **497**
Fonts page, Installation Expert interface, **556**
For Each loops, 478, 516
FOR keyword, SQL, 147
FOR XML clause, SQL SELECT statements, **198**
  AUTO attribute, **198-99**
  EXPLICIT attribute, **199**
  RAW attribute, **198**
for-each elements, XSL, 427-28
foreign key constraints, databases, **153**

Form collection, ASP Request object, **391**
Format property, Masked Edit Control, 111
FormatName property, MSMQ MSMQQueueInfo
  objects, 352, 359-60
forms, 516-19
  controls, **518**
  errors, **517-18**
  events, 516-17
    Load event, **516-18**
    ZOrder method, **519**
Forms collection, **519**
forward-only cursors, ADO recordsets, **78**, 79
Full SQL, **589**
functions, SQL, 610-13
  aggregate functions, **601**, **610**, **621**

G

garbage collection, **497**
General Information page, Installation Expert
  interface, **553**
Generate SQL Scripts dialog, SQL Server Enterprise
  Manager, 154
GET DIAGNOSTICS statements, SQL, **607**, 620
GET method, HTTP, 390
GetChildren method, ADO Record objects, 578
GetChunk method, ADO Field objects, 575
GETDATE function, SQL, 613
GETDATE function, SQL Server, 148
GetDeactivateOnReturn method, COM+
  IContextState interface, 309, 310
GetLastError method, ASP Server object, 402
GetMyTransactionVote method, COM+
  IContextState interface, 309, 310
GetObjectContext function, 243, 307, 308, 309
GetRows method, ADO Recordset objects, 72-73,
  263, **515**, 580
GetSecurityCallContext function, COM+, 244
GetString method, ADO Recordset objects, 580
global.asa file, ASP, **397**, 398, 400, **405**
globally unique identifiers (see GUIDs)
GoF (Gang of Four) design patterns, **35**
GRANT statements, SQL, 598, **607-8**, 620
GUIDs (globally unique identifiers), **220**, 278, 290
  MSMQ queues, **348**

H

HandlerRequired registry key, 186
handunsf.reg file, 187
HelpContext property, ADO Error objects, 574
HelpFile property, ADO Error objects, 574
hierarchical recordsets, 430
Hook subroutine, Win32 API, 510
HTML, 384-85, 411-12, 416-17, **441-44**
HTMLEncode method, ASP Server object, 402
HTTP, 196, 491-92
  GET method, 390
  POST method, 391

T

X

Y

Z

ASPToday - Your free daily ASP Resource . . .

A discount off your ASPToday subscription with this voucher!!! see below for more details.

Expand your knowledge of ASP.NET with ASPToday.com - Wrox's code source for ASP and .NET applications, with free daily articles!

Every working day, we publish free Wrox content on the web:

- Free daily article
- Free daily tips
- Case studies and reference materials
- Index and full text search
- Downloadable code samples
- 11 Categories
- Written by programmers for programmers

And for just-in-time, practical solutions to real-world problems, subscribe to our Living Book - our 600+ strong archive of code-heavy, useable articles.

Find it all and more at http://www.asptoday.com

This voucher entitles you to a discount off your annual ASPToday subscription; to claim your reduced rate please visit:

http://www.asptoday.com/special-offers/

If you have any questions please contact customersupport@wrox.com

C# Today

The daily knowledge site for professional C# programmers

C#Today provides you with a weekly in-depth case study, giving you solutions to real-world problems that are relevant to your career. Each one is written by a leading professional, meaning that you benefit from their expertise and get the skills that you need to thrive in the C# world. As well as a weekly case study, we also offer you access to our huge archive of quality articles, which cover every aspect of the C# language at www.csharptoday.com.

Tony Loton, one of the authors of this book, has written a related case study: "Build a Better Design Tool with Automation", for C# Today, and exclusively for readers of this book, a free PDF copy is available from http://www.csharptoday.com/info.asp?view=ProfessionalUML. In his case study, Tony shows how any Microsoft application can be driven via automation from a C# application, and how Visio can be used to extract information from diagrams (and not just UML) as a more interesting alternative to the usual Word or Excel automation demonstrations. This piece also comes will fully working code.

By joining the growing number of C#Today subscribers, you get access to:

- A weekly in-depth case study
- Code-heavy demonstration of real-world applications
- Access to an archive of over 170 articles
- C# reference material
- A fully searchable index

Visit C#Today at: www.csharptoday.com

Wrox Press
Web Services

A selection of related titles from our Web Services Series

Professional Java Web Services
ISBN:1-86100-375-7
Professional Java Web Services concisely explains the important technologies and specifications behind web services. The book outlines the architecture of web services, and the latest information on implementing web services.

Professional C# Web Services: Building Web Services with .NET Remoting and ASP.NET
ISBN: 1-86100-439-7
This book covers building web services and web service clients with both ASP.NET and .NET Remoting. We also look at the generic protocols used by web services: SOAP and WSDL.

Professional XML Web Services
ISBN: 1-86100-509-1
The technologies presented in this book provide the foundations of web services computing, which is set to revolutionize distributed computing, as we know it.

Professional ASP.NET Web Services
ISBN: 1-86100-545-8
This book will show you how to create high-quality web services using ASP.NET.

Early Adopter Hailstorm
ISBN: 1-86100-608-X
Hailstorm Preview of Version 1.0 - Using SOAP and XPath to talk to Hailstorm - Hailstorm Data Manipulation Language (HSDL) - Practical Case Studies.

Professional Java SOAP
ISBN: 1-86100-610-1
Organized in three parts: Distributed Application Protocols, Sample Application, and Web Service, this book is for all Java developers and system archictects.

Register your book on Wrox.com!

When you download this book's code from wrox.com, you will have the option to register.

What are the benefits of registering?

- You will receive updates about your book
- You will be informed of new editions, and will be able to benefit from special offers
- You became a member of the "Wrox Developer Community", giving you exclusive access to free documents from Wrox Press
- You can select from various newsletters you may want to receive

Registration is easy and only needs to be done once for each book.

wrox

Programmer to Programmer™

Registration Code: 818XYNM236H05W01

Wrox writes books for you. Any suggestions, or ideas about how you want information given in your ideal book will be studied by our team.
Your comments are always valued at Wrox.

Free phone in USA 800-USE-WROX
Fax (312) 893 8001

UK Tel.: (0121) 687 4100   Fax: (0121) 687 4101

Professional Visual Basic 6: The 2003 Programmer's Resource – Registration Card

Name _____

Address _____

_____

_____

City _____ State/Region _____

Country _____ Postcode/Zip _____

E-Mail _____

Occupation _____

How did you hear about this book?

❒ Book review (name) _____

❒ Advertisement (name) _____

❒ Recommendation _____

❒ Catalog _____

❒ Other _____

Where did you buy this book?

❒ Bookstore (name) _____ City _____

❒ Computer store (name) _____

❒ Mail order _____

❒ Other _____

What influenced you in the purchase of this book?

❒ Cover Design ❒ Contents ❒ Other (please specify):

How did you rate the overall content of this book?

❒ Excellent ❒ Good ❒ Average ❒ Poor

What did you find most useful about this book? _____

_____

What did you find least useful about this book? _____

_____

Please add any additional comments. _____

_____

What other subjects will you buy a computer book on soon?

_____

What is the best computer book you have used this year?

_____

wrox

Programmer to Programmer™

Note: If you post the bounce back card below in the UK, please send it to:

Wrox Press Limited, Arden House, 1102 Warwick Road,
Acocks Green, Birmingham B27 6HB. UK.

Computer Book Publishers